Malum

Malum

A Theological Hermeneutics of Evil

Ingolf U. Dalferth
TRANSLATED BY Nils F. Schott

CASCADE *Books* · Eugene, Oregon

MALUM
A Theological Hermeneutics of Evil

Cascade Books
An Imprint of Wipf and Stock Publishers
199. W. 8th Ave., Suite 3
Eugene, OR 97401
www.wipfandstock.com

PAPERBACK ISBN: 978-1-7252-9712-8
HARDCOVER ISBN: 978-1-7252-9713-5
EBOOK ISBN: 978-1-7252-9714-2

Cataloguing-in-Publication data:

Names: Dalferth, Ingolf U., author. | Schott, Nils F., translator.
Title: Malum : a theological hermeneutics of evil / Ingolf U. Dalferth ; translated by Nils F. Schott..
Description: Eugene, OR : Cascade Books, 2022. | Includes bibliographical references and index.
Identifiers: ISBN 978-1-7252-9712-8. (paperback) | ISBN 978-1-7252-9713-5. (hardcover) |
    ISBN 978-1-7252-9714-2. (ebook)
Subjects: LCSH: Good and evil—history. | God—Goodness. | Hermeneutics—Religious aspects—
    Christianity. | Theodicy.
Classification: BJ1403 .D35 2022. (print) | BJ1403 .D35 (ebook)

Translation of Ingolf U. Dalferth, *Malum: Theologische Hermeneutik des Bösen*. Tübingen: Mohr Siebeck, 2008.

To the theological faculty at the University of Copenhagen,
in gratitude for the doctorate *honoris causa*

Contents

CONTENTS

viii

Contents

Contents

Contents

Translator's Preface

THE INSIGHT THAT LANGUAGE is central to all attempts at philosophical understanding is at the heart of this book's methodology. Ingolf U. Dalferth very carefully develops his concepts in dialogue with the philosophical and theological tradition. This hermeneutic procedure has allowed me to follow standard usage and to render philosophical terms in the canonical translations (for editions used, please refer to the bibliography). Dalferth is very clear on where his use of a term differs from everyday meanings or prior philosophical uses. Where this is helpful, he includes the original Greek, Latin, French, etc. in parentheses—a practice I have followed in a number of instances by providing the German term.

I would like to draw readers' particular attention to his rationale for using the term *malum* and the discussion of the words good, evil, and ill—*gut, böse,* and *übel,* respectively—in chapter I.B.

Finally, I would like to express my gratitude to Ingolf U. Dalferth for his generous and patient support.

Nils F. Schott

I

EVIL AS A PROBLEM

A

Disruptions, Problems, and Fundamental Problems

THE SHORTEST PATH IS not always the best. Confronting a problem directly is not always the most successful strategy. After all, what do we really know when we only know what meets the eye? What are we really familiar with when we content ourselves with what we see? How can we understand if we do not keep asking questions, if we do not explore other aspects of what we seek to understand? When we do not take the time to distance ourselves from our perceptions and our experiences, we are unlikely to act successfully. And when we act based only on what we have before our eyes, we will soon be caught up in the thicket of the unexpected and unforeseeable.

1. A Need for Orientation, a Lack of Time, and a Risk

It will never be possible to avoid that danger completely. Only rarely are we able to explore and evaluate all the relevant aspects of a problem, and very often, we know which aspects would have been relevant only later—or when it is too late. Because we want to live and we have to act, we usually cannot wait until we know all the essentials. Not only because we do not have the time. Even if we had all the time in the world, our questions would only lead us from one aspect of a problem to the next. As long as there is time and as long as we can ask, confronting the finite, too, is a process that is never completed, that opens onto infinity at each and every point. Finite problems, too, only come to an end when they are brought to an end by our ceasing to ask questions.

What is to be avoided, then, is not the unavoidable but the avoidable. This sounds trivial only as long as we ignore how difficult it can be to distinguish between what is unavoidable and what is not. We need strategies of coding or representation[1] that allow

1. By "strategies of coding" or "of representation," I mean semiotic procedures in the widest possible sense, that is, all semiotic processes (signs, numbers, models, conceptions, notions, images, words, concepts, styles of communication, genres, etc.) by means of which we orient ourselves in our world in a biological-natural and cultural way. We bring a manageable semiotic order to the world and semiotically locate ourselves in this symbolic order. There is not just one way of doing this. There is a pragmatic and situationally variable diversity and polymorphy that cannot be subsumed under a hierarchical monistic context of orientation. Instead, it differentiates in response to the changing communicative and pragmatic demands of different contexts. In the contexts of the lifeworld, society, science, politics, culture, religion, etc., our localization takes specific forms. Every age and every culture develops strategies for

3

us to make this distinction in ways that are relevant to particular situations, and we must symbolically parse various versions to explore possible orientations and try out options for action, for we always need to orient ourselves. And because as long as we are alive, we cannot not act, we cannot shirk this necessity. Moreover, it is not enough that we have strategies of representation at our disposal to encode the relevant aspects of a situation or a problem in terms of decisive distinctions; it is not enough that, in each case, we are able to order our world in terms of applicable distinctions.[2] If we want to use these distinctions effectively to explore the distinction between the unavoidable and the avoidable in a given situation, we also must be able quickly to dispose of them, to vary them creatively (power of the imagination), and to concretize them critically (relation to life). If we take too long, if we lack imagination or engage with the situation insufficiently, life will have the better of us—in everyday life no less than in politics, academia, or religion.

The scarcity of disposable time (almost always, it's already too late), the inconclusiveness of the imagination (anything can always be imagined and thought differently), and the infinite approximation of the present (anything can be made more concrete and more specific) thus confine us in a dilemma that characterizes human dealings with all biological and cultural strategies of orientation. On the one hand, we depend on procedures of representation that provide us with distinctions applicable across different situations, that serve as points of orientation in the lifeworld no less than in academia, society, culture, or religion. On the other hand, we have to distinguish between the unavoidable and the avoidable in concrete situations that often differ significantly from the regularities and standard situations of the usual orientation strategies: someone used to solving everyday practical problems of orientation by combining visual, acoustic, tactile, and olfactory strategies will be tripped up when limited to the sense of hearing or of smell alone.[3] People who have learned to orient themselves only with the help of map and compass will be lost without them on difficult terrain. People who can think only in terms of social hierarchies will have trouble finding their place in democratic societies. And people who consider irony and reproach, play and mockery, criticism and complaint to be irreconcilable with religious convictions will see religious caricatures as an attack on their personal religious identity, and will act accordingly.

---

encoding and orientation appropriate to the realities of its life: from spatial orientation in relation to the body (in front, behind, above, below, right, left) via social schemata of orientation (relations of kinship, professional designations, titles) and scientific forms of communication (experiments, theories, calculations, dense description) to the search engines we use to orient ourselves on the web. On the concept of orientation I employ here, see part I of my *Die Wirklichkeit des Möglichen*; Stegmaier, *Philosophie der Orientierung*; and the contributions and bibliography in Stegmaier, *Orientierung: Philosophische Perspektiven*.

2. In an environment without movement (a "quiet" environment), an organism biologically disposed only to react to external movements will be bereft of points of orientation, and people whose cultural education was limited to orientating themselves via buoys on the water will be lost in the mountains.

3. This is also true for other biological strategies, human and animal, that work in certain but not in all environments. European bees are at the mercy of Japanese hornets because they engage with their opponents one on one, which works against their European enemies but not against the Japanese hornets. Japanese bees on the contrary pounce on their enemy together and form a dense ball around the hornet, thereby creating conditions (heat and a high level of carbon dioxide) the hornet cannot survive.

We might ignore these difficulties if we did not constantly have to orient ourselves anew. Yet on the one hand, we cannot dispense with remaking and exploring the distinction between the unavoidable and the avoidable time and again because we must act in ever-different situations. On the other hand, we would never get around to acting if we waited until the difference has become clear. Most of the time, we have to act on the basis of insufficient perceptions and explorations of the relevant differences. This is risky but cannot be avoided. If our perceptions and behavior did not take place within the horizons of expectation of inherited experiences and the orientation strategies of others, which they do more than we are conscious of, our life would be even more endangered and our survival even more unlikely than they already are.

2. Orientation Formulas

The fact that we still exist is evidence that the strategies we have inherited are not entirely useless. Yet the risk remains. Entrusting ourselves entirely to our heritage is as unreliable a policy for a successful life as wanting to rediscover and reinvent everything ourselves. We thus manage with *orientation formulas* that have been tried and tested (they are suitable for orienting our lives); that condense the experiences and orientation strategies of earlier generations (they allow access to a contingent set of traditions); that are appropriated with relative ease (they are inherited easily); that can be used in a wide variety of ways (they are flexible and adaptable); and that can be developed differentially and redefined in complex ways (they prompt and provide material for open-ended reflection).

Orientation formulas of this kind include *the good, the true, the beautiful*, but also *the world, the soul*, or *God*. None of them are substantivized predicates that designate experiential differences between kinds or groups of phenomena and could serve, semantically, as definitions. In their formulaic condensation, they instead say something specific about our way of dealing with and our attitude toward the experiential phenomena of our life, that is, they function, pragmatically, as orientation formulas. *The good, the true*, or *the beautiful* do not designate phenomena as distinct from other phenomena but speak to our judgment about and evaluation of phenomena under specific aspects and in specific respects. That is why they are not mutually exclusive but can be combined with a view to dealing with the same phenomena. Similarly, *the world, the soul*, or *God* do not designate objects or phenomena beside or underneath others but condense universal perspectives on all possible phenomena under a certain aspect in a concise formula: that they can be *experienced* (*world*); that they are *alive* (*soul*); that they are *created* (*God*). And these formulas suggest not only a theoretical view of reality from their particular perspective but a practical attitude toward reality as well: What can be experienced is to be *explored*, *used*, and *worked on*; the living is to be *cared for* and *protected*; the created is something to be *thanked for*, its shortcomings are to be *lamented*, and its existence is to be *enjoyed*.

The impact and performance of this kind of orientation formulas can vary. They can function within specialized practices (academia, the economy, religion), in practical everyday life, or in overarching contexts such that they can regulate, for example, the reciprocal transitions between academic, religious, and everyday practices, the way the orientation formula *reason* does, which has to take different concrete forms in each of these domains. They exist above all, however, in those contexts in which a society is particularly concerned with transmitting orienting knowledge and orientation strategies from the past to the present and future, and in which, for that purpose, it provides formulas that can be both appropriated easily and interpreted in complex ways.

3. Orientation Formula "God": Comprehensive Order and Absolute Localization

In the domain of religion, and in Christianity in particular, this is true especially of the *orientation formula of the idea of God*, which systematizes fundamental structures of organization and functions of localization in such a way that reliably orienting our lives becomes possible anywhere and anytime. On the one hand, each understanding of the idea of God comes with a *schema that organizes human beings' relations to the world and to themselves*; that manifests itself in a specific religious semantics (creation, redemption, perfection); that includes everything that can be thought (possibility), that can be experienced (possible reality), and that has been experienced (reality); and that makes it impossible to speak of God without in a certain way speaking about the world and about oneself—and the other way around. And for that very reason, on the other hand, the idea of God also always performs an *absolute function of localization* that makes it possible, at any time and in any situation, absolutely to localize ourselves in the world in relation to God, namely in such a way that we stand in a certain relation to the one who stands in a certain relation to everything else, such that, for example, I cannot conceive of myself as *creature of God* without conceiving of everything else that is different from God as the *creation of God*.[4]

The orientation formula of the idea of God allows for orienting lives but it does not by itself bring about this orientation: the formula has to be *used*, and it is used only when we do not just consider it intellectually but direct our lives toward it and live accordingly.[5] We thus enter into a dialectic that specifically characterizes the religious life. On the one hand, we adopt schemas of orientation found and invented by others, that is, we assume a contingent tradition of orientation. On the other hand, for this tradition to perform its orienting function, each of us must appropriate it on our own account. We thus live thanks to others but at our own risk. Yet it is far from obvious what the questions and the answers of the inherited orientations for life are. We have to ask the questions and seek the answers ourselves. There is no guarantee this will succeed. But it certainly will not succeed if we simply repeat traditional advice without examining the questions it sought to answer. If we content ourselves with oversimplifications (our own or others') that suggest quick answers without sufficiently elucidating the questions and

---

4. On the orienting function of the idea of God, see Dalferth, *Die Wirklichkeit des Möglichen*, 145–68 and 434–548.

5. To avoid misunderstandings: reflectively living one's life cannot do without intellectually considering and exploring the possibilities that do or do not arise. But limiting oneself to this is merely to explore a *possible* life, not *really to live it*. Life is not exhausted by thought. Here as elsewhere, "the proof of the pudding is in the eating."

adequately analyzing the phenomena at issue, we will understand very little and hardly be able autonomously to orient ourselves in our lives.

4. From Disruption to Problem

Usually, disagreement already sets in when we ask which exactly are the questions and phenomena at issue. Everyone will have a slightly different answer. Problems are always problems *for someone*—problems *posed to someone*, trouble *someone is having*. Not just because something that really isn't a problem is made into one (although that happens, too) but because something only becomes a *problem* when we are prompted to notice, when well-rehearsed routines or habits are disrupted in such a way that we no longer know what is going on and begin asking what exactly is different and why it is different.

Problems begin as disruptions of the usual, as interruptions of routines, as deviations from expectations. But these disruptions, interruptions, or deviations become problems only for those who take them as occasions for asking questions. These questions at first only concern the disruption and aim at restoring what we are used to. But in the dynamic of questioning, they soon spread to the habitual and reveal that the habitual is far from a matter of course: not just, *why is this different than usual?* but, *why* is *the usual the way it is and not otherwise?* And once we have started asking these kinds of questions, we are drawn irresistibly from one question to the next.

Only thanks to the questions that provoke them do problems arise from disruptions, and no problem remains solitary when we let ourselves be taken in by the dynamic of questioning. Those who do not let disruptions trigger questions have no problems; those who entirely abandon themselves to the dynamic of questioning will only have problems but will not solve a single one. That is why, to deal with problems, we need both: a sensitivity for questions *and* a sensitivity for the point beyond which further questioning is going to hinder rather than aid the solution of a problem.

Not everyone situates this point in the same place; yet not everyone is asking the same questions, and everyone asks their questions their own way. That is why problems are always *someone's* problems; yet the problems of the one are not necessarily those of the other and certainly not of all the others. Being able to determine what the problems are and to put them on the agenda is thus not just a question of being sensitive to what is questionable but always also a question of power. Not everyone is capable of presenting questions to others in such a way that they are forced, by insight, persuasion, or constraint, to adopt them as their own. But neither do all problems on the public agenda really deserve that everyone—or anyone—make them their own. While a question might irresistibly pose itself to me (e.g., *Why is there so much injustice and meaningless suffering in the world?*), it is often unavoidable to justify to others that, why, and in what regard this question is a problem for them as well. When we designate problems for others to concern themselves with, we have a duty toward them to justify why they should trouble themselves with these problems. That is because disruptions happen, but problems are caused by questions being raised; and since it varies from person to person whether and which questions are posed when disruptions occur, not all problems are generated by each and everyone of us, but every problem is generated by each of us slightly differently.

Not everyone has every problem, but each problem is had slightly differently by each of us.

5. Existential Problems and Fundamental Problems

The fact that they are always "generated" gives problems the questionable and often criticized appearance of being merely intellectual challenges that can be dealt with in the pros and cons of arguments or, if needed, be archived without leaving a trace in an individual's concrete life, independently of whether they have been resolved or not. Life goes on as if nothing had happened.

There is no denying that this danger exists. It exists particularly where those problems of other people are at issue that—rightly or wrongly—do not affect us existentially and, therefore, are (or seem to be) treated as problems of thought, not as problems of life. Existential problems are always individual problems, that is to say, *life problems of specific people*. To ignore this in dealing with them would be to deal with them inappropriately. That is why it is correct to criticize it when turning iniquities in human beings' dealings with each other into intellectual problems renders (or seems to render) them "harmless," or when an atrocity like Auschwitz is banalized by being turned into a readily available topos in ethical debates about guilt and responsibility. There are problems that are of such existential significance that ignoring this aspect makes it impossible adequately to reflect on and remedy them. And there are events that are of such monstrosity that they go beyond everything that could be captured in the terms of a problem and remedied by methodically looking for a solution.

Even if there are no problems without intellectual formatting, not all problems therefore are just intellectual problems. We can think only with our brains, but we are not all brain, and our life is not exhausted by our thinking or by what we are thinking. There are questions with which the events of our life irresistibly confront us, even if those may be different in each life. There are also questions no one who begins thinking about their lives can avoid, even if not everyone must think about their lives. There are questions we do not know how to pose because they are prompted by events that go beyond our capacity to comprehend. And there are questions that cannot be asked without having to be asked again and again, because every answer raises them anew: fundamental questions that articulate fundamental problems without it ever being possible that they be articulated satisfactorily or answered conclusively.

6. The Problem of Evil and Theodicy

All this pertains to what is usually called the "problem of evil" or the "problem of ill."[6] Calling it so is already an interpretation that places "evil" in the methodological context

6. In German, the words *übel* and *Übel*—"ill" as adjective and noun, respectively—are usually employed as general terms. They can be applied descriptively and/or evaluatively to a variety of phenomena and specified to name different kinds of evil (natural, moral, metaphysical) with more precision. The words *böse* and *Böses*—"evil"—in turn, are usually employed evaluatively, that is, in the sense of moral evil. See Häberlin, *Das Böse*, 5–6; Pieper, *Gut und Böse*, 11–17; and Häring, *Das Böse in der Welt*, 3–6.

of *problems and solutions* and thereby imputes enough sense to it for it to be perceived as a—solvable or unsolvable—problem. But what problem is at issue? In few cases has the singular been as inappropriate as it is here.[7] *The* problem of *Evil* (in the singular) does not exist; there are only many problems concerned with many instances of evil. The encounter with evil raises many questions, and only a few have answers that are less questionable than the questions to which they relate.

Nonetheless, the formula "problem of evil" is connected with traditional foregone conclusions that raise certain expectations. In the Anglophone world, the phrase usually refers to the so-called *problem of theodicy*. Unlike the expression "evil" taken by itself, which in moral philosophy designates aggravated human atrocities and unfathomable inhumanities,[8] "problem of evil" names a problem in the philosophy of religion, a problem the experience of evil and ills in the world raises for faith in a good and omnipotent creator of this world.[9] Why did the perfectly good, all-knowing, and all-powerful God create a world in which there are ills and evil in such unimaginable proportions? Would it be impossible for the world to be without ills and evil, or without this unbearable kind of ills and evil, or at least not in such proportions? Yet if that were possible, and if God could create a world in which there were no ills, less ills, or at least no ills that are not necessary for a greater good, how would it be possible still to believe that God is good, to believe in his benevolence,[10] omniscience, and omnipotence, to believe in God at all? If God is omnipotent, he could prevent suffering and ills. If he is omniscient, he would have to know how to prevent them. And if he is perfectly good, he ought to want to prevent them as well. But then, how can there be ills, suffering, and evil at all? Can God not prevent it? Or does he not want to prevent it? Then God cannot be omnipotent or omniscient or omnibenevolent. But if God were not some or all of these, would he still

---

This reflects the history of thinking evil(s), a history of the meaning attributed to the terms, whose refinements have also, as we will see, resulted in oversimplifying problems and reducing phenomena. That is why I summarily speak of *malum* and why I employ the German terms in a way that does not always conform to everyday usage. For me, the fundamental and more comprehensive category (that is, the category that allows us to articulate judgments of sense, truth, and value) is not "ill" but "evil." See Dalferth, *Das Böse*. [This translation generally renders the indefinite *Böses*—something that is evil—as "evil" and, to compensate for the absence, in English, of a direct correlate to *the good*, capitalizes *Evil* to render the definite *das Böse*.]

7. As Plantinga, "Supralapsarianism," 3, rightly notes.

8. See Baumeister, *Evil*; Card, *Atrocity Paradigm*; and Morton, *On Evil*. It is possible to describe phenomena grouped under this heading without knowing how they could be rendered comprehensible as "evil actions" based on evil intentions; see Sereny, *Cries Unheard*. One can also on purpose refrain from using the term to avoid blurring and thereby obfuscating responsibilities for inhuman atrocities; see Clendinnen, *Reading the Holocaust*. Or one can reduce the terms to their emotive and expressive aspect, their capacity for expressing our moral indignation or outrage; see Scarre, *After Evil*, 1–16.

9. See Ahern, *Problem of Evil*. To consider, like Streminger does (*Gottes Güte und die Übel*, 377–78), the phrase "problem of evil" an "inappropriate choice of words" because "the question concerning the origin of senseless suffering" arises "independently of theistic premises as well" is to miss the point. The phrase serves as a formula to convey that the reality of Evil/evils is a problem *for faith in God*. The problem here is not *ill*; the problem is that the fact of evil questions *traditional faith in God*.

10. The expressions "benevolence," or "goodness," and "being good" [*Güte* and *Gutsein*] are used interchangeably here. "Goodness" thus does not name a moral attribute but being-good in the comprehensive sense of *bonum*.

be God? In any case, what we thought would not exist and what might exist would not be what we meant by "God."

This, or some version of it, is how the theodicy problem is usually understood.[11] In that sense, however, it is a problem posed in very precise terms and with many preconditions. This becomes clear when we pay attention to how the problem is formulated and discussed in most cases, where it is presented in the form of various theodicy arguments that fall under the categories of *logical* (deductive or *a priori*) and *empirical* (inductive or *a posteriori*) arguments.[12] From the contradiction between series of propositions about God and series of propositions about ills, the former arguments conclude that God does not exist. They can be refuted apologetically by showing that the two series of propositions do not contradict each other. The latter argue that the facts of ills render it entirely improbable that God exists, and they can be refuted apologetically by citing plausible reasons for the reality and extent of ills in a world created by God, that is, by showing that there is no "gratuitous evil" the way Fred Berthold defines it, evil that is "not necessary or that is avoidable, in connection with God's attainment of his great goal."[13] In the first case, the theodicy problem would be solved by what Alvin Plantinga calls a "defense" that recuses the accusation of contradiction by demonstrating the possibility of reconciling both series of propositions. The second case, in turn, would require a theodicy in the stronger sense, which would have to cite reasons for which God permits ills and evil—and especially why he permits so many unnecessary ills and so much senseless evil—to exist in his creation.[14]

In both kinds of theodicy arguments, the theodicy problem is based on conditions that are not, or have not historically been, or not in this way, given in all contexts.[15] On the one hand, they presuppose a certain, far from self-evident conception of God as *ens perfectissimum*, which does not always and everywhere determine the semantics of the sign "God" or its equivalents, not even in the Christian tradition.[16]

---

11. See Streminger, *Gottes Güte und die Übel*; Kreiner, *Gott im Leid*; Gesang, *Angeklagt: Gott*; Weisberger, *Suffering Belief*, 19–55; and Hermanni, *Das Böse und die Theodizee*.

12. See Plantinga, "Probabilistic Argument from Evil," and "Epistemic Probability"; Alston, "Evidential Argument"; and Howard-Snyder, *Evidential Argument*.

13. Berthold, *God, Evil, and Human Learning*, 7.

14. See Plantinga, "Self-Profile."

15. See Oelmüller, *Die unbefriedigte Aufklärung*, who rightly points out that "theodicy is not an 'eternal' human need and no 'eternal' problem of reason" (194; see also 314n98a). See also Janssen, *Gott—Freiheit—Leid*, 1–16. Sarot, "Theodicy and Modernity," is right to note that the discussions grouped under the heading "theodicy" are not just different ways of engaging with the problem of theodicy, they engage with *different problems*. In modernity, "it is no longer God's nature or God's justice that is the question at issue, it is the existence of God and the truth of theism" (Sarot, "Theodicy and Modernity," 16). What is debated is no longer primarily a theological question of faith but a nontheological question *about* faith.

16. The claim that the problem of theodicy arises "necessarily," as Kreiner, *Gott im Leid*, 41, thinks, "as soon as one understands the semantics of speech about God," is true only against the background of a *very specific* semantics of "God." This applies not just in Christianity but in Islam as well. Compare, for example, Eric L. Ormsby's elaborations in *Theodicy in Islamic Thought* with Navid Kermani's reminder, in *The Terror of God*, of Islam's mystical tradition.

On the other hand, they also claim a certain, not self-evident view of Evil insofar as they assume that it is possible to name a sufficient reason for why everything that is and is being experienced is thus and not otherwise when it could, without contradicting itself, be otherwise. To inquire into evil this way is to assume that it is a *contingent* phenomenon that may occur (because it does in fact occur) but—under the given circumstances or in general—does not have to occur, that could also not be. This conception has not been held at all times and in all places by all people, not even in the Christian tradition.

Third, finally, it raises a certain, not self-evident spectrum of questions that do not pose themselves for everyone who thinks about the ills of the world, that not even pose themselves necessarily for believers confronted with obscure ills and incomprehensible evil. Not always and not everywhere do believers facing ills ask themselves whether these can be reconciled with their conception of God or whether their conception of God can be reconciled with the reality of ills. Most of the time, the experience of ills leads them to cry out for God, to plead for help, to complain about what they are suffering, to accuse a God whose help they had hoped for in vain, to ask what they have done to deserve such ills, to reproach God with abandoning and forgetting them. They seek help and a way out of evil, and for this they turn to God or address their protest, complaint, or accusation to God.[17] But they do not attempt first of all to understand or to show whether and, if yes, to what extent what they believe about God can coherently be reconciled with what they experience. The challenge they face is first of all a practical and existential, not a theoretical, logical, or epistemic, challenge.

Only when these practical-existential religious reactions to ills experienced are reflected on, when their preconditions, contents, and consequences are thought through and thought further, only, that is, in theological and philosophical reflection does a set of questions begin to develop that resembles the problem of theodicy.[18] But theological

17. See Roth, "Theodicy of Protest."

18. That is why I cannot entirely agree with Walter Kern's claim that the "problematic word theodicy is relatively modern" while the "problem at issue" is an "age-old" one (Kern, "Theodizee," 113). What is articulated in the theodicy problem is not and has not always and everywhere been identical with the "problem at issue." Marcel Sarot acknowledges this difference, yet he underestimates its import when he argues that it possible to use the term in ancient, medieval, and modern contexts because it is used vaguely and in a wide sense anyway (Sarot, "Theodicy and Modernity," 25–26). The "problematic word theodicy" can of course be used in a sense different from its modern meaning. Yet the price usually paid for this extension is the loss of its precise historical sense. A prominent example is the wide conception of theodicy Max Weber articulates in his sociology of religion: "theodicy" designates every attempt at rendering suffering and ills rationally comprehensible (Weber, *Economy and Society*, II.VI.viii.518–29; see also *Religiöse Gemeinschaften*, 290–301, and *The Protestant Ethic and the Spirit of Capitalism*). Yet this does not suffice, for example, for giving "theodicy" a sense that would be applicable to the way both monotheistic and Indian religions, for example, are dealing with suffering and ills, as Gananath Obeyesekere has shown. He suggests an alternative definition: "when a religion fails logically to explain human suffering or fortune in terms of its system of beliefs, we can say that a theodicy exists" (Obeyesekere, "Theodicy, Sin and Salvation," 11). Wendy Doniger makes a similar point (Doniger, *Origins of Evil in Hindu Mythology*, 1–2). Yet these attempts are extensions that remain beholden, precisely, to the way the classical concept of theodicy brackets together experience and rational reflection: while they do not insist on the idea of God as a necessary referential horizon, they do not abandon the claim that what is at stake are *rational explanations* for existential problems. What I attempt to do is to take the exactly inverse path, to hold on to the detour via God (and, to this extent, to focus on Jewish, Christian, and Muslim traditions), but to understand this detour not as an attempt at rational explanation but as a rational effort

reflection, too, can take paths that differ from those that have led to the problem of theodicy. It does not have to limit itself to thinking through the reconcilability or irreconcilability of the fact of ills with a given conception of God. It can also begin earlier or at a deeper level and ask *how God is to be understood and thought if the world is the way it is experienced.* Does the fact of ills teach us that we think incorrectly when we think God, because there is not and there cannot be such a thing (as the atheistic solution of the problem of theodicy would have it), or that we think God incorrectly and have to learn to think him differently (as the theological conclusion would be)? In that case, the primary problem for thought is not the *reconcilability* of a conception of God with the experience of ills but the *conception of God* itself.[19]

7. What This Book Is About

These are some of the reasons why the title of this study refers neither to "problem of evil" in the sense of the problem of theodicy nor simply to extreme forms of sociopathic perversion, inhuman atrocities, repulsive cruelties, and disgusting acts of inhumanity,[20] whose mere description exceeds the limits of what can be endured because they can no longer meaningfully be situated on a scale of what is more or less bad.[21] Even if many of them are no longer comprehensible, we cannot ignore how blurry the lines are that in human life separate the unimaginable from the inadvertently or intentionally repulsive, the undignified, and the irrational. There is no lower limit here that we could not fall below, no limit that is not in fact transgressed in all too many cases every single day.[22]

---

to orient oneself in life given the reality of evil.

19. As Johannes Baptist Metz has rightly seen. He emphasizes that the concern is exclusively with "the question of how we are to speak of God at all, given the abysmal history of suffering of the world, of 'his' world. This, to my mind, is 'the' question of theology; theology must neither eliminate nor overanswer it. It is 'the' eschatological question, the question for which theology does not elaborate an answer that would reconcile everything but for which it seeks, each time anew, a language to render the question unforgettable" (Metz, "Theodizee-empfindliche Gottesrede," 82–83). Yet it does not follow that this question must remain only a question and can never lead to any answers, even if these answers in turn can become stale and problematic and thus enjoin us to raise the question once more.

20. That is, the deeds of "nightmare people" such as serial killers (Ted Bundy, Jeffrey Dahmer, Harold Shipman, or Armin Meiwes, the "Rotenburg cannibal"), terrorists (bin Laden, Tamil Tigers, ETA, IRA), tyrants (Hitler, Stalin, Pol Pot, Saddam Hussein), or secret police (Beria), but also of organized crime (mafia), state terrorism (Red Khmer), and ethnic massacres (Rwanda, Bosnia). See Norris, *Serial Killers*; Baumeister, *Evil*, 251–81; Seltzer, *Serial Killers*; and Morton, *On Evil*, 69–103.

21. As Wolf Krötke, "Das Böse als Absurdes," 66, rightly points out, "it is characteristic that on a purely linguistic level, there is no comparison" of 'evil'": "'Evil, more evil, the most evil' sounds ridiculous *per se*. Where there is evil at all, it is unsurpassibly evil." But this does not exclude that among these there are cases, forms, and figures of Evil that, for those afflicted or those observing, are even more extreme than others.

22. The examples from everyday madness are legion and reach the extremes Marguerite Shuster quotes from a report concerning the funeral industry: "In Orlando, Florida, the ashes of a firework expert were blasted with Roman candles into the night sky. The cremated remains of a Marvel Comic editor were mixed with ink and made into a comic book. Villa Delirium Delft Works made cremains into commemorative plates, and another firm (Eternal Reefs, Inc.) offered to turn ashes into 'ecologically sound' coral reefs" (Shuster, *Fall and Sin*, 254n54).

Human beings are not only the beings who discovered dignity and who make an effort to protect it. They are also the ones capable like no one else of debasing other human beings and the ones who time and again humiliate others in terrible and in banal ways. There is no need to recall the great symbols of terror and shame of the twentieth century. Our everyday present is full of behaviors that are so absurd that they ought to provoke indignation or horror—but that happens, if at all, only very rarely. There is no need to look for evidence of experiences of *malum* in human life. The evidence is everywhere around us.

All this will be discussed here but it does not by itself constitute what this book is about. Its title does not refer to a set of questions that would be asked primarily by a philosophy of theodicy or exclusively by a philosophy of morality. Instead, it refers to a *theological set of problems*, namely the *symbolic strategies of religious and particularly of a Christian orientation of life for elucidating experiences of* malum *by going back to God and for elucidating God by going back to experiences of* malum, *that is, for understanding evil with reference to God and God with reference to evil.*[23] Putting the question this way brings up a set of problems I will now briefly outline, which also gives me occasion to lay out some of the analytical categories I will employ throughout the book.

23. Unless explicitly stated otherwise, "theological" in this book always means "Christian-theological."

B

Experiences of *Malum*

IN EVERY HUMAN LIFE there are events that are experienced as *malum*. In innumerable ways, life is harmed, inhibited, disrupted, and destroyed by what it encounters; life's habitual continuities, familiarities, organizations, and structures of meaning are disrupted and ended by the intrusion of the senseless and the irrational; moreover, there are no continuities being prepared, no new beginnings opened up, nor does it become possible to pick up on what came before. The kaleidoscope of evil in human life is infinitely varied, but it always harms and destroys life in a senseless and irrational manner. Evil is not only, negatively, the other of the habitual, the familiar, the ordered, and the meaningful; it manifests itself destructively as a negating negation that does not open up constructive horizons of understanding and of the future. Evil destroys without sense, aim, or reason, and because it harms and destroys senselessly, it is evil.

1. Designations of Evil

I speak of *experiences of malum* whenever that which happens to life is experienced as and assessed to be a senseless infliction of harm, obstruction, disruption, or destruction of life. I use the Latin expression *malum* to avoid, at least initially, the common but oversimplifying distinction, in German, between evil and ills [*Bösem und Übeln*] and to prevent prematurely limiting the discussion of evil to moral evil, that is, to evil actions with evil intentions.[1] If needed, all of this can be inscribed into the meaning of *malum*, but the experiences of *malum* in life are more varied and more disparate than these traditional distinctions suggest.

And yet it was this variety and disparity that led Kant to propose a terminology which became dominant in German-language philosophy and theology. In his discussion of the old rules, *nihil appetimus, nisi sub ratione boni* and *nihil aversamur, nisi sub ratione mali*—"We desire nothing except under the form of the good" and "Nothing is avoided except under the form of the bad"—Kant in the *Critique of Practical Reason* points to an irresolvable ambivalence in the Latin. Is what is meant really a turn toward

---

1. On what follows, see my *Das Böse*. The word *böse* goes back to the Old High German *bôsi*, from medieval Latin *bausia*, "slight" or "bad." Its etymology, however, is not entirely clear; see Kluge and Mitzka, *Etymologisches Wörterbuch*, s.v. "böse."

the morally good and away from the morally evil, or do these rules merely say that we seek what is agreeable to us and avoid what is disagreeable? He continues:

> The German language has the good fortune to possess expressions which do not allow this difference to be overlooked. For that which the Latin denominates with a single word, *bonum*, it has two very different concepts and equally different expressions as well: for *bonum* it has *das Gute* [the good] and *das Wohl* [well-being], for *malum* it has *das Böse* [Evil] and *das Übel* [ill-being] (or *Weh* [woe]), so that there are two very different appraisals of an action depending upon whether we take into consideration the *good* and *evil* of it or our *well-being* and *woe* (ill-being).[2]

In Kant, this cogent distinction nonetheless comes with two particular emphases. On the one hand, the distinction between Evil and ills is a distinction of moral philosophy: *evil* and *good* are moral categories, *ill* and *well* in turn are determinations of our sense experience that designate what is agreeable or disagreeable to us, whatever its moral value may be. The Good and Evil are thus rigorously distinct from, even the opposite of, pleasure and displeasure. On the other hand, Kant determines what deserves to be called evil or good strictly from the perspective of the moral agent. Evil is what is done out of evil or not good intentions, and good is only what is done thanks to individual willing being determined by the universal good will. When we take the phenomena into account, both emphases turn out to be problematic restrictions. We neither experience as evil only what is done to us out of evil or not good intentions, nor is the important distinction between moral and non-moral questions necessarily to be associated with Kant's distinction between sensibility and understanding (or reason).

This suggests that we not follow Kant's terminology. Responsibility for evil deeds does in fact lie with the perpetrators, and with them alone. But what deserves to be called *evil* is to be determined with a view not to the perpetrators but to the victims. Everything that injures, humiliates, and degrades human beings, that creates unnecessary suffering, that senselessly harms and destroys life, that withholds and annihilates possibilities for life, is evil. Everything that counteracts it is good. I therefore use the expressions "evil/ Evil" (as guiding or main category) and "ill" (as concretization of evil) or "good/the good/Good" and "goods" in the wide sense of the Latin *malum* and *bonum* or the Greek *kakon* and *agathon*, which are not from the outset limited to moral phenomena. Instead, I employ the semiotic distinction between types and tokens when, on the one hand, I distinguish between *Evil* (*das Böse*, the type) and *an evil* (*ein Böses*, the token), which I also refer to by the name *ill* (Übel), and, on the other hand, make correlative distinctions between *evils of a specific kind* (type), an illness like asthma, say, and *individual cases of such evils* (token), that is, a particular person's asthma or an asthma attack. The destructive power of evil is not limited to any specific area of life; evil can occur in all of them. Hence the possibility of designating evils linguistically and phenomenally in a greatly differentiated manner, according to the occasions when life is destructively affected and when suffering from such destructions is perceived and experienced as an evil.

2. Kant, *Critique of Practical Reason*, in *Practical Philosophy*, 133–271, here 187–88 (AA 5:59–60); the translations in brackets take up but modify Mary J. Gregor's notes. References to Kant's works are to the Cambridge translations, followed by the standard pagination of the Academy edition (AA).

2. Happening, Experiencing, and Understanding

Human life[3] becomes what it is through what *happens to* it, through what it feels and perceives, that is, through what it *experiences*, what *in experiencing* it makes of itself, what, *in thinking*, it discovers to be real and possible, what, *desiring* and *willing*, it strives for, what, *in communicating* and *acting* in living with others, it actualizes or not. *Happenings* are events from the perspective of those affected by them; *events* are happenings from the perspective of third parties that abstract from the point of view of those affected.[4] *Events* entertain temporal relations with other events, that is, *earlier than*, *later than*, and *simultaneous with*; they have causes and effects; they derive from events and lead to other events and thereby form the ramified and superimposed event series of the empirical world.[5] *Happenings*, on the other hand, are *experienced*; they structure temporal experience according to *past*, *present*, and *future*.[6] They lead to *experiences* in which they are semiotically fashioned and understood in a specific manner—if, that is, they do not end the life they happen to.[7]

That which *happens to* a life affects it in such a way that life becomes what it was not before and comes to be in a way it was not before because it determines the semiotic processes in which and through which life takes place on all levels, and determines them in such a way that every continuation becomes a response and reaction to it (the pathic dimension of life).[8] It *has the experience* [*erlebt*] of what happens to it by having its emotional situation and cognitive conditions changed and characterized in a specific way (experiential dimension of life). It *makes the experience* [*erfährt*] of what it experiences by taking a stance toward this experience—accepting some experiences, refusing others—and thereby appropriating it, that is, it understands both what is experienced and

3. On the concept of life employed here and in what follows, see Dalferth, *Die Wirklichkeit des Möglichen*, 6–46. Eilert Herms's volume *Leben* presents the wide range of aspects of current life discourses.

4. It is possible to speak of events and happenings from a third-party perspective. Yet to say "That has happened to him" is not only to say that an event took place in that person's life: it also says that this event, from this person's perspective and in this particular situation, is of determinative significance.

5. On the temporal problems raised here and in what follows, see Dalferth, *Becoming Present*, 52–85.

6. Happenings are always that from out of which our own experiencing is determined such that our experience can be seen as a response, of varying semiotic intensity, to what has happened to us.

7. Happenings are events in a life that are semiotically processed in a specific manner in experience, namely by constructing that which has happened as a something, constructing it as a particular experience that in responding to what happens to it is (co-)determined in light of what happens to it: each of us experiences what happens to us *in our own way*. This way follows from our response to the happening within a particular life situation (that is, in the context of the individual characterization of a life always already characterized by what happens to it), which in turn leads to a construction of what happens to us that is tinged by and modulated according to the experience codetermined by this happening. Each of us experiences what happens to us in our own way, and similarly each of us understands what happens to us differently and in our own way—in the pre-verbal domain no less than in the verbal. Every understanding, therefore, is irrevocably individual, and every shared understanding is no more than a momentary nodal point within different individual cognitive processes. See chapter 5 of Dalferth, *Auf dem Weg der Ökumene*.

8. The pathic is thus not only a dimension of the physiological but of all levels of life. There are forms of *pathos*, of being determined by happenings, that characterize thinking and acting as well, in enthusiasm (in the Platonic sense of the word), for example, or in being provided with possibilities and occasions for action.

itself in a specific way (experience dimension of life) by making distinctions concerning what is experienced (constitution of the object of experience) and distinguishing between what is experienced and itself (differentiation of object and subject). Whereas it is determined in experiencing, life in making experiences also always determines itself by distinguishing between what it is becoming (experiencing) and the one who is becoming (the self), thereby rendering itself capable of constructing this experiencing as a response to what is happening to it and the self as the active pole of this response. It *understands* that of which it makes the experience insofar that in making experiences, it thematizes both itself and that of which it makes the experience in semiotic processes (understands them as *something*) and determines them within the horizon of linguistic processes against the background of other possible determinations as *this* and as nothing else (understands something *as something*). Taking recourse to a third element (the sign), it thus establishes a distance toward itself and its making an experience such that it can or, as the case may be, cannot understand its experiences (understanding objects) and itself in making experiences (understanding the self) in a specific way. And it *thinks* what it understands by reflecting on its understanding of that which it has and makes experiences of, by determining, in communicating with others, what is real and what is possible about it, and it thereby explores, against the background of what it desires and what it wills, options for actions that will allow it, in its life situations, to behave in a nuanced and purpose-oriented manner.

The process of life thus constantly takes place between the poles of *pathos, logos,* and *ethos,*[9] between a pathic being-determined by happenings to which one cannot react (*pathos*) and an active self-determination in the face of such happenings, through the life activities of *logos* and *ethos,* activities that are undertaken by the self (having and making experiences, understanding, thinking, desiring, willing) or oriented toward an environment (communicating, acting). While in happening and experiencing, the passive moment is preponderant, the active moment dominates, in varying intensity, in making experiences, understanding, thinking, desiring, willing, and acting.

3. On the Analysis of Evil

This allows and enjoins us to give nuanced descriptions and to consider the specific interplay of happening, experience, understanding, and thinking in each experience of *malum.* Thus, for example, an illness (a happening), which a medical diagnosis (a third) enjoins us to think of as a consequence of smoking (an understanding), is also experienced as an evil (an experience). If there were no happening, toward which we cannot not take a stance, there would be nothing to be experienced as *malum.* But understanding a happening (*How did it come to this illness?*) does not at the same time mean understanding the experience of *malum* (*Why was it me who contracted this* malum?), nor does it mean understanding what makes this experience a *malum* (*What makes a happening an experience of a* malum?) or what a *malum* is and how it can be understood (*What is*

9. See Stoellger, *Passivität aus Passion,* which takes up and develops Aristotle's distinction.

meant by "malum"?). All these questions remain open when it has become clear what illness we are dealing with and how it could have come about.

There are thus at least three levels on which experiences of *malum* can be described and analyzed.[10] These are the levels of specific *happenings*; of the *experience* of these happenings; and of *understanding* these experiences: what happens to a life (happening) is experienced by this life as something specific because it constructs what has happened to it (experience) semiotically, and it understands the experience as an experience of a *malum* because and insofar the happening thus experienced is understood in light of a specific understanding of *malum* as damaging, interfering with, injuring, exterminating life, possibilities of life, quality of life, or life-time. *What* is experienced (happening), that *as which* it is experienced (experience), *how* it is experienced (*malum*) and *through which* it is thus experienced (understanding of *malum*) are therefore distinct dimensions of *malum* phenomena that can be analytically distinguished when we approach these phenomena hermeneutically.

There are complex questions to be asked on each of these levels, questions concerning the causes of happenings, the cultural determinations of experiences, the reasons for their being understood as *malum*, and the meaning of the concept of *malum* at issue in each case. Experiences of *malum* have to be questioned in all these respects if we want to understand them, and what may suffice as an answer in one respect may not readily suffice in another: What has happened to us, and why has it happened to us? As what is it experienced, and why is it experienced this way? How is it understood, and why? Through what and in what sense is it understood this way? All of these questions can be asked in a meaningful manner. Yet while the first questions call for scientific and cultural explanations, the others aim at shedding light on evaluations and questions of meaning, which are closely tied to questions of orientation. People who fall gravely ill usually ask not only what has led to this, what their illness consists in, and what can or cannot be done to cure or alleviate it. They also seek to find out how they can live with this evil and how they can—or how they can no longer—understand themselves in light of this evil. They seek not just objective explanations; they confront questions of meaning and orientation of practical relevance for life.

These distinctions allow us to give a more precise outline of a series of points to be considered in grappling with experiences of *malum*.

4. Reality and Illusion

Distinguishing between *happenings* and *experiences* makes it possible to thematize the problem of erroneous or illusory experiences of *malum*. Where something not based on a happening is made out to be an experience, (subjective) experiencing can certainly not be denied; what can be denied, however, is that it expresses something that would grant insight into the makeup of the world in which the one experiencing lives. Experiences

---

10. Paul Weingartner's objectivist theodicy in *Evil: Different Kinds of Evil in the Light of a Modern Theodicy* provides an exemplary case of what happens when these different aspects or respects of the problem are not being distinguished and ills are treated as a certain amount of events or conditions, consistently ignoring the phenomenon's *for-* and *of-*relations.

one has [*Erlebnisse*] can be called experiences one makes [*Erfahrungen*] only insofar as they process happenings. We are thus always justified to inquire into the happening at the basis of an experience, to critically ask whether the corresponding experiencing really deserves being called "experience" [*Erfahrung*].

Having experiences in this narrower sense, too, can have the characteristics of *malum*, and many afflictions confirm this point: a leg amputated many years ago may still hurt, and phantom limb pain is an evil, too. Precisely for appropriately thematizing and, as the case may be, treating such *malum*, an exact identification and description is indispensable. Where it is clear that we are dealing with an experiencing not based on a happening, we will have to seek out different causes for what is being experienced than in the other case: causes that lie in the experiencing itself or in the ones who are experiencing, not in what they experience or in the world in which they experience what they experience. This cannot be read off the intensity of suffering or the evil experienced: the intensity of the pain, the magnitude of the suffering, the extent of the evil experienced do not indicate whether their cause lies in something else or with others. That always has to be established first. And that is why the question concerning the happening is always to be asked and why it is never superfluous either for those affected or for those who seek to help them.

5. Experiencing Evil

A further problem consists in understanding that which is experienced, in understanding it as *malum*. Those affected by a happening may experience and understand it as a *malum* while others may not. And conversely, that which happens to and is experienced by others may be assessed to be a *malum* without they themselves understanding it that way.[11] We thus have to distinguish not only between *happening, experience,* and *understanding* but also between the *understanding of those affected themselves* and the *understanding of others*. From an analytical point of view, therefore, experiences of *malum* always have the following structure: (1) *something is experienced by somebody*, be it as the experience of a happening that can be described as an event affecting the ones experiencing it, be it as having an experience not based on a happening in this sense; (2) this event *is experienced and understood as something*; and (3) that which is thus experienced and understood *is assessed or evaluated as a malum*. Analytically, we can thus always ask about

1. *that which is happening*, which is suffered by someone and processed in an experience of *malum* (*what?*);

2. *the ones affected*, those who suffer and experience it (*for whom?*);

11. That is one of the reasons for the fallacy that holds that ills and evil are merely "a subjective response or a reification of experiences and responses to negativities in the world . . . good and evil are purely subjective." This view neglects the power and fatefulness that characterizes Evil. As Tyron Inbody rightly points out, "*Evil* is a destructive, overpowering menace, an enemy to be resisted" (Inbody, *Transforming God*, 24), not just a subjective evaluation of an objective state of affairs. The fact that others do not regard what happens to me as an evil does not imply that I could do the same. It may be looked at differently, but under the circumstances, I cannot look at it differently.

3. how they understand it (*as what?*);

4. *that through which* they understand it this way (*through what?*);

5. how it is assessed or evaluated (*how?*);

6. *by means of what* it is thus assessed or evaluated (*by means of what?*); and

7. those who thus assess it (*by whom?*).

These questions can be grouped into two sets (1–4 and 5–7) focusing on two different problematic poles. In respect to the first, experiences of *malum* are considered as *experiences*; in respect to the second, as experiences *of malum*. These two aspects are distinct only analytically and hermeneutically. Distinguishing them, however, is important because they give rise to different problems.

As something that *happens* and is experienced in a specific way, experiences of *malum* are embedded in nexuses of causally connected events that can be investigated and explained without such investigations and explanations for all that already accounting for the experience of *malum*. As *experiences* of what happens (2 and 3), they are experiences made in the experiential and practical contexts of particular cultures, in which traditional prelinguistic, linguistic, and supralinguistic modes of understanding and means of interpretation are available (4) with whose help and in whose light something that happens (e.g., an infection) is experienced in a specific sense (as an illness) and understood in a specific sense (as a specific illness). But that does not yet thematize them as experiences of *malum*. They are conceived of as such only when one also considers the adjudication or evaluation as *malum* of that which happens and is experienced in a specific way (5 and 6), that is, when one is talking not only about event, facts, and experiences but about their evaluation and one's attitude toward them as well.

This entails not only an explanation of how this assessment comes about (6), that is, an account of the adjudicative horizon within which the evaluation is made. We also have to distinguish between, on the one hand, the assessment concerning the experience and what is experienced made by those affected themselves and, on the other hand, assessments and evaluation by others (7). The first is the *current evaluation* by those affected from the perspective of the first person, singular or plural ("This is a *malum* for me/for us"), the second a *normative* evaluation from a third-person perspective ("That is a *malum*"). The two can but do not have to coincide. Those affected may have good reasons for assessing something to be a *malum* that we do not see as such, and we, too, for many good reasons, may consider a *malum* what those affected themselves regard differently.

6. Describing and Evaluating

When we want to engage meaningfully with phenomena of Evil, it is important to keep the questions listed above distinct. Explaining something that happens and causes pain and suffering (1–4) does not yet explain the *malum* thereby experienced (5–7). Hatred, hunger, rage, rape, war, floods, earthquakes, unemployment, prostitution, etc., have physiological, psychological, social, historical, economic, political, geological, physical, or chemical causes. But no explanation of this kind shows the phenomenon in question to be a *malum* unless one adds that the world would be better without it than it is with it, and that what could be also ought to be.[12] Conversely, an occurrence like an earthquake or a rape is not explained by naming reasons for considering them a *malum*. The reasons for which a rape is assessed to be evil do not explain why it has taken place; they only clarify why it is considered to be evil. And knowing why it has happened does not provide reasons for it constituting a *malum*. Historical, empirical, economical, or political explanations of evil, therefore, are never sufficient. When they succeed, they tell us why what happened, happened, and perhaps they also tell us why the ones affected experience and describe it as *malum*. But they do not tell us anything about how we are to assess what has happened or about how we are to assess human life in light of what has happened here.

There is thus not only a difference between *giving reasons for* (naming reasons) and *explaining* (discovering causes) but also a difference between *describing and explaining* on the one hand and *assessing and evaluating* on the other. In order to orient ourselves successfully in life, we need both the necessary knowledge and the appropriate value orientations. Neither are always obvious; they have to be explored and investigated. It is usually a matter of controversy which knowledge is relevant and which valuations are appropriate in a given case. But it is not a matter of controversy that knowing what is the case does not yet tell us how to assess this case and what attitude to adopt toward it, nor that knowing how to assess something does not explain why it is happening or has happened.

Assessments (with respect to *what* one has or makes an experience of) and evaluations (with respect to *how* one has or makes this experience) can be distinguished analytically, yet they do not bring out different phenomena (*being* assessed as true or false and *values* assessed as good or evil) but different perspectives on the same phenomena. Experiences of *malum* have descriptive and evaluative components because something is always experienced not only as something but also in a specific way. The first can be articulated as an objective judgment ("*Such and such* is evil"), the second a value judgment ("Such and such *is evil*"). But that does not mean that a *malum* is given only when such an evaluative judgment is made cognitively; rather, such a judgment can be made truthfully only because that which one has or makes the experience of is always experienced and judged within an evaluative perspective. The perception already of what is being experienced is evaluative, not just the judgment about it. For nothing is perceived without being perceived in a specific way, and nothing is lived without being lived in a specific way.[13]

12. This is why it is not enough to determine discourse about Evil only as emotive or expressive, as "an expressive or emotivist way, a mode of registering our moral or humanitarian horror, shock or outrage," as Scarre, *After Evil*, 13, does. That is not only a one-sided emphasis on a single aspect of a complex state of affairs, it also underestimates how intensely cognitive and emotive aspects intertwine in the perception of Evil; see Wynn, *Emotional Experience and Religious Understanding*, esp. ch. 4, 89–122.

13. The analytical distinction between a being-perspective and a value-perspective on experiences of *malum* and *bonum* must thus not be reified in an ontological difference between being and value, between, on the hand, true/false and, on the other, good/evil. The fact that these components or aspects can be distinguished in phenomena says nothing about the structure of these phenomena *per se* but only

7. Factual and Normative Evaluation

There are several reasons why the distinction between the first-person perspective of those affected (2) and the third-person perspective of others (7) is important. It is one thing to be affected, another to describe evil or to think about evil. Of course those affected by evil can think within their first-person perspective about what they experience. But that does not annul the difference between their view of their situation and the view others have on it. There are cases in which this difference plays practically no role because everyone will consider what is happening to be evil. But there are cases in which those affected and involved do not notice or do not want to notice that they are implicated in a *malum*, or in which the ones who assess what is happening as a *malum* fail to capture the experience of those affected. For good reasons, we consider slavery to be an evil, even if slaveholders do not see it that way, and for good reasons, we consider it to be evil when men beat their wives even when the women affected do not complain.[14]

It is thus necessary critically to distinguish between the factual perception and evaluation of situations by those affected or by others on the one hand and their normative evaluation in light of a specific conception of Evil on the other. It is not always and exclusively the view of those affected that alone decides how something is to be appropriately assessed and evaluated. In turn, it is inappropriate to ignore the view of those affected and to judge what happens to them from our particular point of view alone. When we consider to be a *malum* what they do not see to be such or the other way around, the reasons for the diverging points of view have to be communicated if we want the other to understand us, and that presupposes acknowledging the other's point of view.

That is why normative evaluations refer more clearly to explicitly explainable reasons than current evaluations do, reasons that allow for insight into why in certain cases something is judged to be a *malum* contrary to the point of view of those affected. Normative evaluations are always linked with conceptions of evaluation (conceptions of Evil), which for their part may be controversial as well. In many cases, the debate is not just about assessing and evaluating a phenomenon: it simultaneously concerns the question whether the normative conception(s) being marshalled are tenable and persuasive.

Often, however, it would be wrong to regard such controversies only as normative controversies about the evaluative points of view that are, or are considered to be, relevant in a given case. Because these evaluations (assessments) are only analytically distinct from the perceptions (experiences) to which they refer, it is usually a matter of controversy not just how a certain phenomenon or happening is to be evaluated and assessed but also as what it is to be perceived or experienced. When the inhumane situation of another human being is not perceived to be such, its evaluation too is going to be different. But the difference does not have to be that some consider slavery to be positive while others do not; both sides may subscribe to the same normative conceptions yet come to different judgments because they perceive the situation differently. Where an inhumane situation is not perceived to be such, the same value convictions will not lead to the expected evaluation because the situation is not perceived to be one in which

---

quoad nos, that is, it does not differentiate them as such, only the way we look at them.

14. See Thomas, *Vessels of Evil*; Omolade, "Faith Confronts Evil."

such an evaluation applies. Recognizing the inhumanity of slavery thus requires not only a change in value attitudes ("Slavery is an evil") but also a different perception of the situation ("These human beings are being treated inhumanely"). The controversy is not just a normative controversy about value attitudes but a descriptive controversy about appropriate perceptions of situations.[15]

8. Phenomena and Conceptions of Evil

All this addresses a further problem that must figure in any systematic hermeneutic engagement with experiences of *malum*. It is one thing to describe *something as evil*, another thing to define *evil as something*. The first is a process of assessment or evaluation, it manifests itself in an evaluation ("*That is something evil*"); the second is a reflexive process of definition and develops a view or conception of evil ("*evil is such and such*"), which is not itself evaluative but explains how and according to what aspects something is evaluated, within the horizon of this conception, to be evil, or how and under which aspects what is thus evaluated is understood. The description of evil (describing *something as evil*) leads to the question concerning the phenomena that are considered or are to be considered as evil and thus leads to a description and classification of *mala*. The definition of evil (defining *evil as something*) leads to the question concerning what evil is taken to be and thus leads to naming and defining *malum*. Both are evidently connected, because a description of evil (*mala*) presupposes an understanding of Evil (*malum*), and because a definition of *malum* that would not allow for a description of *mala* would be of little help. And yet the description of hunger, illness, suffering, death, catastrophes, wars, disasters, accidents, etc., that are experienced as evils (*mala*) is not yet a definition of Evil (*malum*). And conversely, naming and defining evil is not yet a description of ills.

To do both not just by chance and arbitrarily but in a way that can be justified to others, we must name criteria that allow us to identify evil as evil and ills as ills.[16] These always occur in contingent experiential and practical contexts and are tied to understandings of Evil that are guided by experience and can be systematized in *conceptions of Evil*. Conceptions of Evil do not enumerate phenomena considered to be evil but develop an understanding of evil; they do not describe something as evil but define evil as something. That can take different forms, and it has been done in different ways in the philosophical and theological tradition. But only insofar as we are moving within the horizon of an understanding of evil are we able to describe and evaluate something as evil, and the attempt at systematically developing the understanding of evil that guides

15. The descriptive and evaluative components of experiences of ills are thus not to be thought simply in an additive manner, as if an evaluative perspective were added, externally, to a cognitively determinate content. Rather, the phenomenon understood to be (an) evil is perceived differently from the outset, in light of a different point of view; it is seen as a different phenomenon. On the problem of integrating cognitive and affective components in perceptions of situations and phenomena, see Deigh, "Cognitivism in the Theory of Emotions," 840–42; Goldie, *Emotions*, 59–61; and Wynn, *Emotional Experience and Religious Understanding*, 100–102.

16. See Petersen, *Das Böse in uns*, 13–29.

us or others constitutes the analytical-hermeneutical or systematical-constructive work on a conception of evil.[17]

And yet, knowing as what evil is or has been understood is not to be confused with understanding evil that affects us. Being familiar with conceptions of Evil is something different from understanding evil that overtakes us. We thus have to distinguish carefully between being epistemically versed and being capable of existentially orienting oneself.

9. The Aporia of Experiences of *Malum*

In every human life, there are happenings that are experienced as *malum*. Every human life is thus also familiar with the aporia such experiences lead to; namely, we cannot understand what cannot be understood, and yet we can scarcely avoid trying to come to an understanding of what cannot be understood.

On the one hand, it is characteristic of experiences of *malum* that they do not have any sense, and they defy and avoid any understanding: even if we know everything needed to explain a grave illness, the questions, by no means devoid of sense, asked by those affected—*Why this? Why me? Why now?*—remain unanswered, because our explanations account only for the type and occurrence of the disease but not for how those affected by it (can) understand themselves in the face of the illness, what stance they ought to assume toward it, and how they will be able to live with it.

On the other hand, human life, as a relationship that relates to itself in an understanding, is inexorably confronted with the task of establishing a meaningful relationship to such experiences and to deal with them concretely in practical everyday life. Yet when we try to do this directly and continue with habitual processes of understanding, it is precisely the absurdity of such experiences that comes to the fore. Along the slope of the process that leads from something happening to having and making experiences, to understanding, reflecting, and communicating, experiences of *malum* turn out to be experiences of the senseless and the incomprehensible that condemn our efforts at understanding them to failure.

This does not put an end to our questioning, but questions of the kind indicated do not serve to obtain further objective explanations. They ask questions of sense that are to orient our lives.[18] Explanations and questions of sense both pertain to dealing with experiences of *malum*. Explanations alone do not yet answer questions of sense; questions of sense, for their part, may presuppose and include explanations, but they cannot substitute for them. Yet not only is the relationship between the two kinds of questions asymmetrical, moreover, in dealing with experience of *malum*, we cannot dispense with either one. Asking questions of explanation, and the way they are asked, points to a horizon of orientation in which these questions are assigned relevance for practical life: knowing why and in what way a certain illness has come about is important when we seek to cure, alleviate, or, in other cases, avoid it. And questions of orientation, too, are

17. See Dalferth, *Das Böse*, ch. 1.

18. On the difference between objective questions, questions of action, conceptual questions, and questions of sense, see Dalferth, *Leiden und Böses*, 176–81.

sometimes answered all the better the more precisely we are familiar with the causes and forms of a phenomenon experienced as an ill. In both instances, understanding may reach its limit. We do not know what has happened and why. And we do not understand why precisely this has happened to this person at this point in time. We do not understand the happening at issue. And we do not understand the *malum* thereby experienced.

10. Hermeneutic Tools

We habitually respond to problems of explanation by intensifying our investigation. Yet that alone will not help us advance in the case of questions of orientation, for what is at issue there is not additional knowledge but the stance to adopt toward this knowledge and how we can or ought to live with it. Here, hermeneutic reflection is helpful. As the art of the detour toward an understanding in the face of non- and malcomprehension, hermeneutics offers strategies of thinking to come closer to an understanding of experiences of *malum*. Three of these strategies in particular are worth highlighting.

The first strategy for rendering the incomprehensible comprehensible follows the rule of determining *something as something*. We are all familiar with this procedure. That dot in the sky can be defined *as an airplane*. When it comes closer, that might turn out to be incorrect because the phenomenon might turn out to be more adequately defined *as a bird* and, on a closer look, *as a stork*. We thus determine something by identifying it *as a something*, and we further determine this something by describing it *as something*. Such processes of determination are only possible because we are at a sufficient distance and yet refer to the phenomenon, and because we move within a (conventional) semiotic system that allows for such determinations *as . . . of* what we perceive.

This holds for dealing with experiences of *malum* as well. Those affected by evil must distance themselves from this experience and refer to it in a different way, that is, they must be able to identify and describe what has affected them. They must re-present to themselves what they have experienced in the form of signs, that is, presentify it *as something*, in order to be able to refer to it in an understanding and assessing manner. There is no understanding without such re-presentation in the form of signs, only an affect without distance that in practical life is expressed by their screaming or falling silent. To be able to understand what affects them, they have to distinguish it from themselves and refer to it by re-presenting it, in the form of signs, *as something*, that is, by *designating* it. This does not guarantee understanding it. But such designation is the necessary precondition for making it comprehensible for oneself and for others, for giving voice to it, for being able to articulate and describe it. As long as we do not know where the pain comes from and what triggers it, we are helplessly exposed to it, without distance. When we are able to give the pain a name and to name the illness, we can begin to engage with it.

This re-presenting does not always succeed directly, that is, by categorizing or inscribing something within an already familiar context. In such cases, we must take a detour, that is, we not only have to determine something as something but determine something *by means of something else* or *by referring it to a third*. This second procedure, too, is familiar from everyday practice. Our new neighbor may be entirely unknown to us, and we do not know what to make of him. But when our best friend greets him as his brother, the neighbor, *by means of this reference* as our best friend's brother, is, at the least, no longer entirely unknown. There is a great variety of such determinations of the unknown *via the detour of referring to a third*, when, for example, I recognize a book *as property of the library*, a car accident *as attempted murder*, an illness *as a reason for early retirement*. What may not be sufficiently intelligible when broached directly can become intelligible thanks to this detour via a third if and insofar as this third sheds a certain light on the unknown phenomenon to be understood.

In so doing, and this is the third strategy, we do not only *understand something as something by means of referring to something else*. I thereby also understand *myself* in light of something else. When it comes to understanding what is not understood or not intelligible, we cannot understand by taking a detour via a third without also in that detour understanding ourselves differently. This dialectic between *understanding something (as something by means of something)* and *understanding oneself (as something by means of something)* has time and again been noted in hermeneutics. It owes its importance to the fact that it makes processes of understanding immediately relevant to our behavior and our actions. When we consider someone as a friend, we also understand ourselves as a friend, and when we consider ourselves as someone's friend, we will behave in a certain way when an evil happens to this friend. We help friends, we offer hospitality to strangers (at least we used to), we avoid thieves, we support parents and children—normally. All these are not natural necessities but social conventions that deserve to be cherished as cultural assets because without them (or other conventions to play their role), it is hardly possible to humanly live together socially with other human beings. The *understanding of something* and its correlate *understanding of oneself* perform an immediately orienting function in the practical contexts in which human beings live together.

This correlation of understanding and understanding oneself applies in understanding experiences of *malum* as well: it is impossible to understand the evil one is affected by without correspondingly understanding oneself differently. If we ask not only *why* questions of explanation but also *why me* questions of orientation, we will not be satisfied by any answer that renders intelligible only the ill but not our situation in this ill. Orientation requires not just classifying a phenomenon in an intelligible context (ordering) but also correlating the one affected with the phenomenon in this context (situating). The process of understanding incomprehensible ill is thus always also a process of understanding oneself anew and in a different way—and be it by becoming entirely incomprehensible for oneself. I no longer know my way around—not only because I do not know what has happened to me but because I no longer know who I am to whom it has happened.

11. Religious Approaches to Experiences of *Malum*

Now, it is of course one thing to attempt understanding incomprehensible experiences of *malum* in the way just outlined and quite another thing to understand that there is nothing to understand there. Yet hermeneutically, there are no other paths possible or necessary for establishing a meaningful relation with the absurd and the nonsensical:

we have to take detours via intermediate figures that, on the one hand, distance us in a specific way from what has been experienced and, on the other, shed light on it and allow for perceiving, defining, and understanding or, precisely, not understanding it in a specific way.

In practical life, these intermediate figures may be chosen *ad hoc*, that is, be determined by the situation, be relevant, and enable understanding only in this situation, or they may provide culturally regulated ways of dealing with experiences of *malum* such as they are developed in medicine, law, politics, and religion. Religions do so by means of strategies that attempt, in a variety of ways, to tie the domains of the undefinable, inaccessible, chaotic, senseless, unavailable, incomprehensible, and uncontrollable back to the domains of rationally defined orders and meaningfully comprehensible structures, that is, to thematize them as the other and as the flipside of the meaningful, available, and controllable, a flipside that cannot be grasped for itself and as such.[19] In practical life, in worship, and in forms of thought, religions thus offer strategies for, together, living *with the uncontrollable in a controllable way*.[20]

This does not necessarily imply that we seek to make available that which is unavailable, beyond our control and influence. On the contrary, guiding others in living with the uncontrollable in a controllable way usually means helping them, in the face of the uncontrollable they cannot control, to develop practical, cognitive, and emotional strategies that allow them to live and to survive. The point of religions is not to make the uncontrollable controllable but to allow human beings to live with the uncontrollable in a controllable way.

What intrudes into life in such an unavailable and uncontrollable way can be experienced as *bonum* or as *malum*, as *unexpected happiness* or as *unfathomable senselessness*. One way or the other, human beings find themselves passively exposed to that which happens to them. They can neither bring about nor prevent what overtakes them, nor can they evade it and avoid experiences of unavailable *bonum* and *malum*.

Nor can the unabolishable contingency of experiences of *bonum* and *malum* be abolished or eliminated by religious strategies for living with the unavailable. Their efforts lead us astray, down the wrong paths, where magical, ritual, or intellectual practices seek to abolish or eliminate the unavailability of the unavailable, that is, to discover necessities where there are none and to find meaning where there is only senselessness. When that happens, religions move from being quite rational attempts at living a humane life in the face of the entirely senseless and the unavoidability of the unavailable to being irrational superstitions. But that does not have to happen, and even if it happens in one current of a religion, there usually are other currents in which that does not happen.

All of the more or less complex religions offer different readings of their practices and strategies for controllably dealing with the uncontrollable. They thus understand

19. See Dalferth, "Leben angesichts des Unverfügbaren."

20. Religions perform this function not as systems of ideas or of thought but as *lived communal practice*. Their orienting function in living with experiences of *malum* and *bonum* is inscribed in the practices that religions are. Abstracting from this practice and reflecting on it as taken by itself is not the same as orienting oneself in life by participating in the practice of religion. Orienting oneself in life is one thing, orienting oneself in thinking about orienting oneself in life another.

the third (signs, language, symbols) from out of and through which they seek to shed light on experiences of *bonum* and *malum* in human life, in *descriptive* but also *non-descriptive* ways. The former leads to forms of *transcendence-realist religion*, in which the unavailable is defined, described, and represented positively (*description of transcendence*), the latter leads to forms of *critical religion*, in which it is not understood and used as a definitional concept but as a critical concept for delineating and assessing the available (*critique of immanence*).

Transcendence-realist forms of religion seek to give meaning to the uncontrollable and unavailable by designating it positively and describing it as a transcendental world *sui generis*. They project a *religious counterworld* over against the current world. They offer ritual strategies for establishing a relationship with such a counterworld. And they develop religious forms of thinking for thematizing, representing, and thinking that counterworld with the semiotic means of this world (analogy).

Immanence-critical forms of religion, by contrast, do not seek to give the unavailable and uncontrollable a meaning of its own but try to understand it as the *other* of the meaningful, controllable, and available, by tying or referring the former to the latter in the form of a thinking of negation. Their strategy is not the symbolic development of a religious counterworld and the elaboration of rituals for approaching it in the ambivalence of this world but the discovery of the unavoidable simultaneous presence of the senseless in the meaningful, of the unavailable in the available, and of the uncontrollable in the controllable.

In *tying the unavailable and uncontrollable back to the available and controllable*, both transcendence-descriptive and immanence-critical forms of religion react to a possible threat always present in experiences of *malum*: the possibility, conceivable only as a radical threat to life, of the *absolutely* chaotic, irrational, uncontrollable, senseless, Evil. If the uncontrollable, irrational, indeterminate, and senseless were an independent figure, it would constitute a life-threatening opposite to everything that is determinate, meaningful, and available. Everything meaningful would then not only have to be understood against the background of the always threatening senseless and the possibly invading unavailable, it would also always be in danger of being annihilated, destroyed, exterminated, replaced, and repressed by it.

Religions counteract this danger not by explaining and thereby domesticating the senseless, unavailable, and uncontrollable but by referring it, *in its inexplicability*, to rationally comprehensible structures of sense and by understanding it as the latter's always simultaneously present background. That does not endow the senseless with sense but allows us, within what is meaningful, to adopt a stance toward the senseless and to live with the uncontrollable in a controllable way.

12. Christian Strategies for Orientation

Against this backdrop, what characterizes Christian ways of dealing with happenings in life experienced as a *malum* that has no sense and refuses any comprehension? Which strategies of orientation do we find in the symbolic universe of the Christian faith that allow us, in the face of such experiences of the senseless and the incomprehensible, to understand the world meaningfully (to integrate them into a symbolic order) and to live a humane life in the world thus understood (to situate ourselves within this order)?

Christian strategies for orientation are characterized by their rehearsal of a dialectical double movement that can be traced throughout the history of Christianity and in every Christian life. On the one hand, in experiences of *malum* we refer positively or negatively[21] to God and thereby develop a specific understanding of God and thus also of the world and of our own lives (anabatic theology/atheology). On the other hand, in light of this understanding of God, the world, and ourselves in life's experiences of *malum*, we orient ourselves in a specific way, that is, we understand ourselves, the world, and life in a new and different way (katabatic theology/non- or anti-religious life orientation). Both movements can, at any time, lead us outside a Christian orientation and practice of life because in the face of *malum* that happens to us, we may no longer be able to be oriented by God (the *malum* leads to an obscuring or a loss of God), or because we may, conversely, take refuge in a counterworld's conception of God, in whose light we are no longer capable of reconciling the religious view of life with our practical experience of life and instead get caught in a dualist life practice and an apocalyptic view of the world (that is, we are able to conceive of life with God only as the extermination and destruction of the world of *malum*).

Atheism caused by *malum* (in all the varieties of critical or fundamentalist rejections of religious life-orientations) and dualisms that avoid *malum* (in all the varieties of religious fundamentalism or theories of counterworlds that are critical of experience) are the ever-present dangers and polar concomitants of Christian life-orientations. Yet between them, the spectrum of possible orientations unfolds that this book seeks to trace. How do Christian faith and thought encode a conception of God in the face of experiences of *malum* and a conception of *malum* in light of a conception of God, and how does this help in orientating us in practically dealing with evil in life that affects us or others? In hermeneutical terms, what are the questions to which the Christian conception of God responds in the face of happenings by evil, and which questions does the Christian conception of God raise with regard to dealing with evil in human life?

The background of this way of putting the problem comprises the entire range of questions that are (or can be) raised by having and making experiences of evil, ills, and bad things in human life and that (can) lead to human beings turning toward or against God (or gods or the divine) and to their bringing, in one way or another, God (or gods or the divine) into play in their grappling with evil and ills. In so doing, how do they understand what they experience as evil, ills, or bad things (their understanding of *malum*)? How, in their situation as someone who is affected by *malum*, do they understand that which they refer or no longer refer to as God (or gods or the divine), seeking help or complaining, remonstrating or despairing, optimistically hopeful or negating God in disappointment (their conception of God)?[22] How, again, is this to be described

21. Every religious life-orientation can be negated, and these negations are to be considered when reflecting on each life-orientation.

22. Even when we negate God (God's existence), we connect an understanding with the sign "God," whose referent we negate. This is true even if we consider so-called ontological arguments to be absurd that seek to conceive of the sign "God" in this way: it is impossible to admit this conception and at the

and understood from the perspective of third persons not immediately affected by this *malum*? How, in the Christian faith, does God enter the picture in the face of experiences of *malum*, one's own and those of others (the Christian conception of God)? And how, then, is God to be thought theologically (the Christian idea of God)?

13. The Topics and Thesis of This Book

These question guide the way the present study traces a number of—but by no means all!—central Christian strategies for coding and representing the definitional dialectic between *malum* and conceptions of God, in which *malum* is defined within the horizon of life before God (and not just religious life) and *God* is defined within the horizon of having experiences of *malum* (and not just of religious experiences of *malum*). This book is about the *hermeneutic problem* of understanding *malum* and *God* within the horizon of concrete practical life and orienting one's life toward God. It is not about the *problem of theodicy*, the problem whether or how it is (still) possible, in the face of *malum*, to believe in God, which always already presupposes an answer to these hermeneutical questions. The problem of theodicy is focused on an overly one-sided and secondary debate, in which the pros and cons are critically or apologetically concerned with objections to belief (conceived of in a specific way) in a God (conceived of in a specific way) on the basis of ills (conceived of in a specific way) in the world. It is interested in an experiential criticism of belief in God or in refuting this criticism; it is not interested in what we might call the prototheological questions[23] of how religious life and theological thought deal with life, what role the reference to God, gods, or the divine plays, and how God, gods, and the divine as well as *malum* in its many variations are understood in the process. This does not exclude appeals to God, going all the way to rejecting God in the face of the *malum* experienced, but in religious life, the tension between *malum* and God is not limited to this aspect, which implies a critique of faith and theology. The question is how one can live with Evil,[24] and it is within the horizon of this question that both the turn toward and the turn away from God are to be understood.

In the context of the lifeworld and in the practical situations of life, human beings—and this is the hermeneutical thesis of this book—primarily turn to God, gods, or the divine in order to thank or to complain, to cheer or to call for help, to express their joy and gratitude or to raise accusations, to protest, denounce, or renounce God in the face of what they have experienced or what has happened to others. Their turning toward or against God is never a first but always a second step. They respond to something positive (*bonum*) or negative (*malum*) that has happened to them when they did not seek it out or expect it (nor ought not to have done so),[25] and they cannot respond

---

same time contest that there is a God thus understood.

23. I prefer this expression to "fundamental theology" because I am concerned not with theological foundations or justifications but with hermeneutically showing how questions that determine religious life and enjoin us to think theologically arise from practical life.

24. See the chapter "The Halachic Approach" in Rosenberg, *Good and Evil in Jewish Thought*.

25. It is worth emphasizing explicitly that happenings of *bonum* and *malum* are structurally analogous; theologically, despite all their opposition, they raise complementary questions. This study's

to it because this happening turns everything they do or do not do into a response to this happening. When they turn toward or against God, they do so not in an attitude of theoretical leisure, neutrally weighing arguments pro and contra as to the question(s) of theodicy, but in situations in which they are existentially and emotionally affected.

This can be sensed even among those who, sitting at their desks, conduct a theodicy trial in which God is accused before the tribunal of reason even though they are convinced before the trial even starts that the accusation against God is invalid because the accused does not exist.[26] Even if that were the case, the experiences of Evil and good would persist. "The abolition of God," Kermani carefully points out, is not an appropriate "means of fending off the presumptuous demands of life"; taken by itself, it performs that function "only if one is still able to maintain one's comfortable stoicism in situations of extreme need." To all human beings good and evil happen that they neither sought nor expected, albeit not in the same way and to the same extent. This provokes every thinking human being to ask questions. But besides the experiences in life that makes us happy, "nothing supports God's existence more than misfortune, because this is what evokes the question of the cause in the first place." In Heine's words: "Human misery is too grave. One *must* believe."[27] And the same is true of human happiness.

These, of course, are no proofs for the existence of God, and it is absurd to construe them as inferences from thirst to water or from water to the giver.[28] Instead, they indicate that the real theological challenge of thinking God begins where not only the semantic coherence of predicates and the logical consistency of propositions are at stake but where one speaks in an existentially serious way about God because one cannot but turn toward or against God in supplication, gratitude, or reproach, stake one's hopes on God or no longer put one's hopes in him.[29] God is not just someone or something about

---

concentration on *malum* thus runs parallel to the reflections in my "Leben angesichts des Unverfügbaren" and "Alles umsonst."

26. See Gesang, *Angeklagt: Gott*, 29–30 and 280.

27. Kermani, *Terror of God*, 21–22.

28. As Gesang, *Angeklagt: Gott*, 135ff, has it in his debate with J. Splett. And indeed, "hope in desperate situations is a *psychological defense mechanism*, not an indication for the existence of God." But only an interpreter for whom human speech consists exclusively of statements of fact and of inferences can have the absurd idea of interpreting the call for God in emergency situations as "indicative of the existence of God" or as "an inference of water from thirst" and of then criticizing them for it. Heine was not busying himself with drawing illogical inferences from the misery of his illness; he refused to have the addressee of his anger, his pain, his misery taken away from him. He insisted "that there is someone in heaven to whom I can constantly whimper the litany of my suffering, especially after midnight, when Mathilde has gone to take the rest she often very much needs. Thank God! In such hours I am not alone and I can pray and blubber as much as I want without being embarrassed, and I can pour all my heart out before the Most High and confide to him a good number of things we usually keep silent about even to our own wife" (Heine, *Sämtliche Schriften*, 476). This is not a proof of God's existence from misery but an indication of how God is to be understood and to be thought when we not only seek to reconcile "the suffering and injustice in the world . . . with the image of God that was taught to us" (Kermani, *Terror of God*, 31) but ask what image of God would be appropriate given human misery: How would we have to conceive of God if debating his existence were to be worthwhile? The theological problem raised by situations of misery is not the existence of God but the content and the form of the idea of God.

29. This is correctly recognized by John E. Thiel; see the chapter "Innocent Suffering" in *God, Evil, and Innocent Suffering*.

whom we speak but someone to whom, with whom, and against whom we speak, and not just in such a way that we might as well not do so (that, too, exists) but also in such a way that in those situations it is impossible for those affected not to speak about, to, or against God. Even their silence, then, is eloquent, because they do not simply say *nothing* but specifically and for good reason remain silent *about and before* God.

Such speech and silence is to be explored philosophically and thought (about) theologically. Even in thinking God, we have to be aware that it is about the one to whom human beings turn in situations of happiness and misfortune, of joy and suffering, of gratitude and misery, toward whom they orient their lives or from whom they turn away in disappointment, the one with and for whom, therefore, it is not just about logical and epistemic but about existential and practical problems in life, namely and especially when it comes to experiences of suffering, ills, and evil.

Viewed against this backdrop, the philosophical and theological discussion of theodicy constitutes an explicit and deliberate restriction. It does not just concentrate on the fact of ills to the exclusion of the fact of happiness and joy. Nor is it concerned with how, given the experience of ills that happen to us, God would have to be conceived and thought of. It is solely concerned with the "problem of evil" and its variations.[30] To demonstrate this restriction and in so doing elucidate the different problematic addressed in this study, our first step consists in retracing the outlines of the philosophical and theological discourses that concentrate on the "problem of evil/ill" in this way.

---

30. See McCloskey, *God and Evil*, 3–5, and Weisberger, *Suffering Belief*, 19–55.

C

The Theodicy Problem

1. The Focus of Our Question

THOSE WHO HAVE THE experience of evil or make the experience of evils, that is, who make experiences of evil, do not necessarily think immediately of God. But those who think of God cannot leave evil and evils aside. Experiences of *malum* can be important occasions for turning to God, gods, or the divine. They do not have to be, and those whom these experiences do not refer to God will still have to deal with such experiences.

Things are different when it comes to God. Those who thematize God simply cannot leave *malum* aside. Yet how God and *malum* relate is hotly contested. One of the most acute forms of this contention consists in narrowing the relationship between the two down to a formal contradiction that seems to necessitate the negation of one side or the other: either *God* or *malum*, but not both. Those who do not count on God do not have this problem, just like those who contest *malum*: for opposite reasons, atheists and irrealists are not confronted with any avoidable contradiction, even if they will have other problems. Those who contest *malum* seem to shut themselves off from reality, so much so that their survival is likely to be acutely threatened.[1] Those who consider *malum* to be incontestable can turn it into a foundation for contesting God—*si deus est, unde malum?* (If God exists, where does *malum* come from?)—yet in so doing, they provoke the counterquestions, which may indeed be answered without going back to God, how the reality of *malum*—*si deus non est, unde malum?* (If God does not exist, where does *malum* come from?)—and of *bonum*—*si deus non est, unde bonum?* (If God

---

1. This does not, however, mean that what is considered to be a *malum* is exempt from historical variation or independent of specific social conditions and individual attitudes and sensibilities. See Neuhaus, "Theodizee: Abbruch oder Anstoss des Glaubens?" and "Theodizee und Glaubensgeschichte." The tears of a single innocent child have not always been experienced as making the whole universe tremble, as Ivan Karamazov recounts. A child's early death has not always been seen as an occasion for justified objections against God's goodness. See Kessler, *Gott und das Leid*, 45–50. There is thus indeed a progress of insight into what is to count as *malum*, even if this history is not unilinear and only features protagonists who (like Christianity) both produce suffering and contribute to alerting others to ills that had previously gone unnoticed.

does not exist, where does *bonum* come from?)—is to be explained. Yet they can also turn it into a question concerning God or one's conception of God and ask how God is to be understood, or not to be understood, given the reality of Evil. When this question is addressed to God, it can be articulated as a *plea for understanding—how is malum in your creation to be understood and how are you to be understood given this malum?*; as *lamentation—why do I have to suffer from this malum?*; or as a *demand for justification—how can You, God, exist and let this happen?*

Most forms of the question play a central role in the way believers live their lives. Unlike the attempt at holding God accountable for what he did or for what he did not prevent, believers need not from the outset expect to be refused, as Job was, with an invocation of the infinite difference between creator and creature. Yet the question does not have to be addressed to God, and it does not have to take the form of ordering God to justify his action and inaction before the tribunal of human reason, as if the creature could demand an account of the creator. Instead, it can be a reflexive question on the part of human beings, who consider *malum* to question not God but *their understanding of God* or *their belief* in God. This, then, is not an attempt on the part of human beings to hold God accountable. It is not about a justification *by God* before human beings but about a justification of human *belief in God* given the contradiction between God and the experiences of *malum* in human life.[2] What is up for debate is not God but believing in God or professing God.

It is in this sense that, ever since Leibniz, the so-called theodicy problem has been a *problem of thought*: the question whether and to what extent it is rationally possible to believe in a God in a world full of evils, evil, and suffering.[3] The question arises in this form only under specific conditions, and it does not arise for all who in their lives have to deal with evil.[4] It is a problem "that arises from professing an omnipotent and morally perfect God in a world full of suffering,"[5] that is, it arises (practically) only for believers or (theoretically) for those who confront belief in a good and omnipotent creator-God with the fact of evil. To be sure, atheists and agnostics in their lives have to deal with evil, suffering, and evils like everyone else, but in order to have the problem discussed under the heading "theodicy," one must, at least for the sake of argument, be a hypothetical theist. For believers, it can be a real problem of life, for philosophers "only" a problem of thought,[6] but for both the precondition is that they engage not only with evil but with the way evil questions belief in God.

2. As Kreiner, *Gott im Leid*, 23–24, has rightly pointed out.

3. See Kreiner, *Gott im Leid*, 9.

4. That is also why one cannot say, as Tattersall, "Evidential Argument From Evil," claims, that "the problem . . . why an omniscient, omnipotent and wholly good God would allow the extreme suffering we see in the world" is "thousands of years old."

5. See Kreiner, *Gott im Leid*, 9.

6. As Kreiner, *Gott im Leid*, 35–48, rightly objects to critics like Kenneth Surin (*Theology and the Problem of Evil*, 83–84), Regina Ammicht-Quinn (*Von Lissabon bis Auschwitz*, 230, 254, 282–83, and elsewhere), and others, it is not correct to say that for believers the theodicy problem is not or could not be a real, existentially relevant problem of life because it arises primarily as a speculative and theoretical problem. The opposition between a "theoretical" and a "practical" theodicy (see Surin, *Theology and the Problem of Evil*, 70–141) does not apply if it is conceived of as an opposition between thought and life.

This can be expressed as a formal problem concerning contradictions between propositions about God ("There exists a God who is such and such") and propositions about evils ("There exists an evil that is such and such"). In typical skeptical fashion, Hume in his 1779 *Dialogues Concerning Natural Religion* thus has Philo, drawing on Epicurus, say: "Is he [God] willing to prevent evil, but not able? Then is he impotent. Is he able, but not willing? Then is he malevolent. Is he both able and willing? Whence then is evil?"[7]

When we compare this statement with Epicurus, however, we see that articulating this or similar contradictions does not by any means amount to proffering the same argument.[8] The theodicy problem does not in consist in the (alleged) contradiction between the two series of propositions as such but, more precisely, in what these series of propositions say and in what articulating this contradiction is supposed to demonstrate. Not everyone who, like Philo, raises these contradictions also raises the theodicy problem. Epicurus was unaware of this problem because he had an entirely different conception of god(s) and the world. It is not the exposed contradictions as such that decide which argument is made but *what one sets out to demonstrate with them*. The same (or almost the same) propositions can serve to present entirely different arguments. To show this, let us turn to some classic examples.

2. Epicurus's Questions

The tradition preserves the following argument by Epicurus:

> God either wishes to take away evils and he cannot, or he can and does not wish to, or he neither wishes to nor is able, or he both wishes to and is able. If he wishes to and is not able, he is feeble, which does not fall in with the notion of god. If he is able to and does not wish to, he is envious, which is equally foreign to god. If he neither wishes to nor is able, he is both envious and feeble and therefore not god. If he both wishes to and is able, which alone is fitting to god, whence, therefore, are the evils, and why does he not remove them?[9]

Yet if the theodicy problem is not framed as the theoretical problem of reconciling belief in God and the factual experience of the world, more precisely: of faith in a God understood in a specific way and the undeniable experience of unimaginable and incomprehensible evil in the world, it fails to capture what existentially burdens and challenges believers; and as a theoretical problem, it can also be articulated by those who are not existentially affected the way believers are. For believers who pose the question of theodicy, the "miscarriage of all philosophical trials in theodicy" has thus existential consequences and can lead to a loss of faith or to a deepening of faith in a different practice of dealing with evil. For philosophical theoreticians, in turn, nothing of the kind necessarily follows unless they are themselves believers. As thinkers, what is at stake for them (unlike for believers) is *only* a problem of thought and nothing that is existentially relevant, such that once their work is done, they can easily turn again to other problems or play a game of backgammon (see Hume, *Treatise of Human Nature*, I.IV.vii).

7. Hume, *Dialogues Concerning Natural Religion*, 10.25:74.

8. Weingartner, *Evil*, 127–34, shows the problematic nature of a merely logical reconstruction of both arguments that leaves their entirely different historical contexts and factual backgrounds aside.

9. Epicurus quoted in Lactantius, *Wrath of God*, 92–93; see Epicurus, *Epicuri Physica*, frag. 374, in *Epicurea,* 253. See also Glei, "Et invidus et inbecillus."

Epicurus is going through a number of possible combinations of *mala* and *deus*, all of which lead to aporias. But "god" or "deus" does not refer to the one whom Christians, for example, profess, and Epicurus has a different point in mind than the one in support of which his argument is employed in the context of later theodicies. He is concerned not with questioning the existence of God or gods but with showing the uselessness of religiously taking recourse to the gods in the face of Evil's threatening reality. Human beings have to deal with Evil themselves; taking recourse to God or gods won't be of any help. Epicurus's argument is not one of theodicy but a *protest against the idea of the cosmos in the Greek tradition*. Given the reality of our experiences of *malum*, the idea of the cosmos as a well-ordered and good whole is not tenable.[10] There is no meaningfully ordered cosmic whole. For Epicurus, the universe is a composite of bodies surrounded by a void, without which there could be no movement of the bodies.[11] This universe knows neither beginning nor end, it is a continuous flux of movement and matter, of atoms reorganizing and severing their connections. The existence of gods is not denied, but the gods have no way of influencing either the actual course of things or the life of human beings. They live eternally in the bodyless and orderless spaces between the worlds (the *intermundia*) and do not concern themselves with the world or with human beings.

Against the backdrop of his cosmology (the becoming of the world takes place as a permanent aggregation and disaggregation of atomic elements), the fragment quoted above does not articulate an "accusation against the divinity because of evils in general"[12] but an irresolvable aporia that results from the attempt to explain everything from a single principle. If this principle is a *bonum* to which what is good and beautiful in the world can be traced back, it has to ignore all the *malum* that contradicts it and thereby fails to acknowledge "an essential component of the *world* and an important prompt for thinking."[13]

The answer suggested by Epicurus is thus that in explanations of the reality of the world we ought not to bring the gods into play in the first place. Doing so does not clarify anything but only raises new obstacles: "It is vain to ask of the gods what a man is capable of supplying for himself." Indeed, it does not make sense to expect anything good or evil from them at all. Not only are they factually not responsible for evils; their shortcomings are so great that they cannot be responsible for anything at all. This not only removes fear of the gods as the ones causing human suffering; death, too, loses its terror because for the afflicted, death is not suffering but the end of all suffering. Lack, misfortune, old age, illness, and fear all arise from the concrete constitution of the human being and can be endured in the attitude of *ataraxía*. Those who live this way live "like a god among men," untouched by anything.[14]

---

10. See Schumacher, *Theodizee*, 71–77.
11. See Geyer, *Leid und Böses*, 54–55.
12. Billicsich, *Von Platon bis Thomas*, 70n36.
13. Schumacher, *Theodizee*, 72.
14. Epicurus, *Extant Remains*, 117, 83–85, 93.

That is why the guiding principle of Epicurean ethics is not the *eudamonía*, which Aristotle considered to be "divine,"[15] but the *hēdonē*, which is about human concerns and especially about something that counteracts the fundamental evil of pain.[16] Human beings are earthly, not divine beings. The good gods simply do not have anything to do with Evil in the world—they do not cause it, they do not prevent it, they do not concern themselves with it. Thinking of them as doing so or even as being able to do so is an error. That is simply not what gods are like.

3. Skeptical Intensification: Sextus Empiricus

Whereas Epicurus criticizes human *representations* of the gods but does not question their existence and instead only refuses to admit the gods as causes of evils or as helpers in overcoming them, Sextus Empiricus takes these reflections further and denies the existence of God or of gods.

> Anyone who says that there are gods says either that they provide for the things in the universe or that they do not—and that if they provide, then either for all things or for some. But if they provided for all things, there would be nothing bad and evil in the universe; but they say that everything is full of evil. Therefore the gods will not be said to provide for everything. But if they provide for some things, why do they provide for these and not for those? Either they both want to and can provide for all, or they want to but cannot, or they can but do not want to, or they neither want nor can. If they both wanted to and could, then they would provide for all; but they do not provide for all, for the reason I have just given; therefore it is not the case that they both want to and can provide for all. If they want to but cannot, they are weaker than the cause in virtue of which they cannot provide for the things which they do not provide; but it is contrary to the concept of god that a god should be weaker than anything. If they can provide for all but do not want to, they will be thought to be malign. If they neither want to nor can, they are both malign and weak—and only the impious would say this about the gods.
>
> The gods, therefore, do not provide for the things in the universe. But if they have providence for nothing and have no function and no effect, we will not be able to say how it is apprehended that there are gods, since it is neither apparent in itself nor apprehended by way of any effects. For this reason too, then, it is inapprehensible whether there are gods.
>
> From this we deduce that those who firmly state that there are gods are no doubt bound to be impious: if they say that the gods provide for everything, they will say that they are a cause of evil; and if they say that they provide for some things or even for none at all, they will be bound to say either that the gods are malign or that they are weak—and anyone who says this is clearly impious.[17]

The point is clear: given the reality of evils, the only choice we have is either we conclude that God does not exist, or we act blasphemously. Either *God* is the way he is usually

15. Aristotle, *Nicomachean Ethics*, 1101b35–1102a4:1740.

16. Schumacher, *Theodizee*, 72–37.

17. Sextus Empiricus, *Outlines of Scepticism*, III.9–12:145–46.

thought and conceptualized, that is, he is *good* and *powerful*: then there should be and there ought to be no evils, which, however, do exist. Or God is not that way: then there is no God, at least no God who would correspond to this concept of God.

This makes evils the decisive objection both to thinking God the way he is being thought (that is, a *criticism of the traditional philosophical concept of God*) and to the idea that there are reasons for assuming God's existence (that is, a *criticism of the existence of God*). The two must be distinguished. Evils do not just become a challenge to the conviction that God exists, they already pose a challenge to the *concept of God*: that there are evils is a point not just against the reality of God, it seems to render God *unthinkable*.

4. Gnostic Aporia: Dualism

Or it compels us to think God and the divine in other forms than the traditional ones. If we consistently stick to the Platonic rule that everything that is good is to be explained only through God or the divine and everything evil through something other than God, then Evil in the world cannot be traced back to God but must have another principle. With regard to the relationship of God to Evil, then, one has to agree with the Epicureans: both have nothing to do with each other. With regard to the good, however, one has to side with the Academics and disagree with Epicureans: God conditions, makes possible, and causes everything that is good. When it comes to God and the divine, however, one must, unlike the Academics, abandon the monistic explanation of the world. The way the world is, it cannot exclusively be explained and understood by way of one divine *principle of the good*: that renders comprehensible only what is good in the world. Evil and evils, on the contrary, must be traced back to another, anti-divine *principle of Evil*. For the world is both, *bonum* and *malum*, and neither can be explained by way of the principle of the other.

The result is a *dualism of principles* that characterizes gnostic and other kinds of hermetic thought in a great variety of mythological forms. The world is dominated by two competing powers, Good and Evil, and the human being is the site and the intersection of this power struggle. The right way of dealing with the experience of the reality of evils is thus not to expect of God that he do away with evil but to live differently in the face of it. Those who say that God ought to have freed the world from evils do not know what they are talking about. God could not have freed the world from Evil, nor can he put an end to its reality. That would exceed his powers and his possibilities, for the world consists inseparably of both:[18] Good and Evil, light and darkness, spirit and

---

18. The letter from Hermes Trismegistus to Asclepius emphatically insists on God being the one and unique creator and at the same time the only one to be unreservedly good: "For in god there is only one condition, the good, but one who is good is not contemptuous or impotent. This is what god is, the good, all power to make all things. All that is begotten has come to be by god's agency, by the agency of one who is good, in other words, of one able to make all things" (*Corpus Hermeticus* in Copenhaver, *Hermetica*, XIV.9:56–57). What is bad in the world, on the contrary, is explained by natural changes (*pathos*), which things suffer from the outside and which lead, for example, to their being covered in verdigris like bronze or to get dirty like children. "But the persistence of generation makes evil bloom like a sore, which is why god has made change, to repurify generation" (*Corpus Hermeticus*, XIV.7:56), yet God is not the one to whom these bad things as effects can be ascribed.

matter (in the world), sense and sensibility (in human beings), the domain of the good spirits under the leadership of the highest god and the domain of the evil demons under their anti-divine leader.[19] All that the highest god could do was to equip the human mind with intellect, knowledge, and intuition in such a way that human beings could protect themselves as much as possible against evils and Evil. These faculties distinguish human beings from animals. The only way human beings have of defending themselves against Evil is that they orient their life by the divine principle of the good, not the anti-divine principle of Evil. Like everything in this earthly world, human beings' material bodies will decay, but their souls will be judged by the leader of the demons according to whether they refrained from evils or not, and accordingly they will be assigned a place in the sun or be hurled down into the fiery and watery storms of hell or condemned to continue their "vile migration . . . in[to] other bodies."[20]

While this mythological[21] solution preserves God's unambiguity, his responsibility for the good and his non-responsibility for Evil, it comes at the high price of seeing the world in dualistic terms as the site of the struggle between opposing principles of Good and Evil and, on the level of principles, of not only failing to resolve this conflict but of making it permanent.[22] The fight between light and darkness is as unavoidable as it is undecidable. The world is not a rationally ordered and intelligible cosmos but the site of the never-ending struggle between intelligible order and unintelligible chaos. Within limits, human beings may indeed decide in favor of the Good and against Evil. But the basic dualism remains intact. This "explains" the reality of the world as a mixture of Good and Evil by describing its order and its chaos as the effects of good and evil principles: the world is the way it is because it has the principles it has got.

That, however, is not an explanation but an aporetic repetition, on the level of explanation, of the description of what was to be explained. Where every phenomenon demands its own explanation, nothing is explained at all. Where everything that is good is traced back to a principle of the Good and everything that is evil to a principle of Evil, nothing is rendered comprehensible. Where God is responsible only for the Good and an anti-God for everything that is Evil, there is not even a serious struggle between Good and Evil in the world anymore; the struggle is limited to the struggle for the human

19. See chapter 6, "Gnostics: The War between Darkness and Light," in Rorty, *Many Faces of Evil*, 24–36, as well as Abel and Hare, *Hermes Trismegistus*.

20. See *Asclepius* in Copenhaver, *Hermetica*, 67–92, here ¶12:74.

21. The Gnosis in its many versions is not mythical but mythological, that is, it employs mythical narrative patterns to respond to a (philosophical) problem of thought. It develops a dualist myth of thought in order to resolve a problem of *logos* that, it seems, cannot be resolved monistically. See Koslowski, *Gnosis und Theodizee*; Böhlig and Markschies, *Gnosis und Manichäismus*; and King, *What Is Gnosticism?*

22. After the gods have been chased off the earth and all veneration of the gods has ended, the apocalypse described in the *Corpus Hermeticum* ends with floods, fire, wars, and epidemics, restoring the original state of the cosmos, in which the cosmos is good, like God, its creator: "Such is god, and the world is his image—⟨good⟩ from good" (Copenhaver, *Hermetica*, ¶¶ 24–27:81–84, here 83, Copenhaver's interpolation). Yet because the cosmos is still distinct from the good God, it can at any time become rusty and dirty again and thereby enter the next cosmic cycle, the way Empedocles envisioned it. See Pierris, *Empedoclean "Kosmos,"* and there in particular Primavesi, "Structure of Empedocles' Cosmic Cycle."

being who can and must decide between good and evil: the world is irremediably evil, not only but always also evil, yet humans can and ought to live in such a way that in the end they are guided by the Good, not by Evil, and thus decide in favor of God and against the anti-God.[23]

5. Christian Answer: Lactantius

This is the starting point of the Christian philosopher Lactantius. In his *De ira dei* (*The Wrath of God*), he defends a uniform explanation of the world that takes recourse to God both against the aporias of monism, which it seems must negate or ignore Evil (that is, it does not do justice to the reality of the world), and against dualism, which acknowledges Evil but makes it permanent (that is, it does not do justice to the power of God). He objects to Epicurus that it is wrong of him to demand of God to be immutable and careless, for in that case, he could not be responsible for everything that concerns his creation: "He who takes away all force, therefore, all substance from God, what else does he say except that there is no God at all?" God, he concludes, can only be a principle if as First Cause he remains tied to *all* effects and enters in relation with both sides: "For, in opposite things, it is necessary either to be moved toward each side or toward neither. Thus, he who loves the good also hates the evil, and he who does not hate the evil does not love the good." That is why—against Epicurus and against gnostic dualism—God must be thought in a comprehensive relation to the world: *divine providence* is an essential part of the idea of God.[24]

This relation to Good *and* Evil, however, pertains not only to God but to human beings as well—as Lactantius asserts against the Stoics. Humans, after all, are distinct from all other creatures because God has endowed them with wisdom (*sapientia*), whose entire sense consists in distinguishing between Good and Evil: "It stands, therefore, that all things are proposed for man, evils and goods as well." Evil thus performs the anthropologically decisive function of constituting the human capacity for knowledge: if there were no Evil, there would be nothing to be distinguished as Good or Evil, and there would therefore be no human wisdom, either. Accordingly, Lactantius objects to

23. Human beings are caught up in the dualistic struggle between Good and Evil but—provided they are enabled to do so by the appropriate insight (*gnosis*)—they can choose one or the other to serve as models for their lives without thereby putting an end to the dualism of the two principles. At the site of the human, it is *sin* that provides Evil with the occasion to become active in human life. Evading the power of Evil thus means opening oneself to the power of the Good and putting an end to sin in order to deprive Evil of the ground on which operates. This does not in any way modify the basic dualist structure of the world; it only changes the human being who moves from darkness to light, from the eclipse of God into the light of God, from the domain of the evil to that of the good principle, and who is in this sense "redeemed." In the imaginary of Christian belief, it is possible to speak in quite similar fashion of the need to be changed and redeemed in order to escape the life-destroying consequences of sin by moving from "the contempt, denial, indifference, forgetting, or eclipse of God in us or whatever name we want to give to sin" (Krötke, "Das Böse als Absurdes," 75–76) to believing in God and orienting our lives toward him. The difference lies in the way this "redemption" takes place and how it is thought (through God's loving action in Christ and in faith) and the way in which the world is represented and understood (not dualistically but as God's good creation).

24. Lactantius, *Wrath of God*, 4.2:65–66, 4.6:66, 5.9–10:69, 10.41–53:82–85.

Epicurus that Evil, because of its elementary function in the epistemological opposition, moves us closer to God: the principle, God, is recognized not only through the Good but also through Evil. That is why it is not a contradiction to say that God can overcome Evil but does not want to do so. For in God's permitting Evil, human beings obtain their capacity for knowledge and thereby obtain themselves. Lactantius concludes: "So for the sake of the slight gain of having evils removed, we should be deprived of a very great good, a real good, and one proper to us."[25]

Lactantius's train of thought amounts to the claim that ancient philosophy did not think the concept of principle through.[26] It is precisely the *wrath* of God that ensures that *everything* is connected to the first principle: the principle is that which *effects*, the contradiction between Good and Evil on the side of the human and the world is that which is *effected*.[27] Accordingly, the query *cur malum?*—why Evil?—can be answered by stating "that all things are proposed for man, evils as well as good."[28] Human beings are said to have been endowed with the capacity for distinguishing between Good and Evil because they are called to justice, justice as the creator himself exercises it: in the face of the opposition between Good and Evil, they are called on to do what is right and just, not what is evil.

The argument in its entirety shows the fundamental change in the conception of the world that takes place in the transition from the thought of antiquity to that of Christianity. The world is no longer understood in Epicurean terms as a process of mechanic movements or in Stoic terms as a connection of events determined by reason. Nor is it conceived of gnostically as the site of a struggle between the irremediably opposing basic principles of Good and Evil.[29] Rather, it is seen as the site of divine and human action. All actions take place as decisions between Good and Evil and strive for transforming the current ambivalent world into God's good creation. To explain the world thus understood as a nexus of actions, it no longer suffices to go back to the divine as the ultimate principle of everything and to declare it, in keeping with the Platonic tradition, to be entirely good. If we are to be able to think the divine or God as the only ultimate principle of the world, Lactantius tells us, we must not think it without reference to Evil. The relationship between God and Evil must be defined by something other than a mere reciprocally exclusive opposition. There must be a dynamic overcoming of Evil through the Good that God strives for, and this overcoming requires us to say of God that he is not only different from Evil but that he hates Evil and overcomes it through the Good. God is not good because he is not evil but because he turns against Evil and resists it. God's goodness is his fight against Evil, and because God is the one and only creator of the world, the divine fight against Evil is the overcoming of Evil through the Good.[30]

25. Lactantius, *Wrath of God*, 13.13:91, 13.23:93, 13.25:93.

26. See Lactantius, *Wrath of God*, 6.1:70, and Schumacher, *Theodizee*, 77.

27. On the problem of God's wrath, see Pohlenz, *Vom Zorne Gottes*; on the reception of this idea in medieval theology, see Pinomaa, "Der Zorn Gottes"; on the debate in recent years, see Härle, "Die Rede von der Liebe und vom Zorn Gottes"; Miggelbrink, *Der Zorn Gottes*; and Volkmann, *Der Zorn Gottes*.

28. Lactantius, *Wrath of God*, 13.25:93. Translation modified.

29. Baumeister, "Montanismus und Gnostizismus."

30. We may even put this in terms of a definition: *Evil* is that which God negates through the Good, and *God* is the one who puts an end to Evil through Good.

6. Medieval *Summa*: Aquinas

Building on Augustine and Boethius, Thomas Aquinas has summarized these points and given them a succinct theological form: *si malum est, Deus est*: "If there is evil, there is a God." Far from evils causing the failure of the existence of God, of the idea of God, and of belief in God, in Aquinas even *malum* becomes evidence for God: "For there would be no evil, if the order of good were removed, the privation of which is evil: and there would be no such order, if there were no God."[31] However, it is not *because* evil exists that a God exists, even if theological apologetics tends to instrumentalize the argument that way, only to thus earn ironic applause from a hermeneutics of religious compensations of desire that seeks to criticize religion. Rather, *if* Evil exists, *then* the Good also exists, and if the Good exists, then God exists, without whom there would be no Good.[32] For if evil exists, then something exists that is evil. But if it is good that there is something rather than nothing and if nothing good exists that is not due to God, then God exists if evil exists.

Even those who do not agree with this Thomistic argument would agree that evil exists for us only because and insofar as something else exists as well. Evil could not be negated if there were nothing to be negated. And we would not be able to perceive evil if it did not appear in contrast to something else, and that is not just to say in contrast to other evil. Evil is real not for itself and as such, it is always and exclusively evil on, in, with, or among something else.[33] For evil to become a phenomenon, it takes a real in which it appears by way of contrast.

Aquinas's argument, of course, is more precise.[34] *Malum* stands in essential opposition to *bonum* and because in such oppositions one side cannot be known without but only through the other, *malum* can be known only in its contrast relation to *bonum*.[35] If, however, only everything that is desired or that one strives for is a *bonum* and if every being (*ens*) strives perfectly to realize what it it is and can be by nature, then the intended, fully realized being of every being is a *bonum*, such that "Every being, as being, is good."[36] *Malum* thus contrasts with *bonum* but also with the *esse* of an *ens*, the being of a being. It therefore cannot *be* anything itself, it can only be defined as the lack or absence of *esse* and *bonum*: "No being can be spoken of as evil, formally as being, but only so far as it lacks being."[37]

Yet not everything that a being is not or does not have is a *malum*: unlike birds, human beings do not have wings and cannot therefore take off into the skies like birds. But that is not a defect, lack, or *malum*; it belongs to their essential difference as human

---

31. Aquinas, *Summa contra gentiles*, III.71:177.

32. The concern is thus not with "elevat[ing] the moral experience of evil to the proof of God's existence, as the ethical option this opens up could only be directed at God," as Kermani has it (*Terror of God*, 18). The aim is to discover a condition of the possibility of evil without which there could be no evil. See Sala, "Das Böse und Gott."

33. See Perru, "Le mal a-t-il une réalité ontologique?" and Park, *Das Schlechte und das Böse*.

34. See Hödl, "Die metaphysische und ethische Negativität des Bösen."

35. Aquinas, *Summa Theologiae*, I q5 a3.

36. Aquinas, *Summa Theologiae*, I q5 a3.

37. Aquinas, *Summa Theologiae*, I q5 a3.

beings from other beings. Not every lack of something that is good somewhere and for someone is a *malum*. Rather—as Aquinas learned from Anselm[38]—it indicates that something is missing that one could be and ought to be as the being that one is: "every privation, if we take it properly and strictly, is the lack of something natural."[39] Aquinas thus makes a precise distinction between *negation* and *privation*, between *remotio boni* in a privative and in a negative sense: we are not dealing with a *malum* every time a *bonum* is missing. In that case, it would be a *malum* for human beings that they are not as strong as lions, or as agile as goats, or as perfect as God. These only mark something human beings are *not* (a negation), not something that they are not or do have although *as human beings* they could be it or have it (a privation). Unlike Leibniz later, Aquinas does not consider the fact that creatures are created a "metaphysical evil," evil because they are not perfect like God; this not-being presents itself as a *remotio boni* only in a negative, not a privative sense.[40]

In all of its forms, therefore, the *malum* is the *privatio*, the lack or absence of something that a being, thanks to its essence, *could or should be or have but factually is not or does not have*: "evil is the absence of the good, which is natural and due to a thing." There is thus no *malum* independently of a *bonum* to which it privatively refers. This means, on the one hand, that "Evil cannot exist except in good," and, on the other, that there could never be only *malum* and that Evil could never be explained independently of the Good. Every *malum* can therefore be ended or done away with in two ways. On the one hand, the being whose *malum* it is can overcome this defect by becoming what previously it was not, such that the lack no longer exists. On the other, the *malum* can also be resolved by destroying the *bonum* or being whose *malum* it is.[41] An illness can be cured by the patient regaining his or her health, but it can also be ended by the death of the patient.

The question of the emergence or the cause of evils can thus not be answered without taking recourse to something good.[42] There can be no question that "every evil in some way has a cause," yet it is just as unquestionable that a *causa* can only ever be something that *is* (thus, a *bonum*) and never anything that is *not* (thus, a *malum*). The *causa mali*, too, must therefore be a *bonum*. In the last analysis, every evil is caused by something good, for it could not exist if it were not caused, and it can only be caused by something good. Yet by itself and as such, a *bonum* only ever causes a *bonum*; it cannot therefore be the cause of *malum* as *causa per se*, only as *causa per accidens*. The *malum* emerges *incidentally*, as a side product of the emergence of something good. The reason is that not all that is good can always become real at the same time. Fire (a *bonum*), for

---

38. Anselm (*On the Virgin Conception and Original Sin*, Opera II:146, in *Major Works*, 364–65) had defined *malum* not only as *absentia boni* but in more precise terms as *absentia debiti boni*, that is, not only as something that one does not have but as something that one does not one have although one should and could have it. *Malum* is an "absentia boni ubi debet aut expedit esse bonum," an "absence of good where good ought to be found" (*On the Fall of the Devil*, Opera I.251, in *Major Works*, 210). See also Deme, "'Origin' of Evil."

39. Aquinas, *Summa Theologiae*, I q49 a1, and *Summa contra gentiles*, III.6:12.

40. Aquinas, *Summa Theologiae*, I q48 a3 and I q12 a4.

41. Aquinas, *Summa Theologiae*, I q49 a1; *De malo*, q1 a1 (see also *Summa Theologiae*, I q48 a3); and *Summa Theologiae*, I q49 a3.

42. See Steel, "Does Evil Have a Cause?"

example, causes water (a *bonum* as well) to evaporate, that is, it destroys it, not because it *per se* strives to do so, but because it cannot actualize itself as a *bonum* without depriving the other *bonum* of its form (that is, its actuality). Aquinas makes a similar argument about the failure of an action that is in itself good (for instance, when the fire fails to warm because it is too weak) or a failure caused by unsuitable material (for instance, when wet wood prevents there being a fire).[43]

On the basis of these reflections, Aquinas vigorously rejects any gnostic explanatory dualism that seeks to trace everything good back to a *summum bonum* and everything evil back to a *summum malum*: there is no first principle of Evil the way there is a first principle of the Good. The gnostic way of thinking is a radical mistake because to look for separate principles or causes for separate opposite effects is to overlook that these oppositions are oppositions with respect to something they share and that within the whole of the universe they must agree in a shared principle: "since all contraries agree in something common, it is necessary to search for one common cause for them above their own contrary proper causes . . . and above all things that exist, no matter how, there exists one first principle of being."[44]

This rejection of dualism, however, prompts another danger: turning God, as the ultimate cause of everything good, into the first cause of everything evil.[45] The decisive point of this frequently voiced criticism is not to declare God to be responsible for *specific* evils and *specific* suffering: for every concrete evil we can name concrete causes due to which it emerged or took place. The point of the reproach lies in the question why God created a world in which there are evils *at all*: by taking recourse to particular causes, it may be possible to provide a complete explanation of why this human being contracts this disease without bringing God into the mix, but why the world in general is such that it contains diseases, suffering, and death is a question that also raises questions concerning God.

Aquinas answers them by pointing to the *order of creation willed by God*, an order that, precisely in wanting something specific, excludes something else and thereby results *ex consequenti* and "as if incidentally" in the destruction of certain things as well: it is part of this order that "when one thing is generated another undergoes corruption" and vice versa. "[T]he order of justice belongs to the order of the universe; and this requires that penalty should be dealt out to sinners. And so God is the author of the evil which is penalty, but not of the evil which is fault." And finally, this order also includes the possibility that the created secondary causes fail. God, therefore, is not the one who directly causes evils, for that would presuppose that he wanted or intended them; but unlike the *bonum*, the *malum* can in no way be intended or striven for since that would make it a *bonum*.[46] It can only appear *per accidens* with a *bonum*. The aim is always for a *bonum* because whatever is being striven for is *bonum*. *Malum* in contrast only ever appears incidentally: we enjoy the pleasures of wine and later we have a headache. We

43. Aquinas, *Summa Theologiae*, I q49 a1; *Summa contra gentiles*, III.10:21–26; *De malo*, q 1 a3; *Summa Theologiae*, I q49 a1.

44. Aquinas, *Summa Theologiae*, I q49 a3.

45. Aquinas, *Summa Theologiae*, I q49 a2.

46. Aquinas, *Summa Theologiae*, I q104 a3, I q22 a2 ad 2, I q49 a2, and I q19 a9.

would not strive for a *bonum* we know to entail a *malum* if the good on which the evil appears did not seem more worthwhile than the good the evil deprives us of: we enjoy the wine and accept the headache, but only as long as keeping a clear head does not seem more worthwhile than enjoying the wine.

According to Aquinas, it is in this sense that God is not responsible for such and such an evil but indeed responsible for there being evils in the world at all. God accepts them because they are unavoidable side effects of what a good God wants and strives for. The evil of punishment is willed by God because he wants justice to be done, and the evil of reciprocal annihilation of life is willed by God because he wills to preserve the good order of the world, which cannot exist without processes of living and dying: "the corruption of one is the generation of another, and through this it is that a species is kept in existence." God wills the multitude and variety of species and things, but with it, he wills the inequality that exists between them as well, that is, he wills a plural and hierarchized universe of things differentiated by species and quality. This good order of creation includes both things that are so good that they can never have a defect and things that can lapse from the good, both things that cannot not be things that can also not be. One could only expect of God to abolish these differences and to exclude the evils contingent on and made possible by them if the goodness of the whole would benefit from this abolition. Yet this goodness would be diminished if the evil of certain parts of the whole were eliminated "since its beauty results from the ordered unity of good and evil things, seeing that evil arises from the lack of good, and yet certain goods are occasioned from those very evils."[47]

It would be wrong, however, to conclude that all *malum*, without distinction, is an indispensable moment of the goodness, beauty, and good order of creation. Evils that are unavoidable and belong to the perfection of creation because they support a higher good have to be carefully distinguished from evils that could be avoided and are at best tolerated by God, not only not willed but definitely not wanted (such as human atrocities). That for the sake of the greater goodness of the whole God could not permit himself to exclude the existence in general of evils in the world does not imply that such and such specific evil has to exist for the sake of the goodness of the whole. God wants a creation in which creatures define themselves according to the possibilities of their species. He wants a creation in which human beings are free to want and do Good or Evil because a world in which that is possible is better than a world in which it is not.[48] But God does not want that human beings do Evil; because such actions do not support but diminish the goodness of the whole, he at most tolerates it. The contingency of free acts belongs to the goodness of creation wanted by God; it is one of its perfections, not one of its deficiencies. But that does not apply to atrocities freely wanted and committed, which for that reason rightly incur the evil of punishment.[49]

47. Aquinas, *Summa Theologiae*, I q22 a2 and I q47 a1; *Summa contra gentiles*, II.45:106–108 and III.97:47–51; *Summa Theologiae*, I q47 a 2 (see also Stump, *Die göttliche Vorsehung und das Böse*); and *Summa contra gentiles*, III.71:177.

48. Aquinas, *Summa contra gentiles*, III.71:177 and III.73: 181–82.

49. It is therefore necessary to make a systematic distinction "between that which God fundamentally wants and that which he wants in a given particular case"; see Stump, *Die göttliche Vorsehung und das Böse*, 12.

Unlike Leibniz, therefore, Aquinas does not conclude that we live in the best of all possible worlds. The world is perfect because it is ordered in the most perfect way, yet that does not mean that everything in it is excellent: it means that on the whole it is the best way to serve the purpose for which it was created: the glorification of God.[50] Our world is not the best world because not only could it be different, it could be such that by avoiding avoidable atrocities, it could even more clearly serve its purpose. Nor can it be denied that God can make other things than the ones he is factually making. What God makes he cannot make better (for then he would not be God and creation would not be perfect with respect to the goal he is pursuing with it). But God *can* make better things than the ones he has made: "God can make something better than what he is making."[51] And God will make better things by creating the new world, free of the lapses of sin. That is why the existing world is perfect but not the absolutely best: it is perfect with regard to the goal God pursues with it, but it is not such that God would not have the power to create a world better than this one.

We are obliged, it seems, to conclude that in the new creation, too, there will be evils, namely, the evil that cannot be avoided to achieve other goods and the perfect good of the whole. A creation free of all kinds of evils, like a square circle, is an absurdity. What distinguishes it from the world as it is now, however, is that avoidable evils and Evil will no longer exist, which will put an end to an immense amount of senseless suffering and insufferable evil. The tension, however, that if the good of the whole is to be fully realized there cannot be a life without evils for finite beings, is not being resolved: individuals have to accept suffering, misery, and death for the sake of the greater good of the whole. This precedence of the whole over the part will later have many negative consequences because—put in moral or, rather, immoral terms—it is always possible to say that the realization of the higher good of the whole demands the sacrifice of the individual.

But the main problem of Aquinas's argumentatively impressive solution to the question of reconciling belief in a good God with the reality of evil and evils in the world is likely to be situated at an even more profound level: it is not that Aquinas did not succeed in demonstrating the nullity and reality of *malum* in a good creation; rather, he succeeded *too well*. *Malum* has not only been made understandable, it has become *indispensable*. And more precisely—beyond all the rigorously argued differentiations—it is indispensable not only at the end but already at the beginning for the simple but consequential fact that it is essentially a *contrast figure*:[52] just as there is no *malum* without

---

50. Aquinas, *Summa Theologiae*, I q103 a 1, and *Summa contra gentiles*, III.19:37–38.

51. Aquinas, *Summa Theologiae*, I q25 a5.

52. Hermann Cohen discusses this point: "Even in the most profound of the most profound thinkers, in Plato"—he may well have had *Theaetetus*, 176 a and b, in mind—"we find the offensive careless mistake that Evil must exist as a contrast for the Good" (Cohen, *Ethik des reinen Willens*, 298). This can be conceived of logically-semantically, as a thesis about the contrastive semantics of "good" and "evil"; it can also be seen as a metaphysical thesis about the structure of finite reality, in which *factually* the one does not exist without the other, even if *in principle* it could be otherwise. That it is the latter that applies to the *Theaetetus* is suggested by the advice that "we ought to fly away from earth," from "mortal nature" to "heaven as quickly as we can . . . and to fly away means to become like God, as far as this is possible; and to become like him, means to become holy, just, and wise" (Plato, *Theaetetus*, 176a–b:275).

bonum, so there is no *bonum* without *malum*. Where there are evils, there must be good things, and where there are good things, evils. But is that right? Is it not enough to say: we can only speak of the good where evils are *possible*, not only where they are *actual*? If we do not distinguish between possibility and actuality here, or if we conceive the possible in Aristotelian terms such that it necessarily has been, is, or will be actual, then the contrast figure of *bonum* and *malum* will always lead to neither or both necessarily being actual. And in that case, the problem comes down to the question why it is better for there to be anything at all rather than nothing—a question that cannot be answered, if only because there is no standard or site of evaluation outside of that which is to be assessed. It can only be asked where there is something. And it could only be given a positive answer where it would *per impossibile* be possible that merely asking it would make it impossible to ask.

7. Theodicy Arguments

Not by accident did Leibniz articulate and set out argumentatively to refute the problem he called "theodicy"[53] within the horizon of this basic metaphysical question. Nor is it by accident that he articulated it not as a question concerning the justifiability of belief in a perfectly good, wise, and powerful creator based on our highly questionable experience of the world (the empirical argument, such as we find it later in Hume) but as a formal problem of contradiction between belief in an omnibeneficent, omnificent, and omnipotent God and the experience of Evil and evils in the world (the logical argument): he relates a series of propositions about God ("according to rational insight, God is such and such") and a series of propositions about the experience of Evil and evils in human life ("there are evils," "such and such an evil exists," "there is a significant number of evils in the world") to each other in such a way as to produce, or apparently to produce, a contradiction because both series of propositions are or seem to be incompatible.

The contradiction can be found in a variety of contents and contexts and be construed in different ways. McCloskey, for example, distinguishes between five types of theodicy arguments:[54]

1. *The Classic Contradiction Argument*: The contradiction is seen to exist between the existence of God, of the one perfectly good, all-powerful, and all-wise being, and the existence of evils as such.

2. *The Qualified Contradiction Argument*: The contradiction is seen to exist between the existence of God and specific kinds or amounts of evils (moral evils and natural evils like the suffering of animals).[55]

In any case, the more we emphasize the *contrastive aspect* of Evil, the less we conceive of it as something absolutely negative and see it all the more as the other side of the Good. While this makes Evil a little bit more comprehensible (as the opposite of the Good), it at the same time domesticates Evil in an oppositional bond with the Good.

53. Leibniz, letter to des Bosses, February 5, 1712, in *Philosophical Papers and Letters*, 601.

54. McCloskey, *God and Evil*, 3–5. The designations are my own.

55. For a discussion of typical arguments with respect to the suffering of animals, see Farrer, *Love Almighty and Ills Unlimited*, 77–95.

3. *The Moral Contradiction Argument*: The contradiction is not seen to be a factual or logical contradiction between (propositions about) God and (true propositions about) evils but to lie in the moral incompatibility that arises from the notion that a perfectly good, all-powerful, and all-wise creator could have created, in a morally consistent way, a world containing such evils.

4. *The Unavoidability of a Factual or Logical Contradiction*: The contradiction between the existence of God and the reality of evils in the world cannot be avoided by conceiving of God as omnipotent but not wholly good, or as wholly good but not omnipotent, or as more or less good and omnipotent.

5. *The Unavoidability of a Moral Contradiction*: Even a modification of the attributes of God cannot avoid the moral contradiction between the existence of God and the admission of evils in the world.

Whatever contents are seen to be in contradiction, the contradiction is always construed in such a way that a series of propositions about God is claimed or supposedly demonstrated to be incompatible with a series of propositions about evils in the world.

8. The Core Argument

Hence it is possible to articulate the core argument of the theodicy debate (the basic theodicy argument) in a brief and concise manner:

1. If God exists, then no evils exist.

2. Evils exist.

3. Therefore, God does not exist.

Formally correct, the conclusion follows from the two premises according to the rule *modus ponendo ponens*, provided the terms "God" and "evils" are employed in the same sense in the premises and in the conclusion. The conclusion is true if the premises are true, and the premises are true if that which is understood by "God" and "evils" can be truthfully predicated to something. It is difficult to deny the truth of the second premise,[56] even if one may disagree about what is meant by "evils" and whether the statement "evils exist" is true because of the fact of evils in general (*that* evils exist), of a specific kind of evils (that *these* evils exist), or of the unimaginable extent of evils (that *so many* evils exist). But is the first premise true?

That depends on the *conception of God* employed in the argument.[57] The premise articulates a semantic relationship between the conceptions of "God" and of "evils" according to which both expressions are incompatible when employed simultaneously:

---

56. Which does not, of course, prevent its being frequently contested, for example by "Christian Science, which understands evil as a false perception, an error of the mortal mind," or by presenting it as "really a disguised form of the good." See Wright, *Theology of the Dark Side*, 80–81. Even if these may be true in some cases, as general theses they blatantly contradict people's perception of the world and of themselves. See Stackhouse, *Can God Be Trusted?*, 23–26.

57. See Weisberger, *Suffering Belief*, 19–55.

when we say "God," we cannot say "evils" without contradicting ourselves, and vice versa. Or, to put it in terms of an argument and not of a semantic rule: if we presuppose the classic theistic conception of God in the Western tradition, according to which God is all-powerful, all-wise, and all-benevolent, then it seems we can or must agree with J. L. Mackie[58] that

1. A perfectly good being prevents all evils insofar as it is able to do so.

2. An omnipotent and omniscient being can do everything that is (logically) possible.

3. Therefore, if there exists a perfectly good, powerful, and wise being, then this being perfectly prevents all evils (from (1) and (2)).

4. If God exists, he is a perfectly good, powerful, and wise being.

5. Therefore, if God exists, he perfectly prevents all evils (from (3) and (4)).

It follows from (5) that no evils exist if God exists, and that is the premise of the basic theodicy argument.

Most theists accept (5), but not all: some would like to avoid ascribing *perfect* power and wisdom to God, others implement different limitations to prevent the conclusion of the basic theodicy argument. It is possible to think of several strategies for attempting to do so, which are employed time and again:

1. One may modify the conception of "God" in the first premise and thus argue that God is not all-powerful, only quite powerful;[59] or that God is good not unrestrictedly and in every respect but only quite good;[60] or that God is not all-knowing but, at best, capable of learning, and so on.[61]

---

58. Mackie, "Evil and Omnipotence," 29–30; see also Mackie, *Miracle of Theism*, 150–76.

59. Limiting the omnipotence of God is explicitly advocated in, for example, Griffin, *God, Power, and Evil* and *Evil Revisited*; Kushner, *When Bad Things Happen to Good People*; Hartshorne, *Omnipotence*; or Jonas, "Concept of God after Auschwitz." See also Jüngel, "Gottes ursprüngliches Anfangen"; Henrix, "Machtentsagung Gottes?"; Schiwy, *Abschied vom allmächtigen Gott*; Kessler, *Gott und das Leid*, 60–69; and Berthold, *God, Evil, and Human Learning*, 39–46, 73–90. These different attempts result in an "ecological theology" (Berthold, *God, Evil, and Human Learning*, 73–90) in which God and world are no longer clearly distinct, provided no other way of asserting the difference between creator and creation is found. Pantheistic conceptions seek to mark the difference by considering God's greatness over against the world to lie not only in God's perfection but in the possibility of increasing this perfection: not only is God at any given time the most perfect that exists, but he is also capable at any time to become more perfect than he is. See Dalferth, *Gott: Philosophisch-theologische Denkversuche*, 192–212.

60. David R. Blumenthal thinks that "God is usually, but not always, good"; he even goes so far as to say that a "propensity for evil is inherent in God" and that Evil is "a component of God Godself" (Blumenthal, "Theodicy," 96–98; see also *Facing the Abusing God*). This results in a fundamental ambivalence of God that makes it impossible unreservedly to trust God and may compel us to remain silent about God for religious reasons. See Crenshaw, *Defending God*, 191–95.

61. Harold S. Kushner explicitly argues in favor of God's limitedness: "I recognize his limitations. He is limited in what he can do by the laws of nature and by the evolution of human nature and human moral freedom . . . I can worship a God who hates suffering but cannot eliminate it, more easily than I can worship a God who chooses to make children suffer and die, for whatever exalted reason" (Kushner, *When Bad Things Happen to Good People*, 134). See also Hall, *God and Human Suffering*, 155; Griffin, *God, Power, and Evil*, III.251–310; and Inbody, *Transforming God*, 141–62.

2. One may modify the implicit premise that God is the creator of everything by conceiving of creation not as an act of primary causation by God but as God's participation in creative processes that, in transforming creation, transforms the creator as well.[62]

3. One may modify the second premise by negating the reality of evils in the world;[63] or by defining them as *mala quoad nos*, evils that exist as long as we exist, not as *mala per se*; or by presenting them as functionally indispensable for a higher good (soul-making);[64] or by regarding them as posing a problem not for God but only for us creatures.[65]

4. One may reject the alleged contradiction of the basic theodicy argument as illusory by providing deductive or inductive arguments that show the series of propositions about God and about evils in the world to be compatible. Deductively, one may argue that the experience of suffering and evils does not stand in contradiction to belief in God, such that it is reasonable to believe in the existence of God despite the evils in the world.[66] Or, inductively, one may attempt to show that it is more probable that God exists than that he does not exist, that the experience of evils and suffering does not make the hypothesis of the existence of God any less probable, that no statistical improbability concerning the truth of belief in God's existence could undermine the probability of a belief in God's existence that is founded on

62. Taken together, the first two points (modifying the concept of God and modifying the conception of creation) constitute what Thiel aptly calls "the 'best-of-all-possible-Gods' theodicy" (Thiel, *God, Evil, and Innocent Suffering*, 46–52). Exemplary here are the attempts of process theology to avoid the formal contradiction: neoclassically limiting the classical concept of God (his omnipotence or omniscience, for example), they think God's perfection as capable of increase. God, to be sure, is at any moment in time so perfect that nothing else can surpass him, but he can surpass himself, that is, he can become more perfect than he is at a given moment. See Griffin, *God, Power, and Evil* and *Evil Revisited*; Corey, *Evolution and the Problem of Natural Evil*, 324–27; Baum, *Gott nach Auschwitz*, 128–35. Marjorie Suchocki, however, is right to point out that "[t]o reduce the fact of evil to the myriad choices making up the ongoing universe is to overlook the inevitability of conflict when choices necessarily involve exclusion." The "ambiguity of existence relative to good and evil is real," and that is why a God who is becoming ever more perfect alone does not suffice to solve the actual problem (Suchocki, *End of Evil*, 68). For a critique of Whitehead's attempt at a solution, see my *Gott: Philosophisch-theologische Denkversuche*, 153–212, as well as Nüchtern, *Warum lässt Gott das zu?*; Schiwy, *Abschied vom allmächtigen Gott*; Hoping, "Abschied vom allmächtigen Gott?"; and Kress, *Gottes Allmacht angesichts von Leiden*.

63. See McFarlane, *Grammar of Fear and Evil*, 168–69.

64. This is the much-discussed basic idea of Hick, *Evil and the God of Love*; see also Madden and Hare, *Evil and the Concept of God*; Kane, "Failure of Soul-Making Theodicy," "Soul-making Theodicy and Eschatology," and "Evil and Privation"; Kreiner, *Gott im Leid*, 321–93; Weisberger, *Suffering Belief*, 125–62; and Corey, *Evolution and the Problem of Natural Evil* 202–12, 281–337.

65. See Weisberger, *Suffering Belief*, 59–82.

66. This is the strategy adopted by, for example, James M. Petrik who in *Evil Beyond Belief* argues against Marilyn McCord Adams that it is not only consistent "with God's love and goodness with respect to an individual that the individual's life be engulfed or defeated by horrendous evil" (Petrik, *Evil Beyond Belief*, 130); while inconceivable ills in the world do make a point against unexpectable good, for Petrik, they make an even stronger point in favor of God (137–38). On the category of "horrendous evils," see Adams, *Horrendous Evils*, and the debate between her ("Horrors in Theological Context") and William C. Placher ("Engagement with Marilyn McCord Adams's *Horrendous Evils*").

individual experience,[67] and that, therefore, it is more reasonable to believe in the existence of God despite the evils in the world than it is not to believe.

In these last two cases, the core argument is modified in such a way as to limit neither the conception of God nor that of the world but instead to look for reasons for the world's being evil given that there is a good creator: a perfectly good being prevents all evils *unless there is a good reason for not preventing them*. From this point of view, however, the basic theodicy argument is to be reformulated as follows:

1. If God exists, then no evils exist, unless there is a reason to justify God permitting them.

2. Evils exist.

3. There is no reason to justify God permitting evils.

4. Therefore, God does not exist.

According to Richard Swinburne, this modified version of the basic theodicy argument is the real challenge for theology and the philosophy of religion today. Is there a reason to justify God permitting evils? If the answer is yes, the theodicy argument can be rejected; if it is no, its conclusion has to be accepted.

This moves the focus of interest from logical to empirical arguments. *Logical* arguments seek to show that specific evil matters of fact—for example, *that evils exist in general in the world* or *that this kind or this amount of evils exists*—are, in a strictly logical sense, inconsistent with a central proposition concerning God: *If evils (or evils of a specific kind or amount) exist, then God is not (for example) omnipotent; therefore, there is no God.* Two matters of fact are logically inconsistent if there is no possible world in which both can exist simultaneously or (in the case of propositions) if there is no possible world in which they can both be true. *Empirical* arguments, in turn, say that specific evil matters of fact render the truth of specific propositions about God improbable. Unlike logical arguments, empirical arguments are not bound to claim that propositions about God have to be false in all possible worlds in which these evil matters of fact exist. Whereas *logical arguments* thus typically seek to prove that belief in God in the face of the reality of evils cannot possibly be true, *empirical arguments* typically argue that the fact of evils or of specific kinds or amounts of evil constitutes a good (albeit not absolutely compelling) reason for considering belief in God to be wrong, or at least without foundation.

9. Logical Arguments[68]

In the case of *logical* arguments, the attempt is made to derive a self-contradiction from the conjunction of the two propositions, "God exists" and "Evils exist." Such a contradiction can be avoided only if one or both propositions are abandoned as false. Given

67. See Howard-Snyder, "God, Evil, and Suffering," 114.

68. This section picks up on the discussion in Dalferth, *Die Wirklichkeit des Möglichen*, II.2; see also Weisberger, *Suffering Belief*, 22–40.

the experience of suffering and evils, the reality of evils cannot seriously be contested, which leads critics to conclude that it is the claim about the existence of God that must be abandoned. In opposing all apologetic attempts at modifying or interpreting the two propositions such that they do not end up contradicting each other, they insist that there is no possible world in which "God exists" and "Evils exist" are both true. Since, given the realities of the world as it is, it is not seriously to be contested that evils exist, however, it is not possible that both propositions be false such that rationally one cannot but reach the atheistic conclusion that God does not exist.

To reject this argument (since it is based on deductive logic), it suffices to show that there is at least one possible world in which the two propositions "God exists" and "Evils exist" are true such that a contradiction exacting an alternative decision does not arise. It is in this sense that Nelson Pike, for example, argues that "God, being a perfectly good, omniscient, and omnipotent being, would create the best of all possible worlds" and that "the best of all possible worlds contains instances of suffering as logically indispensable components." Since this cannot be shown to be self-contradictory, it is possibly true, and if it can possibly be true, critics cannot continue to maintain their inconsistency claim.[69]

Such a "defense," as Plantinga calls it, of course, leaves a decisive point unsettled. It does not ask whether such a possible world actually exists, which would indicate that this possible world is actual in the factual world. That would be the task of a "theodicy" that goes beyond a "defense."[70] Nor does it ask what supports or opposes interpreting the propositions "God exists" and "Evils exist" the way the critics do, such that a contradiction arises or is prevented with regard to the real world. And it cannot claim that demonstrating the possibility of such an interpretational world amounts to demonstrating that there is no defensible interpretation of these propositions that would necessarily lead to a contradictory opposition, such that the two propositions could be possible in every possible world, including the real world. That there is a possible world in which both are true does not mean that there is no possible world in which both are not true. Even if one accepts, as some modal versions of the ontological argument do, that the proposition "God exists" must be true in all possible worlds if it is true in one possible world, one does not have to accept that the same holds true for the question of its compatibility with "Evils exist": unlike "God exists," "Evils exist" is not usually considered, not even by theists, to be a necessary truth. Yet if it is neither impossible nor necessary that "God exists" and "Evils exist" together are true, the decisive question becomes whether what can be the case in a *possible world* is the case in *our real world*. And that, precisely, is the problem the empirical-inductive argument addresses.

69. Pike, "Hume on Evil," esp. 46.

70. Alvin Plantinga distinguishes between two kinds of argumentation in engaging with the theodicy problem, which he calls "defense" and "theodicy." While the former aims merely to show that the two (series of) propositions "God exists" and "evils exist" can be reconciled without contradiction, the latter seeks furthermore to demonstrate that the possible world thereby construed does in fact exist. The "defense" limits itself to showing its possibility, the "theodicy" wants to show that it is a reality; see Plantinga, *God, Freedom, and Evil*, 63; "Self-Profile," 42; "Epistemic Probability," 561.

10. Empirical Arguments

As opposed to deductive arguments, empirical arguments tread more cautiously. They argue that given the fact, or the kind, or the amount of evils experienced in this world, it is quite, very, or entirely improbable that a perfectly good, wise, and powerful God exists to whom we owe this world as his creation.[71] The argument is not that there is a logical contradiction between "God exists" and "Evils exist," since this, as has been shown on a number of occasions, is not true as a matter of principle.[72] The claim now is that given the reality of evils, it is more likely that God does not exist than it is that he does exist. For if God is an all-benevolent, all-wise, and all-powerful being, he would prevent all evils that are not indispensable for the sake of a higher good or of preventing even greater evils. Yet there are so many evils that are senseless and unjustifiable in every respect—because they do not in any way enable a higher good or prevent a greater evil, or, if they do do so, they are not indispensable means to this end (that is to say, it is not the case that only this evil could have prevented that greater evil)—such that a lot, even if not everything, suggests that God is not.

The central point of this argument is the claim that many evils in the world are superfluous and excessive, absurd and completely senseless. William L. Rowe has put this point as follows:

> First, I think, is the fact that there is an enormous variety and profusion of in-
> tense human and animal suffering in our world. Second, is the fact that much of
> this suffering seems quite unrelated to any greater goods (or the absence of equal
> or greater evils) that might justify it. And, finally, there is the fact that such suf-
> fering as is related to greater goods (or the absence of equal or greater evils) does
> not, in many cases, seem so intimately related as to require its permission by an
> omnipotent being bent on securing those goods (the absence of those evils).[73]

Stephen J. Wykstra and Alvin Plantinga have objected that these points do not consti-tute persuasive arguments for the truth of "God exists" being improbable because "we couldn't reasonably be expected to know what God's reason is for permitting a given evil."[74] That *we* cannot see any reason why God permits or does not prevent evils of this kind does not amount to God not being able to have any reason to do so, "indeed, it is only *hubris* which would tempt us to think that we could so much as grasp God's plans here, even if he proposed to divulge them to us."[75] According to Plantinga, we as creatures reach a fundamental limit to our insight here—not because we would imagine

---

71. See Draper, "Pain and Pleasure"; "Probabilistic Arguments from Evil"; and "More Pain and Pleasure"; as well as Weisberger, *Suffering Belief*, 40–46; and Otte, "Probability and Draper's Evidential Argument from Evil."

72. See in particular Alvin Plantinga's studies, *Nature of Necessity*, 164–95, *God, Freedom, and Evil*, and "Self-Profile," 36–55.

73. Rowe, "Problem of Evil and Some Varieties of Atheism," 131–132n5; see his "Empirical Argu-ment from Evil" and "Ruminations about Evil."

74. Plantinga, "Epistemic Probability," 562. See also Wykstra, "Humean Obstacle," 152, as well as Rowe, "Evil and the Theistic Hypothesis," and van Inwagen, "Problem of Evil," as well as Hasker, *Provi-dence, Evil, and the Openness of God*, 58–79.

75. Plantinga, "Epistemic Probability," 562.

ourselves to be suffering evils but because we cannot expect to have insight into God's reasons and understand why he permits or does not prevent these evils. If anyone expected to be able to do so, "the creature would be above its Creator and would judge its Creator—and that is completely absurd," as Anselm classically put it.[76]

Yet if this limit to our insight, a consequence of creation, is valid, then the inductive argument loses its foundation. What seems senseless to us does by no means have to be senseless for God. That a large part of evils in the world is superfluous, excessive, and without any sense is by no means as obviously true as it is claimed to be. That is why it does not reliably support the inference that it is probable that God does not exist—independently of the notion of probability one might invoke, as Plantinga demonstrates: there is no basis for such an inference either in personal, frequency-theoretical, logical, or epistemic conceptions of probability.[77] Every evil, no matter how senseless it might appear to us, makes it possible to suggest that it is not impossible that God has a reason for it even if we do not or cannot know this reason.

The suggestion that there might be reasons that we do not know or that we might in principle be incapable of knowing is, of course, of little use in trying to make plausible evils that appear senseless to us. But that is not the task of the suggestion. The argument does not seek positively to demonstrate the sense of evils that appear senseless but only to problematize the self-evidence of the way in which the senselessness of such evils and the probability of God's non-existence are being presupposed. In a purely formal manner, this task is performed by the suggestion that it is not impossible for there to be a divine reason for such evils (even if it is hidden from us) because the notion of a divine reason for evils that appear senseless to us is not self-contradictory. The argument thus does not name any of God's reasons but keeps open the possibility that there are such reasons: it only speaks of a possibility, not of a reality. And the more such possible reasons can be given for a specific evil, the less it can be dismissed as obviously senseless.[78]

This does not provide a better understanding of any given evil, but it is enough to reject the inductive objection to belief in God based on senseless evils in the world. This belief can neither be questioned nor be founded on determining that, given the evils in the world, "God exists" is more probable or improbable than the opposite. That, according to Plantinga, is why the decisive issue for assessing the rationality of belief is not which "*propositional* evidence theistic belief enjoys" but "the degree, if any, of warrant or positive epistemic status enjoyed by theistic belief *apart* from any conferred upon it or its denial by other beliefs."[79] The rationality of belief does not stand or fall on whether it is possible, given the evils in the world, to render the truth of "God exists" more probable than the opposite but on whether this belief itself has the necessary certainty about its truth, and it does not obtain this certainty based on other certain truths or on more or less certain probabilities. Hence Plantinga considers the criticism founded on the inductive argument to fail.[80]

76. Anselm, *Proslogion*, in *Major Works*, 88.

77. Plantinga, "Epistemic Probability," 564–84.

78. See Alston, "Evidential Argument From Evil."

79. Plantinga, "Epistemic Probability," 584.

80. He does, however, consider not just antitheistic criticism but the larger share of the arguments

11. Death as Containing the Consequences of Freedom

For Richard Swinburne, this does not go far enough. He not only wants to reject the criticism articulated in the basic theodicy argument; he wants, in the sense of the expanded argument, to give reasons for why God has created a world in which evils, suffering, and Evil exist to such an extent in the first place. According to him, God not only has, without contradicting himself, the possibility and the right to permit evils, he even has to permit them when and insofar as doing so makes a good possible that even God could not realize any other way.[81] The higher good of free will would thus justify moral and natural evils. For if God wants not just a world of causally manipulable things but of beings that can freely decide, choose, and act for themselves,[82] then he must accept that they choose evil. Swinburne considers it to be a logical self-contradiction to expect that "God could give to men free and responsible choice and also make it the case that they did not choose to do evil. The possibility of men doing evil is a logical consequence of the good of their having free and responsible choice."[83] Freedom, according to him, implies the possibility of being able to do evil.[84] Such a freedom to choose and act on one's own authority, however, could not exist without natural evil: "natural evil . . . is necessary in order that certain free agents, viz. humans, may have the freedom to bring about goods or evils."[85] If it were not possible to inflict suffering on other living beings, or to keep them from suffering or to alleviate the suffering that afflicts them, there could not be any ethically relevant freedom to do good or evil. To choose good and not evil, we must know what consequences our action (can) have and "how to bring about evil or prevent its occurrence."[86] According to Swinburne, however, we can only have this knowledge on the basis of relevant experiences, and this presupposes the existence of many natural evils, for otherwise we would not be able to know what we must know.[87]

Knowledge, of course, is by no means to be limited to what we have acquired and can acquire by way of empirical experience, and to be able to distinguish in an

---

for the probability of belief mobilized *ab extra* by theistic countercriticism to be "shallow, tepid, and ultimately frivolous" (Plantinga, "Epistemic Probability," 558).

81. Swinburne, "Free Will Defence," 586.

82. Be it said in passing that we need to distinguish between freedom of the will, freedom of choice, and freedom of action. Swinburne's arguments focus on freedom of the will. See Wiertz, "*Das Problem des Übels* in Richard Swinburnes Religionsphilosophie," and Kreiner, *Gott im Leid*, 345–50.

83. Swinburne, "Free Will Defence," 588.

84. It is in this concept of freedom that we must look for the central problem, not, as Carl-Friedrich Geyer thinks, primarily in the contradiction between "God's omnipotence and eternal truths of reason that limit this omnipotence" (Geyer, "Theodizee oder Kulturgeschichte des Bösen?," 247). Geyer reads Swinburne the way he reads Leibniz, but Swinburne precisely does not argue deductively, from the concept of God to its compatibility with the reality of the world; on the contrary, he constructs a concept of God by way of an empirical-probabilistic reflection on limits.

85. Swinburne, "Free Will Defence," 594.

86. Swinburne, *Existence of God*, 245.

87. Swinburne, *Existence of God*, 245–46. Eleonore Stump, in "Knowledge, Freedom and the Problem of Evil," rightly criticizes the idea that we can have relevant knowledge of good and ills only on the basis of real ills.

appropriate manner between good and evil, we do not have to be familiar with real evils; it suffices to be aware of their possibility.[88]

Swinburne admits as much, but he insists that ethical freedom would not be possible without knowledge about relevant alternatives and that there is no better way of familiarizing us with this alternative than via the reality of natural evils: "The good of men having a wealth of opportunity for patience, compassion, encouragement and gratitude of particular kinds cannot (logically) be provided in a better way than by the provision of natural evil."[89] Just as without natural evils human freedom would be impossible, so human freedom is impossible without the possibility of moral evil.

This is not to say that human freedom is compelled to realize this possibility. Moral evil is always the result of a free choice for which the human being, not God, is responsible. Nor is it to say that natural evils must exist and that they could not not exist. The claim is only that no human freedom could exist if no natural evils existed and that no such freedom could exist without the possibility of doing evil. Putting aside the dubious epistemological arguments mobilized by Swinburne, the core of the first claim is that factually—whatever else might be thinkable—human beings and their freedom exist only as the product of an evolutionary history that implies pain, suffering, and death in many ways and to many other people.[90] Because the human being did not fall from the sky but belongs to the history of evolution, human freedom does not exist without the reality of natural evils. All earthly living beings live at the expense of other life, and human beings do as well.[91] The possibility of human freedom thus always already presupposes the reality of natural evils—not because these evils would be necessary as such but because human freedom as a product of evolutionary history would not be possible without natural evils.

88. Swinburne, *Existence of God*, 245–57.

89. Swinburne, "Problem of Evil," 26.

90. This constitutes the most difficult problem for theists, as Darwin already emphasized on numerous occasions. "I own that I cannot see, as plainly as others do, & as I should wish to do, evidence of design & beneficence on all sides of us. There seems to me too much misery in the world. I cannot persuade myself that a beneficent & omnipotent God would have designedly created the Ichneumonidæ with the express intention of their feeding within the living bodies of caterpillars, or that a cat should play with mice. Not believing this, I see no necessity in the belief that the eye was expressly designed. On the other hand I cannot anyhow be contented to view this wonderful universe & especially the nature of man, & to conclude that everything is the result of brute force. I am inclined to look at everything as resulting from designed laws, with the details, whether good or bad, left to the working out of what we may call chance. Not that this notion *at all* satisfies me. I feel most deeply that the whole subject is too profound for the human intellect. A dog might as well speculate on the mind of Newton.—Let each man hope & believe what he can.—" (Darwin, "Letter to Asa Grey"). He makes a similar point in his *Autobiography*, 90. On the debate concerning and following Darwin, see Hunter, *Rival Enlightenments*; for discussions within the framework of an intelligent design approach, see Haught, *God After Darwin*, and Corey, *Evolution and the Problem of Natural Evil*.

91. Not just in the economic sense that given the scarcity of resources, the struggle for survival is an essential part of being an animal and of being human but in the biological sense that factually, there is no construction of life without the destruction of other life. In the former case, it is still possible to argue "that material scarcity occasions a more profound participation in God's goodness, holiness, righteousness, and providence" (Barrera, *God and the Evil of Scarcity*, 155) because it makes people open up to that which comes to them from God; in the latter case, that can no longer be rendered plausible.

The reality of natural evils can accordingly be justified by God intending this higher good of human freedom in this and not in any other way. The responsibility for moral evils, on the contrary, lies solely with human beings, not with God, because while God does have to accept the possibility of Evil as a consequence of the human freedom he intends, he is not responsible for the realization of Evil. At most, God could be held responsible if this could be seen as *carte blanche* for unlimited moral evildoing and excessive natural evils. But God, Swinburne tells us, permits neither and instead places a limit on human beings' doing and suffering Evil—especially by means of *death*: "Death is God's safety barrier."[92] Far from seeing in creatures' mortality and death the last and the strongest argument against God's goodness,[93] Swinburne conceives of them as precisely what confirms that, given the evils of the world, God's goodness is always greater.[94] God cannot prevent the natural and moral evils of the world if he wants human freedom, but he contains their excessiveness, intensity, and unlimited propagation by having us, at a certain point, lose consciousness and die. Put differently, on the path of evolution God not only made sure that human freedom becomes possible through evils but also that, despite human freedom, moral evils do not gain the upper hand and natural evils do not increase in such a way as to render human freedom impossible once more.

12. The Free Will Defense

By means of a version of the "free will defense," Swinburne seeks to reject the alleged contradiction between "God exists" and "Evils exist" not just in the case of moral evils but in the case of natural evils as well. Unlike Plantinga, he does not consider natural evils to be a kind of moral evil that can be put down to the activities of non-human agents. But unlike the Augustinian tradition, he does not consider natural evils to be a punishment God imposed for the human being's original sin. Instead, he interprets them constructively as a necessary (evolutionary) condition of possibility of human freedom and thus moves them within the purview of the free will defense. This strategy of argumentation received its name from Antony Flew; Alvin Plantinga has stated it in more precise terms and developed it as the central argument in resolving the logical theodicy

92. Swinburne, "Free Will Defence," 591.

93. To impute to Swinburne with respect to this argument the cynical thesis that "the best way to limit an evil is the next evil," as Hermanni (*Das Böse und die Theodizee*, 299n17) does, is to overlook that Swinburne does not share the premise of this objection, namely that death and "the consequences of inflicting suffering that annul the suffering are obviously themselves evils." The central point of Swinburne's argumentation is precisely the suggestion that death is not *ipso facto* always and everywhere to be regarded as an evil and that it can be coded differently. And what is true of death is true of other things usually categorized as ills or as Evil: what is at issue are always happenings, processes, experiences, deeds that can be coded differently and whose definition, therefore, may include different overlapping perspectives that compel us to treat the phenomena in a hermeneutically and theologically differentiated way.

94. Corey, *Evolution and the Problem of Natural Evil*, 318–19, takes up Swinburne's argument and expands it by suggesting that with death, God created the possibility of many biological forms of life developing on earth. Without dying and death, "the world would have quickly become full of creatures, such that there would no longer have been room for any more" (319). It remains entirely unclear, though, why it should be better "to create a smaller, death infested world, instead of a much larger one containing physically immortal creatures" (319).

problem.[95] Plantinga's core idea is that the contradiction between "God exists" and "Evils exist" can be avoided if there is a possible reason why the perfectly wise, good, and powerful God does not create a perfectly good world but permits or does not prevent certain evils. The existence of free beings is one such reason. If a world in which free beings exist is better than a world in which that is not the case, and if it is impossible in a world that free beings exist but no possibility to do evil exists, then it is not only impossible that God creates a world without free beings (it would not be the best possible world a perfect God could create), it is also possible that God could not have created a world that contains free beings but does not contain the possibility that evil exist in that world. This, however, suffices to reject the alleged logical contradiction between "God exists" and "Evils exist." It is not necessary to demonstrate either that the possibility of freely doing evil is in fact realized, or that God indeed permits evils for the sake of the existence of free beings, nor that it is true or probable that God has created such a world: to reject the logical theodicy problem, it is fully sufficient to show the *possibility* of the proposition that a perfect God create a world in which evils exist, no matter how true or false, probable or improbable, plausible or implausible this proposition might be. For the mere possibility of such a proposition bears out that "God exists" and "Evils exist" are not logically incompatible.

Plantinga's free will defense does not presuppose the actual existence of free beings. For his argumentative strategy, the demonstration that a God-created world of free beings is possible suffices to reject the logical contradiction that allegedly arises from the conjunction of "God exists" and "Evils exist." If it is possible to present a non-contradictory interpretation of these two propositions, the logical problem is resolved and the theodicy-theoretical objection collapses. The consistency of two propositions P and Q is proven if there is a proposition R that can be combined with P such that Q logically follows from the conjunction R and P. Or, as Plantinga writes in general terms: "find a possible state of affairs such that if it were actual, then P and Q would both be true."[96] This, precisely, and only this, is what his version of the free will defense seeks to accomplish.[97]

13. Does God Have Good Reasons?

For many people, that's not enough. They seek not only to resolve the logical theodicy problem; they seek to explain why evils exist at all in a world created by God or why the (kind of) evils exist that we do in fact find in our world. That is, to reject the inference

95. See Flew, "Divine Omnipotence and Human Freedom," as well as McCloskey, *God and Evil*, 117–24; Dore, *Moral Scepticism*; and Weisberger, *Suffering Belief*, 163–207. For Plantinga, see his *God and Other Minds*, 131–55; *Nature of Necessity*, 164–95; *God, Freedom, and Evil*; and "Self-Profile," 36–55; see also Stackhouse, *Can God Be Trusted?*, 70–87.

96. Plantinga, "Self-Profile," 43. And he adds, correctly, that "R need not be true, or probable, or plausible, or accepted by the scientists of our culture circle, or congenial to 'man come of age,' or anything of the sort: it need only to be such that its conjunction with P is possible and entails Q."

97. That is why the criticisms voiced by Hermanni, *Das Böse und die Theodizee*, 292–314, however much they are worth thinking about individually, miss the essential point.

from the reality of evils to the non-existence or improbability of God's existence, they want to give arguments that obtain not only in a possible world but in our real world. The free will defense limits itself to rejecting a formal contradiction (in its negative variants) or to demonstrating that there is a possibility for reconciling the premises of the theodicy argument (in its positive variants). Instead, the attempt is now made to give good reasons for God's having been able to create and for in fact having created the world just as it is, including its evils. Among the most important arguments mobilized to this end are:[98]

1. God wanted to create good, but because good is always the opposite of evils and Evil, God could only create a world with evils and Evil. If no *malum* existed in the world, no *bonum* would exist, either. Epistemically speaking, one could say that *we* need *malum* to be able to recognize *bonum* at all: "God might have made everything good, though *we* should not have noticed it if he had."[99] Yet the first argument does not obtain because there is not only the contrast between *good* and *evil* but also the one between *good* and *better* and, moreover, the observation that *some* evils must exist in order for *some* goods to exist does not justify that *this* concrete evil must exist. And the second argument does not obtain because it posits a reality where a possibility suffices: that a *bonum* cannot be recognized without distinguishing it from a *malum* does not mean that the *malum* has to be real in order for a *bonum* to be recognized as such.

2. God wanted to create a world in which free choice exists because such a world is better than a world without freedom. That is why he had to accept that human beings freely choose to do evil. But on the one hand, free choice could also exist if it were possible to decide to do evil, even if one factually does not do evil, such that the reality of evils in the world would not thereby be justified. On the other hand, free choice can only exist where it is possible to choose between different options but not only where the choice is between *bonum* and *malum*: a world in which the only choice is one between goods of various kinds, too, would be a world in which freedom of choice exists. And finally, the evil that factually exists in the world is in many cases such that it does not allow for and support the free choices of others but precisely makes them impossible and prevents them: as Swinburne objects to himself, "in our world freedom and responsibility have gone too far—produced too much physical and mental hurt . . . God might well tolerate a boy hitting his younger brother, but not Belsen."[100] A world in which "Sophie's choice" is possible cannot be justified this way: although it is *possible* to choose because the concrete alternative exists, *one cannot* choose because every decision is morally and humanly crippling.[101]

3. Because God wanted to create a world in which humans could develop to become morally responsible beings, he had to create a world with evils. A world without

98. On what follows, see Phillips, *Problem of Evil*, 49–94.

99. Mackie, "Evil and Omnipotence," 205.

100. Swinburne, "Problem of Evil," 89.

101. As Phillips, *Problem of Evil*, 75–77, is right to point out in discussing the film, *Sophie's Choice*.

evils would be a world in which there could be no moral character development. Yet such a world would be less good than one in which there could be such development. That is why God had good reason to create a world with evils.[102] That, however, is not a very convincing argument: confronted with evils and innocent suffering, nobody must decide to live a morally good life. And even when that happens, the extent of evils and innocent suffering in the world is so monstrous as to exceed any measure that might be justified this way.[103]

4. Because God wanted to create a world in which his creatures would have occasion to behave in a morally responsible way, he created a world that contains Evil, since "the price of possible passive evils for other creatures is a price worth paying for agents to have greater responsibility for each other," Swinburne thinks.[104] This argument is to be rejected for reasons that resemble those for rejecting the previous argument. It becomes downright cynical when we look at the suffering of concrete living beings (human beings or animals) that is supposed to exist for the purpose of fostering the moral responsibility of others. Even if it could be shown that this suffering does in fact serve that purpose, and that that purpose could not be achieved in any other way, it would nonetheless constitute a morally indefensible instrumentalization of the suffering of others.[105]

5. A similar point is to be made against a further argument of Swinburne's according to which some physical and mental evils may stimulate some people to strive for a better life.[106] These evils do not have to have this effect, and even if they do, it would still have to be shown that this could not be achieved any other way. And even if it could not be achieved any other way, the question remains why so many more evils exist than would be necessary to this end.

6. "A world without evils would be a world in which men could show no forgiveness, no compassion, no self-sacrifice. And men without opportunity are deprived of the opportunity to show themselves at their noblest. For this reason God might well allow some of his creatures to perform evil acts with passive evils as consequences,

---

102. Swinburne, *Providence and the Problem of Evil*, 82–110, 167–71.

103. Thiel, in *God, Evil, and Innocent Suffering*, has rightly made admitting and reflecting on the reality of innocent, senseless, and irrational suffering in the world the center of his theological reflections. Failure to do so easily leads attempts at theodicy to aggravate the problem they seek to resolve. See Tilley, *The Evils of Theodicy*.

104. Swinburne, "Problem of Evil," 88.

105. On what kind of God and of human beings does one base an argument according to which "a creator who gave them only coughs and colds, and not cancer and cholera would be a creator who treated men as children instead of giving them real encouragement to subdue the world" (Swinburne, "The Problem of Evil," 100)? Swinburne does admit: "Now obviously it would be crazy for God to multiply pains in order to multiply compassion. But I suggest that a world with some pain and some compassion is at least as good as a world with no pain" (Swinburne, *Providence and the Problem of Evil*, 161). But what is at issue here is not quantities, a more or less, but the fact that orienting one's life toward or according to God would be done for if the suffering of even one creature were allowed to be instrumentalized the way Swinburne expounds.

106. Swinburne, "Problem of Evil," 96–97.

since these provide the opportunity for especially noble acts."[107] The same counter-arguments apply. If compassion can only exist if and because others are suffering, then would a world in which there is no suffering such that there is no occasion for compassion not be better than a world in which there must be suffering for there to be compassion?[108]

7. Some of what we consider to be *malum* may not be such for God and would not be such for us either if we could grasp the overall context. A physician amputating a leg does not do anything reprehensible even if it may seem so to an observer without a full grasp of the situation.[109] This may be true in some cases. But it is not an argument that obtains in all, in most, or even just in the usual cases. Those to whom evil happens suffer a *malum* if and insofar as they experience it as such, even if they may change their attitude toward and evaluate it differently when they acquire information to prompt them to do so. Whether something is a *malum* or not is decided by those *for whom* it is one. These do not necessarily have to be the ones concretely afflicted, they can also be observers noticing something the ones afflicted might not even notice themselves. But if it is a *malum* for someone, then it is a *malum*, whatever someone else's evaluation might be.

8. God has created a world with evils in order to realize certain goods that could only be achieved that way. But that does not mean that in such a world, every kind of evil would be justified. "There are limits to the amount and degree of evil which are possible in our world. Thus there are limits to the amount of pain which a person can suffer," for what human beings can bear "is limited by their physiology." A good God, therefore, does not have to prevent every *malum* but "a good God stops too much suffering."[110] The argument supposes that evaluating *malum* could be a question of more or less, as if some evils could be compatible with God's goodness while other evils or too much of the same could not. This, however, supposes a standard that would allow not only for judging whether something is a *malum* for some or not but also when there is *too much* of it to still be compatible with God's goodness. Yet such a standard is not available; we can only evoke the *factual* end of a life mistreated by evils. That, however, is not an argument when *this* life is destroyed by *this* evil, for in that case it is not the evil but the life that is ended by the evil. It is one thing to heal an illness, quite another to let the patient die. In both cases, there is an end put to the illness. But everyone thus afflicted will likely want that distinction to be made.

All these arguments attempt not only to prove the *possibility* of the compatibility of God's goodness with the reality of the world but to show that the world must be such as it is to be the world that God wants. Throughout, they commit the error of overinterpreting and

107. Swinburne, "Problem of Evil," 90–91.

108. Swinburne, *Providence and the Problem of Evil*, 161, acknowledges the objection but considers it unsound and seeks to reject it by way of quantification: what is at stake, in his view, is only a *certain amount* of ills.

109. See Swinburne, "Postscript."

110. Swinburne, "Problem of Evil," 89–90.

present what factually is as what necessarily must be if God is to be a good creator and if the world is to have been created by him.[111] These arguments are not convincing because they want too much and achieve too little. They want too much because they seek to prove that what others take to be an objection to God's goodness is a confirmation of God's goodness. And they achieve too little because what is only contingently such as it is can only be necessarily present by going in a circle, as if, given God's goodness, it could not be otherwise or better. This cannot be shown, neither wholesale and generally nor in concrete cases. The cases differ too much to be subsumed under one rule. And the guiding rule of *finite freedom* evoked as a decisive good in order to make the manifold evils of the world compatible with God's goodness cannot perform all it is tasked with in these arguments. Let us consider this question separately, by way of conclusion.

14. The Free Will Argument

Almost all of the arguments just discussed take recourse to the good of finite freedom and the conditions of its realization. They may therefore be read as variants of the attempt to develop the free will defense into an *argument for freedom of the will*. The latter adds the existential proposition: "Free beings exist," that is, "Beings endowed with free will exist," to the two existential propositions of the logical theodicy problem, "God exists" and "Evils exist," in order to prove the consistency of the latter two propositions. The argument can be quickly put as follows:

If God creates free beings, then it is possible that evils exist and thus not impossible that God creates a world in which evils exist. Yet God can create free beings because it is not impossible that a world exists in which beings endowed with free will live. And God must create free beings because he would not be perfectly wise, good, and powerful, that is, he would not be God, if he created a world that would be less good than the best world he could create. If, therefore, God creates a world at all, then the world he creates is one with beings that can freely choose good and do evil. God could not create this world without it being possible that evils exist in it in the form of freely chosen evil. And in consequence, it is possible and neither contradictory nor improbable that the perfectly good, wise, and powerful God creates a world in which evils exist—a world like ours.

This argument is based on a series of premises that are not self-evident but controversial throughout, namely:

1. God creates the best world he can create.

2. A world in which free beings live is better than a world without such beings.

3. A being is free if in identical circumstances it could have acted differently (freedom of action); if in identical circumstances, it could have chosen differently (freedom of choice); if it can accept or reject that which it wants and could want (freedom

111. Kessler, *Gott und das Leid*, 40, rightly notes: "Theoretical 'justifications of God' tend to *justify the existing conditions of suffering and injustice* because they seek to *harmonize* these latter with the idea of God (what kind of God?) and thereby stabilize them." They want to defend God's goodness given the ills of the world yet turn into a defense of the ills of the world before a God "who degenerates, in the best of cases, into a father who doesn't care or, in the worst of cases, into a sadistic monster."

of decision); if it can impose on itself the rules that guide how it decides, wills, and acts (freedom of the will); if it can determine its will according to the standard of what is good and what is evil (ethical freedom); if, thanks to the possibility of choosing and doing good or evil, it determines its will such that it encourages the freedom of others (autonomy).

4. A being is ethically free if it has the possibility to choose and do good or evil and if it cannot avoid this choice.

5. God cannot make any free being freely do something specific.

If all these obtain then God cannot create a world in which free beings always choose and do the good. Yet even if one does not seek to contest that such a world with such free beings exists, even if one stresses that without such freedom, "life would not be recognizably human at all,"[112] why should one believe that such a God exists? Is there a good reason to believe in God's existence, omnipotence, infinite wisdom, and omnibeneficence? Without this basic precondition, the demonstration of freedom of the will and of all its implications would not solve the problem even if all the premises just listed were sufficiently justified. Their validity hinges on the great *if* of the existence of the one omnipotent, infinitely wise, and omnibeneficent God. The justification of this basic supposition, however, remains unresolved in this proposed solution as well. Yet if this conception of God cannot be made plausible inductively on the basis of the real experience of the world, then it does not become any more plausible when it is evoked deductively and shown to be compatible with propositions about the evils and Evil in the world. The basic question then remains why one should believe in such a God or conceive of God in such a way at all. That question, precisely, is not being answered in all the various theodicy debates.[113]

---

112. Phillips, *Problem of Evil*, 108. As Phillips correctly points out, the problem is not the assumption that there are free persons but the use the free will defense makes of that assumption. One assumes the reality of free persons and constructs an argument according to which (1) "A world containing creatures who are sometimes significantly free (and freely perform more good than evil actions) is more valuable, all else being equal, than a world containing no free creatures at all" (Plantinga, "Good, Evil, and the Metaphysics of Freedom," 85) such that (2) a God who creates the best of all possible worlds will create such a world and not a different one. But why should the contingent reality of free persons in this sense be defined as a necessary consequence of a divine decision when no good reason is given why it should be referred to God at all? There are such good reasons, but only *in* the practice of faith, not by bracketing it. Plantinga's argument, too, moves *within* the circle of faith and theology, but he presents his argument as if it could reject the objection *against* faith and theology rather than just render the attitude of believers comprehensible who, in the face of the experiences of *malum* in their lives, nonetheless hold on to their faith in God because it allows them to be grateful for their lives and to thank God not for the *malum* but for the entirety of life with its bona and mala (see Phillips, *Problem of Evil*, 95ff). This kind of theodicy argument thus provides a wrong metaphysical reconstruction of a fundamental attitude of faith and life in dealing with experiences of *malum*—wrong because it insulates this attitude from the life-nexus in which its entire point consists and tries to give it a point it does not have.

113. This is true even where argumentative shortcomings are compensated for by the narrative approach of telling a story that is at least possible, as in van Inwagen ("Argument from Evil," 64–73), for example, where the response to the question "Do I believe it?" is "Well, I believe parts of it and I don't disbelieve any of it" (72). It is possible to argue by telling a story without thereby switching from the register of the philosophical consideration of possibilities to that of theological reflections on experience.

This is where the difference between the theodicy debates and the theological reflections of the Christian faith stand out most clearly. When we look at the basic practical enactments of the Christian faith as a movement of life and as a form of life, not at its derivative theoretical form as a doctrinal system of convictions, Christian faith does not presuppose a ready-made conception of God but *permanently enacts itself as the search for a conception of God that is adequate to our experience*, by critically relating two facts. On the one hand, there is the basic experience of God's salutory becoming-present and the concrete situation of the human beings in whom this experience takes place, that is, the happening, in human life, of a *bonum* that is unexpected and exceeds all expectation. That is why the search for a conception of God that is adequate to God enacts itself as *correction, criticism, modification, and refinement* of pre-given conceptions of God in light of the experiences that count for Christian faith, which it expresses in Christological statements about Jesus Christ and pneumatological statements about God's presence in the Spirit. And, on the other hand, it does not simply start with the experiential reality of evil but with the contrary *reality of God's overcoming of Evil*, that is, with the experience that the *bonum* happening to us does not only uncover and define what deserves being called *malum* but ends and overcomes it in such a way that evil no longer begets evil but good, and good no longer occasions evil but only good.

Christian thought thus assumes as a matter of principle what remains problematic in the thinking of theodicy; namely, (a) that God can overcome Evil by means of Good because the concrete case of the life of Jesus Christ makes it clear[114] that and how God has in fact overcome it in a way that is binding for him and thus for the entire world, and (b) that God can, wants to, and will overcome evil in this way in every case of human life because God has declared what he did in Jesus Christ to be binding, reliable, immutable, and thus eschatologically final for his being God:[115] God is the one who overcomes evil through good, that is, the one who becomes present in every life in such a way that *bonum* comes about for this life where its concrete *malum* lies.[116] For Christian thought, therefore, Evil is primarily relevant not as a problem but as a reality that is present as a passing reality. This takes away nothing of how unbearable it is. But it fundamentally changes what we conceive of as the "problem of evil."

114. Not because it is public and visible for all to see but because in the faith and for the faith that is thereby constituted, it comes to be seen as something that God makes clear through his spirit. Christianity ascribes both—that is, *what* becomes clear and *that* it becomes clear—to the action of God the Spirit and thus to God himself. If one ignores this pneumatological perspective in evoking the life of Jesus Christ, one may have access to a rudimentary and fragmentary story of a Jewish man around the beginning of the Common Era but not to what this special story gives us to see about God's will and action for human beings.

115. Dorner, *Divine Immutability*, already pointed out that this is the point of the concept of God's immutability. On the history of the problem, see Maas, *Unveränderlichkeit Gottes*, and Meessen, *Unveränderlichkeit und Menschwerdung Gottes*.

116. The *malum* is thus not removed, revised, or played down after the fact. There, where the *malum* is in a specific life and in its specific way (every *malum* is a *malum* for a very specific life), God brings a *bonum* to bear that makes *this* life disfigured by the *malum* a good, just, free, and beautiful life by ceaselessly providing it with divine life where it can no longer live by itself. In Christian imagery, this is paradigmatically expressed by Jesus Christ resurrected still bearing the stigmata of the crucifixion, irreversibly and for all eternity: the *malum* is not forgotten and repressed, but God infinitely and incessantly has the *bonum* of his divine life happen to the human being thus disfigured.

D

Dealing with Evil

1. Evil as a Problem and as a Reality

IN HUMAN LIFE, WE primarily encounter evil not as a problem in the singular nor as problems in the plural but as a reality that happens to us.[1] It acts destructively, it does evil, exterminates the good, makes the good evil.[2] As "Nothing in action," it disrupts, injures, shapes, harms, inverses, and exterminates the life of human beings.[3] There is no one who is not affected by it. It seems ubiquitous. We are familiar with it without knowing what it is or being able to name it. We react to it before we reflect on it. We are raised to live with it. In order to be able to live, we have always already come to terms with its reality, socially as well as individually.

Only when evil drastically intensifies or gains the upper hand, when it begins to disrupt and harm human life in such a way that it exceeds the habitual framework of what we are used to and can no longer be ignored by us, only then do we start to pay particular attention. It then turns out very quickly that we perceive or notice "something" we cannot understand and grasp, and it takes a lot of time and much abstraction to learn to distinguish between the *what* and the *how*, the descriptive and the evaluative component of experiencing. What "it" is usually remains unclear because we perceive *that* it is but do not in any specific way perceive *what* it is. No one who is forced to pay attention to evil can doubt the reality of what they perceive. No one is spared making this experience in their own lives. But what it is that draws our attention, drastically or subtly, incrementally or overwhelmingly, in disruptions of and damages to life, escapes our grasp, it seems. We give it names and designate it as "annihilating Nothing," "enemy

---

1. Problems are always something we "cause" for ourselves, something we conceive of and construct as a problem. Evil, on the contrary, we encounter as a reality and thus encounter it pathically, as something we suffer, that affects us, as something we do not cause but that causes us to be the ones suffering it.

2. That is true even for the biological aspects of life when we consider and evaluate what *bona* they make possible and bring about and which *mala* they can cause and trigger; see "Destruktion durch angeborene Fehlbildungen und Defekte," and Peters, "Biologische Anmerkungen."

3. Krötke, "Das Böse als Absurdes," 69.

of the good," "destitution of the true," "devil's work," or "devil" in short.[4] Yet even when everything we can say, everything that can be said has been said, it still seems or is obviously the case that what it is remains unsaid.

2. The Inessentiality of Evil

That is why it has been suggested that the essence "of Evil" is that it has no essence.[5] The reason why nothing seems as indeterminate as the concept of Evil,[6] as is claimed, is that there is nothing to grasp here. Evil is real but it "is" nothing—nothing, in any case, that could be described, understood, grasped, defined as a something. Its essence is thus pithily said to lie in its inessentiality. What it is cannot be known because it does not possess a *what*, and why it is cannot be understood because it is nothing that could be known and understood.

Not that Evil is not being experienced. There is no one who does not experience Evil. But where it is experienced, it is neither Nothing nor a specific Something that is experienced but always that which disrupts, harms, injures, disfigures, destroys a life, whatever form it takes. It can take innumerable different forms and take a different concrete form in each human life. But wherever evil happens, it happens as *id quod nocet*, as "that which is hurtful,"[7] harms a life, damages its reality, limits its possibilities, hurts its feelings, shatters its hopes, offends its dignity. That is why a widely defended and well-founded hypothesis of the philosophical and theological tradition holds that evil is not to be discussed under the category of substance but that of relation: when we inquire into evil, we inquire into what is evil for someone because it damages life or would damage it if it were real.[8]

3. Neither a Science nor a Metaphysics of Evil

As a result, a science of evil seems to be as self-contradictory as a metaphysics of evil.[9] Where there is no *what*, its *how* and *why* cannot be explored. At most, *that something is* can be described and questioned as to causes and effects. In this case, it is possible to investigate how and why (certain) illnesses, natural disasters, accidents, or crimes occur—an important inquiry for understanding their causes and for being able to limit their occurrence and repercussions. But doing so does not explain the evil and harm caused by them. The most perfect of explanations for the fact that an avalanche started at precisely that point in time and buried precisely this child cannot answer the question,

4. See Krötke, "Das Böse als Absurdes," and Jüngel, "Böse—was ist das?"

5. Schmidt-Biggemann, "Vorwort," 8. If that is true here, however, it is true in many other contexts as well. The play on the figure of thought, "essence," must not be overlooked. [*Wesen* can designate both an *essence* and a *being*, as in *Lebewesen*, living being or organism.]

6. Lacroix, *Le mal*, 7.

7. Augustine, *On the Morals of the Manichæans*, 3.5:70; see Häring, *Das Böse in der Welt*, 3.

8. Häring, *Das Böse in der Welt*, 5–6.

9. This is why Knut Berner's title, *Theory of Evil*, is questionable, whatever else the book's merits are (especially in its discussions of Leibniz and Barth).

Why this child? When everything that can be said scientifically about such an event has been said, it remains unsaid what it is that makes it evil.

More than that: the question of Evil becomes particularly acute when it is raised by events that are precisely not inexplicable but have completely been explained: evil always exceeds any measure of explicability. Something is explicable for us when we are able, via a rule, to attribute its reality to another reality that allows us to comprehend why it is and why it is the way it is. This holds for events and conditions as much as for thoughts and actions, for accidents, disasters, and diseases that affect human beings as much as for crimes, acts of violence, and atrocities that human beings commit.

But the fact that something real can be explained in this manner does not explain what (for some, for many, or for everyone) makes it evil. Independently of whether a concrete judgment is made, something evil is always something that in light of the distinction between Good and Evil is to be judged as evil by someone. But whether and why it is to be judged as evil is a question that can be answered independently of whether what is at issue is something real or something possible: the reason for which something is to be judged as evil is different from the reason for which something that is judged as evil is real. An explanation of something real is never already an explanation of the reality of evil.

Conversely, the question of the *why* of evil always includes several questions: What does Evil mean? What does it mean to judge something as evil? Why is this to be judged as evil? Lastly, why is that which is to be judged as evil real? Scientific explanations can only contribute to answering the last question, and as such, they thereby cannot explain Evil. When, faced with experiences of evil, we ask, "Why?" we do not seek a scientific explanation of something real but want to know why something that is to be judged as evil is real for someone even if it were better if it were not real. The question does not merely aim at the reality of something that is evil but at the reality *of evil*, and that is not a question to be answered scientifically alone.

4. The Reality of Evil

The reality of evil, it seems, cannot be explained scientifically, nor does evil seem to have an essence that could be explained metaphysically. Yet if the question *quid malum?*— what is *malum*?—can not only not be answered but not even be meaningfully asked because the *malum* does not possess a *what*, then the question *unde malum?*—where does *malum* come from?—cannot be asked or answered meaningfully either, because that which is but is not a something can at most be explained in terms of its being, not in terms of its being a *malum*. Both of these allegedly "fundamental questions that human beings ask with respect to Evil"[10] presuppose something that does not seem to be the case: that the reality "of Evil" is the reality of something.

But not only what is something is real. Even if "Evil" is not something, it can hardly be denied that something is (or some things are) evil. To try to deny this would mean to negate the reality of evil. But that is so unrealistic that it seems hard to imagine a more

10. Schulte, "Böses und Psyche," 300.

improbable claim. What is questionable is the essence, not the reality of evil. Yet if real is what is although it could also not be, then evil, too, is only real because and insofar as it is something that is evil, although it does not have to be nor have to be such and such. Evil might not be a something, but it is only real because something is evil. That, however, means: evil is always an evil of and about something real that is evil for somebody. This is what its parasitic reality consists in.

5. The Phenomenology of Evil

That is why any phenomenological consideration of evil has to begin with the reality, not the essence, of Evil. But how? If it cannot be said what "Evil" is because "it" is not a "something," then there can be no scientific explanation and no metaphysics "of Evil" but at most a consideration of something real with respect to the way in which it is or is not evil. That implies the possibility that something real be perceived and described as something evil, and this in turn implies starting from some kind of understanding of "evil" that makes it possible to view something real from this point of view. If there can thus be no science and metaphysics "of Evil," can there be at least a phenomenology "of Evil"?

An affirmative answer is possible only if phenomenology is understood in the radical sense: a phenomenology "of Evil" does not describe anything that appears but describes appearances in which nothing appears. It knows evil only as appearances but no appearances of Evil. There is nothing behind the appearances it describes that could be explored or constructed on their basis. What describes them as evil amounts to the appearances of evil: the phenomena of evil *are* Evil.[11]

Which are these phenomena? Which phenomena form part of this group and which do not? Is evil that which the phenomenology of Evil describes as evil or does the phenomenology of Evil describe as evil that which is evil? There would be no need to make much of a fuss about evil if it were evil only because it is described as such. It would then be easy to alleviate. But things are not that simple. The decision about what is evil hinges on the phenomena, not on their description. That Evil is nothing does not mean that nothing is evil. What is being contested is its essence, not its reality. Indisputably, there is something about which it can truthfully be said that it is evil. This something are the phenomena that a radical phenomenology of Evil describes. Yet which are these phenomena? And which are not?

6. Negative Phenomena

Since it is not possible to go back to an essence behind the appearances that would provide answers to these questions, the distinguishing features sought for must be discovered in the phenomena themselves. And most often, these features are seen in a *negative* (in the widest sense): phenomena of evil, we are told, are distinct from others because of

---

11. That is why lying, untruth, stupidity, malice, arrogance, hubris, inhumanity, godlessness, arrogant self-confidence, lack of care, duplicity, etc., are not only indicators of Evil, they *are* evil: each in its own way in its life-nexus and in opposition to what could be and ought to be different in this life-nexus.

their *negativity*, that is, with them, something that would better be real is not real (truth, beauty, health, justice, wealth, happiness) or something that would better not be real is real (lies, ugliness, disease, injustice, poverty, misfortune); without them, the world would be better than it is. In negative phenomena of the lack or absence of something good or the presence or occurrence of something bad, evil is a phenomenon because evil neither is something nor is it nothing, but instead it is a *negative*. For if evil cannot be grasped *as something* and yet is real, it is argued, then it can only be grasped as a *negation* of something that would be better by what exists, as *contestation, impairment, deprivation, prevention*, or *annulment* of something that would be better by what exists. Evil is real because, although it is not itself something, it in one way or another negates *a positive in something* that is, or negates *a positive* that is, could be, or ought to be because the world would be better with it than without it. Yet if evil is real as the negation of a positive, then the phenomenon of evil is that which negates a positive.

But what does that mean? The only way to give *negation* as *negating something*[12] at least some kind of precise meaning is in the form of a negating *judgment*, that is, as contesting that something is true or as claiming that something is not true.[13] Yet evil itself is neither a negating judgment about something, nor is it a mere result of somebody negating something. At most, we might say that evil is that of which it is, or can, or must be truthfully said that it is negative.

It is possible truthfully to define as negative, however, only that which can be specified in three respects: it is a negative *for someone, about something,* and *in a certain respect.* What is not negative *for someone* in the sense that it contradicts what *for this person* is a positive[14] is not *negative* for this person but at most is different from something else. Yet what is *positive* for a person is that whose reality increases their quality of life;[15] *considered to be positive* is that which leads someone to expect an increase in their own or someone else's quality of life; and considered to be *more positive* than something else is that which leads someone to expect that it makes one's own life, the life of someone

---

12. The polysemy of "negation" has left its mark on the history of logic since its origins. At issue in the debate, essentially, is the distinction between four kinds of negation: *propositional negation*, in which the logical form of a proposition is determined by the negating operator "not" (*not:* x *is* P); the *negative judgment* (contesting a positive or claiming a negative content); the *negative copula* (x *is not* P); and *negative predicates* (x is *not*-p); see Menne, "*Malum*," 666–67.

13. See, for example, Bolzano, *Wissenschaftslehre*, §23:3.

14. That does not have to mean that it is a positive *from their own point of view.* Not only what I recognize as positive for me here and now is positive for me, yet nothing could seriously be called positive for me that I could not in principle recognize as such.

15. This includes not only what happens to this good but also what this good does or allows to happen to other life or to the life of others: good is what makes good—makes the one to whom it happens good, the one who does good, or (in the ideal case) both. When we speak of improving the quality of life, we are not to understand it in the narrow sense of maximizing our own advantage. What good we do to others often does us good as well, and many goods that are good for us only on condition that others do not benefit from them are questionable goods. A life is good when it does good to itself and to others, and a life is better when the good that dominates is of the kind that does good to oneself because it does good to others and in which that which does good to others does good to oneself.

else, the life of all others, or the state of the world as a whole better than is the case without it.[16]

Inversely, everything whose realization would impair, prevent, or annul the reality of what is positive for someone stands in contradiction to the positive. To characterize something as negative thus means to judge that it is negative for someone. This presupposes that there is *someone* for whom something is negative: where there is no one, there is nothing negative for them, either. Not only that, though; it also presupposes that there is *something* that is or can be judged to be negative for someone: where there is nothing, there is nothing negative, either. If, however, that which is negative for someone were wholly and exclusively negative in every respect and from every point of view, if, that is, it were impossible to articulate from any point of view any kind of positive judgment about that which is judged to be negative by or for someone, then there would be nothing that would be negative, and therefore nothing negative, because there would be no difference between *not being* and *being negative*. Only where something is in a certain respect negative about something for someone, therefore, is there a negative, and evil is a phenomenon as a negative.

7. On the Shortcomings of Negativity

Is that true only of what is negative? And of everything negative? Is evil at home only in the negative, and is everything negative a manifestation of evil? One thing is evident: if what is negative is evil, then it must always be possible to ask about evil: *What* is evil? *For whom* is it evil? *In what respect* is it evil? What *positive* is negated by it and in what way? *Why* and by what right is this positive considered to be positive and its negation therefore considered to be evil? And what does it mean for a comprehension of evil that an evil is perceived, experienced, or judged *as evil* by someone but not by others?

Yet even this does not exhaust all essential questions. In the negative, evil may be a phenomenon, but is it real only as a negative? There is reason to doubt it. If the reality of evil were always and completely reducible to a negative, that is, to a phenomenon that negates a positive and is therefore definable as a negative, such a rule of negation would practically render evil calculable.[17]

Yet in more than one respect, this does not go far enough. That which harms a life or impedes the improvement of its quality, for example, is by no means always seen, experienced, and judged in this sense by those affected. Does smoking improve the quality of life or does it harm life? Is that a decision to be made by smokers, by physicians, or by health insurance companies? When and where does something that does not improve life but does make it more pleasant become a reduction in the quality of life? At what

16. Evidently, this is where conflicts between competing values arise: what improves our own quality of life is not *ipso facto* what improves the quality of life of others or of everyone else or improves the situation of the world as a whole. The choice of a frame of reference thus determines whether one gives preference to an individual (private), group-related, humanity-related (humane), life-related (biologistic), or cosmic system of values. And one central problem of ethical reflection lies in exploring what, in what conditions, would constitute a morally defensible relationship between these value orientations.

17. Schmidt-Biggemann, "Vorwort," 8.

point does what is positive for a life switch over to become something negative for this life or for others? And how are we to assess something that improves the quality of life of some and simultaneously or even *ipso facto* diminishes the quality of life of others? In all these cases, the negation rule is of no help in determining evil and distinguishing it from phenomena not to be thus determined. Instead, it seems that there can be no determination of evil as negative without a dispute about who has the right to judge and decide whether something is negative or positive for someone and thereby is evil or not evil.

8. The Ubiquity of Evil

That is why keeping an eye out for negative phenomena is not a reliable way to locate the reality of evil. Indeed, seeking evil only in negative phenomena would amount to a dangerous misjudgment of one of its central traits. Evil is not just parasitic. It also has the perverting tendency to render itself invisible, as it were, and to act in the dark and underneath its opposite. Evil is not a "level negation," neither "of the good,"[18] nor the beautiful, nor the true. It occurs in all shades, variations, and disguises. It fascinates and blurs the line that separates it from the beautiful. It impresses and blurs the line that separates it from the good. It scintillates and blurs the line that separates it from the true. By no means is evil real only in such a way as to catch our eye as a negative, as injustice, disaster, accident, distress, or suffering. These are merely cases in which it simply cannot be overlooked, but they are not its only modes of being real. Evil occurs where one does not suspect it, and where we do not perceive it, it later turns out to have been present. We cannot calculate when and where it shows itself. It acts out in the open and in the dark. And it cannot be captured via a fixed rule, including the rule of negation of a positive.

Every attempt at drawing up a typology or categorial table of evil based on the negative and on negation is thus misguided and at best reductive. Evil cannot be registered and classified in an ordered manner because there is simply nothing where it could not in some way be present. That this is true all the way up to God is an issue we will have to address later. In any case, it would be premature and careless to seek evil phenomenally only ever in the negative. Life and phenomena are much too ambivalent for that. Many things experienced and lived as a positive by some are a negative for others: slavery, extorted love, stolen money, plundered property, exploited labor, etc. Would we say that these and similar instances are evil only on the side of the victims but not on the side of the perpetrators? Would we locate evil only where it is experienced as a negative but not where *the same thing* is experienced and assessed positively? Or should we, inversely, not be allowed to call a thing good, beautiful, and true because in a different respect and for others it is not good, beautiful, and true? The world of phenomena can obviously not readily be divided in evil and good, negative and positive phenomena, because one and the same phenomenon can in different respects be one or the other. Only if we see this and take it into account do we get closer to the core of the problem.

18. Schmidt-Biggemann, "Vorwort," 9.

9. Parasitic Reality

It does clarify one thing, however: evil is not everything and not the only thing. It is the evil *of something*, and lives off a twofold contrast: the contrast with something that is and the contrast with whatever else this something is. Evil is not simply identical with the real that is evil (for in that case it would itself be a real something), yet neither is it the only respect in which what is evil is and can be determined (for in that case this something would be indistinguishable from evil). Nothing can be described as evil that cannot simultaneously be determined by a different description. If "Evil" has no essence but instead is real because something real is evil, and if something real is evil although it does not have to be such and therefore is not evil in every possible respect and in every possible description, then evil exists only because something else, and not just some other evil, also exists and because every evil is also accessible via a different description.

That is why it is not only necessary to distinguish between phenomena of Evil and other phenomena. Moreover, *in every phenomenon of Evil* there exists a difference on which hinges not only the perceptibility but the reality of Evil. Evil exists only if there exists something else, not only beside and outside it but also in, with, and underneath it. "Evil exists" means "Something that is evil exists," and while it is possible to negate the predicate ". . . is evil" without annulling that of which it is the predicate, it is not possible to annul this something without thereby annulling the evil as well. Evil thus does not exist in and for itself but only ever as evil *deed*, evil *omen*, evil *person*, evil *intention*: it is always the determination of something that is thereby evil, but it is not that which is thereby determined as evil or which thereby is what is evil. Or, to put it in terms that may but in a way cannot be misunderstood: it makes something evil, but it does not make that which makes it evil.

10. The Relativity of Evil

Evil is thus always the *evil of something*. But it is also always evil *for someone*. There is no evil in itself, neither as an autonomous being nor as an absolute phenomenon. Evil needs the reference to that *in* or *on* which it appears and the reference to the one *to whom* it appears. Its reality is phenomenal in the double sense that it is a *reality of* and a *reality for*: always, *something* is evil, and always, it is evil for *someone*.

Kierkegaard elucidates the problem in his analysis of the phenomenon of anxiety. "Anxiety may be compared with dizziness. He whose eye happens to look down into the yawning abyss becomes dizzy. But what is the reason for this? It is just as much in his own eye as in the abyss, for suppose he had not looked down"[19]—for then, we may continue where Kierkegaard breaks off, he would not have become dizzy. That does not mean that he produced the dizziness himself by looking down, but neither does it mean that the abyss as such produced it. "The abyss is what it is: the other end of a mountain or a peak. Only the eye measuring the distance signals the danger for the human being and lets her become dizzy."[20] Only in the interplay of abyss and eye does the dizziness

19. Kierkegaard, *Concept of Anxiety*, 61.
20. Pieper, "Das Böse: Verhängnis oder Schuld?," 24.

of anxiety emerge, and only in the interplay *of* something real (a phenomenon) and *for* something real (a human being) does evil emerge *if* this interplay leads to (and enjoins us to judge as such) the life of the people affected being harmed, impeded, destroyed, annihilated by this phenomenon. Those affected do not necessarily have to recognize this, which is why they are not always and not as such the best or decisive authority for judging whether something is really evil for someone. But they must in principle be able to recognize it, for otherwise one could not call it "evil." An evil must not only be recognizable as such to those who identify it as evil for the ones affected by it. The former must (be able to) give reasons and render it comprehensible as such to the latter if those affected are not to find themselves exposed to a stranger's gaze that sees them in a way they cannot see themselves.[21]

"Evil exists" thus means not only "Something that is evil exists" but means, more precisely: "Something that is evil *for someone* exists."[22] When we speak of evil, we semantically connect three moments that can be and are to be distinguished and considered analytically: that *which* we call evil (happening); the one *for whom* we call it an evil (the one affected); and our calling it *evil* (mode of concern). If there were no something (a happening) that is or can be a something (an event) for others as well, there would be nothing: without a *happening* (seen from the perspective of the ones affected) or an *event* (seen from the perspective of others), nothing would exist that could be assessed as evil: when we speak of evil, we speak of *something* we call evil. Such a happening or event, however, cannot exist without someone to whom it happens or someone who is affected by this happening in such a way that it is evil for him: without anyone affected, no happening would exist and no one who could be affected by evil. When we speak of evil, we speak of *someone* who is affected by something that is evil for him or her.

Both moments (*happening* and *being affected*) condition one another. Only *phenomena* in which, in the unity of an action, *something appears as something for someone* and *is understood by someone as something* are real and can therefore be evil or not evil.

21. The problem raised here is not just a problem of moral philosophy, it has far-reaching practical and political consequences: Who has the right to judge what is evil for someone? And when is such a judgment sound? Not everyone who complains about evil is really afflicted by evil, as parents and teachers well know. And not everyone who denies that this or that in their lives is evil is right. Here, questions of ethics and etiquette, morality and politics, of the right insight and the right communication of such insights are intricately intertwined. Wrongly communicated, a right insight into evil can destroy itself, and a wrong conviction that something is not evil can render us incapable of recognizing it as wrong. The societal debates about slavery in the nineteenth and about women's rights in the twentieth century are paradigmatic examples of these problems.

22. Not: "There is *something for someone* that is evil." The "something" may indeed be accessible to others, but it does not have to be given for them as evil such that they experience a given situation differently from the outset. At issue is not a relational ontology of phenomena of Evil but an analytical description of the judgment that certain phenomena are evil as a proposition about phenomena within a certain perspective, even and precisely when the phenomena thus described are differently determined for others from a different perspective. Both experience a given situation from the outset in different ways because they experience what takes place within their perspective in a specific and nuanced way that only analyzing abstraction can separate out into "something" and "the specific way in which it is experienced." What is primary in the lifeworld is *the situation experienced in a specific way*; its differentiation into "phenomena" and their modes of perception or experience is a secondary analytical description.

Identical phenomena—landslides, for example—can be evil or not evil depending on whether there is anyone affected. And *one and the same* phenomenon—a stock market crash, for example—can be evil for some and not evil for others or the other way around, depending on whether and how they are affected by it. Yet if no real (something) existed that affected another real (someone) in such a way as to harm it, no evil would exist because for it to be at all, evil must always simultaneously be a *reality of* (*in* a real) and a *reality for* (*for* a real). There must really exist something that happens to someone and there really must exist someone to whom it happens—these are the two necessary (albeit not sufficient) conditions of the reality of evil. Their realization may coincide in one and the same person (e.g., in a nightmare) or distributed among two persons (e.g., in a robbery). But one must really have a nightmare or really be robbed to be able truthfully to say that one is affected by evil. Only where something really exists that happens to someone and only where there really exists someone to whom it happens, and namely happens to him as evil and not as good or indifferent, does evil exist.

Evil thus does not exist in itself but always only *for those affected*. Something is evil *for them* and it is *for them* that it is to be overcome if it is to be overcome. But not everybody finds themselves, in every case of evil, in the place of those affected; not every evil is thus evil for everyone. When evil is described, it is thus always necessary to specify *for whom* it is evil; otherwise, the description remains abstract.

11. Being Affected and the Jargon of Affect

Taking the *for*-structure of (the reality of) Evil into account in describing evil, however, is not to be confused with being affected oneself. When we describe *evil for others*, we speak *about* or, as the case may be, *for* those affected without necessarily being affected by this evil ourselves. When we describe *evil for ourselves*, on the contrary, we speak *as* someone affected. The jargon of affect blends these two modes of speaking; that is why it rings so hollow. Yet just as what is evil for us ourselves does not have to be evil for others and what is evil for others does not have to be evil for us, so it is not impossible that someone who is not affected speak appropriately about the evil that affects others. We do not have to be affected ourselves to identify evil and it is wrong to think that only those affected can speak authentically about evil. We do not always perceive the evil that affects us. Very often, it is only discovered and pointed out by someone else speaking about it.

A phenomenology of Evil will have to describe evil from the perspectives of those not affected and of those affected, yet it will have to clearly distinguish between the two. A theological phenomenology of Evil, in turn, will speak above all from the perspective of someone affected. Not, as is often claimed, because it knows itself to be affected by every Evil or because it would presume in all cases to speak from the position of those affected but because, under the heading of sin, it thematizes such Evil and its consequences as they affect all human beings: evil in the relationship with God who relates to everyone in such a way that they are affected, whether they perceive and recognize it or not.

12. Ambivalent Evil

Even more so than in the case of describing evil, the most difficult problems in attempting to understand the reality of evil and, where possible, to prevent or overcome it, are posed not by the unequivocal but by the ambiguous cases. The phenomena of Evil are often characterized by an irreducible ambivalence insofar as what is an evil for one person is a good for another. Removing evil thus seems *ipso facto* and by necessity to destroy good and diminish goods. One person is compensated for the injustice of being exploited, and justice is done. Another person is thereby deprived of the opportunity to do something many others profit from: creating jobs, building hospitals, supporting museums, financing charitable foundations. Someone receives compensation for the evil suffered in a robbery when the wrongdoer is sentenced; the wrongdoer in turn is robbed of his freedom, his future, or his life.

In such cases, it seems, evil cannot be overcome without doing other evil: to remove evil for the ones, evil is done to the others, and in order to compensate the ones for evil suffered, new evil is committed toward the others. Can this cycle be broken? Can evil be fought with anything other than evil? Is it possible to tackle evil without being infected by it? Is it an evil that perpetuates itself even and precisely when it is fought (and by how one fights it)? Or, in Amos Oz's terms: "How can one be humane, which means skeptical and capable of moral ambivalence, and at the same time try to combat evil? How can one stand fanatically against fanaticism? How can one fight without becoming a fighter? How can one struggle against evil without catching it?"[23] The direct moral approach, as indispensable as it is in the face of Evil, always runs the danger of becoming what it fights against. Evil can "fascinate" even those who turn against it, such that they, precisely in thinking that they wholly and exclusively turn against Evil, no longer see themselves and thereby, exactly, fall into its clutches. To protect ourselves from Evil, we must take detours. And not every detour can serve this purpose in the same way.

13. The Necessity of Distancing and the Ambivalence of Detours

Before evil can be fought, it must be identified, described, and differentiated. That, however, can only be done based on its reality, and this reality is always the reality of Evil *for oneself* or *for others or another*. Yet most often, those affected by evil are, initially, unable to identify and describe what affects them in a way that would allow for a differentiated reaction. Through *time* and *interpretation*, they need to bring about a *distance* from their being affected by evil. There is no precise engagement with evil in direct reactions to it; the evil is much too close to those affected. The task, then, is to bring about *distanciations* made possible by our capacity for employing time and signs to produce a delay in our reaction and a leeway for reflection. Such distanciations characterize not our only dealing with evil in the lifeworld in a number of ways but our dealing with evil in faith and religion as well.[24]

---

23. Oz, "On Degrees of Evil," 289.
24. See Dalferth, *Leiden und Böses*, 214–71.

In hermeneutic terms, this means that in dealing with Evil in thought, we have to take into account the detours that we always already take in our practical dealings with it. Every society and culture is familiar with such detours and distinguishes between *unorganized* (*ad hoc*) and institutionally *organized* ways of dealing with evil experienced, suffered, and committed. The more differentiated a society is, the more differentiated are the detours it has institutionalized in ethics, morality, medicine, law, religion, science, etc., to deal with the different kinds of evil thus distinguished. All of these ways of dealing not only provide hermeneutic schemata for defining and understanding something from a certain point of view as an evil of a specific kind (as greed, revenge, malice, illness, fraud, injustice, sin, bigotry, etc.), but they also provide techniques for taking a specific stance toward it. They all refer to a "third" (an authority, rule, orientation, power, procedure, etc.) according to and with a view to which they define something as a specific evil and thereby allow for and suggest taking a specific stance toward it.

The strength of this hermeneutic procedure is that it thematizes evil by contrasting it with a specific other and thus renders it contrastively definable: as an evil in contrast to a good, a vice in contrast to a virtue, as a misdeed in contrast to a good deed. Its danger lies in that it might be seen as suggesting, erroneously, that such contrastive definition has captured evil in such a way that it can be treated or even eliminated with the appropriate means. The hermeneutic gain that consists in making the indescribable somehow describable and the unimaginable somehow thinkable becomes reductive when the evil thus thematized is equated with its thematization, that is, when the insight is lost that we do not thus grasp Evil but at most thematize it conceptually as ungraspable. Where the contrastive hermeneutic thematization is misunderstood as designation or even conceptualization of the evil thus thematized, perceptional blocks and representational reductions inevitably arise. We no longer perceive what is yet right before our eyes and are incapable of imagining what we are yet familiar with.

This occurs time and again whenever hermeneutic detours for dealing with evil petrify to become schemata for thinking and treating evil and thus take the place of what was to be thematized with their help. Hannah Arendt lucidly points out that eighteenth-century thinkers were unable to conceive "of a goodness beyond virtue, just as they were unable to imagine . . . that there could be wickedness beyond vice."[25] And Susan Neiman similarly brings out how the modern tendency to understand Evil as a product of the will constitutes both a great gain and at the same time a dangerous restriction: "Restricting evil actions to those accompanied by evil intention rids the world of a number of evils in ways that made sense."[26] Yet with Auschwitz, this procedure irrevocably comes up against its limits because the extent and nature of the horror of the Nazi extermination camps cannot be grasped when these ungraspable events are only and exclusively attributed to the evil actions of evil people with evil intentions, as Arendt has irrefutably shown.[27] The detour via virtue, goodness, and good intentions does indeed render some

25. Arendt, *On Revolution*, 82.

26. Neiman, *Evil in Modern Thought*, 268; see Rötzer, *Das Böse*.

27. Arendt, *Eichmann in Jerusalem*; *Men in Dark Times*; *Nach Auschwitz*; and *Ich will verstehen*. This is true even if Evil is thought "transcendentally and as a perversion of the categorical imperative" (Willnauer, *Heute das Böse denken*, 301), for in so doing, one remains caught up in the methodological

evil clearly visible, but it renders other evil invisible because in the light of this detour it cannot come into focus in the first place.

It is thus not just the results that can be problematic: the detours themselves are already ambiguous and ambivalent. They make visible but they also hide. The one cannot be had without the other. That is why hermeneutic detours have to be taken with caution. In engaging with them, their two sides must be taken into account, even in the case of religion.

14. Detours and Dead Ends

In many religions, these detours have long centered on a reference to the divine, gods, God, or, generally, transcendences, which are experienced as accessible in worship, religious practice (prayer, sacrifice), and organizations of life (law), and whose presence or absence (which is always a form of the presence of the divine) suggests a specific orientation and practice of life in dealing with evil one has and makes the experience of. This is true for the Christian faith as well. For Christians, the central detour in dealing with Evil leads via God, whom they understand in a specific manner that distinguishes them from other religious traditions. The *detour via God* is always a detour via a *God who is understood in a specific way*, and *how* God is understood decides the way in which one understands and reacts to evil in light of and in reference to God.[28]

That it could hardly be otherwise is evident already for hermeneutic reasons. If one refers to God to understand evil, that is, if one seeks to understand what seems incomprehensible by referring it to God and shedding light on it from God, then such a step can only make sense if the idea of God is itself not an empty one, if the expression "God" is not devoid of sense. Taking recourse to God, after all, is meant to render the experience of *malum* comprehensible, not to increase its incomprehensibility by something even more incomprehensible. The expression "God," however, is comprehensible and meaningful only insofar as there is a communal practice among people in which the expression is employed in a meaningful way. Only in a communal practice can there be the reciprocal correction and modification without which no functional meaning can establish itself. Yet the constitution and definition of the idea of God can very much vary depending on what form this practice takes.

In the European tradition, this point can be illustrated particularly well in the two different sets of practices in which the idea of God typically plays a role: in the religious practice of prayer and worship (cult) and in the philosophical practice of thinking and giving reasons (reflection). The theologies of the various religious traditions reflect the meaning of "God" in the first practice, whereas the meaning of "God" in the second

---

restrictions of a modernity that can only think as evil that which can be attributed to evil intentions, i.e., that which can be defined as a perversion of good will and situated within the horizon of human actions. Willnauer himself points out that this approach is insufficient (234).

28. In what follows, we will have to pay special attention to the fact that this conception of God has been shaped in very specific experiences of being affected by evil and of dealing with it, such that it is not only the conception of God that (co)determines the conception of Evil but the conception of Evil that (co)determines the conception of God.

practice is the subject of a reflection on theoretical principles in philosophical theology. In each one, however, "God" has a very different meaning. In religious contexts, definitions of God such as "creator," "preserver," "savior," "liberator," "father," or, formally, "the one who is worshipped" predominate, designations, that is, that express the close relationship between God and worship of God. In the context of philosophical reflection, in turn, designations such as "primum movens," "causa prima," "ens necessarium et realissimum," "ground of Being," "the being whose existence is identical with its essence," "the infinite," "the absolute," etc. predominate, designations that obviously cannot be transferred directly into the context of religious practice: one does not pray to the *causa prima* or to the absolute but to the heavenly Father. Yet conversely, one does not explain the validity of the laws of nature in reference to the liberator from captivity but (if at all) by going back to the *causa prima* or the absolute.

Evidently, taking recourse to God in order to understand evil leads to very different results depending on which practice of using "God" one refers to. And although it has time and again been attempted to connect the two and to do justice to both sets of practices in theological thought, the result has usually been that theology itself took different forms: a natural, or rational, version that tends toward giving reasons, and a theology of revelation that tends toward providing explanations. There is thus a tension in the way the expression "God" is defined in theological contexts as well.

Now, religions are not the only detours of this kind on offer, and for an increasing number of people in Western societies today, they are not even the most important ones. But in the history of human engagement with Evil, no other detour has been and continues to be attempted in more intensive and continual a manner than the detour via the divine and via God. No other detour displays more clearly the variety of this procedure of distancing and detour. No other has expressed the meaninglessness of Evil with greater clarity. Yet no other has led to as many dead ends as this approach either. Religions are not only prodigious processes of orientation, they are also very risky and permanently threaten to crash. Their detour via God or the divine, after all, attempts to facilitate a life with and attitude toward senseless evil for people affected by Evil. They do so realistically when they do not furnish this Evil with a false meaning and, thereby, against their better judgment, make it out to be meaningful (even though this, too, happens time and again, which is why religious practice must permanently be accompanied by critical reflection) but when instead they relate it to the divine or God in such a way that, from there and in its light, what is comprehensible about senseless Evil can permanently and always anew be distinguished from what is incomprehensible about it. This makes it possible to deal with Evil in a way that does not force it to yield a meaning it does not have but allows for relating to Evil in its senselessness, incomprehensibility, repulsiveness, and enmity to God. The rationality of this attitude hinges on the way in which this detour distinguishes between what is comprehensible and what is incomprehensible about senseless Evil, and that in turn hinges on how a religion conceives of the point of orientation that is the divine or God, the point toward which or from which it thematizes, differentiates, and symbolizes senseless Evil. This is where the clearest distinctions between religions are to be found, with the most striking consequences even in believers' concrete life practices:

we live the way we understand God, since the orientation toward God orients life in the world, and the conception of God determines the orientation toward God.

All of this leaves its mark on reflections about Evil in theology and the philosophy of religion, which critically retraces the religious detours for understanding what is senseless by means of permanently distinguishing between the comprehensible and the incomprehensible. If in confronting Evil the emphasis is only, for example, on the absolute creative power of a God who is not to be called to task by anyone and does not have to justify himself to anyone, God is turned into an unfathomable abyss of arbitrariness, and human beings are left as alone with their questions and suffering as Job was. If, by contrast, God is only juxtaposed to evil as the one who as a matter of principle has nothing to do with it because he is wholly and completely good, as the followers of Plato propose to do, then the path via God becomes not a detour in dealing with evil but a path on which the view to God's goodness loses sight of evil, which is left to itself. God's goodness in this case is not that which incessantly counteracts Evil and ultimately overcomes it but that which marks the fundamental rift between God and the world because it distinguishes God, who is different in principle from what is worldly, from everything that is or can be evil.

15. The Detour Via God in Christian Faith

Neither corresponds to the conception of God in Christian faith, nor is this the way in which Christian faith in the detour via God opens up the distance toward Evil that allows people to hope and to live despite their being caught up in evil. Confronted with Evil, Christians do not turn to God because God in his absolute power remains untouched by evil or because in his abstract goodness has nothing to do with evil. Instead, they turn to God for just the opposite reason, because they are convinced that God, in the crucifixion and resurrection of Jesus Christ, has presentified himself within Evil in such a way that he suffered its reality in himself without ceasing to be there for others as God and helper. This is what brings Christians, despite all experiences to the contrary, to orient themselves toward God and, via this detour, to engage with experiences of evil. For them, God is the one who, to the point of self-sacrifice, never ceases to do good for those who are affected by evil as victims and perpetrators and cannot by their own efforts resist the reality of Evil. By refusing to be dissuaded, even in Evil and by evil, from acting on behalf of those who are exposed to evil (that is, all creatures) and to do good for those whose God he is and wants to be (that is, all human beings), God limits and puts an end to the reality of Evil *through good*—that is, not by making the senseless meaningful or evil good but by not letting senseless evil be what comes last, at most what comes second to last, and by continuing evil with good.

That is why God's goodness, in the Christian conception, is not only that which distinguishes him from Evil. Nor is it merely the power with which he ceaselessly counteracts Evil. Above all, it is the *way* in which he does so: in taking Evil upon himself and letting those benefit from his goodness who are affected by and caught up in Evil in such a way that they cannot by their own efforts resist it, he does not oppose evil with evil but overcomes the merciless reality of Evil through his inexhaustibly devoted and merciful goodness, which lives not for itself but for the other. God is good because he makes those good who cannot make themselves good. And he makes them good, on the one hand, by letting them benefit from his divine goodness in the way that is best for each of them and, on the other, by taking their evil on himself and having it come to nothing, in infinitely bearing this evil in his unresisting love for them. God does not overcome Evil through evil but through the divine forbearance of his defenseless love. He opens up to the evil of each and every human life. In his divine life, he deprives this evil of its efficacy through his ever-greater devotion to those affected, harmed, and killed by this evil, and thereby imposes definitive limits on it. It is on this selfless patience of God's goodness and love that faith relies in the face of Evil that human beings are unable to resist. Faith thus takes the detour on which God embarked on the cross: the detour to the other. Only on this detour via God's detour to the other is there a way out of Evil. And only a theology that proceeds on this detour toward God's detour will be able to do more than remain silent in the face of Evil.

Yet to avoid misunderstandings, we have to be more precise when we speak of a "detour via God." Christian faith is a *detour via God* that is not abstract but is taken in light of and within the horizon of a very specific understanding of God—of what, precisely, makes it possible to define this faith as *Christian* faith.[29] There is no detour via God that does not take place within the horizon of a conception of God, and there is no conception of God that does not coexist with other conceptions or that could not be better than it is. Only on the basis of a conception of God, to which each instance of the expression of "God" is linked, does God come into focus *as God*, and only in this way and in this marking itself off from other conceptions of God can the reference to God perform an orienting function in human lives.

Conceptions of God, including the Christian ones, are mediated culturally. We grow into them and change them by living with or against them. No conception of God is stable, rigid, or unchangeable, neither historically, nor socially, nor biographically; all are permanently challenged, modified, further specified, and changed by the lived detours of faith, the inquiries of those without faith, and the presence of other conceptions of God. In the process, individuals and religious communities may encounter what is, in the proper sense, *existentially* onerous and trying about the detour of faith via God: when the guiding conception of God becomes questionable and loses its orienting power, *God himself is drawn into one's not-, mis-, and no-longer-understanding*, which this detour was supposed to lead out of. Faith then becomes obscure, the faithful contested, and the detour via God no longer sheds light on life but obscures God.

16. Theological Detours

What is true of faith has a correlate in theology as well, even if differences have to be observed: But what is the reason for this? As lived faith is a detour via God in light of a

29. Recall that the Christian conception of God is one that is always *in becoming* because it does not simply join a number of other understandings of God but plays itself out as their critique, aggregation, modification, or concentration in light of an experience of the operation of God's love in the present. To speak of God and to live with God, it is not even necessary explicitly to say "God."

certain conception of God, so theology—in its modern sense of theoretical reflection—is at most an attempt to explore, on the path of reflecting on conceptions of God, detours toward faith's lived detour via God. Theology does not take faith's existential detour via God by means of a Christian conception of God but takes the reflective detour via a critical engagement with Christian and non-Christian conceptions of God and their implications for faith's detour via God. Its detour, if you like, is not an existential detour via God but a *detour to the detour via God* in critically engaging with conceptions of God that others and Christians form and have formed for us on this path.

Yet when we have to engage with conceptions of God to make theological progress, we quickly come across all the misunderstandings, the half-comprehensions and incomprehensions that constitute the background of every conception of God and are provoked and configured anew at every step of theological clarification. For there is no conception of God that is not a critical continuation, a further determination of a conception that preceded it and that it considers to have been less clear, and there is no conception of God that does not trigger and provoke critical reactions, corrections, or attempts at further resolving its real or alleged lack of clarity. The theological *detour to the detour via God* thus becomes a *critical labor on the idea of God*, an engagement with the strengths and weaknesses of the conceptions of God we encounter and that serve to guide us, a critically interpreting transition from one conception of God to the next.

Theologically, this *detour via conceptions of God to the detour via God* cannot be avoided. Conceptions of God, however, are always culturally conditioned, historically contingent, and part of processes of cultural change in which they become comprehensible or lose their comprehensibility. We have to engage with them if we seek to understand the detour via God of faith.

17. God and Evil

Nowhere does this become clearer than in the way theology deals with Evil. There is hardly any other topic that so undeniably compels theological thinking to take detours as *experiences of evil* do. But hardly is there any other topic that time and again leads both faith's detour via God and theology's detours via conceptions of God toward this detour of faith into such aporias, impasses, and incomprehensibilities: Does evil become better or comprehensible at all when we bring God into the picture? Do sorrow and suffering become more bearable when they are referred to God and God to them? Does speaking of God make the senseless make sense, or is not rather even God infected by and dragged into such senselessness? Does not the detour via God thus lead to an entirely unnecessary exaggeration of the senselessness to which we find ourselves exposed in this life?

We should beware of skipping over such questions with hasty answers. Like faith's detour via God, theological detours must at every step heed the possibility of getting lost in the fog of opacities. These detours are not a theological manual for "finishing" with Evil, evils, sorrow, and suffering, for "coping" with it, "explaining" or deriving a "meaning" from it. Their point, precisely, is that *there is no method for understanding the senseless, Evil, evils, suffering*, that *detours* are all that is left where *nothing is understood any more* and where there is *nothing to be understood*—detours that constitute the only way out in order to live in the face of the senseless, the inscrutable, incomprehensible, and Evil without becoming evil oneself and drowning in Evil.

II

THINKING EVIL

A

Evil Within the Horizon of the Lifeworld

1. Evil Experienced

NOBODY WHO MAKES THE experience of Evil would contest its existence. And because all human beings make the experience of Evil in their lives when something that is evil for them—an impairment, inversion, damage, or defilement of life—happens to them or others, no one would seriously contest the reality of Evil. What is contested, and fundamentally so, is just how this reality is to be understood. What does Evil consist in? Why does Evil exist? Why is it me—or them—who is struck by this Evil? How can Evil be overcome? None of these questions has just one answer, if there are any answers at all, and no answer will satisfy everyone who asks.

The debate about these questions is part of the reality of Evil, for evil is always experienced concretely as a specific ill. An ill, however, is always something that is an ill for someone; not everything that is an ill for one person is an ill for others as well; and what constitutes the overcoming of an evil for one person can be an ill for another.

Because of Evil's essential relationality and concreteness in the lifeworld, the ambivalence of its media, and the contingency of its occurrence in the most varied experiential contexts, there is no unequivocal resolution to the debate about how the reality of Evil is to be understood. Even in cases where there is no disagreement that one is dealing with evil, there may still be disagreement about what this evil consists in.[1] On the basis of different experiences, different answers are given, even if many agree with many others on many things. There certainly is something like a concentration of the experience of evil in specific areas of life (illness, war, the ailments of old age, dying) and a dominance of certain kinds of evil (ills) at the various stages of life. Nor can it be denied that in all

---

1. This thesis is time and again confirmed by the debate about education policy. Everyone agrees that much of what is happening in education today is almost trivialized by calling it a mere ill because it massively restricts the chances a large number of people have in life and needlessly and avoidably harms the reality of their lives. Yet what one side suggests as a solution of the problem is precisely what represents the ill for the other side because there is no agreement about what constitutes the core of the ill—the irresponsible abuse of people's lifetime by ever new regulations or the control of control considered to be ever-insufficient.

its variety, suffering is the site in which we exemplarily have and make the experience of evil.[2] It is just as clear, however, that evil neither is nor can be limited to any area or phase of life; all areas and phases of life can be distressed and perverted by the intrusion and eruption of evil. The reality of Evil can therefore be described in a differentiating manner according to areas of life and kinds of ills, yet it must always be understood in the context of the entirety of life. To get a picture of the full presence of Evil in life, we can thus keep to the structures of orientation that orient us as we live our lives in the lifeworld, that organize our lives and our world and situate us within this order.

2. Means of Orientation in the Lifeworld

Elementary means of orientation in the lifeworld include the spatial orientations relating to our bodies (in front of, behind, above, below, right, left), the temporal orientations relating to experience and action (earlier, later, yesterday, today, tomorrow), and the personal means of orientation relating to communication and interaction (I, you, she, he, we, you, they). They all perform elementary functions in the practical contexts of the lifeworld, yet that is also why they provide the basis and starting-point of more complex symbolic constructions of *spaces* (areas of life that follow different rules but whose relationships with one another are more or less organized, such as family, work, school, sports, religion), *times* (weeks, months, years, seasons, periods of festivity), and *social relationships* (kinship relations, status designations, names of professions) without which we would not be able to orient ourselves in more complex situations. We live in worlds that are organized symbolically because as beings of little instinct, and therefore as highly endangered beings, we would otherwise not survive. By means of signs, language, rhetoric, and technology, we seek to compensate for our biological deficits and shortcomings and to adapt to an unwelcoming world. The means of orientation in the lifeworld are sediments of our attempts at orientation that have become matters of course, and we pick up on them in one way or another even when we move in virtual spaces, times, and social relationships. We go back to them when our world threatens to come unhinged or when we lose track of things. That is why we also draw on all of them to structure the domain of Evil experienced. And all of them suggest themselves especially when we engage with evil experienced, suffered, and committed that takes place within the purview of the experience in the lifeworld.

When we reflect on the different ways of orientating ourselves in the lifeworld with a view to which of their aspects and moments are comparable, a basic structure of orienting organization and of situating ourselves emerges: we live in our respective worlds in such a way that, on the one hand, we belong to them and, on the other, face them and distinguish ourselves from them. In this way, we can on the one hand always describe ourselves as an element of a whole (a *world*) that is structured not by the dialectics of part and whole but by the dialectics of place and horizon: in our place we belong to this world that extends around us as the horizon of our lives, a horizon that is organized into a large variety of temporal horizons (past, present, future), horizons of objects (something

2. See Dalferth, *Leiden und Böses*.

other), horizons of community (other people), etc., without for all that having a definitive inner structure, boundary, or unity. The world in which we live is structured by the way in which we live in it, and it changes just as incessantly as we change within it. On the other hand, we are not just one element in our world (an element that can be defined from the various perspectives of various horizons), we also always simultaneously face our world as its limit and point of reference. Just as the eye does not form part of the visual field but constitutes its point of reference, we are the points of reference of our respective worlds. In communicating, we place ourselves in our world not only as a She or a He but as an I from which and toward which others (or other things) are defined as You and She and He and It. In the enactments of the lifeworld, we thus belong to a *world* that we simultaneously face as an *I* or *We*.

3. What Affects Us and What We Bring About

Within this elementary structure, evil is experienced as something that comes to us from the world or from others and that affects us against our will, and as something that we bring about and see to in the world and in the lives of others, intentionally or unintentionally. We make the experience of evil that intrudes into our lives, and we experience evil as something we cause in our lives and in the lives of others; we find ourselves exposed to evil in our natural, social, and cultural environments (natural ills), and we find ourselves caught up in evil that we ourselves cause or do not prevent in our natural, social, and cultural environments (moral ills). Evil is thus experienced from the outset within the tension between what the world does to our lives and what we do to our lives and the lives of others in our world. It is experienced as harm to which we are exposed but also as injustices and atrocities for which we are responsible; as ills that seem to exist for everyone in one way or another in their worlds but also as ill deeds that would not exist in the world if we did not cause them ourselves. Both aspects have to be kept in mind if we want to understand the reality of evil.

Because evil is experienced in this twofold way, it raises questions that put life in a dialectic light and make it impossible to understand life without acknowledging breaks. Life is experienced both as the site of happenings and as the site where evil originates; the lifeworld is experienced as what perverts our own lives and as what is perverted by our lives, as experiential space of Evil in suffering evil and as practical field of Evil in perpetrating evils. In both respects, evil seems unavoidably to belong to the whole of life, its experience and fashioning of a world. Evil is perpetrated, selectively and willingly, and, neither sought out nor wished for, it intrudes in a life. Life thus finds itself, on the one hand, to be the origin of the evil that endangers and sooner or later destroys it: every life is caught up in evil, it produces ills and perishes because of ills. And it experiences itself, on the other hand, as that which resists evil and opposes evil for the sake of its own preservation, seeking to construct the good and avoid evil—not because life itself ought to be understood as an absolute good or as the highest of goods, of which death deprives us,[3] but because life cannot be lived without defending itself for the sake of its

3. Nagel, "Death."

own preservation against the Evil toward which it is inclined and against the ills that impinge on it. Part of its seemingly unavoidable tragic nature is that life itself, in order to escape the Evil that happens or might happen to it, produces evil and seeks to find in the evil thus produced a way out of the evil it experiences.[4]

Life thus experiences itself as a nexus in which evil takes place, which is harmed and destroyed by evil, and which will, sooner or later, fail because of evil. The experience of one's own life thus inevitably enters into the dialectic of, on the one hand, experiencing life as the site and nexus of Evil and, on the other, experiencing Evil as backdrop, substrate, and endpoint of life. Life appears as the greater whole in which ills occur as disruptions, such that over against these ills, life represents the more comprehensive horizon of the good, while at the same time it turns out to be only an island doomed to disappear in a sea of Evil. On the one hand, life thus comes into focus as the greater whole *vis-à-vis* Evil; on the other, Evil comes into focus as what is greater and threatens life. Both these basic experiences in the lifeworld play a fundamental role when we engage with evil in human life: the struggle against suffering and doing evil belongs to the preservation of life, and insight into what threatens life and into its unavoidable end in death belong to the basic motives at work in all preservation of life.

This entails different procedures, with different emphases and basic orientations, to deal with evil in the multitude and variety of ills. On one side there is the attempt to understand evil within the whole of an experience of world and life; evil, that is, is questioned as to its comprehensibility within the horizon of the whole. On the other side there is the attempt to understand it on the site where it is suffered or produced, there, that is, where it plagues the individual. The *whole of the lifeworld* and the *individual in his lifeworld* thus become the point of reference of the effort to understand Evil.

4. The Whole and Evil

In no way is the lifeworld something given as a whole. It is not a unified and unequivocal ground to which everyday formations of sense, scientific constructions, and institutional regulations could go back at any time, reliably and without contestation.[5] To be sure, there is no unfolding of life that does not have backgrounds, origins, or surroundings in the lifeworld, that does not, in other words, take place in a pre-world, a with-world, an environment that "has not been chosen freely" but which one "can leave only by means of an adjustment" without for all that leaving behind all lifeworld contexts and thus the "at every point in time inexhaustible store of what unquestionably is present, familiar, and, precisely in this familiarity, unknown."[6]

That is why *the* lifeworld does not exist, not for everyone in common, not for specific groups, not even for a specific human being. It is the world lived concretely in each

4. This is the basic problem of life's being intertwined with the process of evolution and its permanent destruction of life in the service of constructing and preserving life. See Hick, *Evil and the God of Love*, 297–304; Griffin, *God, Power, and Evil*; Corey, *Evolution and the Problem of Natural Evil*, 151–66, 281–337; Boyd, *Satan and the Problem of Evil*, 269–92; Dalferth, *Leiden und Böses*, 69–83.

5. Waldenfels, *In den Netzen der Lebenswelt*, 8–9.

6. Blumenberg, *Wirklichkeiten in denen wir leben*, 27, 23.

instance, which changes with life but is not produced by this life; it is that horizon in which implementations of life always already find themselves, without being able to turn this horizon into a ground, a principle, or to fix it as the whole that surrounds it. The "work of structuring and organizing of lifeworld practice can neither be attributed to primary givens nor be derived from ultimate regulations."[7] Our efforts are contingencies that remain concealed because they are contingent, and are therefore not perceived and experienced as something that could also be otherwise. And where that does happen and it becomes apparent that they are not self-evident, it happens on the basis of self-evidences that for their part are equally contingent and not recognized as contingent.

The lifeworld can thus not be thematized as a *whole* in the implementation of life but only on the level where its horizons are symbolized. To be sure, we each live in our lifeworld and presuppose its wholeness, continuity, and homogeneity, presuppositions that have their origin in the fact that our lifeworld universe of self-evidences is oriented toward us as their center and toward the access we always have to our lifeworld. But the unity and wholeness of our lifeworlds, which is instituted in the reference of the implementation of life to a horizon, can be captured symbolically only by distinguishing and pacing out horizons as ensembles of wholes that cannot be reduced to one, and only one, determination of (the) world. They are centered but open wholes, relating to a specific *here* with a manifold of determinative horizons and referential fields as well as the most varied connections and transitions between them, which allow the lifeworld to appear as a network of references and cross-references and only in this way as an ensemble of wholes.

What is one for us in each instance and experienced as a networked whole can be symbolically unified and thematized in several respects, depending on which practical question dominates. Thus in abstracting from certain aspects of the universe of the lifeworld, the world is symbolized as *cosmos*, as an order that makes life possible and sustains it but is always threatened by disorder and disruption by the chaotic; or the world is constituted as *nature*, as the domain of iterative processes and relatively invariant regularities into which we always find ourselves tied without having produced them ourselves or without being able to exercise any real influence over them; or it is conceptualized as the domain of human acting and suffering and thus as *history*; or as *society* and thereby as an assemblage of institutionalized conditions of human coexistence; or as *life*, as that auto-constitutive and self-regulating process in which organic, bodily, and mental processes differentiate, adapt, and re-form as they assimilate and accommodate life-threatening surroundings. The world in which we live can thus be symbolized as cosmos, nature, history, society, culture, or life, and the disruption, injury, or destruction of life can accordingly be described within each horizon as a specific kind of ills, which, by way of contrast, also sheds light on specific kinds of goods. That is why the distinction between good and evil, ills and goods, is never made abstractly but always in centered horizons of wholeness. But neither is it ever made only within one horizon. It is always made within different horizons and thus in irreversibly different manners without letting itself be integrated abstractly into a homogenous horizon of the whole of all horizons, for such a wholeness exists only in the form of multifarious transitions

7. Waldenfels, *In den Netzen der Lebenswelt*, 8.

between the contingent perspectives and horizons in which human life factually takes place and in which the difference between ills and goods is constituted in specific ways.

5. The Individual and Evil

The lifeworld would not be what its designation suggests if it were not *someone's* lifeworld. It is always the correlate of an I or We as whose lifeworld it is constituted and by whom it is lived and experienced as a differentiated whole. In relation to its lifeworld—and thus also in relation to the different horizons of wholeness that can be constructed starting from this lifeworld in regard to specific aspects—this I or We can define itself in different ways. The most important constellations of I and world include:

1. *the undifferentiated unity of I and world*: Genetically, the I experiences itself first of all as *the center of its world,* as that to which others and other things are as if self-evidently referred, as that which merges with its world because this world is nothing other than *its* world: the I *is* the world in which it lives.

2. *the I as part of the world*: This changes to the extent to which the I, in dealing with others, does not experience itself as the only center of a world and thus enters into a process of decentering in which it experiences itself as *an element of its world among and beside others*: it becomes a *part* of the world in which it lives.

3. *the I in the world*: This does not, however, virtually suspend the initial experience; in acting and reacting, the I, rather, experiences itself as a privileged element of its world insofar as it can intervene and change this world: it becomes an *agent* in the world in which it lives.

4. *the I as counterpart of the world*: The more markedly the I experiences itself as the one shaping its world, the more clearly it senses an opposition between itself and its world, the unfolding of its life and itself: in fashioning the world in which it lives, the I becomes the *counterpart* of its world.

5. *the I as counterpart of the You in the world*: Yet what we saw already at an earlier stage repeats itself here, too: the acting I experiences not only the resistance of an environment it has not itself produced but also the presence of other agents in its world, and it cannot choose whether to enter into a relationship with these agents because it always already entertains a relationship with them in which it is itself being determined: it experiences the presence of others in the world in which it lives together with them.

The relationship of an I with its lifeworld can thus be described differently on different levels: as an undifferentiated dyad of I and lifeworld; as part of the world in which it lives; as center of action in its lifeworld; as limit and counterpart of its lifeworld; and as counterpart of others present in its lifeworld. The symbolizations that express each of these relationships, accordingly, take different forms:

1. *animal rationale*: As an element of its world, the I, in its concentration on what it shares with other beings (*animal*) and its specific differences from them (*ratio*), is

inscribed in a comprehensive world nexus projected in a specific way, that is, it is understood as a *human being* and, as such, defined and designated as a *living being of a specific kind*, as an *animal rationale*.

2. *reason and will*: As center of action *in* its world, the I in concentrating not on what it shares with other beings but, exactly inversely, on what it considers its characteristic specificities, is thematized and designated as *reason* and *will*, as point of origin and point of reference of orienting and shaping a world.

3. *I vs. not-I*: When reason and will are conceived of in such a way that everything else, as their counterpart, is unified in an undifferentiated whole, the I positions itself over against its world in the contrast of I and not-I. This contrast can be specified on different levels, according to what operational point of view serves to unify the counterpart of the I into a whole. When the I positions itself over against the world as a cognizing and knowing I, the world is unified as the epitome of what can be known and cognized from the differential point of view of *truth* and *falsehood*. When it positions itself as an acting and willing I over against the world, the world is unified as the practical field of the freedom of the I from the differential point of view of *good* and *bad* or (with respect to morally relevant action in the narrow sense) *good* and *evil*. When the I positions itself over against the world as a feeling and sensing I, the world is unified as the epitome of what can be affectively lived from the differential point of view of pleasure and pain. In all instances, the unity and wholeness of the world is thus constituted via a specific unifying operation by means of which the I relates to everything which it distinguishes from itself as not-I and thereby combines into a whole.

4. *I vs. You*: This is also true when the I recognizes that, as operative center of its world, it exists only because and insofar as it exists through something other, to which it owes not only its being but its being such and such as well. Genetically, the difference between I and You then turns out to be more fundamental than the difference between I and not-I, namely in that the I experiences the counterpart, which refers to it as a You, in its inevitable otherness, from whose claim (Levinas) and address it cannot escape; and just as it experiences the irrevocable otherness of the other at the site of the You, it also experiences the irrevocable otherness of itself over against all the images, representations, and conceptualizations it fashions of itself and its identity. The other is not only a You that is never exhausted by how and as what I experience it, but I myself experience myself as someone other than the one as whom I identify myself (*ipse*-identity) or am being identified and reidentified by others (*idem*-identity).[8]

To the differentiated way in which a first-person singular or plural can refer to its particular world and juxtapose this world as a whole to itself corresponds a no less differentiated way in which evil and ills can occur and take place in these relationships. Already the transition from the undifferentiated dyad of I and world to the decentering of the I as a part of the world can be experienced as an evil, an evil only partially compensated

8. Ricœur, *Oneself as Another*.

for, if at all, by the relative positioning of the animal rationale at the apex of the whole of the world. Accordingly, situating the I in the world as a will guided by reason that is able but also obliged to shape its world can be experienced as a liberation but also as an imposition or as an excessive demand such that some see an ill in what others consider to be the decisive basis for coming to terms with ills. This is equally true for the different ways in which an I refers to the whole of a correspondingly specified world via operations of knowing, acting, or feeling. The differences *true/false*, *good/bad*, *good/evil*, *pain/pleasure* that guide our knowing, acting, and feeling signal the kinds of ills we encounter in these various instances: untrue (pseudo-) knowledge, bad actions, evildoing, painful experiences. There seems to be no other way of constituting the worlds at issue than by means of permanently overcoming various kinds of ills. This holds, finally, also for the relationships between I and other in the world that can be perverted in a multitude of ways and thus give occasion for coming to terms with moral, ethical, and religious ills that arise in such perversions.

6. Faith and Evil

Yet all of this does not tell us anything about the relationship between faith and Evil, which is decisive for the Christian analysis of Evil. Like all human beings, believers, too, live in the structures just evoked that construct, in symbols and in the lifeworld, relationships between I or We and their worlds. Faith, however, aims essentially at God who, for his part, is essentially distinct from the world: distinct as creator from creation (the difference God/created world), as reconciler of the creation that ignores him (the difference God/factually sinful human being), and as perfecter of a creation that fails to comprehend and diminishes itself in this cutting out of God (the difference God/unnecessarily imperfect and inhumane world). To this extent, the world of faith is not sufficiently understood when it is seen as merely differentiating a first-person's (singular or plural) contrastive and correlative world, constituted via specific anthropological operations, or as absolutizing the relationship to others that constitutes the I in terms of a being-constituted by the absolutely Other. Faith is neither one more world-constituting operation in addition to knowing, acting, and feeling, nor can it be reduced to a specific mode of knowing, acting, and feeling, nor is it a projection into heaven of personal and person-constituting basic relationships in the world. Faith is neither an anthropological function nor an anthropological fiction, provided it really is what Christians confess it to be: the human way of implementing the life given as a gift by God in a grateful community with God and his creatures, that is, living the life that God lives.[9]

If we want to do justice to the points Christians make in statements in this regard, then we must not classify faith among the set of human functions and capacities but understand it as the *constitution* within which human beings, with all their capacities and functions, live their lives in this world by explicitly leading their lives before and with God (faith) or by not doing so (unfaith). In the theologically relevant sense of the

9. Luther, *Vorlesungen über 1. Mose von 1535–45*, in *Luthers Werke* (henceforth *WA*) 43.221: "I, the almighty creator of heaven and earth, I am your God, that is, you should live the life that I live."

word, faith is not a particular anthropological phenomenon, not *fides* and not *fiducia*, to use the traditional terms, not *cum assensione cogitare* and not *credere*, which is neither *scire* nor mere *opiniari*; it is a specific mode of human existing. It is a determination not of the *What* (of the essence) but of the *That* (of the existence) of the human being, not an attribute that characterizes a human being ("Peter has faith," that is, "It is a property of Peter that he has faith") but a mode in which human life is lived ("Peter lives as someone who has faith," that is, "Peter lives in his faith" or "Peter lives in having faith"). One lives in having faith or in not having faith: having faith if one also lives the life one receives from the hands of God in such a way that this is being expressed, and not having faith if one does not do so; and no one who lives does not live in either this way or the other.[10]

Those who have faith thus do not do, have, or suffer anything specific besides or among other things they also do, have, or suffer in their lives but live their entire lives in a specific way, and those who do not have faith do as well. The difference between faith and unfaith, accordingly, is not apparent in the human beings who have or do not have faith but in the mode of their life *coram deo*, before God. It does not appear in the relationships of human beings to each other, to themselves, or to their environment but marks the relationship of their lives to God; it is thus not to be identified with any empirical or historical phenomena. In everything they do, have, and suffer in their lives, those who have faith behave differently toward the relation of God to their lives than those who do not have faith. They have the same faculties and skills, limitations and impairments that those who do not have faith can have as well. But they live their lives in a different way insofar as they live them in thanks and appeals, in praise and lament before God. The reference to faith is thus not a reference to something that could be converted into anthropological determinations of knowing, willing, or feeling, or be added to these as one more determination. Faith, rather, is always about the mode of living a human being's entire life before God and thereby about a specific determination of *all* aspects of human life *coram deo*.

The reference to faith thus does not designate a particular element in the set of human capacities and functions but characterizes one side of the basic alternative in which human life *coram deo* is lived, an alternative that comes into focus when human life is examined from the point of view of its relation to God's relation to it: human beings live their lives either *in faith* or *in an unfaith*, and no one can live their life in neither. Faith and unfaith thus mark the *basic existential constitution coram deo*, not a particular human attitude toward life among others. No one knows, acts, or feels, and in addition has or does not have faith. Instead, we live as knowing, acting, or feeling persons before God in one way or the other, either by counting in our knowing, acting, and feeling on God's presence (faith) or by not counting on it (unfaith). That is why with respect to knowing, willing, and feeling, there is always more or less; with respect to faith, there is only an either-or. We can know more or less, will more or less, feel more or less, but we cannot,

---

10. To this extent, we can say that it is impossible for any human being to live and not either have faith or not have faith. This does not mean that it is impossible for him or her to have faith or that it is impossible for him or her not to have faith. No one must have faith or must not have faith; everyone, rather, can have faith or not have faith, but everyone must either have faith or not have faith because no one can live without factually doing either the one or the other.

precisely, have more or less faith: we either live in faith or live in a lack of it. There is no third; rather, if one lives, one cannot avoid either one or the other. It is thus true of all who live that they live *coram deo* and thereby in faith or in an unfaith—whether they know it or want it or feel it or not.

Yet the Christian faith claims not only that all life takes place *coram deo* but moreover that the factual existence of each and every human is lived and implemented *in an unfaith*: human beings first of all and generally live as if God did not exist. *Lived faith* thus only exists as a *transition* from an unfaith to faith, and faith is not lived in any other way than *as this transition*. Judged from the perspective of lived faith—and this is the perspective of the Christian creed—the nexus from which faith *derives* is always an unfaith whereas the nexus within which it *originates* is always *another faith*. For although lived faith *originates* in the Word of faith (the Gospel of God's life-creating presence) alone, faith only comes about when one is called, through this Word, from an unfaith into faith. Just as the site of *lived faith* thus consists in the (never completed and never self-implementing) transition from an unfaith to faith, so the site of a lived unfaith is to be understood as *this side* of the transition to faith; the *goal* of the life of faith, however, is to be understood as the *beyond* of this transition, as the site, that is, where the difference of the basic existential constitution of life on the site of an unfaith and of faith is annulled and where, in that the unfaith has become superfluous, faith has been rendered superfluous as well.

Within the horizon of faith (thus conceived), the problem of Evil and ills becomes unambiguously acute because what is seen as the real evil and the grounds of all other ills is not just anything that is experienced as evil, but it is *unfaith*, as a mode of human living and experiencing, for it is unfaith that shuts human beings off from what God provides them with as *bonum*. In unfaith, humans ignore the overabundant basis of life and shut themselves off from the abundance and surplus without which life will sooner or later have exhausted itself.

In this regard, even human beings' best knowing, willing, and feeling is fundamentally impaired in unfaith by their ignorance of the presence of God: humans do not live up to the possibilities God provides them with, and thus cut themselves off from the good falling to and being allotted to them without which their lives cannot sustain themselves in the long run. This does not exclude having God on one's mind, somehow knowing about God, and thematizing God in a number of ways. Ideas of God can be—and are—conceived in all dimensions of human reference to the world. Within the horizon of knowledge, for example, God is conceptualized as *summa veritas* or *ens realissimum et necessarium*, within the horizon of willing as *summum bonum*, within the horizon of feeling as originary ground and point of origin of all dependence as well as the point of departure of the dialectics of freedom and dependence thus made possible and constituted. But forming an idea of God and a feeling of God within the horizon of one's relationship to the world is something different from living before God in faith and thus something different from living in the existential transition from unfaith to faith, that is to say (judging retrospectively), from being opened up by God to what good God provides one with. This openness cannot be produced from out of unfaith. The transition from unfaith to faith instead always leads via an abyss that one cannot bridge on one's own strength, not by any knowing, willing, or experiencing, an abyss that cannot be sufficiently symbolized and expressed in any kind of knowing, willing, or feeling when it is implemented by God himself in the life of a human being.

The site of human existence before God is not an object of human decisions but the existential site of all decisions and non-decisions, and that is why the change of mode on this site can only ever be experienced the way it is traditionally voiced by Christian faith: as a redirection and reorientation of a life toward God that is due to God alone; as nullification of the old life and beginning of a new life, it always articulates, in images such as *death and resurrection, death and rebirth, captivity and liberation, incurring guilt and redemption,* among many others, the same basic idea: that the life-enhancing and life-saving change of mode from unfaith to faith is due to God himself alone.

B

Christian Attempts at Thinking about Evil

THE THREE BASIC STRATEGIES of attempts at thinking Evil described in the preceding chapter figure in the Christian tradition as well. It, too, tries to understand making the experience of evil and having the experience of ills within the whole of the world; the I, positioned as counterpart of the world, becomes the central point of reference in the analysis of evil; and the basic difference between faith and unfaith comes to guide the discussion of the problem. Yet these attempts presuppose decisions that are of the utmost significance for them and that characterize them as *Christian*.

1. The Starting Point of Christian Attempts at Conceptualizing Evil

Christian faith and Christian thought start from the *reality of evil*, but they understand this reality in a very specific way: it is not an unchangeable reality of human life we have to put up with and which we may at most, in a few cases, avoid, or prevent, or whose evil consequences we might be able to limit thanks to knowledge, provisions, legal rules, and technology. Nor is it merely something that does not have to be but could and ought to be otherwise such that it is not meaningless and futile to try with all available means to overcome it, even if experience tells us that human beings, because of the weakness of their will, the shortness of their lives, and the malice of their hearts, do not reach this goal. Nor is it merely something that, given our own failure, we can only ask God to overcome because we are not capable of doing so ourselves.

The plea that God deliver us from Evil is, of course, inscribed in Christian faith, and the seventh petition of the Lord's Prayer belongs to what Christians have taken over from Jesus and what unites them across all confessional boundaries. But between Jesus's plea for deliverance from Evil and Christians' petition[1] lies Jesus's cross and resurrection, and this changes the point and the basis of the Christian petition. Christians ask God

---

1. More precisely, we would have to say: the experience of Jesus's death on the cross and the appearances of the crucified Jesus that confronted his successors with a fundamental experiential incompatibility ("Jesus is dead"—"Jesus lives") to which they answer by pointing to the resurrection of the crucified Jesus by God (see Dalferth, *Crucified and Resurrected*, 39–82). Bernd Oberdorfer ("'Was sucht ihr den Lebendigen bei den Toten?'") misses the point because the proposition of the resurrected, "I am alive," does not annul but precisely presupposes the truth of "I have died."

for deliverance from Evil not merely because they, like Jesus and the Jewish tradition, expect and count on God keeping the covenant with his people or because they had realized that no matter how closely they scrutinize God's law, they are incapable of really, sufficiently, completely, or even definitively overcoming the reality of Evil such that the only choice that remains is either to put up with the impossibility of overcoming Evil and thereby capitulate before Evil or to ask God to overcome Evil and thereby at least keep some hope alive. Both choices are made by Christians, too, but they do not get at the decisive point of their petition: they turn to God with this petition because they are certain that God not only could overcome the reality of Evil if he willed so but that in the death and resurrection of Jesus Christ God *has overcome* Evil and therefore can and will overcome it in every life, including theirs.

Christians know how much this certainty runs counter to experience. But for them, the plea for deliverance from Evil is not just wishful thinking; they base their confidence on the conviction of their faith that God has overcome Evil. The underlying argument may be summarized as follows: what God has overcome can be overcome such that we may say: "it is possible that evil is overcome"; if God has overcome evil, then he can and wills to overcome it, such that we may say: "God is able and willing to overcome evil"; and that God has in fact done so is proven for Christian faith by its very own existence, which owes itself to the proclamation of God's overcoming of Evil in the death and resurrection of Jesus Christ.

Precisely in the confrontation with the *reality of evil*, Christian faith, taking recourse to the story of the life of Jesus Christ, thus testifies both to the *possibility of overcoming evil* and to *God's ability and willingness to overcome it* because it assumes that *evil has been overcome*. Yet if evil can be overcome by God in principle, as the story of Jesus Christ, according to faith, demonstrates, and if it is overcome by God only because he can and wills to overcome it, then Evil can be overcome in every life story in which God is present in the way he was present in the story of Jesus Christ; and if God is thus present in every life story because every life story corresponds to the life story of Jesus Christ insofar as it would be neither possible nor real if God were not present in it, then there is in every life story the possibility of hoping for and counting on God's overcoming the Evil in it. God's work in the life story of Jesus Christ is thus the reason for Christians' confessing God in a very specific way and for hoping for something very specific for the life story of each and every human being, namely that God overcome the Evil in each story through good.

2. Consequences for Theological Thought

It is starting from this point that Christian theology develops its *understanding of Evil* as well as its *understanding of God* and its *understanding of the human being and its world*. It formally understands *evil* to be that which is overcome by God, as the story of Jesus Christ demonstrates: *everything that and only that is "evil"* (in the sense relevant here) *which God has overcome in the way shown in the story of Jesus Christ: through the good that God is and does.* The definition of *malum* thus does not consist in identifying it with a set of phenomena or the attributing it a certain content but takes place through *the way it has been overcome by God.* This overcoming (put in Christological terms) takes place in the dialectic of cross and resurrection as a discriminating event that distinguishes between *taking up and perfecting* on the one hand and *putting an end to and surpassing* on the other: what *God takes up, continues, and perfects* thereby comes into focus as a *bonum* and what is *put an end to, concluded, and surpassed by bonum* appears as *malum*. Something thus *becomes* a *malum* by God putting an end or surpassing it through the *bonum* of his life. He puts an end to it not by taking it up in the process of his life but by letting it be past, or he *surpasses* it by recalling it only in such a way that it does not leave its mark on his divine life, by muffling it with and tying it into the *bonum* in which he continues and perfects the good of creaturely life in his life. Or, to put it in the terms of the theology of justification: something becomes a *malum* in that God (negatively) condemns it as *malum* and thereby puts an end to it and (positively) acquits human beings disfigured by *malum* of this *malum*, that is, includes them in the relations of his divine life that bring about the new and are no (longer) determined, limited, or impaired by the *malum* that disfigures them. From the Christian perspective, in short, everything on the detour via God that has no future in the life process of God is to be addressed as *malum*, everything, that is, which is not taken up and perfected in him but is put an end to and surpassed through good.[2]

Accordingly, God on this basis is formally understood as the one who *puts an end to and surpasses evil through good*, who is *good* because he does so, and who is *omnipotent* because there is no evil for him (that is, nothing that is evil before him) whose *malum* character he could not and would not put end to and continue it through something new and good: *solely he is to be called "God"* (in the sense relevant here) *who puts an end to and surpasses evil through good and for whom there is no evil he could not put an end to and would not surpass through good.* That God is to be understood and wants to be understood this way is not a generally available rational insight; according to the insight of Christian faith, it has been demonstrated in the life story of Jesus Christ beyond death and thereby in an enduring and binding manner. And because God is present to every

---

2. I speak of *surpassing* because the concern is not with reversing a given *malum*, playing it down, *per impossibile* passing it off as a good, or turning it into a *bonum*: it remains *malum* and it remains a *malum* of the life that is defined by it. But the *malum* of this life is *put an end to* in that, in the life of God, it no longer has determinative power when it comes to what this life disfigured by *malum* is for God and for others. And it is *surpassed* in the life of God in that *this disfigured life* with all its *mala* is included in the life in God and thus exposed to a process of distinguishing between *malum* and *bonum*; this process brings what is good in this life to bear *in the life of God* and renders ineffective what is evil. Just as Jesus crucified, at the right hand of the Father, does not stop bearing the stigmata he suffered on the cross but in exactly this way eternally defines and impresses himself on the life of God because these fatal wounds do not separate him from God but provoke God's greater care and are enveloped by it, so every life that God takes into his life is distinguished by not losing the *mala* that characterize it. These, rather, are surpassed by the *bonum* that is God in that this life is perpetuated *in the life process of the good that is God* in such a way that what becomes good there will always remain a *bonum* and what becomes *malum* there does not, as evil, have a future. Just as the resurrection does not reverse the crucifixion but takes the one crucified up into God's life, so redemption does not reverse the *mala* of life but takes those disfigured by them into God's life community in a way that their life in and with God is no longer hindered and impaired by these mala. Through the *bonum* of his life, which, in Anselm's terms, is "that than which nothing greater can be thought" and at the same time is "greater than what can be thought," their disfigured life is given a future it would not have by itself.

life in the way he defined himself there in order to overcome the Evil of this life through the presence of his Spirit, who creates the new and the good, one is justified in expecting all the best from him and resorting to him in times of trouble. For God is not only good, his goodness consists in his *making good*, that is, in his putting an end to and overcoming evil through good and through good, creating good out of evil.

Finally, therefore, *human life* can formally be understood as that in which God puts an end to and surpasses evil through good: *everything that and only that is to be called "human being"* (in the sense relevant here) *of which it is true that God puts an end to and surpasses evil through good in its life the way he has done in the life story of Jesus Christ.* This does not mean that the difference between the story of Jesus Christ and other life stories is abolished but that God overcomes evil in every life in such a way that he puts an end to and surpasses it through good in this life and for this life. God is present in every present,[3] and because in its enactment, every life is structured by presentness, God is at work in every life such that, as became clear in the story of Jesus Christ, the *malum* of each life is turned, through the greater *bonum* of his life, into a past without a future.

This, however, means that Christian theological thought is always more than an explication of some people's particular testimony concerning God's working in the story of Jesus Christ. In speaking to God eschatologically, that is to say, definitively being effective in this story, their confession makes a universal *theological* claim (that is, a claim concerning the understanding of God): God is such as he has proven to be in this story. And in thus confessing God, it also makes a universal soteriological claim (that is, a claim concerning the understanding of salvation): God is present in every life story in the way thus conceived.

Theological thought thus cannot refer to the Christian confession of faith without thereby thematizing God and God's working in every life story: theological statements never speak only about then and there but always also about here and now because in referring back to confessing Christ, they speak about God as the one who back then and there and therefore also here and now is present as the one who puts an end to and surpasses evil through good. Precisely because Christian theology is decisively oriented by the Christian faith's confession of Christ, it cannot escape into history.[4] It must speak about here and now if it is to say anything worth saying at all.

---

3. See Dalferth, *Becoming Present*.

4. It is thus precisely not the case, as some argue time and again, that Christian theology is a *historical* study because it explains the confession of Christ, or that it could become *relevant for the present* only by giving up on the particularizing orientation by this confession, said to restrict it to a specific religious tradition, or that it could be *academic* only if it held not (just) the views of a religious tradition but instead focused on comparing different religious traditions and the ways they speak of God. All these views suffer from the same prejudice, which consists in the following ideas about the guiding reference to Jesus Christ: that it *particularizes* when in fact, it does the opposite and universalizes, for in speaking of Christ, one speaks about God in a very specific way; that it *historicizes* when in fact, it does the opposite and refers (us) to the present because with Jesus Christ, it is God's working in the present that is at issue; that it is *unscholarly* because it is said to be well-known that other religious speak differently about God and that in questions of religion there is no truth or a different one for each of us—as if the modern dogma, according to which only *speech about* God that can be described historically, sociologically, psychologically, etc., could be the subject of scientific investigation but not *God*, proved anything but the prejudice that God must be understood and construed according to the standard of a given discipline

3. The Fundamental Problem of Soteriology

Yet it is just this specific reference to presence that causes all of the problems theological thought is struggling with. And it does so in the case of the question of Evil, too, for the starting point of all theological attempts at thinking the reality of Evil is thus always a dual state of affairs: the conviction of Christian faith that *God has overcome Evil* and the human life experience that *Evil exists*. There is an obvious tension between the two: How can it be true that God has overcome Evil when evil still exists?

This question marks not only an intellectual problem of Christian theology but a fundamental existential tension of Christian life.[5] It inevitably poses itself when the reality of evil is experienced not just somehow and somewhere but concretely *in one's own life* and when the conclusion we draw from the conviction of faith, for the reasons just discussed, is that God can, wants to, and will overcome Evil not just somehow and somewhere but also and precisely in my own life. For in this case, the reality of Evil in my life seems to question, at least in my case, the effectiveness of the divine overcoming of evil. Yet if what is evil for me is not overcome, then either I am so ill that not even God is able to help, and then God would in my case come up against his limits, or God is not willing to overcome the evil in my life, and then my case would demonstrate that his will is not good but at best arbitrary. Yet if God is not able or willing to overcome Evil in my case, then not only does the question become whether he wills to and can overcome evil at all, but the suspicion arises that the God confessed by Christian faith does not even exist: If God is the one who overcomes Evil through Good, and if Evil in my life is not overcome, then God does not always overcome Evil, or not for everyone, or not always and not for everyone through good, and then the God Christian faith confesses does not exist. For if evil exists that God does not overcome then, as the argument, which in the wake of Epicurus the Christian tradition, too, has stated time and again, has it,

> God either wishes to take away evils and he cannot, or he can and does not wish to, or he neither wishes to nor is able, or he both wishes to and is able. If he wishes to and is not able, he is feeble, which does not fall in with the notion of god. If he is able to and does not wish to, he is envious, which is equally foreign to god. If he neither wishes to nor is able, he is both envious and feeble and therefore not god. If he both wishes to and is able, which alone is fitting to go, whence, therefore, are the evils, and why does he not remove them?[6]

Epicurus is not concerned here with questioning the existence of God or gods but with emphasizing that human beings have to deal with Evil on their own and that appealing to God or gods will not help them in this endeavor. Very much unlike Christian faith, he assumes only the reality of Evil but in no way the *reality of the overcoming of Evil by God*. He sees a fundamental problem where Christian thought sees a fundamental

---

when the whole point of the scientificity of a theology worth talking about lies in seeking, guided by a specific conception of God, *traces of the presence of God* precisely *in* all of the dimensions of human life thus described and, beyond them, in everything not captured by these descriptions.

5. See Janowski, *Ein Gott, der tötet?* 70.

6. Epicurus quoted in Lactantius, *The Wrath of God*, 92–93; see Epicurus, *Epicuri Physica*, frag. 374, in *Epicurea*, 253; see above, I.C.2, 35–37.

presupposition: God is able to overcome evil because he has in fact overcome it in the one case decisive for him and for human beings, and that he therefore can, wills to, and will overcome it in every corresponding case. Yet it is precisely when we take this significant difference into account that we are able easily to apply Epicurus's arguments to the differently constituted case of Christian faith: If Evil in my life is not overcome by God, then the question arises whether it is overcome anywhere at all and whether the basic Christian confession does not miss the mark. For precisely because there can be no doubt that the evil in my life is real, doubt whether the Christian confession of God is true cannot be avoided.

Yet before we give in to this doubt, we should examine our presuppositions. A number of theological questions follow from the problematic coexistence of the statement of the confession with the experience of life, questions that have to be answered before it is possible to draw binding conclusions. If faith lives on the overcoming of evil through God, but if the reality of Evil in life cannot be contested, then the experienced reality of evil can not only be experienced as putting faith in question, but faith can be experienced as an indication that there is a difference between what faith confesses as the *malum* overcome by God and what is experienced in life as *malum*, and that they have to be distinguished: Could the *malum coram deo* professed to have been overcome and the *malum coram seipso* experienced as real not be two separate matters? Can we assume that *malum* means the same thing in both cases? *What is Evil and what does its meaning consist in? Why does evil exist and how has God overcome it? What does "overcoming Evil" mean when evil continues to exist? How does God overcome what is Evil for me here and now? What does the persistence of the reality of evil have to say about what "overcoming" might mean here? And what does the overcoming have to say about what might be addressed here as malum?*

All answers to these questions depend on the answers to the fundamental questions about the meaning of Evil and the meaning of "evil." In the Christian tradition, these questions cannot have a unified answer when it comes to content but, if at all, an answer unified only formally: not only, therefore, is there no unified Christian theory of Evil, there can be no such theory, only an irreducible plurality of Christian attempts at thinking Evil.

4. Three Intellectual Traditions

Even those who contest the second part of the thesis will not be able to contest the first. Christianity has a univocal answer neither to the question of the meaning of Evil nor to the question of the meaning of "evil." Its manifold intellectual traditions take up, connect, and reshape different approaches that not only do not come together to form a unity but cannot even be combined with one another without creating tensions. This is not just a consequence of insufficient intellectual efforts that could be overcome by better and more consistent thinking, brought together in the coherent answer of a unified doctrine; rather, it is due to the *complexity of its starting point*, the *contradictions of what it is tasked with*, and the *divergence of the paths its thinking takes*, which make every answer a selective and unstable combination of aspects that always already contains transitions to other possible answers because other possible and legitimate aspects are not or only insufficiently taken into consideration.

From the very beginning, then, Christian thought has found in its various prehistories complex and barely reconcilable approaches for reflecting on the problem of Evil: in the biblical traditions of the Old and New Testament, these differ from those in the historical environment of Jewish, Hellenistic, and Roman religiosity; in the philosophical conceptions of the ancient Middle East and pre-Christianity, they differ from the practices of Christian life developing in a syncretistic environment. Taking up, picking up on, and appropriating other currents could not take the form of undifferentiated integration but always had to be a selection, and this selection could take different forms according to what aspects of which prehistory were privileged theologically.

This continued and continues in similar ways in every new context into which Christianity enters in the course of its history: it always encounters not just concrete and always different experiences of evil but also views and conceptions of ills as well as notions and hopes for its overcoming toward which it must develop a critically distinguishing relationship without ever being able to do justice to all aspects or to exhaust all relevant possibilities. Yet even if that were possible, there are always diverging paths offering themselves to theological thought, paths on which it can determine the meaning of "evil" and attempt to explain the meaning of Evil. These paths have different horizons that cannot seamlessly be converted one into the others but lead to distinct types of theological engagement with the problems associated with the question of Evil, types that can be articulated in terms of different conceptions of Evil.

The chapters that follow are not concerned with listing phenomena of evil (with the description of *something as evil*) but above all with theological attempts at systematically determining evil as something (the definition of *evil as something*). In the course of Christianity's European history, there have been three particularly consequential attempts at theologically thinking and determining Evil, which Christian faith confesses as having been overcome by God. Each of these attempts has led to a number of variations, and each overlaps with aspects of other attempts in a number of ways. Nonetheless, these three types can be distinguished with sufficient clarity because they seek to determine Evil *guided by different questions within different horizons*: as *privatio boni*, guided by questions of creation theology within an *ontological-cosmological horizon*; as *peccatum*, guided by questions of the theology of sin within an *anthropological horizon*; and as *unfaith*, guided by questions of the theology of justification within a *theological horizon*.

Each of these types of thinking processes aspects of the complex prehistories and ongoing intellectual history of Christianity, and each has undergone its own particular process of secularization in modernity. Within each of these horizons, problems raised in other approaches are refracted. Yet the divergence of horizons does not merely mark different emphases; identical answers may state different things, and different answers may state similar or identical things—and this never ceases to give rise to misunderstandings, both when we think that what is said the same way means the same and when we think that what is said differently does not mean the same. The irreducible variety of theological thinking never lags behind the lived variety of Christian faith. That is what the following pages seek to show by way of a number of examples in which the lines of thought and argument just presented stand out with particular clarity.[7]

7. The discussions that follow are thus concerned with exemplary reconstructions of problems and by no means with even an approximately comprehensive presentation of historical developments and phenomena. Not everything that is interesting and important is to be presented and analyzed here, only what is particularly good at helping us grasp a particular basic approach.

II.1

MALUM AS PRIVATIO BONI

ONE OF THE MOST consequential traditions that Christian theology, taking up and re-casting a long prior history, has appropriated is the response given by Neoplatonism (Plotinus), which says that *malum* (*kakon*) is to be understood as *privatio boni* (*steresis* or *elleipsis tou agathou*).[1] Evil is nothing that exists but only ever a *deficiency of good*, the *lack* of something that could exist and ought to exist, *the absence* of a positive, not the presence of a negative reality.[2]

The notion thus expressed has many facets, and that is one of the reasons why the figure of thought of *privatio* reverberates to this day in theological and philosophical debates but also in the practical conflicts of life, and it often continues to do so even where we are unaware of it. Let us try and clarify the basic traits of what it means.

---

1. See Schönberger, "Die Existenz des Nichtigen."

2. It would be a complete misunderstanding of this point to see in it a denial of the reality of the experience of evil. The *privatio* thesis is an attempt not to deny but to explain the reality of Evil in its incomprehensibility. The "systematic conceptions" of the *privatio* explanation of the reality of Evil have not "disappeared" today, as Lacroix thinks, as a look at Hermanni, *Das Böse und die Theodizee*, shows (to name but one). Lacroix is also wrong when he traces its alleged disappearance back to its "classically" having seen in Evil "*only* a 'lack,' a 'privation,' an imperfection,' an 'absence,' or a 'being-less'" (Lacroix, *Le mal*, 59–60, my emphasis). That is why this tradition cannot, as Willnauer, *Heute das Böse denken*, tries to do, be opposed by citing phenomena "of a cruel and undeniable reality" (21) and demanding a "paradigm shift" in thinking Evil because it is insufficient to "think Evil as a phenomenon of deficiency" (302). Playing the *privatio* thesis off against the reality of Evil is to miss the point of this intellectual tradition, which precisely tries to make the reality of Evil understandable in its incomprehensibility.

A

Privatio boni

1. *Privatio* and *Steresis*

IN PHILOSOPHICAL AND THEOLOGICAL contexts, the Latin term *privatio* serves to translate the Greek *steresis*, which Aristotle employs to take up Plato's notion of *apousia* (*absentia*) and "indeterminate duality."[1] In this duality, two variables do not oppose each other by negating and thereby defining one another; rather, their difference, like that of "lack" and "excess," is that of extreme instances of a more or less, while at the same time, they both differ from a third, from the "good median." The presence of the one indicates the nonpresence (the absence) of the other without the negation of the one implying the positing of the other: where there is excess, there is no lack, and where there is a lack, there is no excess, yet where there is no lack, there is not necessarily excess, and where there is no excess, there is not for all that necessarily a lack. Similarly, *sense* and *nonsense* are not logical opposites but privative opposites marked by the prefix *non-*. *Sense* does not arise from negating *nonsense*, and nonsense is not a mere negation of *sense*, that is, something *without sense*, but the absence, the lacking, the nonpresence of a specific sense.

In the *Metaphysics*, Aristotle subjects the notion of privation to a linguistic analysis that, by describing the common uses made of the term, clarifies and specifies eight different uses of *steresis*.[2] They essentially amount to saying that something is not present that could be present in something (that is, it is not impossible *as such*—for example, *to have eyes*, even if plants cannot have eyes) and that could be present in the thing in question in accordance with its nature (that is, it is not impossible *for this thing*—for example, *to be blind*, which can be predicated of human beings and moles but not of mistletoes, as a privation of seeing). This not-being-present or being-insufficiently-present of a contingent quality or determination a thing could have but does not have now or does not have permanently, can be a mere absence (as in the case of being blind from birth) or

1. See Fritzsche, "Privation," 1378, and Krämer, *Arete bei Platon und Aristoteles*, 244–379.
2. Aristotle, *Metaphysics* V, 1022b22–1023a7:1615.

result from a violent removal (as in the case of being blind after having one's eyes gouged out).[3] In all cases, it is a nonpresence of something possible (here, seeing) in something that could actualize this possibility in accordance with its nature but does not, or not sufficiently, or not at the present moment actualize it. To predicate a privation to something thus expresses a kind of contradiction but not a logical negation: an opposition of negation such as *equal or not equal* applies to everything, the opposition of privation *equal or unequal* does not. Every (logical) opposition, Aristotle summarizes, thus represents a privation, but not every privation represents an opposition.[4]

In the translation of this philosophical term, *steresis*, into Latin, there is a shift of emphasis that is not without consequences. The Latin *privatio* has not only the negative meaning of *deprivation* but also the positive meaning of *liberation*. The *privatio doloris* is not a negative but a positive process; it does not effect a lack by taking a good away, it is the liberation from a lack by abolishing that lack. The basic meaning of *privare*, *to separate from something*, is thus initially open to a positive as well as a negative interpretation. To live *privately* is to live *nonpublicly*, but that is not necessarily to be understood as an evil or a lack.

In philosophical and theological usage, this aspect of privation as the liberation from something evil or the elimination of a lack disappears. This is evidently a loss. For what, then, is the *privation of a privation*? Is it a liberation from an ill or does it increase this ill? Does the removal of inequality, and be it violent, produce a good or intensify an ill? In logical relationships, things seem clear: to negate the negation of something is to posit it. Someone who is not blind (that is, who does not not see) can see, and what is not meaningless seems meaningful. But does the absence of disease already amount to health? Or does being liberated from weakness already amount to producing strength? Since Hegel at the latest, it has been clear that the negation of negation is more complicated a figure of thought than double negation. This is true of privation as well, especially when privation cannot be logically reduced to negation.

2. Negation and Privation

In a decisive manner, privation as a figure of thought is not a concept of logic but of ontology and the philosophy of nature. This is evinced by all ancient and medieval philosophical projects that employ this idea, from Aristotle via Plotinus, Augustine, Maimonides, and Thomas Aquinas to the late Middle Ages when, in the turn away from Aristotelian hylomorphism operated by early modern natural science, the notion of privation, too, becomes less important.

This figure of thought does not owe its persuasive force to strictly logical considerations, even if it is possible to develop it logically from the problem of negating negative predicates ("The water is not cold," that is, not not warm; "God is not idle," that is, not not active). Nor, ultimately, does it derive its force from its philosophical elaboration in ontological and nature-philosophical theories. Its force comes from the figure's ability to

---

3. Aristotle, *Metaphysics* V, 1022b31–32:1615.
4. Aristotle, *Metaphysics* X, 1055a35, 1055b14–15, and 1055b9–10:1667.

shed light on phenomena and from the plausibility and familiarity of experiences of the lifeworld that precede and found ontological and nature-philosophical reflections. It is not by chance that the retreat of the figure of privation—in 1658, Pierre Gassendi notes that it is absurd to turn privation into a principle[5]—joins the decline of a classificatory thinking for which unchanging forms or ideas are the true seat of reality and therefore, as a matter of principle, privileges the given or established order as a manifestation of the good, the true, and the beautiful, over changes and innovations in all instances, from the ever-constant movements of the planets to the fragile and always-endangered realities of human social life.

That, precisely, is why it is important not to misunderstand the privation thesis in terms of a logical or semantic/definitional figure—that could not but miss its real point. It is precisely not as if *privatio* could be treated like *negatio* and as if from the definition of *malum* as *privatio boni*, it could be deduced that "by the same token, the good, too, could be interpreted as *privatio mali* and thereby justify the thesis that all being is negative."[6] If *p* ("It is cold") is the negation of not-*p* ("It is not cold"), then not-*p* is the negation of *p*, whatever one takes "cold" to mean. If, on the contrary, *p* is the privation of *q* ("It is warm"), then *q* is not the privation of *p* because *cold* can be defined as *lack of warmth* while *warmth* cannot be defined in the same sense as *lack of cold*, that is, as *lack of a lack of warmth*, without erasing important differences such as those between *warmth* and *noncold* or *cold* and *nonwarmth*.

That is also why one cannot claim globally that "in all cases in which oppositional pairs such as large/small, long/short, or beautiful/ugly are used," it is possible "to express one pole by a negation of the other" pole.[7] John Hick, to whom Kreiner refers here, argues more subtly: in all such cases, it is possible to use just one side of the oppositional pair and then scale it up or down, that is, "instead of describing objects as larger and smaller, [to] speak of them instead as being more or less large."[8] Instead of speaking of cold, one could thus speak of negative degrees of warmth, or instead of warmth, of positive degrees of cold. Yet what this shows is that scaling just one side of such an oppositional pair does not relieve us of making the positive/negative distinction. That remains the case when the distinction is applied to itself and one seeks to define the negative as a "less" or as the negative limit in the "more or less" of the positive and the negative or, inversely, to define the positive as a "more" or as the positive limit in the "more or less" of the positive and the negative. In all cases, the entire range of distinctions has to be expressed on each of the two sides, and that means that we are always using the same scale. We are merely reading it in opposite directions without being able to "justify" with one reading something we could not "justify" with the other.

For the oppositional pair *bonum*/*malum* or good/evil, this means that defining the Good as limit or degree of Evil in no way implies a justification of the "negativity of all being," but instead claims Evil as a limit or degree of the Good. The scale is always the same, whether it is read as a sequence of increasing evil or a sequence of diminishing

5. Gassendi, "Exercises against the Aristotelians," 97–98.

6. Kreiner, *Gott im Leid*, 133.

7. Kreiner, *Gott im Leid*, 132.

8. Hick, *Evil and the God of Love*, 54.

good. Whether Evil is defined as the zero point of the Good or the Good defined as the zero point of Evil does not tell us anything about the sequence, only about the direction in which we read the sequence. In either case, we must be careful to note that the zero point of the Good is not the same as the negation of the Good and the zero point of Evil not the same as the negation of Evil: denying Good or Evil does not leave us with only Evil ("negativity of all being") or only Good ("positivity of all being") but with nothing at all.

If we want to find the real difference between the definition of Evil as *privatio boni* and the definition of the Good as *privatio mali*, we must neither play it down and regard it as a logical-semantic inversion (and thereby confuse negation and privation) nor play it up and turn it into an ontological alternative between justifying either the "positivity" or the "negativity of all being." We have to take seriously the fact that what is at issue in the figures of thought is *not a difference in the world but a difference in our attitude toward the world*. What is expressed in the *privatio boni* attitude is an experience of the world that is different from that expressed in the *privatio mali* attitude, not in the sense of a mere reciprocal inversion but in a more profound sense that concerns the lifeworld and enjoins us to understand the notion of *privatio* differently in each instance. The first case supposes a prevalence of experiences of the good and describes evil as an infringement of the good; the second case, in turn, supposes a prevalence of experiences of evil and understands the good as a *liberation* from evil. Both can be right, and in every life there is sufficient evidence for both. Yet neither can be reduced to the other, and accordingly, two different sequences of ideas are needed to express both experiences, and not just a univocal concept of *privatio*. The reality of evil we experience cannot always be defined as defect or lack of the good—pain is hardly sufficiently defined as an absence of well-being[9]—nor is grasping the good as a lack of evil anywhere near satisfactory. Inversely, the good may very well be understood as a liberation from evil, yet evil can hardly be understood as "liberation" from the good unless talk of "liberation" is to lose its positive connotation. There is thus no way around expressing the experiential background in the lifeworld of the *privatio mali* and *privatio boni* discourses in two sequences of ideas that interpret the *privatio* metaphor differently. The one-sided fixation on the aspect of lack or deprivation in the range of meanings *privatio* can have has done a disservice to a differentiated development of the problem and thus to the *privatio* thesis. As a matter of fact, only one of the two sequences has been developed, which is why the Christian tradition could take it up but could not stop there.

What both conceptions of *privatio* share, however, is that they do not merely represent semantic problems and cannot be reduced to the logical problem of negation. Where the definition of Evil as *privatio* is concerned, the most important differences between privation and negation may be illustrated by the following points:

1. Privation shares with negation that it can be enounced in a negative judgment whose truth does not presuppose a negative reality. Just as the proposition, "It's not raining," is not true because there would be a negative state of affairs of not raining but is true because the positive state of affairs of rain does not currently apply,

9. See Kane, "Evil and Privation," esp. 49–51, and Kreiner, *Gott im Leid*, 133–34.

propositions about evil are not true because there is a negative reality but because there isn't a certain positive reality: propositions of negation and privation do not posit being, they designate a not-being.

2. Propositions of privation differ from propositions of negation in that they designate a nonbeing in being: they do not say that something is not ("It's not raining") but that something that exists is not, does not have, or is not doing something it could or ought to be, have, or do ("The water is not warm"). Unlike negation, the negative judgment of privation does not designate an arbitrary nonbeing but can be made only concerning something that exists to which what is negated could or ought to be attributable. "There is no water" is a proposition of negation ("It is not the case that there is water"); "The water is not warm," on the contrary, is a proposition of privation ("There is water but it is not warm"). Accordingly, "Paul has no wings" articulates a negation ("It is not the case that Paul has wings") but not a privation because "Paul has wings" could not be true in our world. On the contrary, "The fly has no wings" designates not only a negation but a privation because in our world, an undamaged and uninjured fly would have to have wings. Whereas negations are thus logical operations in judgments concerning arbitrary states of affairs, privations always have ontological implications and can only be stated in negative judgments concerning certain states of affairs.

3. Unlike negation, privation can also be expressed linguistically in positive propositions; these, however, must be understood as implicitly contesting the presence of a positive property in a subject. "The water is cold" means, privatively, "The water is not warm" without implying that "The water is not cold" would mean that it is warm. Accordingly, *cold* can be defined as an *absence of warmth* without *warmth* inversely meaning *absence of cold*.

4. As Kant has shown, there are two further cases to be distinguished: a "lack" (*defectus, absentia*) of something that is not present (the rest, for example, that as not-movement results from a lack of movement) and the "deprivation" (*privatio*) of something cancelled out by something else (the rest, for example, that results from a movement being cancelled out by another, simultaneous and opposing movement).[10]

Accordingly, evil could be specified and conceived of both as *absentia boni* (as nonpresence of something good) and as *privatio boni* (as cancellation or deprivation of a good). Both cases, however—and this is the decisive point—presuppose that both *absentia boni* and *privatio boni* can be said only of something that *is*. Only beings can lack a good (*absentia*) or be deprived of it (*privatio*). What does not exist cannot lack or be deprived of anything, and what is merely possible but not actual can only possibly but not actually lack or be deprived of something.

On this reading, the reality of Evil in both cases means that there is something to which a positive quality (a *bonum*) is not attributable, be it because the cause for developing it is lacking (*absentia*), be it because there is a counter-cause that prevents it

10. Kant, "Attempt to Introduce the Concept of Negative Magnitudes," 217 (AA 2:177–78)

(*privatio*). And accordingly, evil could be overcome, positively, when the absent good is developed or the absent positive quality is acquired (overcoming the *absentia* by causing the *praesentia boni*) or negatively, when the deprivation is terminated and the counter-cause preventing the *bonum* is cancelled out (overcoming the *privatio* by cancelling out the counter-cause preventing the *bonum*).

3. *Privatio* as Loss of Possession

The figures of thought of *absentia boni* and *privatio boni* refer to experiences in the life-world that constitute the plausible background that guides and defines the use and the conception of these figures even in their theoretical elaboration. This is true of both of them, albeit with different emphases.

It is an everyday experience for us that something we are looking for is not there, that something is not as we want it to be, or that something has not progressed as far as we expected. So is having something taken away, withheld, robbed, or stolen from us by others. But it is not the same experience. When we have nothing, we cannot have anything taken away from us, and where there is nothing, nothing can increase or be missing. Every experience of the absence of something or someone presupposes an experience of some kind of being-present. And there can be deprivation only if there are belongings, possessions, or goods we can be deprived of.

We have to go even further and say that there is deprivation only when something is taken from me that really is *my* possession. If someone takes back what he or she lent me, they do not rob me, and something that does not belong to anyone cannot be robbed from anyone. For there to be *privatio*, that which someone takes from me must belong to *me*. This is the idea Aristotle obtains from human circumstances and which he maintains even as he generalizes and applies it to physical and metaphysical matters: everything that is is what it is on the basis of what, in distinction from or in common with other things, it "possesses" (*ousia*), and only what could be expected on the basis of this possession to be "natural" in a being can be defined as lacking or robbed when it is absent. Strictly speaking, only those beings can be deprived of the ability to see, for example, who because of their essence (their *ousia*) could and should by nature have this disposition (*hexis*), that is, human beings and animals but not plants or rocks.[11] That is why for every being, there is, conditioned by nature or essence, a horizon of what it can be, have, and do or what it can lack or be deprived of. Only those who possess something can be deprived of it.

Yet this already constitutes a—by no means unproblematic—philosophical systematization of experiences in the lifeworld. Having and Being, possession and life are not identical; what one is cannot simply be put in parallel with what one has. Someone whose money is stolen from her will possess less than she did before. Someone whose life is taken from him will no longer have any possessions at all but not because he will now have *fewer goods* but because *he* thus has no goods at all anymore. He has not lost everything, it is he who has been lost to everything he possessed. Not only can only those

11. Aristotle, *Metaphysics* V, 1022b26:1615.

who possess something be deprived of it, only those who are can possess. *Depriving of life* is thus different from a *property offense*.

Yet even taken together, the two do not cover everything we may be deprived of. We can lose our possessions not only when we are deprived of them but also because we are chased from the place where they are to be found. *Loss of place* is another kind of deprivation whose consequences are not just economic. Someone who is deprived of their place of life is torn from the social network and the habits of the lifeworld in which he has lived with others. He has lost not only his possessions but his lifeworld. He is thus being torn from what the Greeks call *ēthos*. In prephilosophical usage, *ēthos* (the result of a vowel mutation from *ethos*) designated the ancestral habitat, the abode of living beings.[12] For human beings, this is the lifeworld where they live together with other human beings, where they entertain reciprocal relationships with them, where they reside and are at home with them. This lifeworld is defined by habits and self-evident truths, tradition, morals, and customs, whose familiarity makes this place home. By growing up in(to), adopting, and practicing these habits and certainties, by living with them, they develop moral attitudes that in Latin are called *habitus* (which, like the English *habit*, is related to *habitare*, "to live in") and in German, *Gewohnheiten* (which shares a similar radical, *wohnen*, also "to live in"). To be torn from these habitual lifeworlds is to be deprived of one's social and cultural identities: the who and the what of human beings cannot be captured in a definable "essence of the human" (*ousia*); it shapes itself within the horizons of their concrete lifeworld in the multitude of acts by which they appropriate or distance themselves from their lifeworld's habits, customs, and self-evident truths. They become who they are within the horizon of the *ēthos* of their lifeworld and the habitual contexts of their culture, where they develop basic distinctions such as those between "native" and "foreign," "normal" and "not normal," "self-evident" and "not self-evident," which direct their social lives. While these lifeworld habits and cultural normalities are always contingent, vary in different cultures, and are subject to historical change, each human being shapes their identity in such a nexus, initially adopting and performing it unquestioningly.[13] To be torn from these nexuses, to be deprived of one's cultural and social lifeworld, therefore, is a *privatio* that goes much deeper than a loss of possession and can lead to a fundamental uncertainty about one's very life. What is lost here is not just a *bonum* but oneself.

12. See Aristotle, *Nicomachean Ethics*, 1103a17–18:1741, and Held, "Ethos und christliche Gotteserfahrung."

13. This remains true in principle even in modern societies where the bases of human coexistence become contingent on decisions, and shared habits are replaced by individual decisions. It is not by chance that such decisions initially, and often permanently, take the shape of adopting decisions made by others. Nor is it by chance that modern societies betting on individual decisions give rise to a vast culture of conformity. As clearly as modern societies are characterized by the switch from habitual determination to individual decision, so clearly this very switch creates an "ethos of individualization," in which everyone by, precisely, fashioning their own identity does nothing but what everyone else is doing.

4. *Absentia* as Non-Presence

The figure of thought of *privatio* thus refers us to a lifeworld background characterized by economic ownership relations, social habits, everyday self-evident truths, cultural certainties, and normalcies. Something similar, albeit with a personal and social rather than an economic emphasis, can be said of the figure of *absentia*: a person who could not even be present cannot be said to be absent. Although he was not there, Charlemagne was not absent from Periclean Athens. The absence of things, too, can come to our notice only if we have the idea or experience of their being present. Ancient Greeks did not lack motorcycles since they had no experience or idea of such things. To perceive a lack or defect or to speak of an absence or deprivation, we need a contrasting idea or experience. Without that contrast, talk of *absentia boni* or *privatio boni* remains obscure.

This point is fundamentally relevant. What comes first is not being absent and non-present but being present, not the disruption of an order but its functioning. Until it is disrupted, we may not register it as a self-evident truth we have grown up with. It is thus an experience familiar to us from the lifeworld that Heraclitus aims at when he stresses that "[i]llness makes health sweet and good, hunger does so for satiety, toil for repose."[14] Yet the fact that it is an ill that first makes us realize a good does not imply that the ill does in fact come first. The fact that something is absent or is not there or is different than usual or represents a lack presupposes habits, backgrounds, comparable aspects, contrasting experiences in light of which we can notice that which disrupts to be disruptive in the first place, even if we become aware of them only at the moment the disruption intervenes. Every disruption shows that something familiar is no longer as it was, and this triggers practical and theoretical activity. We ask, *Why? How so? What for?* and seek to react to the disruption by thinking and acting in such a way that it does not escalate.

But in seeking to avoid the escalation of the disruption, our questioning escalates and undermines certainties and habits of the lifeworld. In dealing with disruptions—and this is the point in the lifeworld where the scientific quest for causes and attempts at explanation picks up—we initially seek to understand and remove the disruption to be able to return to the habitual. Yet in the long run, this cannot succeed because the disruption points us to the non-self-evidence and non-necessity of the habits at issue and the question of the cause of the disruption inexorably leads to the question of the validity of the habitual. This dynamic of explanation, which compels every reliable explanation of the disruption of an habitual order to proceed to an explanation of this order, took place at the beginning of European science among the Greeks. In the sciences of the modern period, this dynamic has intensified to become an unstoppable, ever-accelerating process of stripping all domains of life of their self-evidence.

What this process shows, however, is that the starting point is not the disruption that raises the questions as such but the backdrop of habits that allows it to be perceived as a disruption in the first place. Life does not start with problems but with habits we take over from others (parents, family, school), habits whose self-evidence makes human life possible in the first place because they offer orientation and guarantees of what to

---

14. Heraclitus, *Testimonia* D, in Laks and Most, *Early Greek Philosophy*, 3.2.164–65.

expect. Sooner or later, disruptions that arise or different orders we encounter elsewhere and among others will lead us to question them and to seek reasons for their validity. That is part and parcel of becoming an adult. Yet we can only problematize what initially we experienced and lived as unproblematic.

Accordingly, from every disruption we can proceed asking in two directions: we can thematize the fact that the habits of the lifeworld *become problematic,* or we can inquire into the *self-evidence* of these habits. The two cannot be separated, of course, but the dialectic of order and disruption, stability and change, being-such and being-different, Being and Nothingness, Good and Evil, will lead to very different attitudes toward the world depending on which of the two we stress.

5. Ways of Dealing with Privation and Absence

Behind the figures of thought of *absentia boni* and *privatio boni,* we find a clear option in these questions: they speak of absence and lack, defect and deprivation, but in so doing, they do not emphasize the absence but the absent, not the lack but what is lacking, not the defect but its remedy, not the deprivation but the good that has been robbed. They are primarily oriented toward the *bonum* whose *absentia* or *privatio* they indicate. They express no doubts concerning life, no despair concerning the world but on the contrary a fundamental optimism about being and the world, which to be sure knows of disruptions and destructions of life but denies them the significance and dignity of constituting an autonomous reality and conceives of them as local, momentary, or marginal deviations from what is actually valid, good, true, beautiful, and just: the *malum* they speak of is nothing, it merely indicates that a *bonum* that could be and ought to be is not.

By drawing attention away from the *malum* and toward the *bonum,* the formula *privatio boni* signals an essential mode of reacting to disruptions occurring in the lifeworld, the absence of something, or a deprivation: we seek to establish or restore the habitual order, reach the state we expected, obtain the lost possession once more. It is not just the perception of a *malum* that is conditioned by the given context of habits and order; dealing with and overcoming the *malum* is, too: the lack has to be remedied, the absence offset, the deprivation reversed, that is, the habitual order must be restored as much as possible. For if we do not want to be fatalistically exposed to the vicissitudes of the bad and the good in life, we have to see to maintaining the orders that protect us from the irruption of the chaotic, of what endangers and destroys life. In most cases, at least, the established order is thus more important, more valuable, and stronger than any disruption. And if it is not possible to restore the original state, we must at least come to terms with the lack, absence, or deprivation in such a way as to establish a new order that incorporates what is deviant, defective, bad into the habitual course of things.

In the lifeworld, we usually come to terms with experiences of evil according to the following schema: we seek to integrate the evil in the greater context of the functioning habits and the usual procedures as much as possible. Confronted with a disruption, we seek to maintain the habitual order as long as possible or to restore it, that is, to marginalize, relativize, eliminate the disruption and limit its consequences, and when that is not possible, we try to at least find something positive about the evil within the horizon of the habitual: the *malum* then is just *only* an *absentia boni* or *privatio boni*, not an autonomous reality that cannot, as a matter of principle, be integrated into the habitual course of things.

It is not by chance that medicine and the healing of physical diseases became a model for dealing with evil generally.[15] Evil must be treated and cured like a disease, the disruption must be healed, and the habitual state of health must be maintained or restored. This healing process may be painful, and experience suggests not only reacting to diseases that have broken out but preventing as much as possible, in the way we live our lives, that they break out. Curatively dealing with evil, too, may be oriented not just by eliminating evil that has occurred but by preventing its occurrence as well. This applies not only to medicine and thus to physical ills but also with regard to social ills and dangers to communal life, to law. Laws seek to protect the given order of life and thus life under the conditions of this order by regulating that and how violations of this order are to be prosecuted. Their sanctions seek to enforce the orders that are supposed to prevent or minimize the irruption of ills. Medicine and law treat what they consider to be evil by defending, protecting, and effectively asserting the habitual, tried and tested, or established orders of life as a good against disruptions.

6. The Limits of Habitual Ways of Coping with Disruptions

This way of dealing with evil as a disruption of order that gives grounds for asserting the order against its disruption, such as we find it in the lifeworld and subsequently in medicine and law, reaches its limits at three points.

First, where it is not possible for someone to eliminate the disruption and to restore the habitual normal state of affairs, that is, where a loss cannot be replaced or a disease cannot be cured but leads to death. Since this happens constantly and since it will apply sooner or later to everyone, the way of dealing with disruptions that consists in maintaining an habitual order is, in each individual case, only a temporary solution.

Yet what applies to individual cases does not necessarily apply to the whole, or at least not in the same way. The habits and self-evident truths of the lifeworld certainly change but their function does not. The ultimately limited reach of the integrating force of the habitual order of life in each individual life is thus not to be observed in the same way in the life of a community as long as the conditions of economic and political life are more or less stable. A social order and its habits, regulated in the lifeworld and the law, can last for generations even if in each individual case they cannot for long prevent the collapse or interruption of a life. Precisely because every life habit and every order of life is posited against the background of a permanently present danger to life, and because every tried and tested order is permanently endangered by chaos, order is held to be such a valuable good, a good worth protecting and preserving.

Second, the way of dealing with evil that consists in preserving an order reaches its limits, not just for individuals but for an order itself, where disruptions become too massive for the habitual order to be continued or a new functioning order of life to be

15. See Jaeger, *Conflict of Cultural Ideals*, 3–45.

restored. Not just individual life, communal life and societies in their attempt to deal with evil by integrating it into existing or modified orders of life, too, reach a limit where such an order can no longer be asserted against the disruption and collapses. Orders and habits of life are thus not only subject to reforms and modifications but to collapse and revolution as well, even if human life cannot continue without once more rebuilding such orders—usually by going back to many of the elements of the order that has collapsed. Even the collapse of orders in the face of nonintegratable disruptions thus shows that human life depends on orders and highlights their value.

Third, the integrative way of dealing with disruptions also reaches a limit where it is not disruptions that become too forceful for orders but orders become too strong for disruptions, that is, where an order becomes so dominant and self-referential that all it does is confirm itself, that it can no longer be questioned by disruptions,[16] and that it sees both disruptions and their absence as a confirmation of itself. Every order, in nature as in society, tends toward absolutizing and positing itself as a nexus of validity without alternative. Yet where in natural processes, it is contingencies such as illness, death, accidents, or misfortunes that are experienced as chaotic dangers and disruptions and natural laws on the contrary seem to reign without alternative, in the social domain it is the laws that can become problematic when, for example, habits that become overwhelming or the religious sanctioning of traditional orders lead to the inscription in law of particular power relationships or to the suspension or questioning of freedom, change, and renewal. Laws that were supposed to offer protection against social dangers to human life then become dangerous and threaten human life and its development.

In the development of Athens from kingship via aristocratic rule to democracy, along with their perversions tyranny, oligarchy, and demagogical democracy, this ambivalence of the law was not readily apparent because the rule of law was seen as guaranteeing equality, justice, and freedom over against the arbitrariness of tyrants and the autocracy of individuals or groups. It is not by chance that, after the failure of the philosophers' regime in the ideal and just *Republic* and the dashing of his hopes for an ideal philosophical autocrat in the *Statesman*, Plato in his late work, the *Laws*, saw the best guarantee against human corruptibility and the best "protection of each from everyone" in an arrangement in which "neither an individual nor a collective governs but the law, the *nomos*, alone."[17] It was the law-governed state that was to guarantee the connection between equality, justice, and unity with freedom and thus avoid the dangers both of oriental despotism with its suppression of freedom and of demagogical democracy with its propagation of freedom to the detriment of the law. For Plato, there could be true freedom only on the basis of the law, not at its expense. In tying freedom to a more fundamental order, he established a view that was to remain dominant, in numerous versions and with numerous justifications, until the end of the Middle Ages.

It took a long time until it became possible to see something positive in change and the invention of the new, in opposition to the traditional order, and to acknowledge freedom not only as freedom *in* and *through* orders but as freedom *from* and *over against* established orders as well. It took the elaboration of a conception of an individual,

16. See Häring, *Das Böse in der Welt*, 57.
17. Rohls, *Geschichte der Ethik*, 62.

self-determined life Plato did not know and would not have accepted. The notion that individual freedom and individuals' contingent preferences might not be subjected to a binding assessment within a superordinate order of life and values would have been as foreign to him as the modern insight that it is not possible to establish, in a universally valid way, what the good is for a person because what is good for someone must always result from a self-determination that by definition cannot be made by anyone on their behalf. Everyone must determine for themselves what the good is for them or else it is not the good. Law and order can no longer prescribe any content but only formulate the conditions for reconciling individual self-determinations. They outline a legal space by means of principles of freedom to be universally acknowledged, a space in which individual decisions about freedom and life can be legally coordinated. Compared to Plato, however, this in fact inverts the relationship of freedom and order: order is not the basis of individual freedom but is itself the result of individual determinations to participate in the (legally) ordered coordination of individual self-determination. The fundamental reality is not law and order but the freedom of individuals that establish these coordinative orders in free self-determination and secure them by sanctions that apply to all participants. For law and order are only binding when they are willed, and they are only willed when they are founded on the self-determination of individuals to promote and preserve the self-determination of (all, if possible) others.

Plato could not have understood this. He knew freedom *from* and *over against* order as a sophistic and demagogic destruction of law and order, not as establishing them. That is why he staked everything on the law, which was founded on insight into the good and to which all individual freedom had to defer and subject itself. We must not dismiss this as merely a quirk on the part of a conservative philosopher who, shocked by the decay of traditional orders of life, sought to salvage what could be salvaged and to relegitimatize the old order with philosophical arguments. Plato's conception of the polis was anything but an uncritical refurbishing of the tradition; it was a new construction, so fundamentally new that it practically had no chance of being implemented. Only one thing did indeed tie him to the tradition and the lifeworld experience it expressed: a high esteem for the just and orderly nature of the whole as indispensable condition of possibility for a successful human life.

The task was to provide this order with a new philosophical foundation, both avoiding the errors and aberrations of the tradition and taking into account contemporary scientific insights. This effort may be considered an act of practical prudence. In times of upheaval, of uncertainties triggered by economic, social, and political changes, the harrying presence of what threatens and endangers life, the critical review of traditional orders of life and their ethical refoundation may indeed even appear to be a prudential duty. It was not by chance that what centrally occupied Plato, as a social philosopher faced with the loss of plausibility the traditional ethos suffered in the developing democratic polis, the scientific critique of traditional myths and religion, and the socially disintegrating effect of sophistic enlightenment, was a universally valid foundation of justice and equality and thus a just social order. At issue was an argumentative refoundation of the moral, political, and economic orders without which human life is impossible and cannot succeed.

In his efforts, Plato could no longer draw on the origins and on tradition with their confused and obscure views. Their place was taken by scientific knowledge of the world and, after Socrates, philosophical knowledge of the self as the only real path to true knowledge of the good and the just. Binding insight into the true reasons of the orders of the micro- and macrocosm that make life possible can be obtained only via the path of reason. The external world, the cosmos, the order of the stars, the predictable and reliable regularities of natural processes amidst the everyday dangers on land as on water were eloquent illustrations of such orders, but they could only be recognized via the path of self-knowledge ascending to the immutable world of Ideas.

Plato's answer to the questioning of the traditional orders of life (a questioning he shared in many respects) was a foundation in ideas, not a reference to tradition. On this basis, it was possible for him philosophically to absorb the good, tried, and tested order of the habitual, to restore or protect it from the dangers of the unhabitual and disruptive, without falling prey to traditionalism and to assert this order critically in justifying the goodness of a just order against its being questioned by Evil in all its forms. In the orientation toward the idea of the Good, a theoretical and practical orientation toward the immutable order of ideas thus replaced the orders of life that had been guaranteed by the gods. In this way, the reference to the immutable cosmos of ideas dominated by the idea of the good philosophically re-founds the basic tendency in the lifeworld to deal with evil by privileging order over disruption with a new philosophical foundation, and this, precisely, is what manifests itself terminologically in the definition of Evil in the metaphor (coined centuries after Plato), *privatio boni.*

B

Philosophical Elaborations
and Christian Receptions

THIS BACKGROUND IN THE lifeworld and its experiential privileging of order over disruption, the existing over the new, the habitual over the foreign, continues to orient the reflections in the philosophy of nature, social philosophy, and ontology not just in Plato but in the science and philosophy then developing more broadly. For the sake of life, survival, and a better life, the orders of life are to be studied as carefully as possible, and the rules and laws of human communal life are to be designed such that they are as just and as reliable as possible. Conceptions of the right design and just organization of human communal life among Sophists and Socratics differ as much as views on the true causes and orders of natural processes among the pre-Socratic philosophers of nature. Yet as regards nature, society, and human beings, they all share a focus on discovering and erecting the right orders that allow human beings to lead their lives in a good, reliable, and right manner.

1. Guidelines for Dealing with Evil

Political and economic changes, the transitions from aristocratic rule to tyranny and democracy, from agriculture to trade and industry, from a barter to a monetary economy, had shaken the self-evident truths and habits of the traditional ethos and everyday life in the Greek polis. They needed a new and different justification. The right knowledge of nature, the just order of society had to be debated to discover what was right, to preserve what was good, and to correct or minimize what was problematic. To name just one set of problems, we might consider just and good what is proper according to custom and common usage, personified by Themis; or what the gods command; or what Dike and Moira, Justice and Fate, impose even on the gods (Homer); or what courts and the law decide (Hesiod); or what applies equally to gods and humans (Euripides); or what is posited in the polis as valid convention (Sophists); or what attributes to each and everyone what he deserves according to his actions in relationship to others (retributive justice); or what ensures the arithmetic equality of advantages and disadvantages in the relationships among individuals (distributive justice) (Aristotle); or what everyone does when within the cooperative whole of the polis they "do their own business" and do not meddle in what others are responsible and better suited for (Plato).[1] In the microcosm of the individual human life, Evil is avoided and the Good reinforced when the whole of the soul's forces harmonizes thanks to the good order of justice. This is equally true in the social cosmos of the polis or the macrocosm of the universe: everywhere, the Good prevails when the just harmony and order of the manifold whole is preserved and obeyed, everyone has his place and function, and evil is conceived of as momentary lack, local disruption, temporary absence, or irregular deprivation and is overcome as quickly as possible by reasserting the rule and reestablishing the habitual state of affairs.

The background experiences of the lifeworld from which the metaphors of thought *absentia boni* and *privatio boni* derive are thus elaborated, in the tension-filled wake of Plato and Aristotle, to form an entire complex of fundamental theoretical convictions emblematically embodied in the Platonic-Plotinian conception of a comprehensive "hierarchy of being" that was to shape philosophical and theological thinking in Europe until the end of the Middle Ages.[2] The central convictions of this conception include:

1. *Priority of Being over nonbeing*: That something is is more fundamental than that something is not because only where there is something can something also not be, and only something that is can become something that is not yet: *ex nihilo nihil fit*.

2. *Being is better than nonbeing*: That something is is better than that nothing is, and what is is better than what is not because what is can become something better while what is not cannot become anything at all.

3. *Unchangeable Being is better than changeable Being*: However, that everything that is is good does not mean that everything is good in the same way. Rather, what is unchangeable is better than what may be or may also not be and thus only possibly but not certainly reaches and actualizes what it can be. For what is changeable can become better, and what can become better is obviously not yet as good as it could be. What is unchangeable, on the contrary, is everything it can be and can thus not become better. Just as it is therefore better to be than not to be (because one is thus good and can become better) it is better to be unchangeable than to be changeable (because one is thus so good that one cannot become better).

4. *Fullness of Being*: Not only are there many different beings, there are beings of many different kinds. For everything that is possible can be; everything that exists is really possible (and not merely possible in thought, like Pegasus, for example); and everything exists that is real in the nexus of beings as forms of manifestation of Being. The reality of the real is therefore not only necessarily plural because the infinite ground of Being cannot manifest itself in the finite in any other way than as plural. It is plural in a maximal sense because although it manifests itself differently in individual beings, it manifests itself in the totality of all beings and thus in

---

1. Plato, *Republic* 433a.

2. Lovejoy, *The Great Chain of Being*, esp. 24–66; the notion of a "hierarchy of being" is introduced on p. 42.

the whole in the best possible way.[3] Reality thus constitutes a hierarchical nexus of beings of various ranks that goes from the highest, the One and Good beyond all Being, to lifeless matter at the threshold to Nothing, and along a continuous gradation of beings it manifests the infinite perfection of the One and Good in the finite perfection of the fullness of Being.

5. *Infinite perfection of the One and finite perfection of the whole*: The fullness of Being is structured by the basic contrasts between *One and Nothing* and *One and Many*. Only the One, which differs from Nothing in principle and thus differs from it infinitely, is perfect without limitations. The Many, on the contrary, is finite due to its reciprocal limitation and thus stands between the One and the Nothing. It is saved from foundering in the Nothing solely because the One turns it into a unity, turns it from a mere manifold into a differentiated totality. As the effect of the One, this totality manifests the infinite perfection of the One in a finite yet (in contrast to the imperfect manifestation of the One in the individual many and the many individuals) perfect way: the One is the best; the whole is the best possible; every given individual is a good; and every individual being in the graded togetherness of the many in the whole is a good to a different degree.

6. *Priority of order over disorder*: Everything that is (*substantia*) has an essence (*essentia*) that lays out the orders in which it can develop, and there is nothing that does not develop and act in such an order to which it is bound. Grass seeds grow into blades of grass but not into trees, animals, or human beings, and whereas human beings can think and feel, the same cannot be said and expected of rocks and mountains. Each being's path of development is oriented toward entelechy and unfolds within the framework of a nature-given order of goals and goods it can actualize, appropriate as attitudes, or acquire as possessions. And accordingly, the entelechic developmental processes of all beings take place together as ordered connection of their orders of goals and goods within the overall order of the universe.

7. *Priority of the unchangeable order over the changeable order*: The universe of changeable beings and its orders (the visible world) have their foundation in the universe of unchangeable beings and its order (the invisible world). Hence, only what is set up and founded in the order of the invisible is a possible order of the visible world. There cannot be anything really new in this world because everything is ontologically set up in the unchangeable orders of the universe of ideas. The invisible and the visible world do not, however, constitute a duality of worlds but represent a single connected universe in which the fullness of Being actualizes itself in the hierarchical orders of invisible and visible beings.

8. *The universe is more harmonious and beautiful than all disharmonies, defects, and disruptions*: In its double structure as a visible and an invisible universe, the universe is a good order of beings, goals, and goods that actualizes the fullness of Being. This order of the universe is just, beautiful, and good and manifests the activity of reason, which institutes unity and truth. In that all beings in the universe do and

---

3. See Aquinas, *Summa contra gentiles*, II.45:107, III.73:181.

actualize what befits them by nature, the reason (*logos*) that pervades the universe ensures that its manifold processes of actualization unfold in harmonious relationships and that the rational order of the universe integrates the Many as ordered variety and does not let it degenerate into chaotic multitude.

9. *Malum as privatio boni*: Accordingly, in individual beings, a *malum* can occur only as a defect, lack, or deprivation within the applicable framework of the order of possible and real *bona,* such that there is always a fundamental prevalence of the Good, the Just, and the Beautiful over the Bad, the Unjust, and the Disharmonic. Within the universe as a whole, in turn, disruption and lack can only occur in subordinate contexts, not in the whole. In its totality, the universe follows inviolable orders that are prefigured in the unchangeable numeric relationships of mathematics, which can be astronomically observed in the unalterable movement of the stars and manifest themselves in the regular processes of becoming and passing in nature, and whose structure—according to Plato, at least—is to be found in the unchangeable world of ideas in their eternally ordered orientation toward the idea of the Good. As a product and finite form of manifesting the One and Good, the universe as a whole can and must therefore be called *good* and *just*, and within the universe, anything can only be good and just because and insofar as it participates in the goodness and justice of the universe. On this point, all the great schools of ancient philosophy agree, from the Pre-Socratics and Pythagoreans via Plato, Aristotle, and the Stoics to the Neoplatonists and their successors in late Antiquity and the Middle Ages. For them, defects, ills, evils can only ever occur as local marginal and transitional phenomena, not as an autonomous and most certainly not as a fundamental reality. The (neo-)Platonic formula that *malum* is *privatio boni* metaphorically captures this conviction.

2. Plotinus's Monism

This does not aim to downplay Evil.[4] Rather, it seeks to classify Evil within a perspective that always conceives of it in terms of its function and embeddedness within the whole of a greater order.[5] There is suffering and death, misfortune and disease, crime and enmity, injustice, hatred, and violence everywhere in the world. The world, however, does not for all that stop functioning in its good order. Indeed, Evil is the price to be paid for the existence of the cosmic good order. This order can only exist because there are many things that can enter into harmonious relationships: without the Many, there is no variety, and without variety, no harmony and order. Yet where there are many things, ills seem unavoidable, at least when the relationships the Many entertain are not unchangeable and

4. This is an erroneous reproach often made against the *privatio* theory; see Hick, *Evil and the God of Love,* 54; Reiner, "Vom Wesen des *Malum*"; McCloskey, *God and Evil,* 36–41; Kane, "Evil and Privation," 48–52; E. Farley, *Good and Evil*; W. Farley, *Tragic Vision and Divine Compassion*; and Sands, *Escape from Paradise.* For a discussion of some of the reasons given for this reproach, see Weisberger, *Suffering Belief,* 71–82, and Mathewes, *Evil and the Augustinian Tradition,* 75–100.

5. See Geyer, "Das Böse in der Perspektive von Christentum und Neuplatonismus."

unalterable. This, however, can only be the case where every being is already everything it can and ought to be, where the same perfection reigns as in the unchangeable realm of numbers and ideas. But in a world of becoming in which many beings seek to actualize what is possible for them, competition and impairment, reciprocal damage and obstruction, failure to reach one's goals and unsatisfactory development can hardly be avoided. In such a world, all one can do is try and keep damage to a minimum and integrate ills that occur into the goodness of the greater whole as best is possible. To do so, we must explain what evil is, why and in what sense evil can and does exist, and how it remains included in the whole of the good universe.

No one has done so more effectively and coherently than Plotinus, the restorer of Platonism. In his treatise "On What Are and Whence Come Evils," he lays out the procedure for answering the question of the nature and origin of Evil with exemplary methodicalness.[6] If we want to know where Evil has come from, we first have to clarify what that Evil is whose origin we inquire into. If we follow the Platonic principle that "knowledge of everything comes by likeness," we cannot give a direct answer—how could we "know evil"?[7] Plotinus finds a way out of the aporia that seems to emerge here in the observation that Evil is the opposite of the Good. Since "opposites are known by one and the same kind of knowledge," he concludes, "the knowledge of good will also be knowledge of evil."[8] To gain insight into Evil, we must thus look at the Good and answer two questions: What is the Good, and in what sense is the Good the opposite of Evil?[9]

Plotinus's answer to the first question is: the Good "is that on which everything depends and 'to which all beings aspire'; they have it as their principle and need it: but it is without need, sufficient to itself, lacking nothing, the measure and bound of all things, giving from itself intellect and real being and soul and life and intellectual activity."[10] Plotinus thus defines the Good as that without which nothing is what it is: it is the goal toward which every being is, the origin from which and through which every being is, and the existential condition without whose effective presence it could not be. It is that which is indispensably necessary in every respect for everything that is. Inversely, it itself is such that there is nothing it needs: the Good suffices unto itself, indeed, it more than suffices and can therefore give infinitely by effecting what it is: the Good. The Good thus effects what it is: the mind, substance, the soul, life, rational activity, that is, everything that is positive and good in the reality of existing things. Yet for that very reason, the Good itself does not belong to the beings that owe their existence to its efficacy but is "what is beyond existence."[11]

This hints at the answer to the second question: since Evil belongs neither to existing things (which are good) nor to the beyond of existence (the Good itself), it can only

---

6. Plotinus, *Enneads*, I.8.1–15:279–317; references are to the standard numbering of Plotinus's treatises, followed by the page number in the corresponding volume of the Loeb Classical Library for the English translation. See also Schäfer, *Unde malum*.

7. Plotinus, *Enneads*, I.8.1:279.

8. Plotinus, *Enneads*, I.8.1.12–13:279 [modified].

9. Plotinus, *Enneads*, I.8.1.19:279.

10. Plotinus, *Enneads*, I.8.2.4–7:281.

11. Plotinus, *Enneads*, I.8.3.1–2:283.

belong to "non-existent things," where "Nonbeing . . . does not mean absolute nonbeing but only something other than being." Evil is not something, but neither is it nothing; it is the nonbeing of something. And since everything that is is good, since it is only through and because of the Good, Evil can be defined precisely as *nonbeing of the Good* or as "the absence of every sort of good," as "privation" or "lack of good." This "privation is always in something else and has no existence by itself." According to Plotinus, however, this also characterizes matter, which is why he, unlike Aristotle and the Aristotelians, can establish a very close link, if not an identification, of Evil with matter: matter is the "primary evil" that causes Evil in everything with which it is connected.[12]

Like matter, the reality of Evil cannot be contested. For "if anyone says that there is no evil at all in the nature of things, he must also abolish the good." This follows immediately from the oppositional definition of Good and Evil: where there is good, there also is evil, and if there were no evil, there would be no good, either—if the oppositional principle applies. But does it apply? "[W]hat universal necessity is there, that if one of a pair of contraries exists, the other must also exist?" It could be that only its *possibility* exists: where there is health, there is also the possibility of illness. Moreover, experience shows that an individual reality such as *This is a tree* does not have an opposite. Yet a general essence such as Being-a-tree does not have an opposite, either. At most, Plotinus writes, essence has its opposite in non-essence, or the origin of the Good its opposite in the origin of Evil. The origins oppose each other, that is, they are opposing principles. Consequently, the corresponding wholes, all the Good and all Evil, are opposed as well. This is an opposition in the higher sense insofar as the whole opposes the whole, that is, the divine nature opposes Evil. It has thus been "shown that it is not universally true that there is nothing contrary to substance."[13]

All it takes is the step from the level of individual things and their essence to the level of their principles or causes. Nothing that is is without cause; what is different has different causes; and Good and Evil therefore have opposite causes.

Thus if there is good there must necessarily also be evil. For, on the one hand, our universe must necessarily consist of opposites: it could not exist without matter. On the other hand, there is not just the Good but also that which follows from the Good. There must thus be principles for emerging from the Good, and there is a point "after which nothing else can come into being." That is Evil. "Now it is necessary that what comes after the First should exist, and therefore that the Last should exist; and this is matter, which possesses nothing at all of the Good." That is why in the universe, "there must be good, and unmixed good, and that which is a mixture of bad and good," and just as there is more or less good, there is also more or less evil.[14]

Yet the opposition cannot be transformed at will, for what was said about the Good—namely, that it entirely suffices itself and stands in need of no other—can precisely not be said about Evil: Evil entirely stands in need of an other in whom it exists

12. Plotinus, *Enneads,* I.8.3.7–9:283, I.8.1.11–12:279, I.8.1.19:279, I.8.5.1:289, I.8.11.2:307, I.8.14.51:315 [modified].

13. Plotinus, *Enneads,* I.8.15.3–5:315, I.8.6.21–22:293, I.8.6.49–50:295–97.

14. Plotinus, *Enneads,* I.8.7.1–23:297–99, I.8.7.17–19:299, I.8.7.22:299, I.8.15.9–10:315.

parasitically, obscuring its goodness and depriving it of its goodness. While, beyond existence, there is a Good in itself, there cannot be an Evil in itself:

> But because of the power and nature of the Good, evil is not only evil; since it must necessarily appear, it is bound in a sort of beautiful fetters, as some prisoners are in chains of gold, and hidden by them, so that it may not appear in its charmlessness to the gods, and men may be able not always to look at evil, but even when they do look at it, may be in company with images of beauty to remind them.[15]

Yet had Plotinus not argued that Evil first had to exist in itself and then be attached to something else? Yes, but this has to be understood in analogy with matter. Matter in itself is without limit and without shape, such that all shaping presupposes it. But properly speaking, matter "is" not: "matter has not even being—if it had it would by this means have a share in good." It "is" only in a homonymous sense, that is to say, it is posited in and with beings, while in itself it is to be thought not as the essence of beings but only as the definition of the limits of beings, as "being not good" or "pure lack."[16]

3. Plotinus's Achievement

With these reflections, Plotinus achieves several things: unlike Numenius, for whom there is a good world soul and an evil world soul, he consistently avoids any kind of dualism of Good and Evil without downplaying or contesting the reality of Evil.[17] Rather, he makes Evil so strong that, as its necessary contrast, it becomes the permanent companion and shadow image of everything Good and Real.[18] Evil becomes downright necessary for the goodness of the universe. The world would not be the beautiful and good world it is without the shadow of evil that accompanies everything, which makes the outlines of the world's beauty and goodness stand out all the more.

This is not some detached claim made by a philosopher unfamiliar with reality. Plotinus justifies it in his own figurative vocabulary with a rigorous philosophical train of thought. Beginning with the divine One that is beyond even the ideas, he outlines, in a strict deduction, a comprehensive monistic system of the world that does not ignore or negate the reality of evil but seeks to account for it. To recapitulate the main ideas: Plato's divine One and Good is placed above reason (the *Nous* or *Logos*); it is the One from which everything emerges and to which everything returns; it stands beyond all oppositions and is thus elevated above Being and Thinking; it is "suprarational." The Pythagorean conception of the mathematical point, from which line, surface, and body are deduced, may serve to illustrate the thought. The Monas is to the indefinite Dyas, the One to the Many, as the point is to the figures derived from it. The One cannot be identical to the *Nous* because insofar as it is the *thinking* of *something*, the *Nous* always implies a multiplicity. Even if the *Nous* in thinking refers only to itself, there is a duality,

---

15. Plotinus, *Enneads*, I.8.15.23–28:317.
16. Plotinus, *Enneads*, I.8.3.20–24:285, I.8.3.30–32:285, I.8.5.9–12:289, I.8.5.12–13:289, I.8.4.24:289.
17. See Alt, *Weltflucht und Weltbejahung*, 55–81, 112–21.
18. Cf. Plotinus, *Enneads*, I.8.3:283–87.

that of the object and the subject of thinking. Just as it must lie beyond the *Nous*, the One must also lie beyond all beings insofar as all beings are defined by certain forms, by essence, and are thus different in themselves: everything that is is formed matter. Moreover, the *Nous* posits everything that exists, such that the One precedes not just the *Nous* but also all the beings posited by the *Nous*: it is beyond all existence. That does not mean, however, that the One is simply nothing, something merely negative, the negation of Being and Thinking. Rather, it is to be conceived of positively as that which is more than *Nous* and Being, as the cause and the goal of everything and, in just this way, as the indeterminate Good.[19] The One itself, which lies beyond all multiplicity and plurality, cannot be thematized directly, it can only be described in paradoxical formulations as that which causes itself, which as such "is" autarkic and autonomous.

From this One, the first hypostasis, the *Nous*, the second hypostasis, emerges necessarily but freely.[20] The One seeks to understand itself. Yet to develop a concept of itself in an act of mental vision, it must distinguish itself from itself and thus delimit itself from itself. This autodistinction and autodelimitation cannot be on the same level as the One itself: the self-concept of the One cannot be identical with the One. The concept of the One is to be found, rather, in an entity distinct from the One, the *Nous*. As in the relationship between sun and light or snow and cold, this is a question of an overflowing in which the source does not lose anything, a relationship that has been called emanation or emission.[21]

This *Nous* is already structured as a duality, as the thinking of something, as the knowing and the known, as consciousness and object of consciousness.[22] In what it thinks, it contains the archetypes or ideas of everything, including the ideas of individual things. Plotinus identifies this *Nous* with the creator of the world, the demiurge. And from the demiurge emerges—again by emission—the third hypostasis, the world soul that mediates between the spiritual and the physical world. Plotinus associates with the concept of the world soul the Stoic concept of *logoi spermatikoi*.[23] These vivify indeterminate matter and form it into objects of the senses. The metaphor of the sun and the constantly decreasing light it emits, however, suggests that matter, too, is an emission of the One even if it is an absolute privation. This precludes any kind of Gnostic dualism.[24] Reality as a whole is a succession of hypostases conceived of as successive emanations from the One. In the ontological emanation nexus of One–*Nous*–ideas—world soul–world-creating soul–individual souls–objects of the senses–matter, with many intermediate steps, there is a loss of ontological value the further we move away from the One from which everything emerges.

---

19. Plotinus, *Enneads*, V.4.1, and III.8.8–9:385.

20. On the concept of hypostasis, see Dörrie, "'Hypostasis,'" and Köster, "ὑπόστασις [hypostasis]."

21. Plotinus, *Enneads*, V.1.6:29–33, V.2.1:59–61, V.4.1:141–145.

22. Plotinus, *Enneads*, I.8.9–11:303–307.

23. Plotinus, *Enneads*, IV.3.10, V.9.6.

24. Plotinus, *Enneads*, IV.4.14:173.

4. Ontological and Axiological Opposition

Plotinus's argument combines two lines of thought oriented by the ontological opposition between the *One* and the *Many* and the axiological opposition between *Good* and *Evil*. On the one hand, he takes up Plato's opposition between the One and the Many in such a way as to inscribe the entirety of the universe between the two poles of the *One* and *Nothing*: everything that is emerges from the One, the highest Being, and develops in autonomous entities all the way down to matter, which is not autonomous Being but the limit to nonbeing. It is not Nothing, not the negation of Being, but a lack of Being and thus a privation of Being. Unlike Aristotle, for whom privation refers to the form of a thing and thus constitutes a "privation of form," Plotinus identifies privation with matter such that everything associating with matter is infected by its lack of Being. All hylomorphic Being is thus defined privatively and is characterized by a lack of Being.[25]

This ontological diminution has an inverse correlate in the possibility of an increase in Being to be operated as a turn away from matter and the empirical physical world of sense objects and a turn toward the One via a spiritual-mental orientation toward Psyche and *Nous*, world soul and world reason. This elevation and increase in Being, which is an option for all beings endowed with a soul and capable of self-determination, culminates in mystical ecstasy, the becoming-one or unification with the One.[26] Since ecstasy goes beyond all discursive thinking and its distinction between subject and object of thinking, philosophical explication can only insufficiently shed light on it. As thinking is outdone by mystic ecstasy, so philosophy is outdone by religion. And as the association with sensual matter entails a diminution of matter, so a rigorous desensualization and turn away from matter allows for an increase in Being.

On the other hand, Plotinus connects this with the axiological *opposition of Good and Evil*. In the Platonic conception, the One is at the same time the Good, such that all Being that emanates from the One and the Good is good and the entirety of the universe unfolds between the two poles of the *Good* and the *not-Good* as a continuous diminution from the perfectly good to the less good, which can be understood in the inverse direction as a continuous increase from the less good to the better: everything that is is good; in turn, what is not is not good; and everything that is good and is distinct from the highest Good belongs to the cosmic continuous decrease or increase of the better or the worse. On this continuum, Evil does not have a place of its own but is present in a similarly diffuse way as matter is. As matter represents in the universe between highest Being and Nothing the limit of the *privation of Being*, so Evil appears in the universe between the highest Good and the not-good as the limit of the *privation of the Good*: it *is* nothing and hence nothing Good either, but neither is it nothing and hence not the not-good as negation of the good; rather, it is a *lack of good, privatio boni*.

Yet this reciprocal reference or association of *Evil* as *lack of Good* and *matter* as *lack of Being* is problematic. It is questionable, to be sure, whether it is possible simply to identify the two sides and call matter itself "evil":[27] after all, it *is* no *Being* but only a *lack*

25. See Schrödter, *Privatio*.

26. Plotinus, *Enneads*, VI.9.9–10:335–41.

27. Häring, *Das Böse in der Welt*, 80.

of Being. Yet this lack of Being attracts the predicate "evil" when matter becomes, for something that it associates with, a *privation of Being* or *diminution of goodness*, a privation of being-good. As such and taken by itself, matter "is" nothing, hence also nothing evil, but in its cosmic function of depriving of Being, it is so indeed: matter hinders and prevents an increase in Being and thus the becoming-better of the souls associated with it.[28] As "cause of the soul's weakness," it is also the cause of its "vice," and since a cause can only cause what it is itself, matter must in this causal respect be understood as something that is "itself evil before" and something that is "primary evil."[29] Without associating with matter, no soul would have entered into a process of becoming in which its being-good turns out to be capable of increase and it itself thus turns out to be not yet entirely good but at the same time still evil. That is why souls, to become better, must be liberated of their association with matter. And that in turn means that practically and factually, matter and hence sensuality, physicality, and everything connected with them, end up on the side of Evil: if we want to proceed toward the better, we must overcome them.

5. Critique of Plotinus

1. *Unavoidability of Evil*: The first main problem with Plotinus's reflections on Evil is not that they achieve too little, it is that they achieve too much. Plotinus does not take the reality of Evil too lightly, as a superficial interpretation of his formula of Evil as *pivatio boni* might suggest; he takes it too seriously by turning it into an unavoidable determination of the universe. The world *is* not just full of Evil, as he describes in great detail—a good world *cannot be* without evil. The world is good because and insofar as the sun of the Good is shining on it, yet where the sun shines its light on the world, the world necessarily casts shadows—not as effects of the sun but as what necessarily accompanies the effects of the sun. This conjures every danger of dualism: there is only one continuum of Being between the One and Nothing, a continuum that is without counterreality or alternative because it integrates everything, including Evil—yet not as a special, negative kind of Being but as its privation. Ontologically, this depotentializes Evil; cosmologically, however, it establishes and legitimizes it: Evil has a necessary function in the universe, to diversify and multiply the Many. In that sense, it inseparably belongs, albeit as a permanent limit toward nonbeing and non-Good, to the whole that in its totality is well and beautifully ordered: without Evil, the Whole would not be the Whole. And because there is nothing that the Logos of the world does not will to be as it is, there is no evil and no ills that are not a meaningful part of the cosmic order as a whole. Factually, this does not marginalize but instead stabilizes and legitimizes Evil.

2. *Individual Evil and good Whole*: If the whole is always good, then all that and only that which moves away from the whole, which strives to get away from and opposes

28. Plotinus, *Enneads*, I.8.4–15:287–317.
29. Plotinus, *Enneads*, I.8.14.50:315.

the whole, is evil. The whole thus becomes an—abstract!—norm of the Good: the whole is the Good, the individual is what is factually always also evil.

3. *Describing vs. experiencing Evil*: Another problem with the conception of Evil as *privatio boni* lies in the purely factual description of Evil as that which appears as a diminution and lack of Good. This robs the thorn of Evil of its sting and turns Evil into a mere dissonance that contributes to the cosmic harmony of the whole. Yet Evil is too destructive for such a description as a mere dissonance to be satisfactory. No one to whom Evil happens is capable of leaving it at this description: Evil is not, or not only and exclusively, *experienced* as a lack and absence of Good but as a massive, painful, frightening presence of Evil: "As an element in human experience, evil is positive and powerful. Empirically, it is not merely the absence of something else but a reality with its own distinctive and often terrifying quality and power."[30]

4. *Evil for whom?*: A related point is that Plotinus's philosophical definition ignores the *for*-relation: "It is in fact not loss of 'measure, form and order' *per se* that is evil, but only this considered as a cause of pain and suffering."[31]

5. *Tendency toward a topics of Evil*: Furthermore, thanks to the approximation of Evil and matter, which is just shy of an identification, the functions of matter in the universe are described as consequences of Evil. Everything that is specially associated with matter, as opposed to the forms, is thus placed on the side of Evil, especially corporality, the senses, sexuality, drives, etc. This, however, assigns Evil not only a necessary function in the universe but moreover a certain "common place," a *topos* where Evil is encountered in a privileged way: sensibility. The consequences are well known. They demonstrate how dangerous and momentous a decision it is "to assign Evil to specific places in the world or not to counteract a *topics*."[32]

6. *Failure to answer the question Why?*: Plotinus answers *only* the question *where* Evil comes from with reference to matter. Yet the question remains open why the world is such that there is matter and thus deprivation and Evil. Could it not have been different? That this idea is not self-contradictory even to Plotinus's mind is suggested by his notion of the thinkable universe. This, however, only makes the question more urgent when it comes to the world as it is: Why, then, is it such as it is? Plotinus does not really answer the question *why?* and the question *unde malum?* remains open.

7. *The open question of freedom*: But how, then, are we to conceive of Evil that can be avoided: as a consequence of the *universe* or of our *freedom*? The question of freedom appears only as a "marginal problem," and yet "at a closer look" turns out to be "the core of the problem."[33]

8. *Interiorization of the question of God*: Finally, Plotinus's conception of Evil leads to a spiritualization or intellectualization of the relationship with God: the "encounter

30. Hick, *Evil and the God of Love*, 55.
31. Hick, *Evil and the God of Love*, 56.
32. Häring, *Das Böse in der Welt*, 89.
33. Häring, *Das Böse in der Welt*, 91.

with God does not take place in this world but within the innermost being of the spirit."[34] In looking into the innermost being of the *Nous*, the soul "sees God through it."[35] This was to have momentous effects in the way Augustine takes up the *privatio* thesis.[36]

6. Augustine's Transformation in Terms of a Theology of Creation

The interest Christian theology in general and Augustine in particular[37] have taken in the *absentia* or *privatio* conception of Evil is motivated by this ontological integration of Evil into the relationship to Being, which provided them with an intellectual and argumentative tool that allowed for admitting the reality of Evil unreservedly without having to conceive of it as a negative counterreality to God's good creation, a counterreality to be attributed to a negative counterprinciple to God.

The Christian reception of the Platonic-Plotinian conception of Evil as privation thus proceeded explicitly by critically rejecting dualist solutions like the one offered by the Manicheans, who, according to Augustine, to explain the reality of Evil (the *causa mali*) took recourse to a negative counterreality to God (Evil) and thus preferred the idea that God suffered from Evil to believing that they did evil themselves.[38] It is obvious that this approach does not explain anything but merely repeats the contradictions of real experience on the level of principles (God as positive principle in opposition to Evil as negative principle). The Neoplatonic figure of thought of privation, in contrast, allowed Augustine to understand the reality of Evil without having to give up or modify the idea of the good creation of the good and the only God.[39] Since "[i]n the bodies of animals, disease and wounds mean nothing but the absence of health," curing them does not mean that they "go away from the body and dwell elsewhere" but rather that "they altogether cease to exist." And "[j]ust in the same way, what are called vices in the soul are nothing but privations of natural good" such that what we call evils generally are nothing but "privations of the good."[40]

Augustine appropriates this argumentative figure, which he likely first encountered in Ambrose[41] and found elaborated in Plotinus, for Christianity by working it into his conception of the Christian understanding of creation. Let's summarize his argument:

34. Häring, *Das Böse in der Welt*, 81.

35. Plotinus, *Enneads*, I.8.2.25:281.

36. See Jolivet, *Le problème du mal d'après Saint Augustin*, and Evans, *Augustine on Evil*.

37. See Roukema, "L'Origine du mal selon Origène," and Augustine, *Concerning the Nature of Good*, in *Writings Against the Manichæans*, 361–65; *City of God*, 12.1–8:3–37; *Enchiridion*, in *On the Holy Trinity*, 237–76, here 11:240–42; *Against the Epistle of Manichæus Called Fundamental*, in *Writings Against the Manichæans*, 129–50, here 25:140–41, 38–40:145–50; and *On the Morals of the Manichæans*, in *Writings Against the Manichæans*, 69–89, here 2.2–8.11:69–72.

38. "I saw that [they were more] ready to claim that your [God's] substance was vulnerable to evil than that their own perpetrated it" (Augustine, *Confessions* 7.3.4:161).

39. Wyrwa, "Augustine and Luther on Evil," 126–30.

40. Augustine, *Enchiridion*, 11:240.

41. Häring, *Das Böse in der Welt*, 80.

1. *One creator, one creation*: Everything that is and that is not God is created by God: "there is no nature but Himself that does not derive its existence from Him." For God is "the one true God," and "the only cause of all created things . . . is the goodness of the Creator."[42]

2. *Unchangeable goodness of the creator and changeable goodness of creation*: Because God is good, everything he has created is good as well; yet because it is created and is not itself the creator, creation is not "supremely and unchangeably good" but good in such a way that the good in creation "may be diminished and increased": God is wholly and entirely good, what is created on the contrary can be better or worse.[43]

3. *Good creatures and very good creation*: While individual created things are good but changeable, "collectively" they are "very good" and constitute the universe in its admirable beauty. Just as for God there is no *malum* of any kind, so there is no *malum* for creation as a whole because there is no outside to creation from where it could be corrupted.[44]

4. *Origin of malum*: Everything that for us is *bonum* can have its origin only in God; everything that is a *malum*, on the contrary, must have its origin in what has been created, namely in "the falling away from the unchangeable good of a being made good but changeable, first in the case of an angel, and afterwards in the case of man."[45]

5. *The sense of malum in the universe*: Within the whole of the created universe, *malum* as a lack of Good has a double function. On the hand, it serves to bring out what is good even more clearly, and, on the other, it makes the omnipotence and goodness of the creator stand out even more clearly by showing him to be the one who can create the good even from the bad. By intensifying the contrast, Evil increases the beauty of creation and makes it possible to see the real point of God's goodness and omnipotence: to create good from evil.

6. *The parasitic reality of Evil*: Because besides God there is only what God has created and because everything created is good, Evil can exist only as a diminution and lack of goodness in what has been created, never as an autonomous reality. There must always be something good if it is to be called diminished, and where there is no (longer any) good, there cannot be a lack of good (anymore). "[S]o long as a being is in process of corruption, there is in it some good of which it is being deprived," yet "if it should be thoroughly and completely consumed by corruption, there will then be no good left, because there will be no being." Not only can Evil not appear by itself but only in something good; in spreading and intensifying, it also has the

---

42. Augustine, *Enchiridion*, 9:240 [modified].

43. Augustine, *Enchiridion*, 12:240.

44. Augustine, *Confessions*, 7.13.19:174–75: "For you evil has no being at all, and this is true not of yourself only but of everything you have created, since apart from you there is nothing that could burst in and disrupt the order you have imposed on it."

45. Augustine, *Enchiridion*, 23:245.

autodestructive tendency of depriving itself of the basis of its parasitic existence. That is why there is indeed "a good which is wholly without evil," the creator, and a good that "contains evil" and in this respect "is a faulty or imperfect good," creation, yet "there can be no evil where there is no good." Evil does not *exist* (the way a substance exists), Evil only ever exists as a lack of good: "Accordingly, there is nothing of what we call evil, if there be nothing good."[46]

7. Critique of Augustine

Augustine's conception has not only had great impact, it has also been the subject of frequent criticism.[47] Not all criticism, however, does justice to his reflections. Gerhard Streminger, for example, writes: "At first sight, there might be some reality to evils, but in reality, everything is good."[48] But that is incorrect. Certainly, all evil exists as a lack and deprivation of something *in* something good, but that does mean that everything that is real is good. On the contrary, making this distinction is the central concern of Augustine's argument. Nor can it simply be dismissed as a "semantic trick."[49] Augustine's conception of Evil does not elaborate a semantic rule, nor does it offer an empirical description—it provides a "metaphysical view of things."[50] That means it does not describe a state of affairs but develops a particular *perspective on states of affairs*. Hence it is beside the point to object to Augustine that suffering is experienced as real and not only as a lack and that it feels "like ridicule to those suffering" to claim that "suffering is merely a subjective illusion."[51] None of these charges attains Augustine. He does not problematize the reality of these experiences but propagates *a certain attitude toward them*. For the same reason, it is absurd to reproach Augustine's conception with being the "expression of a bad metaphysics because it passes over the fundamental experiences of human beings." Nor is it the case that "the privation theory . . . suggests a deceptive God."[52] Augustine neither denies the reality of suffering and evil nor does he present it as in fact good; what he does do, precisely in the face of the reality of suffering and evil, is develop the possibility of another attitude toward it.

It is true, by contrast, that it does not suffice to understand "There is evil" as "There is a lack of good." While it is sometimes correct, it is not sufficient and only covers part of the spectrum of evil. Instead, we must add, "There is a lack of good *and there is evil*," and that means that "evil" and "lack of good" cannot simply be equated. It is also questionable whether Augustine really succeeds in excusing the creator from responsibility for Evil. It is still possible to ask "why God permits the lack of Being and thus evils in the first

---

46. Augustine, *Enchiridion*, 12–13:240–41; cf. Wyrwa, "Augustine and Luther on Evil," 127.

47. See Battaglia, "Si Deus, Unde Malum?"

48. Streminger, *Gottes Güte und die Übel*, 179.

49. Streminger, *Gottes Güte und die Übel*, 179–80, and Kreiner, *Gott im Leid*, 138.

50. Hick, *Evil and the God of Love*, 54, and Streminger, *Gottes Güte und die Übel*, 179.

51. Streminger, *Gottes Güte und die Übel*, 180, 190.

52. Streminger, *Gottes Güte und die Übel*, 183, 185.

place."[53] It is also correct to say that privation theory offers no consolation.[54] But that is not what it was developed to do. It was meant to serve as a "scientific" theory to explain and account for, in Plotinus's sense, the reality of evil in the universe or in creation.

For Christian thinking, however, the suggested solution of making evil comprehensible by integrating it into the Good cannot suffice. It clearly reflects the background of dealing with experiences of suffering in the lifeworld. Yet this integration of Evil into the totality of the Good is not an overcoming or abolition of Evil. That is why Christian theology has always insisted that this "aesthetic" solution of integrating the counter-orderly into the orderly is insufficient, that what is at issue, rather, is the way in which God by abolishing and eliminating Evil creates something new and good. For this, precisely, is the fundamental experience of the biblical tradition to which the *privatio* doctrine can be joined only with difficulty. As Streminger rightly points out, this doctrine is not of biblical origin, but the implications of his observation are more far-reaching than he realizes.[55]

The fact that the privation theory is no longer compelling philosophically as well has to do with the mechanization and mathematization of the world order in early modernity. The world is no longer a universe in the sense of an ontological-axiological order; it is a universe as a coherent set of laws that determines the functioning of causally organized sequences of events. This world no more features qualities of goodness or justice than it has an intrinsic sense. These questions migrate to the domain of the *res cogitans*, the subject, morality. What is and what ought to be are strictly separated, the objective world of facts is opposed to the subjective world of values. As a consequence, the *privatio* thesis can no longer be articulated in cosmological terms. It migrates to moral philosophy where it must be formulated anew. The best example is Kant's thesis of radical Evil as deprivation of the good order of maxims, which leads to a lack of good will and thus becomes the original ground of all evil acting. The division between metaphysics and morality, cosmology, and physiology is opposed once more only in the temporal and historical conceptions of development articulated in the nineteenth and twentieth centuries (Hegel, Schelling, process philosophy), in which, not by chance, privation theory enjoys a renaissance. Yet all these are overshadowed by the theodicy debates of the eighteenth century, and no one influenced these debates more than Gottfried Wilhelm Leibniz did.

53. Kreiner, *Gott im Leid*, 136; cf. Streminger, *Gottes Güte und die Übel*, 180, 186, and Häring, *Das Problem des Bösen*, 70.

54. Streminger, *Gottes Güte und die Übel*, 183.

55. Streminger, *Gottes Güte und die Übel*, 186–87.

C

Reason and Evil: The Project of Theodicy

Two works, like a frame, mark the development of the theodicy discussion in the eighteenth century. At the beginning stands Leibniz, who in 1697 coins the terms *theodicy* from the words *theou dikaiosyne* in Rom 3:5, and, in 1710, publishes the work that would set the standard for the century to come, *Essays of Theodicy on the Goodness of God, the Freedom of Man and the Origin of Evil*.[1] At the end of the century stands Kant's essay "On the Miscarriage of All Philosophical Trials in Theodicy" of 1791. The development in between the two publications is essentially, if not exclusively, determined by an engagement with Leibniz's thought, which has spread across Europe. This should not, however, lead us to overlook the existence of other widely influential works on the same set of problems—such as the *Essay on the Origin of Evil* (written 1697, published in Latin in 1702 and in English in 1731) by the Anglican bishop, William King; Shaftesbury's *The Moralists* (1709); or Pope's *Essay on Man* (1732)[2]—nor to neglect the importance of the skepticism concerning the question of theodicy spreading in the second half of the eighteenth century in the wake of the work of Hume, Voltaire, Sade, and Rousseau.

Leibniz's own book was occasioned by comments Pierre Bayle makes in his 1697 *Historical and Critical Dictionary*. He had, however, been struggling with the problem of evil and ills in the world from an early age, as he himself writes. He was familiar with the books Laurentius Valla had written against Boethius and Luther against Erasmus but thought "that they had need of some mitigation," which is why their views had been settled "in the moderate opinions of the Churches of the Augsburg Confession."[3] He was thus quite familiar with the position of Lutheran orthodoxy on the question as expounded in the texts on the creation and preservation of the world, the doctrine of

1. The neologism *theodicy* first surfaces in a 1697 letter to Queen Sophie Charlotte of Prussia. See Streminger, *Gottes Güte und die Übel*, 12. In a letter to Des Bosses on February 5, 1712, Leibniz defines the intellectual project encompassed by the term as follows: "For theodicy is, as it were, a kind of science, namely, the doctrine of the justice of God—that is, of his wisdom together with his goodness" (601).

2. To cite but a few of its most famous lines: "All nature is but art, unknown to thee; / All chance, direction, which thou canst not see; / All discord, harmony, not understood; / All partial evil, universal good; / And, spite of pride, in erring reason's spite, / One truth is clear, 'Whatever is, is RIGHT'" (Pope, *Essay on Man*, ep. I.X, ll.289–94:280).

3. Leibniz, *Theodicy*, 67.

the human being (sin), and the doctrine of the predestination for salvation (or, in the strict Calvinist conception, for damnation as well). Let me recapitulate, briefly, both the orthodox background and the concrete occasion of Leibniz's *Theodicy*.

1. The Orthodox Doctrine of *Providentia*

The discussions of orthodox theologians in the age of the baroque did not focus on Evil or on ills generally but above all on the question of the responsibility for sin to be assigned or not to be assigned to God.[4] Even if some, like the Lutheran Johann Friedrich König in his doctrine of the *providentia Dei*, do specify the *providentia circa malum* (which is opposed to the *providentia circa bonum*) with regard to *malum naturale* and *malum morale*, the real interest is in the *malum morale*. König attributes the *malum naturale* to a *comproducere* and *non imbendere* on God's part, that is, he asserts that God participates and does not prevent, but König does not examine the implications of this assertion.[5] The *malum morale*, by contrast, is analyzed quite thoroughly and described with regard to those of God's actions that precede, accompany, and follow on an evil deed.[6] This shows quite clearly that the intentions of Lutheran theology are primarily practical.

Yet asserting God's preserving omniefficacy and developing it in a *concursus* doctrine does not prevent the question of God's participation in or at least partial responsibility for evil deeds. As early as 1559, Melanchthon had added reflections *De cause peccati et de contingentia* to his *Loci communes* that were to prove influential, in which he stated that God cannot be the cause of sins, which must instead be sought in the secondary or intermediary causes.[7] The engagement with the question, however, becomes a standard problem addressed by all Protestant dogmatists.

In Hollatz, for example, this engagement takes place in the lessons on God's cooperation or agreement (*cooperatio sive concursus*),[8] which, alongside *conversatio* and

---

4. This focusing marks the difference between the (Lutheran) *providentia* doctrine and the *praescientia* doctrine. Recent debates tend to be limited to the latter problem alone and to discuss only the question of God's foreknowledge of future possibilities and/or realities (*contingentia futura*) or the question of the modes of this divine knowledge. See Beilby et al., *Divine Foreknowledge*, for an overview of the most important positions in contemporary debates, where the question of providence is almost always equated with the questions of divine foreknowledge, middle knowledge, and God's timelessness in relation to human freedom. The key terms here are Calvinism, Molinism, free-will theism, process theism, and open theism. See Hebblethwaite, *Evil, Suffering and Religion*, 82–94; Geach, *Providence and Evil*; Helm, *Providence of God*; Basinger, *Case for Freewill Theism*; Flint, *Divine Providence*; Sanders, *God Who Risks*; Swinburne, *Providence and the Problem of Evil*; Boyd, *God of the Possible*; Pinnock, *Most Moved Mover*; Hasker, *Providence, Evil, and the Openness of God*, 97–186; and Hasker et al., *Middle Knowledge*. Griffin et al., *Searching for an Adequate God*, provides a detailed discussion of the opposing views, on this point, of process theology and open theism. On process theology, see also Griffin, *God, Power, and Evil* and *Evil Revisited*, as well as Hartshorne, *Omnipotence*.

5. König, *Theologia positiva acroamatica*, pt. I, §§ 281 and 282, 102.

6. See Hollatz, *Examen theologicum acroamaticum*, I.6.21–24:658–62. See also Ratschow, *Lutherische Dogmatik*, 225.

7. See Ratschow, *Lutherische Dogmatik*, 228.

8. Hollatz, *Examen theologicum acroamaticum*, I.6.16:647–49.

gubernatio is one of the parts of the *providentia* theory. Hollatz explicitly refers to the objection: "Whoever agrees to all human actions also agrees with sins. But God does not etc. Therefore."[9] He answers that one must distinguish between human actions and the disorder they effect, between their *effectus* and their *defectus*. God participates in the former but not in the latter: disorder and *defectus* are to be attributed to the intermediate causes alone. God concurs generally and in an indeterminate way—the precise determination of an action is to be blamed on the intermediary causes alone. As an example, he cites Eve: "When Eve reached out for the forbidden fruit, two things are present in the act: (1) the extension of the hand (2) the extension applied to the forbidden fruit."[10] God's cooperation was limited to (1) alone, it did not extend to (2). God works in conjunction with the intermediary causes but precisely only in a general and indeterminate way.

This overly subtle distinction is symptomatic of a seventeenth-century development operative in these passages, which detaches the theory of providence from the theory of creation and highlights different aspects. Whereas earlier, the major concern was with the *disorder* in the world caused by sin and God's reaction for preserving his good creation, the focus now moves, inversely, to the *order* of the world. Traditionally, beside the question of the unity of creation and providence, the problems that followed from the fact of sin and the disorder of the world apparent in evil deeds were at the center of attention. Now, increasingly, there is a reorientation toward the order of the world and its problems.

This is demonstrated exemplarily by the changes in claims about God's concurrence. Initially, in Johann Ernst Gerhard for example, *Deus concurrit* was "the term for God's 'participation' in Evil. . . . Now the frame of reference of the *concursus dei* changes. The *concursus* now responds to the question how God's action on the one hand and the causal nexus on the other relate to each other."[11] Providence thus becomes—as it does in Buddeus's 1724 *Institutiones theologiae dogmaticae*—a doctrine that is no longer tied to the doctrine of creation but is "oriented toward the natural course of the world and toward understanding it," and it thereby allows for "establishing a connection between faith and worldview problems."[12]

---

9. Hollatz, *Examen theologicum acroamaticum*, I.6.17:652.

10. Hollatz, *Examen theologicum acroamaticum*, I.6.17:650.

11. See Ratschow, *Lutherische Dogmatik*, 230.

12. See Ratschow, *Lutherische Dogmatik*, 231. It is in this sense that the problem of providence is absorbed in the general philosophical debate about the possibility and modes of divine foreknowledge. There are, roughly, two parties in this debate, generalists and particularists. The former, as William Hasker explains, argue that "God's governance of the world" "primarily" takes place "in terms of *general strategies*, strategies which are, as a whole, ordered for the good of creation, but whose detailed consequences are not foreseen or intended by God prior to the decision to adopt them," such that it is possible to admit both the existence of senseless evils that do not serve any higher good and a relationship of God to the future of the world that is "open" in the strict sense of the term, that is, takes into account what has not yet been decided. The other side objects that God foresees and has foreknowledge of every single event, that, in other words, "every single instance of evil that occurs is such that God's permitting either that specific evil or some other equal or greater evil is necessary for some greater good that is better than anything God could have brought about without permitting the evil in question" (Hasker, *Providence, Evil, and the Openness of God*, 102–4, and Hasker, "Philosophical Perspective," 146; see also Peterson, *Evil and the Christian God*, esp. 79–99). Gregory A. Boyd characterizes these two traditions as, on the

The problems with this shift are particularly apparent when it comes to the question of the intelligibility of divine providence. How do we know that there is a *concursus Dei* in everything? Hollatz had answered, "from the light of revelation and from the light of reason," for the secondary causes could not be effective at all "unless the first cause cooperates," such that it is clear that "whatever positively is and happens outside of GOD is a being that depends on the Creator," and to depend on God means to be effected by God.[13] The more, however, this cosmologically motivated argument moved away from the physicotheological argument, the more problematic the intelligibility from nature, with the help of the natural light, of God's preserving, coeffective, and guiding providence had to become. That, precisely, is where Pierre Bayle's questions, which provoked Leibniz's *Theodicy*, come in.

2. Bayle's Dualism of Reason and Revelation

In his *Dictionary*, Bayle explicitly defends the thesis that it is impossible for human reason to infer, from the factual state of the world, the existence of a good and just God actively concerned with the world.[14] In the article "Epicurus," he has the philosopher converse with a priest defending providence and repeat the old dilemma: "Answer me, pray; are the Gods pleased with their Administration or no? Mind well my Dilemma: If they are pleased with what happens under their Providence then they delight in Evil; if they are displeased with it then they are unhappy."[15] In other words: either God is not powerful enough to prevent Evil in the world or he is not good enough to want to prevent it. If he is good, he can justify the Good but not the Evil in the world. If he is powerful, he can have founded the factual world but he cannot be good.

It seems, therefore, that the following three principles of (Christian) faith cannot all be true:

1. God is omnipotent.

2. God is good.

3. There is evil in the world.

---

one hand, the (Augustinian) "blueprint model of theodicy" according to which "behind every specific event there is a specific divine reason as to why it was ordained or at least allowed to take place," and, on the other, the "trinitarian warfare worldview, which argues that although there is a *general* reason as to why God made free agents (love), the ultimate reason for why they engage in the *particular acts* they engage in is generally found in them, not God" (Boyd, *Satan and the Problem of Evil*, 418).—The risk of this becoming a circular debate is particularly evident where God's foreknowledge is defined as that which becomes true and thus becomes knowledge in the first place when certain future events become real but which has already previously determined God's providential action in the governance of the world. On this point, see the debate between Hunt, "Divine Providence and Simple Foreknowledge" and "Prescience and Providence"; Kapitan, "Providence, Foreknowledge, and Decision Procedures"; and Basinger, "Simple Foreknowledge and Providential Control."

13. Hollatz, *Examen theologicum acroamaticum*, I.6.16:648–49.

14. See Neuenschwander, *Gott im neuzeitlichen Denken*, 117.

15. Bayle, *Dictionary*, 2.790.

As we have already seen, there are several strategies for resolving the problem: (1) limiting God's omnipotence: God is good but not all-powerful, which is why evil exists as well; (2) limiting God's goodness: God is omnipotent but not good; (3) negating the reality of evil; (4) positing a reason for Evil other than God (which means that God is not omnipotent).

Since Bayle wants to contest or abandon neither the reality of Evil nor belief in God, all that is left to him is the skeptic conclusion that the world as it factually is cannot be reduced to a single, and moreover good, principle. He therefore tends toward a metaphysical dualism, positing a twofold truth and an unbridgeable opposition of reason and revelation: the ambivalence of our experience of the world does not allow reason to explain the world in a uniform manner, that is, to put it down to a single uniform and good principle. Reason, he argues in the article "Manichees," "can only discover to man his ignorance and weakness, and the necessity of another revelation, which is that of the scripture."[16] Revelation, however, cannot be defended against attacks with reasons, it can only be upheld with as it were blind fideism:

> The doctrine which the Manichees oppose [that is, the doctrine of the one good God—IUD], ought to be looked upon by the orthodox, as a truth in fact, clearly revealed, and since it must at last be confessed, that the causes and reasons of it cannot be apprehended, it is better to own it from the very beginning, and stop there, and look upon the objections of Philosophers as a vain wrangling, and oppose nothing to them but silence, together with the shield of faith.[17]

Leibniz comments that Bayle thereby maneuvers himself into a position "wherein religion and reason appear as adversaries, and where M. Bayle wishes to silence reason after having made it speak too loud: which he calls the triumph of faith."[18]

Confronted with an ambivalent reality, Bayle saw no other possibility than to advocate a Manichean dualism in explaining the world. In the "Manichees" article, he has Zarathustra, the prophet of the two opposing world principles, say in a conversation with Melissus of Samos, the Eleatic philosopher:

> [F]or as you surpass me in the beauty of ideas, and in reasons à priori, so I surpass you in the explication of phænomena, and in reasons à posteriori. And since the principal character of a good system is to account for what experience teaches us, and that the bare incapacity of explaining it, is a proof, that an hypothesis is not good, how beautiful soever it appears, you must grant, that I have hit the mark, by admitting two principles, and that you have not hit it, by admitting but one.[19]

The basic problem with this dualist approach is that it does not really explain anything. Leibniz aptly puts the objection as follows: "But, in my opinion, it is not a very good explanation of a phenomenon to assign to it an *ad hoc* principle: to evil, a *principium*

---

16. Bayle, *Dictionary*, 4.96.

17. Bayle, *Dictionary*, 4.527.

18. Leibniz, *Theodicy*, 63.

19. Bayle, *Dictionary*, 4.95.

maleficum, to cold, a *primum frigidum*; there is nothing so easy and nothing so dull."[20] This means that Bayle's dualism is not a constructive approach. It amounts to a critique of a dull physicotheology, pointing to the latter's unsatisfactory capacity for resolving the inconsistencies found in nature. It cannot account for them either, it can only raise them to object to physicotheological optimism. This objection, however, questions the capacity of reason for reaching any uniform conception of the world at all. The theodicy problem thus becomes the touchstone of modern reason: either it proves its claims to an autonomous understanding of the world or it gives up and—like Bayle—takes refuge in a fideist subordination of reason under a blind faith in revelation. This, precisely, is the point where Leibniz's *Essays of Theodicy* set in.

In this debate, Leibniz represents the position of an enlightened Lutheranism. For him, there cannot be an irreconcilable contradiction between the God of revelation and the God of reason: revelation surpasses reason, but it cannot be, as it is in Bayle, irrational. That is why ultimately, there must be a harmony between, indeed, an identity of the God of revelation and the God of reason. For Leibniz, however, this identity is not merely a formal identity but an identification that takes place in a specific way: it must be possible to prove the God of revelation to be the God of reason, not the other way around.[21] Yet this means that Leibniz, unlike Bayle, is not confronted with the problem of demonstrating God's goodness and wisdom on the basis of the state of the world. He claims them as revealed truth and presupposes them in his essay. The problem that occupies him is not the demonstration of God's wisdom and goodness on the basis of the world but the question whether divine wisdom and goodness, as presupposed, are reconcilable with the rational view of the world.

We must, therefore, keep in mind that, at the very outset, Leibniz redefines the problem in a significant and momentous manner that is decisive for what he calls "theodicy."

3. Dealing Rationally with the Counter- and Suprarational

The problem of evil is among the most resistant problems faced by a reason confronting the challenges of the idea of God. Nowhere else do the aporias of efforts at thinking God rationally stand out more clearly: *Si Deus est, unde malum? Si non est, unde bonum?* Every option seems to drive reason to contradictions. Yet the first thing to expect from reason, the faculty of insight into the interconnection of truths, is that it avoid contradictions.[22] It is thus not by chance that the problem of evil has played a key role in modern thought—not only in attempts at thinking of God but also, and precisely, in critically articulating how reason conceives of itself. No other constellation of problems has taught reason more about its limits than the effort to confront questions about the suprarational (God) and the counterrational (ill) on the field of reason.

Modernity has seen elaborations of all the major possible constellations. The counterrational was mobilized against the suprarational, the suprarational against the

20. Leibniz, *Theodicy*, §152:218.
21. See Neuenschwander, *Gott im neuzeitlichen Denken*, 124.
22. Leibniz, *New Essays*, IV.xvii.3:475.

counterrational, both against reason, or reason against both. The opposition between the counterrational and the suprarational has led to fideist (Bayle), agnostic (Hume), and atheist (d'Holbach) conclusions being drawn. Yet there have also consistently been attempts, from Leibniz via Hegel and Schelling to Hartshorne and Plantinga, rationally to shed light on the counterrational within the horizon of the suprarational and philosophically to account for the problems of God, reason, and ill with a uniform conception of reality. And there have been attempts, after Kant had banished the suprarational from theoretical reason to prevent reason from contradicting itself, to limit engagement with the counterrational to the domain of practical reason and to reduce the problem of ill to the problems of (moral) Evil that are to be dealt with anthropologically (morally, legally, politically, psychologically) and to the (in the widest sense) technical aspects of minimizing suffering. The reductionism this entails found a drastic illustration in the catastrophes of the twentieth century, in which all dreams of an anthropodicy failed no less forcefully than all Enlightenment dreams of a theodicy had done earlier.

What has remained are ills and the human need for consolation, the questions of meaning and orientation in the lifeworld that no technology for overcoming ills and dealing with their consequences can answer, and religious and quasi-religious attempts at consolation that take up these basic questions of the lifeworld and the need for meaning. The constellation of problems concerning ill, God, and reason that comes up time and again cannot be ignored by philosophical and theological thinking if only because both, each in its way, relate to experiences, attitudes, and life practices they seek to explain and critically to understand. Nor can they reduce this constellation in such a way that philosophy would exclude the problem of God and concentrate on the relationship between ill and reason, and theology would exclude the problem of reason and focus on the relationship between ill and God. No member of the constellation of problems concerning ill, God, and reason can be taken out without reflection—and this applies to philosophical as much as to theological reflection—losing touch with the problems of the lifeworld it articulates.

The intellectual development of modernity has also shown that the reciprocal provocations of evil, conceptions of God, and conceptions of reason are as insufficiently dealt with by differentiating kinds of reason according to each problem as they are by excluding the suprarational or the counterrational from the set of rational problems to be taken seriously by philosophy or the withdrawal of theology from the debate about an appropriate conception of reason in the face of the experience of ill in life and the experience of God in faith. Philosophically and theologically, the counterrational, the suprarational, and reason must be thought in their interrelation.

To say that this must take place on the basis of reason, because reason is the only medium of thinking available to us, is not to say that philosophy in principle takes precedence over theology, as modernity's juxtaposition of faith and reason generally conceived it. Reason is not a prerogative of philosophy, and the concept of faith not only marks, philosophically, the other of reason but also, theologically, a specific conception of reason: faith is a reason counting on God; reason, accordingly, is either faith or unfaith, but it is not a neutral element beyond either alternative. Those who consider this conception of reason to be inadequate cannot justify their view with reference to its being theological. That would be a relevant objection only if there were a conception of reason that did not rely on a point of view. Yet we have no such conception. If there is one thing the processes in which reason in modernity has sought to understand itself have shown, it is this: insight into the perspectival nature of all reason and all conceptions of reason is the precondition for engaging in the debate about a reasonable conception of reason today.

This precondition, meanwhile, reveals new theological points of interest in early modern attempts at critically reflecting on the constellation of problems of ill, God, and reason within a rational horizon. For if we conceive of reason as essentially tied to a perspective and a horizon, not as the point of view above all points of view (which is unattainable as a matter of principle), it is precisely those attempts that become interesting again which seek to fathom the capacities and limits of reason by critically reflecting on the relationship between the counterrational, the suprarational, and reason within the horizon of reason and thus in reference to the rational point of view without playing down the problems from the outset by reducing the triad in one way or another.

It is in this sense that in the following pages I provide a re-reading of Leibniz's exemplary project. I am not so much interested in presenting Leibniz's work as a precursor of efforts that conceived or misconceived of themselves as overcoming him as I am in taking it seriously as an effort at making the conception of reality that guided the Christian attitude toward life in his time accessible to a critical self-explication, faced as it was with scientific developments that in losing a sense for God also threatened to lose the capacity for shedding light on questions of orientation in the lifeworld, and at doing so by presenting it from the point of view of his conception of reason and in a rationally accessible way. This procedure brings out methodological standards of clarity, consistence, and coherence that apply in such self-critiques even when the self-evidence of the lifeworld and the intellectual means employed in examining this self-evidence have irrevocably changed. Leibniz captured his time, not ours, with his intellectual tools, not ours. Yet in so doing, he came across problems that philosophical and theological reflection cannot ignore in dealing with the constellation of problems of ill, reason, and God even today.

4. Chance and Interconnection

Leibniz thought that if there were such a thing as "blind" chance,[23] which is not and cannot be understood to be anything other than the randomness of an event that takes place "by chance or by accident [*casu aut per accidens*]"[24] and strikes us without any reason when it could just as well not have struck us, things would look bad for reason and for God. Things would go badly for reason, because its efforts at establishing connections and to find reason even in the irrational would come up against a definitive limit and thus enter into a fundamental crisis: an event without *ratio* that forms part of no series whatsoever would not only remain entirely inaccessible to *ratio* but would force reason

---

23. On what follows, see also Stoellger, "Die Vernunft der Kontingenz."
24. Leibniz, "On Freedom," in *Philosophical Papers and Letters*, 263–66, here 263.

to admit that there is something it cannot know without being able to know why it cannot know it. Reason would be unable to see why it does not see, and it would thereby fail as a subject and instrument of enlightenment critique in the very task of self-critique. Those who are not willing to draw the conclusion, as Kant's critique of Enlightenment did later, that reason must limit itself to what it can do and refrain from what it cannot do, must eliminate the scandal chance constitutes for reason—to save reason's claim to enlightened critique.[25] If reality is not rational, then reason is not only not the key to reality but trips itself up, as it were, and thereby promotes irrationality: it cannot know why it cannot know something, and this opens the floodgates of irrationalism and skepticism.

And things would go badly for God, because there would then be something that he could not have known and therefore could also not have willed and done. If, however, only that exists which is made by God and God only makes what he wills and wills only what he knows and judges to be good, then blind chance is reason's litmus test for God: either chance or God, and if chance, then no God—no God, in any event, in accordance with the "most widely accepted and meaningful concept which we have of God," namely "that he is an absolutely perfect being" who "does all in the most desirable way."[26] Yet according to Leibniz, we do "have a more certain knowledge of the existence of . . . God, than of any thing else without us." For if we know that the "idea of a wholly great or wholly perfect being is possible and does not imply a contradiction," then we can be sure that God exists: "*If God is possible he exists*," and because he is demonstrably possible insofar as the concept of a perfect being does not imply any self-contradiction, we must "in the

---

25. Reason does not fail when it sees *that* it cannot know everything; it fails only when it cannot see *why* it cannot know everything. On this point, Leibniz and Kant are in agreement, as they are in thinking that reason can answer this question only by gaining insight into its own finitude in a rational way. Yet whereas Leibniz seeks to demonstrate reason's insight into its own finitude by way of its justified insight into God's superior reason, Kant to this end takes the path of reason's self-critique, in which reason restrains itself to avoid falling prey to autodestructive aporias of reason.

What changes in the development from Leibniz to Kant, therefore, is not only the conception of reason but fundamentally also the conception of reason's finitude: our reason is *finite* not because of the contrast with the infinity of God's reason but because of its incapacity for universalizing itself without restrictions. And it is *rational* not because it knows by rational reasons that God also has reasons for what reason cannot understand but because it is itself capable of understanding how it can escape the aporias of uncritical universalization it itself gives rise to. Given the excesses of irrationalism and enthusiasm and based on insight into the superior capacity of God's reason, Leibniz pleads for an optimistic *self-restraint of reason*; given the objections of skepticism and based on insight into the limits of reason's own capacities, Kant pleads for a critical *self-limitation of reason*. In both projects for saving reason, the attitude they assume toward the ontological argument is philosophically decisive. For Leibniz, it is the rationally irrefutable reason for not only being able but being obligated to count on God's infinite reason and thereby also to realize the strength and the limits of our own reason: everything can be known rationally, just not for us but for God, and *this* we can know rationally. For Kant, on the contrary, the failure of this argument is the occasion for seeking a resolution of the aporias of reason on a path other than via God, making the point that what proves the strength of reason is precisely the insight into the reasons for the failure of reason in the ontological (and thus in every) proof of the existence of God. We can know only what can be known by the means available to our reason, and not only does this not include everything, it also does not include God. Yet the ability critically to know precisely this limit furnishes proof of the strength of reason.

26. Leibniz, *Discourse on Metaphysics*, in *Philosophical Papers and Letters*, 303–30, here §1:303.

present state of our knowledge . . . judge that God exists."[27] Yet if this being exists, then, inversely, chance cannot exist or can exist only because God wills it. Now, as anyone who has ever rolled a dice knows, chance exists but it does not become a scandal for reason: while reason—this was Leibniz's discovery in probability theory—can derive little that is rational from a single roll of the dice, the same is not true for a large or even infinitely large number of rolls. The larger the number, the greater the approximation of a stable limit that can be captured in a rational rule. If chance exists, then, it can be understood as one case in an infinite series and thus also according to a rule, that is, rationally, and if it is not reasonable to contest the existence of God, then the only conclusion is that chance events exist because God wills them to. Yet if God wills chance events, they have the best reason one could wish for: God wills them. Yet what is willed by God thereby ceases to be a chance event without reason and becomes *justified contingency*.

Given the existence of chance events in the world, reason's taking recourse to God thus becomes a question of self-preservation: if it does not want to fail because of the randomness encountered in the world, *randomness* needs to be completely and entirely transformed—not, as Spinoza thought, into necessity: that would be the end of all freedom but—into *contingency*, and on Leibniz's view that is possible, precisely, only by taking recourse to God. Rather than avoid God and contingency, reason fundamentally depends on both: for its own sake, reason must conceive of randomness as contingency, and it can do so only if it conceives of it in terms of God's perfection. Randomness is accessible to reason only in terms of contingency because, as contingent, it is embedded by God in the context of the rational. *Leibniz's project for saving reason consists in the systematic demonstration that all randomness is contingent and all contingency is rational.* And this project stands or falls with God—such as Leibniz conceives of him: the grounds and guarantor of all rational order.

5. Rule, Order, and Interconnection

Randomness is so fundamental a challenge to reason because it questions the very essence of what reason is: the institution of *context*, the connection of individual experiences (*vérités*) the human mind acquires naturally in the process of life to form valid contexts of knowledge, what Leibniz calls the "inviolable linking together of truths."[28] At its basis, reason for Leibniz is that activity of the mind whose basic function is to institute rational connections, that is, the non-contradictory linking and combination of basic units of sense (data, information, truths) into valid sequences of knowledge, justified nexuses of knowledge, and coherent fields of knowledge that allow for reliably orienting ourselves in life and in the world. In so doing, reason can and must distinguish between several levels and kinds of truths such as "'Eternal Verities,' which are altogether necessary, so that the opposite implies contradiction," as is the case for logical, metaphysical, and geometric truths, and *positive truths*, the necessary "laws which it has pleased God to give to Nature" and which we can know *a posteriori* through experience or *a priori* "by

27. Leibniz, *New Essays*, IV.x.6–7:435–38.
28. Leibniz, *Theodicy*, §1:73–74, §23:88.

considerations of the fitness of things which have caused their choice."[29] The difference between these truths lies in the kind of connection they bring about and the validity of the contexts they institute. In turning to these truths and their valid connections, reason's concern is not with knowing individual phenomena as such but with knowing the *rules* that govern individual phenomena, with *combining* these rules in systems of rules, and thus with knowing *organized nexuses* that can be conceived of in terms of the rules for combining individual phenomena into valid nexuses (sequences, networks, fields) and of the rules for combining the rules of individual phenomena into systems of rules. Rational knowledge is a knowledge of complex organization and consists in grasping the rules and systems of rules that institute nexuses.

It is not by chance that reason, as the "inviolable linking together of truths,"[30] is capable of grasping valid nexuses and the rules they are based on. It goes to show, rather, that in reason, the world becomes transparent to itself, that through reason, it is able to grasp its structural principles. In the operations of reason, the world conceives of itself as a controlled, organized, and organizing nexus of rules: reason represents what presents itself in the world but represents it in such a way that it figures the space of possible worlds as the epitome of the truth nexuses established according to inviolable rules, nexuses of which the real world is one, the richest. To that extent, the rules thematized by reason do indeed go beyond the real world, but in its connection of truths, reason—at least "strict and true reason"[31]—does not institute arbitrary nexuses of rules but represents and reproduces those that are actually valid.[32]

The idea of a context organized according to rules is thus fundamental not only to Leibniz's conception of reason but to his conception of the world as well. For Leibniz, the world is a *universe*, that is, not an especially complex object, not a sum of objects, nor the "collection of all possibles," but—as a possible world—"a collection of a certain order of compossibles only" and—as the actual world—"a collection of all the possibles which exist, that is to say, those which form the richest composite."[33] The real world (the world of everything that really exists) is an organized open whole, a nexus instituted by combining the elements of the world into coherent sequences and combining these sequences into networks where everything that is real exists next to and one after the other, in other words, "the whole succession and the whole agglomeration of all existent things."[34] Nothing that is is without connection with everything else that is. There are, to

---

29. Leibniz, *Theodicy*, §2:74.

30. Leibniz, *Theodicy*, §23:88, see §1:73–74.

31. Leibniz, *Theodicy*, §1:73.

32. That reason does so is demonstrated by its reliability in the processes of the lifeworld. A reason that would establish connections in a merely arbitrary way would soon fail in the confrontation with the resistance of the real. The common and, for Leibniz, unlimited reliability of reason in life is proof of its adequacy to reality.

33. Leibniz to Louis Bourguet, December 1714, in *Philosophical Papers and Letters*, 661–63, here 662.

34. Leibniz, *Theodicy*, §8:128. The world is thus not defined as the totality of what is possible but as totality of what is contingent (existing), yet it is in just this way that it constitutes a continuum that (against Aristotle) is *actually infinite* and must not be considered as a very big object, "as an animal or as a substance" (§195:249). See Poma, *Impossibility and Necessity of Theodicy*, 158–59.

be sure, different possible worlds "since all possibles are not compossible."[35] But "in each one of the possible worlds" "all things are *connected*." Hence Leibniz can say figuratively that "the universe, whatever it may be, is all of one piece, like an ocean: the least movement extends its effect there to any distance whatsoever, even though this effect become less perceptible in proportion to the distance."[36] And it is this unbroken, continuous, controlled overall nexus of the world that makes the occurrence of randomness a phenomenon that runs counter to the world and to reason.

6. The Discovery of Contingency

Leibniz thus does not simply assert that "fortune . . . is an empty word," because there are no coincidences. He provides reasons.[37] In doing so—and this is the point of his efforts—he uses reason not only to reveal the irrationality of randomness but to purge them of it by proving that neither are there random coincidences nor is everything necessary but that instead, there is a third beside the necessary and the possible: the contingent. Leibniz reaches this goal in a manner typical of him, by radicalizing the problem. Logically, there are three possibilities: either nothing is random, or everything is random, or some things are random. The notion that nothing is random, i.e., that randomness does not exist, is refuted by every throw of the dice and thus does not represent a serious option. If everything, on the contrary, were random, if there were nothing that was not random, not only would the term lose its significance, reason would be unable to obtain anything rational from the world by calculating either probabilities or limits. Because reason can do so, however, this, too, is not a serious option. Some things, at most, can be random. But what are they? And, above all: What are the others?

Not a coincidence, certainly—but *not by coincidence* can mean many things. To determine more precisely and thereby the better to understand what "coincidence" or "randomness" mean, Leibniz defines the logical universe of modalities by distinguishing between possibility, necessity, and contingency.[38] This distinction, he claims, gives a complete description of the space of modalities, such that there can be nothing that is not defined by these modes. *Necessary* is all that is subject to the principle of contradiction, that is, everything from whose concepts it is possible to infer that it can impossibly be because it is self-contradictory or that it is impossible for it not to be because its negation represents a self-contradiction. *Contingent*, on the contrary, is all that cannot be reduced to the principle of contradiction, all that whose negation thus does not represent a self-contradiction just as it itself does not represent a self-contradiction: it is neither necessary nor impossible, yet it is also not only possible but real. For, it is true of what is *possible*, too, that it is neither necessary nor impossible but can be real, indeed that it *wants* to be real, as Leibniz pointedly puts it: "Everything possible demands existence, and hence will exist unless something else prevents it, which also demands existence

35. Leibniz to Louis Bourguet, December 1714, 662.

36. Leibniz, *Theodicy*, §9:128.

37. Leibniz, "On Freedom," 263.

38. On what follows, see Leibniz, "On Contingency."

and is incompatible with the former."[39] What is *necessary* can thus not not exist; what is *impossible* cannot exist; what is *not necessary* can exist or it can not exist; what is *possible* can exist and would exist if it were not prevented from existing; and what is *contingent* exists, that is, it is not impossible, but it is also not necessary and not only possible but real.

In Leibniz's world of modalities, the interesting case is the difference between possibility and contingency. While each possible thing is what it is and nothing else, what is contingent characteristically could have something else in its place: it is a possibility that has become actual ("actualized"), that has prevented and prevents other possibilities from becoming action because it has "more reason [*ratio*] for existing than others would, were they put in [its] place."[40] What distinguishes the contingent from both the possible and the necessary is that in its place—and that means: *under identical conditions—something else could exist*. For what is necessary is in such a way that it is impossible for it not to exist, such that simply nothing else can exist in its place. What is possible in turn *is* not at all but is something that is not necessary and not impossible and therefore precisely "strives" for what it can be but is not: actual (existing). What is contingent, in contrast, is *actual*, unlike what is possible and, unlike what is necessary, is actual *in such a way* that *under identical conditions, something else* could also be real *in its place*.

This point must be shielded from two common misunderstandings. On the one hand, this does not mean that what is contingent could *itself* also have been *something else*, since that would amount to the self-contradiction of saying about what is that it could also not have been what it is but something else: yet to say that instead of the rain falling, the sun could have been shining, does not mean that the rain could also have been the sun.[41]

On the other hand, it also does not mean that what is contingent could *itself*, under identical conditions, also not have been in its place—a self-contradictory notion: that instead of it raining, it could also not have been raining, does not mean that instead of the rain, there could also have been nothing, or that when it rains it could also not be raining: *If it rains, then it is also possible that it might not be raining* is something different from *it is possible: if it rains, then it does not rain*. Contingency does not imply *being able not to be*, it implies *being able to be otherwise*, namely being able to be otherwise in the sense of *another's ability to be* insofar as in the place of what is, something else could also

39. Leibniz, "On First Truths," 29.

40. Leibniz, "On First Truths," 28.

41. This has an important consequence: for Leibniz, *one and the same individual* cannot occur in different possible worlds. Rather, its concept contains *all* truths about the individual and thus also contains all contexts in which it stands, stood, and will stand. That "Caesar crossed the Rubicon" could in a different possible world also not be true means that what would be real there, if that world were real, would be a being possibly very similar to Caesar but a *different* being. With each individual substance, therefore, the entire universe is up for debate. "If in the life of some person, moreover, or even in the universe as a whole, some event were to occur in a different way than it actually does, there would still be nothing to prevent us from saying that this would be another person or another possible universe which God has chosen. And it would in that case be truly another individual" (Leibniz to Antoine Arnaud, June 1868, in *Philosophical Papers and Letters*, 331–38, here 335). On the problem, see Ishiguro, *Leibniz's Philosophy of Logic and Language*, 171–79.

have been, yet not in the sense that what is could have been otherwise (then it would not be what it is) or could not have been (then what is would not be).

7. The Rationality of Contingency

The definition of the contingent as that in whose place, under identical circumstances, something else could have been, evinces the point and the theological background of Leibniz's reflections—in two respects. On the one hand, what is contingent is thus defined as something (in the literal sense) *factual*: facts are things done [*Tat-Sachen*], that is, the process or result of actions, which differ from mere events or series of events in that under identical circumstances, it would have been possible to act differently. Being able to act differently under identical circumstances is the traditional basic definition of free actions.[42] By defining what is contingent as that in whose place, under identical circumstances, something else could have been, Leibniz conceives of the "contingent truths" or "truths of fact" as *factual truths* and thus as *results* or *processes of free actions*: they are something *freely actualized* and that means: results of an efficacious will and a willed action.[43]

On the other hand, as Leibniz explicitly notes, the contingent and the necessary share something that distinguishes them from the impossible and the possible: there are true propositions about them.[44] While what is *possible* is not impossible but also not necessary, such that there are propositions about it that would be true or false if it were actual, what is *contingent* is real, thus not merely not necessary, not impossible, or just possible, but actual in such a way that in its place, something else could be actual such that there would be true propositions about it. Yet "[e]very true universal affirmative proposition, either necessary or contingent, has some connection between subject and predicate." In identity propositions, this connection is immediately apparent because of the concepts used (*The ball is a ball*). In all "other propositions it must appear through the analysis of terms," that is, it must be possible to bring it out through an analysis of the concepts. Only in this process does it become clear whether something is a *rational truth* or a *factual truth*, a true proposition about something necessary (*veritas rationis*) or a true proposition about something contingent (*veritas facti* or *veritas contingens*): if it is possible to decide the truth of such a proposition solely by means of the principle of avoiding contradiction, that is, to resolve it in "an equation that is an identity," then the proposition is a rational truth; in all other cases, the proposition is a factual truth. Factual truths "cannot be reduced to the principle of contradiction"; rather, "one continues the analysis to infinity through reasons for reasons, so that one never has a complete demonstration, though there is always, underneath, a reason for the truth, but the reason is understood completely only by God, who alone traverses the infinite series in one stroke of mind."[45]

42. See, for example, Melanchthon, *Lucubratiuncula*, esp. cols. 13–14: "Est autem libertas posse agere aut non agere. Posse sic aut aliter agere." Cf. Melanchthon, *Loci communes*, esp. col. 87, ll.15–16.

43. Leibniz, "On Contingency," 28; "On First Truths," 29.

44. Leibniz, "On Contingency," 28.

45. Leibniz, "On First Truths," 28.

In this reference to God, the two series of thoughts join. For God knows the reasons for the contingent (which we can never completely cognize) not only because, as a perfect being, he has perfect knowledge but because these *truths* are due to his *doing* [*Tun*]. They are *factual truths* because they are things he has done [*Tat-Sachen*]: he knows that they are true and why they are true *because* he *willed and made* them himself. What is contingent, especially, shows the world to be *created*, the result of *God's free action*. Just as the rational truths have their reason in God's perfect knowledge, so the contingent or factual truths have their reason in God's perfect will.[46]

8. The World as Nexus of Acts

In thinking the not-necessary reality of the world as contingency, Leibniz thinks it on the model of action as an infinite *nexus of acts*, both micro- and macrocosmically. Every single being is an association of acts, an association of perceptions that, as "internal actions," constitute its identity.[47] Yet the nexus of all beings in the world, too, is a nexus of acts that Leibniz, interpreting the Cartesian dualism of nature (*res extensa*) and mind (*res cogitans*) in the terms of a theology of creation, describes as harmonious agreement of the nexus of purposes and the nexus of effects: what under the aspect of cause and effect presents itself as a succession of events, under the aspect of reason and consequence presents itself as a nexus of acts.[48]

Leibniz thus does not simply revoke the difference between act and event but reconstructs it according to a logic of acts. Because he interprets events, too, as acts, there is the danger that the difference between that which is through us (acts) and that which is for us (events) is being blurred. He therefore distinguishes, within the category of act, between acts to be ascribed to God and acts to be ascribed to us. Everything contingent is a deed and thus the result of a free decision of the will. Yet, neither is everything contingent our deed alone, nor is it God's deed alone; neither might we say, like "some

46. Leibniz's argument in the *Monadology* (*PPL* 643–53) that "[t]here must be simple substances, since there are compounds" (§2:643) supposes a definitive and unambiguous analysis of what is complex. There is little to speak in favor of such an analysis, however, when it is detached from its unnamed theological-metaphysical precondition, which is that there is nothing that is not either necessary or contingent because it can be traced back either to God's wisdom and his perfect knowledge of all "truths of reasoning" (§33:646) or to God's will and perfectly good willing of all "contingent truths or truths of fact" (§36:646). An analysis of the complex must be finite, be unequivocal, and result in simple elements because it is something known, willed, and effected by God. That alone, too, yields confidence in considering the principle of sufficient reason to apply even where we cannot find or cognize final reasons and first elements (§32:646). Only because everything that exists exists through God's wisdom and will, "the sufficient or final reason will have to be outside the sequence or *series* of these detailed contingent factors, however infinite they may be" (§37:646). To surrender the premise of God is to destroy the persuasive force of the principle of sufficient reason, turning the principle from a manifestation of confidence in the rational penetrability of reality founded on a theology of creation into an at most heuristic principle of finite cognition.

47. Leibniz, *Theodicy*, §17:644.

48. Leibniz, *Theodicy*, §79:651.

modern philosophers" (the Spinozists) do, "that God is the only agent,"[49] nor is any of our deeds such that it would be independent of a deed of God's.

This leads to two fundamental problems, only one of which, the *problem of freedom*, Leibniz thinks through intensively. If everything actual is contingent, that is, is a deed and thus the result of a free determination of the will, but if at the same time, not everything contingent can be traced back solely and exclusively to the will of God but some contingent things can also be traced back to the will of creatures, how are we then to define the relationship between divine will and creaturely will? No human *factum* would exist if God did not want that. This does not mean, however, that everything humans do is willed by God. There would be no creaturely deeds if God did not want that. But that God wants there to be creaturely deeds at all does not mean that he wills the concrete deeds of his creatures. A crucial abyss opens up here between divine freedom and creaturely freedom. God wills *that* there be finite freedom, for since it would not be self-contradictory to think that it might not exist, it would not be if God did not will it. But God does not inevitably also will *what* finite freedom wills. If God wills finite freedom, as indicated by its contingent actuality, then he wills that what is willed is being willed *freely*, and then God can indeed wish but he cannot effect that creature's will and do what is *freely determined*. Freedom is unavoidable, and not God's creative freedom alone but also the creaturely freedom it has made actual. According to Leibniz, then, that everything actual is contingent and thus a deed done excludes neither that there is finite freedom nor that God is present as willing and acting in the practice of finite freedom. What is excluded is only that everything that is (although it could also not be) is effected by God: there are things we effect that God does not will, although he wills that we will *freely* what we will, and that we freely will *what is good for us*. Yet *effecting* that *we freely will and do what is good for us* is something even the omnipotent God cannot do: the free willing of something determinate cannot be forced, and if we want freedom we must concede the freedom to determine oneself because everything else would abolish freedom. That is why Leibniz is of the "opinion that our will is exempt not only from constraint but also from necessity."[50]

And from this, precisely, results the other, the *cosmological* problem. If everything actual is a *factum*, then there exist not only *facta* that go back to a creaturely willing that is not inevitably congruent with the divine willing, which gives rise to the question concerning the relationship of divine and creaturely will; then it is also true that God's willing and doing in each case picks up on what is *contingently actual*. God can only ever make actual what is compatible with what is in each case already actual. And that is why every *factum* of God's picks up on the already existing facta in such a way that each such divine operation is a *cooperation* between God and creation. God wills the good in each case and in picking up on what is already actual in each case, he effects the best among all the possible consequences: "Thence it follows that God wills *antecedently* the good and *consequently* the best."[51]

49. Leibniz, *Theodicy*, §32:142.
50. Leibniz, *Theodicy*, §34:143.
51. Leibniz, *Theodicy*, §23:137.

This is the point where process philosophy takes up and develops Leibniz's reflections.[52] If every action is interaction, as Hartshorne says, then reality is not just a nexus of acts but a *process* of interaction.[53] God picks up on the contingent actualities already existing in each case in such a way that he seeks to link them up with and to actualize those possibilities that continue to determine creation in the direction of what his will for creation is. Since it belongs to this will, however, that his creatures *freely* decide in favor of what is good for them, God's continuing determination of creation in the direction of the goal he is aiming at cannot be described as a coercion but only as an *enticement* of the creatures to themselves freely will and do what is good for them. God works not through coercion but through persuasion and enticement to do what is good. In every cooperative actualization of something contingent, God thereby picks up on two aspects of contingent reality: on the one hand, the existing *reality* but also, on the other, *his own earlier willing and doing* that, although it has made the existing reality possible and code-termined it, may not or only somewhat shape it because that which is the case concretely is conditioned by the free action of creatures who do not as a matter of course pursue the same goals as God does. The process of reality as a nexus of contingency can thus always be described on two levels: on the level of the willing and doing of God who always wills the good and achieves the best possible; and on the level of creaturely willing and doing, which never represents God's willing and doing alone. The first descriptive level marks the continuity of the process of reality in divine willing, a continuity thanks to which the association of acts on the second level does not take place arbitrarily but in such a way that the aim always remains to actualize the best possible, that is to say, in such a way that reality does not only change but develops, and develops toward the better.

9. The God of Reason

With his thesis that truths of reason have their reason in God's perfect knowledge whereas contingent or factual truths have their reason in God's perfect will, Leibniz positions himself both against Spinoza and against Descartes. Against Spinoza, he defends the view that there are contingent truths that go back to the choice or decision of a will, be it the will of humans or the will of God, truths, that is, that exist only because they were willed and something different possible in their place was not willed. Not everything that is can be necessary in Spinoza's sense, that is, be the consequence of a "blind necessity" and exist exclusively "through the necessity of the divine nature." For, as Leibniz says, taking up an argument of Pierre Bayle's, the impossibility that Spinoza did not die in The Hague is something different from the impossibility that two times two equals six: the latter contains a logical contradiction, whereas the former is excluded

---

52. Whitehead, *Process and Reality*, cannot be understood without Russell, *A Critical Exposition of the Philosophy of Leibniz*; the same is true of the *Principia Mathematica* they wrote together, and of the relations theory developed there in particular.

53. Hartshorne, *Reality as Social Process*, concludes from this that freedom itself must be thought as a dynamic tiered process that runs through all levels of reality, from the most elementary natural processes to the free decisions of human beings. Accordingly, divine interaction with these various actions presents itself in a variety of forms as well.

only factually but is not impossible logically. This difference cannot be revoked with the argument that "all things exist through the necessity of the divine nature" because not everything that is not impossible but possible (because it contains no contradiction) exists necessarily. Even a Spinozist, according to Leibniz, would not want to claim "that all the romances one can imagine exist actually now, or have existed, or will still exist in some place in the universe."[54] If, however, there are possibilities that are not actualized, then "existing things cannot always be necessary" either, for "otherwise it would be impossible for other things to exist in their place, and whatever never exists would therefore be impossible."[55] It is therefore unavoidable that we distinguish between necessary and contingent truths. Then, however, God too must be thought differently from how Spinoza thinks him. If nothing is without God, as Spinoza rightly asserts, then the difference between what is necessary and what is contingent must apply also in the reference to God. And that means that with regard to God, we must distinguish between God as the source of what is necessary (his understanding) and God as the origin of what is contingent (his will).[56] Precisely because it is correct that everything that is is thanks to God's power, we must distinguish between God's understanding and God's will because otherwise the indispensable difference between what is necessary and what is contingent, between necessary truths and contingent truths, would be abolished.

Against Descartes, who does not deny God's understanding and will, Leibniz emphasizes that his will cannot be entirely indifferent and uninterested toward the good and toward ill. In the *Objections and Replies*, Descartes argued that God's omnipotence required that God's will "from eternity" be indifferent "with respect to everything which has happened or will ever happen; for it is impossible to imagine that anything is thought of in the divine intellect as good or true, or worthy of belief or action or omission, prior to the decision of the divine will to make it so."[57] God did not consider whether it would be better to create the world in time or to create it from eternity and then decided in favor of a temporal creation as what was better but the inverse: because he willed and made a temporal creation, this creation is better than an eternal creation.[58] For Leibniz, this means nothing other than "that God established good and evil by an arbitrary decree," which he considers to be absurd and an insult to God. For if the will of God is not oriented by the good, if God thus does not will what is good but what God wills is good, that would mean that God had enacted the good and the just "by a kind of hazard." And if we "assert that there was something good and just before his decree, but that he is not required to conform to it," then there is no reason why he should be bound by his decree or change it and revert it into its contrary. "There is nothing to prevent such a God from behaving as a tyrant and an enemy of honest folk, and from taking pleasure in that which we call evil."[59] Just as Spinoza abolishes the difference between what is necessary and

54. Leibniz, *Theodicy*, §173:234–35.

55. Leibniz, "On Freedom," 263.

56. See Leibniz, *Theodicy*, §7:127–28, and *Monadology*, §§43, 46–48:647.

57. Descartes, "Replies to the Sixth Set of Objections," 291 (AT 7:431–32), see also 292 (AT 7:432): "the supreme indifference to be found in God is the supreme indication of his omnipotence."

58. Descartes, "Replies to the Sixth Set of Objections," 291 (AT 7:432).

59. Leibniz, *Theodicy*, §175–77:236–37.

what is contingent by declaring everything to be the necessary consequence of God's necessary nature, so Descartes abolishes it by making everything look like an arbitrary positing on the part of God's will. But just as we must not invert contingent truths into necessary ones if we do not want to abrogate reason by means of self-contradictions, so we must not turn necessary truths into arbitrary postulates if reason is not to be replaced by arbitrariness and randomness. Accordingly, Leibniz stresses against Descartes that "[w]e must not imagine . . . that since the eternal truths are dependent upon God, they are arbitrary and dependent on his will. . . . This is true only of contingent truths, whose principle is fitness or the choice of the best; necessary truths, however, depend solely on his understanding and are its internal object."[60] Because for the sake of reason, the difference between what is necessary and what is contingent must not be eclipsed—for otherwise blind necessity (Spinoza) or nonrational arbitrariness (Descartes) come to characterize reality—God as the principle of all being must be thought in a differentiated manner *for the sake of the reasonableness of reason*. On the one hand, what is necessary (eternal truths) must be traced back to his understanding, what is contingent (factual truths) back to his will. On the other hand, his will must be thought in such a way that God is not indifferent toward what he wills but determines himself as perfect goodness according to the principle of choosing what is best, that he wills that which is the best of all available alternatives he (thanks to his perfect understanding) knows to be possible. God knows everything that is possible because he is perfect wisdom; he wills the best because he is perfect goodness; and he creates the best possible because he is perfect power.

This also defines God's work of creation in greater detail. God can create only what does not contradict, "among truths of reason, those which are identical." Yet by definition, these *veritates rationis identicae* are not contradicted by what is possible, that is, by what is not necessarily not. Yet although every possible demands to exist, "it does not seem possible for all possible things to exist, since they get in one another's way." Among the "infinite number of series of possible things" only those can be actual, therefore, that are *compossible*, and since "one series certainly cannot be contained within another" because "each and every one of them is complete," not all, and neither some, but only one or no series of possibles can be actual. If any one of them is actual at all—and given our experience *a posteriori*, there is no reason to doubt this—then there must be a reason why precisely this and none of the infinitely many other series of possibles is actual. And because "nothing happens without a reason" and because "that which has the more reason always happens," that which is actual must have the best reason, namely the reason that is "greater" than all the reasons in favor of other series of possibles. But nothing possible would be actual if God had not actualized it. The reason why there is anything at all and not rather nothing, and the reason why precisely this contingent something exists and not rather something else in its place, can therefore only be the one and identical reason by which God has freely determined his will (that is, himself) to actualize that which is factually actual. There is no other reason for that which is actual being actual instead of something different that could have been actual in its place than God's free decision which possibles are to be preferred in their urge for existence to others and are thus not to be hindered by the latter in their becoming actual. They "have more reason

---

60. Leibniz, *Monadology*, §46:647.

for existing than others would, were they put in their place," because God willed that they and not the others become actual.[61]

10. The Challenge of Ill

This finally brings us to the real problem. For if all facts exist only because God willed that they exist and not something else in their place, then why is the world as ill as it is? Once more, Leibniz renders the problem more acute by excluding all the answers that readily suggest themselves.

While it is correct to say that God willed it to be that way, it is also misleadingly imprecise. It leaves open the possibility that God is as ill as the ills he effects. That however is an impossible possibility. For if God is the absolutely perfect being that not only cannot not be (i.e., that is necessary)[62] but that also "always acts wisely, that is, in such a way that anyone who knew his reasons would know and worship his supreme justice, goodness, and wisdom," then God can neither determine his will to do ill nor not determine it at all; he cannot act either ill (for an evil reason) or arbitrarily (without a reason). "[I]n God there never seems to be a case of acting purely because it pleases him to act in this way, unless, at the same time, it is pleasing for good reason" because such a case would contradict his concept and thus himself, that is, it would conflict either with his wisdom, his goodness, or his power. Leibniz thus strictly excludes any modification of the concept of God—and thereby puts the problem of ill in the world in terms that could not be more acute: How can there be ills in a world that, as the creation of the perfect God, necessarily is such that God chooses the good and actualizes the best possible?[63]

Leibniz is no less resolute in his rejection of the attempt to exonerate God that consists in pointing out that a different world is not even imaginable. The opposite is the case: "It is true that one may imagine possible worlds without sin and without unhappiness, and one could make some like Utopian or Sevarambian romances." Yet if a world without sin and without suffering could have existed, then why did God not create it? Because it would not be better than the factual world: "I deny that then it would have been *better*."[64] A world without ills is imaginable, but it is unimaginable that it would be better than the factual world.[65] This view seems not only to be extravagant but entirely

---

61. Leibniz, "On Contingency," 29, 30, 28.

62. Leibniz, "On Contingency," 28. We cannot trace here the conviction, which is decisive for his argumentation and expressed in Leibniz's various versions of the ontological or *a priori* argument, that the actuality of the suprarational can be proven rationally. See, among others, Blumenfeld, "Leibniz's Ontological and Cosmological Arguments." Without this conviction it is impossible to follow not only his proposed solutions but already the very question he addresses in his theodicy. The loss of this conviction, precisely, is the most consequential objection to his engagement with ill. That is why for theological thinking, which cannot simply assume this loss even if it does not base its conviction about the actuality of God on ontological or cosmological arguments, the merely pragmatically, anti- or atheologically motivated rejections of Leibniz are not very convincing, and it is why the problem and the argumentation of his theodicy remain a challenge.

63. Leibniz, "On Contingency," 29, 30.

64. Leibniz, *Theodicy*, §10:129, §9:128.

65. See also Rasmussen, "On Creating Worlds without Evil."

counterintuitive: Is a world with n−1 ills not better than a world with n ills? And would a world with n=0 ills not be better than one with n=1 ills? We might grant Leibniz that "if the smallest evil that comes to pass in the world were missing in it, it would no longer be this world."[66] Yet the question, precisely, is whether a different world would not be better than the factual world, and if it were better, why God created not it but the factual world. Leibniz makes several arguments, but his central and decisive argument is this: "since God has chosen this world as it is," it must be, despite all imaginable alternatives or desirable improvements, the better world "since he does nothing without acting in accordance with supreme reason," and if he has created this world and not a different possible world, then it follows that it was this world that, "with nothing omitted and all allowance made, was found the best by the Creator who chose it." The factual world is the better and thereby the best possible world, because God created it and not any of its possible alternatives.[67]

Leibniz thus rejects the two ways out of the dilemma that suggest themselves, a modification of the concept of God and a problematization of the factual world as God's creation. If reality is really to be rationally comprehensible, reason must understand precisely the contingency of this factual world with all its ills; and it will understand it only if it does not conjure the offensive contingency of ill in the world away and busy itself only with imaginable but merely fantasized alternatives, only if instead it conceives of this world in its offensiveness as God's good creation. God's being God and creator is decided in this world, not in a different world, and the rationality of reason is tested by understanding this reality, not a different reality.

11. Ill as a Fundamental Problem of Reason

From this standpoint, it is possible to conceive of Leibniz's philosophy entirely as an effort at philosophically dealing with the problem of ill. From beginning to end, his reflections on contingency are reflections on theodicy, and because the problem of theodicy poses itself in the first place only where God's goodness, human freedom, and the reality of ills are taken equally seriously, Leibniz's entire philosophy is shaped by preconditions in which reason, contingency, and God stand in an undissolvable relationship.

None of his basic metaphysical principles can thus be understood without heeding their theological preconditions. This is true already of his guiding question, *Why is there something rather than nothing?* The justification Leibniz gives for this question— "nothing is simpler and easier than something"—cannot convince unless one presupposes that for everything that is, there must be a reason why it is and does not rather not exist and unless this presupposition, insofar as it makes sense at all, makes sense only in those cases where the "Being" at issue is understood as an *action* or the *result of an action*, that is, as something based on a will such that it could also not have been done or something else could have been done in its stead.[68] That which is thus demands a reason

66. Leibniz, *Theodicy*, §9:128–29.

67. Leibniz, *Theodicy*, §8–10:128–29.

68. Leibniz, *Principles of Nature and of Grace*, §7:639.

why it is and not rather is not and why it is the way it is and not rather otherwise only if it is a *factum* in Leibniz's sense, and not a fact or "brute fact" in the now-common sense of "something which one just has to accept as being the case, and of which no explanation can be given."[69] If the world is everything that is the case, there is no reason to ask for reasons. This changes only if everything that is the case is a deed done, that is, the result of a willing and doing that under identical conditions could also have willed and done something different. This presupposes that the distinction between events determined by causes and actions guided by reasons is made in such a way that events, too, are to be understood as actions. And because that does not make sense as long as we know humans only as beings of action, the abolition of the difference between actions and events presupposes the theological thesis that everything that is is either *with* God or *through* God, in other words, that it is either an eternal truth or that it is a reality willed and actualized by God, or a reality willed and actualized by a reality willed by God.

Only within this theological horizon does the real point of Leibniz's basic metaphysical question reveal itself. In a world in which everything is with God or through God, the questions, *Why is there something at all rather than nothing?* and *Why is what is such as it is, and not something else in its place?* are easily answered by referring to God's wisdom, goodness, and omnipotence. By contrast, it seems hard, even impossible to answer the questions, *Why are there ills at all rather than there being no evils?* and *Why is what is ill, and not rather something else in the place of the ill?* It is not the first but the second set of question that represent the real challenge for Leibniz's thought. And that is why the problem of theodicy is not a sideline of Leibniz's philosophical efforts but their very core.[70]

12. Reason Dealing with the Irrational

It cannot seriously be contested that there are ills. But must they be? Or could they also not be? If, however, they could also not be, would not the world be better without them? And if it were better, why did God create not it but our factual world?

These are some of the questions Leibniz finds himself confronting. But they are thus put in terms much too vague to be answered. The first step in the attempt to confront these questions with reason must therefore consist in rendering them precise as problems, that is, in defining in more detail the conditions under which what questions pose themselves as what problems and in what way. The second step is to spell out the method with whose help we may hope to solve these problems. The third step is to treat the problems along the lines thus indicated and to attempt to find a solution.

To render the problem more precise, Leibniz proffers a series of conditions on which he turns to the questions raised by the ills in the world. The first is to suppose the *reality of these ills*: a world without the ills that factually exist within it would not be the world we are dealing with. The second is to suppose that *this world is created*: the world in which we live is God's creation. The third is to suppose the *concept of God* as the

---

69. Parkinson, "Philosophy and Logic," 216.

70. It is not a coincidence that the *Theodicy* was the only book Leibniz published himself.

absolutely perfect being: God is the only, perfectly wise, good, and powerful origin and the first reason of all things.[71] It follows, however, that everything he knows, wills, and does, he knows, wills, and does in the most perfect way, for "[t]o act with less perfection than one is capable of is to act imperfectly."[72] This yields, as the fourth condition, the *unsurpassable quality of this world* as that which God could not have made better: although other worlds are imaginable and possible, they would not be better than the present one, which is evident *ab effectu* precisely from God's having created the present world and no other.[73]

In light of these conditions, it becomes possible to articulate the problem Leibniz is seeking to solve in more precise terms. His concern is *not* with proving the probability or improbability of God's existence or goodness or omnipotence or wisdom on the basis of the reality of this world: he presupposes that God exists and that he is the absolutely perfect being.[74] His concern also is *not* with glossing over the reality of ills in this world or playing it down: that ills really exist is the impulse and starting point of the entire

71. See Leibniz, *Theodicy*, §7:127–28, and *Discourse on Metaphysics*, §1:303.

72. Leibniz, *Discourse on Metaphysics*, §3:304.

73. See Leibniz, *Discourse on Metaphysics*, §3:304–5, and *Theodicy*, §10:129.

74. He proves it another way, namely *a priori* from the noncontradiction of his concept and *a posteriori* from the existence of contingent beings. "God alone, or the necessary being, has the privilege of necessarily existing if he is possible" (Leibniz, *Theodicy*, §45:647). This follows from his being *the only God* (§39:646). For if everything that is possible strives to exist and does not exist only if prevented from existing by something else, then there is a possible that is necessarily actual or existent and "ha[s] nothing outside of it which is independent of it" (§40:646) and could prevent it in its striving for existence. And since "nothing can prevent the possibility of that which is without any limits, without any negation, and consequently without any contradiction, this fact alone suffices to know the existence of God *a priori*" (§45:647). The necessity of God must thus not be confused with the necessity of *verités éternelles* that belong to God's understanding (§43:647). God is not necessary the way a mathematical truth is. A mathematical truth is necessary because its opposite constitutes a self-contradiction. God is necessary because if God did not exist, there would be nothing that could or could not be in contradiction. Even the eternal truths and possibilities "are" necessary or possible only because they are "founded on something existent and actual" (§44:647, cf. §43:647). They "are" not in themselves and as such but are "dependent upon God" (§46:647) or, more precisely, dependent on God's understanding, the way contingent truths are dependent on God's will. That is why we must understand Leibniz as Hartshorne has suggested: *p is necessary* means *p is known by God as necessary*; *p is possible* means *p is known by God as possible*; and *p is contingent* means *p is known by God as possible and willed as actual*. The necessity of God, however, cannot be understood along these lines. God is not because he is the object of his knowledge; rather, because he is, he is an object of his knowledge. God is not one of the "necessary truths" (§46:647) but the "necessary being" (§45:647), that is, not a necessary truth but a *necessary reality*, namely the *only* necessary reality (§39:646), the "actual" being (§44:647). Leibniz's argument that God must exist if he is possible is thus entirely correct in inferring "the *existence* of God" (§45:647, my emphasis), that is, a *reality*, not a necessity: God is the *singular limit case of the actual* that is *neither something contingent* (a truth of fact) *nor something necessary* (a truth of reason). He is the limit case of that possible that is *actual* without being chosen by God's will because God's will, like God's knowledge, presupposes the reality of God. And he is the limit case of that necessary that is necessary precisely *as this singular actual* insofar as "without him there would be no reality in possibilities—not only nothing existent but also nothing possible" (§43:647). God, we might put it, is the only possible of which it is true that there is no possible world in which it would not be true that God is actual. In other words: it is impossible that something is actual, possible, or necessary and God is not actual. Whatever is actual, possible, or necessary implies God's reality. And that is why for Leibniz, the only convincing answer to the basic metaphysical question, *Why is there something at all and not rather nothing?* is: because God is.

intellectual effort. *Nor* is he concerned with contesting that a world without suffering and ill would be possible and could have existed: it can very well be thought, but it would not be *this* world, and it would *not* be a *better* world.[75] What he is concerned with, very precisely, is proving that there is no irrational contradiction, which would paralyze reason, between the following convictions held to be true:

1. God is the absolutely perfect being.

2. The present world is his creation and thereby, such as it is, is that beyond which something better could not have been created.

3. There are ills in the world.

The problem Leibniz confronts is thus to *prove the compossibility or compatibility* of these three (complex) convictions. For if it is possible to show that they can be reconciled without contradiction, it may not get rid of the irrationality of ill, since ill continues to intrude irrationally in life and disrupts or destroys the nexus of life, but reason can at least gain insight into the relationship between ill and creation as a whole and God—reason does not simply have to capitulate. And for this to succeed, the following questions have to be settled: What are ills and where do they come from (with reference to (3) above)? In what respect is the present world the optimum of creation despite and given these ills (with reference to (2))? And given this world and its ills, in what respect is the creator really perfect such that, "although, generally speaking, he could have avoided all these evils," the reality of ill in creation does not derogate "his holiness and supreme goodness" (with reference to (1))?[76]

This specification of the problem and the task also specifies the *method* with which Leibniz seeks to solve the task. It is the same method he developed for dealing with randomness. Just as reason cannot rationally comprehend (determine or predict) the individual roll of the dice but must take into account as great as possible a number of rolls to search out the regular rationality of chance, so, to search out the rationality of the irrational, it must not fixate on the individual ill but must, in keeping with the law of large numbers, take ills into account within the horizon of the world as a whole, namely the world understood as the optimal creation of the perfect God. If reason does not want to fail, it must not concentrate on *individual ills* and try to find their meaning but must, rather, turn to the *relationship* of the ills to creation and to God. A rationality of the irrational can be found out not by looking at the individual case but only by looking at large numbers in the entirety of creation such that the search for it must take the shape of determining the limit of the optimal relationship between ill and good in creation. Yet since ills, unlike rolls of the dice, are not homogenous nor all of one and the same kind, we must first obtain a precise and differentiated notion of what "ill" means if a differentiated view of the phenomena is to be possible. For in not just describing individual ills and distinguishing possible ills but conceptualizing factual kinds of ills, reason lays the foundations for stripping the offensive contingency of ill of its strict irrationality.

75. See Leibniz, *Theodicy*, §9:128.
76. Leibniz, *Theodicy*, 61.

13. Kinds of Ill

In §21 of his *Essais de Théodicée*, Leibniz differentiates the basic concept of ill (*le mal*) into three kinds of ill, namely *le mal métaphysique*, *le mal physique*, and *le mal moral*:

> Evil may be taken metaphysically, physically and morally. *Metaphysical evil* consists in mere imperfection, *physical evil* in suffering, and *moral evil* in sin. Now although physical evil and moral evil be not necessary, it is enough that by virtue of the eternal verities they be possible. And as this vast Region of Verities contains all possibilities it is necessary that there be an infinitude of possible worlds, that evil enter into divers of them, and that even the best of all contain a measure thereof. Thus has God been induced to permit evil.[77]

The first thing to be highlighted here is the distinction between ills that are necessary and ills that are not. Ills are *necessary* if there is no possible world in which they do not exist; by contrast, they are *not necessary* (that is, not only are they not necessarily not, that is, *possible*, but they are not impossibly not, that is, *contingent*); if on the one hand there is no world in which they would have to exist and on the other there is at least one world in which they do exist: these ills can be but they do not have to be, and that they can be is shown by there being a world in which they are actual. Or, as Leibniz specifies: that ills are not necessary only means that there is no specific world in which they would have to exist, but it does not mean that they could not exist in any world or that they would not exist in at least one world. On the contrary, since they are not impossible but are possible "by virtue of the eternal verities," it is necessary that in the "infinitude of possible worlds" there be some in which they would exist if these were actual. It is true of no possible world that in it these contingent ills are necessary, but it is true of the totality of possible worlds that there necessarily are some in which they would be actual if these worlds existed. In this regard, these ills are not necessary; yet because they are neither impossible nor merely possible but precisely are only possibly not, it is necessary that there be some possible worlds in which they would exist if these worlds were actual.

Leibniz, however, does not stop even there: these non-necessary ills are not only unavoidable in some possible worlds, but even "the best of all" must contain some of them—not the best of all worlds but the best of all possible worlds. For not all possibilities are compossible, such that not everything possible in a world can be actual at the same time, and because not everything possible that is good is compossible, not everything possible that is good in a world can be actual at the same time. Every good world must therefore include a selection of compossible goods and thereby also contain a selection of unavoidable ills, and the best possible world is the one that combines a maximum of compossible goods with a minimum of unavoidable ills. Not the best, only the best possible world can therefore be actual, but it also must be actual if God really is its creator.[78] For the creator would not be God if he created something lesser than the

---

77. Leibniz, *Theodicy*, §21:136.

78. On the origin of the concept of the best possible world, see Knebel, "Necessitas moralis ad optimum," and Ramelow, *Gott, Freiheit, Weltenwahl*.

optimum that—given unavoidable ills—is possible.[79] And the optimum is the world with the most compossible goods and the least compossible ills.

14. Ill's Function in the World

The judgment about the created world in Leibniz is not, as in the story of Genesis, "very good" but "the best of all possible ones given the unavoidability of ills." Belonging to these unavoidable ills there are both those that are necessary, i.e., that cannot be missing in any possible world, and those that are not necessary, i.e., that taken by themselves may be missing but that cannot be missing in the best possible world because a world without them would not be better and thereby not be the best possible world. *Metaphysical ill*, which "consists in mere imperfection," that is, in nothing but creatures being creatures and not the creator, is necessary and unavoidable. Just as the creator is the absolutely perfect being, so the creature is an imperfect being as a matter of principle: "God could not give the creature all without making of it a God." And just as the absolute perfection of the creator is founded on God being that possible being that is the only one not to have beside and outside it anything independent of it that could hinder its urge to exist, such that his existence is "a simple consequence of possible being," that is, actual simply because it is possible, the fundamental imperfection of creatures consists in their being possible but many and therefore only ever one possible among others such that it takes an external decision for the one possible and not another possible to become actual, a decision whose result can only ever be a contingent actual whose place could have been taken by another. Just as God must essentially "be incapable of limits," so inversely "the creature is limited in its essence." God is *the actual* whereas the creature is always only *an actual*. This difference is not one of degree but of principle. It is not a more or less of perfection as we find it among creatures, it is the absolute difference between *essential perfection* and *essential imperfection*.[80] God is essentially *perfect* because he is actual already by being possible and therefore represents *the actual* that is due to no other actual while all other actuals are due to him. Creatures by contrast are essentially *imperfect* because by being possible they are by no means also actual; their actuality is due to a decision which of them are to be actual and which are to be not actual, such that every creature is *a contingent actual* in whose place another one could have been but is not actual due to the decision of the divine will. The imperfection of creatures and thus the *metaphysical ill*, however, is for them not so much a lack or a deficit than it is, on the contrary, *an infinite gain*: the gain of existing at all and not rather not being, namely *existing as a contingent being*.

The same cannot simply be said for non-necessary ills. They may indeed be missing, but not in the best possible world because a world without them would not be better but less good. *Malum*, and precisely the non-necessary *malum physicum* and *malum morale*, is thereby *functionalized*, and in a twofold manner: on the one hand, it constitutively

---

79. Leibniz, *Theodicy*, §8:128.

80. Leibniz, *Monadology*, §9:128–29, §21:136, §40:646 and §45:647, §40:646 and §20:135, and §50:648.

belongs to the *identity* or "numerical individuality" of the world because "if the smallest evil that comes to pass in the world were missing in it, it would no longer be this world." This world, however, is the one that has been created and that has therefore been considered the best by the creator: "if there were not the best (*optimum*) among all possible worlds, God would not have produced any." That there is something at all and not rather nothing thus proves that what exists is the optimum. Then, however, on the other hand, both the necessary and the contingent ills of this world must contribute to the goodness of the whole reaching the optimum, that is, they must be included teleologically in the optimum of creation, be it because without them, the world would not be a creation and thus not be at all (as in the case of necessary ills), be it (as is true with regard to contingent ills) because every other possible world would include even more ills or because the actual world would possess fewer goods without these ills. For it is the case, as Leibniz stresses in taking up relevant traditional arguments which he explains with examples, "that often an evil brings forth a good whereto one would not have attained without that evil." Nor is it possible to complain "that evils are great and many in number in comparison with the good," since that is an erroneous view due to insufficient attention being paid to the great number of goods. In order to see that "it may be that all evils are almost nothingness in comparison with the good things which are in the universe," it suffices to realize that "the proportion of that part of the universe which we know is almost lost in nothingness compared with that which is unknown." Good and ill cannot be played off each other quantitatively. On the contrary, the more ill there is, the more good there must be, since good and ill correlatively refer to each other: "For as a lesser evil is a kind of good, even so a lesser good is a kind of evil if it stands in the way of a greater good."[81] That, however, means that God, who because of his perfection, creates only the best that can be created, would have created nothing or at least not this world if ill were preponderant or if ills and goods were fully balanced. It is therefore possible to infer from the mere fact that the world exists that despite all indisputable ill the good must be preponderant, that therefore it is better that this world exists than that another world existed in its place or that there were no world at all.[82] Ill thus belongs to

81. Leibniz, *Theodicy*, §9:128–29, §8:128, §10:129, §13:130, §19:135, and §8:128.

82. The notion that there could be no world at all makes sense only on the theological condition that the world is God's free creation, i.e., that it is only because God *wills* it and does not rather not will it, and that God did not have to will and create it, i.e., that he could also have been without creation. And this in turn is not to be understood as an attempt to undermine the existential certainty of creation but on the contrary to reassure creation about God's care for, love for, and interest in it: that it is although it could also not have been shows that God willed it. It is precisely the discovery of and emphasis on its *contingency* that assures creation of its being willed by God and its proximity to God: God could have been without world whereas the world could not be without God, and that is why the fact of the world is proof and confirmation of God's interest in the world—not in the sense of an experiential basis for hypothetically inferring God's existence from the world but in the sense of theologically interpreting the world as creation. From the theological perspective, that is, on the supposition of God, the mere existence of the world is reason to praise and thank God, yet this perspective on the world can be assumed only by those who see themselves as God's creatures: that the world is *creation* can be derived from its *contingency* only if this contingency is interpreted, as it is by Leibniz, as a fact, namely as a *factum dei*. Yet to interpret it this way means that the one interpreting understands himself to be God's creature: without understanding oneself as God's creature, the world cannot be understood as God's creation, either. It is clear to Leibniz that his interpretation of contingency *is tied to* a theological stance, but that is not a problem for

the *existence*, the *identity*, and the *optimum* of this world as God's creation, and to each of these it contributes in different ways.

15. No Creation without Ill

Leaving aside the specific theological framework of Leibniz's theodicy argument, his basic notion of functionally including ill in the world to enhance its goodness to the optimum of the good and the minimum of the bad can be spelled out in a variety of ways. The logical-ontological version of his monadology then is only one of its possible forms. When we think the functional integration of the *malum* into the whole of as much good as possible and as little bad as possible not only *logically*, as compossibility, and *mathematically*, as the integral of the two limit movements of maximizing the good and minimizing the ill in the optimum of the best possible, but *temporally* as the *connectability of the new* (new actions and new knowledge) with what is already there (present knowledge and completed actions) for the sake of optimizing the state of the world by diminishing ill and increasing good, then the whole is no longer understood as cosmos or universe but as *world history*. Leibniz's basic notion thus leads to modernity's *philosophy of history* where, as in Hegel, *malum* as the negative becomes the driving force of progress toward the better or, as in Hegel's antipode, Schopenhauer, the *bonum*, said to be nothing but a *privatio mali*, precisely blocks true progress because it presents us with the illusion of not living in the worst possible of all worlds. Either way, it seems to lead to what Odo Marquard has called the great "uneviling of evil,"[83] be it because evil becomes the engine of the better (Hegel) or be it because it is being turned into the truth of the actual (Schopenhauer). For whether the bad is understood as something good that is missing and therefore as driving the striving for the better or, inversely, one subscribes to the idea that "[t]he good, and this one ought to know, is always the evil one lets go"[84]—in either case, evil or ill is deprived of its fundamental offensiveness by being functionally referred not only to something good but to an optimal whole of good and ill.

This can be said of Leibniz only with a number of reservations, even if that has become difficult since Voltaire's caricature of his position.[85] But with his distinction between *malum metaphysicum, physicum*, and *morale*, he suggests, precisely, that every wholesale discussion of *malum* as positive or negative driving force in the universe is incorrect: if we seek to solve the riddle of the reality of evil and give a meaningful answer to the question whether and how ills can or cannot be avoided, we must differentiate ills.

him. This characterizes his conception as a modern intellectual project, albeit one of pre-modernity. Yet that, precisely, allows it to become interesting once more in post-modernity if we take its being tied to the stance and horizon of a specific theological perspective seriously, that is, if we do not dismiss it as a metaphysical conception of the world whose combination of a descriptive and a normative view of the world is no longer possible for us today (see Janssen, *Gott—Freiheit—Leid*, 39) and instead understand it as elaborating a theological-philosophical stance exemplary in the rigor of its argumentation precisely and especially under conditions in which a metaphysics without positions is unavailable.

83. Marquard, "*Malum*," 655.

84. Wilhelm Busch, *Die fromme Helene*, quoted in Marquard, *In Defense of the Accidental*, 29.

85. Janssen, *Gott—Freiheit—Leid*, 40–50, correctly brings out just how little the Popean equation, in the discussion after Leibniz, "Whatever is, is right," has to do with Leibniz's creation-theological philosophy of contingency.

His answer is that metaphysical ill is unavoidable because it is founded on the essential imperfection of creation and that this imperfection, precisely, is the unavoidable reason for all physical and moral evils. The latter may be avoidable in each concrete case, but they cannot be avoided completely: if we want creation, we cannot exclude the existence of ills.

16. No Justification of Ill

It would therefore be a complete misunderstanding to confuse this functional inclusion of ills in the identity and the optimum of creation with an attempt at justifying ills as necessary. On the contrary, with regard to necessary ill, Leibniz is concerned with showing that one cannot live in a created world without being affected by it, because as "mere imperfection," it marks the difference between the created and the creator and is nothing but that which distinguishes the non-perfect creature from the perfect creator: that it *exists contingently*. And with regard to non-necessary ills, he seeks to take *the contingency of ill* seriously, that is, to conceive of ill as actual, though not as necessary but precisely as not necessary. *Deus necessario eligeret optimum, non ideo tamen optimum foret necessarium*: that God necessarily chooses the best—"it is necessary for God to choose the best"—does not mean that the best thereby is necessary—"it does not follow that what is chosen is necessary"—but rather that it is freely chosen by God, that it is *contingent*.[86] What follows from Leibniz's argument is not "the best is necessary," but "it is necessary that the best exist." And accordingly, the ills of this contingent world are not necessary, but it is necessary that the best of this world also include ills. For *necessary* is all that, and only that, which is contained in the eternal truths of divine reason; *actual* but not contingent is God alone; *contingent*, in turn, all that, and only that, which is due to the good will of God who wills that it be even if something else could have been in its place. The ills that exist in the world are facts, not eternal truths. There must therefore be reasons for them, yet these are not necessary but sufficient reasons that explain why these ills exist and not rather something else in their place. These reasons, however, can be found only in a will, and while for some ills, this is the will and willing of human beings (moral ills), this cannot be true of all contingent ills (physical ills). The reason for the reality of at least some ills and the reason for the possibility of all ills, it seems, must therefore be sought in God's will, for as his "understanding is the source of *essences*," so his "will is the origin of *existences*."[87] What Leibniz's argument renders problematic is thus not the contingency of *evils*, but God's will and thus the conception of God that guides his reflections.

17. The Justifications of God in the Face of Ill

Leibniz was well aware that it was indeed the *conception of God* that was at issue. He even says, explicitly, that his intention "is to banish from men the false ideas that represent

---

86. Leibniz, "On Contingency," 30.
87. Leibniz, *Theodicy*, §7:127–28.

God to them as an absolute prince employing a despotic power, unfitted to be loved and unworthy of being loved."[88] He sees such a false image of God both among Spinozists and among Cartesians, among those who regard everything that is actual as a necessary consequence of God's nature and thereby negate all freedom and among those who regard everything that is actual as arbitrarily posited and thereby confuse freedom with arbitrariness. The one who forces everything under his power and uses this power in pure arbitrariness does not deserve being called God. Leibniz—clearly echoing the "We must fear and love God" of Luther's catechism—gives a theological justification: "the essence of piety is not only to fear him but also to love him above all things."[89] Hence, it is possible to specify his problem: Given the reality of ills, how can we think God such that we can not only fear but love him?

Leibniz can take up the traditional answer of the Platonic tradition—we simply have to hold God responsible only and exclusively for all that is good and hold everything but God responsible for ill[90]—only with reservations. It does not touch on the essence and origin of ill and is difficult to reconcile with the Christian conception of creation and of God. If the world is entirely and exclusively God's creation because nothing would be if God were not, the question of the relationship between God and ill cannot be answered simply by pointing to the mere opposition: even if God, as the creator of everything, is not himself responsible for the ills, he nonetheless seems to be responsible for those who cause them. For either he is himself the author of ill or someone else is, and since no one who is not can be the author of ill, and there is no one whose author is not God, it seems that either way, God cannot be dismissed from the question of the authorship of the ill in the world.[91] If God really is the only and perfect creator of this world, then to avoid reason contradicting itself, it must be possible to argue with reasons both that "evil has a source other than the will of God" and "that it has been possible for God to permit sin and misery, and even to co-operate therein and promote it, without detriment to his holiness and his supreme goodness."[92] And this means: *God can be loved only if it is possible to understand that and how the origin of evil is not God's will and yet that God cooperates and participates in the sin, the misery, the ill of this world without ceasing to be God.*

18. Ill as Privation

Leibniz justifies this thesis with a new kind of answer to the old question, *Si Deus est, unde malum? Si non est, unde bonum?* In keeping with the tradition, he holds that without God, there would be no good and that "God is the cause of perfection" in creation. Yet against the Cartesians' view, he holds that what is good is not good because God wills it, but inversely God wills what is good because his will is not arbitrariness but lets itself be determined by what he knows to be good: the good is founded not in God's will but in

88. Leibniz, *Theodicy*, §6:127.

89. Leibniz, *Theodicy*, §6:127.

90. Plato, *Republic* II, 379c:224; see also X, 617d:494.

91. Lactantius already was well aware of this point and insisted on it (Lactantius, *On the Wrath of God*).

92. Leibniz, *Theodicy*, 61.

his knowledge, for God does not create blindly, his willing is oriented by "the primitive form of good" in his understanding.[93] God wills what is good as he knows it, and nothing else, and he does what he wills and nothing else. That is why God wills only the good, and he does only the good.

Yet that is precisely why the question *unde malum?* becomes more acute. In keeping with the Augustinian tradition, Leibniz answers *negatively* that "God is not the cause of evil."[94] His *positive* answer, however, significantly differs from the traditional theological view according to which *malum* is fundamentally *malefactum* and *peccatum*, creatures' willing and committing of ill in violation of divine commandments and therefore self-incurred guilt (*culpa*) or a punishment (*poena*) God has imposed in consequence. Creatures here are seen as malicious authors of all ill, the creator as arbitrary legislator and punishing judge. This is precisely the false image of God Leibniz wants to liberate us from because it represents God as an absolute and despotic ruler, "unfitted to be loved and unworthy of being loved."[95] All it sees in God—the Lutheran background is impossible to ignore—is a God of the Law who must be feared, not a God of the Gospels who can be loved.

Leibniz's justification for the partial negative answer that God is not the cause of ill is not just founded on the conception of God as the absolutely perfect being who wills and does only what is good but also on a conception of ill that sees ill strictly as *privation*. God cannot be the author of ill because "the privative nature of evil" makes that impossible. Ill is not a negative good but the absence or lack of good; it exists not independently but only parasitically on something else. It is a defect of creation but not an effect of the creator. If, as Leibniz does in keeping with the Christian tradition, "we . . . derive all being from God," this defect cannot be blamed on matter, as the Neoplatonists would have it. Rather, in keeping with the Augustinian scholastic tradition, we must say that "God is the cause of the material element of evil which lies in the positive, and not of the formal element, which lies in privation." God is always the cause of what is positive and perfect in creation; the defects of creation by contrast arise because of "the limitation of the receptivity of the creature." Ill is nothing that is effected but, as privation, consists precisely in the inverse, "in that which the efficient cause does not bring about."[96] The creator wills and effects the good, but because creation is as it is, ills, too, always arise in the process. Ill is the unavoidable shadow of the contingency of creation.

Not what God wills and does is thus the origin of ill (as Leibniz says in keeping with the tradition), but neither is it what the creatures will and do (as he argues against the tradition); rather it is something that lies beyond divine and creaturely willing and doing: "the source of evil . . . must be sought in the ideal nature of the creature, insofar as this nature is contained in the eternal verities which are in the understanding of God, independently of his will."[97] The *causa mali* is not a willing of ill by God, nor is it, later,

---

93. Leibniz, *Theodicy*, §20:135, §30:141, §20:136.

94. Leibniz, *Discourse on Metaphysics*, §30:322.

95. Leibniz, *Theodicy*, §:6:127.

96. Leibniz, *Theodicy*, 61, §20:135, §30:141, §20:136.

97. Leibniz, *Theodicy*, §20:135. See Geyer, "Theodizee oder Kulturgeschichte des Bösen?," 244–45, 247. Geyer sees in this a fundamental limitation of God's omnipotence, which, according to him, defines

the willing and doing of evil by creatures: "even before," before they sinned and lost their innocence, "there was an original limitation or imperfection connatural to all creatures, which makes them capable of sin or failure."[98] The reason for all ill is the "*original imperfection in the creature* before sin, because the creature is limited in its essence."[99] The reason of all ill lies in *being a creature*: the privation of ill is the limitation of the creature.[100]

19. Supra-Responsible Evil

This answer aggravates the problem. For how, then, can the creator be acquitted of responsibility for the ill his creatures do and suffer? If all physical and moral ill is possible only because of metaphysical ill, which in turn is not a *malefactum* on the part of the creature but the precondition of all its *male velle* et *bene nolle*, its willing of what is not good and not willing of what is good, and which can therefore be characterized neither as *culpa* nor as *poena*, then God, it seems, must take responsibility at least for this fundamental *malum metaphysicum*. Does exonerating the creature not come at the price of incriminating the creator?

Leibniz says no. Responsibility exists only for what one wills and does although one could also not have willed it or done something else. Yet this, precisely, cannot be said about God with regard to ills in general and metaphysical ill in particular. Yes, God has freely decided to create a world different from himself. But he thereby also decided in favor of something good, not of something ill. That creation exists is good; that it cannot exist without ills is the price to be paid for the existence of creation: ill precisely is *not* the price of freedom but the price for the existence of creation. God must accept the possibility of ill and cannot prevent its actuality, not because he wills *free creatures*, as modern theism, in the footsteps of Augustine, argues time and again in the free will defense; it is *because he wills the creation* that *God cannot avoid ill* and create an entirely good but can create only the *best possible* world: "Thence it follows that God wills *antecedently* the good and *consequently* the best."[101] In what regard?

Because willing a creation means willing something imperfect, because God wills something other than himself, he cannot avoid ill. He can will a creation only if he accepts its imperfection and thereby accepts metaphysical ill. This is not a lack worthy or capable of correction, it comes with the concept of creation: creation—and this is true *of every conceivable and possible creation*—is *imperfect as a matter of principle*, for if it were not imperfect, it would be indistinguishable from God and thus not a creation.

God "more in analogy with Plato's 'helpless' demiurge" than as the free creator-God of the Jewish-Christian tradition. Yet the reference to God's being tied to the ideas that exist in his divine understanding independently of his will is not proof of God's dependence on anything but himself; on the contrary, it is an analytical statement about what characterizes God's creative understanding: he is what he brings forth such that the "ideas" are nothing but the shape the implementation of his divine understanding takes.

98. Leibniz, *Discourse on Metaphysics*, §30, 322.

99. Leibniz, *Theodicy*, §20:135.

100. See Heinekamp, *Das Problem des Guten bei Leibniz*, 148–56.

101. Leibniz, *Theodicy*, §23:137.

That there is a world (and not rather none) and that there is *this* world (and not another one in its place) are contingent states of affairs concerning which we not only can but must ask about God's responsibility. That is not the case when it comes to the world as creation being different from God, that is, *imperfect*, and to its essential imperfection becoming concrete in the imperfections we describe as physical and moral ills. In both regards, therefore, *that* the world is and that it is *so*, Leibniz vehemently rejects the view that God "could have acted much better." Proponents of this view do not know what they are saying when they talk about creator and creation.

But how are we to speak of creator and creation? By realizing that there need not be a creation: the world, understood as God's creation, is *contingent* because, although God could have been without the world, the world could not have been without God. If we leave God aside, the proposition becomes meaningless: that there are contingent states of affairs *in* the world is one thing, that *the world* is a contingent state of affairs is another. If contingency is to be ascribed to what would not have existed had something else existed, then this can be said at most about states of affairs "within the world," but not "for the world as a whole," as has been critically noted not just by John L. Mackie. Yet Leibniz does not infer "the contingency of the whole from the contingency of every part."[102] He does not infer from contingency *in* the world the contingency *of* the world, and God from there; he precisely argues inversely from God as creator to the contingency of the world as creation. For if *contingent* is the name of something that is in the place of which something else could have been as well, then the world can be called contingent only if another world could have been in its place. This requires seeing the world as one of various possible worlds from which the creator chooses and actualizes the one that best corresponds to his willing the good. These possible worlds, however, do not exist as options floating freely in nothingness, they exist *in God himself*, more precisely: *in God's infinite understanding*. God is necessary not because there is a contingent world but there is a contingent world only because God is perfect and hence the only being to be actual simply because of its being possible. If we leave the creation-theological horizon of Leibniz's entire argumentation aside, we miss the point.

Within this horizon, however, it is true that nothing that is is without God: where there is something, there is God, and if God did not exist, it would have no existence. When God is being thematized under this aspect as the reason of the being and existence of what is different from him, he comes into view as *power*: God is omnipotence because everything that is is only because God is. That, however, must be defined in more detail. To be sure, there is something different from God in the first place only because God wills it, and because he could also not have willed it, it is contingent. But when it comes to what is contingently created, we must distinguish with more precision between what could not have been different and what could have been different. Thus the *eternal truths* are not made by God but absolutely necessary, that is, they are such that God, too, cannot do anything contradicting them "without being led into absurdities"—not because he would thereby be subjected to an alien norm external to him but because the divine will cannot act in contradiction with the divine understanding without putting God at odds with himself. The *positive truths* of the rules and laws valid in this world, by

102. Mackie, *Miracle of Theism*, 84–87.

contrast, are posited by God as those that within the frame of the eternal truths allow for the best possible organization of the world. They go back to God's will, not to God's understanding, and for that very reason they are based not on blind arbitrariness but on a targeted willing: "God gave such laws not without reason, for he chooses nothing from caprice and as though by chance or in pure indifference."[103] God's *power* does not act blindly but actualizes his *will*, which in turn is oriented by his *understanding*. God's understanding, however, is the realm of eternal truths, that is, the perfect knowledge of everything that is possible. This includes the knowledge that not everything that is possible is possible together. Hence, God knows that more than one world of compossible possibilities would be possible of which, if any at all, only one can be actual. He must therefore select one; he selects the one that best corresponds to his will to do what is good; and this best of all possible worlds is the one he actualizes. God's creation is thus not an exercise in shaping a given matter. Rather, "the *Region of the Eternal Verities* must be substituted for matter." And there, precisely, we must look for the origin of ill as well: the realm of eternal truths "is the *ideal cause* of evil (as it were) as well as of good."[104] Because not everything that is possible is compossible, and because only one world of compossible possibilities can be actual, God can create only an *imperfect world*, and as *perfect God*, he will create the optimal imperfect world containing a maximum of perfections and a minimum of imperfections. Because God is *creator*, he creates the *imperfect* world and because God is *perfect*, he creates the *best possible* imperfect world.

The origin of evil is thus *not* to be sought in God's will but in the limitations that inevitably arise when not everything is possible at the same time and when not everything possible at the same time can be actual together. God wills only the good and chooses only the best possible. That is not a restriction of his perfection but the way in which he as creator deploys his perfection. God holds on to every point of his perfection, to his perfect power, wisdom, and goodness.[105] If there is a creation, then it is good that it exists because it would not exist if God did not will it and God only wills the good. Yet if God as creator wills a world different from him, then he wills it because it is good that there be not just the perfect but the imperfect as well: that is the fundamental, creation-theological premise of Leibniz's entire argument. If there is cause to speak of "optimism" at all, then this is the place to do so: it is good that this world exists because it would not exist if that were not good. That there is anything at all besides God already speaks for his goodness, but so does that which exists and so does the way God relates to what exists. Thus God, because he is good, wills not just any but the best possible of the imperfect worlds, that is, the one with the maximum of perfection and the minimum of imperfection. And because he knows that imperfection is unavoidable in all cases because it consists "in the privation or limitation of creatures," he comes to the aid of his creatures in their unavoidable metaphysical imperfection and the physical imperfection that results from it by means of "that degree of perfection which it pleases him to give."[106]

103. Leibniz, *Theodicy*, §2:74.
104. Leibniz, *Theodicy*, §20:136; my emphases.
105. Leibniz, *Theodicy*, §7:127–28.
106. Leibniz, *Discourse on Metaphysics*, §30, 323.

Leibniz thereby stresses God's goodness in three respects: God is good because he wills and creates a world at all. He is good because he creates the best possible world. And he is good because he comes to the aid of his necessarily imperfect creatures by compensating for their imperfections in an act of free grace: as *will*, he seeks to compensate for what as *understanding* he cannot avoid: his creatures' imperfection. Thus it is especially with regard to the actuality of ill that God comes into view not as a despot and judge who can only be feared but in every respect as the one *to be loved*: loved for the fact *that* he has created a world, for creating *this* world, and for *coming to the aid* of his creatures in this world. God the creator is not a punishing but a helping God, and his goodness does not consist in being good by himself, letting ill be ill, but in making what is not good as good as possible, in reaching out with his grace to what cannot be better but is not good, and in his grace correcting what could be better than his creatures are making it.

20. Kant's Criticism

All this, of course, does not mean that Leibniz's proposed solution is without problems or convincing in every respect. Yet the most pertinent objections to Leibniz are not, as is generally supposed, the ones Kant puts forth in his essay, "On the Miscarriage of All Philosophical Trials in Theodicy," which miss the point of Leibniz's argument on a number of decisive points.[107] Leibniz stresses not only that metaphysical ill is unavoidable because it is founded on the essential imperfection of creation and that this, precisely, is the unavoidable reason for all physical and moral ill; not only, too, that God out of moral necessity and according to the determination of his will in keeping with his wisdom and goodness is forced according to the rule of the optimum to permit creatures' moral ill; but also that God the creator in his essential perfection comes to the aid of his essentially imperfect creatures by compensating in free grace for what they cannot avoid. For while physical and moral evil can be avoided in every concrete case, albeit not as a matter of principle, and can accordingly (in the case of moral ill) be imputed to the perpetrator as guilt, this is not the case for metaphysical ill: it is to be imputed as guilt neither to the creature nor to the creator. That moral ill is possible only on the basis of metaphysical ill, that is, on the basis of creatures' essential imperfection, does not mean, as Kant thinks it does, that it is not to be understood as evil but as an "ill" that "must inevitably be sought in the essence of things, specifically in the necessary limitations of humanity as a finite nature; hence the latter can also not be held responsible for it," for the explanation of its possibility does not amount to a justification of its actuality.[108] Nor does it follow that a God "who would be forced to permit evil and ills in his creation" could "not seriously be venerated as holy, benevolent, and just God" because he would then be a "God impaired in his creative freedom," that is, no God at all.[109] For Leibniz, the reason for the love and worship of God lies precisely in the creator *willing* a creation *at all* and, given the

107. Kant, "Miscarriage."
108. Kant, "Miscarriage," 27 (AA 8:259).
109. Janssen, *Gott—Freiheit—Leid*, 51.

unavoidable imperfection of creation, in moreover *coming to the aid* of his creatures to compensate for their imperfections in free grace. God is holy, benevolent, and just precisely in gracefully helping where ill cannot be avoided—an aspect that is decisive for Leibniz but that Kant's reflections do not consider. Leibniz rigorously knows God not only as creator but also as helper and savior, and from the outset, in a properly theological way, he understands God's being a creator as an expression not only of his power but also of his wisdom and goodness.

The real problems of Leibniz's argumentation are to be sought out elsewhere. I will highlight three of them.

21. The Distinction between *malum physicum* and *malum morale*

The distinction has a long tradition, but Leibniz clearly takes it up via its articulation in Cartesian philosophy as between the ill that affects us in the world of *res extensa* (*malum physicum*) and the evil that the *res cogitans sive actans* itself produces (*malum morale*). Yet it only makes sense to call something taking place in the world of extension a *malum* if we do not lose sight of the relation of this happening to the one *for whom* it is a *malum* because it harms him or causes suffering. The aspect that differentiates between *malum physicum* and *malum morale* would then be that, in the first case, *events* cause suffering that are not actions and for whom no one is responsible (natural events); in the second case, by contrast, suffering is caused by *actions* that go back to a free decision of the will and for which responsibility must be taken because they could have been avoided under identical conditions (human actions). The commonality between them would be that they cause suffering; the difference would be that in the one case, suffering is an avoidable consequence of freedom (*morale*), in the other, by contrast, an unavoidable effect of natural necessity (*physicum*).

This suggests a common concept of *malum* according to which everything that (and only this?) is ill that either is being encountered by someone as suffering or is being done by someone to someone as harm: "To do evil is to make someone else suffer," as Paul Ricœur puts this view.[110] This leads to difficulties not only in the case of the *malum metaphysicum* but also has other consequences to be taken into account. First, an ill is something that and only something that is an ill *for someone*, more precisely: that causes suffering for someone. The history of ill would then have begun with the history of life, because in a world without life there is no suffering and therefore no ill either. This means not only that, to our current knowledge, ill and evil exist *on our earth alone*; it also means that on this earth only that is an ill which harms someone and causes suffering: mudslides that do not kill anyone, floods that do not harm anyone, earthquakes that only cause rocks to tumble, they and many other things would not be ills.

Second, it is often difficult to decide whether an event harming someone is a natural event or an action: Is a flu a *malum physicum* or a *malum morale* for which someone can be held accountable? Is globalization, are the effects it has on the unemployed, a *malum morale* or a *malum physicum*? Similar questions can be asked concerning many social,

110. Ricœur, *Evil*, 66.

economic, political realities and the effects they have on human beings. The distinction cannot be made neatly in every case, but that is not necessary. For it becomes relevant only where specific questions of responsibility come up—in matters of insurance, for example. In such cases, there are always ways of making the distinction with sufficient precision.

Third, suffering can be produced only where there is a capacity for suffering, and this capacity exists only where there is life. This, however, poses two problems. On the one hand, the transition from life capable of suffering to beings not yet capable of suffering is fluid, such that the scope of ill in the world cannot be fixed clearly. On the other hand, the capacity for suffering can increase or diminish, such that life of different kinds and qualities can be distinguished by the degree to which a life is able to suffer. It does not follow from this, however, that ill would have to be graduated accordingly, that ills that presuppose a greater capacity for suffering would be greater or graver than those that affect living beings on a lower level of the capacity for suffering. Insects might be less sensitive to suffering than vertebrates, and "with the greater development of the intellect," the sensitivity to suffering may increase until it "reaches its highest pitch in human beings, and even there continues to grow in proportion to cognition and intelligence; the man in whom genius dwells suffers the most."[111] There is good reason to doubt this last inference: intelligence is not *ipso facto* a guarantee for a higher sensitivity to suffering, nor does it prevent one from being prone to a higher degree to imagined suffering or to exaggerating small sufferings as great tragedies. It might be argued that intelligent people are prone to sufferings like doubt, narrowmindedness, touchiness, arrogance, intellectual and moral disgust, among many others, that do not plague others or not in the same way or to the same extent.[112] But being prone to *different* suffering than others does not in any way mean suffering *more*: intelligent people do not suffer *more* than others, especially since according to this "logic of suffering," the one to be suffering the most would not be intellectuals but God, the pure intelligence, a view Schopenhauer hardly intended. Rather, it is generally true that what humans compared to other vertebrates and vertebrates compared to insects suffer is different in each case, but never such that the ones would therefore suffer greater ill than the others. A change of temperature that humans have little trouble with can be fatal for an insect. It is therefore not an ill for the human being but a fatal ill for the insect. Correlating suffering and ill within the horizon of life must not therefore tempt us into assessing the magnitude of ill on the standard of a given organism's capacity for suffering: the magnitude of an ill is always to be judged within the life-horizon of those affected itself, not in a comparative context abstracted from it.

Fourth, finally, one of the central objections to Leibniz, from Voltaire to today, is that he focused more on the problem of moral than that of physical ill and expressed an unacceptable lack of sensitivity to concrete suffering that is said to render his reflections abstract and unfit for practically dealing with suffering. But this objection misses the point in more than one regard. Leibniz at no point contests, minimizes, or declares physical ill to be irrelevant. On the contrary, he explicitly defines it as pain and is capable

111. Schopenhauer, *World as Will and Representation*, 336.

112. Kreiner, *Gott im Leid*, 34.

of unsparing descriptions and depictions. However—and this, as is so often the case, such criticism overlooks—for the *task* he sets *himself*, namely to think through the question of "the origin of evil *in its relation to God*" in order "to reconcile reason with faith in regard to the existence of evil,"[113] the salient problem is not physical but moral and metaphysical ill. For it is more than obvious that physical suffering has its origin not in God but in what is created. With regard to God, it only becomes a problem insofar as it provokes the question concerning creation precisely in this world with its glaring sufferings—a question that is also posed by moral and metaphysical ill and can therefore also be discussed under those headings, as Andrea Poma rightly notes: "Leibniz recognises suffering as a concrete, real problem, but the fact that it cannot be imputed to God finds a relatively simple conceptual justification in theodicy."[114]

22. The Identification of *malum morale* and Sin

A further problem is the identification of *moral ill* and *sin*, which Leibniz makes almost as a matter of course but which is far from self-evident. It manifests the tendency, typical of modernity, of moralizing sin, a tendency that in turn derives from the (complex) Augustinian tradition's old attempt at defining sin as a problem of the will and describing it as an inversion of willing from *bene velle et male nolle* to *male velle et bene nolle*, from willing what is good and not willing what is not good to willing what is not good and not willing what is good. It designates a willing of ill that is an ill in that it shuts itself off from God's will, and this shutting off already, not only the deed committed, is the real ill. This willing of ill becomes manifest, however, in ill deeds toward others and toward oneself, and catalogs of sins and vices provided pastoral-theological instructions for seeking out and naming these ills. The more the manifestations of inverted willing in ill deeds served as a guide, the more easily the moralizing reduction of the conception of sin suggested itself. Here, as so often, the attempts at pastorally concretizing theological insights were not too unsuccessful, they were too successful such that the evidence was identified with the thing it was evidence of. Sin disappeared behind the sins, which could be depicted so drastically, evil was obscured by fascination with sensational ills such that it was all the more undisturbed and effective. That is why it is erroneous to think that the theodicy problem does not even pose itself "if we defined evil intentions as ills. . . . The mere intention to defraud someone, steal from them, lie to them, injure them, or kill them is as such neither necessarily a sin nor necessarily an ill in the sense relevant to theodicy."[115] The opposite is true. Not the ill deeds committed but the wrong determination of the will at their basis is the decisive problem of sin, precisely the *incliniatio ad malum* and not only the deeds committed. Anselm would have countered such attempts at seeking sin only at the surface but not in the depths of willing with his dictum, "You have not

---

113. Leibniz, *Theodicy*, 61, 67, my emphasis.

114. Poma, *Impossibility and Necessity of Theodicy*, 171.

115. Kreiner, *Gott im Leid*, 30.

considered how heavily sin weighs."[116] Evil intentions are the ill because without them there would be no ill deeds.

The problem is not that this definition of sin centered on the will is going too far, it is that it is not going far enough. If the decisive point is the misguidedness of human life with regard to God, then sin must centrally be understood *theologically* as (intentional or factual) contradiction of God's love and care. Sin is not the morally ill deed toward others or oneself but that which makes it possible and presupposes it: the human's turn away from God. But this turning away manifests itself not only in ill deeds but also in humans' good or well-intentioned deeds with their often anything-but-good consequences. The *malum morale* cannot theologically be equated with sin because it dismisses humans' intentional or real doing good from the perspective of sin and thereby downplays sin. To prevent anyone being defrauded, robbed, lied to, injured, or killed, the appropriate enforcement of laws would suffice. But that would not chase sin from the world.

23. The False Definition of Metaphysical Evil

The real problem of Leibniz's attempted definition, however, is what he calls *malum metaphysicum*: the ontological imperfection of the created compared to the perfection of the creator. Here above all, Leibniz is still in the grip of the *privatio boni* tradition and, against the intention of his theological claims, holds on to a description of the world in a normative perspective that soon, albeit unjustly, made his approach irrelevant in the mind of contemporaries. Where the tradition of Neoplatonism and its Christian reception describes the humans' being creatures and not being God as imperfection (in contrast to the divine perfection) and finitude (in contrast to the divine infinity), it conceives of it as a *lack* and something *negative* when it should be seen as something *positive* and as a *gain*. The point of creation is not that humans have the deficiency of not being God, but that they have the good fortune of existing although they do not have to exist and could also not exist. Being a creature is an "ill" only if we think finitude in contrast with God's perfection and infinity and thus categorize it as *privatio*, or if we call it an "ill" because we conceive of it as the condition of the possibility of physical and moral ill. If, however, we define the human not in contrast with God but, say, with animals, the *deficiency* of the human *is being defined differently* as well: not as finitude but as a reduction of instinct that threatens and challenges the life of the human and to which we owe our drive to shape our lives, to develop technology and rhetoric (Blumenberg). Being a creature is not *ipso facto* a lack, and if it is understood as a deficiency, it can consist in very different things, depending on the horizon of reference.

Indisputably, the creatureliness of human beings also shapes the way they misdetermine themselves. Yet the reason for physical ills, moral evil, and theological sin is precisely not human creatureliness but its inversion and obfuscation. Humans are sinners not *because* they are creatures but they are sinners *as* creatures. And they also do not commit morally ill deeds *because* they are *finite*, but they harm themselves and their neighbors *as* finite beings. It is not finitude that is a *malum* but perverted finitude. And

116. Anselm, *Cur Deus Homo*, in *Opera* II:88.

it is not the creature that is a sinner but the creature perverted, blinded to its creator. The theology of creation must therefore not take the path of the *privatio boni* tradition continued by Leibniz and describe the whole of creation as a togetherness of *bonum et malum*. As Aquinas rightly writes: while we must say that the finite creation is an internally differentiated diversity, there is no reason for understanding this diversity as something structured by the relationship between good and evil.[117] The existence of finite differences is not identical with the difference of *bonum* and *malum*, and the improvement from *good* to *better* is something other than the one from *bad* to *good*, even if we distinguish only between degrees of perfections and argue as Leibniz does: "For as a lesser evil is a kind of good, even so a lesser good is a kind of evil if it stands in the way of a greater good."[118] For this ignores that nothing is good or ill in itself and that it is not better or worse only in relation to something else but that it is good or ill in relation to the one *for whom* it is a good or an ill. That is why *one and the same thing* that is an ill for one person can be a good for another, and vice versa.

This has fundamental consequences that cannot be tied in with Leibniz's view of reality as a continuous more or less of good or ill in which the best still represents a minimum of ill and the most ill still a minimum of good such that, strictly speaking, there can be in reality nothing completely new but also no complete ending.[119] The essential *for-relation* of the good and the ill, rather, signifies that the phenomena of our experience of the world cannot be sorted out unambiguously and "objectively" according to *evil* and *good* not because they feature only a more or less of good or ill in relation to each other but because this definition characterizes their value relation *to us* or *to God*, not their ontological relation to each other. In the relation to us, however, every phenomenon can be experienced and viewed not only from one but from different perspectives. Even death (that of others or our own imagined death) is not always and fully to be judged negatively but can very well, as a moment of finite creation, be assessed positively. Theologically, it becomes negative in that through sin it becomes the definitive separation from God, and philosophically, it is feared for example because of regret about a botched life and the definitive removal of the possibility of yet giving one's life another direction and a meaningful content.[120]

In both these regards, the contingent facts of life in relation to us enter into an evaluative perspective within whose horizon they are described and assessed as evil or good *for us*. This is true for the individual phenomena, it is true for the totality of phenomena in relation to each individual (each individual's specific world), and it is true for the world as a whole, that is, for "the whole succession and the whole agglomeration of all existent things."[121] Defining them as good or bad, evil or good, means to locate them in relation to someone within a specific horizon, and if this definition is to be understood, neither this relation nor this horizon can be ignored: the world is not good or ill or a mixture of both, but it is good or ill always only for someone and within the

117. Aquinas, *Summa Theologiae*, I q48 a1 a5 and elsewhere, e.g., a4.

118. Leibniz, *Theodicy*, §8:128.

119. See Leibniz, *Monadology*, §73:650.

120. For a secular account, see Tugendhat, "Gedanken über den Tod."

121. Leibniz, *Theodicy*, §8:128.

horizon where the contingent phenomena are being unified into a world for this person and defined as good or ill for this person.

That is why Leibniz's definition of the factual world as the best possible creation, too, is not a judgment without point of view and horizon but, precisely to the contrary, it can be grasped only on its theological preconditions: it is a judgment that views the world's contingent reality strictly before God, and in so doing strictly understands God as the one who as perfecting creator is actively working to overcome the imperfections of creation by teaching us to avoid ills that can be avoided and through his grace comes to our aid where ills cannot be avoided. That the contingent world is the best possible creation thus includes not only that whatever is present in a given instance is regarded as to its perfectibility within the whole of God's creation, that is, it is not taken by itself and in its concrete situation, which is always relatively deficient, but viewed as to its intended perfection as a moment of the entire creation in its becoming. It also includes—and necessarily so—that it is not being judged directly but in the *detour via God*: only in this relation can the world be judged the way Leibniz judges it. If we leave God aside, if we replace God with another reference, or if we do not understand God the way Leibniz understands him, as the one who is creator out of goodness and in his goodness comes to the aid of the creatures where they, because of their creatureliness, cannot be as perfect as the creator, then Leibniz's claims become as offensive as they were soon felt to be.

To this day, "Leibniz's solution" is admitted to be "theologically sound" but reproached for seeming "to fly in the face of common-sense experience of natural disasters, misery, disease, cruelty, poverty and so on."[122] But if Leibniz's solution is indeed theologically sound, then the objection is not convincing because the recourse to "common-sense experience" is precisely not a concrete and close-to life attitude toward the ills of this world but an abstract one since it ignores God and leaves God's relation with ill aside. Leibniz's solution stands in need of improvement not because, in confronting ill, it brings God into play but, on the contrary, because it does not bring him into play even more intensely, namely not just as regards the whole of the world and the great number of ills in the limit calculation of maximizing the good and minimizing the ill but as regards each individual ill in the place where it occurs as an ill for someone.[123] Precisely if we understand God and take him seriously the way Leibniz presents him, then God is a creator and helper at every point of reality, committed to overcoming ill and actualizing the good. The actual world is the best of all possible worlds only because and insofar as it is the site of the permanent overcoming of ill toward the good—not through us but through God, yet through God in such a way that it does not happen without us. Because we lose ill from sight when we leave aside *for whom* it is an ill, ill must be taken into focus and overcome at the place where it occurs.[124] If, theologically, there is a "solution" of the problem of ill, then it is not an abstract one, a calculation within a whole of an experience of world as such, but the problem is solved in such a way that each and every ill of each and every person is identified and overcome for each and

122. Ross, *Leibniz*, 104.

123. Stump, "The Problem of Evil," 417; see also Penelhum, "Divine Goodness and the Problem of Evil."

124. This is the correct thesis of Adams, *Horrendous Evils*.

every one in their place. Yet the very definition of God that is set up in and suggested by Leibniz's reflections is that he is present for each and every one in their place in such a way that in the process of overcoming ill through good, the best life possible for them is being actualized: God is really thought as God only when he is being thought for each and every one in their place as the one who overcomes their ills and actualizes what is good for them. God is not only generally the creator of the world, he is creator only because and insofar he is the creator *of each individual world of each individual person*. The ill must always be overcome *in my life* toward the best possible life, not just in the greater whole of the process of the world. And if this can be said about and expected from anyone at all, then it is God.

That is why what shows Leibniz's efforts to be "abstract vis-à-vis concrete suffering"[125] is not the recourse to God, but it is precisely the loss of God that renders the ill anthropologically opaque and impenetrable in its irrationality and nonsensicalness. That is why it is necessary to intensify and amplify Leibniz's detour via God in the confrontation with evil, not dismiss it for the sake of allegedly practical shortcuts. The direct confrontation of reason with ill seems regularly to end in noting that evil is irrational and reason at a loss. Even those who have no use for theological attempts at consolation must consider what Leibniz suggests: that the recourse to God is the key for understanding the ill as the shadow of the world's structure of contingency, differentiated as to unavoidability and avoidability. Because we are actual in no other way than contingently, ill for us is both: contingently unavoidable in principle and contingently avoidable indeed in concrete cases. In the place of every ill, there could be something *else* and at the same time the world could *not be without* ill. There is no life without ill, but no ill is such that a life could not also be without it. In the practical living of life, this urges a sober distinction between avoidable ills, ills we are to avoid, and ills we cannot avoid. But this rational differentiation, according to Leibniz, can be obtained only through the detour via God, without whom neither the contingency of ill nor the distinction between avoidable and unavoidable ill can be rationally explained.[126]

125. Janssen, *Gott—Freiheit—Leid*, 39.

126. After Leibniz, it was the late Schelling and process theology that saw most clearly that the Christian reception of the notion of the *privatio boni* requires, above all, working on the concept of God. Both tie *malum* into the process of creation, which they think as God's self-actualization, even if their models differ widely in their details. See Schulte, *Radikal Böse*, 195–246, and Dalferth, *Gott: Philosophisch-theologische Denkversuche*, 153–212.

D

The Inadequacy of the *privatio boni* Tradition

DESPITE THE ENORMOUS WEIGHT of the Augustinian tradition, Christian thought has never really accepted the notion of *privatio boni*. There are good reasons for this, namely the difference between the conceptions that underlie the orientations of the world and of life as well as the differently accentuated guiding interest of Christian attempts to think evil.

1. Cosmo-Theological vs. Creation-Theological Thought

The conception of evil as *privatio boni* derives from a cosmological and ontological intellectual framework that differs from Christian convictions at key points. The juxtaposition of a cosmo-theological and a creation-theological monotheism succinctly expresses the difference:

Cosmo-theological monotheism	Creation-theological monotheism
1. There is only one God.	1. There is only one God.
2. God's relation to the world is correlation; the relation of the world to God is participation.	2. God's relation to the world is creation; the relation of the world to God is dependence.
3. That there are ills in the world is a necessary fact.	3. That there are ills in the world is a contingent fact.

Both conceptions agree that there is one and only one God. However, they conceive of the divine in extremely different ways, conceptualizing the one God either as the "absolute true Being" over against whom everything else is less true and actual or as the "absolutely good Will," by whom everything else is conditioned and on whom everything else depends.[1] While cosmotheology and its pan(en)theistic successors think the relation between God and world as participation or correlation, such that there can be no world without God and no God without world, creation theology stresses the constitutive dependence of the world on God but at the same time also God's creative freedom over against the world: the world exists only because God wills that it exist, whereas God could also exist without a world existing. Yet if the world is due to God's will and

---

1. See Dalferth, *Jenseits von Mythos und Logos,* and *Theology and Philosophy,* pt. I.

decision and if what God wills and does is entirely good, then it is entirely good that the world exists and the world that exists must, with regard to the one who willed and made it, be called good without restrictions.[2]

If, then, there are ills in the world, for cosmo-theology, it is impossible that they not exist: the intricate relationship between God and world is such that what can exist sooner or later will exist (because that is possible which was actual, is actual, or will be actual) and such that what does exist must exist and cannot not exist (because it must occur sooner or later if it can occur at all). For creation theology, by contrast, ills need and indeed ought not to exist: they ought not to exist because the world is due to a good resolution of God's and as such is good. And they need not exist because the world, had it remained such as God willed and made it, would have remained good and without ills. If, then, there are ills, it is possible that they could also not be, and if that could be, it also should be.[3]

Within the framework of cosmo-theological thinking and its pan(en)theistic successors in the nineteenth and twentieth centuries (Hegel, Schelling, Schleiermacher, Whitehead, and Hartshorne),[4] the *privatio boni* theory is able to explain existing evil as a lack of good on the part of individuals within the whole: nothing that is different from the absolutely One, True, and Good is as perfect as, taken by itself, it could be and should be. Deficiency is unavoidable because this constitutes the difference between the infinite One (God) and the finite Many (world). Yet deficiency is unavoidable also because in the many, not everything can perfectly be what it potentially could be, such that under conditions of finitude there will always be deficiency and thereby *malum*.[5] Within the framework of creation theology, both answers are insufficient because they do not explain why ills that need not exist factually do exist. The *privatio boni* conception explains why ills must exist when they exist but not why ills exist that need not exist. That is why, taken by itself, it has always been insufficient for Christian thinking.

2. Unlike the cosmotheological attitude toward the world, the Christian relationship to the world is thus *not tragic*: for the latter the world and life are not unavoidably ensnared in evil and ills, things *could and should be different*. On the difference between the two attitudes, see Patzer, "Humanismus und griechische Tragödie," 172–85.

3. Let me simply note that this also settles the question where the origin of evil is to be sought: it cannot be sought in and with God because everything that is from God is good and not evil. Nor can it be sought to lie with some counter-God because there is one and only one God and everything else that exists is created by him, that is, it absolutely depends on him in what it is and is capable of. Rather, it can only be sought in creation, and this is not a self-contradictory endeavor only if creation is such that through God's decision something comes into being that on the one hand can decide in the relative sense, that is, choose between good and evil, and on the other hand cannot not choose, that is, that must decide: a free creature. That it *can* decide characterizes this creature as *free*; that it *must* decide characterizes it as creature. The creature *differs* from God because it must do what it can do (it is not free as concerns its own ability); the free creature *shares* with God the ability to choose between good and evil, to decide in favor of one or the other (what it wants to do, it also can do).

4. See Janssen, *Gott—Freiheit—Leid*, 71–126; Hermanni, "Die Positivität des *Malum*," 55–72; and Hügli, "Die Instrumentalisierung des *Malum*." Mathewes, *Evil and the Augustinian Tradition*, 149–97, shows how this tradition shapes Hannah Arendt's thought.

5. Both arguments stand behind the category of the ill Leibniz calls "metaphysical."

2. Privation and Perversion:
Evil in the Cosmos and Evil in Human Life

Yet there is also another, entirely different reason for this. What is front and center in Christian attempts at thinking evil is not the definition of evil in the whole of reality but the effort to understand its occurrence in the life of human beings. In the experience of individuals and of the community of human beings, evil is not encountered in the reflective figure of a lack of good (ontological *privatio*) but as an ill being we suffer or evil we do or that is being done to us (anthropological *perversio*).[6] For those affected, *malum* always manifests as *male pati*, an ill suffered, be it that it happens to them from someone else (as deed) or from something else (as event). For those who *do* it or to whom it is *done*, by contrast, it is always a *malefactum*, the ill deed of an evildoer who causes misery and suffering by what he does or does not do.

That evil is being experienced as *malefactum* does of course not mean that all evil can be understood this way. Just that, however, has been tried time and again by attempts to make the act-theoretical conception of evil deeds into the frame and basic figure of a theological explanation of all evil. Such a procedure suggested itself in a view of the world that saw the world as divine creation and thus as based in a divine decision without which what is would not be. If the world as a whole is the result of acting and deciding, then the evil occurring in it, too, is to be understood within the horizon of action and decision. And if it cannot be understood as the direct consequence of the creator's acting and deciding without dissolving the difference between creator and creation, it must be understood starting with the decisions and actions of the creatures. That, however, raises not only the question of what the deciding and acting consists in that results in evil but also of how the creator's good action can lead to a creation in which evil can be willed and done and good can be not willed and not done. How is it possible that in a good world there are evil deeds if this world is the good creation of the good creator? The theological tradition sought to answer this question by referring to the human's *peccare* and *malefacere*.

---

6. It is not by chance that *privatio* (*boni*) and *perversio* (*humanae naturae*) are the two basic notions of the Augustinian tradition and its engagement with evil. See Mathewes, *Evil and the Augustinian Tradition*, 75–103.

II.2

MALUM AS MALEFACTUM

TAKING UP THE NOTION of evil as *privatio boni* has always been only one, and not the central one, among Christian attempts at thinking evil. Evil happens not only when life is irrationally harmed, humiliated, and destroyed by ills; evil is also committed by people intentionally or unintentionally. Ills are encountered as *ill deeds*. That is why *malum* must (also) be thought as *malefactum*.

A

The Human Being as Perpetrator of Evil

1. Ills as Ill Deeds

EVIL DOES NOT ONLY just happen to human and other living beings, it is also done to them. As *factum*, *malefactum* is an *evil deed*: not just something that exists in the world, nor just something that happens or takes place in the world but something that *is done by someone*. As a deed, it has a perpetrator who is responsible; as an ill deed, it raises the questions of the *guilt* (*culpa*) the evildoer thereby incurs and of the *punishment* (*poena*) to be expected for it. For in human coexistence, guilt demands atonement, and punishment is the form in which an evil deed is being atoned for, precisely because it cannot be undone.

A *deed* differs from an event not only in that, under identical circumstances, it could also have been effected differently or not at all, in that it is an *action* and not mere behavior (freedom of action) but also in that it is based on a free will that, under identical circumstances, could have determined itself differently, that could have willed something different (freedom of the will). Accordingly, a deed is *bad* when it does not achieve or effect what it seeks to achieve or effect; it is *evil*, in contrast, when it is based on a will that does not will what it could have and ought to have willed: the good (in a given context); and it is *morally evil* when the perpetrator does not will what is morally good (whichever way this is defined) or wills what is morally evil.

In the unfolding of life, willing and the will are not independent factors but rather always occur in connection with needs, wishes, interests, opinions, knowledge, expectations, and so on, that influence and codetermine what is being willed.[1] All traditions of ancient philosophical anthropology thus think the will as something that does not itself will (something) but as something whose willing is determined either by *reason* or by *desires*, and it is a *good will* only to the degree in which the former is the case; in the latter case, it is an *evil will*. The main reason for this lies in their conception of reason as that which has its eye on *the whole*, cosmologically and anthropologically as well as socially and politically: reason is oriented toward the general and the shared, the well-being of

---

1. See Bieri, *Das Handwerk der Freiheit*, 36–42, esp. 39–40.

all, the best for each, the harmony of each and all individuals in themselves and with the social and natural environment surrounding them. Desire by contrast has its eye only on what is its *own*, its own interest, the particular, what isolates, what is not shared. That is why, if we want to will the good, we must not let ourselves be determined by desires but be guided by reason.

Against this background, a *malefactum* can be defined as ill deed in two ways: it is an *ill* insofar as it represents and effects an ill *for someone*, that is, causes damage or suffering for them. Such an ill becomes an ill *deed* (and not just an accident, an unfortunate blunder, an inadvertence with ill consequences), moreover, by being based on an evil willing and a wrongly determined will.[2] While human actions, as regards their factual consequences, are in many ways to be described as *mala*, these *mala* are *malefacta* only if they are based on a wrong willing and thus on a wrong determination of the will. And just as every ill deed is founded on a specific ill willing, so every ill willing is founded on the wrong determination of the will to will ill: the reason and foundation of all ill deeds and the real *malum* is therefore *that wrong determination of the free will that makes free will a willing of ill and thereby entails all ill deeds.*

2. Freedom and Fact: The Burden of the Deed Done

The mainstream of Western theology, represented by Augustine, however, did not stop at this conception of the will. It has conceived of human beings not only as the ones who can freely choose between good and evil and who must make this choice, for else they would not be human. It has moreover held that the free choice of evil, once made, permanently damages human beings (each individual human being), be it because it prevents them from choosing the good, be it because they are in no way able to undo the evil they did. Humans' freely caused self-damage can thus be conceived of in two ways: as *factual loss of the ability freely to choose the good* or as *inability to revise the evil factually done (chosen)*, that is, as *factual inability to do good* or as *fundamental inability to free oneself of guilt.*

Both cases must be kept well distinct. The second case aims at a hard-to-dispute phenomenon: the experience and the insight that human beings cannot by any free act of the will undo evil freely chosen and done: *malum* as *factum* remains out of reach for human *facere* because action in the present can only ever shape and transform what is to come but not what is past. What is decisive here is that the *malum* is a *factum*, not that the *factum* is a *malum*; what makes the evil irreversible is that *it has been done and willed*, and this is as true of the ill we have committed as of the ill we have only willed, despite all the morally and legally relevant differences between willing and doing. While legally,

---

2. The atrocities of Nazism have made it impossible to overlook that there are ill deeds that cannot be understood this way and that thereby reveal the fundamental limitations of the Western tradition of thinking. Here, *actions* effected and did unimaginable evil *without it being possible, in many cases, to identify clearly graspable evil or criminal intentions*, that is, without it being possible concretely to identify these actions as *evil deeds* in the traditional sense. See Neiman, *Evil in Modern Thought*, 267–80. The more humans move in worlds constructed together that in group processes transform their self-evidence in such a way that what previously has been unthinkable becomes quotidian, the more easily they become perpetrators of evil *without evil intentions*. See Welzer and Christ, *Täter*.

only the deed that can be *proven* counts, morally, already the deed that is *done* matters, and religiously, the deed merely *willed* is relevant (see Matt 5:28). The real *malefactum* in the sense at issue here is not only the deed committed but already the resolution to commit it: not only the one who acts evil but already the one who wills evil *is evil*, is someone who wills the evil and does not will the good. An evil person, too, can fail, that is, not enact the willed ill. Yet a failed wrongdoer is not someone who really is good. He *willed* the evil—and this is enough to make him an evil person. For—this is the existential truth content of the Fall—even if in other cases he may again determine himself to do good, he could *no longer undo the fact of the wrong determination* of his will: where once a *malum* has become a *factum*, has become the fact that I willed or did something evil, it cannot be abolished or erased by any deed. Where an evil deed has been done, indeed, where something evil has been willed or intended, *evil has happened*, and this cannot be undone in any way. Hence there is guilt, and guilt demands atonement through punishment.

Only from this vantage point is it possible to understand the first case. For if we conceive of the choice between good and evil as a choice between apples and oranges, one that can be made one way this time, another the next, it seems absurd to consider that the human being, seen as a will, had by its free choice of evil permanently forfeited its ability freely to choose good. Of course, we are all familiar with situations in which a decision came up that never comes up again the same way and that, when we decided in favor of one thing, permanently excluded another. Yet the decision between good and evil comes up again and again in our lives in changing situations. How then is it possible to say that someone who has *once*, freely, wrongly determined himself to do ill is *forever* thus wrongly determined, that this fundamental decision dominates and perverts all other decisions in his life?

The decisive point here is that, strictly speaking, two things are being said: someone who wills evil once, whether he does ill or not, thereby confirms that he is not good but evil, and the best deed of someone evil at most appears to be good because it stands under the sign of the proven wrong determination of his will. This only seems to be contradicted by our ability to decide, from case to case, to do or not to do good and by our in fact doing good as well: Is not what we do good when it does not harm others or opposes what harms them? But it is not the being good of the deed that is at issue, it is the being good of the doer, and this determination takes up other salient phenomena in life: just as a deed can seem to be good because it does not cause any ill although the will it is based on is not good, so a deed can effect ills although the doer willed something good. Just as the doer's willing good cannot be inferred from a deed's being good, or his willing ill from his doing ill, so the being good of a deed cannot be inferred from willing good, nor can it be inferred from willing ill that a deed cannot entail any good consequences: there is always a hiatus between willing and implementing that prevents this inference. That is why good can also arise from willing ill and ill from willing good. And that means that in both cases, doers lose control of their deeds: willing the good does not reliably lead to the goal intended and willing ill does not necessarily entail the evil willed. On the one hand, this gives rise to permanent disappointments; on the other hand, there is also reason for hope: doers are not the masters of their deeds and human beings are not the masters of good and evil in the world.

I would like to highlight four aspects of the approach to defining evil just sketched.

1. *Consequences of freedom*: In being understood as *malefactum*, *malum* is being conceived of as the result of self-determination and freedom of the will: ill deeds are not a coercion from outside and not a mere fate but consequences of *our own ill willing*.

2. *The weight of the factual*: Our own free decision in favor of the ill corrupts every human life such that it is faced with an irreparable damage: it cannot undo what has happened but only try to live with what has happened. The factual results of the free determination of the will cannot be abolished or rendered undone by any free determination of the will: when once we have willed ill and done ill, we will not be able to undo it by any other willing or doing. This includes two things:

3. *Nonnecessity of Evil*: On the one hand, a *malum* as *malefactum* did not have to be. The Christian definition of *malum* as *malefactum* objects to all *ontological pessimism and dualism*. The *malefactum* did not have to be committed, and the *malum* accordingly is thought as contingent. It could be different, it would be desirable if it were different, and it is—in principle, at least—avoidable.[3]

4. *Guilt and fate*: On the other hand, the facticity of factual ill excludes any revisability of what has been willed, what has been done, and what has happened. By having happened, that which did not have to be can no longer be eliminated. This results in the indisputable *guilt* of the wrongdoer and, in connection with it, the *fate* of never being able sufficiently to remove or abolish this guilt by oneself. The irreversibility of the *malefactum* is the condition for the doer's inability to undo what has been done. The asymmetry of the *malefactum*'s contingency—that it did not have to happen and can now no longer be made to not have happened—irreversibly ties *malum* in with the problem of guilt and punishment, *culpa* and *poena*.

3. Augustine's Questions: *Malum* as *male velle et bene nolle*

To define Evil, Augustine did not stop at taking up the notion of *privatio boni*.[4] Instead, he undertook the definition on the basis of a different conception with which he linked it, the definition of *malum* as *malefactum*. The fundamental question the definition of *malum* as *privatio boni* leaves open is precisely the one it is meant to answer: *Unde malum?* It gives an answer as to *what* Evil is (the lack of Good) and *where from* Evil comes into the world (from the combination of matter with the forms), but it does not say anything about *why* there is Evil, why—to put it in the terms of Neoplatonism—there are not only pure spiritual beings but sensuous beings as well, why besides the *hylē noetē*

---

3. See Weingartner, *Evil*, 43–58.

4. Häring, *Die Macht des Bösen, Das Problem des Bösen*, and *Das Böse in der Welt*, 94–105; Evans, *Augustine on Evil*; and Tilley, *Evils of Theodicy*, 113–40.

there is also a *hylē aisthētē*. The principle of the "plenitude of being" explicitly does not provide an answer. It may indeed be better that there are not only one or two but many colors, and the same can be said about languages, cultures, arts, landscapes, animals, human beings, and many other things. But it does not follow that the same could be said of Evil, on the contrary: it cannot be said that it is better that there is Evil than that there is not Evil, already because there "is" no Evil in the sense of being relevant here in the first place: Evil is not a *bonum* but precisely its *privatio*. Yet why is there this privation?

4. *Materia mala?*

In the *Confessions*, Augustine recounts how this question of the *causa mali* haunted him. Especially if we suppose (1) that there is only one true God (*deus verus*), and not two originary beings or substances, a good God and an evil Countergod, as Augustine takes the Manicheans to claim; (2) that this God is "subject to no defilement or alteration, and . . . in all respects unchangeable," that is, that he is not sometimes good and sometimes different, thinks, wills, and acts now this way and now another; and (3) that this God "made not only our souls but our bodies too, and not only our souls and bodies but people everywhere and all things," then the reality of Evil turns the question of the *causa mali* into a fundamental problem. For if we look for the cause of Evil in a principle other than God, then we suppose that the unchangeable divine substance "suffer[s] evil," which is self-contradictory. If by contrast we seek it in God himself, then we suppose that the entirely good God could cause evil, which is no less self-contradictory.[5] This blocks the Manichean way out—to regard the soul as the work of the good God, the body, the bodily and material in turn as the work of the powers of darkness—as much as the Neoplatonic attempts at making matter pass for the cause of ills. If the good God has really created everything, then were do ills come from?

Augustine describes the difficulties thus raised with precision: while everything the highest good (*summum bonum*) has created is a lesser good than it is itself, it is still good as well. God, the highest good, can thus not himself be the *causa mali*. Was it, then, a *materia mala*, an evil originary material from which he created, such that the good he willed did not come about because of the ill matter from which he created? That would presuppose a very restricted and problematic conception of creation. In that case, God "formed" the material

> and disposed it in order [yet] he left in it some element that was not turned to good . . . But why? Did he lack the power so to convert and change it all that no evil would remain, he who is omnipotent? In any case, why would he have chosen to use it for making things, rather than using this same almighty power to destroy it entirely? Or could it have existed against his will? Or again, if matter was eternal, why did he allow it to exist so long, from infinite ages past, and then at last decide to make things out of it? Or, if he suddenly decided to act, surely he, being almighty, could have acted in such a way that it should cease to be, and he alone should exist, he, the complete, true, supreme, infinite Good? Or, supposing that it was unseemly for him who is good not to fashion and build something

5. Augustine, *Confessions*, 7.3.4–5:161–62.

good as well, ought he not to have done away with all the bad material and destroyed it, and himself originated some good matter instead, which he could use
to create everything? If he were able to construct good things only with the help
of material he had not himself constructed, he would not be omnipotent.[6]

If God is the omnipotent creator of heaven and earth confessed in the Creed, then, according to Augustine, the recourse to a *materia mala* does not offer a viable answer to
the question of the origin of Evil: it would then be necessary to modify the conception of
God's being the creator, of his omnipotence, of his goodness, or of everything together
in such a way that not much would be left of the content of the creed.

5. The *liberum voluntatis* as *causa mali*

Yet if the *causa mali* can be sought and found neither in God, in the *summum bonum*,
nor in an alleged *materia mala*, then where? The traditional Christian answer Augustine
was familiar with was that "the cause of evil is the free decision of our will, in consequence of which we act wrongly and suffer your righteous judgment."[7] We *do* ill because
we *voluntarily will to do ill*, and we *suffer* ill because as ill doers we have incurred guilt
and are rightly punished for it by God.[8] We are thus responsible ourselves not just for the
ill we do but also for the ill we suffer: it is the just divine punishment for our doing ill.

Yet this answer is more complex, multifaceted, and offensive than it may already
seem at first sight. What Augustine writes is true not just for him: while he heard this
response and did try to understand it, it did not really become clear to him. What he
finds helpful is the reference to the *will* (*voluntas*). It provides him with an indisputable
place to start, since "I was as sure of having a will as I was of being alive." At this point,
the question of the *causa* and thus of responsibility is unambiguous: I am the only one
responsible for my willing. "When I wanted something, or did not want it, I was absolutely certain that no one else but I was wanting or not wanting it." Yet if the cause of the
willing is the one willing, and he alone, then it is also the one willing, and he alone, who
is the cause of his willing ill, whether he wills a *malum* or does not will a *bonum*: in the
case of our own willing ill—and it is not by chance that Augustine here switches from
the vocabulary of *malum* to that of *peccatum*—the answer to the question concerning
the *causa peccati* is clear: *I myself am the origin of my willing ill.*[9]

Augustine gives a precise analysis of this willing ill.[10] It is *not a willing of an ill*, for
the ill is not anything to orient us but the absence, the lack, the *privatio* of something. It
is, rather, *an ill willing*, a willing that wills not the good but, in an act of self-love, wills
something other than the highest good: "The lapse [of ill willing] is not to what is bad,
but to lapse is bad. In other words, the natural objects to which there is a lapse are not

---

6. Augustine, *Confessions*, 7.5.7:164.

7. Augustine, *Confessions*, 7.3.5:161.

8. Or, as Augustine has it: "natural things are not evil. Rather whatever is called evil is either sin or
the punishment of sin" (Augustine, *Literal Interpretation of Genesis*, I.3:146).

9. Augustine, *Confessions*, 7.3.5:161.

10. See Bracht, "Freiheit radikal gedacht."

bad, but to lapse is bad because the will lapses against the natural order from what has supreme being to what has less being."[11] It is an *ill willing*, that is, a willing in the wrong way, not a willing of ill. What is wrong is not (primarily) what is willed, but the mode of willing is wrong, and this precisely corrupts that which the willing aims at. Were it otherwise, the *malum* would have to be given ontologically in order to be willed and chosen by the will. Yet that would precisely situate the *malum* within creation and render its origin incomprehensible. The recourse to willing only helps if the willing is corrupted intrinsically by the very mode of its willing and not by the objects of its willing. Only then is it evil *of itself* and in this way makes what it wills evil. It does not have a *causa efficiens* different from itself, it is itself a *causa deficiens*, a lapse from a good willing of the good to an evil willing of something other than the good: "No one then should look for an efficient cause of an evil will, for the cause is not one of efficiency but of deficiency even as the evil will itself is not an effect but a defect. For to defect from that which has supreme being to that which has less is to make a start in having an evil will."[12]

Augustine calls such a willing that is evil of itself *peccatum*. Sin is not primarily and originarily a doing of ill but a willing of ill, a not willing of what is good (*bene nolle*) and a willing of what is not good (*male velle*) in the indicated sense of *not willing in the right way* or *of willing in not the right way*; and there is no other origin for this sin than myself. I might be forced into doing ill. But nobody can force me to will ill. For the ill I do, there can always be a cause that coerces me and that may serve as my excuse. For the ill I will there is no such thing: according to Augustine, I am the master of my willing, and that is why I alone am responsible for my willing ill. *The origin of sin is always and exclusively the sinner himself.* And the sinner becomes a sinner precisely by willing and doing in the wrong way that which he can will and do.

Augustine even goes a step further: he accepts responsibility not only for the ill he wills but also for the ill that he does not will but does. To be sure, doing something against our will (*invitus facere*) is more of a suffering (*pati*) than a doing (*facere*) and is therefore not to be seen as our own guilt (*culpa*) but only as a punishment, that is, not as *culpable ill* but as a *punitive ill*. But in thinking of God's justice, Augustine writes, he quickly had to realize that he was not suffering this punitive ill unjustly.[13]

6. *Velle* and *Facere*

This admission is based on an unspoken train of thought that includes three sets of problems. First, the phenomenon of willing is differentiated: I am master of my willing, but I am not master of my doing. I am master of my willing because my willing or not willing has no other reason and no other cause than that I will or do not will something. But I am not in the same way master of my doing because not everything I do or do not do is being done or not done because I will or do not will it. It is not the case that everything I will is also done by me, and everything I do not will is not. Rather, it is very

---

11. Augustine, *City of God*, 12.8:36–37.
12. Augustine, *City of God*, 12.7:32–33.
13. Augustine, *City of God*, 12.7:33–35.

much the case, and indeed much too often, that I do not will something I do or that I will something but do not do it. While there is thus no difference between me and my willing (I am my willing), there is a gulf between my willing and my doing (I am not my doing) that again and again leads me into the contradiction that, as someone who wills, I will something other than what, as someone who does, I do.

I can bridge this gulf neither by my willing nor by my doing: even if I only will to do what I will to do and do not will to do anything I do not will to do, it cannot be excluded that I do what I do not will; and I precisely cannot control whether I only do what I will to do or do not do what I do not will because I have final say only about my willing but not my doing. Only in willing am I in agreement with myself; in doing I am not, and that is why it is precisely in not doing what I will or in doing what I do not will that I experience myself not as competent doer but as incompetent sufferer. And that means: although I am the *causa mali* as regards my willing ill and the ill deeds resulting from it, I alone am not the *causa mali* as regards my doing evil: even if I do not will any ill, that does not exclude that I do ill. I am caught up in ill not only through what I have to take responsibility for (my willing ill and its ill deeds) but also through what I do without having willed it and thus without being able to take responsibility: I always experience ill in the twofold shape of a *guilt I am responsible for* and a *fate I cannot escape*. I will evil (in an evil way) and incur guilt, and I do evil I do not will, and even if I could put an end to the first (which I cannot, according to Augustine, because under the conditions of fallen existence, I cannot will in a way that would not be a *male velle* or a *bene nolle*), the second would not thereby be abolished.

It is precisely the evil consequences of good deeds (that is, deeds willed by me as good) which prove the notion that evil is always and unavoidably tied in with evil intentions to be a fallacy. Augustine's shifting of the question from the *ill deed that harms someone* to the *ill will that wills doing damage to someone* does indeed move the problem of freedom to the center of debate in an important and consequential way that opens a path modernity has resolutely continued to follow. At the same time, however, it also suggests an alignment that holds evil always to be the result of evil intentions and incompetent willing—a supposition led *ad absurdum* by the industrial destruction of human life in the twentieth century.[14] Augustine was not unaware of the problem. He saw it and sought to respond to it in his own way.

7. *Aut culpa aut poena*

This brings us to the second set of problems. If we are to distinguish between my (willed) ill deeds and my (unwilled) ill doing, then not all *malum* in my life is a *malefactum* I am responsible for because I will it, and there is also ill that I am involved in and in which I participate through my doing without my willing it and therefore without my being able or obliged to take responsibility, ill that I cannot avoid even if I do not will it.

Augustine tries to do justice to this problem with the thesis that all ills are subject to the alternative *aut culpa aut poena*: if a *malum* is not to be addressed as *culpa* (as it

14. See Neiman, *Evil in Modern Thought*, 267–80.

must be in the case of ill willing and the ill deeds arising from it), it is to be understood as *poena* (as in the case of the unwilled doing of ill) and there is no *malum* that is neither the one nor the other nor both. That all ills are subject to this alternative is clear, according to Augustine, from the fact that ills in my life manifest as *male facere* or as *malum pati*, as *ills done* or as *ills suffered*. If they are *ill deeds*, they are based on a *male velle et bene nolle*; if that is not the case, an ill I do is not an ill deed but a suffering of ill. An ill deed can exist, like all deeds, because and insofar as it is based on a free willing that is responsible for this deed and bears the guilt for it. The reason for the ill deed and what makes it an ill deed is not alone the *freedom of action*—under identical circumstances, I could also have acted differently—but *freedom of the will*—I did not have to will what I did will and do because I did not have to will it as I did will and do it. Freedom of action is also the condition for willed or unwilled ill doing and thus of suffering ill, yet willed ill deeds exist only on the basis of a freedom of the will that wills what is not good by willing in a not good way (*male velle*) and does not will what is good by not willing in a good way (*bene nolle*).

On the one hand, then, there would be no *malefactum* without *liberum arbitrium*, and for every ill deed we can and must ask who bears the guilt for it because they willed the *malum* and did not will the *bonum* or willed in an evil rather than good way. For ill deeds "are" not nor do they "happen," they are *done* and *willed* and someone must take guilty responsibility for them. On the other hand, it is by no means evident from the outset that an ill doing is an ill deed and thus a *malefactum* for which someone must take guilty responsibility: that depends on the willing it is based on, and if this willing is not an ill willing, then that which has been done against the will is not an ill deed but a suffering of ill. The question about the willing at the basis is thus the touchstone for whether a *malum* falls under the category of *male facere* or that of *malum pati*. When such ill willing is absent in me, then my own ill doing falls under the category of suffering just as much as when an ill must be described as an evil deed done to me by someone else because it is based on his ill willing.

That is why the case of the ill suffered is more complicated than that of the ill done. All ill I suffer is either my fault or that of someone else. If it is incurred by me, if it is either a willed ill deed (as when I do harm to myself) or an unwilled ill doing, then, according to Augustine, it must be traced back to someone else, namely God, and be understood as punishment. If by contrast it is the fault of someone else, then it is either an injustice she does to me, that is, an ill deed done to me that makes her guilty, or a deed that does not make her guilty because she neither willed to commit injustice nor committed injustice against her will but imposes it on me or executes it as a just punishment. In this respect, what a judge or executioner does is indeed an ill for the one affected, but it is neither an ill deed nor an ill doing on the part of the judge or executioner because they do not will ill nor do they do ill against their will, but they give the law its due. They punish me but they do not commit ill, although I experience it as an ill for which, however, not they but I myself am responsible. Whatever I suffer as ill is therefore *another's injustice toward me* or *punishment imposed on me*—*tertium*, it seems, *non datur*.

The reason it seems that way lies in a problematic symmetry between *facere* and *pati*. It is indeed possible to say that there is a suffering of ill (*pati*) to correspond to every ill deed (*facere*) insofar as a deed is an ill deed precisely in that it inflicts suffering on someone and causes someone to suffer. Yet on the one hand, Augustine does not define the ill deed via what it does to others but through the ill willing on which it is based: a deed is an ill not because it causes suffering to a victim but because it is based on willing to inflict suffering on someone. Otherwise, the doings of judges and executioners would have to be defined as ill deeds, too, because for those affected it is an infliction of suffering or ill. Even if every ill deed means a suffering of ill, that cannot mean, according to Augustine, that every suffering of ill is to be understood as the ill deed of a perpetrator. On the other hand, moreover, there is no symmetry between victim and perpetrator to correspond to the symmetry of ill deed and suffering of ill such that every perpetrator of ill would also be a victim of ill. Someone who does ill to others inflicts suffering on them, and someone who suffers ill has ill inflicted on them by someone. Yet it does not follow that both not only can be but in fact are true of everyone: it is possible that someone does ill but does not himself suffer any, and likewise it is possible that someone suffers ill but does not himself inflict ill. In Augustine's theology, both are relevant cases and not just theoretical possibilities.

In a monogenetic history of humanity, the first would have been the case for Adam or Eve or both Adam and Eve if they had not been punished by God for their ill deed. That God punished them and thereby inflicted something on them that they suffered as an ill does not make him an ill doer: judges and executioners are not villains but exercise just judgment, and God does not incur any guilt by what he decrees but practices punishment for those who have incurred guilt.

The second is the case of Jesus Christ who has suffered ill but according to the creed of the Church has not done any ill: he is *only* a victim, not a perpetrator of ill, and more precisely a victim who *voluntarily* suffers these ills although he could have evaded them. Like all other human beings, he is affected by and suffers ills, but unlike all other humans he is not himself a doer of ill, and that is why the ill he suffers is in no way a punishment imposed on him, because he himself bears no guilt. The ill he suffers, rather, is, on the one hand, the ill *others do to him* and, on the other, the ill he suffers *in their stead*, the ill, that is, that is intended as punishment for their guilt: Christ is not only the one who *suffers innocently* but the one who *suffers voluntarily*, and he is such not only insofar as he does not evade the suffering others inflict on him (passive obedience) but also insofar as he takes on the punishment they deserve and receive for their doing and suffers it for them and in their stead (active obedience): he not only suffers the ill they do to him but also the ill they have to suffer as punishment for what they are doing to him—he not only dies the death they inflict on him but also the death they thereby deserve. That is why *his* death is *their* death. But why do they deserve death?

8. The Unfathomability of the *causa mali*

This is where the third train of thought sets in. It takes the form of an inference from the notion of God's justice. If God is just, then what he imposes on me as punishment is not unjust. That is why it cannot be unjust when he lets me suffer the ill of doing something against my will. For it is not culpable behavior to suffer something ill, and Augustine includes in suffering ill not only what others do to me but also the experiences of willing something good but not achieving it and doing ill instead, or of not willing ill but none-theless doing it, having to do it, or being unable not to do it. Augustine's argument, then, is not that it is just to be punished also for deeds one has committed against one's will: that would be a highly problematic argument. His argument, rather, is the more subtle thesis that it is a punishment that we commit ill deeds we do not will: Why do we do evil even though we do not will it at all? Why do we inflict harm on ourselves and others although we will what is good or even the best? That is the question that occupies him, and he answers it for himself by pointing to a punishment of God's: that we have such experiences shows that the world is not as it should be. It is not as it should be because in the world there is *male velle et bene nolle*. And that the world is this way shows an inversion that goes beyond our individual ill willing and that cannot therefore be traced back to my guilt alone but to a punishment imposed by God: the origin of my ill willing am I myself, and I alone, but the origin of my suffering ill seems to be more complex.

The questions have thus not been settled. If the *causa peccati* is my not willing the good and willing Evil, then why am I in such a way that this kind of willing is possible?

> Who made me? Was it not my God, who is not merely good, but Goodness itself [*summum bonum*]? Whence, then, did I derive this ability to will evil and refuse good? Is it in me simply so that I should deserve the punishment I suffer? Who established that ability in me, who planted in me this bitter cutting, when my whole being is from my most sweet God? If the devil is responsible, where did the devil come from? If he was a good angel who was transformed into a devil by his own perverted will, what was the origin of this evil will in him that turned him into a devil, when an angel is made entirely by the supremely good creator?[15]

To be sure, then, I myself and nobody else am responsible for my ill willing. But I cannot be responsible for my being in a situation to will ill in the first place, neither as regards the very possibility of willing ill and willing good nor as regards this being an option I have access to.

9. Open Problems

With regard to the actuality of ill willing, then, we must answer three different questions: Why is it possible at all, rather than impossible, to will ill or to will in an ill manner? Why is it not impossible for me to will ill but rather possible? Why do I will what is possible—what is ill—by willing in an ill way rather than will what would also be possible—the good—by willing in a good way?

The three questions evidently are related but must be kept distinct. It is one thing that it is possible to will ill—"it is not impossible to will ill," that is, it is not self-contradic-tory for ill to be willed and done. It is another that I have the capacity for willing ill—"it is not impossible for me to will and to do ill," that is, "I will ill" is not a self-contradiction. But I can be blamed for neither, no more than I can be blamed for existing. I am not responsible for the fact *that* I exist, I am only responsible for *how* I live, and likewise I

---

15. Augustine, *Confessions*, 7.3.5:161.

am not responsible for the fact *that* ill can be willed and done, or *that I can* will and do ill but responsible only for in fact doing it. But why do I do it? Why am I someone to whom the *male velle et bene nolle* truly applies? Even if there were an explanation for why there is the possibility of willing ill at all and why it exists for me, why do I actualize this possibility? Why do I not always will and do only the good when the ill does not have to be willed but merely can be willed? Why am I someone willing ill and not willing good when I could also have been someone willing good and not willing ill?

That is the real question to plague Augustine, and he makes it clear that recourse to either God or the devil is of no help. If God is the entirely good creator who does not do and effect anything that is not good, then how can I be created by him in such a way that I not only can but in fact will ill? The answer that God wills it in order for me to be punished justly rather than unjustly is not an answer because no punishment would be necessary if no ill were willed and committed and because it would be absurd (because it would contradict God's being good) to suppose that God, in order to be able to punish me justly, would ensure that I in fact will and do ill: a judge who would command committing the crime for which he judges the accused in order for his judgment to be just and not unjust would not only be an absurd figure, he would be a criminal figure. God cannot be thought this way without it no longer being God who is being thought.

Yet strictly speaking, it is not only this answer that is absurd, the question already is: if nothing and no one but I is and can be the subject of my willing, if therefore I can be entirely certain, as Augustine stresses,[16] that when I will or do not will something it is in fact *I* who wills or does not will and not someone else, then not only can the question of the cause of my ill willing only have one answer—*I myself, and I alone*—but the question, too, of the cause of my willing ill and not good, although I could also have willed good and not ill, can only have one answer—*because I will it*. The reason for my willing ill and the reason for my willing ill although I could also have willed good cannot be different from each other. If I and I alone am responsible for my willing because no one but I myself can decide the mode of my willing, then I and I alone am also responsible for my decision to will ill and not good, that is, for willing this way and not another. Augustine's question can thus only concern why I am such that I not only can but must make this decision, why God has created me in such a way that I face this decision and cannot evade it (and this is what his *theory of freedom* responds to). Yet I cannot meaningfully ask why God has created me in such a way that I will ill and do not will good, that is, decide in favor of the ill and not in favor of the good. The question is not meaningful because God did not create and could not have created me that way: if the ill willing is *my free decision*, then it would not only be wrong but impossible to name any other author for this decision than, precisely, me. Even an omnibenevolent and omnipotent creator cannot create me in such a way that I freely decide to be someone willing good and not willing ill or someone willing ill and not willing good.[17] As my creator, he is responsible for my

16. Augustine, *Confessions*, 7.3.5:161.

17. This problem also brings up short the attempt of deterministic Calvinism to solve the problem of Evil by declaring God himself to be the one to cause Evil but absolving him from responsibility for doing so. See for example Gordon H. Clark, according to whom "God is not responsible for the sin he causes . . . for the plain reason that there is no power superior to him; no greater being can hold him

being such that I must decide between the willing of good and of ill because I cannot will without doing so *bene* or *male*. Yet he cannot be responsible for my freely deciding in favor of ill (or also freely in favor of good): the author of my ill willing is always and exclusively I: "I alone have sinned" (2 Sam 24:17).[18]

Neither does the recourse to another author, the devil, say, offer a way out—it only shifts the question.[19] If *per impossibile* the devil were the author of my willing ill and not willing good, then where does this willing ill and effecting ill come from in his case? The myth of the fallen angel does not give an answer but rephrases the problem.[20] How is it possible that an angel, created entirely good, wills and does ill? For if angels are creatures that have been created by "the supremely good creator"[21] in such a way that they can will only the good but not Evil, then a devilish angel is a self-contradictory impossibility: it cannot exist. If angels by contrast are creatures that are created in such a way that they only ever will the good but never Evil although they could will it, then a devil is not an angel; but if he is created by God entirely an angel, then it is incomprehensible how someone who only ever wills the good but never Evil nonetheless does not always will the good but sometimes or at least once wills Evil, too.

The recourse to the devil and the angels common in popular piety—a recourse Augustine was well familiar with[22]—not only does not explain anything but makes the problem even more pressing for human beings. For it now turns out that it is possible to be able to will or not will ill but to will and do only the good. The angels show that it is not self-contradictory for someone *to be able to do* good or ill and yet *to do only good*. But if that is possible, the question becomes more pressing why someone (be it a human or a devil) who does not have to will and do ill nonetheless wills and does it. Precisely if it is correct that no one except *I myself* can be the author of my willing ill and not willing good, the question remains why I became this author when this did not have to

---

accountable; no one can punish him; there is no one to whom God is responsible; there are no laws which he could disobey" (Clark, *Religion, Reason, and Revelation*, 240–41). Not only is it a contradiction to say that God causes sin but "the sinner alone is the author of sin" (241), even if this is justified with the sophistic claim "that God's causing a man to sin is not sin" because "[b]y definition God cannot sin" (239). It is also an error to think that it is possible to deny God's responsibility for what he has allegedly caused by pointing to the absence of any responsible authority above him. That would have the absurd consequence that those to whom ill is done through God either suffer unjust ills for which the ostensibly just author is said not to be responsible such that it becomes completely obscure what God's "justice" is supposed to mean here, or that they must even be held responsible for these ills. Moreover, it completely overlooks that the basic responsibility at issue here is not toward another or a higher authority but toward those affected or harmed by Evil.

18. See also Augustine, *City of God*, 12.6.

19. This applies to more recent attempts, such as Boyd, *Satan and the Problem of Evil*, which consider the recourse to Satan to be indispensable to an explanation of "natural" ills that are not due to free human decisions: "no explanation that ignores his activity is adequate" (18). It must be objected that recourse to Satan's activity does not explain anything, as Anselm already showed in *Cur deus homo*. In Boyd, too, Satan thus is but the placeholder for a freedom-theoretical account that includes natural ills: "My argument here is that there is in fact nothing 'natural' about it. Ultimately, it is as much the result of free agents exercising their will as is 'moral evil'" (Boyd, *Satan and the Problem of Evil*, 18n4).

20. See Auffarth and Stuckenbruck, *Fall of the Angels*.

21. Augustine, *Confessions*, 7.3.5:161.

22. See Jung, *Fallen Angels*, and Russell, *Satan*.

be. If being able to will both good and ill really belongs to the essence of willing, why do humans then will not only what is good but what is ill?

The three questions—Why is it not impossible to will ill? Why is it not impossible for me to will ill? Why do I will ill?—thus demand different answers, and Augustine cannot provide them all.

10. Why Is It Not Impossible to Will Ill?

Why is the world not created by God in such a way for it to be impossible to will ill? If a world without ills is better than a world with ills, as will be readily admitted, would then a world in which there could be no ills not be even better than a world in which there are no ills only as a matter of fact? And if so, then why did God not create such a world? "Why doesn't God cause us to have a wholly virtuous free will?"[23] Augustine's answer to these questions is familiar from Plotinus: a world in which there could be no ills would be a world in which there could be nothing good, either. If there is to be good, then ill cannot be impossible. That follows from the contrast relationship between *bonum* and *malum*: someone who wills good thereby wills no ill. If it were impossible to will ills, it would also be impossible to will no ill and thereby also impossible to will good. A world without ills is thus better than a world with ills, but a world in which ills are possible is better than a world in which ills are impossible because only there can there also be good.[24] If, then, God wants to create a world in which there can be good, he must create a world in which there can be ills.

11. Why Is It Not Impossible for Me to Will Ill?

Why am I not created by God in such a way that it would be impossible for me to will ill? Even if willing ill does not represent a self-contradiction, if it is not impossible but possible, and even if it is true that this possibility exists only insofar as it exists *for someone*, it does by no means follow that it exists or must exist *for me* or for any other human being. If a world with the possibility of willing ill and thus also of willing good is better than a world without this possibility and if this possibility exists only if there is someone who can will ill, it also does not follow that this possibility exists or must exist for me: Would the world not be better than it is if the possibility of willing ills existed only for those who do not will ills but only will good? Would a world with angels who freely always will good although they could also will ill not be better than a world with human beings who could indeed will good but freely will ill? Insofar as the question suggests that God could have created a world in which it would be possible to will good or ill but what is willed freely is always good and not ill, it suggests, for the reasons cited, an impossible

23. Berthold, *God, Evil, and Human Learning*, 19.

24. This possibility, not the actuality of ill, is the point of "contrast theory"—otherwise, it could be refuted as easily as Berthold, *God, Evil, and Human Learning*, 10–18, proposes to do. The problem, however, is that Augustine does not clearly distinguish *ill* and *good* on the one hand and *good* and *better* on the other. Not every possible enhancement of the good presupposes ills to be actual, for otherwise protological remembrance of and eschatological hope for a good creation would be self-contradictory.

possibility: God can create a world in which good or ill can be willed freely but he cannot create a world in which only good is ever freely willed. To be sure, a world in which it is always the good that is freely willed would be better than a world in which that is not the case; but such a world can only ever exist *contingently* and *factually*: while it is possible freely to will good only where it could also not have been willed, it is actual only *in actually being willed*.

This is made clear both by the myth of the fall of the human and by that of the fall of the angels, which tell of ill actually being willed and done freely. As the story shows, it is not impossible for the humans in paradise to will ill; rather, they live beyond good and evil as long as they do not will what they do and do not not will what they do not do. A world in which humans do live freely, however, is better than one in which they are only able to live freely, and that is why a world in which humans freely will good and evil is better than one in which that is not the case. Although it would be better if they willed good and not ill, as is factually the case, for Augustine, a world in which there could be neither good nor ill would be less good a world than one in which ills factually exist, because in this one, there could be good, in that one, not. God can thus will that what is freely willed is only ever good and not ill. But he cannot effect that, he can only make it possible by creating creatures that can freely choose between good and ill by willing in a good way or not willing in an ill way even if he thereby also creates the possibility that they may choose and will ill. Whether good or ill is chosen, however, depends entirely on those who chose because that is an act of freedom and thus contingent. If, then, God had wanted to create a world in which it is impossible for humans to will ill, he would have had to create a world without humans. And this means, conversely: because God willed a world with human beings, it could not have been impossible for them to will ill.

12. Why Do I Will Ill?

Up this point, Augustine's argument holds. But the third question still remains unanswered: If for God a world with humans is a better world than a world without humans, and if being human is tied in with the ability to will ill or good, *why then do human beings will not good but ill*? Why among the possibilities they have is it this one that becomes actual? True, it is possible to will good only where the contrast between good and ill exists, for otherwise, that which is being willed could not be defined as good. But it does not follow that it would be self-contradictory to will only good and precisely not ill, that is, to actualize only the willing of good and not the willing of ill. Regarded both positively and negatively, it would be possible, after all, that human beings only will what is good (thus always do good), or that they cannot will what is good (thus never do good), or will what is not good (thus do evil), or that they cannot will what is not good (thus never do evil).

But possibilities are one thing, reality another. Like all realistic thinkers, Augustine does not start from mere possibilities but from actual life. The enigma of human existence, however, that he, too, is unable to solve is the *contingency of human freedom*, which freedom does not find itself confronted with abstract options of Good and Evil but has factually decided in favor of ill willing and ill doing. Augustine sees this, but his forceful attempt at bringing out humans' responsibility for their own willing and doing leads him, for all evil—the evil we do and the evil we suffer—to ask about a responsible perpetrator, that is, to try and understand the entire actuality of human life on the pattern of action. The contingency of human freedom—that human beings have decided in favor of ill willing and ill doing, and not otherwise—thus necessarily raises the question about a necessary perpetrator. Only if that perpetrator is the human being itself can the human be held responsible and punished. And this compels Augustine to think free human existence throughout as *contingent*, that is, as something that factually is the way it is but does not have to be this way and could be otherwise. Were that not the case, it would be impossible to think a liberation of the human from its having fallen into *malum*.

Yet since this is precisely what he is concerned with, Augustine rearticulates the contingency of human freedom in a *theology of sin* and seeks to resolve it in a *soteriology*. Salvation would be impossible for human beings if human life could be only the way it factually is. Yet it does not have to be evil, it could also be otherwise. How, though, can it become what it could be but is not? To understand Augustine's answer, we must understand his conception of sin.

B

Sin and Sinner

1. The Human Being as Sinner

WHEN, FROM THE PERSPECTIVE of the ill deed, we try to think *malum* as *peccatum*, we must ask about the subject of the free act of the will that has led, and leads time and again, to the *malefacere*. Among all the creatures, humans are the only beings whom we know to be able to act freely. For us, freedom as the faculty of self-determination is a fundamental characteristic of the human because it allows us to derive the central particularities of human life when compared to other organisms. Not all human beings are free, but all humans have the faculty freely to determine themselves to freedom. And what is true of freedom, according to Augustine, is true of sin as well.

The figure of speech in the singular—*the human being* is the subject of the *malefacere*—means a number of things. Neither are only *some human beings* sinners and others not, nor is a human being only *sometimes a sinner* and sometimes not. Instead, there is a fundamental alternative: either the human being is a sinner (and then everyone always is) or it is not (and then no one ever is). Now, there is sin and thus a sinner (at least one). If there is *one* sinner, however, then *everyone is a sinner*, for either *no* human being is a sinner or *all human beings* are sinners.

The reason is twofold. On the one hand, anyone who speaks of *being a sinner* always speaks about himself; on the other, he always speaks about the *overcoming of sin through God's grace*, that is, he refers to something good that happens to the human through God and is experienced as coming from God. That, however, means: if there is any sinner at all, then there are only sinners. If there were human beings who are not sinners, then there would be humans for whom God's grace would not be something good, who would thus not belong to those to whom God, in free care, renders good. For that is what *God's grace* means: God *makes* those who are not good (just, free, living the fullness of life), or are not good in the way they could and ought to be, *good* (just, free, gifted with the fullness of life)—not because they had deserved it in any way but because God is what he wills and does what he wills.

The theological thesis about the factual universality of sin is thus the flipside of the thesis in justification theology about the factual universality of divine grace. That is why its point is not negative but positive: God's care about some—indeed, already God's care about just one, from whom he could not withdraw his care again without ceasing to be God, as in Christian belief is proven centrally by Jesus Christ—shows his care about all: there is no one whom God as savior from Evil would not care about, nor is there anyone who would not experience good through this care of God's. And this, precisely, is what theology expresses in the designation "sinner": God does good to the humans in the *malum* of their ignorance of God, and humans are "sinners" insofar as that is true of them.

The theological argument behind this thesis can be briefly summarized: the fact *that* human beings are sinners is not salient with regard to them or any aspect of their lives but shows itself in God's care for them. The *contingency of this care* (it does not have to be actual) manifests the *contingency of being a sinner* (the human being does not have to be such that it requires God's care as something it lacks) in the first place: that the human being is a sinner is not self-evident, and it becomes understandable not with regard to the human but only with regard to God's care.

God's care, however, is no less contingent. The fact *that* God cares about the human is not self-evident either (contingency of care), nor is the fact that God cares about *every* human being (universality of care) and that his care *effects a good* for everyone that no human could effect for themselves (goodness of care). According to the Christian conviction, this only becomes clear in and through the story of Jesus Christ, which irrevocably (namely, revocable only at the prize of God abolishing himself) manifests what God wills (not so much from as much as) for human beings: that, in the communion with God, they become able in the fullest sense to be what as humans they can and ought to be.

The fundamental Christian creed therefore (1) refers essentially to the particular contingent events summarized in the expression "Jesus Christ" (historical contingency). It (2) expresses the universal point of this particular history by conceiving of these events as the end of history (and not only as events in history) or as the end of the world (and not only as an event in the course of the world) because it irreversibly reveals how God wills to act and does act toward human beings (eschatological contingency). And it (3) expresses the by no means self-evident fact that God wills only good for the human in the metaphor of Jesus's resurrection from death (soteriological contingency): God's care effects a *good* that humans can in no way effect for themselves. For—and this, precisely, is what the metaphor of resurrection from death highlights—where humans can no longer do or not do anything, where it is no longer possible to decide one way or the other, God himself creates the addressee of his care anew. This addressee thereby *is* entirely and exclusively through God's care for him, and he remains entirely bound to God's care without which he would be nothing and would sink back into nothingness. If God were to withdraw again, God himself would destroy the life addressed. But God would not be God if he again destroyed life that he himself freely created. That is why Christians confess the resurrection of Jesus Christ to be the pledge *that* God continues to care for everyone he cares for (God is faithful); that he cares about *every human being* (God is God for everyone); and that he continues to care for everyone *in the way that* he proved to be God in Jesus Christ (God is good). God remains faithful to himself and maintains his willing and effecting the best for each and every human being, for everything else would be nothing but the self-abolition and self-destruction of God. Everyone can thus bet on God caring for him with a good that makes it possible for and enables them to be human the way they could and ought to be in communion with God. That is why the orientation toward God becomes relevant for the orientation of our lives: it is not reconcilable with everything and everyone but leads to a mode of life that differs from other modes of life with the distinctions articulated in the Lord's Prayer, the confession of Christ, and the commandment of love.

2. The Nature of Sin

With these reflections, however, I have consciously gone beyond the conception of sin in the Augustinian tradition. We ought to return to this tradition, for its conception of sin contains a number of further salient aspects that have by no means been restricted to Roman Catholic thought but have shaped popular piety and exercised their influence widely across Protestant theology as well. It is by design, therefore, that I discuss it by way of a late testimony from the early eighteenth century, roughly contemporaneous with the theodicy debate between Bayle and Leibniz we explored earlier.

Sin here is defined as enacting and following the *Fall*, the *lapsus primorum parentium*. The *consequence of sin* is the transformation of the entire relationship between God and human beings, and that means that human's physical, spiritual, mental, mental, and moral condition changes. The dogmatic tradition describes this as the change from the originary state of justice (*iustitia originalis*) to the state of moral vitiation, which it conceives of as the loss of the image of God and the most profound deprivation of the human being's entire nature. It describes the action for which responsibility is to be taken in precise terms as the loss of the state of justice through original sin, which in turn it views as *peccatum originale originans*, that is, as enacting the turn away from God, and as *peccatum originale originatum*, that is, as the state of vice that follows from this turn away. Because this original deed depraves the *nature* of the human, it has consequences not just for the perpetrator but for all human beings.

On the other hand, the conception of sin just sketched is problematic because it presupposes an essentialist conception of human nature that is highly questionable not just philosophically but theologically as well. Sin there is thought not relationally as an impairment of the relationship with God but qualitatively as damage to the substance of the human. It is a privation, a loss of the state of justice and it is—which, factually, is of even greater consequence—a reorientation of the human toward the non- and counter-divine that manifests in carnal concupiscence, that is, the inclination toward evil. The human is *constantly inclined to Evil*, as evil thinking, evil willing, and evil deeds permanently prove. Sin manifests in innumerable sins, which, however, are being located in human life in places where the turn away from God is said to be particularly clearly in evidence: in the domain of sensuality, sexuality, immoderation, envy, boasting. God's anger, however, does not aim only at the sin in deeds committed but already at the *constant inclination to Evil* from which they start. It is thus not only the *deeds* committed that are sin but also the *thoughts* and the *intentions* (will) that never become deeds; and what is being punished is not only what is done, thought, and willed but already the *basic inclination to evil thoughts, evil willing, and evil deeds*. That is why the human being is wholly and entirely sinner and not just somewhat sinful in only some of the dimensions of human life.

The pastoral and theological consequences are devastating.[1] Every illness, every accident, every misfortune not only entitles but practically compels us to ask what offense those affected and thus punished have committed. The victims of evil are thereby, in addition to being victims, held responsible for the evil. Of course this does not always happen in so direct a way. But the tendency to seek the reason for someone becoming the victim of evil with the victim is thereby established and for centuries has terrible consequences. Not only does every *malum* in the course of the world become a punitive tribunal of God's; those who become its victims, moreover, are held (at least co-) responsible for it. This was not the least of the good reasons and the indisputable justification for Enlightenment thinkers' revolt against this view of the world and against the dogmatic tradition's anthropology of sin on which it is based.

3. The Cosmic Dimension of Sin

The approach that begins with the *evil deed* and proceeds to inquiring into the *will* it is based on and investigating the conditions under which the will determines itself as *willing ill* or *willing good* comes up against limits when the attempt is made to turn it into the exclusive and comprehensive explanation of the reality of Evil. The human is only one factor in the whole of reality, the scope of life is wider than human life, and not everything ill that happens and takes place in the organic world can be traced back to humans' ill willing as its cause.

The step already from an individual human being and its ill willing to other human beings or even the totality of human life and human history is problematic. When taking ill willing and ill deeds as one's guide, a spreading of one person's ill to others can only be thought in terms of her ill deed's *having an effect on others*. Yet this seems to be able to connect only those with the individual ill doer who *simultaneously with her* or *later than her* can be affected and influenced by her deeds. And it is not by chance that for this very reason Augustine and the tradition he represents take the step from the evil individual to humanity as a whole via the historical-mythical construct of Adam and Eve who as *the first human beings* brought ill into the world, an ill that has a lasting effect in the continuity of human history and turns this history into a *total nexus of ill willing and ill doing*. This takes place in two stages, both articulated in doctrine, namely in the theory of the original sin of the human being or of the *fall,* and in the theory of the continuing effect of the original sin or of *hereditary sin*. Both are to be understood as theological attempts to make the view of Evil obtained from the ill willing and ill doing of the individual fruitful for understanding Evil in the history of humanity as a whole: the history of humanity is a total nexus of ill deeds that continuously produce new ill deeds; these ill deeds are based

---

1. As Volkmann, *Der Zorn Gottes*, 12, rightly points out.

on an always-new ill willing; and there are no human beings who would not be subject to this total nexus of ill acting and ill willing.

Yet at most, this approach can explain Evil in human history, not the ill in the total nexus of life or of the world in general. In concentrating on the individual human being and on the total nexus of humanity, the Augustinian tradition has thus sought to account for the *cosmic dimension of ill* in two contexts.

The first is the attempt to relate all ill that *cannot* be immediately traced back to human ill doing and ill willing to it *indirectly* by conceiving of it as a *punitive institution of God's for the human ill doers*: all ill either results from an ill willing and is thus guilty (*culpa*) or it is a divine punishment for the ill doers and thus just (*poena*). The centrality of the human being for understanding Evil is thus consolidated by understanding all ill in general to be an *ill for human beings* and, moreover, understanding all ill for human beings either as the *result of their own free ill willing* or as *punitive consequence of their own free ill doing*. This anthropocentric total view not only presupposes that ill only ever exists as *ill for human beings* but also that *there are always already human beings*, namely *human beings who will and do evil*. Since the Darwinist revolution, this view has become untenable as an empirical-historical conception. Auxiliary constructs like the notion that already prior to the human being, ills existed for other organisms—for dinosaurs, for example, who went extinct, or for other living beings—in preparation of the punitive ills that would become necessary for the predicted ill doing of human beings are unacceptable not only as *post festum* retroprojections but also in their fundamental tendency. The suffering of others cannot be related to human ill doing this way. It is ill not only *for humans*, and neither is it a pure making possible of ills that were able to become ills for humans when humans were to be punished: it is *ill for other living beings*. Reading the totality of ills in the evolutionary history of life as *making possible and implementing the punishment of the human being for the ills it willed and committed* is theologically obsolete. Not only are not all ills punishments; not all ills have something do to with humans: the cosmos of ills is more comprehensive than the cosmos of humanity and the nexus of actions of human history.

The theological tradition was indeed aware of this, and it attempted to think it in a doctrinal context that today is no less obsolete: the theory of angels. I read this doctrine as an attempt to obtain once more, from the concentration of ill willing and ill doing, the *dimension of the reality of the world as a whole*, that is, to operate an extension not to the whole of human history but to the universe as such.

4. The Theory of Angels

Just as all ill in the human world and in human history is due to human beings' *male velle et bene nolle* and the *male facere* that results from it, so all ill in the world and world history in general is due to the *male velle et bene nolle* and the *male facere* on the part of suprahuman creatures: the angels. Like human beings, angels are *creatures* and thus distinct from the creator, but unlike human beings, they are creatures who are free from the dangers of sensuality and sensuous matter. That they, too, are not spared from Evil shows that not sensible matter (as the Neoplatonists think) but something else must be the *causa mali*.

Accordingly, the dogmatic tradition has developed a differentiated theory of angels, whose main points can be summarized as follows: angels are understood to be spiritual substances in accordance with Scripture (Ps 104:4; Heb 1:14); that means that like humans, they are *created* and therefore *finite* beings; but unlike humans, they are (put positively) entirely *spiritual* and *intelligent* beings and thus (put negatively) are *non-corporeal* beings.

Their typical properties are inferred from this: as non-corporeal beings, they do not have all the restricting properties of corporeal beings, that is, they are invisible, immortal, everlasting, not tied to specific places, and indivisible, in short: they are atomic spiritual beings that are and can be everywhere and always. Yet precisely as such spiritual beings, they are not merely a privation of corporeal being but defined positively as *intelligent beings*, that is, they possess knowledge and freedom of the will. As creatures of God, however, they possess all this not just like that or for their own use but for a very specific purpose: being created means being created for a specific purpose and with a specific destiny, and the purpose and destiny of angels is *to glorify God* and *to serve God*.

This outline sketches the preconditions that allow for describing the history of angels. The dogmatic tradition does so by distinguishing three scenarios it derives from each other: *status gratiae*, *status gloriae*, and *status miseriae*. The *status gratiae* is the originary state of the angels created by God. They are all equally good, equally just, equally holy, and have the same basic determinations, thus freedom of the will as well. Since, however, this freedom is understood as *freedom of choice*, and namely as freedom of choice between good and evil, it does not exclude the possibility of disobedience toward God. For only, we are told, if they could do evil but do not do it do they do the good they do freely and of their own will and thus in a way that corresponds to their destiny as spiritual beings for the glorification of God. Yet some angels made ill use of their freedom of the will: they decided in favor of disobedience toward God and thus entered into contradiction with their destiny as angels. This changed all of reality and transformed the *status gratiae* of angelic existence into two subsequent forms: the *status gloriae* of the *good angels* and the *status miseriae* of the *evil angels*.

The disobedience of some angels changed the state of all angels: the good angels, too, changed through the fall of the evil angels because the action of the others demanded of them to decide either to act like they did or not to do so and maintain what they were created to do. They were compelled to decide and to act. And this is always the first consequence of evil doing: that others are coerced into a decision about their own doing and willing. Yet only this decision makes angels *good* angels, and God rewards them for it by transforming their *status gratiae* into a *status gloriae*: they are strengthened in the good in favor of which they have decided in such a way that they can no longer even run the danger of resolving otherwise and falling. Because they have decided not to sin, they are rewarded with no longer being able to sin: the *status gloriae* differs from the *status gratiae* in that the possibility of being able to sin no longer exists. The good angels can no longer commit sins and evils.

The objection readily suggests itself: Is this really an improvement and not rather a fundamental loss? If freedom is to consist in being able to choose between good and evil, then is not the loss of the possibility of choosing evil the loss of freedom as such? The doctrinal response is that this is to be seen not as a loss but as an *enhancement of their freedom*, for being able to choose only good is said to be better than being able to choose good or evil. This seems to be none too convincing an answer if we base ourselves on the contrast relationship between willing good and willing evil from which the entire argument starts. For does this relationship not mean that the loss of the possibility of willing evil also abolishes the possibility of willing good? That is admitted. Yet the objection is qualified as an abstract one said to ignore the context of the entire argumentation: God abolishes the possibility of being able to will evil on the basis that the angels (or some angels) have decided to be *good* angels, that is, to will the good: they act well not out of compulsion but *freely motivated and resolved*, and it is to this decision that the abolition of the possibility of willing evil refers. *Because they freely decided in favor of the good, they can no longer decide in favor of Evil.* The possibility of willing evil as condition of the possibility of being able to will good is thus not simply negated; it is *present as memory and precondition of their own decision in favor of the good*—but precisely only as *memory* and *precondition* of the decision *made* and no longer as the possibility of *future* (different) decisions. Because they have freely decided in favor of the good, they can no longer—not on their own initiative and on the basis of their decision as such but through God's grace and reward—decide otherwise than in favor of the good. In abolishing the possibility of willing evil, God commits the good angels to their own history, that is, to the decision in favor of the good.

The situation of the evil angels is analogous: they, too, through their decision in favor of Evil, fundamentally change their *status gratiae* into a *status miseriae*, and in complete analogy, this state is defined as the divinely ordained abolition of the possibility of willing and doing good. To the loss of the possibility of sinning among the good angels corresponds the loss of the possibility of not sinning among the evil angels: they can no longer do anything but ill because they freely and without compulsion decided in favor of willing ill and doing ill and are committed by God to this free decision in favor of Evil. Unlike the fallen human beings, the fallen angels can thus not be saved: they have chosen Evil, and God respects that. The consequence is a fundamental tarnishing and obscuring of their angelic powers such that they think about themselves and about God and everything divine in a fundamentally inverted manner: along with their willing, their knowledge, too, has been inverted into wrong knowledge.

Behind the narrative structure, we must see the theoretical point of this mythical story: even as it holds on to the sin character of all evil, it seeks to give an explanation of the fact of *malum* that cannot be found directly in the recourse to the sinning of human beings. To do so, it must not only understand the entire universe as a nexus of actions that allows for understanding every event as a doing that in turn makes it possible to ask about the intentions (the willing) it is based on. As a Christian approach, it must also be careful not to obscure the created character of the universe with its explanation of cosmic *mala* by the sin of the fall of the angels, that is, not to question God's judgment that what has been created is good. Hence the dogmatic theory of angels has argued that while the exact number of fallen angels is uncertain, it is absolutely certain that the greater number did not fall: the angelic world as a whole is more strongly defined by Good than by Evil, Evil is marginal over against Good. Were it otherwise, the world of the human would not only be threatened, it would be lost.

The cosmological consequence of the worldview laid out in this narrative is a universe of different ontological and axiological levels. The reality of the world is divided into the world of the good angels above, the world of evil angels below, and the human world that lies between them. This has the anthropological consequence that since it can move up or down, depending on how humans live and act, the human world is being understood as the arena where good and evil angels fight over the human souls: humans are everywhere dealing with angels but always also with evil and fallen angels who seek to seduce them and blind them, to inspire them with false notions about God and everything else and tempt them into a wrong determination of their will.

Compared to a theory of *malum* focused on human acting and sinning alone, the theory of angels represents not only an expansion that allows for including the entire visible and invisible universe in theological theorizing. It also has the effect, in one important respect, of being more adequate to experience than modern attempts at restricting Evil entirely to moral Evil and at focussing this moral Evil entirely on human acting and willing. Devils and demons *symbolize the suprapersonal power of Evil* over against the offenses of humans.[2] We not only *do* Evil because and insofar as we will it, but we also find ourselves *caught up in evil* that we cannot evade and that leads even our best-intentioned deeds to have evil consequences we not only did not expect but would under all circumstances have sought to avoid. Just as good does not happen only where we will good, so evil is not avoided where we do not have evil intentions. The reality of the world is more abysmal than the modern, morality-focused view of the human suggests. This must be considered even when we no longer describe this aspect of tragic entanglement in Evil as *God's punishment* or as the *action of demons*, as the theological tradition just outlined does.

Finally, soteriologically, too, the theory of angels makes an important point: the overcoming of Evil must be thought not just futurally but cosmological-universally and therefore at the place of each and every individual. The liberation from evil must not be limited to correcting human willing, that is, be thought only as the giving of a new will. It must comprehend the liberation from the burdens of our history, that is, save us from the consequences of our evil deeds. And it must take place as care for the victims of this history, that is, obtain justice for them. Only a conception of God that allows for understanding and thinking God in such a way that he overcomes Evil in the world in these three respects can represent a soteriologically acceptable answer to the reality of Evil. Every merely private salvation is thus excluded from the outset. This, too, the theory of angels has inscribed in the Christian intellectual tradition.

2. That much at least is brought out in Bernhard Claret's study, *Geheimnis des Bösen*, which leaves many things unclear. He does not succeed in developing a useful and precise set of concepts to thematize these phenomena. Not so Jürgen Bründl. He shows that in the figure of the devil, this suprapersonal power is interpreted *personally* and therefore *addressable*: "Without the devil, the reality of Evil remains without a face and without an addressee. . . . In this way, the figure of the devil interprets the phenomena of an evil reality as a mystery in the theological sense" (Bründl, *Masken des Bösen*, 401).

The world, however, is today no longer being experienced and understood as the arena of angels and demons but as a law-governed nexus of natural forces whose exploration is the task of the sciences. This is, on the one hand, a consequence of the Christian faith, which de-demonized the world and rendered it, as God's good creation, accessible to human research. On the other hand, however, it is also a development that in the Renaissance and the Enlightenment worked against Christian faith insofar as scientific inquiry focused not on exploring the world as *creation* but as *nature*, as it increasingly explored the functional nexus of the forces and laws of nature without there being any meaningful reference to God in its hypotheses and theories to explain the reality of the world: "We don't need that hypothesis."[3]

The consequence for Christian faith was that it had to give expression to its belief in the good creator under conditions that no longer allowed for speaking of God in scientific terms. Following Schleiermacher, Kierkegaard, and Bultmann, this has been attempted in ever-different manners by asserting God no longer cosmologically but anthropologically, which resulted, especially in the second half of the twentieth century, in warnings about the threatening loss of the cosmological dimension of the Christian faith. The efforts at countering this danger in Idealist philosophies of the absolute or in process philosophy and process theology can be understood as attempts at regaining the cosmological horizon of the Christian faith. Yet here and in other efforts, it is important not to fall back into the opposite extreme, to avoid throwing the de-demonization of the world promoted and effected by the Christian faith into doubt, that is, to avoid replacing a theology of the world with a new mythologization of the human experience of the world. Just how great this danger is is evident in the manifold fundamentalist currents that propagate an antimodern version of modern theology. To counteract the scientific de-deification of the world, they fill up the world, in a spiritualist or fundamentalist manner, with forces, spirits, and gods that human life is said to have to deal with.

In confronting all this, Christianity today is challenged to resist both the secularizing de-deification of the world and its re-mythologizing deification. This includes in particular asserting the basic attitude of belief in creation—God's creation is good—against neo-Manichean dualizations of the world as the arena of the struggle between Good and Evil. While these latter do highlight the power aspect of Evil and the moment of lapse into Evil, they very inappropriately minimize human beings' individual responsibility. Here, too, it is important to maintain the correct balance between not releasing humans from the responsibility for the Evil they will and do, on the one hand, and not falling into the error of always and everywhere tracing back all ill and evil to someone's *guilt and intention,* on the other: as certainly as there is guilty doing of ill, so certainly there are experiences of anonymous Evil that is *supraindividual* and cannot be attributed to any single doer caught up in it alone.

The theory of angels draws attention to a final important point: the liberation from Evil cannot be thought and represented in all cases. While the Christian tradition thinks the liberation of the human being from *malum* such that the human *sola gratia* becomes *a new human being* open toward God and turned toward God, it does not provide for such a renewal for the fallen angels. For them, salvation from their self-chosen turn away

3. See Antommarchi, *Mémoires du docteur F. Antommarchi,* 282.

from God *is not at all conceivable*: evil angels eternally remain evil, their wrong decision remains fixed in eternity. This is not only one of the main reasons for the eschatological dualism of church tradition, which has the world enter heaven or hell. It is also a notion with immense pedagogical consequences because it emphatically holds free beings responsible and commits them to the consequences of their freely chosen actions. As much as this underscores the importance of one's own decisions, it also becomes a highly problematic means of exercising pressure where the ill consequences of one's own free actions cannot be repaired and cannot be forgiven even by God. Human beings are surrendered to their own willing and doing as victims, victims not just of another's doing but victims of their own. And this, precisely, is one of the points where the secularization of this tradition in Kant's ethics sets in.[4]

4. See Rommel, *Zum Begriff des Bösen bei Augustinus und Kant.*

C

Will and Moral Evil: The Project of Freedom

1. Doctrinal and Authentic Theodicy

AT THE END OF the age of theodicy in the eighteenth century, nobody stressed more emphatically than Immanuel Kant did that when it comes to understanding Evil, the human being is thrown back entirely on itself. In 1791, with regard to the preceding century's rationalist efforts in the wake of Leibniz and Wolff, he unequivocally diagnoses "the miscarriage of all philosophical trials in theodicy." All theoretical arguments that seek to prove that the fact of ills and evils can be reconciled with the notion of an omnibenevolent and all-wise creator fail not only in fact but in principle, because reason can acquire reliable knowledge only about objects of sense experience. Yet neither *God* nor *freedom* nor the *world* are possible objects of experience. The theoretical function these "ideas" have is different: they do not designate transcendent "objects" but indicate how we, as free finite beings, situate ourselves in the whole of what we can know and shape through our actions and, in so doing, understand ourselves as members of a shared world that is structured not only by the rules of natural causality (natural world) but also by the rules of the causality of freedom (moral world).

Kant does not think that we simultaneously live in two distinct worlds, even if some of his statements might give that impression. We live in the one and only world there is. But in our lives, we have two irreducibly different experiences of reality, which he calls "nature" and "freedom." The first, nature, marks the experience that we are conditioned by something other than ourselves: we would not exist, and we would not exist the way we exist, if something else were not the case. We are conditioned by conditions over which we have no control. The second, freedom, by contrast, marks the experience that we can condition something other than ourselves and are able to determine ourselves one way or another: some things in our world would not exist, and they would not exist the way they exist, if we did not exist, and not only because we are there but because we effect them on our own initiative. We can get actions going and create works that are conditioned on us and our doing. Indeed—and this goes even further—we can act in such a way and determine ourselves to act in ways that can in no way be derived from something else or that seem in any way to be conditioned by anything but themselves: we can act freely (freedom of action) and we can freely determine ourselves to act (autonomy). What Kant conceptualizes as "nature" and "freedom" are these experiences of being conditioned and dependent on the one hand, and of being independent and capable of self-determination on the other: both belong to human life, neither can be reduced to the other, and we cannot live as humans without being both natural and free beings.

Precisely because both these experiences are to be found in human life, it is important not to blend and confuse them but rather to clearly distinguish between them and not let ourselves be led into wrong inferences from nature to freedom or vice versa. Seen as a natural nexus, our world of experience is a law-governed linking up of causes and effects that yields no information about any intention that guides it or any good will to creation it is based on: (what we perceive as) the good order of nature does not speak in favor of them, and what is inappropriate (which we experience as ills) does not speak against them. That which is (nature) does not yield insight into what ought to be; at most we can come to understand why that which is is the way it is when we begin to grasp the laws in force behind the phenomena. Yet inversely, too, insight into that which ought to be (freedom) does not yield knowledge of nature but only the discovery of what life could be if it were as it ought to be, that is, if it were good.[1]

Kant thus takes up an insight of the Enlightenment tradition and restructures it for his purposes. Nature is not an open book in which the will of the creator could be recognized, as seventeenth- and eighteenth-century physico-theologians had tried to prove. On this point, Kant agrees with theological orthodoxy, which had justified it via the theory of sin: in principle, God's will can be recognized in creation (it is recognizable *per se*), but through sin we have become blind for it (it is unrecognizable *quoad nos*). Yet Kant cannot take the theological way out, which consists in trusting Scripture to come to know God's will and on that basis decipher nature as creation. The Book of Scripture is not a viable key for understanding the Book of Nature. Nature, as Galilei emphasized, is written in the language of mathematics, and it has to be understood on its own or it is not understood at all, as Newton showed. This, however, makes the natural world in every respect "a closed book" from which no form of "God's *final aim*" (which is always moral) can be obtained by "*ratiocinating*." All attempts at a "doctrinal theodicy" are thus, as Kant says, doomed to failure as a matter of principle, because "at bottom . . . our presumptuous reason fail[s] to recognize its limitations."[2]

Yet the experiences of Evil, ill, and suffering remain, and therefore also the question concerning God the creator of the world and his will for human life. With regard to these questions, the world as nature (natural order) might be a closed book for us, but that does not exclude that they can be understood on the basis of insight into the world as the place where humans live and the moral order of freedom thereby posited.[3]

1. See Kant, *Critique of Pure Reason*, 540–41 (A547–48/B575–76).

2. Kant, "Miscarriage," 31 and 24 (AA 8: 264 and 255).

3. This addition is decisive: what the world as nature is can be understood only from nature, and that is what the natural sciences seek to do. Yet what the natural world is *for the human being* and for how human life is lived in it cannot be stated if the human moral order of life and orientation by freedom is

We live in the world by shaping it, and we shape it by determining ourselves to relate to what determines us in a determinate way and to deal with what we seek to determine in a determinate way. All our interests, including reason's interest in knowledge and our efforts at maximizing our knowledge and minimizing our ignorance, are thus ultimately motivated practically and, seen in isolation, are incomplete and ultimately incomprehensible: even the interest of "speculative reason is only conditional and is complete in practical use alone."[4] We want to know what is true because we must live and act, and what does not help us to that end is useless. According to Kant, that is true of all knowledge. "Mathematics, natural science, even the empirical knowledge of humankind, have a high value as means, for the most part to contingent but yet ultimately to necessary and essential ends of humanity."[5] We thus learn something not only about the world but above all about ourselves and our lives in this world. And that is what counts.

It is in this sense motivated by practical life that Kant, as regards understanding Evil, cites Job and calls for an "authentic theodicy," in which God "through our reason . . . becomes himself the interpreter of his will as announced through creation." We thus no longer seek with our reason theoretically to interpret the world with a view to God but conceive of our reason as an instrument of God's interpreting himself: it is not us who make the world understandable for ourselves, but the world makes itself understandable to us. For this self-interpretation of God's "is not the interpretation of a *ratiocinating* (speculative) reason, but of an *efficacious* practical reason which . . . can be considered as the unmediated definition and voice of God through which he gives meaning to the letter of his creation."[6] God's good will is not to be recognized in nature but solely in receptive reason or in conscience.

At the core of his conception of reason, we might say, Kant thus discovers a point at which reason comes into view no longer actively, as a comprehending (*logos*) and a self-determining and self-fashioning (*ethos*) factor, but passively, as *hearing, receiving,* or *pathic reason.* The power of reason as *logos* and *ethos* is due to a *pathos* in which it becomes what it is for us: the voice of conscience in which we are not talking to ourselves but God's will immediately and authentically discloses itself as God's will and not merely as the hypothetical result of inferences from something else. As conscience, reason hears that through which it is constituted in the first place. Without this fundamental being conditioned by something other than the natural conditions of the natural world, it could not in the first place establish an active relationship with the phenomena of the natural world in theoretical cognition and ethical self-determination. It comes from something other than itself, and this enables it to determine itself not only conditionally but freely to know and act in dealing with the natural phenomena of the world. Reason can be theoretically and practically active only because and to the extent that, as conscience, it

---

ignored. The exploration of the order of freedom thus does not convey any knowledge of nature (what nature is *as such*) but insight into what the natural world and its scientific exploration signify for human life (what they are *for us*). Both questions have an irreducible significance of their own and cannot be transformed one into the other.

4. Kant, *Critique of Practical Reason,* 237 (AA 5:121).

5. Kant, *Critique of Pure Reason,* 701 (A850/B878).

6. Kant, "Miscarriage," 31–32 (AA 8:264).

becomes what, as cognizing and will-determining reason, it is: the place where human freedom is experienced in knowing and acting.

2. Nature and Freedom

The presupposition of Kant's opposition of doctrinal and authentic theodicy is thus his distinction between a *theoretical* and a *practical* use of reason, a distinction to be viewed against the backdrop of the pathic constitution of reason as *hearing reason* or *conscience* and the critical restriction of the theoretical use of reason Kant operates there to the "realm of nature," as opposed to (in Leibnizian terms) the "realm of grace" or "realm of freedom."[7] If the question concerning the sense of senseless ill is to make any sense at all, the world must be described in light of this distinction in differentiated terms: if the world were only nature, there would be nothing to understand. As natural beings, humans would be subject "to all the evils of poverty, illnesses, and untimely death, just like all the other animals on earth, and will always remain thus until one wide grave engulfs them all together . . . and flings them . . . back into the abyss of the purposeless chaos of matter from which they were drawn."[8] Natural processes have no meaning even if, in a teleological perspective, we suppose the functioning of nature to have such a meaning. But that is no more than a subjective way of seeing things that may be unavoidable for us but should not lead us to seek in nature what we see in it: *meaning for us*.

For us, there can be such meaning in nature, but it can exist without reservations only in the domains where we act and posit meaning: in the domain of moral action. Only because there is such action can we meaningfully ask about meaning, but because we can do so, we must do so. Free action includes not only willing something that is not but ought to be; it also includes supposing that what ought to be can be and hoping that it will be. Now, freedom strives to actualize the morally good, an actualization that for us consists in the virtuousness of the morally good life. Under the factual conditions of the wrong life, this cannot be actualized; we concretely encounter it, therefore, only as what ought to be, not as what is. Moreover, for the *animal rationale* we as human beings are and remain even as moral persons, there can be such a *good life* only if we do not just *live* but also *live happily*, that is, actualize the maintenance of life (existence) and happiness (well-being) we strive for naturally as rational animals. Who does not live cannot live well, and who does not live happily will not live the good life as a matter of course but only ever be able to experience it as an always-alien contrast to guide the actualization of human wishes and hopes. The shared actualization of virtuousness (good life) and happiness (happiness) can thus not exist in this factual life, but only if the world in which we live is as it could be (a world in which we can live happily) and ought to be (a world in which we can live well), that is, if the difference between what is and what ought to be in our life is abolished because we, *on our own initiative* (and no longer just in obeying an imperative), do what we ought to do and *factually are* (and not just imagine and hope to

---

7. See Kant, *Critique of Pure Reason*, 680–84 (A812–19/B840–47).
8. Kant, *Critique of the Power of Judgment*, §87:318 (AA 5:452).

be) what we can be. In this life, we are very far away from that, but only the actualization of these improbabilities would render a good and happy life probable.

These reflections allow us to understand why for Kant not only the postulate of God but the postulate of eternal life remains immediately tied to the notion of freedom. Who wills the good also wills that it become actual and remain actual. This is conceivable for us human animals only if the world as it is as nature (being), as it would have to be for a happy life (well-being), and as it ought to be for a good life (being good) does not exist with "is" and "ought to be" juxtaposed yet unrelated—as on the one hand it really is (factual existence in the world) and could be possible (possible being well or happy in the world) and on the other hand as it would have to be if good life really ought to be possible within it (normative being good in the world)—but with "is" *and* "ought to be" organized in relation to each other. If there really ought to be freedom, its actualization requires a world that even as the natural nexus that it is and as the good order that it could be, not only as the moral order that it ought to be, can be understood to "intimate . . . the foresight [*Vorsorge*] of a wisdom in command of nature" to be at work in it such that "the existence of a cause of all nature, distinct from nature"—which, in theory, is not properly to be articulated as such—is not a self-contradictory definition.[9] It is precisely the notion of God, to which Kant takes recourse here, that guarantees that the human being's will to freedom (being good) and the striving for happiness (being happy) can be actualized insofar as the world of freedom (in actualizing what ought to be and what is willed to be) and the world of nature (in the actualization of what is wished for and what is hoped for) can be transformed one into the other or represented one by the other.

What is thought here and developed in the ideas of God (theology), freedom (cosmology), and immortality (psychology) is thus not something alien forced onto human reason from outside, or a merely speculative fancy, but the innermost and unavoidable insight of reason. After all, "reason . . . by means of the *theological* idea"—that is, the idea of God—"frees itself from fatalism—from blind natural necessity both in the connection of nature itself, without a first principle, and in the causality of this principle itself—and leads the way to the concept of a cause through freedom, and so to that of a highest intelligence."[10] It thinks God because only that way can it think the reality of freedom, the actualization of good that ought to be and is willed to be, and the fulfillment of the happiness wished for and hoped for in human life.[11] There is no freedom without God, at least no freedom that is understood as not merely the conditional faculty to choose between options it is presented with yet which it has not produced, but a freedom that is autonomy, that is, the unconditional faculty to set purposes for one's life that are not just opportune or helpful but morally good. Only those who are autonomous can be morally

9. Kant, "To Perpetual Peace," in *Practical Philosophy*, 311–51, here 331n (AA 8:361), and *Critique of Practical Reason*, 240 (AA 5:125). The concept of cause here is obviously used differently than in the strictly governed context of the theoretical use of reason, that is, not as a category of the understanding applied to phenomena.

10. Kant, *Prolegomena*, §60:152 (AA 4:363); see also Heimsoeth, "Zum kosmotheologischen Ursprung der kantischen Freiheitsantinomie."

11. On this point, see especially the work of Josef Schmucker, *Die primären Quellen des Gottesglaubens; Das Problem der Kontingenz der Welt; Die Ontotheologie des vorkritischen Kant;* and *Das Weltproblem in Kants Kritik der reinen Vernunft.*

good (and morally evil), and no one is autonomous without being oriented by the notion of God without whom the being happy that is wished for would not be an actualizable possibility in this world, and the being good that is hoped for would not be a possible reality of this world.

3. Freedom and Natural Causality

Kant does not doubt that there is freedom, namely freedom understood as the capacity of finite rational beings to set purposes for their actions themselves and to realize these purposes. In their conduct, human beings are not only determined by what the natural causal processes are, they can also orient themselves by what ought to be, which plays no role in the causal nexus of nature, cannot be obtained from it, and cannot be tied back to it. In the way they live their lives, humans are dealing with what is *and* with what ought to be, and "ought" is in no way comprehensible as a modulation or manifestation of "is."

This has implications that go in two directions. On the one hand, it means that nature can be explained scientifically without science being able or having to take recourse to freedom, even if explanation, as a human action, points beyond the nature thus explainable: freedom is not a natural phenomenon and thus not a possible object of scientific explanation. On the other hand, however, it also means that freedom cannot be thought in such a way that its actualization would contradict nature. Freedom is neither a derivative nor a negation of natural phenomena: "the ought, if one has merely the course of nature before one's eyes, has no significance whatever."[12] This does not mean that the ought as such is of no significance, quite the opposite. It just cannot be explained in the nexus of nature but must take recourse to a different kind of reality. And that presupposes that the phenomena of our knowledge of nature, which are defined and governed by causal mechanisms, are not everything, that they, in Kant's terms, as "appearances," are precisely not "things in themselves": "For if appearances are things in themselves, then freedom cannot be saved."[13]

The condition of the possibility of freedom is thus that two critical differences apply: the difference between *nature* and *freedom* and—with regard to both sides of this difference—that between *appearance* and *thing in itself*. Both are categorial differences whose two sides do not differ by degree. They can therefore not be demonstrated in any domain of real phenomena because phenomena are always characterized by transitions. There is no *nature* and besides, within its horizon, *freedom* as well, and there are no *appearances* and besides, within their horizon, *things in themselves* as well. Rather, this way of distinguishing is required if, as free beings, we want to orient ourselves in the world, live in it, and act in it. For in doing that, we not only have to take into account the experience that we can initiate modes of conduct and sequences of actions that in crucial respects are not only effects of determining causes (experience of *freedom*: actions are not only effects of natural causes but appearances of freedom) but also the related experience that no concrete mode of conduct and action is exclusively and completely determined

12. Kant, *Critique of Pure Reason*, 540 (A547/B575).
13. Kant, *Critique of Pure Reason*, 535 (A536/B564).

freely, that is, that no conduct or action immediately and directly actualizes the "will" or the motivating intention. This actualization is always codetermined by givens that only ever let the result be approximately what it ought to be (*experience* of freedom: appearances of freedom are not exclusively results of free determination but always also effects of other events and consequences of other actions).

If on the level of appearances, that is, with regard to everything that can be scientifically observed and described, no phenomenon can be unambiguously and exclusively identified as a phenomenon of freedom, if it comes into view as such only if the causes that motivate and effect it are being considered, then there can be appearances of freedom only if there is not only a causality of nature but also a causality of freedom that is distinct and can be distinguished from natural causality. There is only one world in which we live, but this world takes place as a succession of *events* of which some, not all, can simultaneously be understood as *actions*. But is that the case?

In the third antinomy, Kant articulates the problem in pointed terms and discusses it in detail.[14] According to the thesis, "[c]ausality in accordance with laws of nature is not the only one from which all the appearances of the world can be derived. It is also necessary to assume another causality through freedom in order to explain them." And according to the antithesis, "[t]here is no freedom, but everything in the world happens solely in accordance with laws of nature."[15] Kant justifies the thesis in the manner of the classic cosmological argument: the chain of causations for each individual phenomenon cannot progress to infinity but must be complete if this phenomenon is to be rather than not be. The completeness of the series of causations must lead to a first cause that possesses the "faculty of beginning a series of successive things or states *from itself*," a cause, in other words, that is free.[16] And that means: either there is freedom or no phenomenon can be explained or comprehended completely as the effect of its causes.

Kant justifies the antithesis with the corresponding opposite train of thought. Suppose freedom exists: then it remains obscure how a causal chain could arise from it, how a "non-dynamic" state could transform into a "dynamic" state. The dialectic of the two theses follows from a shared presupposition: that every appearance is the effect of the totality of the causes that condition it. This totality, however, is never given; it is not an object of possible experience but always an *idea*. Yet ideas are not appearances and are not apt to explain appearances. They instead compel us to suppose a categorial difference between *appearance* (which can be explained) and *thing in itself* (which is not an apt explanatory reason but is to be supposed systematically in order for the explanation of phenomena to be possible). Without this critical difference, neither the possibility of explaining natural phenomena nor the possibility of freedom are comprehensible. Yet since both are realities (we can in fact explain some things, as Newton has shown, and we really can initiate actions, as we know), the distinction between causality of nature and causality of freedom is a supposition that systematically cannot be avoided if we want to understand the world in which we live and the reality of our life in this world.

14. For a discussion of the most important interpretations of this set of problems, see Natterer, *Systematischer Kommentar zur Kritik der reinen Vernunft*, esp. 503–40.

15. Kant, *Critique of Pure Reason*, 484–85 (A444–45/B472–73).

16. Kant, *Critique of Pure Reason*, 486 (A448/B476).

4. Free Will

Freedom is thus to be defined not only negatively as that which cannot be explained by taking recourse to natural causality and empirical being. That, rather, is merely the flipside of the positive definition as an ought that represents "a species of necessity and a connection with grounds which does not occur anywhere else in the whole of nature."[17]

The place where this non-natural causality of freedom is experienced is what Kant, taking up the philosophical tradition, calls *free will*. It is a will determined in the two respects mentioned. On the one hand, "such a will must be thought as altogether independent of the natural law of appearances in their relations to one another, namely the law of causality."[18] This is not an impossible notion, as Kant shows in resolving the third antinomy, provided we critically restrict natural causality to the domain of the appearances of the sensible-phenomenal world and do not extend it to things in themselves or the noumenal world. If we negate this difference, the possibility of freedom collapses; if we critically admit it, the consequence is that there can be no theoretical knowledge of the freedom of the will: free will is not a natural phenomenon, theoretical reason has nothing to say about the theme of freedom, either positively or negatively. On the other hand, however, free will is to be thought not only negatively as something that cannot be explained as an effect of natural causes but at the same time positively as something that—as *will*—can get effects in the sensuous world started by itself (spontaneously)[19] and that—as *free* will—can in so doing refer to itself in such a way that as the initiator of such effects, it can orient itself by the good and thus determine itself to do what is good or to do what is evil.

5. Event and Action

We must therefore carefully distinguish between the two moments of the *will* and of *freedom* in the concept of free will: we must speak of *will* to be able to differentiate between *events* and *actions*, and of *freedom* to prevent the distinction between *free* and *unfree actions* to lose its meaning.

Both are indispensable to comprehending our experiences in the lifeworld. Only actions, not events, can be meaningfully attributed to responsible doers. And only free, but not unfree actions can be meaningfully judged in moral categories such as good or evil, meritorious or guilty. *Unfree* actions are not events that are caused by other events, but *actions* that have an author even if this author does not freely commit them or has not done so freely.

Events can be explained by causes; actions, by contrast, cannot be explained via recourse to causes alone. *Causes* are events that make other events (their effects) more probable than these would be without them, because it is impossible that there are effects but not their causes, and because it is improbable that there would be these events if they were not effects of those causes. *Authors* by contrast do not make actions more

17. Kant, *Critique of Pure Reason*, 540 (A547/B575).
18. Kant, *Critique of Practical Reason*, 162 (AA 5:29).
19. Kant, *Critique of Pure Reason*, 537 (A541/B569).

probable but are, on the one hand, the reason why there are these actions at all (here they join the causes of events); moreover, on the other hand, they are the reason why these actions could also be otherwise than they factually are (here they differ from the causes of events). Nothing that happens is an action if it can be explained without recourse to an author. This recourse, however, differs from the recourse to causes precisely in that it is not impossible in the case of actions that their authors exist but they themselves do not. When something is identified as the action of an author, it does not for all that become more probable; it remains improbable. While the recourse to causes explains something as an event, the recourse to authors explains something as a decision between options for action.

The two do not have to exclude each other. Actions can always also be seen as events, but not all events can be seen as actions. Something that happens is an *action* (and not an event) when what happens does not only have *causes* but an (or at least one) *author*. As effects of causes, events would not be if these causes were not, but when these causes are, they must be as well. Actions by contrast require going back to a will or author without whom they would not be, but if this author is, they could also not be or something else could be in their place. While, therefore, events, relatively to their causes, *must be*, actions, relatively to their author, *could be otherwise* or *could not have been*. The recourse to causes thus increases the probability of events while the recourse to authors underscores the improbability of actions.

Now, an *action* is one thing; a *free* action is another thing. An action is not free already by being an action, that is, by differing from events in that, under the same conditions of authorship, they could also not have been (this way). That relatively to its nexus of conditions, an action did not have to be does not mean that it could in fact have been otherwise. It differs from an event insofar as, as a matter of principle, it might have been otherwise even if, as a matter of fact, it could not have been otherwise. As an *action*, it might have been otherwise, yet as *this specific* action, it could not have been otherwise. Yet only an action that could be otherwise not only in principle but also in fact (because its author could also do something other than what she factually does) is free. It is an *action* insofar as relatively to its author it could also be otherwise, if it represents one option among other possible options for its author. In contrast, it is a *free* action insofar as its author is free also to do something other than what she in fact does, that is, not only free to choose the option she chooses but also free to choose another. In short, actions have authors, free actions have free authors: they could not only be otherwise, but their authors could also have done something other than them.

6. Will and Arbitrariness

Insofar as we are being thematized in this sense as authors of free actions, we come into view as beings who not only *have* a will (that are able to will one thing or another) but who *are* will (that are able to conduct themselves freely toward their willing). We are beings of will because, as *authors* of actions, we can change the state of the world by initiating actions that cannot sufficiently be explained by the causes of the events through which they take place: we effect not only *events* that have causes but *actions* we initiate as authors.

This formal definition, however, only says *that* we act as beings of will, not *how* we do so, and it leaves the difference between *free will* (which determines itself to pursue purposes) and *irregular arbitrariness* (which follows arbitrary interests and needs) un-clear. Kant therefore specifies the faculty of initiating actions (spontaneity or the faculty of action) by inquiring into the faculty of determining oneself one's faculty of action in a determinate way, that is, of conducting oneself freely toward it and to posit oneself purposes for one's acting. Only thanks to this faculty of self-determination, called "au-tonomy," does the *will* distinguish itself from arbitrariness and becomes *free will*, that is, "a faculty either of producing objects corresponding to representations or of determin-ing itself to effect such objects."[20] Not only can we choose between given options (which would maintain us dependent on what we have available as our options), we can posit purposes for ourselves and pursue aims that only "exist" because we posit them. We have the faculty not only to make decisions and to act (capacity for choice) but also to posit options for decision and to act freely (capacity for freedom).

7. Good Will

That alone, however, does not make free will good. To that end, free will must determine itself *to do what is good,* and that is not the case when it wants to actualize something very specific (that is, certain pre-given "moral" options) but when it wills to actualize all options it is considering *in a very specific way.* Free will is *good* not by willing and doing specific good deeds (*bona*) or not willing and doing evil deeds (*mala*) but by willing and doing everything it wills and does *in a good way.* That, however, is always and only the case if it does not let itself be determined by the object of its willing (that is, if it does not act depending on pre-given options its willing or not willing aims at) but is oriented in everything it does and does not will by the moral law and determines itself in its willing or not willing of something through "*the mere form of law*" (that is, it determines itself and acts freely).[21] Not *what* we will (the object of willing) but *how* we will it (the form of determining the willing) decides whether it is good or evil. And something is *good* only if it is willed the way the categorical imperative commands: "act only in accordance with that maxim through which you can at the same time will that it become a universal law."[22]

By "maxim," Kant understands the "subjective principle of volition," that is, that through which someone determines their will independently of all objects at which this will could aim or does aim in such a way that their concrete willing and doing in different

20. Kant, *Critique of Practical Reason*, 148 (AA 5:15); compare the corresponding definition of the "faculty of desire" in the book's preface, 143–44 note (AA 5:9).

21. Kant, *Critique of Practical Reason*, 164 (AA 5:31).

22. Kant, *Practical Philosophy*, 37—108, here 73 (AA 4:421). On the different articulations of the cat-egorical imperative, see Ebbinghaus, "Die Formeln des kategorischen Imperativs"; Kaulbach, *Immanuel Kants "Grundlegung zur Metaphysik der Sitten,"* 94–100; and Geismann, "Die Formeln des kategorischen Imperativs."

life situations acquires a uniform character.[23] Although in every life situation, we always pursue in our willing and doing very specific objects, we do not act differently in each situation, but we act in each situation in a way that, according to the principles we have chosen, seems to be appropriate in this situation or in situations of this kind. If these principles (the maxims) are good, we act well, if they are evil, we act evilly. Yet they are good only if they do not systematize our private interests but correspond to the practical moral law, that is, when they make that which should and could serve as instruction for action for everyone else in the situation at issue into the decisive instruction for our action. They are evil, by contrast, when they do not do so, that is, when we egotistically pursue our own well-being or even altruistically the well-being of others, when we are interested in increasing happiness and decreasing unhappiness for ourselves and for others, but do not choose our own being good and the "ought to be good" and "can be good" of all others to determine our will and instruct our actions, when we do not orient everything we will and do toward promoting and not hindering the moral education of the person of every human being. For as certainly as human beings want to live in such a way as to be as happy as possible and as little unhappy as possible, this does just as certainly not distinguish them from other animals that, each in its own way, strive for the same thing. Unlike them, however, human beings can also try to live not just happily but to live well, and the more they work for their own being good and becoming good and that of everyone else, the more, that is, they make an effort to promote their own freedom and that of others to determine themselves autonomously, the more perfectly they actualize what characterizes them as humans: the ability to live as a free person.

8. Autonomy

A will (a person)[24] is thus *free* not only in the *negative* sense, when it does not let itself be determined by what it wills (its object), but in the *positive sense*, when it determines itself, on its own, to do what it wills or does not will. Yet it cannot do this without determining itself *in a determinate way*, and because of this way (and not because of its

---

23. Kant, *Practical Philosophy*, 56n (AA 4:400); see also *Critique of Practical Reason*, 153 (AA 5:19).

24. In what follows, "will" can always be replaced by "person," because the issue is not one particular faculty of the human being among others but the human being with all her emotional, cognitive, and volutative faculties as a being capable of free self-determination. The "faculty of autonomy" is thus not to be understood in the terms of an anthropology of faculties as one of the capacities of the *animal rationale* that the human *is* but as an indication that *as a person* the human being always experiences its animal rationality and rational animality within the horizon of an *ought* that cannot be derived from its *being* as human animal but is contained in its ability to conduct itself toward everything it is and can be in such a way that it lives its being human in this way or that, in a way that is good or one that is not, one that must be called evil. When we understand free will merely as an ability to decide for or against something in a way that is more or less uncoerced, intentional, and voluntary, as Duggan and Gert argue ("Free Will as the Ability to Will"), we miss that point. And we also miss it when like Berthold, *God, Evil, and Human Learning*, we define free will, in Augustine's footsteps, as a "mental act" (49–50) that "must be intentional" (50–57), "uncoerced" (57–59), "voluntary" (59–62), and "autonomous" (62–63). This reduces free will to the autonomous unfolding of a mental act, which indeed does allow for establishing that "there is no absolute and sharp difference between the human and the animal world" (96n9) because it describes a biological ability and not the human being as person.

object), it is either *good* or *evil*. And it is *good* and not evil when, in how it wills what it wills, it orients itself on its own by what it shares with every other free will: the categorical imperative of duty or of the moral law. For in that case, it measures the particularity of its concrete willing by the universal criteria of willing what everyone else in this case ought to be able to will and will it in such a way that everyone else in this case ought to be able to will it in this way, too. This does not abolish the fact that a will always wills something determinate and is thereby concrete. Yet only a will that wills the determinate thing it wills in the determinate way articulated by the categorical imperative is not only a free but a good will, and thereby a will that actualizes rather than fails to achieve the point of its autonomy.[25]

On the one hand, every concrete will shares with every other concrete will that it differs from each other concrete will. This commonality is of such a kind that every concrete will must have it if it is of the kind it is said to be, a *concrete will*. On the other hand, in its unrepealable difference from every concrete will, it can share with others that it wills what it wills concretely only in such a way that the others, too, in its place could have willed it in this way. This commonality—which constitutes the *good will*—is something it can have but does not have to have. If it has it, then it has it only by willing what it wills in such a way that it wills it in this mode, and if it does not have it, then it does not have it because it does not will what it wills in this mode. In the first case, it is a good will; in the second case, an evil will. Whether it is the one or the other is a contingent question that depends on its concrete moral decision. But it must be one of the two because we cannot concretely will anything without willing it in a morally relevant way, that is, in such a way that the will thereby determines itself as good or not good. The free will therefore does not have to be good, but it must be *either* good *or* evil. It is good only if it wills what it wills in the way the categorical imperative prescribes. For then it wills what it wills in such a way that it could have and would have to have been willed in this way by every other human being in the same situation, and only if it wills what it wills this way, is the free will oriented by what it can have in common with every other free will without ceasing to be a concrete will. The common feature of a freedom distinct from natural causality lies not in the object of the willing nor in the non-notion of an object-free willing but in the orientation of the will by the ought of the moral law alone.

Only in this orientation is the will not only determined but determined to do what is good. For according to Kant, nothing in and nothing outside the world can without restrictions be considered good, to be a good will alone.[26] Actions are good only insofar as they are based on a good willing; a willing is good only insofar as it arises from a good will; yet the will is good solely by its willing the good, and it wills the good solely when what it wills is such that everyone else would have to be able to will it in this way, everyone, that is, who wills what they will in such a way that everyone under the circumstances would have to be able to will it in this way. Put differently: only that willing is free and good that is oriented by a maxim of action that can claim to be obligating everyone else as well because it says that only that is good which is freely willed in such a way that everyone else can freely will that everyone freely wills it in such a way that

25. See Rommel, *Zum Begriff des Bösen bei Augustinus und Kant.*
26. Kant, *Practical Philosophy*, 49 (AA 4:393).

everyone else can freely will that everyone else wills it in such a way that. . . . It is not a determinate content but this formal quality of a universalizable rule alone that decides a willing to be good or not. Only that willing is good that is determined by a good will, and only that will is good that in everything it wills is oriented by the moral law alone. For precisely in doing so, it does not subject itself to an alien law but posits by and for itself the purpose of willing only what is good, that is, not to will anything it wills in any other way than thereby to promote the autonomy of everyone freely to advance the promotion of everyone else's autonomy.[27] True autonomy is not just self-determination but self-determination to do *what is good*, and *good*, in very formal terms, is everything, exclusively, that we will in such a way that it promotes the autonomy of others freely to determine themselves to promote the autonomy of others.

9. Limits of Autonomy

This has three important implications to be highlighted. First, nobody is free simultaneously to will good *and* evil, that is, to will the same thing simultaneously and in the same respect *both* as something good *and* as something evil. Autonomy implies an either-or in the self-determination of the will, or else there is no moral determination of the will: either the will is good or it is not, but it is not both simultaneously and in the same respect.

Second, nobody is free to will *neither* good *nor* evil, that is, to live without distinguishing and deciding between good and evil: autonomy is not a faculty we can have without practicing it. If someone can live autonomously, they must live autonomously, and they do so even if *per impossibile* they try to determine themselves not to live autonomously. If there is a will that can be good or evil, then it is either good or evil, but neither neither of both nor both simultaneously and in the same respect.

Third, finally—and Kant's theory of radical Evil articulates this point in a way many find offensive[28]—nobody is free freely to decide in favor of good *or* evil, that is, freely to will *either* Good *or* Evil: autonomy is not a self-determination of the will in which the will would in a morally neutral way determine itself to determine itself either in a good way or in an evil way; rather, it *is* the moral self-determination of the will as good or evil. I am not autonomous such that I then autonomously determine myself as good or evil; rather, I am autonomous *in determining* myself in a good or evil way. Autonomy does not consist in the autonomy of the will *to* determine itself, it consists *in* the self-determination of the will. Every iterative step back here produces the illusion that for self-determination, there could be a neutral situation prior to self-determination. But there is no such situation. We do not decide to decide ourselves, we decide ourselves. And we do not determine ourselves to determine ourselves to will Good *or* Evil, we determine ourselves to do *what is good* or we do not. There is no self-determination to self-determination that would not already be a self-determination to effect Good or Evil, just as there is no moral self-determination to refrain from every moral self-determination

---

27. "Hence the will is not merely subject to the law but subject to it in such a way that it must be viewed as also *giving the law to itself* and just because of this as first subject to the law" (Kant, *Practical Philosophy*, 81 [AA 4:431], my emphasis).

28. See Rogozinski, "Kant et le mal radical."

that would not be a moral self-determination. If we are autonomous, that is, if we have the capacity to determine our will to do what is good, to determine it not to do what is good, or not to determine it to do what is good, then we also do so, and there is no situation in which we would not already have done one or the other: when we are beings capable of autonomy, we *are* good or we *are* evil, because we cannot be capable of autonomy without in fact being good or evil. Someone who can be good or evil *is* good or *is* evil. In principle (though not necessarily in fact), they could also be the other if they are the one. But they could not be both, nor neither, if they can be and live one or the other.

Autonomy in Kant's sense precisely does *not* consist in being able freely do determine oneself to decide either for or against the Good, as if we could freely choose *either* to determine or not to determine our will by the moral law *or* not to do so. We cannot freely determine ourselves *either* freely to determine ourselves to effect Good or Evil *or* not to do so. That would not be a free will but an abstract willing that in fact is never available to us this way. We can will this or that, we can posit these or those purposes for ourselves. But we cannot freely determine our will to will not to be a free will: that would be a self-contradiction that would dissolve free will and abolish the difference between nature and freedom.

That we are not free to be free or unfree does not mean, however, that we could not abuse our autonomy by determining ourselves to effect not Good but Evil. Just as we are not abstractly free to choose between Good and Evil, we are not free *not* to conduct ourselves autonomously, that is, not factually to actualize one or the other option of autonomy. We are not free to be not free and thereby not responsible for the way we live our lives. For not only when we *decide against what is good* do we freely determine ourselves, we do so already when we *do not decide in favor of what is good*. Because we are determined to have autonomy, we cannot not conduct ourselves autonomously: where we do not freely decide in favor of what is good, we thereby freely commit to the opposite of what is good, to what is evil. Not deciding in favor of the good is factually deciding in favor of what is evil, for in this case not deciding is itself a decision. While according to Kant, it is impossible to decide in favor of what is evil for the sake of Evil (he grants this possibility to diabolic will alone), it is not just a possibility but a reality for us that we do not decide in favor of what is good but thereby in favor of what is evil. It is a reality because at issue here are not *two* decisions (for or against what is good or for or against what is evil) but *one* decision, insofar as in one and the same act we either choose what is good (and thereby do not choose what is evil) or do not choose what is good (and thereby choose what is evil).

In this sense, Kant stresses that "a free will and a will under moral laws are one and the same,"[29] not because a free will is always a good will but because a free will cannot be without being *either* a good will *or* an evil will. Only that will is truly free that freely wills the good but that can also fail to do so and thereby, precisely, can also will and do evil. For just as only those will the good who determine themselves solely by the moral law,[30] that is, will everything they will in such a way that it promotes the autonomy of

---

29. Kant, *Practical Philosophy*, 95 (AA 4:447); cf. 99 (AA 4:452).

30. "What is essential in every determination of the will by the moral law is that, as a free will . . . it is determined solely by the law" (Kant, *Critique of Practical Reason*, 199 [AA 5:72]).

others freely to promote the autonomy of others, so those will evil who do not will the good—not only because they explicitly have evil in mind but also because they do not explicitly determine themselves to do what is good. We are good only if we will what is good ourselves, but we are already evil when we do not will what is good—be it intentionally, out of negligence, stupidity, or malice.

10. Radically Evil

This is the key to understanding Kant's contentious discussion of *radical Evil*.[31] Freely willing the good is what we ought to do always and everywhere if we really seek to distinguish ourselves as beings of freedom from the determination by nature, but it is not what we do always and everywhere. On the contrary, in every concrete case we can see that we precisely do not determine ourselves that way. Our willing and the maxim of our action is thus not such that it is oriented decisively by the good will, that is, the determination of the will by the good alone. We would be good if only we willed what the free will wills in being oriented by the moral law. But because we do not will that, we are not good in what we will but are evil. For *evil* is the will that could be and ought to be good but is not good, that fails to live up to its own possibilities of doing what is good.

This, however, leads to a dilemma: supposing that we are able freely to choose between good and evil, that is, able freely to determine or not determine our willing according to the principle of the good will (if we had premoral freedom to determine ourselves morally positively or negatively), and supposing it is not possible for us to not freely determine our will one way or another (we are not free not to determine ourselves morally), the question is why we freely decide in favor of what is evil and not in favor of what is good. If by contrast we are not free to choose or not to choose between what is good and what is evil (that is, if we must choose) but also not free freely to determine ourselves oriented either by Good or by Evil (that is, if we cannot freely determine ourselves in a morally good or a morally evil way), if instead we can and must note in every situation that we are always already not just determined in a good or an evil way but in fact in an evil way, then the question is whether we can be held responsible: if it is a fact that we are evil and will what is evil, then this is either a result of our moral self-determination, for which we are responsible, or it is not, in which case it is not a moral matter that could be ascribed to us. We thus face the dilemma of either not knowing any reason why we freely decide in favor of what is evil and against what is good or not knowing if our being evil is the result of our self-determination (that is, morally relevant) or not (and thus, strictly speaking, not even to be referred to as "evil").

The precondition of the entire reflection is that it is in fact true that we always will evil and not good, that (1) the situation is in fact a morally relevant one, not a pre-, extra-, or non-moral situation, and that (2) this situation is characterized by our being not good but evil because we will not what is good but what is evil. If we are evil, then we are so because of free self-determination, or else we are not evil; we can only be evil

31. See Kadowaki, *Das Radikal Böse bei Kant*; Schulte, *Radikal Böse*; Lichtenberg, "Über die Unerforschlichkeit des Bösen nach Kant"; and Willnauer, *Heute das Böse denken*, 53–166.

because of free self-determination, however, if we could also have been good. Yet if there were no situation in which we could freely choose between one and the other, then this choice would not only be pre- or extra-moral (because it would not itself be determined by the good or evil will but would operate this determination in the first place), it would not even be possible yet to see why we determine ourselves to effect evil and not good. Being morally determined, however, cannot result from a non-moral determination (a non-moral "is" never gives rise to a moral "ought"); being morally determined to effect evil can only be the result of a moral determination to effect evil. If, though, as Kant emphasizes, "Evil can have originated only from moral evil," then "there is no conceivable ground for us . . . from which moral evil could first have come in us."[32]

Kant develops the dilemma in his theory of *radical Evil*. At every point in their lives, humans can see that they will what is evil although they ought to will what is good but cannot trace this to a free decision in the past between the will to effect good or to effect evil. Going back in time is thus not a solution to explain the evil will. Rather, "[e]very evil action must be so considered, whenever we seek its rational origin, as if the human being had fallen into it directly from the state of innocence."[33] *What* the malice of the action consists in can be clearly stated: it follows from the maxims of actions that are not oriented by the moral law of practical reason, maxims in which other purposes than willing the good determine our willing and doing instead. Yet *why* that is so remains incomprehensible for Kant: we can only note the matter of fact of evil, we can say that it lies in the wrong determination of our will not to will what it ought to will, but we are unable to explain why that is so. The fact of the wrong determination remains as impenetrable to us as the fact of freedom that makes us aware of our free will.[34] We can because we ought to, but at the same time we cannot because we do not will. In principle, we can will the good (because we ought to will it); concretely, however, we precisely do not will it (although we ought to).

11. What Drives Animality, Humanity, and Personality

Kant discusses this in a line of thought that can be succinctly summarized as follows. Whether our concrete will is good depends, as we saw, on whether in what it wills it is oriented by the moral law (the standard of the good will) or by sensibility (the occasion of orienting the will by something other than the moral law). This presupposes (1) that not only sensibility but morality, too, can become an incentive of our willing; (2) that there are no other kinds of incentives; and (3) that we concretely always determine our willing by these two incentives of the will. Every human being qua human being possesses three originary predispositions that "belong with necessity to the possibility of this being," namely predispositions to animality, to humanity, and to personality. The

32. Kant, *Religion*, in *Religion and Rational Theology*, 39–215, here 88 (AA 6:43).

33. Kant, *Religion*, 86 (AA 6:41).

34. That at least is the basic point of the argument in the *Critique of Practical Reason*, which followed the failure of Kant's attempts to deduce freedom in the *Groundwork for the Metaphysics of Morals*. The recourse to the fact of freedom replaces the attempts at deriving this fact as being principled from a principle, since none of these yielded a convincing result.

"predisposition to the *animality* of the human being, as a *living being*" includes the driving force of "physical or merely mechanical self-love" that serves self-preservation and the preservation of the species through procreation. The predisposition "to humanity" consists in the rational capacity, "in comparison with others," to "judge oneself happy or unhappy." From this arises the drive to win out over others to produce, secure, and enhance one's well-being, but this is nothing but a concretization of (biological) self-love that aims not only at maintaining life but at making life as happy as possible.[35]

Not so the "predisposition to personality," which consists in "the susceptibility to respect for the moral law *as of itself a sufficient incentive to the power of choice.*"[36] Kant thus conceives of the human not only as *animal rationale* whose behavior is essentially determined biologically by self-love, with regard to both animality and rationality. He adds to this biological view of the human as a special kind of animal the decisive aspect that the being human of the human being is not decided solely by how the species "human" is factually defined in comparison with other animal species but essentially contains a normative moment of how the human being wills to be and understand itself as human. We are not only what we are in comparison with other animals (*rational animals*), but we are who we, as animals of this special kind, can be, will to be, and ought to be: *persons*. The predisposition to personality enables us to determine ourselves, our willing, and our doing by the *idea of humanity*, that is, to be oriented by the idea that we ought to be and that we can be free and morally good beings. Human beings are not only what they are as rational animals in the nexus of life, they are always also those they will themselves to be in this nexus. We are who we are not independently of how we understand ourselves and what we determine ourselves to effect.

Our will is therefore always determined by two incentives: the biological incentive of animal and rational self-love, which aims at self-preservation (existence) and well-being (happiness), and the moral incentive of determining oneself in willing and acting as a free person through an orientation by the idea of humanity (being good).[37] Only once we include the respect for the moral law as an incentive in our maxims do we live not only biologically as rational animals but morally as self-determining persons. Only then are we free not only to conduct ourselves this way or another (freedom of action) but to determine ourselves to follow this conduct or another, that is, freely to posit purposes for ourselves through which we actualize not just something but ourselves as moral persons (autonomy).

35. Kant, *Religion*, 74–76 (AA 6:26–28).

36. Kant, *Religion*, 76 (AA 6:27).

37. If the human will were not always determined by both incentives, the moral law would not have to appear in the form of a categorical imperative. A will that would always already be oriented by the morally good would not have to be presented with a command to do so. And a will that would be entirely incapable of orienting itself by it and followed only animal and rational self-love would be unable to follow the command. Yet because and insofar both applies to the human being, namely, on the one hand, that it does not always already will what is good on its own initiative but also, on the other, that it is not the case that it can orient itself only toward self-preservation and well-being and not also toward being good, the human stands between God and animal, between the good will that without exception wills the good and therefore is good and the animal willing that wills neither good nor evil and can therefore be defined neither as good nor as evil.

Yet that is still putting it in too weak terms: we can not only freely determine ourselves to effect moral good, but because we are beings who can do so, we ought to as well, and because we ought to, we also can and must. This means that as human beings we live in such a way that even where we do not explicitly decide, we have in fact made a decision: those who do *not* determine themselves to effect the good but insist only on their self-preservation and well-being (happiness) have thereby determined themselves to do evil because they do not actualize their capacity for personality in the way it could exist and ought to exist in the orientation by the good. For there is no possibility for human beings to do neither the one nor the other, to live "morally neutrally." Because we have not only the predispositions to animality and to humanity (rationality) but also to personality (autonomy), we cannot actualize the first two without factually also actualizing the third in a concrete way. Not only can we act wrongly, that is, endanger or destroy our life or well-being (within the dimension of our biological *being* as rational animals), we can also determine ourselves wrongly, that is, fail to live up to our human possibilities of personality (within the dimension of our moral "ought" as persons); and we cannot do the first without simultaneously also always having done the second. The first are errors that harm our life and well-being ("being" as existence and happiness), the second are offenses that do not allow us to be the persons we could and ought to be ("ought" as ought to be free and good). But we cannot live without, factually, in all three dimensions *either* committing these errors *or* not committing them (*tertium non datur*): whoever lives actualizes, *in one and the same act*, albeit each in different ways, their predisposition to animality, humanity, and personality. No human lives only as *animal* or only as *rational animal* but as such always also as *person*—be it by actualizing this predisposition the way it wills to be, ought to be, and can be actualized, be it by failing to do so.

The peculiarity of personality over against animality and rationality is that no human being is a person without living as a person on their own initiative, that no human being can live as person on their own initiative without living as a good or evil person, that, in living, no human being can avoid living, even as a person, in being determined one way or the other. No human being is a person the way she is a rational animal, as the product of an evolutionary history in the course of which she became what she is. At most we might say that it thereby becomes *possible to be able to be* a person. We become persons by living as persons; that is, by in fact becoming what we as rational animals can be. Every human being can become a person by freely—that is, not just compelled from the outside or the inside (by drives, needs, desires) but on their own initiative (conscience)—living as a person, that is, by determining themselves (their will) in such a way that they live as good or evil human being. For just as the *free will* is that will that makes me free in that I practice it, so the *good will* is that use of free will that makes me good in freely deciding in favor of what is good and against what is evil, and the *evil will* is that use of free will that makes me evil in freely not deciding in favor of what is good.

12. Evil Will

That, precisely, is the case when respect for the moral law is not the decisive incentive in determining our willing and acting, that is, when we do not decide in favor of what is good, although we could and ought to do so, but of something else. Then we *are* evil because we *do not make ourselves good*, that is, do not decide in favor of what is good. Only those are evil, but then they are indeed evil, who do *not* decide in favor of the good in whose favor they could decide and as moral person ought to decide. It is not just those who are not good who are evil, but those who are not good *although they could be good*: animals and plants that cannot be good (in the moral sense relevant here) also cannot be evil, whereas we are good or evil because we can be both and are incapable of being neither. We can be evil only because and insofar as there is the incentive of respect for the moral law, and we are evil when we do not let this incentive play a decisive role within the construct of our maxims but subordinate it to the incentives of self-love. If, however, we not only are able to orient our wills by the two incentives but are unable to avoid doing so because the human is always both a being of the senses and of reason,[38] and if the two incentives can only ever determine our willing not in equal measure and in parallel but in a relation of subordination, then there are only two basic possibilities: either we subordinate the actualization of our moral being a person to the actualization of our self-love; or we subordinate the actualization of our self-love to the actualization of our being a person. In the first case, we are guided by our striving for happiness in the effort to preserve our life and live as happily as possible (being). In the second, we are guided by the duty to consider, in striving for our happiness, not only other people's striving for happiness but also and above all to make our and their duty to be and to become persons the decisive determination of our willing and acting (ought). The decisive moral principle is not just the greatest happiness of the greatest number but the duty of allowing ourselves and others to be the persons we as human beings can be.

It is therefore possible to speak of evil in the morally relevant sense only within the horizon of respect for the Law as the principle of human being a person, not within the horizon of human self-love as *animal rationale*. Just as a good will is the one and only one that can be called *good* without restriction, so an evil will is the one and only one that can be called *evil* without restriction. Yet a will is evil when it wrongly organizes the internal complexity of the driving forces that determine it, that is, if it does not make the free determination of the driving forces of self-love to promote its own and others' being a person the highest determining reason of its willing but lets itself be guided by motives of self-love. Doing so, that is, not freely determining itself to do what is good, however, is a matter of the will as well: the evil will, too, is a free will that can be assigned responsibility, but it is a free will that in a self-contradictory way is caught up in the negation of its freedom as freedom to do what is good and that misconceives of and practices this freedom as freedom from what is good: those are evil who pervert the freedom to do what is good as freedom from what is good by not determining themselves to do what is good although they could do so or determine themselves to do evil although they do not have to do so. To be an evil will, there is no need to will Evil for the sake of Evil (that, as Kant says, would be a diabolic will);[39] it suffices not to will the good one could will and ought to will. Those who do not will the good they could will fail to attain what as good will they ought to be.

38. Kant, *Religion*, 82–83 (AA 6:36).
39. See Kant, *Religion*, 82 (AA 6:35).

Yet this is precisely what for Kant is not just a possibility but a reality, and not an occasional reality of human being but one that characterizes not only each individual human being in every concrete situation but the entire human species. The human being, Kant writes, "is evil *by nature*," and he explains:

> "He is evil *by nature*" simply means that being evil applies to him considered in his species; not that this quality may be inferred from the concept of his species (that is, from the concept of a human being in general, for then the quality would be necessary), but rather that, according to the cognition we have of the human being through experience, he cannot be judged otherwise, in other words, we may presuppose evil as subjectively necessary in every human being, even the best.[40]

The human is evil not necessarily but only naturally. That is why it is not self-contradictory to think the human in such a way that it would not be evil: the human being is evil but does not have to be so. And for that very reason, inversely, we cannot fathom the malice of the human in thinking about it, or discover it in the concept of the human, but must perceive it in experience: that the human being is evil cannot be deduced from principles but can only be noted as factual reality.

Yet in the experiential reality of human life, it is not even possible to avoid perceiving it. Wherever "the exercise of freedom in the human being" is manifest, corruption "is detectable."[41] It consists not only in some people sometimes or always or all people in one situation or another acting evilly. The point of this corruption, rather, is that humans always and everywhere act according to evil maxims of action, that is, they determine their will by principles that are not due to a free orientation by the good but are determined by the driving forces of their self-love: they are oriented by a basic principle that makes not their being a person but the needs of their rational animality the guide of their willing and acting. This, however, affects not only some but all situations of their acting, and thus not just sometimes but always. Those who in their willing and acting follow this amoral guiding maxim are therefore not just evil but cannot on their own initiative stop being evil.

Kant thereby supposes several things. First, he assumes that all human willing and acting is determined by the driving forces of sensibility (striving for happiness) and morality (striving for virtue), that there are no further determining grounds, but also that there is no willing and acting that would not be thus determined. Second, with regard to morality, he assumes that every maxim of action, that is, every subjective principle of willing is "either *morally good* or *morally evil*," that there is no third possible determination, and that there is no maxim that would not be either morally good or morally evil. For "[i]t is of great consequence to ethics in general . . . to preclude, so far as possible, anything morally intermediate, either in actions . . . or in human characters."[42] What is not good is evil, and there are no gradations between willing the good, not willing the

---

40. Kant, *Religion*, 80 (AA 6:32), interpolation Gregor.
41. Kant, *Religion*, 84 (AA 6:38).
42. Kant, *Religion*, 71–72 (AA 6:22); my emphases.

good, and willing evil: not willing the good is evil because it is not willing what as a person one could and ought to will.

Yet what is true for each individual maxim is true for a human being's entire construct of maxims. It either is good because the individual maxims are good and all maxims are organized in a good way, that is, oriented toward the actualization of the morally good. Or it is evil because that is not the case. In this latter case, however, human beings are not only evil but *radically* evil because they determine their will in such a way that they not only factually do not act well but can no longer act well at all: those who consciously do evil, that is, who know that what they do is evil because it follows the principle of self-love and not morality, can no longer undo it, nor can they have any illusions about the character of their willing and acting: they are not just *perhaps* but *actually* evil. And "[t]his evil is *radical*, since it corrupts the ground of all maxims; as natural propensity, it is also not to be *extirpated* through human forces." Salvation from evil can therefore in no way be thought as auto-salvation. For that to be the case, we would ourselves have to choose maxims that make the good the guide of human willing and acting. This, however, is factually impossible, because it "could only happen through good maxims—something that cannot take place if the subjective supreme ground of all maxims is presupposed to be corrupted."[43] On our own initiative we can at most conduct ourselves legally, but we cannot live morally.

13. Evil by Nature

For Kant, the human being is thus characterized by the double determination of having a *predisposition to good* and of being *evil by nature*: humans can be good and ought to be good, but they are factually evil and thus incapable on their own initiative to in fact be what they could be and ought to be.[44] The fact, however, that their will in decisions about what is to be done in a given situation is determined not to will what is good but what is evil, that is, to decisively orient themselves by self-love and not the moral law, is not on the same level as the human predisposition to the good. Only *because* humans have this predisposition—that is, because they are predisposed to live their lives as the rational animals that they are *as the persons* they can be and ought to be—can they be factually evil: if they were not predetermined to determine themselves to do what is good, they could also not find themselves determined to do what is evil. And if they were not only in fact but in principle predetermined to do what is evil, they could not only not make the change from evil to good by themselves, they could not make it at all: the turn to the good, which humans must await *ab extra* because in their factual situation they cannot make it themselves, would be impossible if the human as such were not only factually evil but could not be anything but evil.

According to Kant, then, humans find themselves in the existential conflict that, on the one hand, they ought to be good and know that they can be so because they ought

43. Kant, *Religion*, 83 (AA 6:37).

44. This means, conversely, that the human, as Wimmer, *Kants kritische Religionsphilosophie*, 112–13, rightly emphasizes, is good in principle but in no way by nature. See also Claudia Card, who underestimates the significance of this point (Card, *Atrocity Paradigm*, 73–95).

to be so, and, on the other, they cannot be good because they factually are not good and know that they cannot by themselves become what they ought to be. With regard to the ought, then, the difference between *being* and *ought* is amplified and an abyss has opened between *ought to be good* and *cannot be good*, such that humans live not only in the tension between sensibility (being determined by nature) and morality (determining by freedom) but, as moral beings, also in the tension between the predetermination in principle to do what is good and the failure in fact to live up to this predetermination in their lives as evil persons.

This means, on the one hand, that the human being is never good but must always walk a path toward the good. And it means, on the other, that this path to the good for humans is always one that begins neither in a morally neutral place where they could decide between the orientation by the good or by evil, nor in a place where they would already have decided in favor of the good; it begins in a place where they live in a way in which they ought not to live if they sought to live up to their predetermination to be persons. The goal of the good must always be reached from the initial situation of evil, and because this evil characteristically is moral evil, that is, consists in the wrong determination and wrong orientation of the maxims for action at issue, there is for those affected no path to the good they could take by themselves: no acting can make them good if they are not already good, yet they would only be good if they had determined themselves to do what is good, and that precisely is what they can note at any time by looking at themselves and at everyone else: the decisive human principle of orientation is self-love (both within the animal horizon, aiming at the preservation of life, and within the rational horizon, aiming at happiness), not the respect for the moral law and thus the effort to live as person among persons and not only as *animal rationale*.

Kant can no more say why that is so than he can say why humans are free and predetermined freely to decide in favor of the good: both are facts that can be stated but that cannot in turn be explained on other grounds. It is not specific actions that make humans evil, but the way in which they act at all proves their orientation by self-love and not by the moral law. And it is not specific actions that prove humans to be free, but it is the fact of their being in a position to act at all and to orient themselves not only by what is but also by what ought to be that manifests their predetermination to freedom. Just like the freedom of the human being, the fact of evil will cannot be deduced but only stated. The grounds of our being evil is comprehensible to us: we have subordinated the incentive of respect for the law to the incentives of self-love. The "origin, however, of this disharmony in our power of choice with respect to the way it incorporates lower incentives in its maxims and makes them supreme" is inscrutable to us: "there is no conceivable ground for us, therefore, from which moral evil could first have come in us."[45] We know the way in which we are evil, but we do not know why.

14. Shadows of Freedom

Kant's entire engagement with the reality of evil is based on his philosophy of freedom, and just as in Leibniz, ill is the unavoidable shadow of contingency, so in Kant, Evil

45. Kant, *Religion*, 88 (AA 6:43); see also 80 (AA 6:32).

is the shadow freedom cannot shake off: if there is freedom (which does not have to exist), then there is evil (which does not have to exist) as well, and if freedom exists only as underivable fact, then the shadow of evil that accompanies it exists only as an incomprehensible fact. That means: evil need not exist but it does, and evil could not exist if there were no free will, but free will exists. Free will is the form in which freedom becomes concrete in human life, the form that makes good and evil alike possible and understandable. It also allows for explaining why evil can exist and what evil consists in but not why that which can exist but does not have to exist does in fact exist.

If we start from the reality of free will—and this is a central basic feature of Kant's reflections on evil—there is a far-reaching consequence: if there were no evil (anymore), then there would not only not be anything evil, there would be good. Kant sets up his treatment of the entire problem so as to construct a complete alternative within the horizon of free will: the will is either good or evil, it is never both (simultaneously and in the same respect), nor is it ever neither. With regard to the experiences of life in this world, we might want to avoid talking about good and evil and only distinguish between agreeable and disagreeable, pleasure and displeasure, happiness and unhappiness. This, according to Kant, would be restricting ourselves to inserting the human as *animal rationale* into the nexus of a life it leads in passion, action, and reaction by seeking to maximize what is agreeable and minimizing what is disagreeable. All of this does not require viewing the human being in any other but the biological nexus of nature. Such conduct is possible because and insofar as human beings possess emotions, understanding, and will, namely the will (choice) to be able to act this way or another, the understanding rationally to weigh different options for action against each other, and the emotions to turn toward what is agreeable and away from what is disagreeable.

With all of this, however, the human being does not yet come into view as a person capable of freedom. Humans do not have to make their (egotistical or altruistic) particular interests as *animal rationale et sociale* the standard of their actions. Rather, they are able to subordinate these interests to the orientation by the Good, because they are in a position freely to conduct themselves towards that which is useful for them as agreeable and harmful for them as disagreeable. We do not have to follow what we consider agreeable but can also decide differently. And we do not have to avoid what is disagreeable to us but can conduct ourselves toward it in this way or in another. Self-love, self-interest, and usefulness can, but do not have to, determine us. We are free to let them play themselves out or not to let them. We do not have to follow our animal drives and rational considerations but are able to distance ourselves from them. And when we do the one or the other, we can assess it this way or another, agree with it or disagree.

What shows itself here is a freedom that is more than the freedom of choosing between pre-given options guided by the maximization of the agreeable and useful and the minimization of the disagreeable and harmful. How we live is not only conditioned by our emotions, our understanding, and our will, but also determined by our conscience. We can be addressed as to ourselves in our animal and rational behavior, we can distinguish ourselves from what we will and do, and we can also do something we do not by ourselves will, not because of external compulsion but simply because we ought to. We are capable of codetermining that which conditions our conduct by determining ourselves to conduct ourselves in one way or in another. We do not have to follow either our drives or our emotions or our rational considerations but are always able once more to distance ourselves from them and act differently than they suggest.

These are experiences we are familiar with for which the view of us as rational animals does not sufficiently account. These experiences are the base point of Kant's talk of the human as "personality" or "person." Viewing human beings only under the aspect of their animality, emotionality, and rationality does not come to see them as persons. When we concentrate on humans being persons, however, then we must talk about free will, and when we talk about free will, according to Kant, then we cannot avoid talking about good and evil. Both condition and call for each other: the basic moral alternative between good and evil is given with freedom of the will. For what is at issue here, unlike in the case of the agreeable and disagreeable, is not just something that occurs in degrees and smoothly transitions from one degree to the other. Something good is not wished for or something evil not avoided because it is agreeable or disagreeable, or useful or harmful, whatever it may be for others. The good is chosen, if it is chosen at all, because it is the good and not just because it is good for someone, and Evil is avoided, if it is avoided, because it is Evil and not only because it is evil for someone. We *will* what is agreeable and we *do not will* what is disagreeable. But we *ought to* will what is good and *we ought not to* will what is evil, not because it is agreeable to will what is good and not to will Evil but because we ought to will and we can will what is good even when it is not agreeable and because we ought not to will Evil, although we could, when it is agreeable. Despite all my unpaid bills, I do not in the packed streetcar take the wallet bulging with cash from the negligently open bag of the person next to me, not because it would be disagreeable to possess this money or agreeable to possess it, or because I fear getting caught, or because I calculate rationally that on the whole we are better off when we do not steal each other's wallets, or because it would be unwise in this case because that person has invited me to dinner and it would then be up to me to pay, and so on; I do not do it because it would be an injustice and not good—or at least, to put it more cautiously, I *cannot* do it *for this reason alone*: I do not have to follow my needs, emotions, calculations, and prudent considerations but can orient my conduct by other aspects, other models, and other maxims.

15. Nonetheless and Notwithstanding, Against and Instead

Kant's experience of freedom is thus an experience of the "nonetheless" and the "notwithstanding": we are not tied into the meaningless and desolate course of nature alone to which we belong as rational animals. If that were the whole truth about human life, then human beings, as noted above, would be subject

> to all the evils of poverty, illnesses, and untimely death, just like all the other animals on earth, and . . . always remain thus until one wide grave engulfs them all together (whether honest or dishonest, it makes no difference here) and flings them, who were capable of having believed themselves to be the final end of

creation, back into the abyss of the purposeless chaos of matter from which they were drawn.[46]

But that is not all we know, we also know the experience of "not this way," of being able to do otherwise, of the ought, of the conscience that we ought to live not this way but otherwise, the freedom of not being lost in the chain of natural processes, of being able to initiate by ourselves new chains of processes, of doing that in a determinate way, and even of determining ourselves to engage in conduct that contradicts what self-love, self-interest, and considerations of usefulness suggest to us. For all of our being tied into the natural nexus, we are to conduct ourselves toward this nexus in one way or in another. We thereby do not step out of this nexus, but we are the place where the starting point emerges of an order of freedom that is distinct from and differs from the natural nexus and cannot be reduced to it. We experience this order as resistance and opposition to the natural conditionedness of our life, as liberation from the fetters of nature, but also their abolition, enfranchisement, and completion in an order through which we are not simply being determined but which we (co)determine and through which we determine ourselves, and this is what Kant has symbolized in the objection of the ought to being.

This oppositional character of freedom, that is, freedom *from* and *against* and *as different* from natural necessities, also shapes Kant's conception of the (morally) good. We are good when against our natural inclination toward evil, we orient our will by the good and determine it by good. Nobody becomes good simply by opting for the good; we must assert the good against evil. Being good is never accessible to us directly and without obstacles, it is, rather, always attained only by overcoming evil. We are not good, we must become good. Yet we do not become good simply by willing so, but the good must come into play against the resistance of the reality of evil, and this reality prevents the good not only in others (they are evil) but in ourselves (we are evil).

16. Conflict of the Will as Life Conflict

On this point, Kant was much shrewder than his optimistic contemporaries. If the good is always the free self-determination of the will to do what is good, then it can never be achieved other than through conflict with and opposition to evil. If we were good from the beginning, we would not have to determine ourselves to do what is good. Yet if we are not good from the beginning, then—because there is only a strict alternative here—we are evil from the beginning. To become good, we must determine our will in a new and different way from the way it is determined, that is, change our evil will into a good will.

Yet such a change is not at all possible. A change of will is not just a modification but a self-modification of the will and takes place by the will determining itself differently. But an evil will cannot on its own initiative determine itself to do what is good because it is evil precisely in and through not doing so. Only a free but not an evil will can become good through self-determination. If it is evil, then it cannot change for the good but only be superseded and replaced by a good will. A change of will is not a conflict

---

46. Kant, *Critique of the Power of Judgment*, §87:318 (AA 5:452).

of determining or self-determining one and the same will but a conflict between two differently determined wills. This conflict, moreover, is not to be found in the will but takes place in life: not the will but life must change. We do not become good by replacing in the will that we are the determination "evil" with the determination "good"—that is impossible already because this determination must be a *self-determination*, and we never find ourselves in a pre-moral situation in which we would not already have morally determined ourselves. We become good solely in that *another will*—and namely a will that determines itself differently, namely in a *good* way—takes the place of the evil will as the decisive determination of our life.

On the path to the good will, a person's evil will is thus not only determined differently, it is replaced by another will: where previously there was an evil human being, there is now a good one. This does not happen through an evil will transforming into a good will but through an evil will being replaced by a good will, that is, through one self-determination being superseded by another. Evil and Good are incompatible self-determinations that cannot occur in one and the same will but only as conflict between differently determined wills in the succession of time in one and the same life. Self-determination is a creative process in which it is not something that is already there that is determined or regulated in one way or in another (regulating determination) but in which something that was not there before is determined or constituted in one way or in another (constituting determination). In the self-determination, the will makes itself free to be what it thereby then factually is: an evil or a good will. The decisive change from Evil to Good thus does not take place specially in one and the same will but in the conflict of different wills and thus in the concrete unfolding of a life. It is not a conflict of the will (a conflict within one and the same will) but a life conflict (a conflict in one and the same life), and it unfolds in the conflict between the self-determination to do what is evil (which constitutes the evil will) and the self-determination to do what is good (which constitutes the good will) as a conflict of the fundamental moral orientation of this life.

That is why we must say that insofar as it is viewed as a person acting morally, the human being does not *have* free will but that the human being *is* free will. Free will is not a particular aspect of or in the human that could be demonstrated by neurobiology, it is the human being viewed in all its dimensions and in the entire unfolding of its life as morally responsible person. Accordingly, the good or evil will is not a particular aspect of the human being as *animal rationale* that could be studied on its own and investigated scientifically; it is the moral mode of a human life that orients or precisely does not orient itself by the good and thereby unfolds as the life of a morally good or evil person. Like free will, good or evil will as the concrete form of the free will cannot be pinned down in some part of the human organism and studied as a biological phenomenon; rather, it says something about the way a human being lives her life (moral mode). When we seek to address evil or good free will, we must look at the moral mode of a person's entire human life in all its relations, not just at its biological substrate. Freedom cannot be measured and weighed, nor can good and evil: they appear only as determinations of a life which thereby expresses how it determines and understands itself.

D

The Inadequacy of the *Malefactum* Tradition

1. How Can Evil People Will What Is Good?

IT IS STRIKING HOW Kant, in philosophically taking up and recasting the Augustinian *malum* tradition, puts the accent entirely on the *male velle* and *bene nolle*, that is, articulates the problem entirely within the perspective of the *perpetrator* of evil but not of the victim of evil. But especially at the base point of his analysis, it turns out that the perpetrator of evil is someone who has "always already" and fundamentally decided in favor of the wrong order of maxims—not because there was some point in time at which he explicitly made that decision but because there is no point in time at which he would not act such that his action would not be based on this wrong order of maxims. Accordingly, everybody finds themselves to be someone lapsed into evil. And not because they explicitly decided in favor of it but because they did not explicitly decide in favor of the Good.

Kant's entire argumentation depends on conceiving the situation of the moral decision between Good and Evil in such a way that not deciding in favor of the Good represents a decision in favor of Evil. Human beings never find themselves in a neutral position but always already in morally qualified situations, namely in negatively qualified situations. The problem thus does not consist in how it is possible for humans to will the Good and not will Evil but, more precisely, how it is possible for humans *who will Evil* to will the good and not will Evil. The path to the Good is always a path out of Evil. And this path, precisely, is one evil persons cannot take by themselves. They thus find themselves challenged to do Good in a situation in which they do not even will to do the Good. Not only are they incapable of doing Good, they are unwilling to will it. Or, put differently: Evil manifests as a self-contradiction of the will not willing what it can and ought to will, and instead willing what it cannot and ought not to will.

2. The Price of Freedom?

This is something different from the "price of freedom" evoked time and again. We could not be free, we are told, if we did not thereby also have the possibility of abusing freedom, and we could not freely choose what is good if we did not thereby also have the possibility of freely choosing what is evil. This, however, also includes the ability to actualize this possibility. Therefore, the argument goes, if we are to be in a position freely to determine ourselves to do what is good, then we must also be in a position freely to determine ourselves to do what is evil, and if we can do that, we have to reckon with us—or some of us—doing so. "That is why Evil is the risk and the price of freedom."[1]

The problematic step in this argument is the inference from the possibility of being evil to its actualization. Why should what is not impossible become actual and not just remain possible? Kant does not provide an answer but only states that we factually are that way. He does so, however, by placing two striking accents. On the one hand, he emphasizes the universality of this fact, that is, he highlights that there is no one of whom it would not be true to say this. On the other hand, he considerably attenuates the point by defining it, to be sure, as factually not willing and not doing the good but *not* as willing Evil *for the sake of Evil*. Humans can and ought to do the good for its own sake, but according to Kant, the same cannot be said of Evil. It is impossible for humans to will Evil for the sake of Evil: it would turn humans into devils.

It has often been objected that Kant's view here has been overtaken by reality.[2] We might respond that, in entirely formal terms, everything that is willed is a good because it is striven for, be it as a means, be it as an end or purpose. Yet this answer is insufficient because it leaves open the question whether a good striven for is something good or something evil. This question is not without meaning already for the simple reason that it cannot be inferred from something being striven for and from its, in that sense, being *a good* that this something *is good* unless we illicitly turn a blind eye to the fact that humans are very capable of wishing for, willing, and striving for evil.[3] Kant's position does not declare to be impossible what we are factually doing. He does not exclude that we factually act that way; he contests that this fact can be understood not only as evidence of factual conduct but as the expression of autonomous self-determination: choosing Evil oneself as the moral goal of one's action would not be a moral option but the abolition of morality—which cannot be excluded for humanity. For Kant, we cannot choose Evil as an end in itself to determine our willing and acting—not because that would not be possible *per se*, nor because it would in principle be impossible *for us*, but because it is an option we could exercise only at the price of destroying our humanness as such—we would diabolize ourselves and that means: dehumanize ourselves.

3. Human and Inhuman

Understood this way, Kant's denial of humans choosing Evil for Evil's sake does not make a factual claim refuted by the history of the twentieth century but marks a boundary: it states what no longer falls within the spectrum of moral options of human self-determination because we thereby determine ourselves in such a way that the result is no longer a good or a bad human being but no longer a human being at all. And that means

1. Safranski, *Das Böse oder das Drama der Freiheit*, 193.

2. Safranski, *Das Böse oder das Drama der Freiheit*, 194.

3. See Stocker, "Desiring the Bad."

nothing but that human beings are *able to act in such a way* as to dehumanize themselves: humans are capable not only of being evil but of ruining their personality. They can destroy their *lives* by violating the conditions of their animality. They can destroy their *rational* lives when they live in contradiction of the conditions of their rationality. They can ruin their *moral* lives when they negate their personality. An evil person, too, is a person and to be appreciated as such. But someone determining themselves to pursue Evil out of pure malice is no longer someone to whom dignity could be attributed: they are not only evil persons but Evil personified.

When at this stage of the argument, both Safranski and Neiman[4] bring in the Marquis de Sade, their discussions thus do not in fact do what they are meant to do: refute Kant's thesis that humans do not choose evil for the sake of evil by presenting a case in which evil is precisely chosen only for the sake of evil, extensively and in a great variety of ways. The opposite is the case: it affirms the boundary of being a moral person Kant establishes. For what is shown by the reference to Sade is nothing other than what Kant notes: someone determining himself to pursue evil this way squanders his being a moral person. Kant does not deny that we could at all times live only as *animals* or act only as *rational animals*, he only denies that we would then still be *persons*. We can ruin ourselves as living beings (by violating our animality). We can ruin ourselves as acting beings (by violating our rationality). And we can ruin ourselves as persons (in violating our personality). The first and second point may be obvious in suicide or self-enslavement (rendering ourselves immature). The third point is not for all that any less dangerous, on the contrary: suicide and self-enslavement are human actions that have a correlate in murder and enslavement, which humans commit not on themselves but on other human beings. Depersonalization by contrast is something *we can do to ourselves* and that can be done to us by no one else. Those who squander their being a person do so themselves. They do not thereby have to stop living (qua *animal*) or acting (qua *animal rationale*), but they are no longer persons autonomously determining themselves and instead surrender to the processes of their animality or rationality without once more assuming a moral stance toward them. Just as it is not possible to read in a person's face whether and to what extent they are a person, it is not possible to tell whether and to what extent they are no longer such. Both are apparent for others and for oneself *in acting alone*, in *how one lives*. Their acting shows whether someone is a good or a bad human being or inhuman. Kant did not consider it impossible that inhumans might exist; he considered it inconceivable that humans would by themselves (and that is the only way they could) will to become inhuman.

4. The Incompleteness of the Perpetrator Perspective

The notion that it becomes apparent in action whether a person is good or evil, even if the decision whether they are one or the other is made not in action but in the self-determination to action, has further important implications. We cannot read off any action

4. Safranski, *Das Böse oder das Drama der Freiheit*, 194–212, and Neiman, *Evil in Modern Thought*, 170–96.

whether it is the action of a good person or an evil person; that is something we come to know only once we measure it by the universalization criterion of the categorical imperative. But this criterion fails when someone makes evil the maxim of their living and acting for Evil's sake. To exclude this and maintain the functionality of the criterion, Kant marks the boundary to a no longer human but diabolic will. Only if this is excluded is it possible and justified at any time to ask what *moral* will a human being's action is based on, that is, whether it is a good will or not a good will.

This, however, has the problematic consequence (1) that evil is seen and defined exclusively within the perspective of the perpetrator and (2) that behind every evil doing, an evil will is to be sought out. Yet only if the first is true, the second applies as well. If, however, we understand that which is evil no longer within the perpetrator perspective as wrong or omitted determination of the will to do what is good but, starting from those affected by it, as that which harms their being human with respect to their life possibilities as *animal, rational animal,* and *person,* then the second consequence, too, becomes implausible because it is by no means a matter of course that everywhere evil takes place, evil must be willed. Evil then manifests in *deeds and events* that do evil to others without this allowing for inferring an evil will on which they are based. Not only where ills take place for which no human being is responsible but also where evil takes place that is done to someone by human acting or not acting, an evil willing cannot necessarily be inferred: *evil also happens where no one specifically and intentionally wills evil or specifically and intentionally omits willing what is good.* It is possible to do evil not only when we do not will the good but also when we do will the good: willing good and doing good do not exclude that something is being done that is evil for a human being. Even someone willing what is good can do something that is evil for others. But—and this is the comforting aspect of this discomforting rule—those who do not will what is good can do good for others. In both respects, the inferential connections between will, willing, and doing are loosened.

This, however, shows Kant's taking up and recasting of the *malefactum* tradition to be, at a decisive point, a problematic reduction and oversimplification: Evil cannot be completely reduced morally to the cases where ill deeds are based on evil willing or a not-good will. Evil also happens where only good is willed to be done. Whether evil happens is not decided in the autonomous person's self-determination but in what concretely happens to the other person. The touchstone for the reality of evil is the other, not the autonomous self.

The victims of evil in the form of ills not only include those surrendered to a perpetrator. Evil is always suffered, but the evil suffered is not always done by a perpetrator to whom it can be attributed as a responsible or irresponsible deed.[5] The perpetrator perspective, to be sure, is ethically decisive, and theology, too, must not lose sight of it to avoid overlooking responsibilities where they do exist and where they must be addressed. Yet the perpetrator perspective alone is often an inappropriate reduction in dealing with the reality of Evil. Theology is thus well-advised to orient itself explicitly by the victim perspective: Evil is to be ended and overcome at the place of the victim.

---

5. That is why it is an inappropriate reduction to see evil only where evil is done to subjects by subjects; cf. Petersen, *Das Böse in uns,* 162.

The perpetrators are always affected by their ill deeds themselves as well. The group of victims is thus larger than the group of perpetrators, in several respects: not all victims are also perpetrators, and not only those are victims of evil to whom evil is done as the deed of a perpetrator.

5. Questionable Partialities

A reduction of evil to evil done by someone can be supposed only if we abandon the modern difference between event and action, nature and freedom, law and rule, science and morality, and interpret everything that happens as a deed done, as *factum* in the literal sense, as the doing of a doer or perpetrator. This would be to interpret the entire reality of the world in all its dimensions and aspects in the terms of the theory of action and freedom. Yet that means nothing but entering once more into the aporia which the distinction between event and action, between natural causality and freedom was supposed to lead out of, the aporia that the ills not caused by and responsibly attributable to humans, too, are assigned to someone freely deciding and therefore responsible who causes them, namely God the creator or a satanic counterpart acting against him.

This consequence, precisely, has in recent years increasingly been drawn again.[6] All ills are "the result of evil intentions and activity of human and angelic agents." Little children buried alive in mudslides or washed away by waves are to be seen not as victims of natural events but as "victims of war" for which we must "assign the blame to human or demonic beings who are opposing God's will," for "[t]he world is literally caught up in a spiritual war between God and Satan." This means two things. On the one hand, there are no merely natural events and processes but only actions where it is always possible meaningfully to ask about the intentions that guide them. On the other hand, these actions are not always, wholly, and exclusively to be traced back to God, for that would render God entirely equivocal. But while "Scripture emphasizes God's ultimate authority over the world," it "does not teach that God controls all the behavior of free agents, whether humans or angels. Humans and fallen angels are able to grieve God's Spirit and to some extent frustrate his purposes. . . . While his *general will* for world history cannot fail, his *particular will* for individuals often does." That, however, means that no ill that happens is willed by God, never mind "part of God's 'secret plan,'" such that we would have to or could look for reasons of God's we do not (yet) understand. On the contrary, these ills are caused not by God but by "Satan and other evil agents," and "God fights these opponents precisely because *their* purposes are working *against his* purposes." The world is a battlefield of divine and anti-divine powers, and just as all that is good is to be traced back to God, so everything ill and evil is to be traced back to the evil intentions

---

6. See above all Boyd, *God at War*; *Satan and the Problem of Evil*; and *Is God to Blame?* The quotations that follow are drawn from Boyd, *Satan and the Problem of Evil*, 15–16. Similar views are advocated by Robinson, *Devil and God*; Lewis, *Creator and the Adversary*; Stuermann, *Divine Destroyer*; and Bloom, *Lucifer Principle*. For a critical discussion of such attempts, see already Farrer, *Love Almighty and Ills Unlimited*, 132–60, who notes that it does not make sense to take recourse to the devil to explain my doing ill: "the devil is one thing, original sin is another" (133). Even if I bring in the devil as the one who tempts me, "I still need not choose the devil's way; yet I do. The whole mystery of iniquity lies in my perversity, a mystery which the supposition of diabolic malice does nothing to clarify" (140).

of Satan and other evil demons who abuse nature and human beings for their struggle against God.

Everything that happens in this world is thus understood as God's fight "against human and angelic opponents who are able in some measure to thwart his will."[7] In this worldview, there is no neutral nature and there are no contingent historical processes, everything is "caught up in a spiritual war between God and Satan." "Nature" is not a domain with its own laws but a system of natural forces influenced by "spirits" and "evil agents": "When nature exhibits diabolic features that are not the result of human wills, it is the direct or indirect result of the influence of diabolic forces."[8]

This worldview goes much further even than the dissolution in process philosophy and quantum physics of the distinction between event and action and the ensuing transformation of all laws of nature into the regularities of action theory. Natural processes are not only indeterministically open and chaotic, such that human freedom is not impossible on higher levels of complexity;[9] they are the intentional actions of good and evil agents. "Nature has no will of its own with which to oppose God. But if we accept that there are spiritual agents who can influence the objective world just as humans can, then we can begin to understand how nature could become hostile to God's purposes, even though it has no will of its own."[10] The world is not only to be understood throughout as a nexus of actions (freedom-theoretical worldview) but as a battlefield of good and evil powers (neomythical worldview).

Both views are compelled to extend the consequences all the way down to the sub-atomic domains of reality, that is, draw comprehensive cosmological and nature-philosophical consequences from their methodologies. From the point of view of a theory of freedom, quantum mechanical processes are thus not only understood as conditions allowing for free decisions on more complex levels of reality.[11] The totality of natural processes is interpreted "in a variation of the free-will defence, applied to the whole created world. One might call it 'the free-process defence.'"[12] And both taking this notion up and going beyond it, the neomythical view can interpret this as the intentional action of spiritual agents: "Beings other than God must have a say-so in what transpires. The origin of everything the Creator opposes must lie . . . in the irrevocable free wills of spiritual agents who have been given some authority over nature."[13]

---

7. Boyd, *Satan and the Problem of Evil*, 15; cf. Boyd, *God at War*.

8. Boyd, *Satan and the Problem of Evil*, 15 and 247. In chs. 8–10 (242–318) of his book, Boyd seeks to show that only such a "warfare" view of the world allows for a theologically appropriate understanding of natural processes.

9. An argument proffered, for example, by Bartholomew, *God of Chance*; Penrose, *Emperor's New Mind*; Murphy and Ellis, *On the Moral Nature of the Universe*; and Kane, *Significance of Free Will*.

10. Boyd, *Satan and the Problem of Evil*, 283.

11. See Russell, "Quantum Physics in Philosophical and Theological Perspective," 362: "Since quantum chance is involved in the production of order and life, this suggests that even the random character of elementary processes contributes something essential to the greater panorama out of which emerge the conditions for genuine alternatives, and eventually the reality of free will and authentic relationship characterized by love." See also Murphy, "Does the Trinity Play Dice?"

12. Polkinghorne, *Science and Providence*, 66.

13. Boyd, *Satan and the Problem of Evil*, 283.

To be able to understand all ill as the ill deed of an ill doer, the neomythical world-view postulates spirits as agents. This thesis, however, remains a mere *ad hoc* postulate; it is discussed with reference to passages in the Bible and figures of thought from the early Church but is not made plausible as regards the possibility, the reality, or the probability of such agents.[14] This is done explicitly to excuse God from being reproached with responsibility for the natural ills not caused by human beings. Yet Boyd's entire elaborate argument cannot hide the fact that introducing these anti-divine spirits is in no way able to give a better response to the problem of irrational ill than the supposition of natural processes that effect ills unintentionally. Faith in the creator-god is thereby no less confronted with the question of why God does not already put an end to the action of these powers now, especially if "[i]t is clear that God shall someday vanquish this rebel kingdom."[15] Why only "someday"? Why not now? And, generally: Why does all ill have to be the ill deed of an ill doer? Without this supposition of Boyd's, which he never questions, there would be no occasion for his neomythical speculations. Yet even granted this occasion, these speculations do not render anything comprehensible; they explain what is obscure with something that is even more obscure.

The freedom-theoretical approach, too, raises fundamental difficulties, but these are of a different sort. Its core problem is the danger of evacuating the notion of freedom and leading it *ad absurdum*. Not only is there nothing that would not be construed as a free decision; to be able to operate this expansion, it is also necessary to conceive of freedom minimalistically, to reduce it to the choice between alternative options. To be sure, this allows for finding freedom wherever there is an either-or. But it also creates an unnecessary vulnerability to the currently forming cultural countermovement of behavioral biology and neurobiology, which take the diametrically opposite path and seek to reduce all freedom processes to causal natural, environmental, and neuronal processes.[16] What is seen to be at work everywhere in nature is not freedom; on the contrary, with reference to Libet's experiment, it is claimed inversely that what appears to us as "freedom," too, can be exposed as a subjective illusion about objective causal processes in nature.[17] Just as freedom-theoretical universalism seeks to reduce natural processes to the decisions and actions of agents, so nature-theoretical universalism inversely reduces the freedom phenomena of human life to deterministic natural processes and thereby reveals them to be subjective illusions.[18] When we think we make a decision,

14. See Boyd, *Satan and the Problem of Evil*, 29–49. It is one thing to postulate such spirits, forces, and powers; making them philosophically or theologically plausible is another thing entirely. To do so, merely referencing passages from Scripture does not suffice.

15. Boyd, *Satan and the Problem of Evil*, 15.

16. See Brooks, *Free Will*; and Double, *Non-Reality of Free Will*; on the other side Thorp, *Free Will: A Defence*; Searle, *Minds, Brains, and Science*; and Weatherford, *Implications of Determinism*.

17. See Libet, "Time of Conscious Intention to Act"; and "Unconscious Cerebral Initiative and the Role of Conscious Will" in Libet, *Neurophysiology of Consciousness*, 249–68 and 269–79; Keller and Heckhausen, "Readiness Potentials"; Haggard and Eimer, "On the Relation Between Brain Potentials and the Awareness of Voluntary Movements"; and Miller and Trevena, "Cortical Movement Preparation and Conscious Decisions."

18. See Walter, *Neurophilosophy of Free Will*; Pauen, *Illusion Freiheit?*; and Beckermann, "Neuronale Determiniertheit und Freiheit."

neuroscientists and philosophers of mind such as Wolfgang Prinz, Gerhard Roth, and Wolf Singer conclude from the results of Libet's experiment, the decision has long been made by our brain.[19] Our consciousness is always lagging behind our brain's decisions; we do not do what we will, we will what we do.[20]

That of course is a problem only when the concept of freedom has been downplayed the way it is done here: freedom is exhausted by deciding in favor of one thing or of another. But that does not even begin to address the choice between good and evil. The concept of freedom that comes together in Kant's notion of autonomy cannot be rendered comprehensible with recourse to causally determined or undetermined decisions between alternatives; it requires a recourse to reasons and thus requires showing what makes reasons valid. What is decisive is not the ability to choose and do *this or that* but the ability to establish a relation to these processes and possibilities that allows us to *determine ourselves* to determine ourselves this way or that. Even if the misleading talk of the "deciding brain"—the (alleged) fact that it is not we who decide but our brain that has already decided—were meaningful and viable, it would only be an objection to the autonomy and capacity for self-determination of the human if the option for the good could be and would have to be construed on the model of the decision to move a finger. That, however, does not apply in any way. Nor is decision in the sense relevant here free in the sense of a negative conception of freedom if I am able, at a minimum, to stop before the decision and reflect *and* my decision is determined by the result of these reflections. Rather, I am free if *I am able to determine myself* to act and live in a certain way that does not have to be this way but could also be otherwise. What makes me free is not that when faced with alternatives for action, I can determine *what* I do; rather, that I can determine *myself* to do what I do *in a certain way* manifests my freedom. This freedom includes the ability to recognize what something is and what it counts as, that is, the capacity to judge it as something good or evil, beautiful or not beautiful, true or false. These judgments and evaluations cannot be sufficiently grasped as causal processes, but they are an essential and indisputable aspect of human life. That is why freedom cannot be dissolved in actual causal processes against the background of a decision between alternatively possible causal courses of events; rather, it is the ability to begin new causal processes not only by continuing already existing causal chains but *oneself* starting new ones.[21] In this sense relevant to understanding autonomy, there is freedom only there where the issue is *to determine oneself*, taking such distinctions, judgments, and

19. See Prinz, "Freiheit oder Wissenschaft?"; and Roth, *Aus Sicht des Gehirns*; see also Bieri, *Das Handwerk der Freiheit*, and Geyer, *Hirnforschung und Willensfreiheit*. Prinz writes: "The idea of freedom of the will expects us to accept, in an otherwise deterministically constituted view of the world, local holes of indeterminism. . . . Yet at issue here is not . . . merely the absence of determination . . . but something entirely different and considerably more radical: nothing short of replacing the usual causal determination by another form of determination that cannot be explained causally. This form of determination assumes a subject conceived of as autonomous that is itself free, that is, not determined. . . . The idea of freedom of the will demands of us that we see in every subject an independent, autonomous source of determining action" (Prinz, "Freiheit oder Wissenschaft?," 92). And this assumption, precisely, is said to have been disproven by Libet's experiments.

20. See Prinz, "Freiheit oder Wissenschaft?," 98–100.

21. As Kane, *Significance of Free Will*, 79–101; Clarke, "Toward a Credible Agent-Causal Account," 203; and O'Connor, "Agent Causation," rightly emphasize.

evaluations into account. Such freedom, however, does not even enter the picture if we start from the ability to move a finger.

This is the point where the partialities of the naturalist view of freedom and the freedom-theoretical view of nature meet: both must reduce, simplify, and dilute the conception of freedom in such a way that it coincides with the choice between alternatives. Understood this way, however, it no longer allows for comprehending the rich conception of freedom as self-determination (autonomy). Not just neurological naturalizing approaches, freedom-theoretical interpretations, too, that reconstruct everything that is and happens as processes and realities of free action and decision, dissolve the specifically human concept of autonomy. It is not the mere choice in facing alternatives that is the core of Kant's notion of freedom, it is the determination to perform good actions, which are good not because of their consequences but because they are willed and determined solely by a good will. This notion cannot be reduced to the contingent choice between two options without dissolving it: this reduction leaves open the very thing at issue: identifying what is responsible for the occurrence of contingent and thus, in principle, avoidable ills in the life of human beings and in their world. Where everything is conditioned by decisions, the decision against what is good or in favor of evil and ill has no longer a distinct character. Then all *facere* is *male facere* or *bene facere*. And that transformation is none other than the transformation from the worldview of the theology of creation to the worldview of the theology of sin, which does not understand sin beginning with God's acting grace overcoming sin but on the model of moral and nonmoral decisions. This reduces the conception of sin to the terms of the theory of action and fails to grasp the concept of freedom.

II.3

MALUM AS UNFAITH

IT IS A DISTURBING fact that more evil happens than is willed and done intentionally. This blocks the way out that would consist in restricting evil, in a moralizing manner, to evil willing and evil doing. Holding on to this moralization as an achievement of modernity requires expanding the category of non-moral ill to include the evil consequences of good or well-intended deeds. In any case, the point of view changes: now, what is evil or acts an ill is no longer decided by what I will or how I will it but by *how it affects others (including myself)*.[1] The crucial site for evil to manifest is not the willing, planning, and acting subject but the one affected by *malum*—be it a human or another living being.

This changes the situation of the argument. It deprives the subject of the competency to decide the good or evil of its action: the question is decided not with me but *at the site of the one affected*—and that usually means *at the site of the other*. This is not a flight from responsibility for Evil, a responsibility that Kant went to such great intellectual lengths to preserve. It is, rather, the expression of the insight that even the greatest effort at living up to our duty to be responsible cannot prevent that we do evil to others. We are not masters of our deeds, because even our well-willed and well-intended deeds (can) have effects that are the opposite of good. Kant knew that, and that is why he shifted the decision about an action's being good to the guiding intention and to the will determining this willing.

Yet we are also not masters of our intentions, because willing what is good according to our reason does not guarantee that it is also good according to the reason, stranger to mine, of the other. This would be otherwise only if there were grounds to suppose a common good will and a common practical reason that morally obliges me *and* the other in the same way and speaks with the same voice in every conscience. Here, however, there is a discrepancy both between possibility and actuality and between what is and what ought to be. To be sure, the notion of such a shared reason is not impossible and self-contradictory *per se*, yet *a posse ad esse non valet consequentia*—that it ought to be such and could be such does in no way mean that it also is such, as Kant well knew.[2]

---

1. Compare the inverse approach taken by Zagzebski, "Agent-Based Approach to the Problem of Evil."

2. Kant, *Lectures on Metaphysics*, 320 (AA 28:555).

Trying to avoid the problem by sidestepping a reason determined by contents and moving to a "pure" and merely formal reason as determining grounds of a pure willing said to be the same for every rational individual by virtue of its mere formality, like Kant tried to do, does not change the situation. Such an attempt achieves both too much and too little. It achieves too much because it avoids contradiction in content at the price of no longer being able to develop a normative ethics at all, as Giovanni B. Sala has pointed out. Only because "an action is good according to its essence (that is, from the perspective of its object, which morally qualifies it)" can it "become universal, that is, become the content of a moral law. The inverse path—because an action displays the form of universality, it is good—cannot be taken. For it lacks an objective criterion for finding out which ways of acting can take this form and which cannot."[3] Kant's attempt achieves too little, in turn, because practically, it is not an advance. That the voice of my conscience is also the voice of the other's conscience and vice versa can be problematized at any time, and is to be problematized in each concrete case, without there being a neutral site for doing so. It is not possible to postulate such an identity of reason and of conscience without doing so from one's own position or from that of the other, and these positions never coincide. The question whether what each side postulates really converges in the relevant aspects always remains to be explored and tested. Even where both sides take recourse to reason and conscience, the difference between one's own reason and that of the other, one's own conscience and that of the other, remains indelibly inscribed in this recourse. Even when everyone wills what is good, that is, determines themselves in the way that, in their conviction, everyone else in the other's place would have to determine themselves, they do so *each where they stand* and *from where they stand*. This, however, makes any Platonic supposition of the unity of the Good problematic. For it does not exclude that the two orientations by what is good contradict each other, that they, for good reason, deny the other's good will, and that they lead to actions that inflict evil on others or on those acting themselves.

If this is correct, it has far-reaching consequences. If even the best of intentions offers no guarantee that no evil is inflicted on others, then the evil that happens cannot in a regular manner be traced back to an evil intention it is based on. However, establishing a constitutive tie between evil deed and evil attention thus leads to the dilemma either of no longer being able to define much of what is done to human beings as evil, although it indisputably is evil, or of no longer being able to trace back some of the evil others do to their evil intentions. In the first case, the Augustinian-Kantian definition of Evil does not go far enough and becomes implausible in the lifeworld because it does not allow for calling something evil although it is evil for those affected. In the second case, to be sure, this is avoided, but at the price of shedding doubt on this definition of Evil in general because its decisive point, the bond between the evil deed and the evil intention, is being dissolved. Yet if Evil needs no evil intentions, if it can result from stupidity, thoughtlessness, self-pity, and even the best willing, then it is no longer possible to take the path of orienting oneself by inferring evil willing from evil doing, and the situation becomes morally unclear.

3. Sala, *Kants* Kritik der praktischen Vernunft, 104.

A

Faith and Unfaith

IN THE TIME BETWEEN Augustine and Kant, Reformation theology thought through the consequences of this dilemma with provocative incisiveness. Not only some of human acting is evil, and not just all of human acting is not as good as it could be and ought to be, but *both* the morally evil *and* the morally good actions of human beings are sin as long as the human being is a sinner. If "[g]ood works do not make a person good, but a good person does good works,"[1] then the good works of people who are not good persons are not good in the sense relevant here, and not just their (morally) evil but their (morally) good action, too, is sin.

1. The Reformation's Revolution in the Way of Thinking

The argument presupposes a revolution in the way of thinking that has far-reaching consequences. The human being is a sinner. The theological tradition says so, too, and to reject Manichean over-radicalizations with their doubtful fatalistic consequences, it adds that the human being is *not just a sinner* (and thereby under the power of Evil) but *even as* sinner is and remains a *creature* (and thereby under the power of the Good).[2] If humans were entirely and exclusively sinners, they would be—from the protological point of view, before and after the fall; from the soteriological point of view, as sinners and as saved; or, from the eschatological point of view, as living toward death on this earth and as someone eternally living out of death—something so radically different in each instance that the expression "human being" could be employed only equivocally, on both sides of these contrasts. That is why the tradition says that, essentially, the human is God's creature (for it is impossible that the human being exist and not be a creature), yet factually, the human is a sinner, that is, a creature who ignores God although it does not have to and ought not to ignore God, a creature that, as human being, also could not be a sinner (for it is not impossible that the human being exist and not be a sinner).

Up to this point, Reformation theology follows the traditional view. But they part ways when it comes to the question of what sin is at its core and of what makes the

---

1. Luther, *Freedom of a Christian*, 514.
2. See Dalferth, "How Is the Concept of Sin Related to the Concept of Moral Wrongdoing?"

sinner a sinner. Where the tradition says that sin is an active *turning away from God* (to emphasize the guilt aspect of sin and the responsibility of sinners), the Reformers tend to say that sin is the *inability and unwillingness to turn toward God* (to emphasize the power and doom aspect of sin as well as the soteriological dependence of the human on God). Both paradigms of the conception of sin could be regarded as compatible variants of a single view only as long as *turning away from God* and *not turning toward God* were understood as an active doing within an anthropology of action that defined the human being exclusively via its *actiones* and the *passiones* that corresponded to them. Just as the human as creature is the result of God's working, so as sinner the human is the result of its own actions. And just as God is responsible exclusively for humans' being creatures but not for their being sinners, so humans are exclusively responsible for their being sinners but not for their being creatures. They are creatures because God makes them so, and they are sinners because they make themselves so.

This makes sense as long as sin is thought primarily as *turn away from God*. If it is thought primarily as *not turning toward God*, however, another perspective suggests itself. Doing nothing is not always a doing but sometimes just what it says: no doing at all. Someone who in an emergency does not help someone else, although they are present and could help, omits giving assistance, that is, by not doing anything, they do something. Yet someone who is not present in that situation or is unable to help does not, by not doing anything, do something but, precisely, does nothing. In the one case, doing nothing is a doing, in the other, by contrast, it is not.

In looking at such morally relevant problematic situations, it seems we must distinguish between three kinds of cases: a *doing*; a *doing nothing* that can be interpreted as a doing; and a *not-doing* that cannot be interpreted as a doing on the part of human beings. From the traditional perspective, only the first two but not the last case is relevant to the theory of sin. That makes sense when sin is understood in analogy with morality, that is, when sin is found and can be found only where there is free and responsible action (doing) or where free and responsible action would have been possible (doing nothing that can be interpreted as a doing). But the perspective of sin would thereby be restricted to cases of the first and the second kind, that is, allow for life situations that do not fall within this perspective because they are neither a doing nor a doing nothing to be understood as a doing but a not-doing. That, however, cannot be reconciled with the Paulinian-Augustinian conviction that, factually, all of human life is infected with sin.[3] There is—Jesus Christ excluded—no human situation that could not be defined as sinful.[4] And to guarantee this point, not-doing, too, has been interpreted—illogically and against the phenomena—as a doing nothing and the human being understood always, everywhere, and exclusively as an acting being defining itself through its acting and making itself a sinner through its sinning.

3. Paul and Augustine provide different rationales. Augustine presupposes a "fall" of angels and of humans that Paul does not know of as such.

4. Classically, this is being explained and justified, following Augustine, with the concept of hereditary sin. Yet this concept, of course, does not begin with human beings' factual situation and way of life but with the human and the story of its origin. This puts it on the wrong track when it tries to think the ubiquity and transmorality of sin. See Freund, *Sünde im Erbe*; Gestrich, *Die Wiederkehr des Glanzes*; and Kleffmann, *Die Erbsündenlehre in sprachtheologischem Horizont*.

Quite evidently, we reach an entirely different, more radical, and fundamentally offensive conception of sin when we do not exclude the possibility of sin-neutral life situations by interpreting all not-doing as doing nothing but, inversely, place the emphasis on the paradigm that not just humans' doing and their doing nothing that can be understood as doing but their not-doing that cannot be understood as doing, too, proves humans to be sinners. The human being is fully and entirely a sinner: in what it does (by doing or omitting) *and* in what it does not do.

In this case, however, the human's being a sinner can no longer be rendered comprehensible by taking recourse to human doing alone. That, precisely, is the methodological consequence Reformation theology draws in a number of ways. Human beings are sinners not through what they do in acting or omitting but where and how and as who they do so: they, as God's creatures, live as though they were not God's creatures. Not the moral quality of their deeds but the basic existential constitution of their lives— the mode in which they conduct or constitute their lives—shows them to be sinners.[5] In their existential place, they live before God with all their doing and omitting (doing nothing) and not-doing in such a way that they ignore God, their creator, and thereby also their own being created, and they behave toward God, others, and themselves such that they neither appreciate their creator nor their fellow creatures in a fitting way but violate the first commandment and thereby also all the others.[6] In this existential-modal sense, sin cannot be restricted to humans' morally evil acting. Sin is not what humans do by sinning, and their sinning is not what makes them sinners, but what sinners do is sin, be it good deeds or evil deeds (judged before the world), and they are sinners because before God, they live as if they lived only before the world and themselves but not before God. The Aristotelianizing Scholastic tradition argues that humans are sinners because they sin; the Reformation counters by arguing, citing Augustine and Paul, that humans sin because they are sinners.

This is not just a logical inversion of the justification; behind it, there is a different guiding conception of sin. Sin is not to be understood starting *from human doing* and thus in analogy with morality but starting *from faith* and thereby as that which, in faith, is overcome by God himself. The perspective guiding the conception of sin is not *sinning* but the *forgiveness of sin*: *sin is that which is forgiven in having faith.*

This, however, also presupposes a conception of faith different from that of the inherited theological tradition. Faith is not to be understood either cognitively (in the category of the *logos*) as a doxastic attitude between opinion and knowledge, nor morally (in the category of the *ethos*) as a determination of the intellect by the will and a determination of the will by the intellect to adopt a certain mode of action but rather in entirely passive terms (in the category of *pathos*) as that which happens to humans in such a way that it makes them what they are as people of faith.[7] Faith is thus not to be understood logically or morally but pathically and affectively. It is that which, as God's

---

5. Körtner, *Wie lange noch, wie lange?*, 17–18.

6. It was Luther especially who "in a theretofore unusual way emphasized" that everything depends on how humans relate to the first commandment. See Ebeling, "Theologie zwischen reformatorischem Sündenverständnis und heutiger Einstellung zum Bösen," 182.

7. On the history of the problem of *pathos* and the pathic, see Stoellger, *Passivität aus Passion.*

action and good deed, comes to the human *mere passive*; it is nothing they would have to implement themselves as *fides* or *assensus* or *voluntas* to counteract sin. That, precisely, is an entirely impossible possibility for sinners. If they were *only* sinners, they would not only be unable to act, they would not exist at all: being a sinner is not a positive but a privative determination of being that cannot occur in and by itself but only ever in and with something else. Humans can act only as *sinful creatures* but for that very reason never *only* as creatures or *only* as sinners. Because humans are not only creatures but also sinners, they cannot act *merely as creatures* nor *merely as sinners*; their acting is always only one whose possibility is founded in their being creatures and whose determination is founded on their being sinners. Wherever they act, they act as sinners even if as sinners they can act only insofar as they are creatures and remain such even as sinners.[8]

Yet if humans defined as sinners can never act only as creatures but must always simultaneously act as sinners, then there is no possibility for them to counter their sinning by means of what they are doing since everything they, as sinners, do is sin. Sin therefore is not overcome by sinners turning against sin or actively omitting sin but—if at all—by *their being forgiven their sin*. Those who *as sinners* try to counteract sin by trying to do what is good and omitting what is evil will never be able to overcome it. They will only ever have the experience of failure and of the incapacity of overcoming it because with everything they do, they continue and do not put end to what they are and how they live.

But even if *per impossibile* they succeeded and no longer sinned here and now, they would not be able, by what they are doing now, to undo what they have done before. In that respect—as Anselm saw exactly—*one* sin causes an entire life and *one* sinner causes all of creation to go awry. A sinner can no longer escape his sin because as someone who acts, he can only act forward toward the future but never backward toward the past. And once sin has occurred in creation at all, the sinners can no longer erase it from creation. No creature is capable of undoing or abolishing it for themselves or for others, neither in the history of creation as a whole or in an individual life.[9]

Sin can only be overcome, not erased, by God forgiving it.[10] Forgiving is that mode of God's dealing with the irreversible reality of sin that—put negatively—neither ignores sin in defiance of reality (that is, acts as if it did not exist) nor *per impossibile* attempts to undo it (that is, acts as if what has been done could be undone) nor ignores the victims and no longer distinguishes between perpetrators and victims (that is, renounces justice) but—put positively—in explicitly acknowledging the reality of sin and the responsibility of perpetrators, contains the effects of sin by strengthening the good and no longer lets the relationship with his creatures be burdened by the reality and consequences of sin:

8. In his *Wie entsteht christlicher Glaube?*, Oliver Pilnei does not even begin to address such differentiations. He writes about the constitution of the Christian faith guided by epistemological questions and leaves almost all essential aspects of the topic aside. He reduces the category of annunciation to verbal communication in an entirely inappropriate manner; he fails to understand the Reformation's emphasis on the passivity of faith; and he does not even perceive sin as part of the problem of how faith arises. He does not see that Christian faith is constitutively about overcoming the sinner's distance from God, and as a result, the "phenomenology of the Christian faith" he postulates is meaningless.

9. Compare Trillhaas, *Dogmatik*, 190: it is part of the essence of sin "that it can no longer be undone. While I can repair damage and correct an error, I cannot correct sin."

10. Compare Scheiber, *Vergebung*.

what has happened remains what has happened, but it no longer stands between the one who forgives and the one who is forgiven.

This means concretely: in that on his own initiative, God reaches out to the sinner in his distance and thereby, on his own initiative, suspends the consequences of sin for himself and for the sinner, the sinner is *mere passive* opened by God toward God and toward his neighbors and thereby enabled to live a new and different life before God.[11] The sinner thus gains a differentiated view of himself and of God by, on the one hand, recognizing himself as a creature who has ignored its creator and, in so doing, acknowledging God as his creator, and, on the other, exposing himself as a sinner who has failed to live up to his destiny and is permanently dependent on God's forgiving care to be able, despite what has been done, to live in a new and different way and thereby confesses God as his savior. He begins to conceive of himself as creature and thereby of God as his creator to whom he owes everything without having thanked God for it and in this way precisely begins to understand himself with a view to his life thus far as a sinner and thereby God as his savior who protects him from the consequences of his sin and through his forgiving allows him to live in a new way. In this new life of the *homo iustificatur fide*, the human justified by faith, the justifying God and the justified human cooperate in such a way that good prevents evil that has occurred from continuing to exercise its effect and the victims and perpetrators obtain justice in a differentiated manner. For in forgiving the sinner without forgetting his sin, God ensures that Evil has the last word neither in the life of victims nor in the life of perpetrators but instead is corrected, ended, and outdone by the good in the sense relevant to each of them.[12]

Only someone who in this sense lives from out of the forgiving of sin, which turns him from a sinner into a *iustus* and *cooperator dei*, can also actively omit sin. For just as only sinners sin, so only those who are no longer burdened by but freed from their sin can no longer sin. They live *in the faith* because they have been forgiven their being sinners, and they thereby no longer have to try doing what they cannot do (to undo or to end their sinning) but, knowing that it is impossible to escape their being sinners on their own, they can live *from out of the forgiving of sin* and do without the impossible attempt to turn against sinning while sinning.

If we think sin this way, not starting from sinning but from the forgiving of sin, then everything is sin that does not happen from faith (Rom 14:23) but picks up on something other than the forgiving of sin, and nothing is sin that happens from faith and thereby starts from the forgiving of sin. Yet all that and only that does not happen from faith which ignores God's sin-forgiving care and is thereby done in unfaith, while inversely all that and only that which does not happen in unfaith is done in the faith. *Faith* and *unfaith* [*Glaube und Unglaube*] are thus the two existential determinations under which everything in human life before God is taking place when viewed in light

---

11. See Dalferth, "Mere Passive: Die Passivität der Gabe bei Luther."

12. If sin were merely forgotten, the victims would not obtain justice, and the forgiveness granted the sinner would thereby be meaningless. Sin, rather, cannot be forgotten but must instead be recalled by God already because without that, it would be unclear what concrete good comes from God to the victims to obtain justice for what has been done to them. God cannot simply forget the sin not because of the sin but for the sake of concretizing the good with which God seeks to end the history of the sin in the lives of the victims and of the perpetrators.

of the forgiving of sin. There is no human life that is lived *neither* in the faith *nor* in unfaith. But neither is there any life in the faith that would not have become such in the transformation from unfaith to faith, and that is why no one who lives in the faith is a stranger to life in unfaith.

2. On the Grammar of "Having Faith"

We cannot capture the full force of the Reformation's conception of faith if we start from the colloquial ways of understanding "having faith" and "believing" we are familiar with. Faith is not a particular instance of belief. This is not immediately self-evident, especially not in German, where the expression *glauben* is generally used either in the sense of *doxastically considering something to be true* ("I believe something to be the case"); of *fiduciarily trusting someone* ("I believe someone"); or of *personally having confidence in someone* ("I believe in someone"). These usages entertain certain relationships with each other. There is no personal confidence and fiducial trust without doxastically considering something to be true, nor is there personal confidence without fiducial trust. It might be possible to conceive of Christian belief as a *doxastic considering to be true* that assigns more probability to one state of affairs than to its opposite. But it is not possible to do so in the case of *faith in Jesus Christ* (the paradigm the following sections will explore), because this faith is held without restrictions, not just hypothetically and provisionally until the opposite is proven. Yet neither is it possible to capture this faith sufficiently in terms of *personal confidence* or *fiducial trust*, because it is not just a practical human attitude like the belief of Christians that ends with death at the latest. Rather, it, as justificatory faith, associates human life with God's life in such a way that this connection cannot be interrupted even by death.

In the Christian self-conception, then, faith in Jesus Christ cannot be understood by any of the three ways to conceive of believing just named, taken by themselves or in combination. However, insofar as it cannot be confessed without expressing itself in human life as a specific considering to be true, trusting, and having confidence, this faith entertains (factual, not conceptual) relationships with all three moments that we must clarify, even if it cannot be sufficiently defined through them. To obtain an appropriate concept of faith in Jesus Christ, we cannot therefore start from our colloquial preconceptions and usage of "believing" and "having faith." This view contradicts a significant theological tradition, but without heeding this objection, we cannot understand the point of the Reformation's conception of faith.

3. Doxastic Faith

Common philosophical and theological analyses of belief that start from our usual understanding of the term follow Kant in defining belief as a type of considering to be true that features the certainty of subjective conviction but not the security of objective knowledge. In continuing the tradition that dominates Western intellectual history from antiquity (notably in Plato's *Theaetetus*) via Augustine to the present, *belief* is thus epistemically situated between *opinion* and *knowledge*.

In *On Lying*, Augustine takes up classical thought and characterizes opining (*opinari*) as an attitude that is always associated with some "false thing." Those who opine think they know what they do not know. They therefore stop looking and thereby fail to try and obtain knowledge. Knowing (*scire*) is always without error, that is, always true. Should something we think we know turn out to be false it would therefore clearly turn out to have been an opinion, not knowledge. Believing (*credere*), by contrast, differs from knowing in that believers know that they do not know even if they have no doubt about what they believe.[13] The difference between having an opinion, having a belief, and having knowledge, therefore, is this: with a false sense of certainty, those with an opinion do not make the effort of testing their opinion and of thereby specifying it further as knowledge. Believers in contrast know that they do not know what they believe even if they do not doubt its truth. For that very reason, they try to turn their belief into knowledge. Knowers, finally, know what they know to be true and know that they cannot go wrong.[14]

Medieval theology adopts the basic traits of this analysis of the relationship between *scientia*, *fides*, and *opinio* and bequeaths it to Western thinking in a great many variations. For Hugh of Saint Victor, "[f]aith is certainty in things absent, established beyond opinion and short of knowledge." And in Aquinas's definition: "Faith is a mean between knowledge and opinion." While faith does not have the certainty of provable knowledge, it goes beyond mere opinion insofar as it "implies assent of the intellect to that which is believed." Faith becomes this assent on the one hand "through being moved to assent by its very object," that is, by what it aims at and what it has faith in; yet on the other hand also "through an act of choice, whereby it turns voluntarily to one side rather than to the other." If such a choice is made in doubt or with the concern that the other side might be the correct one after all, it is an opinion; if it is made without such concern, it is faith. That is why, although it is impossible to know and have faith in the same thing at the same time, it is by no means excluded that one person knows what another only believes.[15]

At the end of the Enlightenment, Kant takes up this tradition of analyzing faith in a now-classic way in the Transcendental Doctrine of Method of the *Critique of Pure Reason*. He presents it as distinguishing between three kinds of considering matters or propositions to be true. "*Having an opinion*," he writes, "is taking something to be true with the consciousness that it is subjectively *as well as* objectively insufficient." This means that someone who has an opinion about something considers it to be possible (that is, not self-contradictory or impossible), but they are convinced that it is in fact (so) neither with respect to the matter (that is, objectively) nor with respect to themselves (that is, subjectively). Having an opinion is a "problematic" or "preliminary" judging that can turn out to be false or correct. "If taking something to be true is," in turn, "only subjectively sufficient and is at the same time held to be objectively insufficient, then it

13. Augustine, *On Lying*, in *On the Holy Trinity*, 457–77, here 3.3:458/CAG 1.3:414–15.

14. See Löwith, "Knowledge and Faith"; Mandouze, *Saint Augustin*, 265–88; and Flasch, *Augustin: Einführung in sein Denken*, 314–26.

15. Hugo St. Victor, *On the Sacraments*, 168, and Aquinas, *Summa Theologiae*, IIa IIae q1 a2 [modified], a4, and a5; see also a1.

is called *believing*." When I believe something, I am indeed subjectively convinced that it is not only possible but also actual, yet I do not have objective grounds also to assert the truth of my conviction as generally valid knowledge. Believing therefore is an assertory judging of a state of affairs I consider to be true without being able to prove it. "Finally, when taking something to be true is both subjectively and objectively sufficient it is called *knowing*." Someone who knows something is not only subjectively convinced that it is true (possible and actual); there are also objective grounds for it that can be made evident to others. Knowing is an apodictic judging that articulates the justified certainty that the matter at issue is true.[16]

More recent analyses of doxastic belief have further elaborated Kant's attempt to bring together, in a logic of belief, having an opinion, believing, and knowing as kinds of taking to be true that have different strengths. They define belief as a propositional attitude. This attitude is relative to case-specific alternatives, one of which is considered to be more probable than the other(s) and is said to be captured in the terms of probability theory and specified by a logic of decision.[17]

Richard Swinburne's work is exemplary of this approach, widely adopted today. According to him, believing something to be the case means believing that it is more probable than its opposite.[18] Someone who believes that today is Thursday believes that it is more probable that today is Thursday than that it is any other day of the week. Knowing and having an opinion thereby become limit cases of believing. If we suppose, the way objective theories of probability do, that matters can be situated on a probability scale from 0 to 1, then to have an opinion is to believe more improbable matters and to know is to believe (almost) certain matters: someone who knows something believes the matter at issue with a probability of 1. Analogously, subjective theories of probability assign matters a subjective probability between 0 and 1, depending on how inclined we are to act on their basis. Where having an opinion, as believing matters subjectively considered to be less probable, offers a bad basis for rational action and knowing, as believing matters considered to be (almost) certain, offers a rather good basis, belief is a more rational basis for action than having an opinion but a less rational one than knowledge. That is why it is always advisable to transform belief into knowledge or to replace believing and having an opinion with knowing in order to be able to live and act more rationally. Yet this transformation and replacement is not a transition to something categorically different from belief but an increase in the certainty of belief that guides our action.

This simple basic approach immediately leads to complicated questions the moment we inquire into the relationship between different beliefs, into the relationship between beliefs and action, beliefs and evidence, and so on. Nonetheless, the basic approach already makes clear that, in sidelining all affective and fiducial aspects, a doxastic conception of belief is not only useless in trying appropriately to characterize religious belief,[19] it is entirely insufficient in attempting to grasp what Christian theology calls *faith in Jesus Christ*. What is meant is not probabilistic knowledge but an eschatological

16. Kant, *Critique of Pure Reason*, 686 (A822/B850).

17. See Lenzen, *Glauben, Wissen und Wahrscheinlichkeit*.

18. See Swinburne, *Faith and Reason*.

19. See von Kutschera, *Vernunft und Glaube*, 123–28.

reorientation of one's entire life that is due to God himself and is experienced passively by the human being.[20] This new orientation of life, to be sure, finds expression in the confessions of faith of individuals or communities, but to understand these confessional propositions in probabilistic terms is very much to misunderstand them: the probability of beliefs that can be captured this way must not be confused with the orientation of life that finds expression in them. There are several reasons for this, among them:

1. Doxastic belief is gradual, relative to alternatives, and, compared to these alternatives, more or less certain. Not so faith in Jesus Christ: there is no gradual transition between *having faith in Jesus Christ* and *not having faith in him*, which are complete alternatives. Christians do not have faith in Jesus Christ because they consider that to be relatively more probable than faith in Moses, Mohammed, or Buddha.

2. Doxastic belief differs from subject to subject and from time to time. It is dependent on context, time, and person. That is also true of *Christians' believing*, of the life-practical forms in which they live their faith, but not of *faith in Jesus Christ*, that is, of what they experience coming from God as reorientation of their lives and what opens up to them a new life in the orientation toward the one to whom they owe this reorientation of their lives. If this happening were not in a decisive respect the same, even across different times, different places, and different persons, the Christians of different times and places would not have the same faith in which they lived and would therefore not be justified or saved by the same faith. They would thus not just confess their faith in different ways in their creeds but confess different things.[21]

3. Our doxastic beliefs are the products of our causal-cognitive interaction with our environment. For that very reason, they refer to their times and are subject to changes. By contrast, Christians understand their faith to be the self-presentification of God in their lives, which gives their lives a fundamentally new orientation by orienting them toward God's presence. And because this faith that reorients them is, in a soteriologically decisive way, due to God, it is in decisive respects the same faith, in all the variety and difference of its exemplifications.

4. The decisive point of this aspect is that human beings are justified (saved, enriched, spared, brought onto the right path, etc.) by faith and thus by what God does for them, not by (doxastic or fiducial) believing, and thus not by what they do or what they actively participate in. Justifying faith is not a gradual having more or less belief or confidence and therefore is not an act of belief humans could perform, nor must it be confused with what humans do, think, will, or feel when they have faith.

20. See Dalferth, "Mere Passive: Die Passivität der Gabe bei Luther."

21. *Faith in Jesus Christ* is becoming affected by and being included in the eschatological reality, constituted by God in Jesus Christ, of the change from unfaith to faith, which opens up for human beings—*all* human beings—a possibility that they do not have by themselves (it becomes *possible* for everyone to believe); that they are concretely given in the Gospel (it creates the concrete *occasion* to believe for everyone reached by the preaching of the Gospel); and that is *actualized* by the Spirit as a reorientation of their lives in the change from unfaith to faith (everyone who believes thanks God for it).

5. Death will end all human believing and eradicate our beliefs as it will our emotions, feelings, doubts, and certainties. But if what they believe and confess is true, namely that God presentifies himself in them the way he becomes present in Jesus Christ, then death will not put an end to, it will not eradicate God's life-renewing self-presentification that Christians in confessing faith in Jesus Christ express as reorientation of their lives. Believers will, as they hope, live precisely because of this faith, even if they die.

The differences thus noted are sufficient evidence that the faith in Jesus Christ must in no way be confused with belief in the sense of a gradual doxastic considering to be true that can be developed probabilistically. The fact that the German language uses substantivized forms of the verb *glauben* for both of them—*der Glaube* (faith in Jesus Christ) and *das Glauben* (belief in states of affairs or persons)—thus confuses matters more than it sheds light on them. It does not follow from the differences enumerated, though, that there is no connection between them: factually, there is no faith in Jesus Christ that as a reorientation of life would not also manifest (doxastical) knowledge of faith, (psychological) (un)certainty of faith, and (probabilistically justifiable) action in faith. When it comes to its crux as justifying or saving faith, however, it cannot be identified with these historically contingent figures of expression.[22]

Faith in Jesus Christ is the God-given sharing in the change from unfaith operated in Jesus Christ. It is not to be equated with an individual or communal consciousness of faith. While faith and unfaith, for the reasons cited, are exclusive and complete alternatives without gradual transition one to the other, consciousness of faith exists only ever as a certainty of faith that is more or less perfect, tinted individually, and always exposed to contestation. Accordingly, the *genesis of faith* as the step from unfaith to faith (in the life of Jesus Christ and—thereby made possible, and actualized by the Spirit of Christ—in the life of the individual human being) and the *genesis of the consciousness of faith* as the step from the uncertainty to the certainty of belief must be described differently. According to the Christian conviction, *faith* is grounded in the Christ event, which has taken place once and for all and is valid universally. Through this event faith becomes possible for all human beings and through the Spirit it becomes actual (if it becomes actual) in the concrete life. *Consciousness of faith*, in turn, is grounded in the communication of the Gospel[23]—which must be undertaken ever anew and is necessarily particular—in which God's Spirit, in freely presentifying, lets the truth of another's testimony of faith become evident to the hearer. It is the same Spirit who actualizes the God-given possibility of changing from unfaith to faith in the concrete life of a human being *and* brings it to consciousness. Only faith thus brought to consciousness can anthropologically manifest as experience of faith, knowledge of faith, and action in faith, yet still, these historical manifestations must not be confused with faith. In the theologically relevant sense, faith is not what persons feel, know, or do when they have faith, but it constitutes the persons

22. This is also the correct intuition at the basis of Schleiermacher's attempt to separate faith from both knowing and from doing and at the same time specifically to refer faith to them by associating faith with sentiment.

23. In the comprehensive sense I lay out in Dalferth, *Evangelische Theologie als Interpretationspraxis*, 90–113.

who testify the faith when it becomes evident to them. This means that faith is the basic constitution into which human beings find themselves, against all expectation, placed from out a life in an unfaith that ignored God and closed itself off from God, a constitution in which they as God's creatures live as they can and ought to live: open toward their creator and their fellow creatures and thus in the fullness of the concrete relations of life in which the being a person of human being consists.

4. Fiducial Faith and Personal Confidence

Similar points apply to the two other basic forms of the colloquial understanding of faith, *fiducial trust* ("I believe someone") and *personal confidence* ("I believe in someone"). If faith is thought in strictly theological terms as the *opus dei* (that is, described with a view to the determination thus operated of the humans concerned) through which God justifies human beings, that is, places them in the correct and, for them, the best relation to him,[24] then faith in Jesus Christ is not a case of human trust that differs from other cases only by the object at which this trust is directed. It is then sufficiently grasped neither by a trust in others or a trust in oneself that does not lose its assurance about others ("I believe in you") or in oneself ("I believe in myself") even despite signs to the contrary, nor as a basic trust that always already encounters the environment and other persons in particular with a credit not backed up by experience. Theologically, there are essential aspects missing when faith in Jesus Christ is said to be "an interpersonal act of trust, of confidence, of committing-to." It is true, of course, that "[b]elief in God is primarily a personal act which is situated in the relation of I and You."[25] The dominant character of the relation of faith is indeed not that of a subject–object or an I–He relation but that of an I–You relation in which a *personal inclusion* is front and center. But seen as justificatory faith, faith is not just a human "attitude of confidence." It is believers' being founded, thanks to God, precisely not on other people or even themselves, or on the reliability of the world but on God alone.

Because it aims at God in such a way that it knows itself to be constituted by him, Christian faith is being diminished and inverted where it is reduced, propositionally, to a human taking to be true or, personally, to a human confidence and relying on. Faith in God is not a case of such belief but a phenomenon *sui generis*. To put it in the terms of the logic of language: "faith in God" cannot be analyzed as a general relation of "believing in . . ." where the place of the ellipsis can be taken, among many other things (Goethe, the current government, justice, and so on), by God; it must be analyzed as a relation of "believing in God" that cannot be analyzed further but must be understood as such.

The inverse, too, then becomes absurd: just as faith in God is not a case of belief understood generally, all belief is not a reductive concretion of faith in God. Yet that is

24. Faith (logically speaking) is the converse of the relation of justification, that is, the description of the justification of the human through God from the perspective of the human justified through God; and (phenomenologically speaking) it is the responsively thematized happening of God's becoming present in the life of the human being ignoring its creator. See Dalferth, *Existenz Gottes und christlicher Glaube*, 238–76.

25. Neuner, "Der Glaube als subjektives Prinzip," 23, and Fries, *Fundamental Theology*, 17.

precisely the thesis prominently advocated in recent decades by Wolfhart Pannenberg, who, in the methodological footsteps of Spinoza and Schleiermacher, postulated that all human trust is directed, implicitly and beyond the specific people it *prima facie* addresses, at God. When we trust our parents, we manifest a basic trust directed at God. All trust on this reading exemplifies this fundamental anthropological structure of a *basic trust* that always and everywhere, consciously or unconsciously, is aimed *at God*, the actuality that determines everything.

> Even though basic trust is placed first of all in the persons who are the closest points of reference for the child, this trust is, by reason of its lack of limits, *implicitly* directed beyond mother and parents to an agency that can justify the unlimited character of the trust. This agency must be proportionate to the limitlessness that is the unique mark of basic trust.

Yet the inverse is also true:

> To the limitlessness of basic trust, which looks beyond the mother to God as its primary object, corresponds its reference to the wholeness of the self. Basic trust in the proper sense is directed to that agency which is able to protect and promote the self in its *wholeness*. For this reason, God and welfare are very closely tied together in the living of basic trust.[26]

This argument not only raises the factual question whether this alleged fundamental anthropological structure exists at all but also the methodological question of how knowledge of this structure is obtained. It is obviously opened up by the factual relations of trust that do in fact characterize human life. But must these relations be read and understood as exemplifying such a basic structure? Does this not "ontologize" a theological interpretation of these anthropological facts, that is, reduce them to a theologically interpreted structure of possibililization, and does it not make a *theological interpretation* pass for an *anthropological fact*? Methodologically, it is one thing to interpret anthropological facts theologically; it is another thing to declare theological interpretations to be anthropological facts. The first case seriously allows for the possibility of other perspectives of understanding; the second defines them as views that fail to see reality as it really is.

Put once more in the terms of the logic of language, Pannenberg's suggested interpretation, too, follows the tradition of attempting to understand faith in God and belief practiced in the life-world in one and the same sense of "believing," even if he does not regard faith in God as a special case of the general structure of life-world believing but interprets all life-world phenomena of believing as more or less successful concretions of the general structure of faith in God. But "I believe in God" is not a case of concretizing "believing in . . ." and "I believe in . . ." is not a reductive form of "I believe in God." Not only do the two (structures of) propositions have different implications, they differ above all on one central point: life-world believing is said of persons who are also differently determined and determinable: as people who know, act, suffer, think. Faith in God in the sense relevant here, in contrast, *posits* persons as persons with the totality of

---

26. Pannenberg, *Anthropology in Theological Perspective*, 233, 234.

their references, that is, it is not said of persons already constituted but constitutes their being a person.

That, however, means that the logical structure of these propositions is different. Whereas "A believes (in) . . ." is a proposition *about A*, namely that A believes, "A believes in God" in the theological sense relevant here is not a proposition about A but *about God*, namely that God effects A (or something in or with regard to A). The colloquial phrase "A believes in God" is thus systematically equivocal because it suggests a double conception: colloquially it is said of A that he believes in God, theologically it is said of God that he constitutes A as believer. When Christians confess their belief in God, they do not speak of what they do but of what God does in them. Their colloquially articulated confession, "I believe in God," is thus to be developed theologically as follows: "I believe in the one who makes me as a believer/brings me to faith/locates me in faith," shorter: "I believe that it is not I who believe but God makes me as believer," or, as Luther puts it in the explanation of the third article in the Small Catechism: "I believe that by my own reason or powers I cannot believe in Jesus Christ my Lord or come to him. But instead the Holy Spirit has called me through the gospel, enlightened me with his gifts, made me holy and kept me in the true faith."[27] In this sense, faith in God is a phenomenon *sui generis*, and this point must not be lost from sight when this faith is expressed in the colloquial forms of speech of life-world believing.

For even if the faith in God that constitutes believers as believers is a phenomenon *sui generis*, it factually does not occur in the way people live their lives without phenomena of *doxa* and *fiducia*. These, however, must not be equated with it if we do not want to fail to understand faith: faith in God is neither one concretion among others of a fundamental anthropological structure of trust, nor is it this fundamental structure of trust itself such that all human phenomena of trust would be more or less clear manifestations of faith. That is why talk of faith as personal relationship of trust becomes problematic where faith is not rigorously thought as *fides creatrix*, as constitution of the human person through the word of God. Faith is the way a deed of God's—which makes human deeds and attitudes possible and provokes them in the first place—takes place and expresses itself in human life. This deed creates something new because it places a human being from a state in which she lives her being a person only in a reduced way and in ignoring the possibilities that could and ought to characterize her as a person (unfaith), into a new state (faith), in which the fullness of the relations with God and with the fellow creatures can be actualized, relations in which human being-a-person actualizes before God.

Faith is thus personal not as an attitude of the person but as what constitutes the person as person. That is why Christian faith wants to and must be conceived of strictly from its ground and object *God*, through whom it is what it becomes, namely in the way God, according to the Christian conviction, has revealed himself in the history of Israel but above all in the story of Jesus Christ. It is for this reason that faith, in an elementary way, voices itself as *faith in Jesus Christ*, that is, as faith in God such as God has revealed his being God in and through Jesus Christ and defined his being God as love that ends evil through good. Rather than follow the colloquial conception of believing and its

27. Luther, *Small Catechism*, 225.

philosophical and anthropological specifications, a theological explication of faith in Jesus Christ must follow this faith's own self-conception, that is, develop the particular grammar of this faith.[28]

5. On the Grammar of Faith

The evangelical grammar of faith developed in Reformation theology can be succinctly outlined in four points:

1. No human being lives neither in faith nor in unfaith, and only human beings—or only beings who can, like humans, believe or not believe in God—live in one or the other. With respect to God's presence, there is no neutral human existence, but the difference between faith and unfaith is applicable only to human life and not to all life. Animals, for example, live neither in faith nor in unfaith, even if their lives are factually affected by the consequences of unfaith or faith in the lives of humans.[29] Only beings that in principle can freely orient themselves toward God can be reproached for not doing so. Those who cannot love God on their own cannot be accused when they do not love him on their own.

2. Every human being at some point lives in unfaith, but not everyone also lives in faith: no one has to have faith, but there also is no one of whom it could not at some point truthfully be said that she does not have faith. For while it is necessarily true that every human being lives in faith or in unfaith, it is neither necessary nor true that every human being necessarily has faith or necessarily does not have faith; rather, when someone has faith or someone does not have faith, that is only ever factually true. No human being has to have faith, but no human being has to not have faith, either. Yet because on the one hand, every human does and must do one or the other and, on the other hand, no human being has faith who has not before this not had faith, it is true of every human being at some point that she lives in unfaith but by no means also true that at some point she lives in faith. Everybody who lives lives in unfaith, but not everybody who lives lives in faith, and neither the one nor the other has to be.

3. Everyone who lives in unfaith can also live in faith: no one is excluded from faith.

---

28. I speak of *grammar* in this context because the issue is to find out what the factually efficacious structures and rules are that define the unfolding in reality of the faith and constitute its particular intelligibility, not to take recourse to standards of rationality that are brought to bear on faith from the outside and measure it by something other than what actually defines and characterizes it. While the grammatical structures of different languages can certainly be compared, the grammar of English just as certainly does not furnish a useful standard for assessing the grammar of German. Instead, every explicit grammar is an attempt at presenting the implicitly efficacious rules of a language in a certain way. And that is true of theology as well, which sees its task to be the presentation of the grammar of faith.

29. That is why talk of "fallen creation" should refer to human life and not, without differentiation, to all life, and the suffering of animals should not be associated wholesale with humans' unfaith, as is done time and again. See Boyd, *Satan and the Problem of Evil*, 246–48, for whom the mass suffering of innocent animals is one of the main reasons to identify nature not with creation but with fallen creation and to see not just natural life processes to be operating in it but the struggle between good and evil spirits.

4. No one who lives in faith is a stranger to living in unfaith: everyone who believes can always, albeit in different respects, be defined as believer and as sinner. That he is a sinner is a true judgment about him as regards his past, which determines him (*per se* he is a sinner); that he is a believer, by contrast, is a true statement about him as regards God's efficacious presence in him (*per deo* he is a saved sinner).

The difference in the exististential constitution of the places where life is led in the presence of God (faith vs. unfaith) and the difference in the determination of those who live in these places (believers vs. non-believers) thus must not be confused. Of the human beings that live in these places it is possible and necessary to say what cannot be said of the places themselves. As alternative constitutions of life, the place of unfaith and the place of faith mutually exclude each other. Yet while it is possible to live only in the place of unfaith (and thus be a sinner), it is not possible to live only in the place of faith because one lives there always as a sinner who has made the change from unfaith (old life) to faith (new life) not by oneself but through God alone. There is no new life (life in faith) without contrast to the old life (life in unfaith), yet the old life is characterized precisely by not knowing this contrast and therefore not recognizing itself as old. Only from the place of faith is it thus possible to speak of unfaith because unfaith, not knowing faith, is unable to designate itself as such.

This, however, gives rise to a dialectic with significant consequences as regards the defining relationships between *bonum*, *malum*, and sin. In the *place of unfaith*, even humans' good willing and doing remains a doing and willing of sinners, and in the *place of faith*, even humans' evil doing and suffering of evil is nothing that would separate them from God and could prevent God's presence in them that makes them good. Yet humans are thus sinners not because of this or that evil deed or this or that evil willing but because they *do not have faith*, that is, they do not live before God in the place opened up to them through God and in the way made possible by his presence. They ignore what they are provided with (unfaith) and thus squander the chance they are being offered (original sin). This unfaith is the original sin, and it infects all of human life in such a way that good as well as evil willing and doing do not put an end to and eliminate unfaith but confirm and emphasize it. Humans who do not have faith remain the sinners they are, and they confirm this not only in their evil but also in their good deeds.

6. Faith

The offensiveness of this notion is not a coincidence but results from the evangelically specified Christian conception of faith. In the theologically relevant sense, *faith* is always and exclusively *faith in God* because it aims at the one who constitutes it: only a faith that has faith in the one who constitutes it is *faith* in the sense relevant here. If it is not directed at God, it is not faith, and if it is directed at something or someone other than God, it is superstition.

Insofar as God, at whom faith is directed, is present to every present, all human beings are at every point in time in a situation in which they can be determined by this presence. Nobody is able not to conduct themselves toward it, everyone factually conducts themselves toward it, consciously or not. Yet there are exactly two basic alternative possibilities to conduct oneself toward it, *faith* and *unfaith*. For everything that is not faith is unfaith and everything that is not unfaith is faith. Every human being accordingly lives either *in faith* or *in unfaith* in God. Just as faith (as regards its object) is always and exclusively *faith in God*, so (as regards the believing human being) it is always and exclusively *life in faith*. And just as only *faith in God* opens up the possibility of defining superstition as superstition, so only *life in faith* liberates the possibility of defining its opposite as *life in unfaith*. Only *faith* lets *superstition* appear as such, only *life in faith* differs from *life in unfaith*.

Viewed from faith, then, all human life is defined as *faith* or *superstition* (under the aspect of reference) or as *life in faith* or *in unfaith* (under the aspect of living one's life). Viewed from non-faith, by contrast, there is neither a difference between faith and superstition nor a difference between life in faith and life in unfaith but at most a variety of human ways of believing (under the aspect of reference) or of forms of life (under the aspect of living one's life). The distinction between *faith* and *superstition* and the distinction between *life in faith* and *life in unfaith* are available only from the point of view of faith and cannot be rendered systematically plausible in any other way. Nor is there any position beyond the difference between faith and non-faith that would in fact represent the standpoint of faith or of non-faith. That is why in the Christian perspective, human life is either a life in faith or in unfaith, and it is lived, with respect to God's efficacious presence, as faith or as superstition.

7. Christian Faith, the Faith of Christians, and Faith in Jesus Christ

All this is true of *Christian faith* as well. Christian faith is faith insofar as it is directed at God, and it is Christian insofar as it is directed at *God understood in a specific way*, namely the way in which God has defined himself, according to Christian conviction, in the story of Jesus Christ, in the history of Israel culminating there, and in the way in which he becomes comprehensible to human beings through his Spirit time and again in the history of the Church: as a love that saves, that is merciful, that brings back onto the right path.

The biblical and Christian confessions of God's love, goodness, justice, power, and presence are not a "projective reflex of people in happy situations or naturally optimistic people. Rather," in many cases, "they arose *in* the distress and defeat of the good, *in* the suffering of the innocent, *in* the non-arrival of help from God." They are indeed not "descriptions of a *given* benevolent-omnipotent God at one's disposal, a God one could include in one's calculations—in a theory about the reconcilability of God and suffering, for example." But they are also not just "assertions and promises whose truth is disputable and must yet be found."[30] Rather, they are asserted and confessed because there is good reason, thanks to the happenings the Christian community recalls not only on Easter, Good Friday, and Christmas but every Sunday, to hope that God is such as he showed himself to be there, and that therefore he wills to and will end and overcome Evil

---

30. Kessler, *Gott und das Leid*, 121.

by the Good even where it is not experienced this way.[31] Christians trust that God will prove to be love for everyone because in the cross and resurrection of Christ he proved to be such. The homological reference to Jesus Christ is thus the indication of the end of the world entangled in Evil because God in the event of the cross and the happening of resurrection committed himself eschatologically and thus definitively to overcoming the Evil of the world through the Good as saving, merciful, corrective love. That is why for Christians, the word "God" indicates the power of love that overcomes Evil through Good in such a way that it no longer leads to Evil but only to Good. And it is why for Christians, all propositions of faith about God's love, goodness, justice, and power are *propositions of hope and promise* that attribute to God what he will do and effect in and for everyone because he himself committed himself to it in Jesus Christ and promised it.

Christians confess and live this faith, and that is what makes them recognizable as Christians. As the *faith of Christians*, the forms in which Christian faith has been expressed have changed time and again in the course of history, yet as *faith in Jesus Christ* it was and always and exclusively is faith in God in this specificity. *Faith in Jesus Christ* is thus not a Christian supplement to or expansion of faith in God but the concrete form faith in God takes in light of the gospel.[32] And that this faith in God shapes and determines Christian life as *hope* is not a mere consequence of faith in Jesus Christ but the form in which this faith is confessed and lived. Verbally, this takes place exemplarily in the confession of Christ, nonverbally in the ways of living one's life that correspond to this confession and whose determinacy is noted in the double commandment of love. *Confession of Christ* and *action of love* in the service of God and of one's neighbor are the two corresponding basic figures, in which Christian faith manifests itself in the life of Christians communally and individually as lived hope.

Now, Christians would misunderstand themselves if they sought simply to equate *their* faith with *faith*, that is, dismiss all *non-Christian faith* as *superstition* and all *non-Christian life* as *life in unfaith*. Faith exists not only where it is explicitly confessed and lived as Christian faith but everywhere people have faith in *God in the Christian conception* (in God as he is understood in a Christian way), that is, where people live in such a way that their life is determined by the reference to God such as Christian faith knows and confesses him, and is lived in this determination. To have faith in God in this way and live accordingly, it is not necessary explicitly to know and confess this conception *as* the Christian conception of God. Those who live in such a way that in everything, they count on God and hope for and expect everything good from God, who in all distress seek shelter with God and rely on his help, who have their hearts set on nothing that passes but entirely bet on God's reliable loyalty and care—they live the faith that Christians confess because they rely on God the way Christians do.[33]

---

31. Kessler, "Christologie," 411–23; see also Menke, "Der Gott, der jetzt schon Zukunft schenkt."

32. This must be recalled time and again in the conversation with Judaism and Islam.

33. See Luther, *Large Catechism*, 300–4. That Luther in these pages interprets the first commandment does not contradict what has just been said but confirms it: this commandment speaks of no other God than the one whom Christians confess in the Creed (352–66), to whom they pray in the Lord's Prayer (366–87), in whose name they are baptized (388–402), and in whose presence they congregate for communion (402–15).

Christian faith is thus not simply identical with faith in God, but neither is it a special kind of faith in a Christian God who has existed only since Christians have existed. Rather, it is the explicit form of *faith in God in the Christian conception*, a God who exists and who can exist also where he is not explicitly confessed as such. It is possible to have faith in God in the Christian conception even if one is unable explicitly to express this conception as such, be it because of a lack of *capacities for articulation* (as in the case of severely disabled, injured, or sick persons) or because of a lack of *possibilities for articulation* (as in the case of people living in times or areas in which the Christian faith and the message of the gospel are unknown). What is decisive is that *God*, at whom the faith is directed, *is such* as he is being understood explicitly in the Christian creed, *not* that one *explicitly believes that* God is such or that one *explicitly knows and confesses God in this conception*. That faith exists only if it is entirely directed at God does not mean that God exists only if faith is directed at him. As Luther emphasizes, faith does indeed create divinity, but it does so in us, not in the person of God.[34] Even where the issue is faith, the most important issue is always God. The point of the Christian conception of God, however, is precisely that *God* in free love puts himself in relation with the human such that humans as creatures live through the creator and with the creator, in the presence of the one to whom they owe more than they ever dreamed of, wished for, or sought, even when they do not refer themselves to their creator or in their relationship with God do not explicitly know and confess him to be the way that he, according to the basic Christian creed, conducts himself toward them and all other creatures: as a loving father.

Theologically, then, *faith* is always insufficiently defined when it is understood in such a way that it is impossible to have faith in God unless one asserts a *very specific conception of God*: in that case, *God* is replaced by a *conception of God* as the decisive criterion of faith, and instead of *living the faith in God in one's life, knowledge* about living this life takes center stage. Yet as certainly as it not possible consciously to refer to God and to live before and with God without a conception of God, so it is certainly not the case that faith is lived in life only when or only where God is conceived of in a certain way. Faith does not exist without knowing and doing, but it cannot be reduced to either one or the other, as Schleiermacher, in his own way, knew. That is why *Christian faith* is not to be identified with *faith in God in the Christian conception*. *Christian faith* is an explicit (not a special!) form of *faith in God* who in the Christian conviction has definitively determined himself in the cross and resurrection of Jesus Christ as the one who only wills what is good for his creatures and on whom we can therefore call and rely in all distress. Just as *faith in Jesus Christ* is one of but not the only form in which Christians manifest the Christian faith, so the *Christian faith* is an explicit but not the only form in which the *faith in God in this conception* exists.

Not everything that calls itself "faith" is thus faith *in God*, not every faith in God is faith in *God in the Christian conception*, and not every faith in God of that kind is *Christian faith*. Faith in *God in the Christian conception* exists everywhere faith is *factually* directed at God with the determinacy that Christian faith *explicitly* confesses in referring to Jesus Christ and his Spirit. But in order *factually* to have faith in the one who is thus understood the Christian way, it is *not* necessary to know and confess God that way

---

34. Luther, *In epistolam S. Pauli ad Galatas Commentarius*, in *WA* 40.1, 360, lines 5–6.

explicitly. Such faith exists not only where the conception of God is explicitly defined by the relation with Jesus Christ but wherever that is expected and hoped for from God which Christian faith expects and hopes for from him, that is, wherever life with and before God is lived the way that God, according to the Christian insight, has determined himself in and through Jesus Christ. *Faith in Jesus Christ* (Christian faith) is thus not a special faith but a special, namely, Christian expression of faith in God in the determinate way indicated by the name "Jesus Christ." This marks a *specific conception of God* in whom one has faith (the Christian conception of God as creative love) and it points to the *specific life practice* of those who have faith in God in this way (the Christian life of faith of those who because of God's love must attempt to live, in the false life of the world of unfaith, a true life of love for God and one's neighbors). In the faith in Jesus Christ, a conception of God and a relation with God thus combine in the unity of a specific, precisely a Christian, living of life.

8. Faith and Unfaith as Existential Determinations

According to the differentiation of the Reformation conception of faith as developed so far, *faith* is not an anthropological determination beside or among others (reason, understanding, will, sense, emotion, feeling, and so on) or a succinct formula for the human as rational being or free being of will; it is an *existential determination* that marks the constitution of one of the two existential places in which a human being with all its determinations factually lives and can live: the place of *faith* and the place of *unfaith*. *Faith* ("A believes") and *unfaith* ("A does not believe") are not defining predicates of the human but localizing predicates, they do not say what (among other things) humans are but where and how they, with everything they are and can be, live before God.

On the level of language, this means that propositions like "I believe" are not to be understood and analyzed like "I think" or "I take to be true" or "I will" or "I feel" or "I trust." They are to be analyzed in a *locative* sense, the way "I live in Berlin," "in prison," or "with my family" are, or in a *modal* sense, the way "I live unhappily," "in pain," or "like a king" are. "I believe" thus means "I live *in faith*" or "I live *having faith*." Neither is added to the determinations of my concrete living of life as another determination but qualifies them as a whole by indicating *how and where I live*. Those who have faith live their lives in the place of the presence of God in such a way that it is oriented and determined positively by this presence. They live *having faith* insofar as they are oriented by this presence, and they live *in faith* insofar as in time and space they live in the place that God, through his concrete presentification, makes the place of the eternal presence of the believer with God.

This structural proposition can be concretized in more than one way, as the texts of the New Testament already show in many and exemplary ways. Since God according to the Christian faith presentifies in the determinate way pronounced in the confession of Christ and variously accentuated in the confessions of God's love, mercy, justice, rule, friendship, liberation, and so on, Christian life *in faith* can be stated, in a theological equivalent, as life *in Christ, in the Spirit, in the body of Christ, in God's love*, and many other ways. Each of these metaphors foregrounds another aspect of life *in faith*, but they all share that they do not name separate aspects or dimensions of Christian life but, each in a specific way, designate the place and the mode that shapes the life of believers in all its aspects and dimensions and could shape every human life before God.

This is decisive. *Before God* is not just a formal indication of place but a modal qualification of the place in which the human being lives. Since God acts always and everywhere, the existential place of the human being comes into view as a situation in which humans are affected by God's action always and everywhere and therefore have no choice but factually (not consciously!) to conduct themselves toward God's action in having or not having faith: however humans live, whatever they experience, do, or suffer, they thereby assume an attitude toward God dedicating himself to them (such that they exist and do not rather not exist) and toward how he dedicates himself to them (such that they live in one way or the other, having faith or not having faith), toward how, that is, God relates to them. They can take up this communication (live in faith) or ignore it (live in unfaith), but they do one thing or the other, they must do so (they cannot not communicate), and either way they continue it and react to it. Anyone who lives lives in faith or in unfaith, and no one who lives lives neither in one way nor in the other. For each and every human being lives only because and insofar as God dedicates himself to them. Yet in living, they also conduct themselves toward this dedication, namely in such a way as to either appropriate or ignore it in the way they live their lives.

The existential place of the human being before God is thus constituted by God's dedication to the human: human beings are who they become and can become through God's effective presence in their place in the world. As the place in which they lead their lives, the existential place of the human before God is modally defined in a strict alternative as the place either of appropriating (life in the mode of faith) or of ignoring (life in the mode of unfaith) God's dedication to which they owe themselves, and therefore as the place of everything that God effects in the place of human existence. The decisive thing effected by God in this place, however, is on the one hand that he enables humans to live in this way or that in the first place—this characterizes God as creator who distinguishes the being of the human from its (possible) not being; yet on the other hand also that he does not let humans live in unfaith but makes it possible for them to live in faith by placing them from unfaith into faith—this characterizes God as savior, who changes the human from being a sinner to being good and just.

9. Nonbeing vs. Being and Unfaith vs. Faith

Both the change from not being to being and the change from being a sinner to being good take place *in* and *for* the human being but not *through* the human because humans become what they are only through this change: living beings that cannot live without living in unfaith or in faith (change from not being to being) *and* that do not have to live in unfaith but can live in faith (change from unfaith to faith). When they do not exist, humans cannot live either in unfaith or in faith; but they also cannot exist without living either in faith or in unfaith. The fact that humans come into being from not being does not mean that they also have obtained the possibility of living in unfaith or in faith, it means that they do in fact live in this way or that. But they can also only live in unfaith if the contrast with faith exists, and this contrast exists actually and not just hypotheti-cally when a life in faith is in fact actual.[35] Just as we cannot distinguish between being and not being when no one exists, so we cannot distinguish between unfaith and faith when no one has faith. Both do not have to be the case in all cases and in all places. But if nobody exists at all who believes, then the point of the opposition between faith and unfaith, too, is void, and if no one exists, there is no point in thinking about their faith or unfaith either.

The existential place of the human being is thus defined by the double difference of *not being vs. being* and *unfaith vs. faith*. There is no third term to either of these alterna-tives, not even that of being neither the one nor the other. The decisive thing God does in and for the human being is that he places them from not being into being and from unfaith into faith: those who live benefit from the *change from not being to being*, and those who have faith benefit from *the change from unfaith to faith*. Given the reality of the world and of human life, both changes are so improbable that something more improbable can hardly be thought.[36] Why should someone exist who does not exist and does not have to exist? And why should someone live in faith if they also live when they do not live in faith?

There is no general answer to either question. But just asking them suggests itself only because what does not have to be *is* (namely that there are lives being *lived*), and because what does not have to happen *happens* (namely that there are lives being lived *in faith*). Where the one or the other is the case, those affected know that they are not themselves the cause of the fact *that* they live or that they live *this way*. Both changes lie beyond their own possibilities, and because they are neither impossible nor self-evident nor necessary, Christian faith and thought (and not just they) attribute them to God. The first change cannot be operated by anyone on their own because someone who does not exist cannot on his own come into being (*ex nihilo nihil fit*), and someone who exists has become not through himself but through something else (something becomes *ex nihilo* only through *creatio*, which is initiated not by not being but by the creator). Yet the other change, too, cannot be operated by anyone on their own—not by the nonbeliever who does not see any reason for such a change, even if he imagined it (or else he would not be a nonbeliever), but neither by the believer, for the believer is always the result, not the subject of this change and can assess it only *post festum*. Where the change happens, it is regularly attributed not to one's own willing, ability, and doing, but to the unexpected and entirely improbable action of God. That is why faith is always faith *in God*, that is, faith in the one who calls human beings—to talk just about them—from not being into being (Rom 4:17) and places them from unfaith into faith.

Faith in the sense relevant here is thus not some minimal form of knowledge or cognition, not an instance of cognitive taking to be true, but neither is it a version of a moral determination of the will or an emotional definition of one's life. Faith is con-nected to all of these, but unfaith is no less so. There is a more or less of cognition and

---

35. That is why Karl Barth highlighted Jesus Christ as the reality of a life in faith, as the decisive point of reference from which human life in unfaith and faith can be thematized in the first place.

36. There need not be any life in this universe. Yet although, improbably, life exists, it is not in any way probable that I exist.

feeling and willing *in faith* and a more or less of cognition and feeling and willing *in unfaith*, but there is no faith that would be an increase of the knowing and feeling and willing of unfaith and no unfaith that would be a decrease of the knowing and feeling and willing of faith: between unfaith and faith, there are no gradual differences that could be bridged by continual advances in knowledge, by intensifications of feelings, or by increased willing; there is only the abyss of an opposition that is as deep as the one between the death of Jesus on the cross and his resurrection through God and that therefore can be bridged, as was the case there, by nothing and no one but God himself.

The change from unfaith to faith thus is no more founded on the one who *becomes a believer* than the change from not being to being is founded on the one who *becomes*; both are founded solely in God's conduct toward those whom he calls into *life* as humans or into a *life in faith*. This change cannot be demonstrated in any special aspects of human life compared to other aspects but only be clarified via the difference that God as creator posits between not being and being, possible and actual (as modes of being), and unfaith and faith (as modes of human being's actuality or existence). Only where something exists is it possible to distinguish between possible and actual, and only where a human being actually lives, between unfaith and faith. But just as the difference between being and not being cannot be demonstrated via the possible alone but requires recourse to the actual (for otherwise, all that ever appears is a *being able* to exist or not to exist), so the difference between unfaith and faith cannot be demonstrated in the actual life of a human being alone (since this could at most bring the difference between ways of leading a human life into view); it requires recourse to the one to whom, according to Christian faith, the reality of faith and its distinction from the reality of unfaith is due: God.

Put differently: faith is not preceded by any neutral, general reason proper to each human being, no shared feeling and no willing planted in every human being whose imperfect forms faith would perfect. Faith, rather, is preceded on the one hand by *unfaith*, which it overcomes because and insofar God constitutes the believer in the change from unfaith to faith, and on the other hand by *God*, who also maintains those within being who live in unfaith because he determines himself to help them to a life in faith.

10. The Genesis of Faith

Faith in God does not arise from nothing, and faith in God in this determinate form certainly does not. It emerges as Christian faith because of concrete processes of communication of the Christian community, processes in which this determination of God's is explicitly confessed as God's irrevocable self-determination and communicated, presented, expressed, and lived as God's good news for humanity. This always takes place in ways that can and deserve to be improved. Yet without this Christian communication of the gospel, there is no Christian faith because it cannot emerge without this practice of communication and cannot continue to exist without its being practiced. Communication precedes faith, and faith continues communication.

But it is true not just of this explicit form of faith in God that it concretely arises in the life process of human beings only as a modification, criticism, correction, remodeling, or removal of another faith, of a faith in another god, or of non-faith in one of its many variations. It is thus always possible to ask from which background of a life this faith emerges, how it modifies, specifies, criticizes, corrects, and changes this background. *Faith* in God in this determination can be grasped only with reference to a process in a life from which or in consequence of which it concretely emerges, and it can only be defined in contrast with—articulated from its perspective—*unfaith* definable in many ways from each of which it diverges in specific ways. No one is born a believer. One becomes a believer only in the change—which can be described as such only ever retrospectively—from unfaith to faith. This change takes place concretely in a human being's life process and thus in specific communicative contexts under ever-different conditions. And that is why one *is* a believer in *becoming* a believer in the change from unfaith to faith.

That the change from unfaith to faith takes place in human life is never an unavoidable consequence of the prior course of life, whatever it may have looked like. Faith is never only the answer to open questions of human life, as if these could determine what faith would have to be, but rather the inverse: faith prompts many questions in the first place, by answering them (questions that retrospectively presuppose the answers given by faith) and by the way in which it answers them (questions the answers of faith raise prospectively), and by answering and raising many questions that would not have been posed without this answer; in a dynamic profusion, it goes beyond what humans expect, wish for, and hope. It falls to human beings, not in a way that leaves them as they are and gives them what they do not yet have but in such a way that they become what on their own they could never have become and discover that they live from what they previously did not miss and did not seek: God's good-making presence.

That we *live*, and that we live *in faith*, is not only entirely contingent, it is also due to entirely contingent events: the *intrusion of the good* (that is, of that which *makes good*), which improbably makes life actual and makes good and evil distinguishable in the first place, and the *intrusion of the better* (that is, of that which *makes better*), which not only outdoes evil with good but also outdoes what is good with what is better by asserting true life in individual actual lives. For it thereby becomes inescapable to distinguish between *old* and *new life*—which from the point of view of the old cannot even be expected—and permanently to make that distinction in actual life, in thinking and acting, by critically asking what in this life is life in unfaith (old life) and what in it anticipates and indicates the true life in faith (new life) and what in one's own life, accordingly, ought not to be continued but ended or to be strengthened and promoted. Those who become aware of the intrusion of the good and the better and thus of the basic contingencies of their lives can no longer naively take the world and life as they appear but are constantly being referred to distancing detours for critically interpreting and shaping them in light of the guiding difference between old life and new life, including the question what we can do and ought to do to live the actual life as the new life and what we cannot and do not have to do because it is already done and happening.

No one has to become aware of the contingencies of their lives, but those who do have gained not merely theoretical knowledge but a practical insight that changes their lives. We live differently when we know that we could also not exist and sooner or later will no longer exist. We also live differently when we discover that while we may live well without God, we live better with God. We can continue to ignore what we paid no attention to earlier. In order to live contentedly and well as a human being, no one has to become a believer. But no one is excluded from it in principle, either. For when faith does arise, when people do begin to live and to understand themselves in the way God distinguishes them by conducting himself toward them as—to use the familiar biblical images—their God, helper, savior, liberator, comforter, friend, giver of life, heavenly father, then this is always an event for which they thank not themselves or others but God alone. Yet they thank God not because he arbitrarily saves the ones and rejects the others but because he is being experienced as someone who proves himself to be merciful, loving, helping, saving, comforting, friendly, strengthening not only in a hoped-for and prayed-for way but moreover in an entirely unexpected way that exceeds everything hoped for and prayed for, that is, proves to be a God who wills humans' happiness and not unhappiness, what is just and not what is unjust, freedom and not unfreedom, life and not death, a God who not only gives what is missing but gives much more than what had even been registered as missing. God's mercy is more than solving human problems and removing human ills and difficulties. It is not only the end of human misery nor is it merely strengthening the good over against the bad in human life. It is all that as well, but it is not exhausted by it. It promises something better than the best, more than what can be thought up and hoped for as an increase of what is relatively good over against what is evil and ill. It is the profusion of what is not just relatively better and perhaps the best, the profusion of what is wholly and unrestrictedly good that in and through God's presence falls to human beings entirely unexpectedly and undeservedly, unasked for and gratuitously.

If God, however, is merciful at all—and the reality of faith lives on this experience of undeserved overabundance—then God is merciful always (for his mercy is based solely on his own benevolent conduct toward humans and not on any kind of goodness on the part of those toward whom he conducts himself benevolently),[37] and if God conducts himself this way toward one human being, he does so toward all others as well. That is why according to the Christian insight, not just believers but all humans are destined and chosen to live in faith. For faith means nothing but *living from the profusion of God's mercy*, that is, being determined by the good God effects in a life.

11. The Possibility and Actuality of Faith

This has consequences for the theological conception of the human being. Humans can be defined as the beings who can have faith because God relates to them in such a way that they do not have to remain in the unfaith of forgetting about God but can live in faith in God's good presence. That does not mean attributing to humans the *ability* to

---

37. That is why God's mercy is entirely *without grounds* when we look at those to whom it turns, and it is *identical with God himself* when we look at him who thus turns toward humans.

have faith but rather, given the actuality of faith that is due to God alone, not denying any human being the *possibility* of faith.[38]

This thesis is not shown to be true by proving anthropologically that there is no human being who does not believe something because all human beings, by orienting themselves in the world in having opinions, beliefs, and knowledge, prove that they are grounded in a relationship without which they could not have opinions, beliefs, and knowledge. That would be nothing but a functionalizing reduction and downplaying of the fullness of the mercy God allots to the human. The truth of the thesis, rather, is founded on *that faith actually exists*, that is, that people really live the way God conducts himself toward them.[39] For on the one hand, its actuality evinces its possibility;[40] on the other hand, this actuality would not be possible if a God did not exist at whom faith is directed as its ground and object, and God would not be the God in whom faith has faith if he were the God only of some and not of all. If, therefore, there is faith at all, then faith is possible not only in the case of this one life but of every life, such that it is true for every human being that it is possible that they have faith. If faith is actual at all, then it is not impossible for any human being that they become believers and live no longer in unfaith but in faith. That we can have faith is not an anthropological ability but a possibility we owe to God, as is shown where in the life of a human being, with all its abilities and inabilities, the change from unfaith to faith takes place. For while faith is possible and actual *for* the human, it is never possible and actual *through* the human.

Where, then, the change from unfaith to faith takes place, it is always a freedom event in a double sense, an event in which faith is freely given to humans by God (as believers confess) as a gift (although God would not have to do so) and, against their unwillingness and their disinterest in having faith, is actualized for them as redetermination of their lives and through them as free, voluntary reorientation of their lives (although no human has to do so). This freedom event can neither be effected (faith cannot be methodically produced because neither God's freedom nor the freedom of others is something we can dispose of), nor does it happen without a prior history (faith does not emerge "just like that" without reference to something that preceded it), nor does it always presuppose the same kind of prior history (faith arises not only in lives structured on the pattern of Paulinian conversion or Pietist rebirth stories). Faith instead can emerge in *every* life and as redetermination of *every* prior life history, however long or short, happy or unhappy, religious or nonreligious this history may have been. Yet wherever faith does arise, it does *not* do so *from* the prior history of a given life but is due to very specific events *in* this life that condition and determine it: the *communication of the gospel*. And because these events always precede faith in such a way that it would not exist without them, and because it cannot understand itself without being aware of

38. In analytic terms: "The human can have faith" does not mean "The human has the ability to have faith," but "For every human being it is true that it is possible that they have faith."

39. What is decisive is not the plural but the actuality of this faith: even if only one human being lives the way God conducts himself toward her, that is, exists from the profusion of his mercy, the actuality of faith is thereby evinced. In the Christology of his *Church Dogmatics*, Karl Barth develops this notion systematically.

40. Inferred according to the rule *ab esse ad posse*: if it is actual that human beings have faith, then it is possible that they have faith.

it, faith in all its forms is always *responsive faith*, that is, a faith that (when it becomes aware of it) understands itself to be an answer to a communicative event it confesses as *God's gospel*.

In the responsive perspective of faith, the point of this event is that God presentifies himself in the concrete and noninterchangeable givens of a human life (that is, in *this* life), in a comprehensible way (that is, *communicates himself*), and in that determinacy (that is, *as gospel*) that makes it possible to have faith in him and leads to faith in him. This happens not only where the gospel is *explicitly communicated as gospel* (that is, within the horizon of Christian communication practices)[41] but everywhere human beings come to have faith in God through God's Spirit, that is, where God's presence is opened up for them in the way it was opened up in and through Jesus Christ and has since been explicitly confessed by Christians: as the presence of unconditional divine love. Wherever such faith arises, it is based on God's self-presentification in evangelical determinacy, that is, God communicating himself *as* gospel or, in short, the communication of the gospel (divine communication of the gospel). And wherever this gospel is *explicitly communicated as gospel*, that is, expressed in a *Christian* way, the faith in God then emerging is *explicitly Christian faith* that confesses that God presentifies himself via this communication of the gospel in such a way that one has and can have faith in him (Christian communication of the gospel).

12. The Genesis of Christian Faith

According to the Christian conviction, there would thus be no *faith* without the divine communication of the gospel (God's self-presentification in the determinacy of the gospel), and without the Christian communication of the gospel, there would be no faith that could explicitly articulate and would confess itself as *Christian* faith. The former can exist without the latter (as Romans 4 is not the only text to recall), but the latter can exist only in relation to and distinction from the former. The two must therefore be clearly distinguished precisely in their relationship.

The first is an explicative judgment of the faith that in responding names that to which, on its own conception, it owes itself: *faith* is the all-determining *becoming concrete of the gospel in a human life*. This becoming concrete takes place as the effective reorientation of a life in which through God's effective presence, it is opened toward, anchored in, and made sensitive to God and his presence in such a way that it no longer can and no longer wills to live and shape its relationships with others, with the shared environment, and with itself without taking God's presence into account. *Gospel* thus

---

41. When Lutheranism stresses the tie between the Spirit and the *verbum externum* of the Christian communication of the gospel, this is not an inappropriate "pneumatological reduction" or bondage of the Spirit but a reminder, grounded in experience, that with regard to the Spirit communicated through this external word at least we can be certain that it is *God's Holy Spirit*: those who say *Amen* to the gospel owe their doing so not to themselves or some kind of spirit but to the Spirit of the God who presentifies himself in the gospel. God's Spirit is efficacious here in a perceptible manner and in a way that allows for identifying it as God's Spirit, but it is not the only place where God's Spirit is efficacious.

means the *force of changing a life through God's presence* through which a life becomes a new life, open to God and one's fellow creatures, that is, becomes a *life of faith*.

When we seek to address the gospel, we must speak of this *dynamis* of a life becoming new, opened up to God and those close to God, reoriented and thereby renewed by God's becoming present. It is not by chance that in the New Testament, this is done narratively, by the Gospels telling the story of Jesus as God's history with humanity (God comes to the human beings) and as stories of human life becoming new through God's becoming-present (humans becoming mended and new through God coming to them). Only in intertwining these references to the history of God and the biography of human beings is it possible to speak of the gospel in a comprehensible way, because the gospel is always the gospel of *God's presence salutarily intruding in life* and equally is gospel *in and for the life of specific human beings*.

Both references and thus the biographical concretion of the gospel must be preserved not only in kerygmatic narrative but also, as Paul's or John's texts show exemplarily, in theological argument. For if the gospel exists only as gospel *of God* and *for specific human beings*, then it can only be told and developed as *the story of the experience specific human beings have of God's presence in their lives*. And if the gospel communicated in the Christian manner exists only in this way, then the faith thereby conditioned exists only in being multiply conditioned by what the gospel *is about* (God's creative presence); by what those *for whom* it became gospel report and confess (the symbolizations of their experiences of becoming new through God's presence); and by the life *in which* it is effective as gospel and whose becoming new it effects (the life situation of those to whom the gospel in a specific symbolization is being communicated). Like the gospel, faith too exists only in ever-new biographical concretizations, and only in this continuing variety can both be addressed.

The second is a descriptive judgment about faith that outlines the typical communicative structure of the situation in which Christian faith as the consequence of Christian communication of the gospel articulates itself, in the form of thanks and petition, prayer and confession. Yet the Christian communication of the gospel takes place in manifold ways, not only through the living of Christian lives of faith (through Christians living in a specific way) and this living interpreting itself *as* living a Christian life of faith (through Christians saying why they live this way) but essentially also through explicitly making a distinction between the gospel and faith and through thereby addressing the gospel as the ground and object of faith. It is only in (verbally) *symbolizing* (and thereby *interpreting*) the gospel that the gospel is not only being communicated but becomes communicable *as gospel* in a Christian manner.

Such symbolizations always posit a difference between what is being symbolized and the way in which it is being symbolized. Not verbal communication alone, but verbal communication especially is creative insofar as the *what* is being interpreted by the *how* in a specific way and can thereby become more, but also less, comprehensible. This inevitable difference between the what and the how in symbolization is not only the reason for the danger that the reception of the gospel can fail when the *how* is mistaken for the *what*. It also yields the possibility of further explicit communication of the gospel in a different way, that is, of entering into a process of symbolization or interpretation in which the semiotic tension between *how* and *what* becomes the engine of continuing communication. This is true of all human communication of the gospel, including the Christian one.

Christian communication of the gospel can take place through individuals or groups, when the occasion arises or in a regular way, in institutional or individual forms. Just as faith is lived in community, so the gospel that constitutes faith is communicated not only by individuals but also by the community, and not only on occasion but in institutionally regulated forms. Without institutions of communicating faith, there would be no Christian community of faith; without this community, no Christian testimony of faith; without this testimony, no Christian communication of the gospel; without this communication, no Christian faith and no life of faith; without faith and life of faith, no Christian theology.

Christian theology thus exists at all only because there is something other to which it refers: the Christian *communication of the gospel*, and this communication on its own conviction exists only because there is what it calls the "gospel": *God communicating himself as gospel* or (more succinctly) *the self-communication of the gospel*. This is the short formula for—to say it in the language of the theological tradition—a process of human life becoming new that is grounded *extra nos* (in God himself) and takes place *pro nobis* (in our favor), unfolding *in nobis* (in the actuality of our human life in this world)[42] in a way that can be paradigmatically summarized as *dislocating interruption* (through the gospel), *liminal redetermination* (in faith), and *reorienting reshaping* (in the life of faith).

13. Dislocation and Reorientation

From a formal point of view, human life becomes life of faith in that a human being, in being included in the communication of the gospel, is placed from the position of the third person (HE/SHE/IT/THEY) in the participants' position of the second (YOU) and first person (I/WE), that is, from being a non-participating third party becomes someone affected by and participating in communication. Where faith comes about, the attitude toward life changes from the ground up, because humans begin to understand themselves essentially from first- and second-person perspectives of God's personal relationship with them, perspectives through which they become what they are in the first place. They understand their new life personally as life in faith in God, whom in the basic Christian prayer they address as their Father, and from there, they also understand their prior life in a personal perspective as life in unfaith, in which they ignored that and how God relates to them. Even in the third-person perspective, it is thus possible to speak about life in faith appropriately only by taking the constitutive significance of the first- and second-person perspective for the living of human life in faith into account. That is

---

42. And thus not only in a neo-Protestant "interiority" that would first have to turn "to the outside" to become noticeable for others and actual in the world. Rather, the *in nobis* in particular refers to the *living of community and shared practical life before God* where the concrete processes of communication take place without which the biographical actualization of the gospel does not come about, through which we become those whom God makes us to be by communicating himself to us as gospel.

why it is possible to talk about people who have faith adequately only in "second-person accounts," as Eleonore Stump puts it.[43]

The systematic consequences of this pragmatic–existential-ontological change are immense. Because of the kind of communication at issue, the change of the communicative position from HE/SHE/IT/THEY to YOU and I/WE entails a fundamental dislocation of the human. This is evident in that in this communication, we as you are compelled to say I/WE not just once but twice, that is, we find ourselves in a tension between I and I (I before and without the communication of the gospel, and I through and in this communication) or belong to two contrasting WE (to the WE of those who ignore God and to the WE of those who because of the communication of the gospel can no longer ignore that they are not being ignored by God). Since both WE stand in the contrast relation of being other, the contrasting line of being other runs not simply between me/us and the others but right through me/us ourselves: believers are others to themselves in that through the gospel they as humans are being dislocated (with respect to themselves) and relocated (with respect to God). Only across this abyss, which they have not effected themselves and which they can therefore never bridge or abolish despite all biographical continuities, can believers understand themselves to be "the same," whether they schematize this "temporally" (before–after) or "spatially" (the one and the other at the same time) or "perspectivally" (as *simul* of two irreducible determinations). They can no longer univocally understand themselves as I, self, or subjects who attribute what is other "to themselves" but only as beings fundamentally determined by difference, beings whose center of identity is in no way to be found in or with themselves but only *extra se* in God's effective presence, which joins what cannot communicate itself in an identity-preserving or identity-forming manner into the unity of a biography.

The fifth article of the Augsburg Confession presents this point succinctly, stating that "by the Word and Sacraments, as by instruments, the Holy Spirit is given: who worketh faith, where and when it pleaseth God, in those that hear the Gospel."[44] What is given through word and sacrament is thus nothing that would somehow come to be disposed of by humans or could even approximately be captured as anthropologically determined: neither a faith nor a will opening itself to God, nor a heart seeking God, nor the tendency to count on God more than before, nor any other capacity one might now have. What is given, rather, is God the Holy Spirit, without whom no human becomes or remains a believer because faith is wholly bound to the effective presence of the good, just, merciful God the *verbum externum* of the gospel is about. With the Spirit, God himself enters into the life of the human, becomes its determining interlocutor, and thereby reorients it from the ground up and in all dimensions, opening the human up, out of its God-ignoring and God-marginalizing self-reference, to God's presence. Put differently: one is placed into a situation of God's personal presence and thus located within a communicative event, evoked by the expression "Spirit," where it is no longer possible

---

43. Stump, "Second-Person Accounts and the Problem of Evil"; "Evil and the Nature of Faith"; and "Narrative and the Problem of Evil." For similar reasons, I have spoken of the "situation of address" as the basic situation of faith. See "Christian Discourse and the Paradigmatic Christian Experience" as well as *Religiöse Rede von Gott*, 393–494.

44. *Augsburg Confession*, 10.

to determine and understand oneself without constitutively taking the relationship with the interlocutor, God, and the dynamic of the communication with God into account.

That is why faith in this present God is not a merely cognitive, voluntative, or fiducial event in the human; faith is human life being determined anew through God's effective presentification in this life, which does not change just one aspect of this life but reorients this life as a whole, opens it up to God's presence and the presence of those who are close (that is, all those who like oneself are close to God). Human life is changed from the ground up in that God becomes present in it as the decisive interlocutor of the human, such that one no longer understands and must understand oneself before oneself or before the world but before this presence of God without ever or in any way being able to attribute or ascribe this presence to oneself as a predicate. It is not God who in faith becomes a predicate of the human—a misunderstanding not just of Feuerbach—but through God's becoming present in the life of humans, human beings are distinguished from themselves in such a way that in faith, they must say "I" in multiple ways. They become someone they previously were not and could not by themselves have become (a new human being). As such, believers differ fundamentally from their prior history which they nonetheless have to accept being ascribed to them as their own. Both, this break and this continuity, characterize the life of believers. They relate to both by learning critically to distinguish in their own biography between that which has been rendered old, been overtaken and overcome by the new and definitively consigned to oblivion (the old human being), and that which is taken up and continued, set straight and deepened in the new life and retrospectively appears as anticipation of the new. In dogmatic terms, believers know themselves not only to be justified sinners, they also begin to grasp that even as sinners, they were always already God's creatures.

That is why believers can talk about themselves only ever in differential formulas: someone who has faith is—to employ familiar, albeit not the only relevant distinctions—*simul iustus et peccator*; someone who is just is just through the *aliena iustitia Christi*; someone who is a sinner is *simul peccator et creatura*. They never are what they are only before themselves or before the world. They are what they are always also and above all before God. Yet because there is nothing that would not be before God, humans before God always come into view in both regards, namely as the ones they are insofar as they ignore God (sinners) as well as the ones they remain although they ignore God (creature) or as the ones they become because God for his part does not ignore them (justified). All these differences are consequences of the basic difference of faith in that God the Spirit indisputably asserts himself to humans as the actuality that determines them such that they cannot but relate to it—in faith or in unfaith. Those to whom God presentifies himself do not remain who they are but become the ones they are through what happens to them.

14. Gaining an Identity

The one who says "I" in faith is therefore someone other than the one who (as she knows retrospectively) said "I" in unfaith. In this regard, faith is the opposite of an "interiority" of the subject that would differ from the "exteriority" of the living of life. It is, inversely, the opening up of a communicative vis-à-vis of God and human that is not less but differently and more fundamentally "external" than the life-relationships between human beings in the world—more fundamentally because the relation with God does not simply join the relationship of the human to the world and to itself but comprehends them. Faith is tied to the effective presence of the Spirit in the life of the human being, a presence that is initiated, opened up, and given through the word of the gospel and that compels the distinction in life between faith and unfaith.

In faith in God, the human is thus not only placed in a new and different public and finds itself in two publics irreducible to each other (*coram mundo* and *coram deo*). Both, moreover, are qualified by the difference between faith and unfaith in such a way that believers before the world and before God must speak within two horizons also with regard to themselves (*coram seipso*) and thus must say "I" twice: who they are is defined by the irreducible difference of their lives before the world and before God (that is, it must be answered differently as regards their relation to the world and their relation to God), but, moreover, both lives are qualified by the even less reducible difference between faith and unfaith that is due to God's presentification in a human life (that is, it must be answered differently once more and in a whole new way as regards their relation to the world *and* to God as lived faith or as lived unfaith). In insisting not only on the impossibility of abolishing the difference between the relation to God and the relation to the world but even more so on the impossibility of abolishing the further difference (with which it is not to be confused) between faith and unfaith, the Reformation theory of justification is not the proto- or original form of the neo-Protestant theory of subjectivity but definitive proof of the latter's theological failure: the subject-theoretical recourse to an "I" always to be presupposed completely misses the fundamental differentiation and dislocation of the believing sinner that justificatory faith operates.

Believers are thus those who they become through God making himself present to them as gospel. This "them" does not refer to those to whom this happens although it could also not have happened, such that they would at most be determined by it contingently. Rather, it designates that which *becomes* through these events in the first place: the new human before God. Those who in their lives *become believers* know that they have their identity *extra se* in God's evangelic presence.[45] As such, they cannot but retrospectively identify with their biography *as sinners* and ascribe it to themselves as well as let it be ascribed to them, yet—and this is decisive—this biography is a history overcome by and, despite all continuing effects, concluded by what they become and have become through God's presence. It is not sinners who become believers, nor does a self-identical I understand itself both as sinner and as believer; rather, only believers who have their identity in Jesus Christ can understand themselves as sinners, and for that very reason, they can understand themselves as sinners only within the horizon of the actualized

---

45. More precisely we would have to say that they know *negatively* that they owe their identity not to themselves and that they cannot identify it with any image they or others have of them. They know *positively* that they owe their identity to God alone and that this identity consists in how God views and judges them. Yet what this includes is something they can know only approximately and say indirectly by taking recourse to the one in whom, according to Christian faith, God's judgment of every human being has become manifest: Jesus Christ. And that is why they cannot concretely talk about their identity without regarding this identity to be anchored *extra se* in the identity of Jesus Christ.

forgiveness of their sins. The "I" of sinners is what believers retrospectively unmask as the self-misunderstanding of taking their identity to lie in themselves, not in the relation of God to them. And that is why believers confess their sin not as what *they* have overcome but as what has been *forgiven* them by the one to whom they owe who they are.

The life of human beings is thus interrupted through God's communicative presentification in his efficacious word and good Spirit as *their God* (God for them) in such a way that they are being dislocated from the habitual indifference, ignorance, and uncertainty toward God and placed in a different nexus of determination and orientation in which they live and understand themselves, their lives, and their world. For in that it becomes clear who and what God is and what he does and wills for them and for all human beings, they are being enlightened about what—in universal-inclusive terms—our actual situation before God is and what possibilities our life thus has or does not have. Insofar as God as God thereby opens up his presence through Word and Spirit *as gospel*, humans are not just negatively dislocated from their situation of ignorant indifference toward God but are, above all, positively located in God's presence in such a way that they (can) have faith in God, trust God, and place their hopes in God, that is, in such a way that human life is liberated from its self-referential navel-gazing, oriented toward God, opened up to others, and thus renewed from the ground up.

The result of the dislocating interruption of human life through God's self-communication as gospel that is at issue in the Christian communication of the gospel is thus a new attitude toward God, world, others, and oneself in which life proves to be redetermined from the ground up. Where in the responsive reference back to the gospel life is lived *in faith*, *everything* is exposed to the critical light of the fundamental distinction between the old and the new. To be sure, this distinction becomes possible only through the appearance of the new, for it is only this that establishes the contrast with the old and defines the old as old (without the new, there is no difference between the old and the new). And it becomes comprehensible only for those who have insight into the new, that is, who understand themselves in light of this new and thereby bring the critical distinction between the old and the new to bear first and foremost on themselves (without the new for me the difference between old and new does not make sense). Yet where this difference does appear because God communicates himself as gospel, it covers everything and does not leave anything in a state of indeterminate neutrality. There is then nothing that would be neither old nor new, but everything—this is the reorienting reshaping that is permanently taking place in and as life of faith—is viewed and judged differentiatingly in light of this distinction.

It is thus necessary to distinguish critically between discontinuities and continuities in one's own life process, that is, for the sake of responsibly shaping the present and future life with and before God we must, in recalling our past biography, pay attention to what is old and can no longer be continued given the new, and to what was an unnoticed announcement, preparation, and trace of the new. Only in this differentiating redefinition of our own *ipse* and *idem* identity is there a Christian biography, not in a unilinear narrative of a human identity preserving itself in psychological-physical continuity. Christian identity is an identity allotted to us and granted to us *ab extra* that appears in the continuity of human living as a crisis and conflict of orientation because it leads to irreducible differences.

Believers thus understand themselves *as believers* (and not in some other determining respect) from the perspective of the intrusion of the gospel in their lives through which they are irreversibly placed in the liminal in-between of faith in the biographically ungraspable eschatological difference between old (unfaith) and new (faith). That is why they can understand their own past, present, and future only in an eschatological differentiation as a past of the *simul creatura et peccator* (of the creature that time and again becomes a sinner); as a present of the *simul iustus et peccator* (of the righteous who cannot by herself cease being a sinner); and as a future of the *homo iustificatur fide* (of the human being who as creature and sinner lives on God making her righteous). And they cannot live their lives in this world in any other way than as a process in which what the gospel effects (a life in faith) wins against what opposes it (life in unfaith)—not as continuous progress in time but across all setbacks, dead ends, and breaks as a biography on which the last word is spoken not in it, by it, or by others, but by God alone.

A life of faith is nothing but a life in faith in God. Having faith in God means nothing but living in trusting what God communicates as the gospel of his becoming-present, which makes good, just, and whole, and in which his judgment about the life of his creatures unfolds. And communicating the gospel in a Christian way is nothing but testifying in word and deed, communally and individually in living one's life, testifying to this self-communication of God's, which reorients a human life and makes it good in all its breaks, guilt, and incompleteness.

15. Unfaith

If faith is the path out of sin, then unfaith—in all its forms—is sin. Every life is sinful that is not shaped, enriched, and reoriented by faith. Before that happens, there is no need to know what one is missing, nor does one have to consider it a lack not to be something of which one does not even know one is missing it. Human life is sinful not only in intentionally turning away from God but also in unintentionally not turning toward God. Both are godless, albeit in different ways. But both also are possibilities of human life only because God is present, not only to the *iustus* but to the *peccator* as well.

This presence of God is decisive for defining sin not only because sin could otherwise not be defined via its being forgiven but because its actuality and its content always consists in inverting the relation to the present ground of our own existence and thus regularly results in a life that is not shaped by the hope placed in God and his promise. This is true whether we define sin, with Luther, as *unfaith*; with Kierkegaard, as *despair*; or, with Tillich, as *estrangement*.

16. Sin as Unfaith

Luther's decisive insight in defining sin as *unfaith* is that sin designates not just a certain (morally) wrong conduct by human beings, nor only a disruption of the assemblage of human forces and faculties, that is, an anthropological defect *in* the human; it designates human beings' wrong position in the relation with their creator. It is the *entire human being* with all its faculties and their successful and unsuccessful employment, its morally good and evil deeds, who does not conduct itself toward its creator as would be expected given the way the creator conducts himself: thankful for what it receives as goods for life; lamenting what it sees lacking in itself and others; turned toward God in fear and love as to the one who not only works everything in everything but has promised to effect what is best for his creatures. Unfaith means living as if this relation of God's to us to which we owe everything we are and have did not exist.

This unfaith manifests in many, indeed, in all modes of human life that unintentionally or intentionally, willingly or factually, ignores God: by not thanking the one whom it would be appropriate to thank, and instead placing one's trust and confidence in what does not deserve them because it is at best a means and medium but not the ground of what is good in life. The sin of unfaith can occur in the shape of *not having faith* in God, as ignoring and not paying attention to God, or in the form of *superstition*, as belief in a false "god"—in an entity, that is, that strictly speaking does not deserve the designation "god" because it is itself a created reality. Yet it can also take the form of explicitly *refusing faith* and of *contesting faith*, which closes itself off from and rejects faith.

As differentiated as the assessments of all these forms may have to be, this changes nothing about the fact that they are all versions of unfaith, that is, forms of the wrong life that those who live that way—that is, all human beings—cannot by themselves evade because everything they do and can do in this situation is always a continuation and repetition but not an abolishment and ending of this false life. Even what is good can be done for a great number of reasons, and it may not matter much to those who benefit from it for what reasons and from what motivations good is done to them. But the doing of good is not thereby *ipso facto* an ending or overcoming of sin; it can even represent a particularly clever aggravation of the false life before God: one does—intentionally or in fact—good for the sake of another end than the doing of what is good alone, that is, subordinates the good to other interests and purposes and thereby turns it into a means of asserting oneself in the wrong life and not a means for or path toward overcoming the wrong life. That is why the sinfulness of the wrong life is not evinced by enumerating good or evil life phenomena. This sinfulness consists in the contingent, that is, not necessary but only factual and therefore in principle changeable fact of its basic orientation, which is self-referential and closes itself off from God. This orientation is not self-evident but becomes apparent in the encounter with God's will in the law and in the gospel. For the law makes clear what a life in faith would and ought to look like, and the gospel makes clear how such a life can and does come about. The law thus opens up the counterfactual alternative to the wrong life before God, and the gospel actualizes this alternative by ending the wrong life and in it beginning the right life.

Like unfaith, however, faith is thereby not an anthropological determination beside or among others (reason, understanding, will, emotion, feeling, and so on) but qualifies the human being with all its determinations under the aspect of what God does in and for it. The decisive thing God does in and for human beings is that he places them from unfaith into faith: faith is *the change from unfaith to faith through God*.

This change cannot be made by the nonbeliever (or else he would not be a nonbeliever), yet also not by the believer (for the believer is always the *result* but not the *subject* of this change) but by God alone. That is why faith is always faith *in God*, that is, faith in the one who places believers from unfaith into faith. For Luther, unfaith and faith thus do not mark phenomena in or about the human but mark the human's factual relation to God: there is no one who would not live in this relation (everyone alive who is not God is God's creature), and in the case of the human being, who unlike other creatures could know its creator and should thank him, this life relation is always soteriologically qualified, namely either as unfaith or as faith or, each in different respects, as both but never as neither. Every human *creatura* lives either as *peccator* or as *iustus* or as *iustus et peccator*, and not to live one of these three ways is not to live at all.

This indicates how the soteriological determinacy of the relation of the human to God leads to existential determinations of human life that can be enumerated in human life itself. Luther's soteriological dialectic of relation, which situates the human being within the referential horizon of its relation with its creator, thus becomes an anthropological dialectic of existence, in which this referential horizon manifests only in qualifications of existence or modes of existence of human life.

17. Sin as Despair

This happens most impressively in Kierkegaard. Kierkegaard reconstructs Luther's soteriological analysis of the reorientation from unfaith to faith, from the wrong life to the right life, which humans cannot actualize themselves, as a dialectic of human existence and elaborates Luther's soteriological-relational analysis of unfaith in the relation to God in the terms of an existential analysis of *despair*.[46]

Kierkegaard as it were reads the relational analysis of the human being's relationship to God into the human living of life by describing the human itself not only as a being who lives in relations but as one who, as a self, is itself a being of relations:

> The self is a relation that relates itself to itself or is the relation's relating itself to itself in the relation; the self is not the relation but is the relation's relating itself to itself. A human being is a synthesis of the infinite and the finite, of the temporal and the eternal, of freedom and necessity, in short, a synthesis. A synthesis is a relation between two . . .
>
> Such a relation that relates itself to itself, a self, must either have established itself or have been established by another.
>
> If the relation that relates itself to itself has been established by another, then the relation is indeed the third, but this relation, the third, is yet again a relation and relates itself to what which established the entire relation.
>
> The human self is such a derived, established relation, a relation that relates itself to itself and in relating itself to itself relates itself to another.[47]

46. See Sack, *Die Verzweiflung*; Davies, *Human Sacrifice*; Schulte, *Radikal Böse*, 288–314; Theunissen, *Das Selbst auf dem Grund der Verzweiflung* and *Kierkegaard's Concept of Despair*; Cioran, *On the Heights of Despair*; and Decher, *Verzweiflung*.

47. Kierkegaard, *Sickness Unto Death*, 13–14. See also Ringleben, *Die Krankheit zum Tode*.

As the synthesis of the temporal and the eternal, the human being is an always-precarious relation, since it never simply is this paradoxical synthesis of what is infinitely different but always has to become it, yet because of the paradoxical structure of the synthesis, the human cannot become the synthesis such that it would ultimately simply be the synthesis but only ever such that, in becoming the synthesis, it simultaneously relates to this becoming. Yet in relating to the paradoxical relation it is becoming without ever being it, the human at the same time relates to the other of itself to whom the relation that it is becoming is due and without whom the becoming it is engaged in would not exist. In becoming a self, the human being therefore not only never reaches the goal but always also, simply by becoming, relates to an other of itself, to its creator.

Kierkegaard's analyses thus start from three presuppositions that are by no means self-evident: that the human is a synthesis of the infinite and the finite; that it must become a self by trying to produce this synthesis; and that it cannot succeed in doing so without conceiving of itself as a self-in-becoming and a becoming-self posited by God.[48] Under the heading of *despair*, Kierkegaard inscribes what Luther called unfaith in this structure. In all its versions, despair is an imbalance, a disruption, a misdetermination of the relation that a self is in relating to itself, to the other of itself, and to the relation thus posited. For the self is always a *fact*, namely the fact *that* it is a relation that relates to itself. Like all facts, this fact, too, could be otherwise or something else could be in its place. Not every way in which the self is is thus *ipso facto* also the only possible or right way, and it is not the way it could be or ought to be whenever the relation that relates to itself and in relating to itself relates to another tries to live against the logic that determines these relational structures, that is, whenever it lives as a self in a self-contradictory way. Whenever that is the case, Kierkegaard speaks of *despair*.[49]

This self-contradictory determination of the self can take different modes, and like Luther in his presentation of unfaith (not having faith, superstition, refusal of faith), Kierkegaard, too, distinguishes between three versions of despair: not being aware that as a human being, one has the peremptory duty to be a self; wanting to be a self one is not; and not wanting to be the self one is. *Despair* is either the manifestation of the dreaming innocence of not knowing about one's own being a self and the obligation thus imposed of becoming one's self: one lives without consciousness of the self and thus also without consciousness of the duty to become a self and accordingly in an unknowing despair that does not even know itself as such. Or, having become conscious of this, it is the expression of the simultaneously unavoidable and entirely absurd attempt of willing to be a self by breaking away from the process of becoming a self and ignoring that one is a self only

48. According to Theunissen, *Das Selbst auf dem Grund der Verzweiflung*, these three presuppositions are mere hypotheses articulating necessary conditions that, according to Kierkegaard, humans must fulfill to be able to despair. They are initially unfounded and justified only later in the analysis of despair. Behind their supposition, however, stands a theological view of the human being that is elaborated in strict analogy with classic Christology and plausible only against that background. See Dalferth, "'Die Sache ist viel entsetzlicher': Religiosität bei Kierkegaard und Schleiermacher," and "Becoming a Christian According to the 'Postscript.'"

49. For Theunissen, the decision that despair is always a not-being-self is thus already made, and made in a way that blocks the phenomena of life. See Theunissen, *Kierkegaard's Concept of Despair*; similarly already Sack, *Die Verzweiflung*.

through becoming a self and that one becomes a self only through relating to the relation one is becoming in such a way that one is simultaneously also relating to its ground, that is, God. The attempt by the individual awoken from its dreaming innocence at not wanting to be a self or at being an absolute, independent self not tied into relations and not committed to the unreachable becoming of a paradoxical relation of infinity and finitude can result only in an escalating despair: one desperately wants not to be oneself and desperately wants to be oneself. The self comes upon itself as a posited self-relation and wants to break away from this positing by trying to posit itself. It desperately wants not to be what it is, a heteronomously posited self-relation; and it desperately tries to become what it can never become, a self-relation not posited heteronomously but positing itself autonomously. All its life, the self unceasingly vacillates between these two movements, which are impossible and therefore drive to despair; that is its "sickness unto death."

What is thus described existentially as despair is the mode in which what, in Christian terms and in explicitly locating human life before God, is called *sin* is being lived in the practice of life. Just as human beings are desperate, whether they know it or not, whether they are conscious of their task of becoming a self or whether they try to actualize this the way it cannot be actualized, they are also, unconsciously, consciously, or intentionally sinners; and just as they exist their whole lives in despair, so they are sinners their whole lives before God: we are sinners without knowing it, we are sinners because we factually live by ignoring that we owe ourselves to God, and we are sinners by explicitly rebelling against God and wanting to be an autonomous self without and against God.

On the one hand, then, sin is distinguished rigorously from morality; on the other, it is consistently thought as despair. The theological category of sin is not to be restricted to the moral category of Evil but also includes, along with this category, its opposite, the Good. The counterconcept to sin is not the Good but forgiveness and thereby faith. Faith, too, is thus not defined morally. It stands in opposition not just to Evil but equally to the Good or, more precisely: to the entire moral opposition of Evil and Good. Good and Evil are moral, sin and faith in contrast are nonmoral categories. Yet the highest sin, too, is therefore something other than radical Evil. According to Kierkegaard, it is the sin against the Holy Spirit, which is the case when the self's aporetic wanting to be an autonomous self is directed against forgiveness itself. It is the rejection of the one without whom we would not even exist and could not become a self: we reject the condition of the possibility to reject the condition of possibility. It is the existential aporia in life, which thinking tries to think in the ontological argument: denying what in denying one must claim and contesting in living that without which we would not and could not live.

By bringing despair to a head in this existential aporia, Kierkegaard not only thinks despair as sin but sin as despair. Aquinas, too, saw *desperatio* as sin, namely as the state in which someone abandons the hope of sharing in the divine goodness and mercy. Yet for him, *praesumptio*, the arrogant erroneous notion that humans could reach the future good by themselves, or *infidelitas*, unfaith, or *odium dei*, hatred of God, are sins, too. *Infidelitas* is sin because it does not take the truth of God to be true; *odium dei* is sin because there the human will contradicts the goodness of God; and *desperatio* is sin because the human gives up hope of sharing in God's goodness. Sin is thus differentiated according to the theological virtues of faith, love, and hope and the anthropological distinction between knowing, willing, and hoping. The sin in the domain of the understanding or the intellect is *unfaith*; in the domain of affect, it is *despair*; and in the domain of the will, it is *hatred of God*. And just as affects can have an effect independently of the intellect, so despair, too, can occur independently of unfaith, that is, not only in people who do not have faith but also in people who do.[50]

In Aquinas, *desperatio* is thus only one, and not the gravest, form of sin. In its own way, though, this is also true of unfaith, which doubts God's truth. In Luther, this shifts such that unfaith becomes the fundamental and main sin, that is, not just one case among many but the basic case of sin, which determines and tinges everything else in the life of the sinner. And Kierkegaard, picking up on Luther, continues this shift by equating not sin with unfaith but unfaith with despair. Unlike Aquinas, he sees despair to oppose primarily not hope but faith, and thus sees it to occupy the place taken in Luther by unfaith. And just as unfaith is the lived self-contradiction of the human being closing itself off from and refusing what it is, God's creature, so despair is the lived self-contradiction of not wanting to be what one is as a self posited by God and instead wanting to be what one is not, a self that is not a self posited by God.

If the self is the contingent fact that the relation relates to itself, then in all its forms, the despair Kierkegaard analyzes amounts to denying one's own contingency. And since this denial is itself contingent and made by an essentially contingent and not necessary self, this desperate being thus exists in a self-contradiction it cannot itself abolish: it denies what it is by not wanting to be what it is and instead wanting to be what it is not. And this contingent denial of its contingency manifests not only actively in willing, thinking, and acting as a self (in contradicting God) but also factually in living its existence without being conscious that it is and ought to become a self (in not knowing and ignoring God). Either way, we live as if we were not contingent selves although that is precisely what we are: we exist in contradiction.

18. Sin as Estrangement

All attempts at thinking sin theologically are characterized by taking recourse to an elementary self-contradiction in thinking and living. This applies to Paul Tillich's definition of sin as *estrangement* as well.[51] The figure of thought of sin presupposes an originary unity of human beings with God that manifests in the unity of the essence and the existence of the human being. What in God, the infinite power to be or "being-itself,"[52] is indistinguishably one (*being*), in creatures splits into essence (*what*) and existence (*that*), and in sinful creatures leads to the estrangement of existence and essence. The estrangement from God (*before God*) at the same time estranges the human from itself (*before itself*). "Man as he exists is not what he essentially is and ought to be. He is estranged

50. See Aquinas, *Summa Theologiae*, IIa IIae q20 a1–3.

51. See Schepers, *Schöpfung und allgemeine Sündigkeit*; Schrey, *Entfremdung*; Eichinger, *Erbsünden-theologie*; and Kleffmann, *Die Erbsündenlehre in sprachtheologischem Horizont*.

52. Tillich, *Systematic Theology* 1:237.

from his true being. The profundity of the term 'estrangement' lies in the implication that one belongs essentially to that from which one is estranged."[53]

The concept of estrangement thus marks a non-unity of the human's existence and essence as a consequence and expression of the non-unity of human and God, and it marks both against the background of a unity that is not (is no longer) but can be and ought to be. If the relation between God and human being were destroyed completely, this would mean the destruction of the human, and the split into existence and essence would deteriorate and fall apart into something that actually exists but is not human (a nonhuman reality) and a being human that does not but at most could exist (a merely possible being human). Nothing that is can be without God, nothing possible and nothing actual. All being is ontologically dependent on the creator, including the human being ignoring God. Sinners, too, are creatures that live on the care of God. The estrangement of the human from God is thus a split in the human being between its essence and its existence, but it is not an ontological separation of the human from God. God maintains his relationship with his creatures even where they turn away from him, he is faithful even where humans ignore God's care.

In this regard, God is the supporting ground even of estranged being. Yet God is not the reason for the estrangement.

> If what is beyond essence and existence participates in existence, then it can participate in it only in the form of overcoming the split between essence and existence. The way in which the divine participates in existence is the overcoming of estrangement, the creation of the New Being. . . . Possible participation in existence is the creation of the New Being. God cannot participate in it in any other way because he does not participate in estrangement.[54]

This means that God does not enter into the estranged existence but participates in it only ever in such a way that he transcends it by overcoming it. On the one hand, he is the reason that the estranged being is at all and is not rather not. On the other hand, he relates to the estranged being in such a way as to overcome the estrangement, that is, he reconciles the estranged human being—both with itself in the sense of overcoming the split between essence and existence in human being but also with himself in the sense of overcoming the estrangement of human being from the divine ground of being. Both together characterize what Tillich calls "New Being": a being that leaves the estrangement behind, as past, because God as power of being and ground of life has reconciled the estranged creature with himself.[55] The new being is being in God in whom the estrangement between the essence and the existence of the human is abolished in that the human is fully included in God's presence and thereby, precisely, becomes who it can be and ought to be.

It is not by chance that Tillich calls this position "panentheism":[56] everything is in God insofar as God actively participates in everything while creation, inversely, is

---

53. Tillich, *Systematic Theology* 2:45.

54. Tillich, "Das Neue Sein als Zentralbegriff einer christlichen Theologie," 230.

55. See Mugerauer, *Versöhnung als Überwindung der Entfremdung.*

56. See Repp, *Die Transzendierung des Theismus,* 308n13, who quotes this self-description of Tillich's from an unpublished 1956 lecture, "The Method of Theology and our Knowledge of God."

passively included in being-itself. What is being described from the perspective of God as "universal participation" is to be defined from the perspective of creation as "the passive experience of the divine parousia in terms of the divine presence."[57] All activity in overcoming estrangement thus lies with God. Human beings are affected by it in a purely passive way. They do not even have to be conscious of the divine participation as such. Where they do become conscious of it, it manifests in the overcoming of the estrangement of essence and existence in the human, in achieving what as humans they are intended for. On this path of overcoming his estrangement, "man discovers *himself* when he discovers God; he discovers something that is identical with himself although it transcends him infinitely, something from which he is estranged, but from which he never has been and never can be separated."[58] The path to overcoming the estrangement, to discovering God, and to actualizing what they are intended for thus leads entirely from God to the human being, ontologically and noetically: only where God makes himself manifest (reveals himself) do humans become aware of him, and they become aware of God in no other way than in overcoming the estrangement of their existence from their essence.

Without recourse to God—Luther, Kierkegaard, and Tillich demonstrate each in his way—neither the reality of the human being nor that of its possibilities can be understood. God is the actuality of the possible; without him, the possibilities of the human being cannot (ontically) become actual and (epistemically) be understood. The recourse to God not only makes clear what humans are intended for and what they can be but also what they factually fail to be although they could be it. Only in the relation to God do we see what is really Evil in the life of humans and what both precedes and forms the basis of all their doing ill and suffering ill: their estrangement from God and the estrangement from themselves it conditions, which makes them live and suffer in Evil without hope for God and the overcoming of what is Evil through what is Good.[59] To understand the reality of Evil in human life, we are theologically being referred to the hermeneutic detour via God.

57. Tillich, *Systematic Theology* 1:245.

58. Tillich, "Two Types of Philosophy of Religion," 10.

59. The fundamental *malum* of the human being is thus not its finitude and creatureliness, as Leibniz thought, for whom this is the *malum metaphysicum* to which all other *mala* are due, but the *estrangement* of the creature from the creator. Being a creature means community of creature and creator; being a sinner, in contrast, means missing the sense and the possibilities of this community by ignoring its reality.

B

Faith and Evil: The Project of God

THE DETOUR VIA GOD is not a path readily traced out. We do not know in advance where it leads. Even if we do not understand it, the lived reality of evil is uncontested, yet only rarely is what we understand by "God" clearly thought out in advance. The detour of thinking via God is thus essentially a path of discovering God in thinking. This could be shown on a great number of points. In what follows, I will limit myself to three trains and elaborations of thought in which Christian thinking engaging with the reality of evil has defined the outlines and contents of the notion of God: the discovery of *God's goodness* (of his *being good*), of his *justice*, and of his *love*.[1]

The focus on these aspects of the notion of God follows the traces of three ways of dealing with Evil in taking recourse to God or the divine that have been of great consequence for Christian thinking and that outline as well as concretize both the conception of *malum* and the conception of God in reciprocal processes of determination.[2] These

---

1. This does not mean that other definitions of the notion of God such as *power*, *faithfulness*, or *wisdom* would be of lesser or no significance: similar stories of discovery and elaboration could be told about them as well. But they are not at the center of what follows because within the horizon of the questions debated here, theological reflections on the Christian way of dealing with the experiences of *bonum* and *malum* in life, they appear as specifications of God's goodness, justice, and love.

2. Even if the path traced by the following reflections leads via God's goodness and justice to his love because love is the central summarizing and theologically most productive metaphor for the Christian conception of God, this hermeneutic construction does *not* suggest that the three developments addressed here constitute a goal-oriented story of progress in which the truth contents of earlier insights are "sublated," preserved, and processed. On the contrary: each of these stories of development continues in later periods and to this day by engaging the other stories or not, and represents not just an obsolete step preparing what follows later. The complex stories of development that have entered into the Christian conception of God can also be reconstructed in such a way that they converge in specifying the metaphor of God's goodness or of his justice. Doing so, however, will only contribute to clarifying the *Christian* conception of God if it also includes and considers what the metaphor of God's love is employed to say and think. For, inscribed in this metaphor, more clearly and harder to ignore than in other cases, is the reference to the message, the life, and the suffering of Jesus Christ, and not granting this reference a decisive role would deprive a Christian conception of God of its particular features. This theological hermeneutics of Evil thus opts for God's love as the central notion of a Christian orientation of life on purpose—also because the problem of existentially dealing with evil becomes acute in the hermeneutic detour via God's love with unparalleled intensity. In what follows, however, all three paths of reflection are concerned above all with thinking through theological perceptions of problems and trains of thought by way of exemplary constellations in order to clarify the procedures of orientation

processes can be described as a complex movement of thought that concentrates on three sets of problems that build on each other: the discovery of central attributes of God in engaging with the reality of Evil (*process of the theology of experience*); the integration of these attributes in a unified notion of God (*process of reflective theology*); and the unification of the manifold experiences of *malum* in a unitary conception of *malum* (*process of the hermeneutics of experience*).

1. *Process of the theology of experience*: In a first step, typical and central attributes of God are discovered and defined in engaging with the reality of Evil by going back to God. When the *bonum* is understood as the opposite of the *malum*, God typically comes into view as *the good God*. When the *bonum* is understood as a fight against the *malum*, God is thematized as *the just God*. And when the *bonum* is understood from the perspective of the overcoming of the *malum* through the *bonum*, interest focuses on God as *God of love*. What manifests itself in the divine attributes of God's goodness, justice, and love is thus a complicated and variegated history of dealing with experiences of *bonum* and *malum* by taking recourse to God. In what follows, reconstructing these processes will take center stage.

2. *Process of reflective theology*: In the context of the monotheistic orientation of life by the one and only God, however, these divine attributes do not remain juxtaposed without connection but are referred to each other so as to maintain the unity and uniformity of the notion of God. Factually, this happens by "sublating" the problems in dealing with experiences of *malum* left open by the individual definitions of God, that is, by further defining them in the definition of the notion of God. God's being good is thus defined by and understood in terms of his justice, his justice by his love. It is not by coincidence that this definition of God has become the central definition of the notion of God in Christian thinking.

3. *Process of the hermeneutics of experience*: Yet bringing different definitional threads together in the central notion of God's love not only makes the theologically important point that what is being understood by "God" thereby obtains an unmistakable outline and determinacy. It has also had, and time and again has, the theologically dubitable consequence that what is here understood as the last and decisive step in determining this notion of God is also taken to be the last and decisive determination of what is understood or is to be understood by *malum*: because the overcoming of unfaith is the key to insight into God's love as the creative force to overcome evil with good and make new what is old, everything that is lived and experienced as *malum* is reduced to ignoring, misunderstanding, and denying God's love in unfaith. Unfaith is being understood as the source of all evil, and faith, inversely, is understood as overcoming all evil through the good.

This, however, leads to what we might call the *fallacy of theological oversimplification in dealing with the experiences of* malum *in human life*. For while there are good religious and theological reasons for preserving the unity and uniqueness of the God to whom, confronted with experiences of evil and ill, we take recourse to understand what is happening to us and to be able to live with what we cannot understand, there are no

---

and the strategies with whose help theological thinking engages with the reality of Evil via the detour of working on the notion of God.

religiously or theologically good reasons therefore to describe all experiences of *malum* undifferentiatedly in one and the same way and always and everywhere to see only one and the same *malum* at work. As correct and as important as it is to form a differentiated but unified and consistent notion of God on the anabatic path of thinking from the reality of manifold experiences of *malum* to the conception of God, so absurd is it, in katabatically going back from the notion of God to the lifeworld's manifold of experiences, not to preserve the phenomenal differences of experiences of *malum*, equating different moments of *malum* in a theologically and religiously dubious way and treating them in a uniform manner. That those who are affected by *malum* turn to the one and only God for help in no way compels us to therefore understand all evil that affects and can affect humans in one and only one way as well, to make it pass for one and the same *malum* and define it as effects and consequences of the same *malum*. God is one; life in contrast is irreducibly manifold when it comes to what affects human beings as *malum* and as *bonum*.

The theological gain of hermeneutic insight into different determinations of *malum* obtained in the detour via differently accentuated conceptions of God is thus gambled away once more where the integration and unification of the different definitional views on God in the notion of God's love is misunderstood in such a way that one would think it possible to use it as a notional tool for reducing all experiences of *malum* to one and the same *malum* that manifests in them. When the emphasis on the unity of the notion of God leads to a standardizing view of all experiences of *malum* and thus to blurring and dissolving the differences by which, precisely, a differentiating engagement with them must be directed, the recourse to God loses its orienting function in life. Where all questions receive the same answer, no question is really being answered anymore.

That is why it is wrong to suppose one is strengthening faith by responding to everything by pointing to unfaith. The opposite is the case: faith is thereby robbed of its point. Given the manifold and multilayered reality of Evil, the recourse faith takes to God offers orientation in life only if it does not blur the phenomena but "saves" them, that is, outlines them more clearly and lets them appear in greater differentiation and in more precise resolution. Orientation in life succeeds best not when everything is painted grey in grey or white in white but when contrasts come out as clearly as possible. This is what recourse to God can and ought to procure: it is meant to make us sensible for what, with regard to life with God, is damaging in life and thus is *malum* and what is not. But that does not mean that everything that in human life is experienced as *malum* deserves being called *malum* in this theological sense or that the overcoming of what stands between God and human as *malum* would have to entail the abolition or elimination in every respect of any and all evil. Life is not monochrome, and faith does not help us orient ourselves in life by painting everything the same color; rather, in the recourse to God, it sheds a light on everything that brings out and highlights differences and oppositions also with regard to experiences of *malum* and *bonum*.

B.1

The Other of Evil: The Discovery of the Good God

WE DO NOT ALWAYS encounter evil in drastic ways as misfortune, accident, or catastrophe. Sometimes it spreads in a life almost imperceptibly, like a disease whose symptoms we have gotten used to until one day it can no longer be overlooked. Yet be it that evil unexpectedly intrudes in a life, be it that it gradually breaks open, human beings always find themselves surrendered to something that seems unavoidable and incomprehensible, something that changes their life from the ground up, and that they cannot at first or in the long run make any sense of. What just now seemed to be alright goes awry, and what we long chose to overlook can no longer be ignored. Evil can exist in a life in uncounted ways, but there is no life in which there would be no evil at all.

1. The Experience of Evil as the Origin of the Difference between *Is* and *Ought*

Where evil becomes actual in a life, contradictions and oppositions arise that can escalate into conflicts and deep rifts. They enjoin us to relate to them in a differentiated way. This presupposes establishing a mental distance toward them to be able to explore their causes and horizons of possibility. That is not possible without symbolizing them. Hermeneutically, such representations have a peculiar structure, for the issue is not to symbolize a "something" ("Evil") but *events* (the changing of a life affected by evil) and to symbolize them from a point of view *after* the appearance of the evil. This takes place with the aid of contrasts such as fortune/misfortune, joy/suffering, light/dark, good/evil, and so on, that not only describe an opposition but express a decline in value between the state before and the state after the appearance of the evil in life as worsening, damaging, destroying life.

Hermeneutically, the figures that represent the contradictions having erupted in a life therefore regularly present three features: they *distinguish*, they *evaluate*, and they make use of a concrete *life-world semantics*. They thus mark a contrast (A vs. B, or A vs. not-A); they evaluate the two sides of this contrast positively and negatively under the aspect of pleasure and displeasure, good and evil, true and false, beautiful and ugly, and so on; and they express this evaluative contrast in a medical, political, economic, moral, legal, aesthetic, etc., semantics taken from the domain of experience and life in which the evil has been encountered and in which the contrast in question is to make orientation possible.

Typical differences of orientation in the human life world and practice of life feature this structure of contrast, evaluation, and specific semantics. They thereby refer to what generates them, to experiences of Evil in specific life-nexuses and their symbolization for specific purposes of orientation: suffering is contrasted with joy, illness with health, injustice with justice, war with peace, loss with gain, unfreedom with freedom, death with life, the depressing with the cheerful, the dark with the light, night with day, cold with warmth, the alien with the familiar, the unpleasant with the pleasant, the bitter with the sweet, the chaotic with the ordered, and so on. In each case, there is an indication of what was disrupted (second element of the contrast) by the intrusion of evil (first element of the contrast) in such a way that what might previously not have been perceived explicitly as such (joy, health, justice, peace, gain, freedom, life, the cheerful, the light, day, warmth, the familiar, the pleasant, the sweet, the ordered) is now understood explicitly as something to strive for, while the evil that has occurred (suffering, illness, injustice, war, loss, unfreedom, death, the depressing, the dark, night, cold, the alien, the unpleasant, the bitter, the chaotic) is understood as something to be avoided.

This leads to a peculiar interlocking of a double directionality toward origins and toward goals in lifeworld nexuses of orientation, in which an original state allegedly as yet untouched by Evil (*being*) is presented as the state to be aimed for once more (*ought*) after the intrusion of Evil. Usually, only that which is experienced as disruption of the habitual comes to the foreground. But the contingency of this process also brings out the contingency of what had previously been considered self-evident. Not only the intrusion of Evil but also the Good that has thereby become distinguishable from Evil thus turns out to be questionable and to stand in need of explanation. It is no longer enough to make only the occurrence of suffering, illness, injustice, unfreedom, war, death, and so on comprehensible. This must also be done for the state of joy, health, justice, freedom, peace, life, and so on, which can thereby be thematized retrospectively or *ex post* as *what is lost* and prospectively or *ex ante* as *what ought to be*, as what one seeks to restore or to actualize in a new and perhaps better way by overcoming, containing, or dissolving the intruding Evil.

Each of the orienting contrasts cited—suffering/joy, illness/health, injustice/justice, war/peace, loss/gain, unfreedom/freedom, death/life, depressing/cheerful, dark/light, night/day, cold/warmth, alien/familiar, unpleasant/pleasant, bitter/sweet, chaotic/ordered—thus sums up the structure of how a history of experiences is lived, a structure that comprises what is past (joy, health, justice, freedom, peace, life, and so on), what is present (suffering, illness, injustice, unfreedom, war, death, and so on), and what is to be gained anew (joy, health, justice, freedom, peace, life, and so on). They do not only state what *has been* (good) and what *is* (evil) but evaluate it in such a way that the good that has been is *what, in the face of, against, and despite evil, ought to be.*

In these contrasts, although they are structured as dualities, the good thus always occurs twice: as the good whose self-evident presence has become past because of the occurrence of Evil and as the good that for this very reason is to be obtained anew, against Evil. The positive side of the orienting contrasts is thus always to be understood simultaneously as statement and postulate, descriptively and normatively. It says what was good and which good ought to be. These contrasts therefore fulfill not only a descriptive function (being) but also serve to orient conduct and guide action (ought). They not only sum up what has happened but signal how humans understand themselves and their life in the face of evil with respect to their past, their present, and their future, what they seek to avoid (evil) and what they will to live toward (good).

Good and *evil*, however, are thereby determined from the outset in a difference heavy with consequences that results from their being viewed from two irreducible perspectives: *good* is that which has been made past by the evil that has occurred (the good as the *contrast* to Evil), yet that is *good*, too, which is to be obtained anew, against Evil (the good as *overcoming* of Evil). Accordingly, *evil* is that which hinders what is good, removes it, makes it past (Evil as *ending* the good) but also that which is to be overcome by what is good (Evil as *challenge* to the good). The merely dual contrast between good and evil thereby becomes a succinct formula for a history in which *the good* moves from being the merely semantic opposite of Evil to becoming the dynamic overcoming of Evil, while *Evil*, in turn, moves from ending the good to being ended by the good. Both "concepts" become formulas of development that no longer allow for simple oppositions because what is inscribed in the semantics of the good now is being overcome by Evil (as present being) and is overcoming Evil (as the future that ought to be), and inscribed in Evil is the overcoming of the good (as present) and being overcome by the good (as future).

For the good, then, the temporal modes of the past and of the future are decisive: without the recollection of a past that is no longer and without hope for a future that ought to be, it is not possible to talk about the good. The decisive temporal mode for Evil, by contrast, is the present—albeit a present that is being referred to a past it has replaced but also to a future that will or ought to replace it. That is why we cannot talk about the good without looking at its being damaged by Evil (passively) and its overcoming of Evil (actively); and we cannot talk about Evil without thematizing its damaging of the good (actively) and its being overcome by the good (passively).

2. Advantages and Limitations of Mythical Life-Orientation

All these traits shape not only the biographies and narratives of the lives of individuals, they also characterize the myths in which shared experiences have long expressed themselves in ways that were the standards of a community.[1] Myths mark the horizon within which it is possible in a culture meaningfully to gain understanding and outside of which it is not.[2] They thus provide the hermeneutic guidelines by which attempts at understanding and agreement must be oriented for their questions and answers to remain comprehensible.

1. Klaus Koch is right to point to the "close connection between the sense experience of the world and mythical language" (Koch, "Vom Mythos zum Monotheismus im alten Israel," 98).

2. Burkert, *Savage Energies*; Vernant, *Mythe et religion en Grèce ancienne*; and Bremmer and Brodersen, *Götter, Mythen und Heiligtümer*. See also my *Jenseits von Mythos und Logos* and the contributions in Brandt and Schmidt, *Mythos und Mythologie*.

This also applies to dealing with the contradictions in which life is caught up when *kakon*, *malum*, or evil intrude in the form of ills, misfortune, disaster, injustice, misdeed, and so on. These contradictions are experienced as something that does not have to be, as something that has not always been thus in one's life and therefore is questionable and requires explanation: it is not necessary that these contradictions exist in life, at least not in these concrete forms in the concrete life of a specific human being. It is not necessary for anyone to experience the injustice of being cheated by their neighbors, even if it is not surprising that there is injustice in life in the first place, given that we obviously no longer live in a golden age. Evil in its various forms belongs to the reality of life. It can thus occur in each concrete life even if it does not have to occur in this life precisely or in this form. Yet when that which does not have to be but can be happens, it is experienced as something that is practically unavoidable: the elementary contingent experiences of Evil take place via occurrences that overtake a life in so unexpected or seemingly un-avoidable a manner that in them we experience ourselves as if surrendered to a foreign power. They do not have to exist, but we are surrendered to them. It is not by chance that the myths of traditional cultures symbolize these life experiences by telling of gods.

These myths of gods are not merely fabulistic play with possibilities, nor do they just develop merely fictional counterworlds. Gods are neither very imaginative fictions, nor are they independent transcendent realities; they are life experiences condensed in contingency formulas and interpreted according to a logic of action. Mythic narra-tives about gods thus have the life-hermeneutic and life-orienting function of making processes and events in human life comprehensible by interpreting them as the conse-quences of divine decisions and thus as *actions*. Human beings do not live in a world of blindly efficacious natural processes; they are woven into contexts of meaning that suggest and authorize inquiring not only into effective causes but into the meaning, purpose, and goal of events in their lives. For mythic experience and thought, events, including the seemingly senseless and incomprehensible happenings of Evil in human life, can always be read as actions that are due to decisions and that can therefore, in principle, be understood.[3]

Human beings thus live—and that is the achievement of these myths—in *a world that is in principle comprehensible*, even if that is often difficult and sometimes impossible to recognize, and even if what they can recognize makes clear to them, above all, that not they themselves but other powers and forces determine their lives.[4] By interpreting the world as a meaningfully ordered whole (cosmos), and human life as a nexus of actions and decisions whose principles can be found in the decisions and actions of the gods, myths do two things. On the one hand, they allow human beings to orient themselves in a seemingly chaotic world in a somewhat reliable way with regard to the gods. On the other hand, the reference to the decisions of the gods makes clear that human efforts at understanding can never go further than realizing that the contingency of human life is

3. Myths thereby determined the path the European experience of world has taken to this day. "Our idea of the world is the idea of a *comprehensible* world. It is the idea of a world in which we can under-stand *why* something is happening" (Bieri, *Das Handwerk der Freiheit*, 15).

4. See Graves, *Greek Myths*; Kirk, *Nature of Greek Myths*; Bremmer, *Interpretations of Greek Mythol-ogy*; and Bruit-Zaidman and Schmitt-Pantel, *Religion in the Ancient Greek City*.

founded on the contingency of divine decision-making.[5] What humans experience does in principle have a meaning, even if it may be difficult to recognize, but why it has this meaning, precisely, and no other, is ultimately unanswerable because humans can never get further than the divine decisions that make life this way and not otherwise. They know on the one hand why their life is the way it is (namely because of the decisions of the gods), but on the other hand, they also know that the reasons for these divine decisions are no longer accessible to them, be it because they are known to the gods alone, be it because they elude the gods themselves insofar as their divine decisions are bound by fate, which even the gods cannot evade. There are thus reasons that can be given for the contingencies of human life, namely, the decisions of the gods. For these divine contingencies, however, no more reasons can be given; these contingencies can, at most, be noted.

Within the horizon of the mythic orientation of life, the happenings of human life thus have a meaning, but why they have this meaning and not another remains obscure. In principle, humans can know why they are the way they are. But why they are *this* way, precisely, and not otherwise, they can in principle never know. The ultimate thing to know about human life within the horizon of the mythic orientation of life is that ultimately nothing can be known on this point. At the apex of its self-reflection, the mythic orientation of life flips over into Socratic philosophy. Yet prior to this apex, it in many ways allows for comprehendingly conducting oneself in the living of one's life toward what is incomprehensible in life, that is, for understanding it neither completely nor not at all but understanding it at least to the point of being able to live with what is senseless in life in a sufficiently meaningful way. The will to understand just must not be taken to the extreme of wanting to understand *everything*; but neither must meaninglessness go to extremes and become the experience that determines *everything*, for in both cases, the orienting force of mythic thought collapses. That is why the highest insight of thinking consists in learning to understand what one cannot understand: the questions concerning the limits of understanding are the beginning of philosophical thinking. And to this end, engaging with the Greek myths has become paradigmatic in Christian thinking as well.

3. The Mythic Detour via the Gods

Hesiod and Homer, Herodotus writes, "taught the Greeks the descent of the gods, and gave the gods their names, and determined their spheres and functions, and described their outward forms."[6] They thereby constructed the intellectual ordering context in which the Greeks oriented themselves as an order of the divine world according to kinship relations. In the form of gods, their family trees, and family relations, it became possible to inquire into and address the order of a reality experienced as threatening and chaotic. It is not a coincidence that the word *theos* is originally used in Greek as a predicate concept, not as a noun. It characterizes an event that brings order, structure,

5. See Burkert, *Savage Energies*.
6. Herodotus, *History*, 2.53.

calculability into the chaos of the experience of world. Where such order takes place in the chaos, the Greeks according to Károly Kerényi invoke *theos*, and where this happens, where the world proves to be *kosmos*, humans must speak in the terms of myth.[7]

The divine becomes a god who can be addressed where it brings order to a specific domain of life, bans the chaos, and turns this space into a cosmos. This makes this domain of reality reliable, and this precisely is what the community's public religious ritual recalls regularly.[8] Humans can deal with the god, even if in these dealings they always remain dependent on the unavailable god as guarantor of order. Thanks to the ordering god, fear of the chaos diminishes and confidence in the order of the cosmos grows. A domain of reality thus becomes a space of human action precisely by being thought as the space in which a god rules.[9]

Human life is lived in many domains. They all are characterized by something genuinely chaotic and threatening, be it the power of sensual love, sudden horror, the intoxication of wine, motherhood, the mystery of growth, or the order of communal life. In each of these domains, the Greeks recognize an ordering god who deprives it of its chaotic threat and makes it a space for human life. Aphrodite thus stands for the elementary power of sensual love, Hera for marital motherhood, Pan for panic horror, Dionysus for intoxication, Demeter for the growth of grain, and Athena for practical reason. Each of these divine figures stands for the ordering of a domain of reality and possibility in the world, but taken all together, they stand for the world as a whole, for the world as cosmos. That, precisely, is the reason for their permanent conflict. Later criticism has mocked the constant fighting on Mount Olympus. But conflicts like the one between Hera and Aphrodite are emblematic of the elementary and continual tension between two realities that cannot be sublated into each other. The conflicts of the gods signal elementary tensions of human reality. And just as Zeus, the father of gods and humans, time and again must arduously defuse the conflicts between the gods, so the oppositionality of the world can be held together only in ever-renewed processes of obtaining unity.

Within this horizon of orientation, we also find attempts to understand the contradictions that are due to the intrusion of Evil in human life. By themselves, these contradictions are irrational and incomprehensible. Relating to them meaningfully requires detours that allow for rendering the incomprehensible comprehensible.[10] The mythic narratives about the gods in Homeric culture try to do so by tracing the contradictions in human life back to divine decisions: what humans suffer has been allotted to them by the gods whose life, in contrast, is free of such contradictions. "For on this wise have the gods spun the thread for wretched mortals, that they should live in pain; and themselves

---

7. Kerényi, *Griechische Grundbegriffe*, 17–18, and "Theos: 'Gott' auf Griechisch."

8. See Parker, *Athenian Religion*, esp. chs. 4–7.

9. In this sense, the gods of the Greeks are "portfolio gods," that is, "*innerworldly* suprahuman powers thought to be personal and intelligent," as Harald Patzer rightly stresses (Patzer, "Die dichterischen Formgesetze der Gattung 'Tragödie,'" 488).

10. This does mean trying to obtain, *per impossibile*, sense from the senseless; it can also mean relating *to the senseless* in a way that makes sense and living in a way that makes sense *in being confronted with the senseless*.

are sorrowless."[11] It is the contrast, precisely, between the human world and the world of the gods that makes this point.[12] Unlike human beings, who live only a short life, mostly in misery, and no sooner flourish than they are carried off, the gods live without aging and in eternal youth. They are distinguished by the beauty and greatness of their appearance, by the strength and knowledge of their mind, and they live free of suffering on the ethereal heights of Mount Olympus. There are no worries there and no pain, no old age, no infirmity, and no death, and when the gods fight—and they do so often and violently, especially because they favor different human beings and peoples—it does not last too long. At the end of the day, they gather serenely and joyfully feast together. The lived contradictions of human life are thus made comprehensible by being traced back to the gods to whose intrigues they are due, but in that world, unlike in the world of the humans, they do not leave any permanent traces but time and again dissolve in the all-reconciling serenity of the gods' Olympian world.

It has not always been this way. The world of the gods, too, has not always been sheer pleasure alone. Zeus, the Greek myths tell us, dethroned his father Chronos and the titans and confined them to the darkness of Tartarus.[13] At this point, the history of the gods links up with the history of humans, as narrated exemplarily by the myth of Prometheus.[14]

Prometheus, the brother of Atlas and Epimetheus, is said to have been one of the most ingenious titans. He created the human beings and always helped them. In the struggle between Zeus and Chronos, he foresaw the result and preferred fighting on the side of Zeus. He persuaded his brother Epimetheus to do the same. One day, a fight broke out in Sicyon about which part of an ox was to be sacrificed to the gods and which part consumed. Prometheus was asked to act as arbiter. He dismembered the ox, and from its skin he sewed two sacks. In one of them, he placed all the meat, hidden in the stomach, in the other, all the bones, hidden under a rich layer of fat. He offered Zeus the choice. Zeus chose the sack with the bones and fat (which has since been the share of the gods). Prometheus laughed at him, and out of anger, Zeus punished him by taking fire away from the humans, shouting, "Let them eat their meat raw!" Yet Prometheus, with Athena's help, succeeded in stealing fire from the sun's chariot on Mount Olympus and gave it to the humans. Since then, humans have had that without which there could be no culture: fire.

Zeus took revenge. He ordered Hephaestus to form from clay a woman who was then adorned by all goddesses on Mount Olympus: Pandora. This woman he sent as a gift to Epimetheus. Warned by his brother, Epimetheus refused the gift. Angrily, Zeus chained Prometheus naked to a column in the Caucasian mountains, where day by day, a vulture eats from his liver, which grows back every night. Prometheus thus suffers endless pain. Shocked by his brother's fate, Epimetheus married Pandora, whom Zeus had made stupid, malicious, and lazy. As Hesiod presents it, it is from her that women descend who are nothing but a source of suffering for men. She opened a little box that

11. Homer, *Iliad*, 24.525–26.
12. See Otto, *Homeric Gods*, 129.
13. Homer, *Iliad* 14.203–78, 8.479; in more detail, Hesiod, *Theogony*.
14. See Graves, *Greek Myths*, 1:143–49.

Epimetheus had received from Prometheus along with the warning to keep it closed. Prometheus had confined there all the ills that afflict humanity: old age, labor pains, sickness, madness, vices, passions. They all immediately escaped the box, attacked Epimetheus and Pandora, and have since then plagued all mortals. According to this myth, then, as Wolfgang Schadewaldt points out, suffering, evil, and illness are attributed to the most beautiful of human possessions, to culture. They are the flipside, as it were, without which there is no culture. According to Hesiod, only hope, which could have helped humans deal with the ills, remained in the box. With culture, then, not only did all Evil enter the world through human stupidity; at the same time, the one thing that allows for living with Evil in the world did not: hope.

4. Good and Evil among the Gods

Yet even the gods do not simply stand above all evil. They do not suffer but do evil. They argue and fight with each other, lie to and cheat each other, seek to take advantage of each other and to impose their interest against the others' among the humans, and in all this they time and again inflict evil on human beings. In that sense, the gods are one-sidedly free from evil: unlike human beings, they do not suffer from it. Inversely, this means that while the gods are serene, without age, and immortal, no Olympian is only and exclusively good. They all have their often rather dubious origin and past, they can behave this way or that, and none of them is a stranger to the difference between good and evil.

This asymmetry of being able to do but not to suffer evil, however, is not the only remarkable thing with regard to the gods here. They are all also subject to fate (*moira*), and their domains are clearly limited. They cannot do everything but are limited to the domain of life whose ideal order they represent: Poseidon to the sea, Hera to motherhood, Aphrodite to love, Artemis to hunting, and so on. Above all, however, no god can act beyond death or bring someone back from death to life. Beyond death lies the realm of shadows, and there even the Olympian gods of life have no say.

That is why recourse to them allows for orientation in life only up to a point. Insofar as a domain of life can be addressed in a specific god, the human being can orient itself in its weakness and its being surrendered to the powers of nature; for example, because they know that in a storm at sea, the one to call on for help is Poseidon (and not Hermes or Pan). But this orientation is always precarious. A god can at any time also become an opponent, and among the Olympian gods, there is always some game being played. In that regard, only those can rely on a god who know the current constellation among the gods, and no one mortal does so sufficiently.

Yet even if one knows what gods to turn to in what life situation, their competence is limited not only by subject matter but in time as well. With death, it definitively reaches its end. Here at the latest, it becomes evident that the life of human beings is determined not only by the Olympian gods but by the *power of fate* as well. While the gods, despite all ambivalence, are there to help humans and thus essentially stand on the side of the good, with fate things are the other way around:

Sometimes it may appear that the decree of fate [necessity, *ananke*—IUD] allots some positive good to man; but from the totality of its functions there can be no doubt that its character is not positive but negative. It sets a boundary to limit duration, catastrophe to limit prosperity, death to limit life. Catastrophe, cessation, limitation, all forms of "so far and no farther," are forms of death. And death is itself the prime meaning of fate [imposed by Moira].[15]

Death thus depends not on the gods but on another power.[16] That is why the Olympian gods in their fullness of life simply do not have anything to do with death, and their effective power is limited to life. Unlike humans, the gods know what Fate has determined. Yet they cannot stop the course of things, they cannot prevent or reverse fate. They can only lament: "Behold! The gods weep, all the goddesses weep, / That the beautiful perishes, that the most perfect passes away."[17] When Fate arrives, the gods must step aside. Their power over human life is limited to the restricted span of human life. When Fate wills to end it, the gods must yield.[18]

Remarkably, Fate in Homer is *never a person or personality*. It is an ungraspable power, the idea of an inviolable order of death that even the living and personal gods cannot unsettle but must respect. "Death is determined for all living things, and on this principle even the power of the gods is frustrated." In that regard, Fate "denotes the negative in the world of life, whereas deity denotes the positive."[19]

The basic opposition that determines everything and characterizes the life-orientation of Greek myths is thus the one between the *realm of life* and the *realm of death*. Yet in the figure of "allotting" Fate, this realm of death projects into life, while inversely, the power of the gods does not reach into the realm of death. Not the gods' Olympian serenity is thus the more fundamental and more comprehensive, the truly dominant reality in the world but the negative, that which refers to death. In the realm of life, it is only pushed back, into the margins, into the background. But it is there and will ultimately be determining, while life is only a passing brightening in this all-comprehensive darkness.

Viewed this way, the Homeric religion of Olympian gods is a great and simultaneously futile protestation against death. It focuses entirely on the light side of life but always against the background of this night side. And because it knows that death can ultimately not be eliminated and overcome, its serenity is shot through with a tragic melancholy that, as a kind of *basso continuo*, accompanies the joy of life and pleasure of existence it celebrates.

---

15. Otto, *Homeric Gods*, 264–65.

16. As dark powers of determining death, the *moirai*, daughters of Zeus and Themis, belong to the old Earth religion displaced by the revolt of the Olympians. See Otto, *Homeric Gods*, 266–67.

17. Schiller, "Nänie."

18. Otto, *Homeric Gods*, 273.

19. Otto, *Homeric Gods*, 276–77.

5. Good Gods and Evil Gods

It takes just a small step, and "this counter-play of light and dark can turn into a definite dualism."[20] In Homeric religion, the negative falls like a shadow into life, and therefore comes into view *in life* only as darkening or deficiency—that will be the point where the *privatio boni* tradition sets in. But here already, a suspicion remains active that it could be the other way around, that the light is only flaring up briefly in the dark, that life is only an interruption of death, that being is only a flareup in nonbeing. The opposed tendencies stabilize in a basic opposition when oriental religions introduce to Greece a strict dualism that distinguishes between the competence of certain *gods for Good* and certain *gods for Evil*. In the permanent struggle of these gods against each other, the experience of contradiction in human life continues on the level of divine powers. For just as the good gods are responsible for the good in human life, so the evil gods are responsible for Evil in human life. Human life is thus not only defined by divine decisions of limited scope; it is also the arena of the conflict between competing and fighting divine decisions. The human being does not only execute the decisions of the gods; as long as Fate permits, it becomes the place where the gods' permanent fight plays out.

The myths of Homeric epic show that and how the gods of Greece each are responsible for different domains of existence. They represent these domains in such a way that humans seeking help can turn to them when they want to survive the manifold threats to life. In confronting the intrusion of Evil and the contradictions of life, the recourse to the gods thus allows for orientation in life in the service of life, and at the same time, the detour via the gods leads to a fundamental religious alternative. Either the gods move entirely to the side of the good, light, and positive and must thus be opposed to a dark negative power (Moira, Fate), because human life is determined by both the positive and the negative, and also and especially because with death, the negative will win in the end. Or positive and negative gods are being opposed to each other. Then divine events become events of a permanent conflict between Good and Evil. This entails the hermeneutic gain of being able to represent and narratively treat of Evil at all, by describing the contradictoriness of human life once more among the gods and discussing them in the mode of divine competencies. At the same time, it has the problematic consequence of, as it were, eternalizing Evil in the conflict between the gods, unless the one side carries off a definitive victory.

The orientation provided by the Greek myths, in contrast, consists of two things. On the one hand, they point humans to a state that makes it clear that life does not have to be the way humans experience it. On the other hand, they bring out that even Evil is not simply the opposite of the world's good order but belongs, along with the gods as its opposite, to the whole of the cosmos. Just as Evil does not have to be, so it is not just the other of the cosmos. Mythic thinking, rather, tries precisely to give expression to the whole by way of contrasts, to articulate it as heaven and earth, day and night, good and evil. This is a considerable achievement of rationalization and orientation: the world is not a blind chaos but a structured whole of opposition and order that can guide the living of life. We are not surrendered to an ungraspable and therefore only threatening

20. Otto, *Homeric Gods*, 285.

manifold but live our life in a structured unity, presented as the unity of Good and Evil in the whole of the world.

This allows for orienting oneself in the world, but only at first sight: where gods are in charge of good and evil, and where there are good and evil goods, we must stick with the right ones at the right moment and know how to keep the others away. On closer consideration, myths' orienting achievement does not solve the problems, it intensifies them and aggravates the experience of our powerlessness: we are now dealing not only with ills in our lives but moreover also with evil gods. Where there are only good and evil gods toying with us, what is revolting about this life is traced back to the life of the gods, but it is not eliminated or stopped: there is a *shifting of the problem* that cannot satisfy in the long run.

Two possible solutions suggest themselves. One may try and remove the ambivalence by amplifying the divine to become the entirely and exclusively good and opposing it as the One to the Many in such a way as to contrast it, the one Good and the good One, to the Many, a mixture of good and evil—that is the path of Platonic monism. Or one may turn the ambivalence into a principle and dissolve the unity of the cosmos in an ultimate duality that thinks the opposition of cosmos and chaos not only as potential contradiction and permanent threat of order by chaos but as the struggle between two irreconcilable realities—that is the path of Manichean dualism. Both are paths thinking has taken to be able to deal with the experience of Evil and the oppositions thereby erupting.

6. Tragedy and Theory

Paths of thinking exist only in the plural, they unfold in exploring possibilities and weighing alternatives, and they are rarely taken in thinking alone, especially when they are intended to be taken by others as well. In Greek antiquity, too, attempts at developing a differentiated conception of and relation to Evil by reflecting on individual and collective experiences of Evil are not restricted to the philosophical tradition alone. Instead, philosophical theory and Attic tragedy take characteristically different paths.

Attic tragedy explores the existential implications of the mythic tradition by elaborating myths' anthropological aporias and presenting the unavoidable tragedy of human existence in a life determined by an other in a way that is comprehensible for viewers and that they can experience for themselves.[21] It positively takes up the mythic tradition as a reservoir of images and problems and treats of suffering, entanglement, blindness, catastrophe, guilt, and death, in other words, of evil that is unavoidable in an existence subject to the inscrutable action of alien powers. Evil is less the intentionally committed evil deed of individual human beings than it is the tragedy of being entangled in supra-individual inevitabilities no human life can evade.

This entanglement in tragically suffered inevitabilities leads to an experience of life that, along with knowledge about an order of the whole entirely ungraspable for human

---

21. See Bierl, *Dionysos und die griechische Tragödie*; Zimmermann, *Greek Tragedy*; Latacz, *Einführung in die griechische Tragödie*; and Schmitt, "Wesenszüge der griechischen Tragödie."

beings, includes human self-knowledge as knowledge of a being pathically exposed and surrendered to the consequences of its being entangled in the incomprehensible and the inscrutable. This is the foundation of the proverbial connection of *pathein* and *mathein*.[22] This connection of suffering and learning is not a coincidence but an eternal law for the human being. Aeschylus traces it back to Zeus himself, "who sets mortals on the path to understanding, Zeus, who has established as a fixed law that 'wisdom comes by suffering.'"[23] Through pain and agony, the human is brought to acknowledge the order of the world and its laws, which humans did not make and cannot govern but in which they are inextricably caught up.[24]

This insight echoes in Plato's theory of the soul in two ways.[25] On the one hand, the theory of affects in the *Gorgias* instrumentalizes it rhetorically insofar as speech is meant not to intellectually teach the listener but pathically move him, that is, prod him in the direction desired by the speaker through the production of *pathēmata* in the soul. *Pathos* is thus coupled with inciting and exciting the imagination and thereby attributed to a specific faculty of the soul. This undoubtedly reduces the tragic experience of entanglement and suffering to a rhetorically produced passion.

Yet that is only one of the ways in which Attic tragedy's insight into *pathos* continues to have an effect in Plato. For, on the other hand, he takes it up and reworks it in his theory of poetry. Poets, he says in the *Ion*, do not sing "by art . . . but by divine influence," they are "merely the interpreters of the gods" and "possessed."[26] Entirely in keeping with this point, art in the *Phaedrus* is said to arise from enthusiasm, from "being-in-God," which is one of the four kinds of divine madness (*deia mania*), beside the religious-cathartic, philosophical, and prophetic mania.[27] In all these kinds of divine madness, humans find themselves surrendered to something other than themselves.[28] This can be read as a philosophical continuation of the tragic experience of being caught up in a decreed fate to which the human is surrendered. Yet it can also be read as a theory of the soul attributing to the human the special ability of the soul to experience, precisely in *pathos*, the highest insight and divine wisdom. The soul's power of imagination is the place where the human being is not itself sensibly or intellectually active but open to being determined by the divine. It is not by coincidence that ancient theories of the prophetic picked up on this point, theories then taken up in Islam, medieval Christianity, and the Renaissance.[29] The soul's faculty of imagination is not arbitrary fantasy and unfounded

22. See Dörrie, *Leid und Erfahrung*, 10–17, 312–19.

23. Aeschylus, *Agamemnon*, ll. 176–78.

24. See Reinhardt, *Aischylos als Regisseur und Theologe*, and Taplin, *Stagecraft of Aeschylus*.

25. According to Bremmer, *Early Greek Concept of the Soul*, the Greeks prior to Homer knew of two souls: a *free* soul that had no psychological predicates, acted outside of the body, and became apparent in dreams, for example, and a *body-soul* that endowed a person with life and consciousness. The two amalgamated in a single concept of the soul only gradually, as the philosophical doctrine of a soul differentiated into different faculties exemplarily shows.

26. Plato, *Ion*, 534c, e.

27. Plato, *Phaedrus*, 249b–250e:155–57.

28. See Pieper, *Begeisterung und göttlicher Wahnsinn*.

29. For the reception of these theories in Al-Farabi, Avicenna, and Averroes, see Kermani, *Gott ist schön*, 335–56; for the middle ages, see Decker, *Die Entwicklung der Lehre von der prophetischen*

construction but the place where in the *pathos* of enthusiasm, a comprehensive reality is being experienced that is more than what people in their everyday lives are able to perceive through their senses and grasp with their intellect. It consists in being overpowered by something against which we cannot protest but which we experience ourselves as surrendered to. This is not the least of reasons why the Stoics later considered the soul's *pathēma* to be not a mode of knowing reality but the irrational mode in which dependences, which the wise man was to liberate himself from, entered into life.

Against the background of the entanglement without guilt of excellent humans in particular in supraindividual inevitabilities that Attic tragedy reflected, evil was conceived of less as the intentionally committed evil deed of individuals than as a tragic fate humans cannot evade.[30] Philosophy sees it differently. It does not dispute that human life is tied into nexuses its actions cannot influence. But while in acting, we are bound by the inevitabilities of life, in thinking, we can rise above them. In a critical reaction against myth and tragedy, philosophy is concerned with overcoming, through theoretical contemplation, suffering in a life that does not contest the reality of suffering in the world but changes our attitude toward it. To be able to live well in a world of suffering, we must understand what Evil is and how it can be part of the cosmos.

The answer given in the wake of Plato is a philosophical theory of the good as the beyond of all being (*to epekeina tōn ontōn*) and the corresponding ontological theory of Evil as that which itself is really nothing but can be determined only as a deficit, as a lack of being. The purely Good must exist because otherwise, nothing would exist at all. The merely Evil cannot exist because it itself is nothing. Between these two poles, our human existence unfolds. For us, then, everything that exists is determined by the Good, without which it would not be, and damaged by Evil, without which it would not be the way it is. The former makes it capable of improvement, the latter worthy of improvement. And this why we ought to be what we can be (good) and not remain what we do not have to be (evil).

Behind this stands the experience of the world as cosmos, as a whole of well-ordered opposites, constantly threatened by the intrusion of the chaos that could destroy this cosmos. The fundamental task of philosophical theory then consists in knowing the reasons to which good order and disorder in the world are due, that is—in Parmenides's terms—to distinguish what is from what is not in order not to confuse truth and being with opinion and appearance. Human life and the cosmos are shaped by the fundamental difference between that which is, is true, and is good, and that which only appears to be, is not true, and is not good. The former is what is constant, permanent, and thereby truly actual and good, the latter what is variable, transient, apparent, and evil.

Offenbarung, 13–29; and for the Renaissance, see Curtius, *European Literature and the Latin Middle Ages,* 372–78.

30. Patzer is right to point out that the issue is "not so much a *'guilt'* that demands its *'punishment'* than an objective disruption of the divine order that inevitably makes the perpetrator 'susceptible to reparation.' . . . 'Tragic guilt' thus has a double aspect. It is incurred by someone who has committed a violation of a divine law, which according to *divine* law makes him 'susceptible to revenge,' while according to *human* law, he must be considered innocent and may indeed have simultaneously committed the deed in obedience to another divine law" (Patzer, "Die dichterischen Formgesetze der Gattung 'Tragödie,'" 490).

The question to be answered in thinking, accordingly, is how, given this difference, the unity of the cosmos can be preserved. How is it possible to distinguish the true from the false, good from evil, the constant from the transient? If "[t]his is the same: to think and the thought that 'is,'"[31] then being and appearance, truth and falsity, and good evil can be distinguished in thought by showing appearance, falseness, and evil to be incompatible with being, truth, and good. The good is the standard of Evil, and that is why we must first come to know the good to be able to uncover Evil.

This is the basic notion Plato stringently develops in his philosophy. In doing so, he does not take up either the mythic tradition or the critique of myth in the philosophy of nature directly but, following the Socratic reorientation of philosophical thinking, critically turns against both. The new methodological approach of Socratic philosophizing consisted in the insight that true knowledge of the world can be had only via the path of self-knowledge. To know why the world is the way it appears to us, we must know who we are, we to whom it appears this way. Reasons are never only reasons *for something* but also always *for someone*. Those who do not know who they are cannot know whether they really know the reason for something or not. Only self-knowledge offers the criteria for doing so. Yet self-knowledge cannot be obtained from knowledge of the human being as part of the nexus of nature, which persists in a third-person perspective and sees the human as a "something" of a specific kind. It can only be gleaned from the human inquiry into itself as self-knowledge that manifests itself in the life of the soul and is expressed in the first person. Only a logos that is grounded in the pathos and ethos of the soul and thus knows that the human soul is referred to a reality beyond itself not just in the knowledge of ideas but also in the enthusiasm of the imagination, can reliably bring out the difference between being and appearance, truth and untruth, good and evil.

7. From Mythology to Theology

In rigorously following this path, Plato develops a philosophical theology that is not a continuation of mythology by other means but arises from a criticism of both the mythological tradition and the pre-Socratic critique of myth. From the outset, then, theology in European thinking is a critical counterproject to mythology, opposing the mythic theory of gods with a cosmologically founded theory of God.

In its very first known appearance already, the concept *theology* stands in a telling contrast to the concept *myth*. Likely the oldest instance of *theologia* occurs in a passage in the *Republic*, which outlines Plato's ideal state, that discusses the right education of the children destined to join the ranks of the guardians.[32] Socrates stresses to his interlocutor, Adeimantus, that their education must begin not with gymnastics but with music because the soul must be formed before the body. He answers the question whether "music" also includes "narratives" (*logoi*) by pointing out that children indeed are formed by true and false *logoi* but first of all by false ones: the first thing they are told

---

31. Parmenides in Laks and Most, *Early Greek Philosophy,* 5.2.3–151, here D8.39:47.
32. Plato, *Republic* II:379a:223.

generally is stories (*mythoi*) that, "though not wholly destitute of truth, are in the main fictitious."[33]

This poses a problem that is always a delicate one for state planners. Especially in educating children, getting off to the right start is decisive if the "young and tender thing[s]" are not to be spoilt from the outset. It is thus not to be permitted that in listening to random myths, children let opinions enter their souls that are "the very opposite of those which we shall wish them to have when they are grown up." State planners must therefore exercise strict supervision over the mythopoets who compose the myths. According to Socrates, from the pedagogical point of view, many of the myths currently told are to be rejected. Most of the myths Hesiod, Homer, and the other poets present are pedagogically dangerous because they depict the gods as entangled in immoral actions. It is not exactly helpful for those who are to defend the city and "to regard the habit of quarrelling among themselves as of all things the basest" to hear about "the wars in heaven, and of the plots and fightings of the gods against one another." Nor does "the narrative of Hephaestus binding Hera his mother, or how on another occasion Zeus sent him flying for taking her part when she was being beaten" really impress upon the children the behavior expected of them in the family. This is—how could it be otherwise—where the legislator must step in. A pedagogical framework is needed, critical outlines of the right kind of stories about the gods (*typoi peri theologias*) that mythopoets and mythologists have to abide by. These types have to present God in such a way as he essentially is, namely good and perfect in every respect, that is, precisely not entangled in immoral actions. That is why their basic rule is that "the good is to be attributed to God alone; of the evils the causes are to be sought elsewhere, and not in him."[34]

The *theologiai* at issue here are thus none other than the myths of the gods told by the poets in their epics, songs, and tragedies.[35] These narratives must be critically evaluated if they are to fulfill their pedagogical function. While they are lying discourses, their vividness gives them an important role in the formation of children's souls. To ensure this purpose, according to Plato, the mythopoets or mythologists need critical outlines of the right type of stories about the gods that can function as paradigms for them. There is no distinction made yet between theologians and mythologists.[36] Both are being opposed to the philosophers who, as founders of the state, are forced to deal critically with the tales about the gods always already abounding. The point of this critical conduct is apparent in the drift of Plato's argumentation, which, starting from mythopoets and mythologists, is directed, via theoilogists, at theologians.[37] Thus Socrates initially talks about the *mythopoioi*, the makers of myths who compose new myths, "lesser" ones in comparison to the "greater tales" presented by Hesiod and Homer.[38] Socrates thus distinguishes between the mythopoet and the mythologist, between the inventor of new myths and the herald of old myths. Yet he does not admit the traditional *mythologia* without

33. Plato, *Republic* II:377a4–6:221.

34. Plato, *Republic* II:377b–379c:221–24 [modified].

35. Plato, *Republic* II:379a8–9:223.

36. Compare Aristotle, *Metaphysics*, I:983b29:1556, III:1000a9:1579, XII:1071b27:1693.

37. Kerényi, *Griechische Grundbegriffe*, 12–13.

38. Plato, *Republic* II:377c7–d6:221.

restrictions, either. It is, first—as indicated by the phrase, *typoi peri theologias*—restricted to that which refers to the gods. Not struggles between giants and the exploits of heroes are objects of a pedagogically responsible mythology but narratives about the gods: the *mytho*logist must become a *theoi*logist. Yet the narratives about the gods, too, require critical review. They must conform to the critical *typoi* that in turn have their standard in how *the God* (*o deos*) is.[39] Only where there is *theology* in the strict sense of speech about *the God* can there be a pedagogically acceptable mythic speech about *the gods*, *theoilogy*. Such a speech about God as distinct from speech about the gods, however, is the reserve of philosophers and thus of the logos. It alone is able to provide not only a problematic theory of the gods but a true theory of God. Without the philosophical theology elaborated by the logos, there can thus be no acceptable poetic theoilogy elaborated by myth. Only philosophical theology makes it possible to deal with mythology critically.

Plato's pedagogically motivated concept of theology thus represents an agenda of demythification with two emphases. On the one hand, it restricts traditional mythology to that which refers to the gods. On the other hand, the stories about the gods must be guided by critical *typoi* whose standard is the way the God is. The stories about the gods, therefore, are not the result of a critical reduction of traditional mythology to its rational core but pre-given paradigms necessary in order to be able to discover such a core in the first place. That is why they cannot be obtained via a rational historical or allegorical interpretation of traditional mythology. That—as the Socrates of the *Phaedrus* emphasizes—can at best lead to a confused variety of probabilities but not to knowledge of the truth. Instead, the philosopher—and this constitutes a Socratic metacritique of the pre-Socratic critique of myth—must first attain knowledge of the logos, and thus also of true theology, via the path of self-knowledge. Only then can he discern in myths, too, the truth they contain.

8. From the Gods to the Idea of the Good

Plato, Aristotle says in the overview of the history of philosophy that opens his *Metaphysics*, started from Socrates's inquiry into the general and his search for definitions and had reached the conclusion that definitions

> applied not to any sensible thing but to entities of another kind—for this reason, that the common definition could not be a definition of any sensible thing, as they were always changing. Things of this other sort, then, he called Ideas [*ideai tōn ontōn*], and sensible things, he said, were apart from these, and were all called after these; for the multitude of things which have the same name as the Form exist by participation [*metexis*] in it.[40]

Plato thus follows Socrates in turning from nature to soul and thereby also in his striving for knowledge of the true as knowledge of the general. We cannot reach such knowledge on the path of sense perception since everything perceptible by the senses is subject to change, to becoming and passing away. What is true and generally valid, by contrast,

39. Plato, *Republic* II:379a7:223.
40. Aristotle, *Metaphysics* I.6, 987b5–11:1561.

must be invariable and abiding. Yet what is invariably and abidingly true cannot be perceived by the senses, it can only be grasped in thinking or contemplated in the mind. Those who seek to know it must liberate themselves from being determined by the body and fully enter onto the path of the soul. This path leads—via the four levels of knowledge that are conjectural knowledge through the hearing of words, sense knowledge through perceiving of one's own, intellectual knowledge in concepts, and rational knowledge through insight into the being of the ideas—to the ideas as the originary images in the mind for everything that is, and at their summit, the idea of the Good. The ideas are the true causes of what sense objects really are. When we seek to know a specific object the way it is, we must heed not the phenomenal aspects of the individual thing (for example, a human being) but the ideas (for example, humanity) that make this object what it is and to which definitions refer.

Such knowledge is possible because there exists, between the idea(s) and individual phenomena, a causal relationship that Plato describes with concepts such as "participation," "depiction," "imitation," or "communion." Each thing is what it is on the basis of the ideas that it represents more or less perfectly. When Plato calls these ideas in themselves true or existent, then this does not mean that the idea of humanity, for example, possessed a higher degree of existence than the individual human being. What it means, rather, is that humanity, for example, is human to a more perfect degree than individual human beings since the latter, because of their participation in other ideas, are always simultaneously something else (for example, black, white, short, tall, and so on). That is why Plato can emphatically call the idea that which really is, that itself which is (*ontōs on*), where "is" can be read as predicate or as copula. The ideas are thus the principle of unity for their respective domain of variety. The complex idea (that is, composed of different distinguishable ideas) "humanity," for example, is the principle of the unity of the variegated and different human beings, that is, that which all these share despite all their differences and makes them human beings.

Plato thus conceives of all the phenomena of our world of experience as effects of causes and thus looks at them from two sides. As composite, and that means decomposable, variable, and visible, individual phenomena, they are what they are because and insofar as they participate, each in determinate ways, in non-composite, that is, indestructible, invariable, and invisible ideas. The ideas are thus being granted divine attributes. The attributes of self-identity and unity especially show the connection between Plato's conception of ideas and Parmenides's teachings. Plato, though, now conceives of what truly is in the plural and no longer opposes it abstractly to not-being as that which is not in this way: the ideas are the principles of the variable individual things. Just as there are no phenomena without ideas, so there are no ideas independently of phenomena. To speak of causes without there being effects would make no sense, and neither would speaking of effects without there being causes.

That is why dualistically attributing a two-world theory to Plato misses his point. The separation of invariable ideas and variable phenomena does not mark a difference between an intelligible and a phenomenal world but two aspects of the objects of our world of experience: that which they are (ideas) and that as which they appear to us (phenomena). These aspects relate to each other in such a way that ideas are to their corresponding individual phenomena as an "original" is to its "copy."[41]

It remains unclear, though, how exactly this copy-relation is to be defined. How do individual things participate in their ideas? Is there something that connects them? If there is to be similarity between original and copy, it seems that some kind of link must exist. Yet such similarity mediated via a third can exist only between objects of the same type, and that, precisely, is not the case here: humanity is not a human being, wisdom is not wise, the idea is another, namely an abstract type of object over against concrete individual phenomena.

Plato does not succeed in fully clarifying this point because he is able only ever to understand every relation between two entities as participation (which blurs the difference in type) in a third that they share. Yet supposing that an idea F and the individual phenomenon F are F only because of a shared third F obviously leads to an infinite regress. If, however, we interpret the relation of participation not as similarity but as an element-class relation (for example, the individual human being is an element of the class of human beings), then the idea (humanity) is an abstract object but not a general essence, since classes, like concrete individual objects, are individualities, albeit abstract ones. In Plato's concept of the idea, then, two differential relations combine in an unclear way: the opposition of *the individual and the universal* (predicable being), and the opposition of *the concrete and the abstract* (ideal being). For this very reason, it remains obscure what kind of relation connects idea and individual thing.

Because of the amalgamation of the problem of abstractness and the problem of universality, the separation Plato asserts of idea and individual phenomenon, too, raises problems. On the one hand, knowledge is always knowledge of what is universal, general, invariable, true, timeless, and necessary, that is, it is knowledge of ideas. On the other hand, all knowledge implies something that knows, namely the soul. The soul belongs neither to the phenomena nor to the ideas but is, over against them, a third. Since it does not obtain its knowledge via perception but via knowledge of the ideas relevant in each case, the soul can either always already know or it can know nothing at all. Under these conditions, Plato can only explain that we know something by means of his theory of *anamnesis*: there must have been an originary state in which the soul, independently of all perception, that is, separated from the body and its functions of sense perception, has "viewed" the ideas; it has forgotten this again upon entering a body; but what it has forgotten represents a potential of knowledge that can be activated by snatching what has been known from oblivion; and this, precisely, is what all of the soul's learning and knowing consists in.

This has a series of momentous consequences. First, this conception presupposes the pre- and post-existence of the soul, which Plato, accordingly, professes in the *Phaedo*. Second, this argumentation demonstrates that Plato constructs knowledge in analogy with perception. Yet knowing that something is true or false is different from perceiving an object. Perception is relative to an object ("I perceive something as something"); knowledge is propositional ("I know that p"). When knowledge is understood to be a

---

41. Plato, *Timaeus*, 29a:715; see also Runia, *Philo of Alexandria and the 'Timaeus' of Plato*, and Verweyen, *Philosophie und Theologie*, 80–85.

non-sensible kind of perception, ideas must be (abstract) objects and cannot be universal concepts (which can be predicated in judgments). The recourse to ideas, therefore, does not solve the problem of truth in knowing concrete individual phenomena; moreover, the problem is raised in addition, and in a different form, in the context of knowing abstract individual things as well.

Third, while the soul must be distinguished from the ideas as the organ to know them, it must also somehow resemble these invariable, eternal, indestructible entities, for otherwise it could not come to know them at all. It belongs neither to the phenomena nor to the ideas, it is a third over against them. Just as, for Plato, the body resembles the transient individual things, so the soul resembles the abiding ideas, and from their abiding nature, as the arguments of the *Phaedo* seek to show, their immortality and eternity follow immediately.

Finally, human beings have a soul only in their bodies. Their knowledge, accordingly, is as distinct from the ideal knowledge of ideas as individual phenomena are distinct from the idea. Only God himself can completely know the truth of the ideas, as Plato demonstrates in the *Parmenides*, whereas humans can know them only approximately.[42] Since God, however, can know the ideas but because of the separation cannot know individual things, human knowledge, referring to individual phenomena, and divine knowledge, aiming at universal truth, are fundamentally different.

The knowledge of ideas can thus not be constructed in analogy with knowledge of individual phenomena. The ideas are not simply juxtaposed, without connection, but are organized into groups of ideas or in a pyramid of ideas.[43] This organization is such that hierarchical relations exist between (to use later terminology) genus, species, and individual concepts (e.g., plant/tree/fir) and such that the highest of the basic ideas (being, movement, rest, the same, the different; Aristotle will speak of "categories") join to form a cosmos structured by connection and separation.[44] To know something, it is thus necessary to reconstruct the inner connection of ideas that is relevant to a specific state of affairs, and this is done by applying the method of *diairesis*, that is, by classifying a concept completely according to its species and subspecies.

Ultimately, the entire cosmos of ideas is constituted by an idea that is superordinate to all other ideas as their basic principle: the *idea of the Good*. For Plato, this is an ontological and epistemological, not only (as it is for Socrates) an ethical principle. "[T]hat which imparts truth to the known and the power of knowing to the knower is . . . the Idea of the Good . . . what is known receives from the Good not only its being known but its very being and essence, although the Good itself is not being but exceeds being in dignity and power."[45] The good is beyond being. As such, it neither can be fully grasped by thinking nor does it belong as an idea to the cosmos of ideas. It therefore is not really correct to call it an "idea," and Plato also calls it "brightest and best of being."[46] It is not completely withdrawn from knowledge but can be known as precisely that which

42. Plato, *Parmenides*, 134c:679.

43. Plato, *Parmenides*, 130a–c:672–3.

44. Plato, *Sophist*, 245e–255e:397–410.

45. Plato, *Republic* VI:508e–509b:371 [modified].

46. Plato, *Republic* VII:518c.

cannot be known and can be said as that which cannot be said. It is an entity captured sufficiently neither in the mathematical construction of *dianoia* nor in the conceptual dialectic of *noēsis*; it is the originary principle to which every attempt at foundation must ultimately take recourse and from which the entire cosmos of ideas can be derived.

The good is thus something that lies beyond being and knowledge, it is the Unsayable One that can be claimed as the Good but cannot itself be said: "the one is not at all," we read in the *Parmenides*. "[T]he one does not exist in such way as to be one; for if it were and partook of being, it would already be; but if the argument is to be trusted, the one neither is nor is one. . . . [T]here is no name, nor expression, nor perception, nor opinion, nor knowledge of it."[47] The entire cosmos of ideas and via this cosmos everything that is at all can thus be traced back to a basic difference, the difference between the One and the Many, the limit and the unlimited, which Plato, unlike the Pythagoreans, characterizes as the difference of the great and the small, that is, as an indeterminate duality.[48] And because the One brings structure and order to the Many and thus forms chaos into a cosmos, the One is the Good and thus is the principle of what is good, while Duality is the principle of what is bad, since everything perfect is formed, thus delimited, and, through the limitation, it is good and beautiful.

9. The Absolutely Good

The connection thus sketched between soul, ideas, and the Good forms the basis of Plato's philosophical theory of God. He does not obtain this theory from the mythological theory of the gods and the pre-Socratics' criticism of that theory but bases it on the Socratic theory of the soul. The distinction made there between the body and the *psychē*, the human being's true self, offers him the key to the systematic distinction between the variable world of sense phenomena and the invariable world of ideas accessible only via the soul. That this permanent spiritual reality behind the change of appearances does in fact exist is evinced by the order of the stars and by mathematics. Yet, as the allegory of the cave shows, it can be known only on the arduous path via the soul to the ideas (as the paradigmatic images in the mind for everything that is) and to the idea of the Good at their summit. Like the ideas, God too belongs to the domain of perennial being and the invariable. God, however, is not identical with any idea, not even the idea of the Good, but, as the absolutely Good, God is as it were the grounds both of the ideas and of phenomena's participation in the ideas.

That is why Plato subjects the pre-Socratic criticism of myths to an explicit metacritique in which he attempts to show that gods exist; that they care about human concerns; and that they cannot be bribed.[49] His arguments on the first point especially have exerted decisive influence on the subsequent course of philosophical theology. Confronted with the criticism of the natural philosophers, Plato holds, the naive recourse to the order of the cosmos and to "the fact that all Hellenes and barbarians believe in [gods]" cannot

47. Plato, *Parmenides*, 141e–142a:688.

48. Compare Aristotle, *Metaphysics*, I.987a29–988a17:1561–2, and III.998b10:1577.

49. Plato, *Laws*, X.885e7–8:452, 899d–905d:470–77, and 905d–907d:477–79.

be maintained: the sun, the moon, and the stars are not gods but "earth and stones only, which can have no care at all of human affairs, and ... all religion is a cooking up of words and a make-believe."[50] Nonetheless, such criticism starts from a fundamental inversion of before and after: it explains the sun, the moon, and the stars, organisms, plants, and the soul by the basic elements fire, water, earth, and air instead of acknowledging that in truth, the soul is "the first" and has come into being "before all bodies."[51]

Plato justifies this thesis with an inquiry into the essence of movement. There is no denying that movement in the comprehensive sense of becoming, varying, growing, change of place, and so on, exists. Movement prompted by something else, however, must be distinguished from movement that prompts itself. Only things that move themselves live, and the principle of life is the soul. All movement, however, goes back to such a "motion which can move itself": the *psychē* is the cause of any and all change and movement.[52] Yet souls are either capable of good and evil and thus variable, like human souls, or they are invariably good and thus divine. Gods are nothing but such soul-principles of perfect movements in the world, and in that sense, Plato thinks, no one will "tolerate the denial that all things are full of gods."[53] The most perfect movement, however, namely the one most similar to the movement of reason, is the cycle of the heavens. It must thus be based on the most perfect soul, "a principle of wisdom and virtue" that brings about the entire cosmos and "ought by every man to be deemed a god."[54] Behind the gods in the cosmos, there is thus for Plato the God who, as the one who is spiritual, good, identical with reason, and moving himself, holds in his hands the cosmos as a whole. God is the soul of the cosmos the way the gods are souls of individual processes in the cosmos. The sun, the moon, and the stars are not gods, but their orderly movement is the visible sign of the divine.

Plato's theory of God, too, thus reacts to the problem of cosmic order. Unlike in Xenophanes, though, its guiding difference is no longer the difference between the cosmos as a whole and the processes within the cosmos;[55] it is the difference between the spiritual reality of the soul and the world of sense appearances. The invariable world of the ideas is accessible only via the soul. God, however, is neither appearance nor idea, not even the idea of the Good. Instead, transcendent like the ideas, he is simultaneously immanent to what is becoming as dynamic powerfulness, as world-soul. He is the being above being that cannot be grasped even at the highest level of human knowledge, *noēsis*, but can be discerned "only with an effort."[56] For knowing also always means knowing the causes of something. Yet when it comes to "the supreme God and the nature of the universe," it does not make sense to inquire into causes.[57] Causes are always causes of phenomena and thus are ideas, whereas ideas are always existing and thus nothing

50. Plato, *Laws*, X.886a:453 and 886d:454.

51. Plato, *Laws*, X.891c:459, 892c:460, and 892a:460.

52. Plato, *Laws*, X.896a–b:465.

53. Plato, *Laws*, X.899b:469.

54. Plato, *Laws*, X.897b–c:467 and 899a:469.

55. Xenophanes in Laks and Most, *Early Greek Philosophy*, D16–19:33–35.

56. Plato, *Republic*, VII.517b8–9:379.

57. Plato, *Laws*, VII.821a1–2:389.

whose cause could be inquired into since they do not change. As regards God, then, the philosophical inquiry into causes and grounds fails.

That, precisely, is the reason why Plato, mythomachian in matters of pedagogy, becomes mythopoetic in matters of philosophy. Human speech cannot express God, the dynamic *psychē* principle of all that is, in the logos, that is, neither in the mathematical science of figures of dianoetics nor in the dialectic conceptual science of noetics, but only in myth, which is the product of the creative philosophical imagination. Time and again, at decisive points of his elaborations, Plato therefore recounts artificial myths that suggestively express what even the dialectic logos cannot grasp. At the summit, as it were, of Plato's metaphysics, a transition takes place to a theology that in turn is able to present itself only mythologically. And this means that Plato's philosophical theology is *demythifying* (as regards the traditional myths about the gods) but not *demythologizing*. At the limit of the logos, mythological speech and thereby the enthusiastic imagination assert their inalienable theological right.

The Platonic *psychē* theology thus doubly refers to myth: on the one hand, it is a criticism of and an alternative to traditional mythology, which—in purified form—it can also grant pedagogical value. On the other hand, in order to present theological truth, it itself requires a new mythopoetics, a "New Mythology."

10. The Basic Rule of Speech about God

The basic rule of this new mythology is that one may trace all that is Good entirely and exclusively back to God alone, all that is ill entirely and exclusively only to what is other than God. God absolutely has nothing to do with Evil in all its forms. He is absolutely Good, yet thereby also absolutely different from everything else, and that means both from the Good whose reason he is and from the Evil that stands in opposition to it. In God's absolute being-Good, two differences thus converge: the difference between Good and Evil, and the difference between the Good and its grounds. The first marks the fundamental opposition between God and world, the second marks their being related despite all oppositeness. That God is Good means that everything that is Good is ultimately Good through God: the reference to God is the last answer to the question *unde bonum?* That God is Good, in turn, means that God absolutely has nothing to do with everything that is not Good but bad or Evil: the question *unde malum?* can be answered with anything but the reference to God.

This rule stands in tension not only with traditional myths about the gods but also with the religious experience of Jews and Christians and with the processes of understanding God that have sedimented in the biblical traditions.[58] Plato introduces his rule explicitly as a philosophical-scientific corrective to equivocal mythic speech about the

---

58. Not at all unlike Plato, the rabbis in engaging contemporary gnosis sought to establish that God creates everything but not Evil. The Talmud, Berakhot 11b, thus comments on Isa 45:7—"Who forms light and creates darkness"—for example: "Let him say the following formula instead: *Who forms light and creates brightness. . . .* But if so, what about the continuation of the verse: "Who makes peace and creates evil"? Do we say this blessing as it is written in the Bible? Rather, it is written evil and we euphemistically recite the blessing all things to avoid mention of evil." See also Thoma, "Gott im Unrecht," 89–90.

gods in popular religion and tragic poetry. God is thereby unmistakably defined, but at the price that while God is the unequivocal point of orientation for humans fashioning their lives, he is also no longer a possible object of human experience. In the world, the good God can be discovered only indirectly via weak refractions of the good but can no longer be experienced as the presence of the good. God is no longer to be found in the world but only in the soul, and moreover in a double ungraspability: on the one hand, in the merely negative determinacy of that which cannot be conceived by means of finite conception (negative theology); and on the other, in the positive indeterminacy of what one finds oneself exposed to in rare moments of enthusiastic being-lifted-out-of the conditionalities of the finite world (mystic-ecstatic theology). Negative theology and mystic ecstasy are the only modes in which one can, not grasp the good, but open oneself up to its presence.

Between God and life-world experience, a distance, a deep rift even, opens up of a kind the mythic tradition was unfamiliar with. Plato's discovery of God's absolute being good distances God from the experiences not only of the lifeworld but of religious practice as well. No religious experience, neither that of the Greek myths and tragedies nor that of the biblical traditions of Judaism and Christianity, speaks of God in this philosophical, unequivocal, and one-sided manner. Nor do any of them content themselves with speaking about the Good that is God in the modes of negative theology and mystic ecstasy alone. It is not surprising that in taking up Plato's basic rule of philosophical discourse about God and using it as a hermeneutic rule for theologically interpreting Christian experiences and biblical texts, Christian thinkers run into significant complications: a "good God" understood in these terms does not exist in the biblical texts.[59] Only Islam, at least in its orthodox main traditions, will come to describe not only the notion of God but also the experience of God in faith exclusively according to this rule.[60]

11. Good and Evil in the World

According to Plato's basic rule, God remains entirely and exclusively on the side of the good and thus enters, as a matter of principle, into an opposition both to Evil (the bad) and to any "mix" of good and evil (bad). While *God is entirely good*, the *world is both good and bad (evil)*, namely a cosmos that, through its good and harmonic order, tames the chaos breaking out time and again in various forms and keeps it under control in the various domains of life. There is, by contrast, *no entirely Evil*, since evil can only ever occur *in something*, that is, it itself is nothing but appears only ever as something good missing and lacking.

---

59. It is remarkable that all the way to the most recent debates, the theological recourse to God in light of the tragic dimensions of human life experience leads to views that do not advocate a personal conception of God. See Sands, *Escape from Paradise*, 1–16; E. Farley, *Good and Evil*; and W. Farley, *Tragic Vision and Divine Compassion*.

60. There are also other traditions that know not only of ambivalent experiences of God but experiences of an evil and malicious God who spreads terror and fear, in Islamic mysticism, for example. See Kermani, *Terror of God*.

Platonic thought thus excludes a dualism of Good and Evil but not a dual opposition between God, the entirely Good, and the world, which is both good and bad. This dual opposition of God and world has a correlate within the world in the opposition of the invariable world of ideas and its formal shadow images (mathematical objects) on the one hand and the variable world of appearances on the other. The Good thus appears in the world of experience as a formative and shaping force doubly refracted: it is the unified and ordered structure of the ideas and it is, mediated by the ideas and by the mathematical forms, the force that institutes unity and order in the transient world of appearances as well.

The world of experience—and this is the orientation the philosophical discovery of the good God achieves—is thus structured in dualities between (on the side of ideas) being, being one, being true, being good, being beautiful, being eternal, and (on the side of appearances) the oppositions or "mixtures" that condition and cause change and transience, namely being/not being (that is, beings), unity/multiplicity (the manifold), true/false (the actual), necessary/impossible (the contingent), good/evil (the living), beautiful/disordered (the worldly), eternal/temporal (the finite), and so on. Beings, the manifold, actual, contingent, living, worldly that can be experienced in the world, can thus in each case be understood as "composite," which explains their variability and transience but which also at the same time situates them "between" being and not being, being one and unstructured multiplicity, between what is true and what is false, necessary and impossible, good and evil, beauty and chaos, eternity and nothingness.

This is not merely a description of the state of the world in terms of contrasts but an attempt at understanding the world in the way it is being experienced: as an incessant dynamic process of opposing forces and tendencies, constantly threatened by the descent into chaos and maintained against chaos only with difficulty. While the positive side of these oppositions is oriented toward true being, the negative side tends toward not being. Against this always-threatening background, the harmony of the cosmos is mirrored in the simple proportions of numbers, and its visible expression is the movement of the stars on simple, ever-constant paths. To this macrocosmic harmony corresponds, in the microcosm of human life, the harmonic correspondence of body and soul. All that is negative in life (illness, death) results from the disruption of harmony caused by the human being, and in the cosmos, too, all that is evil, bad, and harmful occurs as deficiency and damage to its harmonious orders.

This avoids any kind of dualism of principles because there is an entirely Good (God) but no entirely Evil. What does arise, though, is a problematic series comprised of all that is nonbeing, many, false, impossible, evil, disordered, and null, and which is summed up in the concept of indeterminate matter. This matter is the questionable reason for why there are many different instances (trees) of a specific kind (tree).[61] According to a remark of Aristotle's, Plato saw the cause of the negative and of the

61. This reason is questionable insofar as Platonic thought distinguishes between two principles of differentiation. The variety of ideas is due to the fact that all of them, each in its way, are perfections that can neither be derived from nor reduced to each other. The manifold of individual phenomena, in contrast, is a multiplicity of imperfections that in each case represents only an approximate actualization of what it could be and ought to be as the complex of ideas that it concretizes. Every idea is perfectly what it is while each individual phenomenon could be what it is in a better way.

dysteleological in the opposition of *One* (Good) and *Many* (Bad).[62] Everything perceivable by the senses thus becomes negative because it does not live up to the original (the idea): negativity or evil is defined as a *deficient mode of being*.

God's unrestricted and exclusive being good is thus being developed entirely from the contrast with the unclear situation of the world of experience: only in being considered entirely good can God be distinguished from the world and serve to explain the unity, goodness, and beauty of the Many. The question *unde bonum?* is thus being answered. The question *unde malum?*, however, remains unanswered within this system of thought. Evil is what is required to distinguish between that which is of the divine and that which is of the world in order to make the difference between God and the world and thereby also between the world of ideas and the world of appearances in general plausible. While Evil is thereby not attributed an actuality of its own, it becomes downright indispensable for understanding the cosmos: ontologically, it is nothing, yet cosmologically, it is necessary.

This leads later Platonism (Plotinus, for example) to call matter (*hyle*) the lowest and most deficient and therefore the real evil.[63] Matter is what quite actively resists being shaped by ideas and only ever allows for their deficient actualization.[64] The Good, in contrast, consists of the ideas (in Aristotle, *eidē* or forms), that is, of that which in change guarantees continuation, validity, truth, and order. While being, what is true, necessary, beautiful, eternal, and so on are *good*, nonbeing, what is false, impossible, variable, chaotic, finite, null, and so on are viewed as bad or *evil*. In the world, these opposites are bracketed together such that the cosmos is understood as the cosmos of the oppositions between Good and Evil: unlike the divine, which stands entirely on the side of the Good, the world is the place, full of tension and conflict, where the mutually opposing tendencies toward the Good and toward Evil battle it out. The one world consists of what is good and what is evil, and Evil is the lack of the Good that could exist and ought to exist in a particular place of the cosmos.

12. The Aesthetic Legitimization of Evil

It is, of course, one thing to say that Evil has no independent reality but all Evil is tied into the well-ordered cosmos as a lack, and another thing to declare Evil, as that which in all its forms contrasts with the Good, downright to be the condition of the possibility of the harmonic order of the whole. What is disruptive in the world and is experienced as lack and deficit is thus determined in thought as what makes the ordered variety of the cosmos possible in the first place (cosmological monism). No cosmos without *malum*. If this thesis is understood not descriptively but normatively, we find ourselves in a different world.

---

62. Aristotle, *Metaphysics*, I.988a14:1562.

63. See Corrigan, *Plotinus' Theory of Matter*, and above, II.1.B.2, 124–25.

64. Compare Happ, *Hyle*, who says of matter that in this respect it is "essentially active" (802): it is what *counteracts* the Good.

Evil is then thought not only as a factual but a necessary moment of the world, insofar as without it, the harmonious order of the world as contrastive nexus of good and bad would be aesthetically and ethically impossible. That is not only a questionable aesthetic legitimation of the reality of Evil. It is also very difficult to explain persuasively in terms of lack or privation. It is not by chance that in the Hellenistic age, taking up Asian systems of thought, the juxtaposition of good and bad in the cosmos is ontologically radicalized and explained by taking recourse to two different principles, that is, by doing exactly what Plato had tried to exclude because he considered it to endanger the unity of the world. The place of cosmological monism is taken by a dualism of principles, and *Good* and *Evil* are understood as opposed and opposing principles of reality (ontological dualism).

This signals a profound change in the way the world is understood and life is felt to be. The world is no longer experienced and understood as a cosmos but as an arena of opposing forces and powers. It is no longer experienced as a harmonious order in which *malum* is conjured by being tied in with *bonum* but rather as a place of permanent conflict between *malum* and *bonum* that plays out in the entire macrocosm but especially in the microcosm, in the place occupied by the human. As long as Evil has no ontological status of its own but occurs only as deficiency and lack of what is good, it is contained as a matter of principle by being able to occur only in coexisting with the good in the whole of the cosmos: as *dis-order*, as *disruption* of order, as *lack* in being. Macrocosm as well as microcosm are *cosmos* as long as there is a guarantee that Evil is tied in with the Good and dominated by it.

Where this whole falls apart, however, where the world is attributed two souls that determine it, a good soul and a bad one,[65] thinking essentially has four options. Either the world is and remains what it is: an ambivalent arena of opposing principles. Or Evil wins and destroys the Good but thereby simultaneously destroys itself: Evil alone cannot exist. Or the Good wins by not only eliminating the deficits and lacks of the world but by overcoming the forces that work against the Good. *In* this world, this can formally be thought and implemented as a path of de-materialization, de-variabilization, de-temporalization, de-pluralization, that is, as the reduction of the finite, temporal, and variable world of phenomenal becoming to the infinite, eternal, and invariable *world of ideal being* in which everything that is exists in the perfection, truth, beauty, and goodness it is capable of. If, however, one supposes that a world of ideas cannot endure in itself and as such but must always appear in shaping a sensible-variable world, then all that remains is the fourth option of assuming a succession of worlds. Either, then, Evil is accepted as a permanent trait of this world; or it destroys itself along with everything else; or it is overcome by replacing the temporal world of the senses with the eternal world of ideas (end of the history of the world); or it is overcome by this equivocal world being replaced by a new and better world (succession of worlds). If, in contrast, it is deemed impossible that the struggle between Evil and Good be ended cosmologically because the world's ambivalence proves to be unavoidable, then the attempt of orienting oneself by the good becomes, anthropologically, an *escape from the world*, that is, a retreat from

---

65. Cf. Plato, *Laws*, X.897a–d:466–67.

the temporal, variable, evil world of sense appearances to the eternal, invariable, good world of ideas.

13. Escape from the World, Willpower, and Freedom of the Will

To achieve this, one must try to live a life in which the Good dominates Evil. This requires, oriented by *the Good* (God), promoting the properties of life that stand on the side of the Good (unity, truth, beauty, necessity, eternity, and so on) and avoiding or repressing the properties that stand on the side of Evil (the temporal, sensual, false, variable, unnecessary, and so on).

Plato's theory of the faculties of the soul spells out how this can happen. As the driving and creative force of human life, the soul is not an undifferentiated something. It is itself a microcosm of mutually opposing forces and faculties, namely: the faculty of desiring aiming at the physical-sensible world; willpower aiming at human knowing and willing; and rational willing or wisdom and insight aiming at the eternal world of ideas and mathematical forms. Justice, virtue, or welfare (*sōtēria*) are always to be found where the good (justice, virtue) dominates the other parts of the human soul; where the opposite is the case, chaos and disorder reign. If the soul is entirely determined by the faculty of desiring, it is immediately exposed to the sensuous influences of the environment and defined by pathos and affect. If it is dominated by willing, it seeks to shape the environment and not just be defined by it, and it thereby places itself under the rule of ethos and imagination—with the one positive exception that in the enthusiastic *eupathein* of the imagination, the soul is open to the reality at which the logos, as the good, is aiming.[66] Yet if it wants to do this responsibly and rationally and avoid that its imagining and willing becomes subservient to its desiring, it must control and define the pathos and ethos of the soul by means of the logos, that is, in shaping its life, it must not be oriented by what is sensually harassing it in the constant changing of impressions, passions, and affects, but by what is always valid, invariably and eternally: the ideas of the good, the true, the beautiful, and the eternal. Only a life of the soul thus defined makes human beings relatively independent and free from their bodily finitudes and puts them in a situation where they can orient their lives toward what is good, true, beautiful, and eternal. Only in this way do they not only live but live as humans.

It is thus precisely because of its differentiation that the soul is the central organ of shaping human life. Human beings are not just functions of their environment but can relate to this environment because and insofar as they can relate to their soul: we shape our lives by shaping the life of our soul and thus influence that through which we influence our relating to the world. The soul is the microcosm that, unlike the macrocosm and the forces at work in it, is not entirely inaccessible to being shaped by the human.[67] While humans can exercise only conditional influence on the environment surrounding

66. Plato, *Phaedrus*, 247d:154.

67. As Socrates and Plato knew, chasms open up within the soul itself because the soul is more than it at any point knows and can know of itself. Augustine rediscovers this in a whole new way (Augustine, *Trinity*, XIV:370–94), and under the changed conditions of the twentieth century, it is being recalled in Freud's analytic figure of the unconscious and Jung's differently accentuated analysis of archetypes.

them, in which their life is always threatened and endangered, they can to a certain extent shape the lives of their own souls by granting reason dominance over their desiring, imagining, and willing, or by letting their willing and imagining be defined by reason and not the affects of desiring. And humans are capable of this because of the differentiation of the soul and the ability to relate to the soul to shape it: that is freedom of the will. They often do not succeed because it is difficult to assert reason as the determining grounds of the will against the often stronger forces of desire: that is the weakness of their wills. Because of their freedom of the will, humans are able to shape their lives themselves insofar as they shape the lives of their souls. Because of their weakness in making reason (and thus the orientation by what abides) the decisive determination of their willing against the wishes and affects of desiring (and thus the orientation by the transient and changeable), they most of the time do not shape themselves the way they could and ought to if they were determined exclusively or decisively by reason. They remain surrendered to pathos and thus to the sensual world instead of making themselves free over against this world by means of the logos, being oriented in the living of their lives by the world of ideas, thanks to logical insight, and by the hyperreal reality of the good, thanks to the enthusiastic imagination.

The degree of independence from sensibility is thus the measure of freedom, and sensibility is characterized by the directness with which it ties the human into the process of its sensually experienceable environment. Yet both freedom and sensibility—and only this distinguishes them as *human* specificities—are always understood as mediated and mediating. They do not manifest as such but in and through determining the *willing* through which humans manifest in actions in their environment: because of their willing, humans *can* distinguish themselves from animals. Yet they only *do* so if they do not let their willing be determined by affect, pathos, and sensual desiring and behave like irrational animals; only if instead they determine their willing through the logos and thereby direct it by what lies beyond the situation, by the universal, the true, the good, and so on, which is impossible for animals, bound as they are by their situation. For if the pathos determines our willing, then *we are being determined*; we in contrast *determine ourselves* if we determine our willing through the logos. The first of these, humans share with all other organisms; the second distinguishes them as *rational* organisms. For if *to live* is to act and change one's environment, then this presupposes that the soul, as the *movens* of action, determines the human to effect a certain action. To do so, however, it must itself be determined. If it lets itself be determined by the pathos of the desiring faculty, then the human acts like all other organisms do, guided by sensibility. If the soul, in contrast, determines itself through the logos of the rational faculty, it relates freely and creatively to its being determined by sensibility and brings the human truly to live as human in being oriented by the good.

14. Outlines and Basic Problems of Dealing with Evil

The tradition of Platonic thought, for which God is entirely good, cannot deal with evil theologically, only either *cosmologically* or *psychologically* (anthropologically). In any case, the good God is to be distinguished from the world in such a way as not to be infected by the world's ambivalences and to remain unequivocal as the point of orienta-tion of human life. This one-sidedly commits God to "being"[68] *wholly other* than Evil, but it does not say that God is *against* Evil: if God is thought the way the Platonic tradition thinks God, it is impossible to say or think that of God. The Good that is God stands in contrast to Evil but does not struggle against it, it is not the elimination or overcoming of Evil. The notion of the absolutely good God thus takes up only *one* strand of the differen-tiation of good and evil, namely that the Good is *wholly other* than Evil, but not the other strands, that the Good works against Evil or that the Good ends and overcomes Evil. While the good God is entirely different from Evil, and Evil entirely different from the Good, the Good is not impaired by Evil (God is beyond all good and evil) and Evil is not ended or overcome by God. God does not impair Evil, but—and it must be put in such stark terms—he makes it possible in the first place: without God there would be no evil, not because God would effect evil but because without God there would be nothing that could be good or evil. In short: God is absolutely good and everything stays the way it is.

The discovery of the good God is thus above the discovery that God is *wholly other* than everything else, and that is referred to as "good" because this absolute otherness renders God absolutely attractive for all others: at the center of Plato's thinking is not the epistemological rule, cited time and again, that "like must know like" but, quite the inverse, the rule that the greatest opposites attract each other the most. His thinking is concerned with *increasing the difference between God and world*, not in connecting the two in the supra-idea of the Good. It is dominated by a negative theology of difference, not by a theology of increase.

This is clearly evident in its Neoplatonic continuations. To guarantee the unequivo-calness of the notion of God, Neoplatonism finds itself compelled not only to distinguish God as entirely good from the equivocal world but to situate God as the Good beyond being, that is, not merely to distinguish him from the world but to conceive of the dis-tinction in such a way that in the world, it is only ever possible and admissible to speak of God's being good if the rule of negative theology is observed: the Good that God is is distinct from all worldly good in such a way that every similarity is dominated by an even greater dissimilarity. This dissimilarity is not only the dissimilarity conditioned by the difference between good and evil but also the dissimilarity conditioned by the difference between what is good and *the* Good, that is, the originary ground of all that is good. In both respects, however, God is separate from Evil as a matter of principle. He absolutely has nothing to do with it.

Evil is found not with God but only in the world and in the lives of human beings, and that is where it must be dealt with, in being oriented by the incomprehensibly good God. There are different paths for doing so that suggest themselves. The attempt at deal-ing with the existential challenge of Evil *cosmologically*, that is, in the form of a theory of the world, consists in

---

68. In the Platonic tradition—unlike the Scotist tradition—it is not even possible to attribute "being" to God and the world in the same sense.

1. thinking Evil as being tied into the greater whole of the Good (Plotinian monism);

2. expecting the present transient world to be replaced by a coming eternal or differently temporal-eternal world (succession of worlds);

3. intensifying the difference between good and evil to become an opposition of principles that sees the world as the arena of the struggle between Good and Evil (Manichean dualism); or

4. inversely, conceiving the world only as a continuous process of material atoms connecting and disconnecting again and no longer describing it as a cosmos according to the categories of good and evil (Epicureanism).

From the cosmological perspective, then, the consequence of the discovery of the good God is either that the world is understood fundamentally *gnostic-dualistically* or that it can only be understood as *free of God*. In the first case, orientation by the good God leads into the opposition between God and material world or God and counter-god, in the second case into the dismissal of God as a point of orientation for life in the world: the world is being experienced as a place of distance from God, as the place where the conflict between God and counter-god is being played out, or as a world without God.

This changes the view of the world from the ground up, because the world is no longer understood as a cosmos in which Evil is tied into the greater nexus of the Good. Either the world moves entirely to the side of Evil, or no reference to evil is made at all. When these traditional lines of ancient thought were taken up again at the beginning of the modern period, both of them affected the modern cosmology then being elaborated in the form of hermeticism and mechanism. Yet neither the one nor the other puts an end to the human experience of evil and of ills. That is why the attempt is made to confront evil and ills *anthropologically* and *ethically* (that is, in the practice of human life) by

1. focusing, as the Academy does, on the good world of the ideas (turn away from the sensible world and turn toward the eternal world of ideas);

2. orienting one's life, like the Stoa advocates, by the all-penetrating principle of the logos thanks to which macrocosm and microcosm enter into correspondence and agreement; or

3. participating, as the Manicheans demand, in the struggle of the Good against Evil.

To each of these ways of dealing with Evil corresponds a view of the world that is not easily made compatible with the others. The world is experienced Neoplatonically as the opposition of the world of ideas and the world of the senses; Stoically as spiritually permeated nexus of necessities that determine the macro- and the microcosm; or dualistically as the arena of the struggle between good and evil powers such that one can defend against the evil powers only by allying oneself with the good counterpower.

Cosmological ways of dealing with Evil thus vacillate between aesthetic legitimation, dualist exaggeration, and systematic exclusion, which in disregarding Evil also disregards the good God and leads to a secularizing view of the world. Anthropological ways of dealing with Evil in turn run the dangers of withdrawing from the world (escape from the world); of identifying with the processes of the world, which are declared to be necessary (identification with the world); or of experiencing oneself only as surrendered to the struggle between the powers of Good and Evil (despairing of the world).

Both approaches suffer from failing to distinguish between the descriptive and the normative components of experiences of *malum* and from understanding all events axiologically. They thereby miss the specificity of human life, which consists in putting ourselves in a judging and evaluating relation toward the happenings of the world and of life. Good and evil are thus sought and found in the happenings of the world as such, and not in the human relationships to the happenings in the world in which we live. Yet if it is possible in human life to relate to everything in the world under the differential aspect of good and evil, then it is a questionable and unlegitimized transgression to project the difference of good and evil into the world itself and to turn the way one relates to the world into a trait of the world itself. That precisely is a basic characteristic of the entire intellectual tradition discussed here, and for this reason, precisely, it is so dubious to take this tradition up and continue it under the conditions of modernity. For under these conditions, it has become clear that a systematic distinction must be made between, on the one hand, that which is and, on the other, how one relates to it in judging, evaluating, and acting, and that this distinction must be made even if this relating-to in judging, evaluating, and acting itself belongs to what exists in the world: human life actualizes possibilities that are *valid in* human life and *possible for* it. Yet these possibilities must precisely not be read into and projected onto all that human life can relate to and deal with, assuming we seek to avoid a metabasis that causes confusion and has momentous consequences. This is apparent in the contradictions into which it leads.

15. The Aporias of Explaining Evil in Recourse to the Good God

That God is entirely good is not a religious experience but a philosophical positing to explain the good. In the wake of Platonic thought, given an ambivalent world in which both good and evil are being experienced, the notion of God is being elaborated in such a way that, against the backdrop of the basic contrast between good (*agathon*) and evil (*kakon*), God rests entirely and exclusively on the side of the good: the only one to be entirely and exclusively good is God. Everything else is only good insofar as it can be explained in recourse to God. For in the recourse to God, only that can be truthfully explained which is through God, and only that is also good.[69] Everything that cannot thus be explained, by contrast, is ill or evil because it is not through God. The discovery of the good God thus allows not only for explaining the good but also for unambiguously distinguishing it from Evil: all that and only that is good which can be explained through God, everything else by contrast is evil.

This argument, which seems so evident, presages the failure of this approach. For either evil is thus inexplicable because it is nothing that could be defined and explained as a *what* (definable essence) or a *something* (existing being), or it requires another explanation that takes recourse to something other than God. This, however, means

---

69. This presupposes that an explanation is true only if it cites as the reason for a thing (a state of affairs) that which is in fact the reason for its being or being-such. Obviously, that is not a matter of course.

either that not everything that is being experienced in the world is explicable or that it is explicable only if there are explanatory principles besides God. Since God is of no use in explaining the reality of Evil, this reality is either inexplicable or else explanatory principles other than God are required. The solutions this approach attempts play out between these two poles: evil either is *inexplicable* or is only *explicable otherwise*.

Both sides are being argued in more than one sense. That evil is *inexplicable* is being understood in at least four different ways, each in different versions:

1. Either the scope of explanatory orientation in the world that takes recourse to the good is restricted to what is good as a matter of principle (restriction of the explicable to what is good), simply noting, as regards evil: *there is something inexplicable*. Evil then turns, in a critical interpretation, into the limit concept of the good (*there are limits to what is explicable*) or, in a metaphysical interpretation, into the gateway for a negative ontology of the inexplicable (*there is something that cannot be explained*) about which one cannot speak but only remain silent. While in the first case, we must remain silent because there is nothing we could talk about, in the second case, we must remain silent because there is something we cannot talk about. While the two are mixed up time and again, they are evidently different things.

2. Or Evil is defined as a defect in the good and is thereby not explicable but describable as a lack: *what can be explained is not as good as it could be and ought to be*. Evil is understood as privation of the good and its reality is interpreted as an indication that the goodness of reality can be enhanced (*privative interpretation of Evil*). The focus is thus not as much on Evil as it is, via Evil, on the possible enhancement of the good.

3. Or thinking compels a counterexperiential correction of experience insofar as thinking denies the evil being experienced: *there is nothing there to be explained*. Where explicability functions as a criterion of reality, Evil becomes, in thinking, an erroneous experience that deems itself to be experiencing something although there is nothing explicable it is experiencing, although nothing is really being experienced (*denial in fact of the reality of Evil*). For what does not exist is not evil, and what is evil does not exist. Yet only what exists can be explained, and only what can be explained exists.

4. Or Evil is defined as something that can neither be explained nor not explained. It is possible to do so to emphasize that something like this cannot exist: *there is nothing that would be neither explicable nor not explicable* (*denial in principle of the reality of Evil*). It is also possible to do so, however, to say that Evil is not in this way and thus does not fall into the domain of what can be scientifically explored: *what is evil is neither explicable nor not explicable* (*denial in principle that science is competent to deal with Evil*). Evil is marked in thinking as being beyond thinking, running the twofold risk of either becoming indistinguishable from nothingness or becoming distinguishable from nothing anymore.

To consider Evil, in contrast, to be something that is only *explicable otherwise* leads into a twofold aporia that makes explanation impossible in different ways, be it because a contradiction is produced in the explanation, be it that a contradiction is produced through the explanation. Where evil is being explained, or where the attempt is made to explain evil by something other than God that is itself not evil but good, by something that is explicable through recourse to God, then that would indeed be an explanation—if it were possible *per impossibile*—because only what is good can serve as explanatory reason for something else. But it cannot *de facto* be an explanation because it is impossible to explain evil through good. If Evil, in contrast, is being explained by something that is itself evil, by something that is not explicable through recourse to God, and if this explanation is accepted, then irreducibly different principles of explanation for the good and for Evil exist, and in explaining the world, the unity of the world threatens to fall apart dualistically. A unified principle of explanation does not allow for explaining Evil even if to do so, recourse is taken to something other than God; and dual principles of explanation in thinking cannot preserve the unity of the world in which good and evil are being experienced.

The path of thinking that posits God as what is absolutely good and thus absolutizes God *qua* good in order to explain what is good in the world thus ends in two contradictions equally incapable of explaining anything: if the attempt is made to explain good and evil unitarily via recourse to what is good, one either enters into an explanatory contradiction (what is evil could only be explained by what is good, but it is impossible to explain what is evil by what is good) or one must restrict the domain of the explicable to the good and declare Evil to be inexplicable. If the attempt, in turn, is made not to explain good and evil unitarily but each based on its own principles, then the dualism of principles of explanation does not, in thought, preserve the unity of the experienced world. It thereby, moreover, does not strictly speaking explain anything but only repeats in thought the contradictoriness of experience. Either way, in its search for explanation, this path of thinking flounders on the experience of life: the discovery of the good God renders God as explanatory principle of the equivocal reality of the world of experience impossible.

On the one hand, this results in the reality of the world being explained scientifically without recourse to God and thus in the attitude of atheism as a methodological principle: God as a scientific entity is eliminated from modern explanatory thinking, both as something that is able to explain what is real and as something accessible to and in need of explanation. The tradition discussed here had tasked the notion of God with too much, used it without differentiation to explain being and being good and thus also, contrastively, to explain not being and being ill. It prepared the ground for eliminating the notion, through a critique of this excess, entirely from thinking and for conceiving of scientific explanatory thinking in systematically atheistic terms. As so often happens when one undifferentiatedly seeks too much, one is in the end left with nothing.

On the other hand, all of this changes nothing about the reality of experiences of *malum* in human life. This reality of evil in life, however, is not to be dealt with in the mode of scientific, philosophical, or theological *explanation* but in another way. What can be explained is only ever the happening on the basis of and through which there is an experience of evil. That this happening is being experienced and assessed this way, however, cannot be made comprehensible through an explanation of the happening alone.

Dealing with evil in life demands more than scientific explanation, and the recourse to God as detour to an understanding of the reality of evil is of no use in explaining what cannot be explained otherwise.

This renders the recourse to God superfluous only if we think that reasonable discourse about God is possible exclusively in the mode of explanation or of ultimate explanation. The opposite is the case: in this mode, it is not possible to talk about God reasonably. That is why the detour via God in order to deal with evil must be constructed differently than as a search for an explanation of evil. The notion of the good God leads to aporias if recourse is taken to the goodness of God as an explanatory principle of what is and what is not, and of judging and evaluating it as *bonum* or *malum*. These aporias can be avoided when the notion of the good God is taken up and further defined in a nexus of life and of thinking concerned not with explaining the world but with orienting life. And that precisely is the case where God comes into view not only as the wholly other of *malum* but as fighter against *malum*. For the "discovery that God, too," cannot "explain Evil but that at most we can experience God as liberating power against Evil" is by no means an insight only of secular modernity.[70] It accompanies biblical and Christian experience and thought in all their phases.

70. Häring, *Das Böse in der Welt*, 173.

B.2

The Struggle against Evil:
The Discovery of God's Justice

THE PATH OF THINKING God guided by the opposition between good and evil was never the only path of thinking him, nor has the detour via the notion of the good God been the only detour for thinking Evil. Instead of the effort to explain Evil, the *struggle against Evil* can be the center of interest, too. The good is then no longer only the opposite of Evil but the counterforce to Evil: the good is the enemy of Evil, and Evil the enemy of the good (and the beautiful and the true).[1] God, too, is then no longer only the one who is wholly other than Evil but the one who struggles against Evil.[2] Good is not only that which is good but the "one who is good" (Matt 19:17), the one who not only is absolutely other than Evil but stands in the most rigorous conflict with Evil in all its various forms insofar as he, for his part, fights the enemy of the good not with evil but—and only this makes God *absolutely* good—with good.

1. God's Active Justice

That God is such and is active in this way is, of course, not obvious. In a long historical process it first had to be discovered and experienced in upheavals that changed people's lives from the ground up and compelled them to engage in reflections that led to, along with a different conception of God, a different understanding of themselves and of the world. Thinking this dynamic of resistant and mutually resisting realities of evil and good requires taking into account not only opposites but *counterforces* and *counterpowers*, and this, precisely, characterizes the path religions take in thinking Evil.

Judaism, Christianity, and Islam are thus guided by the opposing actions of what is just and what is unjust and try to think Evil on the detour via the notion of the just God

1. Compare Jüngel, "Böse—was ist das?," 124, and Boyd, *Is God to Blame?*, 60: "we must see God as fighting evil, not willing it." This is true even if one does not draw the apocalyptic consequences Boyd associates with it (Boyd, *God at War*). In a different and theologically more tenable way, Nigel G. Wright stresses the tradition of the *ecclesia militans* and the view it implies of "God's Holy War" against Evil, against those who are evil, and against the one who is evil (Wright, *Theology of the Dark Side*, 183–95).

2. See Mettinger, "Fighting the Powers of Chaos and Hell."

as the injustice against which God is committed to fight in order definitively to put an end to it. God for them is not only the one who does right by those who suffer wrong and holds those who do wrong responsible; they hope that God will abolish injustice and assert justice in such a way that the struggle against wrong and for right will become superfluous because justice will reign. Evil, in this way of thinking, is thus not only the other of the good; it is the unjust working against the just. The good is not only the other of Evil; it is the just that overcomes injustice. And God is not only good but just, in that he not only differs from Evil but fights and overcomes the unjust with the just.[3]

That God is just and fights against what is unjust is an insight obtained only gradually against widespread experiences to the contrary. The biblical record documents in many and varied ways that God has been experienced and understood as by no means entirely good but as himself a responsible author of evil and ills.[4] Even where people had placed their hopes in God's justice, the experience that it is the unjust who flourish and that the just not only suffer but suffer *through God* and *from God* led to crises that time and again confronted them with the alternative of either stopping entirely to orient their lives by God or asking, even entreating him to explain himself in less ambiguous terms.

The history of thinking Evil documented in the biblical texts and continued in different ways in the religious and theological thought of Judaism, Christianity, and Islam is a history of conflicts with God and crises in life that manifest the struggle of opposite forces one tried to designate under the heading "Evil" and *per impossibile* to think and understand.[5] This multipronged history held in store not only the discovery *that* God is just (the fact of God's justice) but also the discovery of *what* God's justice consists in (the essence of his justice) and of *how* God actualizes this justice (the mode of its actualization). And all this did not remain a one-way street. Along with the image of God, the discovery of God's justice, rather, also changed the conception of justice and the insight into how a human life before God becomes just.[6]

This history of discovery was not a linear one but developed differently in Judaism, Christianity, and Islam: not just between these traditions but within each of them, too, God's justice is thought and understood differently.[7] In any case, though, the discovery

3. It is thus an inadequate reduction on the part of Schleiermacher that, in taking up Aristotle's distinction between retributive and distributive justice, he dogmatically restricts the concept of God's justice to the concept of retributive justice and attributes distributive justice to God's wisdom as a creation of order; see Schleiermacher, *Christian Faith*, §84:345–52. In the biblical tradition, God's justice includes not just his rewarding and punishing actions but essentially also the establishment of the harmonious order of creation against the threats of chaos that intrude time and again.

4. As Crenshaw rightly notes, "a cruel streak exists in the biblical depiction of God" (Crenshaw, *Defending God*, 178). See also Crenshaw, *Whirlpool of Torment*, and Penchansky, *What Rough Beast?*

5. See Oberhänsli-Widmer, "Schafft Gott das Böse?"

6. In that sense, it is only conditionally correct when Häring says that "Scripture in its entirety knows of no theology of Evil." Scripture is indeed no theological treatise, and taken by themselves, the "experiences of what is good and what is ill, pleasant and unpleasant, useful and dangerous" mirrored in the biblical texts do not constitute a theology (Häring, *Das Böse in der Welt*, 19). Yet a theology begins to emerge when we do not look at these experiences as such but ask how engaging with them has changed the conception of God and how this, in turn, has led to changed attitudes toward such experiences.

7. Even if these developments partly overlap, it would be a mistake to think that the Jewish, Christian, and Muslim conceptions of justice—each internally differentiated in turn—could be reduced to a

of God's justice led not only to thinking Evil in a specific way[8] but also to understanding the essence of justice and the mode of becoming just in a new way.[9] The discovery of God's justice led not only to a new conception of God but at the same time also to a new conception of the meaning of justice.

2. Multivocal Experienced-Based Imagery of God in the Bible

The biblical traditions of the Old and New Testament have not only friendly things to report about God.[10] There are worlds lying between their image of God and Schiller's optimistic *Ode to Joy*: "above the starry canopy there must dwell a loving father." Their image of God has terrifying features nourished by experiences in which God was encountered not only as a friend but as an enemy, not only as helper but as opponent, not only as consolation and rescue but as threat and horror.[11] God is not to be trifled with. He is a jealous God and a wrathful God who can destroy lives and annihilate nations, who commits violence and exacts revenge where his will is being resisted, who insists on his right and does not shrink from killing the guilty and the innocent in his wrath. Hatred and glory, merciless fury and merciful patience characterize the image of him.[12] Just as the gods of the Greek myths do not correspond to what Plato's critical correction opposes to them in the entirely and exclusively good God, the God of the biblical traditions cannot be equated with this Platonic Good. He is not beyond being, without affect; even when he is furthest from the human, he remains a very lively God close to life.[13] The full contradictoriness of a profoundly ambiguous and contradictory experience of

common mainstream with certain particular additions. Each of them includes preceding developments in a new total context, leading to a thorough reinterpretation of earlier insights that can therefore not be passed off as the common roots of different conceptions. Despite shared biblical backgrounds and references, "God is just" means something different in the contexts of Jewish, Christian, and Islamic theology.

8. This is mirrored in the terminologies of Evil and sin; see Knierim, *Die Hauptbegriffe für Sünde im Alten Testament*.

9. In what follows, I demonstrate this point in the biblical tradition; on the Muslim view, see Kermani, *Terror of God*.

10. See Crenshaw, *Whirlpool of Torment* and *Defending God*, and Penchansky, *What Rough Beast?* That is why Verweyen feels compelled to speak of processes of "demythologizing" and "demagicking" belief in God in Israel (Verweyen, *Philosophie und Theologie*, 26–38). Arguing against Jon Douglas Levenson's *Creation and the Persistence of Evil*, Yair Hoffman attests the Hebrew Bible an "inattentiveness to the comprehensive problem of evil." Biblical thinking, he says, focuses on "divine retribution" and marginalizes the cognitive "problem of evil": "Indeed, from a purely logical point of view, even the certainty of divine justice does not offer a satisfactory thorough solution to the problem of evil, yet it reduces the dilemma to the degree of existential irrelevance" (Hoffman, "Jeremiah 50–51 and the Concept of Evil," 28).

11. Tyron Inbody describes just how difficult it is for traditional Christianity to acknowledge this: "I taught my course in theodicy three times before I would include this material in the syllabus" (Inbody, *Transforming God*, 197n4).

12. See Tasker, *Biblical Doctrine of the Wrath of God*; Korpel, *Rift in the Clouds*; Herion et al., "Wrath of God (OT)"; Dietrich and Link, *Die dunklen Seiten Gottes*; and Schüle, "Der dunkle Gott."

13. On the history of the problem, Pohlenz, *Vom Zorne Gottes* (1909), remains important.

life is mirrored in the images of God of the biblical traditions, not only in the Old but in the New Testament as well.[14]

This does not make them an unusual exception among religions or in the history of religions. Quite the opposite: it is precisely in this that they show themselves to be tied in with the nexus of life and experience of the ancient Middle East.[15] The gods of Mesopotamia, Egypt, and Canaan were not beings free of affect but could compete with each other in wrath and love, envy and conflict. This is true not only as regards natural phenomena, weather gods and gods of vegetation, but also where the gods' affects could be perceived only as mediated by the divinely instituted political and cultic authorities. In Egypt, for example, the god's anger about injustice was perceived and experienced in the just anger of the king and his officials about injustice.[16] This divine anger could also be directed at the failures of specific individuals, as testimony from the fifteenth century BC shows, and after the Amarna period, all of history is seen as subject to the wrathful tribunal of the gods.[17] Yet the figure of thought of finding the wrath of god represented in an experienceable way in the wrath of the king remains dominant.

These and similar traits can be found in the biblical traditions as well, even if the prohibition of images critically spelled out that all direct identification was a no-go. The religious thought of Israel does share with the conceptions and images of God in its surroundings many traits and motifs that are taken up to interpret Israel's own experience and to orient it in a confusing world: the creator's struggle against Evil; the divine ruler's jealousy and arbitrariness; the god of war's potential for violence and the thirst for revenge; the wrath against the enemies of Israel and against the nations but also against Israel itself; the retribution and punishment by a God who does not tolerate his will being ignored and his rights being spurned; the inexorableness of the judge of the world whose judgment no one will escape and who demands of everyone to answer for themselves.

All these interpretations of God—and this applies to the positive determinations of the image of God as well—are not records of timeless divine predicates that, taken together, would define what the biblical tradition understands by "God." Instead, they are time and again taken up critically, elaborated, corrected, and recast in light of new experiences, a hermeneutic process that continues throughout the entire history of Israel as theological labor on the image of God and the notion of God both within and outside of the biblical texts.[18] It is also pursued in, alongside, and in engaging with the texts of the New Testament, in what Austin Farrer has called the critical "rebirth of images" in Christianity.[19]

14. Hanson, *Wrath of the Lamb*; Eckstein, "'Denn Gottes Zorn wird vom Himmel her offenbar werden'"; Travis, "Wrath of God (NT)"; and Limbeck, "Zürnt Gott wirklich?"

15. Van der Toorn, *Sin and Sanction in Israel and Mesopotamia*; Emmendörffer, *Der ferne Gott*; and Groß, "Zorn Gottes: Ein biblisches Theologumenon."

16. See Assmann, *Politische Theologie*, 87–99.

17. See Assmann, *Politische Theologie*, 96.

18. See Fishbane, *Biblical Myth and Rabbinic Mythmaking*, and Crenshaw, *Defending God*.

19. Farrer, *Rebirth of Images*.

3. Crises of Comprehension

These processes of interpreting and reinterpreting the images of God do not represent a continuous development. Experience prompts nodes and layers to develop in them that give rise to enduring features in the image of God, to exaggerations that open up profound insights without being universally shared, but also to wrong paths and dead ends that cannot be continued because they end up, intellectually, in contradictions or, practically, in a loss of orientation in life. It might still be comprehensible that a God from whom one hopes and expects to receive what is good is being associated with war and violence, murder and revenge, obduracy and retaliation, disease, epidemics, and raging against the enemy. But that he works himself into a frantic rage; that he indiscriminately strikes down "all the firstborn in the land of Egypt, from the firstborn of Pharaoh who sat on his throne to the firstborn of the prisoner who was in the dungeon, and all the firstborn of the livestock"; that he executes his destructive ban on entire cities and exterminates them to the very last person; that he inflicts epidemics, famines, plagues, disease, and death on entire nations; that he has them massacred and their bodies eaten by vultures; that he toys with the pious and treats them worse than their worst enemy would; all this and much more goes beyond anything one could in any way render comprehensible (Isa 63:1–6; Exod 12:29; Deut 7:2, 7:20–26, 28:16–44; and Job 30:21).[20] A God experienced and represented this way takes on sadistic and diabolic traits that cannot be justified or even merely understood in any way. From such a God, one can only flee and escape to safety; such a monster does not exist and cannot exist.

What is challenging about the biblical imagery of God, then, is not the fact alone that God is also portrayed as the author of ills but the fact that he orders, executes, and demands ills and evil of so excessive an extent. As long as that is happening only to others, to the enemies of Israel, the adversaries of the pious, and the sneerers of God, short-sighted confidence in God may not yet take offense. But where it concerns Israel and the pious themselves while the opponents of God's people and those who flout God's commandments are doing well, it leads to fundamental crises in life and with regard to God.

These crises intensify to the point of becoming unbearable where faith in God enters into contradiction not only with the experiences of life but with itself. In being confronted with experiences that contradict the traditional image of God, there are, hermeneutically speaking, three basic possibilities for reacting: one can understand differently either these experiences or God or both, that is, modify the conception of the experiences in question or that of God or both. Each of these possibilities can be actualized in different ways. These range from attempts to assign the experiences and the images of God another sense by including them in new contexts (approaches of immanent hermeneutics) to efforts at opposing what is experienced and what is thought as God with an alternative, another and better reality (transcendent-realist alternative). Confronted with contradicting experiences, one can thus modify or completely abandon the traditional *image of God*, that is, think God differently (new theology) or no longer think him, be it because one concludes that God is beyond all that can be thought (negative

---

20. See Inbody, *Transforming God*, 80–84.

theology), be it because one comes to believe that there is or can be nothing that could be thought under the signifier "God" (negation of theology). Or one can maintain the traditional image of God against the *experiences* and subject them, in light of this image, to a reinterpretation that derives a sense from them they did not at first seem to have (new conception of the reality being experienced) or make them pass for experiences of a preliminary reality in need of improvement that will be overcome by another, future, new, true reality (experience of a new reality). The former leads to reinterpretations of what has been experienced, the latter to hoped-for or expected eschatological alternatives to what has been experienced.

Both, labor on the image of God in light of given experiences and on the conception of experience in light of a given image of God, usually do not happen separately but in dynamic association. One's image of God cannot be conceived anew or dismissed without also changing one's conception of what has been experienced, and experience cannot be reinterpreted and confronted with alternative possibilities without also changing the conception of God. The dynamic of this association is brought out with particular clarity by the crises that compel a religious tradition to reassess the relationships between its conceptions of God, of the world, and of itself.[21] For religion lived in community is always tradition, and the organ of tradition is language (in the widest sense of a shared use of signs), in which it seeks to symbolize, think, and understand what is being experienced. In the language of a religion, and that means in its traditions, texts, and rituals, these crises take shape in the changes made in the conception of God, world, and self.

Such changes take place all the time, but all religious traditions are familiar with especially notable crises by which they have been durably shaped more than by others. For the conception of God in the biblical traditions of the Old and the New Testament, there are two exemplary crises with far-reaching consequences. For Judaism, it was above all the *crisis of exile* that compelled Israel's traditional faith in God to re-form itself with regard to monotheism and a theology of divine promises. Without this crisis, the Old Testament would be inconceivable. For Christianity, it was the *crisis of the cross*, which taught that Jesus's proclamation of God to Israel is to be understood in its universal eschatological significance. Without this crisis, the New Testament would not exist. In both cases, a complex tradition is subjected, in light of a subversive crisis, to a trenchant reinterpretation that permanently defines the image of God, world, and human being in Judaism and in Christianity. These crises were subversive because they were experienced not only as a contradiction between an experience and the traditional image of God but as a contradiction in the underlying basic conception of God itself. Israel could no longer hand down the traditional image of God and of itself after it seemed as if God, in destroying his people and deporting what remained of it into exile, had himself made

---

21. This is true not only of religious traditions but of individual experiences as well: where evil intrudes on our lives, what we understand by "God" changes, and this changes how we understand ourselves in the face of incomprehensible, senseless, irrational experience of Evil, which cannot be rendered comprehensible via the recourse to God but with which we try to live in relating to God without being able to understand it. As Nicholas Wolterstorff puts it: "To live without the answer is precarious. It's hard to keep one's footing. . . . To the most agonized question I have ever asked I do not know the answer. . . . I am not angry but baffled and hurt. My wound is an unanswered question. The wounds of all humanity are an unanswered question" (Wolterstorff, *Lament for a Son*, 67–68).

the actualization of the promise he had given Israel impossible and become unfaithful to himself. And the disciples could not hand on Jesus's message about the imminent coming of the kingdom of the heavenly Father unbroken after the one who had proclaimed this message had been killed on the cross and his message thereby seemed to have come to an end. Only against these crises and in living and working through them were Israel's faith in God and Christians' faith in God able to re-form, and the traces of these crises are durably inscribed in each of these traditions.

4. The Crisis of Exile and Its Effect on the Image of God

Crises of the traditional faith in God have occurred time and again in the lives of the pious. Their traces are found in many texts, especially in the Psalms and in the novella of Job. For Israel's thinking of God as a whole, however, one of the most decisive crises was the catastrophe of 587/586 BC, the destruction of Jerusalem and of the temple, the loss of autonomous statehood, the fall of the dynasty of King David, and the ensuing period of the Judaic upper classes' exile in Babylon between 586 and 539 BC. This crisis, which, with the end of Judea following the conquest of the Northern Kingdom by Assyria in 722–21 BC, seemed to signal the final exit from history of the people of Yahweh, compelled like no other a further development and reshaping of the inherited conception of God and left its traces in many texts of the Old and then also of the New Testament.[22] The simple oppositions of earlier times that drew on the experiences of the exodus and on the Sinai and had been elaborated in the Jerusalem theology of Zion—God is with us and against our enemies; our God is more powerful than the gods of the others; God is with the just and against the unjust—had failed and could not be continued in this form. What Israel had experienced and suffered had compelled the insight that God punishes not only the ill deeds of others but those of his people as well; he punishes not only proportionally to the wrong committed but in an inscrutable and no longer comprehensible excessive way; not only does he himself commit evil, he entices good people to do evil by making them obdurate in order then to punish them for it; he is not only the unrelenting opponent of the enemies of Israel but seems himself to be its worst enemy. His arbitrariness seems limitless and his wrath without measure. He rages not only against the enemies of Israel but against Israel itself, he punishes not only the perpetrators of ill but the pious as well—not everywhere and always but still in such a way that it is no longer possible to know what to make of him, how to live with him, what to believe about him, and whether he can still be relied on.

---

22. This does not mean that *all* further developments are to be seen *only* in light of these crises or that they were concerned solely with working through these theologically. Both in Israel and in Christianity, there have been many and varied developments that in facing the challenges of their times outlined and elaborated the conceptions of God anew. In the texts of the Old Testament, for example, this applies to the traces left by the engagement with Persian religion. In the New Testament, this applies to the different accents with which Pauline, deutero-Pauline, and Johannine texts unfold the conception of God. And it applies to the consequential developments of Christian theology of the early Christian and Imperial period that led to the formation of Trinitarian doctrine and Christology. See Dalferth, *Jenseits von Mythos und Logos,* and Markschies, *Gnosis.*

In light of these experiences, Israel's exilic and post-exilic theology and history of the faith could not avoid rethinking, from the ground up, the conception of God and of itself it had inherited. In the Priestly Source (on the Aaronite side), in Deuteronomy and the books of Kings (on the Zadokite side) scribes wrote their genealogy anew in engaging with the theme of Evil.[23] The previously marginalized Latter Prophets were rediscovered and their message updated in light of the events that had occurred.[24] Authors and commentators felt compelled to think and understand God—a God who had become vague beyond recognition—anew and differently in light of the events experienced. And that was not possible without understanding themselves anew and differently. God had become obscure, and only against the background of this obscurity was it still possible to think God in order to shed light on one's own life, experience, and suffering in the recourse to God.

What the biblical texts report about God hence remains shot through with tensions and contradictions that cannot be resolved without losing sight of the fact that the biblical efforts to understand a God who cannot be conceptualized referred to concrete historical experience. All of this does not come together in a uniform image of God of the kind theological and philosophical thinking attempt time and again to construct. The omnibenevolent, omniscient, and omnipotent God is an intellectual construct of later ages with little support in the experiences the biblical text testifies to.

Since the Babylonian exile, however, the God of the people of Israel Yahweh had increasingly been understood monotheistically as the one and only God of the entire world.[25] As the God who "fill[s] heaven and earth," he ever more clearly shifts into a world-transcending beyond and moves away from human beings' concrete life experiences (Jer 23:24).[26] God is not only one, he increasingly becomes "entirely different." This

23. With the destruction of the Davidian dynasty and of the Jerusalem temple, the legitimation of those among the Jerusalem priestly scribes who traced their genealogy back to Zadok, the high priest in Solomon's temple, entered a fundamental crisis. In response, a group of priestly reformers sought to go back further than the Jerusalem tradition and legitimize itself by invoking Aaron, brother of Moses, whom Yahweh, according to pre-exilic narratives about Moses, had installed as priest. It is this group to whom the Priestly Source is attributed. Conceived in exile, its narrative goes from creation (Gen 1) to the installment of the Aaronites at Sinai (Lev 9). The Zadokites countered with a revision of Deuteronomy, first written already before the exile (chs. 12–25, 28), adding a frame that traced the text back to Moses who had received the Law not on Mount Sinai (as in the Aaronite Priestly Source) but on the Mountain of God called Horeb (chs. 5, 9–10, 26). See Otto, *Mose: Geschichte und Legende*, 42–54; Rüterswörden, "Das Böse in der deuteronomischen Schultheologie"; and Thiel, "'Evil' in the Books of Kings."

24. Jeremias, "Das Wesen der alttestamentlichen Prophetie," 3–5.

25. On pre-exilic developments toward Yahweh monolatry, see Beck, *Elia und die Monolatrie*, and Miller, *Religion of Ancient Israel*, esp. 1–45.

26. In this case, as becomes clear in Deutero-Isaiah, it is not even necessary anymore to polemicize against the gods of other nations and people because they are but Nothingnesses anyway—and they are such because unlike the one and only true God, they *do not effect anything*; see Hermisson, "Gott und das Leid," 14–15. The one and only God has absolutely nothing to do with the statues of gods that are made by goldsmiths, carried around, and erected in Babylon. These statues are being erected, then they stand there and no longer move. They are being shouted at, but they do not respond and do not help anyone in their distress (Isa 46:1–7). Not so for Yahweh, who is the only godhead that really exists. He cannot be seen, he knows no image one could make of him, carry around, or erect somewhere, and he cannot be confined in any location. But what he says will come about, and what he intends to do, he does. He can be relied on, one can place one's hope in him. The rescue he has promised is imminent and

in turn results in the ever-expanding space between God and the world of the human becoming populated with intermediate beings, angels or messengers of God who mediate
between him and the humans. This allows for clearing up ambiguities of the traditional
imagery of God by distributing the different traits among God and other entities. While
in the books of the Kingdoms, the census conducted by David is attributed to God's
wrath flaring up against Israel, the description of the Chronicler written two hundred
years later attributes the same event not to God but to Satan: "Satan stood up against
Israel." The "negative functions that up until then God fulfilled himself" are transferred
to Satan: "While earlier, there were no apprehensions about ascribing incitement to sin
to Yahweh, this role is now being saddled on Satan" (2 Sam 24:1; 1 Chr 21:1).[27] Yet even
in the Chronicles, this attempt remains an exception and is not suitable to explain the
ambivalence of the traditional images of God generally.[28]

Similar things can be said about other attempts at clarification. The biblical images
of God cannot be rid of their ambivalence, either, neither by hermeneutically distinguishing in them, as Philo of Alexandria does, anthropomorphic representation and
truly philosophical content, nor by theologically separating them, as Marcion of Sinope
does, into images of an allegedly dubious Old Testament tradition of a passionate God of
the Law and images of a good New Testament tradition of a philosophically calm God of
Love. Philo, for example, says with regard to God's regret about having created the human
(Gen 6:3) that some people "suppose that the Existent feels wrath and anger, whereas He
is not susceptible to any such passion at all. For disquiet is peculiar to human weakness,
but neither the unreasoning passions of the soul, nor the parts and members of the body
in general"—which are required for such an affect—"have any relation to God."[29] But
he then runs into significant trouble in trying to explain why the biblical texts so often
and at such length talk about God's affects. And Marcion's approach, ascribing all that is
incomprehensible, offensive, and unacceptable to a redundant Old Testament God and
finding in the New Testament only a good God of love and mercy, can be accomplished
only through violence and leaves behind a theological ruin in which neither the Old
Testament's nor the New Testament's experience of God could recognize itself.[30] Irre-

---

is already beginning (Isa 46:8–13).

27. Haag, *Vor dem Bösen ratlos?*, 74–75.

28. Despite his being mentioned later in the vision of Zechariah (Zech 3) and the prologue to Job
(1–2), Satan in the Old Testament remains a marginal mythological figure who fulfills narrative rather
than theological functions; see Day, *Adversary in Heaven*. Satan becomes the epitome of Evil and the
archetype of the one who seduces and tempts into Evil only in the New Testament (Matt 4:1–11; Luke
4:1–13; 22:3–4; John 13:27; 1 Pet 5:8; Eph 4:27). Herbert Haag succinctly describes the historical developments in religion and theology leading up to this (Haag, *Vor dem Bösen ratlos?*, 77–105). See also
Jung, *Fallen Angels*; Horst, "Teufel II"; Böcher, *Christus Exorcista*; Russell, *Satan*; Ferguson, *Demonology
of the Early Christian World*; Garrett, *Demise of the Devil*; Arnold, *Powers of Darkness*; Twelftree, *Jesus
the Exorcist*; Martinek, *Wie die Schlange zum Teufel wurde*; Pagels, *Origin of Satan*; and Watts, *Isaiah's
New Exodus and Mark*, 137–82.

29. Philo, "On the Unchangeableness of God," 11.52:37.

30. The attempt is made again and again, to this day. See, for example, Ray Embry, who piles reference onto reference to show that "Israel's God of wrath and the Christian God of Love" (Embry, *Enigma
about Divine Love*, back cover) must be strictly separated. "*The Creation of Evil* by Jehovah (Isa 45:7)
completely disgraces the concept of *Divine Love*" (Embry, *Enigma about Divine Love*, 7). The teachings

solvably interlocked, there is evidence of both in the biblical texts, and although striking developments and shifts of emphases have taken place, these must never be considered only from an analytical distance as a historical development from the dark to the light and from evil to good such that what comes later is also what is better. An unequivocal and clear image of God cannot be found in any biblical texts but can only ever be found (or precisely not found) in engaging with these texts. Both the cruel and the good that is being reported and confessed of God, to acquire an orienting function, equally compel our taking a position; and not relating to them, too, is a way of taking a position.

The path from the doubtful ambivalence of the image of God to an image sufficiently unambiguous to serve to orient one's life must thus be taken anew time and again and by each person for themselves.[31] God cannot be confessed as good without thereby taking a position on how God is good for someone or for oneself.[32] Nor can God be feared and accused as terror without giving expression to the terror of those affected and to their fear of God. Because the image of God entertains an elementary relation to concrete life experiences—and this, above all else, is what the biblical traditions bring out—what is at issue in this image is always simultaneously the image of the human via which we understand ourselves: image of God and image of self are indissolubly connected. We cannot take a position on the image of God without at the same time taking a position toward ourselves: how we understand God shows how we understand ourselves, and vice versa.[33]

5. God as the Author of Evil

The ambiguity of the image of God in the biblical traditions results from precisely this connection. If the image of God were entirely unequivocal, it could hardly be related to the entirely equivocal life of human beings (God would be *entirely* different), yet if it became entirely equivocal, it would no longer be of use for orienting oneself in human life (what is actually meant by "God" would no longer be understandable) and the reference to God would lose its life-practical point. The image of God must be developed theologically between these two poles, and to exercise its orienting function, it must in different respects be both—entirely *different* and entirely *similar*.[34] To demonstrate

---

of Jesus and the tradition of the Old Testament are said contradict each other throughout: there is thus no commonality between the Jewish Jehovah and the Christian Abba.

31. Only that is at issue here, not a forever unattainable absolute unambiguousness. This suitability for orienting lives on the part of the image of God centrally includes the experientially tested reliability of the orientation of their lives, on the part of the community and the individual, toward a God thus understood and represented.

32. Without decisions, there is no theology. What characterizes theologians is not that they cite biblical texts but that, in engaging with these texts in the context of the realities of life in their own time, they distinguish between the Law and the Gospel. We can see this in the biblical texts themselves; it is the reason why they continued to be (re)written and why they cannot be fixed to a certain current state of development as a canonical norm without losing one of their most important points. The canon is not the text; the canon is what these texts, in ever new attempts, try to understand and interpret.

33. Chr. Janowski, *Ein Gott, der tötet?*, 72, rightly insists on this point.

34. See Dalferth, "Leben angesichts des Unverfügbaren".

this point, let me trace, by way of example, some of the fault lines that have shaped the biblical thinking of God in the wake of the catastrophe of 587/586 BC.

That God is the author of everything, that is, not only of the good but of Evil as well, follows for Israel from the faith in the one and only God expressed in the first commandment.[35] Pre-exile, this was a matter of course that prompted no further questions; the catastrophe of 587/586 turned it into a fundamental challenge to Israel's faith. "Does disaster befall a city, unless the Lord has done it?" Amos (3:6) asks in the eighth century, and he can presume that no one will contest the point. For Israel, God was by no means in charge of the good alone, with all evil put to the charge of others than God, even if fear of demons and belief in spirits were not unknown to Israel.[36] But God's opponents are always his creatures, that is, not independent from but dependent on him. When they do evil, God in a way does evil through them.[37]

This is not an unbearable notion for faith because there can be reasons for it. That God effects evil can be seen, for example, as just punishment of ill doers who violate his will: God's wrath is directed at those who turn away from him. The one to whom evil happens from God must then of course also have incurred guilt, as everyday religious logic suggests, and the book of Job at the very latest shows how this view comes up against its limits: that the unjust must suffer through God might be understandable, but when that happens to the just, the limits of what can be understood seem to have been trespassed.

But it does not have to be like that when God is thought differently. Even if God's wrath ruthlessly crushes everything and by far exceeds any comprehensible relation to actual guilt incurred by those affected, if God—as Lamentations 2 deplores after the destruction of Jerusalem[38]—destroys the land, the city, the palace, Zion, the temple, his priests, and his own cult; if God punishes not only the guilty but in extreme ruthlessness tears down everything and has women and children, priests and prophets, young boys and old men, young women and young men massacred, that is no reason to become skeptical about one's faith and question his divine power or divinity, no reason not to turn to this God in lamentation and accusation of his excessive wrath.[39] On the contrary, such sinister doings of God's can very much be understood as expressions of his being God: "I am the Lord, and there is no other. I form light and create darkness, I make

35. On what follows, see also Hermisson, "Gott und das Leid," 4–5. Christine Janowski systematically takes up this insight: "It is *not* possible to *begin* with talking about the destroying God if God is not to become a Satan or Devil and thus a corruptor. . . . One must begin with God the creator" (Janowski, *Ein Gott, der tötet?*, 70)

36. See Schmidt, *Gott und das Leid*, 7–8.

37. It is this notion that Luther's arguments in *De servo arbitrio* pick up on. If we start from God's uniqueness and exclusive efficacy, then there is nothing that is and happens in which God would not be efficacious. "Since . . . God moves and actuates all in all, God necessarily moves and acts also in Satan and ungodly humans. But God acts in them as they are and as found by God" such that "evil things are done, with God setting them in motion. It is just as if a carpenter were cutting badly with a chipped and jagged ax" (Luther, *Bondage of the Will*, 225). See also Reinhuber, *Kämpfender Glaube*, and Wyrwa, "Augustine and Luther on Evil."

38. Compare Greenstein, "Wrath of God in the Book of Lamentations."

39. Lamentations 2; see Westermann, *Lamentations: Issues and Interpretation*, 158–59, and Emmendörffer, *Der ferne Gott*, 63.

weal and create woe; I the Lord do all these things," the exile prophet Deutero-Isaiah proclaims (Isa 45:6–7). Against any kind of dualism that feels it needs to protect God from the accusations of those affected by suffering and seeks to hold someone other than God's own will responsible for it, Deutero-Isaiah relates God's being creator not only to the domain of light and welfare but also to that of darkness and calamity.[40] As the one and only God, Yahweh is not only the creator of heaven and earth, he is also responsible, without limitations, for good and evil, welfare and calamity.[41]

This is meant not just in the sense that God only does evil to punish Evil (that is, really acts in a good way), or that he creates calamity for the enemies of Israel but welfare for Israel. Israel, of course, is familiar with that as well, as the Song of the Sea about the miracle in the sea of reeds exemplarily shows: "Sing to the Lord, for he has triumphed gloriously; horse and rider he has thrown into the sea" (Exod 15:21). Yahweh has left the Egyptian pursuers to perish in the sea along with their horses and chariots. This is not only an act of saving Israel, even if that is the tenor of Miriam's song. The Egyptians are overtaken by a calamity they incurred, as the narrative of Exodus explains, only because Yahweh has made Pharaoh obdurate, which leads him to order his troops to chase after Israel on its way out of Egypt. Yahweh himself prompts the evil that he punishes with calamity. He creates welfare for Israel by chasing others into calamity.

Deutero-Isaiah does not stop at this traditional point of view. For him, Yahweh is the one who creates welfare and calamity *for* Israel. He speaks in the situation of exile after the destruction of Jerusalem. None other than Yahweh himself has brought this calamity on for Israel. In earlier times, it would have been concluded that the Babylonians' victory over Jerusalem was the victory of the Babylonian gods over Yahweh, that is, that Yahweh perished along with his people. Deutero-Isaiah counters by claiming that none other than Yahweh himself effected this collapse. In the same breath, however, he also stresses that after the end of David's dynasty and the demise of the Jerusalem kingdom, it is none other than Yahweh himself who raises the Persian Cyrus to the level of the anointed in order for him to carry out, with Yahweh's help, the task of subduing Babylon and liberating Israel (Isa 45:1–7). Israel's calamity and Israel's welfare are effected by God who makes not only the Babylonians but also the king of the Persian empire his instruments. Yahweh, the God of the annihilated and exiled people, thereby proves himself to be the absolute Lord not only of Israel but of the entire world.

Few claims will ever have sounded more absurd. The defeated claim that their God is the Lord of the victors, that the victors function merely as his tools. Yahweh, the God of the annihilated Israel effects welfare and calamity, in Israel and in the other nations; he is the only Lord of the entire world, of its light as well as its dark sides. This comprehensive view of God's power of creation purposively goes beyond what the Priestly Source ascribes to God (Elohim): that he created *everything in a good way* and created *only what*

---

40. See Hoffman, "The First Creation Story," and "Jeremiah 50–51 and the Concept of Evil," 26–27.

41. Lüthi, *Gott und das Böse*, 152–53, and Groß and Kuschel, *"Ich schaffe Finsternis und Unheil!,"* 43–46. That this time and again created problems for Jewish thought as well is apparent in Shalom Rosenberg: "Our Sages, when they formulated our Morning Prayers, changed 'creates evil' [Isa 45:7] into 'creates all,' to prevent us from reciting a blessing over the creation of evil" (Rosenberg, *Good and Evil in Jewish Thought*, 13). See also Thoma, "Gott im Unrecht," 89–92.

is good but, precisely, did *not* create *everything* (Gen 1:1–2, 4a).[42] God's creative order-ing is preceded, according to the narrative of Genesis, by a given chaotic earth that is desolate and empty and must first be shaped into a space for life by separating water and land as habitats for aquatic and land animals. That is possible only once the creation of the skydome separates the primordial waters from the waters under the sky, even if they remain a constant chaotic threat and can break through the sky at any point that God no longer holds them back, as the story of the Flood recounts. And the darkness above the primordial waters, too, is pregiven for the creator; only the creation of light integrates it into creation in such a way that it in the alternation with day, darkness becomes night. Unlike the day, however, the night is not a time of life, such that in the alternation of day and night, the darkness of pre-creation maintains a threatening presence in the night. That is why God judges only the light to be good but not day and night together. Accord-ing to the Priestly Source, then, God's creation is entirely good, but it is not everything, because chaos, primordial waters, and darkness are pre-givens that are conjured in and through creation only with great effort and remain present as permanent threats (Gen 1:2–10 and 6).[43]

This could not but raise the question of the scope of God's creative power. Deutero-Isaiah answers it by declaring the darkness, too, to be a work of God: Yahweh has cre-ated the light and the darkness, and he is thus responsible not only for welfare but for calamity as well (Isa 45:7). Proverbs does not go that far, even if the speaker, Wisdom, refers to itself as having been instituted by Yahweh and born before time and before the beginning of the earth and the existence of the primordial waters. The primordial waters, too, have thus not always existed. While it is not said that Yahweh had created them, he and wisdom are said to preexist them (Prov 8:23–24).[44] This leaves open the possibility of concluding what Deutero-Isaiah had concluded and asserted for darkness: the primordial waters, too, are due to God. But in any case it raises the question of God's responsibilities for the orders of creation, which not only allow the human being to live but in which "young lions roar for their prey," where the chaos monsters Levia-than (crocodile) and Behemoth (hippopotamus) threaten the lives of humans, where animals endanger and fight humans, humans animals, and humans each other, where constantly one life for the sake of its self-preservation threatens and destroys another life (Ps 104:21; Job 41, 40).[45]

Where God's being creator is not restricted to the establishment of the good order against the threats of chaos, primordial waters, and darkness, where instead these, too, are traced back to him and God's good order is itself being experienced as an inter-locking and coexistence of life and death, welfare and calamity, there God seems to be

42. See Groß and Kuschel, *"Ich schaffe Finsternis und Unheil!,"* 35–43.

43. See Levenson, *Creation and the Persistence of Evil*, esp. chs. 2, 4, 9.

44. See Levenson, *Creation and the Persistence of Evil*, 38–43.

45. How the expressions "Leviathan" and "Behemoth" are to be understood is a matter of contention. Gordis, *Book of God and Man*, 119–20, like many others, interprets them naturalistically as designating crocodile and hippopotamus, whereas Fyall, *Now My Eyes Have Seen You*, 117–37, 157–74, takes them to be "embodiments of the powers of death and evil" (129). He thereby follows Wakeman, *God's Battle with the Monster*, 113–17, who identifies Behemoth with Mot and Leviathan with Yam. Newsom, *Book of Job*, 248, too, gives such a symbolic reading.

responsible for everything and thereby to become ambivalent.[46] Orientation by God is thus rendered impossible. David, who given his sin can choose between three years of famine, three months of fleeing from his enemies, or three days of plague in the land, would rather "'fall into the hand of the Lord, for his mercy is great; but let me not fall into human hands.' So the Lord sent a pestilence on Israel" (2 Sam 24:14–15). While God also sends ill and calamity, his mercy is great. In the pre-exilic texts, it was possible even during a plague sent by him to feel safer with God than with unpredictable human beings. God was known not only to give life but to kill as well, yet his mercy was known to be great. All this has become obscure for the survivors in the Babylonian exile after the all-destroying catastrophe of 587/586. Are the promises God has given still valid? Has God's mercy transformed into mercilessness? Even if God is the Lord of the world, as Deutero-Isaiah says, how is it to be possible to orient oneself by him when he, in a way no longer comprehensible, effects welfare *and* calamity?

Remarkably, the attempt at theologically working through the catastrophe in Deutero-Isaiah does not lead to a simple restitution of the pre-exilic image of God, which knew God as the one and only God of Israel without thereby contesting the existence of the gods of other nations. What comes about instead is a monotheistic universalization of Yahweh: the God of Israel is thought as the God of the entire world and thus as the only true God. The old Israel has perished, but its God, precisely in no longer one-sidedly representing good for his followers and evil for his enemies but instead himself effecting welfare and calamity with regard to Israel, has proven to be Lord not only of the history of Israel but of world history as a whole.

6. Rereading History

Now, it would be a misunderstanding to infer that this rids human beings of their responsibility for evil: If it is willed and effected by God, is it not God, then, and not the human who is responsible? And in that case, is there still any need to be concerned with God since he does whatever he wants, in good as in evil? The expansion of Yahweh's power in becoming the God of world history who creates welfare and calamity as he pleases leads into the aporia that he can no longer serve to orient human lives. If everything comes from God, good as well as evil, and comes without differentiation to both good and evil people, then there is no need to be concerned with God. Everything comes as it comes, whether we orient our lives by God or not.

It is not a surprise that, against the background of these possibilities, post-exilic theology mobilizes everything to exclude this consequence. It tries vigorously to adjust

---

46. What is preparing itself here is a profound change in the guiding religious and theological categories that can be described, in the terms of the history of religion, as the switch from the cosmological orientation figure *order vs. chaos* to the monotheistic orientation figure *God vs. world*. See Stolz, *Weltbilder der Religionen*, esp. 139–72, and *Religion und Rekonstruktion*, esp. 248–67. While in the former orienting context, God is situated on the side of order against chaos, he now confronts both order and chaos. As a consequence, God can no more be claimed, without adducing further reasons, for the *bonum* of the good order than he can be for the *malum* of chaos—and thereby becomes deeply equivocal.

the distribution of responsibility between God and human being, namely with regard to the history of Israel, to the individual human being, and to God himself.[47]

In the books of Kings, shaped by the deuteronomistic theology of the Zadokites, the catastrophes of Israel and Judah are unambiguously traced back to the renunciation of God.[48] Second Kings 17:2–23 gives a detailed list of the offenses of Israel (and Judah) that have led to the catastrophe—that of Samaria first, but then also of Judah, as the insertion 2 Kings 17:19–20 makes clear. Other gods had been worshiped, other laws followed, other cults practiced; the warnings of the prophets had been cast to the wind, idols been fabricated, fortune-telling and magic pursued, in short: everything that God had forbidden had been done, none of what he had commanded been obeyed. The guilt for the disaster that occurred thus in no way lies with God but only and exclusively with Israel itself and its representatives. Thus, in the view of the author of the books of Kings, the behavior of the kings especially shows that Israel had been inexorably sliding toward doom because since Solomon (1 Kings 11:4), the actions of all kings, with very few exceptions, had been displeasing the Lord and thus led Israel toward ruin. The message is unequivocal: it is not God who turned away from the people, the people turned away from God. The old image of God does not have to be revised; it is the key to correctly understanding the reasons for the history that led to the catastrophe.

Two hundred years later, the author of Chronicles confirms this view when he tersely notes that Zedekiah, the last king of Judah, too,

> stiffened his neck and hardened his heart against turning to the Lord, the God of Israel. All the leading priests and the people also were exceedingly unfaithful, following all the abominations of the nations; and they polluted the house of the Lord that he had consecrated in Jerusalem. The Lord, the God of their ancestors, sent persistently to them by his messengers [admonitions—IUD], because he had compassion on his people and on his dwelling place; but they kept mocking the messengers of God, despising his words, and scoffing at his prophets, until the wrath of the Lord against his people became so great that there was no remedy. (2 Chr 36:13–16)

The ensuing catastrophe was thus not an arbitrary act of calamity on the part of God but just punishment for the renunciation and unfaith of his people. What needed to change was not one's view of God but one's view of the history of Israel.

7. Reinterpretation of Individual Lives

The books of Kings and Chronicles assign responsibility for the history of renunciation leading to the catastrophe to the people's political and religious leaders in particular. But it does not suffice simply to shift responsibility to others alone. One must accept it for oneself if there is any sense to be made of God punishing even those who were not perpetrators but victims tempted by others, if God is not to have acted in unjust arbitrariness.

47. On what follows, see Haag, *Vor dem Bösen ratlos?*, 54–57.

48. See Thiel, "'Evil' in the Books of Kings," 2: "The books of Kings are dominated by the theme of evildoing."

Psalm 51 in an exemplary way documents this step from ascribing guilt to others to ascribing it to oneself. Judging from its language and content, this psalm is likely to have originated in the "wisdom-oriented milieu of scribes," of the pious and righteous.[49] In his prayer, the speaker does not talk about others but about himself: "For I know my transgressions, and my sin is ever before me. Against you, you alone, have I sinned, and done what is evil in your sight, so that you are justified in your sentence and blameless when you pass judgment" (51:3–4). For the speaker, the destructive action does not mark a darkening of God but constitutes a just punishment for his sins. "Indeed, I was born guilty, a sinner when my mother conceived me" (51:5).[50] This is not a speculation about the origin of sin but the expression of the speaker's acceptance of full responsibility for it. "The speaker of the prayer is sinful from the beginning and thus entirely sinful."[51] There is nothing good in him himself and nothing evil in God. The situation is unequivocal: God does right even where he effects calamity because the person affected by it is himself responsible and cannot talk his way out of it. His guilt cannot be shifted to others (kings, priests, princes) but must be borne and taken responsibility for entirely by himself. He is in no position to will, say, or do what is good by himself. For him to be able to do so, God in a new act of creation must create a pure heart for him, give him a certain spirit (51:12), and open his lips for him to be able to praise God (51:17) and teach the other transgressors the paths of God (51:15). Only God can do the good, whereas the speaker is by himself incapable of it and can do good only insofar as God enables him to.

8. Return to the Old Image of God under Different Circumstances

God alone is responsible for all that is good in the human being, but it is entirely incorrect even just to try and hold him co-responsible for Evil. Jesus, son of Sirach, makes this point with great clarity in the context of Hellenistic culture around 180 BC.[52] "Do not say, 'It was the Lord's doing that I fell away'; for he does not do what he hates. Do not say, 'It was he who led me astray'; for he has no need of the sinful. The Lord hates all abominations, and he does not let it happen to those who fear him" (Sir 15:11–13). Nothing could be more absurd than trying to see in God not only the author of welfare but of calamity as well. "All the works of the Lord are very good" (39:16). The fact that, within creation, there is both good and evil corresponds to the purposiveness of the order of creation—conceived here in downright Stoic terms—in which what is good serves those who are good and evil is required to punish those who are evil (39:24–34). For humans have a choice: "If you choose, you can keep the commandments, and to act faithfully is a matter of your own choice. He has placed before you fire and water; stretch out your hand for whichever you choose. Before each person are life and death, and whichever one chooses will be given" (15:15–17). God's created order gives humans

---

49. Pfeiffer, "'Ein reines Herz schaffe mir, Gott!,'" 306.

50. This verse—erroneously—counts among the central sources of the theory of original sin; see Suda, "Psalm 51,7 als Belegstelle für Augustins Erbsündenlehre."

51. Pfeiffer, "'Ein reines Herz schaffe mir, Gott!,'" 299.

52. See Crenshaw, "Problem of Theodicy in Sirach," and Gilbert, "God, Sin and Mercy."

a choice between good and evil possibilities (fire and water), and they have the freedom to decide in favor of one or the other.

When evil happens to someone, it is thus always the consequence of their own decision. No one has to do evil, but when they do evil, they must expect that God punishes them with evil. That is something to count on with certainty; we should not speculate on God's mercy: "Do not say, 'His mercy is great, he will forgive the multitude of my sins'" (5:6). The one thing that is certain is that evil people are punished because humans do what they do freely on their own and on their own responsibility. God is in no way to be dragged into this doing: he has not co-caused it, and one should not expect him not to do what is to be expected of a just God in this case, namely punishing. The human has the freedom to violate God's commandments but must expect God's punishment. This may not be immediately obvious in every case. Yet we should not be misled by the lucky fate of the unjust; their true destiny will assert itself on the day they die at the latest (9:11–12). The consequences of their deeds will in any case catch up with the unjust, and the end of someone's life shows whether they have lived righteously or not (1:13 and 23, 2:3, 6:28, 7:36, 16:22, 21:10).[53]

The old relations have thus been restored under new conditions: God punishes those who are evil but does not himself commit any evil. The calamity he wreaks, too, is part of his just effecting of welfare. For in this way, he ensures that the unjust suffer their just punishment, that is, that injustice does not remain without consequences.

This seems to preserve the order of creation—but only as long as we look only at the big picture and do not look too closely. For is it really the case that evil happens only to evil people but not to good people, or that those who are evil experience only as much evil as they deserve for their ill deeds? What about all the excessive calamity that seems to bear no proportion to the crime committed? What about the excess of a punishment that eliminates not only those who are guilty but the innocent as well? It may be understandable that the unjust receive their just punishment, but how could it be possible to understand that calamity unjustly strikes the just?

Theologically, that cannot be the last word, and it has not remained the last word.[54] The Old Testament is familiar with different responses and has thought through the problem of thinking God in relation to Evil and of thinking Evil through the detour via God in more than one way. Time and again and in too many different situations, authors were affected by evil in ever-different ways. To be able to orient oneself in these different circumstances, certain typical situations, *topoi* or *loci* of thought crystallized over time in religious memory and in the theological tradition, for which model narratives were elaborated.

Exemplary instances are the narratives of Adam, Noah, and Job, each of which differently conceives of and represents both the evil they describe and God's justice they thereby illustrate.[55] Thus, according to the narrative of Genesis, the *malum* that strikes

---

53. See Forster, *Begrenztes Leben als Herausforderung*, 235, 241–43.

54. On later developments in Judaism, see Neusner, *Theology of the Oral Torah* and "Theodicy in Judaism," as well as Chilton, "Theodicy in the Targumim."

55. It is not a coincidence that from this perspective, the narratives of Adam, Noah, and Job are all versions of the story of creation.

Adam is an alleviated punishment for his inappropriate and unjustified misconduct toward God. The *malum* Noah escapes, by contrast, is the punishment imposed by a God disappointed by and angry about the never-ending injustices humans commit toward him and toward each other. And the *malum* that overtakes the undisputedly righteous Job is in no way due to any known or concealed injustice, it is a test that God has set for him without his knowledge. In the first case, God is just because he reacts with such restraint to Adam's failure toward himself (which contradicts Adam's own human rectitude) that it simultaneously puts the creator's enduring care for his creature on display: God punishes and spares the unjust.[56] In the second case, by contrast, the limits of his care and justice, which are not willing to accept anything and everything humans do in the long run, are on display: God punishes the unjust and saves the just. And in the third case, it is no longer clear for the one affected, Job—although not for the reader of the Job novella, who knows more—whether one still can, whether one still ought to speak of God's justice or whether one is just left exposed to his arbitrary power: God drowns the just in ills. The three narratives mark exemplary cases on the spectrum along which the Old Testament thinks through God's justice with respect to Evil and through Evil in the light of God's justice. They deserve a closer look.

9. The Experiment of Creation: Adam

God created a *good* world—that is the tenor of the narrative of creation with which the Priestly Source once more depicts, to the exile generation, the starting point of the entire history that led to the current misery. Creation here is not yet understood as creation from nothing. There is no evidence of that notion before the time of the Maccabees (2 Macc 7:28), and it plays no role yet in the Genesis narrative. God's creation, rather, is described in terms of ordering and shaping, manifest in separating and distinguishing, categorizing and setting of boundaries: between light and darkness, day and night, heaven and earth, land and see, plants and animals, animals in the land, the sea, and the air, and the human being distinguished as "image of *God*" from all other creatures and as "*image*" from God. Creation is narrated as bringing order to what is disordered, unlimited, and unseparated, and it is a good creation because it creates a world ordered by boundaries in which humans can live and orient themselves.

This creation is threatened whenever these boundaries are damaged, blurred, or destroyed. Wherever this happens, there is "wrong," something is being done that is "not right" because it questions the orders that make life possible in the first place. Inversely, "right" or laws are made where life-promoting order is created. Doing so is "just" or "righteous," and those who comply live "righteously." Just as creating and maintaining life-promoting order is thus *justice* or *righteousness*, so endangering and damaging this order is *injustice* or *unrighteousness*. For the thinking of the Priestly Source, this begins

---

56. This analogously applies to God's reaction to the fratricide, Cain (Genesis 4): God does not impose, as one might have expected, the death penalty but spares and protects the murderer. See Dietrich and Link, *Die dunklen Seiten Gottes*, 152–53.

with the creation of the world and finds its summit in the Torah, in the Law that God, through Moses, has given to Israel for maintaining and shaping its life.[57]

That this order exists is what is astonishing and remarkable, not that there is disorder, repulsiveness, injustice, and evil. The Priestly Source's theology of creation is concerned not with the question *unde malum?* but the question *unde, cur et a quo bonum?* Evil is that which is always probable and to be expected; what is astonishing and improbable, by contrast, is what is good. God is to be thanked for this, not for everything there is. God bears responsibility solely for the orders he institutes and promulgates but not for the disorder he thereby shapes, limits, and pushes back against. Just as God did not create "everything" without qualification, so he is not responsible for "everything" without qualification. He is *just* and *good* because he creates life-promoting orders, but this justice and goodness is from the beginning directed against something else, from which it is arduously obtained and which it actively puts in its place. Creation is the struggle of order against disorder, and just as the justice of order can be maintained only in the fight against the injustice of disorder, so it is permanently threatened by the destructive counterpower of the disordered, unjust, and repulsive.[58]

Already the creation of the world as such, then, is a process that shows God to be originally just because he fights against the repulsive. In creating, God establishes a harmonious order in which the dangers of chaos, the primordial waters, and darkness are conjured by the order of space (primordial waters and cosmos, heaven and earth, sea and land) and time (day and night, the cycles of sun and moon, week, year). This order has been threatened from the beginning, but without the human being, things may have gone well. To be sure, at the end of the sixth day, having created the human and assigned him his task in creation, God says that everything had turned out "very well" (Gen 1:31). Yet the last editor of this text knew that this version of the narrative did not tell the whole story. That is why he added a further, a different version of the story of the creation of the human in which it becomes clear why things did not go as well with this being as they could have. The human is a being of possibilities that fails itself because it seeks to be something other than itself and thereby is less than it can be.

This is first of all and above all a judgment of the biblical author on the contemporary reality of human life. The life of humans could have been different and better than it is now. That it is not has its reasons not in defects or deficiencies of the created world in which they live. It is due solely to the equivocalness of the human being itself, which is why at least two stories have to be told about it to capture its problem. Humans, as the psalm emphasizes, are neither God nor animals but "a little lower than the angels" (Ps 8:5). Their intermediary position in the construct of creation endows them with possibilities every animal is lacking but also confronts them with dangers no animal faces. Unlike all the animals, which are what they are and are called what humans call

---

57. On the conception of "justice" or "righteousness," see Rad, "'Righteousness' and 'Life' in the Cultic Languages of the Psalms."

58. This struggle has been actualized and reached its goal "in heaven," that is, in the domain where God's just rule has comprehensively imposed itself. It remains yet to be actualized definitively, though, "on earth," where humans live together. Accordingly, the third petition of the Lord's Prayer asks that "Your will be done, on earth as it is in heaven." See Berger, *Wie kann Gott Leid und Katastrophen zulassen?*, 42–43.

them, humans are what they make of themselves by understanding themselves the way they understand themselves, and they are always different yet again from how others know them and call them. Among all creatures, humans alone can miss themselves by understanding themselves as what they are not: as God, who they are not, or as animals, which they are not exclusively.

This missing of themselves, which leads humans to live short of their possibilities, forms the story of the second account of creation.[59] As described there, the human being is made, brought to life, placed in a beautiful garden with trees bearing good fruit (Gen 2:9), and warned about the fruit bad for him (2:17). But defects remain, and God makes improvements. He comes to see that it is not good for Adam to be alone (2:18) and gives him animals for companions. But the human is still not satisfied (2:20). That is why God makes a companion for Adam, from a piece of Adam himself (2:21–22), and only now is the latter satisfied for the first time: "This at last is bone of my bones and flesh of my flesh" (2:23). But this satisfaction does not last. Rather than be glad about the possibilities they have (2:24–25), enjoy the luxuries they are being offered (2:16), and content themselves with the tasks they are given (2:15, 2:19–20), the human couple want more than they are due. They want to take the place of God himself, become like God, know what is good and what is evil (3:5), and they let themselves be prompted by the snake's insinuation to rebel against God to become what, however, they already are: not mortal (2:8, 3:4–5). Thereby, however, the point is reached where God must react in order to maintain the basic condition of the good order of creation: the difference between creator and creature. For the properties by which God is distinct from his creation are the knowledge of good and evil and eternal life (3:22). The human beings are the only ones among his creatures to whom God has shown what they must do in order not to die: they must not eat the wrong fruit (2:17). He thereby has elevated them above all other creatures and moved them closer to himself in such a way that the only difference between him and them is the knowledge about what is good and what is evil, that is, knowledge about what is conducive to the order of life of creation and what is not. That is why he could place them above all other creatures and make them the ones who cultivate and maintain the garden (2:15) and assign names to all other creatures (2:19–20). Yet when they abolish the last difference between themselves and God, by appropriating knowledge of good and evil, God is left with only one choice to maintain the good order of creation, which the humans have, unwittingly, fundamentally threatened, namely with reestablishing the difference by depriving them of the other thing they have shared with him: eternal life. He does so by chasing them from the garden into a life of toil and pain, of desire and oppression, of fighting against the other creatures, of labor, of arduous survival, and of inevitable death (3:14–19).[60]

Because in its naive foolishness, the human, an uncomprehending and obstinate "glutton and wannabe,"[61] endangers God's entire good creation, God, to prevent worse from happening, must remove the human from his proximity. While it has preserved the creation, it has come at the price of keeping the human alive as a permanent disruptor

59. Wolde, *Semiotic Analysis of Genesis 2–3*.

60. See also Dalferth, *Das Böse*, 79–85.

61. Krochmalnik, "Das Böse in der jüdischen Tradition," 14–15.

of the orders of creation. For even where they live the now-limited span of their lives, they arrogantly continue to endanger creation and damage life as wannabes and gluttons (Gen 3), jealous fratricides (4), good-for-nothing ill-doers who trespass against God (6), shameless rapists (9), and overly confident conquerors of the skies (11), as the narrator of the Priestly Source recounts in the expanding series of "lapses" of humanity in the primeval history of Genesis 1–11.[62] As chapter follows chapter, the never-ending misconducts of the human turn God's original judgment about his creation, that everything was "very good," into its opposite. Already half-way through the primeval history, God reaches the point where he regrets having created humans in the first place and ponders their destruction: "I will blot out from the earth the human beings I have created—people together with animals and creeping things and birds of the air, for I am sorry that I have made them" (6:7). All of created life is to be annihilated because humanity is unable to control its arrogant and creation-threatening conduct and way of life. From this point on, humans struggle not just against their environment: God himself is their opponent. At the beginning of their exile from his proximity, God still made garments for them before he released them into their new lives. Such caring acts are out of the question now. Humans have used up their credit with God. God himself has become their opponent.

10. The Second Experiment of Creation: Noah

If it weren't for Noah. As the Priestly Source presents the primeval history, Noah is the only one among all human beings whom God considers to be just and without reproach (7:1). Unlike the others, Noah does not contravene creation and shed doubt on the differences between God, human, and animal, whose non-observation has chaotic consequences and destroys the orders of creation that make life possible. He does not join in the transgressions of the others who as humans mix with what is above the human (6:1–4) or behave in ways indistinguishable from animal behavior because they no longer fulfill their task of preserving and caring for creation (6:11–12). Noah is "righteous," that is, he lives right and behaves in a way that befits the special position of the human between the divine and the animal: he "walked with God" (6:9), that is, he lives in the correct relation with and distinction from him. He begets the sons Shem, Ham, and Japheth (6:10), that is, he lives up to the task of the humans chased from Paradise to preserve humanity, despite the self-incurred limitation of individual human lifespans, by continuing the succession of generations. And, as charged by God, he cares for creation, tasked not only with naming the animals, as Adam was (2:19–20), but with sheltering them—in pairs and thus capable of reproduction—in the ark and thereby with saving them from the disaster of the flood (7:1–9). And he not only tends the garden and tills the field, as Adam did (2:15 and 3:17–18), he becomes the first cultivator and the first drinker of wine (9:20–21).

For the sake of his righteousness, Noah is spared from the flood with which God destroys a human species spurning its destiny and abusing its position when he allows the primordial waters to break into creation once more. In the contrast between

---

62. See Goldstain, *Création et péché*; Scharbert, *Prolegomena eines Alttestamentlers zur Erbsünden-lehre*; and Dexinger, "Alttestamentliche Überlegungen zum 'Erbsünde'-Problem."

antediluvian and postdiluvian humanity, there is thus a new beginning of creation, not only with a *not yet just or unjust human being* (Adam) but with a *just human being* (Noah). The first attempt at creation failed because Adam misunderstood himself and acted wrongly, a wannabe and glutton who by seeking to rise above his station fell short of his possibilities. This misguided conduct, according to the narrator of the primeval history, continued via Cain, intensifying and spreading in the misguided conduct of all human beings, and thereby provoked God's resolution to destroy them.

Now, with Noah, God undertakes a new beginning under different conditions—although "the inclination of the human heart is evil from youth," that is, the postdiluvian human being is still a wannabe and a glutton, doing no good and willing evil, as God notes without illusion, and that won't change in the future, either. Humans as human are permanently threatened by their precarious position between God and the animals that time and again pushes them beyond themselves and has them fall behind their possibilities. According to the author's insight, that cannot and will not change. What does change is God's conclusion from what humans make of themselves. God "will never again curse the ground because of humankind" (8:21), that is, he commits himself to no longer threatening all of creation with destruction because of human misconduct. Despite the evil inclinations and deeds of humans, the good order of "seedtime and harvest, cold and heat, summer and winter, day and night, shall not cease," that is, creation will be preserved (8:22). The covenant he establishes with Noah seals this new beginning. While it does not guarantee the justice and right life of human beings, it does guarantee the reliable harmonious order of all living creation. Never again is human conduct to be the occasion for extinguishing life on earth in its entirety. God will no longer aim his bow at his creation, but he sets it in the clouds for all to see as a sign of the covenant (9:12–17).

All this does not mean that humans had become better, as the continuation of the narrative shows. For the sake of Noah's righteousness, creation as such has survived, and it is in the future no longer going to be threatened by God as a matter of principle. But humans immediately begin behaving in a way that runs counter to creation, that is, not right and unjust, as Noah's drunkenness and the behavior of his son demonstrate (9:18–22). And once more, misconduct concerns not only individuals, once more, the conduct of all humanity becomes misguided, as the narrative of the construction of the Tower of Babel shows, which concludes the cycle of the primeval history (11). Yet while before the covenant with Noah, God still reacted to human arrogance with disappointment and anger and sought to undo his work of creation, he now just reacts with irony. Excessively overestimating themselves, the humans think they are building a tower to reach the heavens, but God has to come "down to see the city and the tower, which mortals had built" (11:5). Human arrogance to him now is but clueless child's play, nothing more, and with the confusion of languages, his reaction is as to a child's play gone overboard. It is no longer the others and the rest of life on earth that have to bear the consequences of the humans' arrogant actions but only they themselves.

While the new beginning of creation has not thereby made humanity better, it *has* changed God's attitude toward his creation and toward human misconduct. The human can no longer become a threat to all of creation. By themselves, they could not become such anyway, only by prompting God, through their conduct, to react in a massive way.

But that will no longer happen, not because human beings have changed but because God no longer allows things to get to that point. God no longer reacts to human provocations in a way that would endanger all of creation. In interacting with his creation, he has made himself independent of the human and reacts calmly to its provocations. As creator of just orders, he has not grown insensitive to the injustice of humans, but he restricts his reactions entirely to them: the consequences of human conduct must be borne by humans, not by creation as a whole.

11. Divine Justice and the Harmonious Order

This is the first stage of the discovery of God's justice: it founds and guarantees a reliable harmonious order. From the beginning, God wills and effects what is good (Genesis 1). He does so even where, in order to preserve the good orders of creation that make life possible and preserve it, he must remove the human beings with their excess and overconfidence from his presence and proximity. The humans are not, as announced, killed (2:17); only the life of the individual is restricted, while the life of the species is continued and preserved in the succession of generations (4). While God distances himself from the humans, he still makes garments for them to cover their nakedness (3), creates means of life for them in the form of agriculture and livestock breeding, development and civilization (3 and 4), and protects even ill-doers and fratricides from the feared consequences of their wrongs (4:13–15). And this care continues in God's conduct toward the offenses of Noahide humanity: God is just because he reacts to offenses and does not let them go unpunished. Yet even in punishment, he still seeks to do justice to the punished and to have his punishing not be excessive but just and conducive to life.

God's justice as the Priestly Source describes it thus establishes an order of creation on which all creatures in the water, in the air, and on land can rely according to their capacities and particular properties in the alternation of day and night, summer and winter. And he gives special rules to the human beings, the most problematic creatures in this order, that allow them reliably to orient themselves even under the conditions of being removed from the closeness to God. Adam thus exemplifies that God does not tolerate injustice and that the unjust must expect to suffer the just consequences of their actions: injustice is punished by God. And Noah exemplifies that God does not ignore righteousness, and that the righteous can expect to enjoy the righteous consequences of their actions: God rewards righteousness.

The actions of humans thus determine their predicament, in good as in evil. Yet they do so not by themselves, as if naturally, but rather through God instituting a just connection between the actions and the predicaments of human beings: what is unjust is followed by evil, what is just is followed by good (connection of action and predicament). No human being lives only and exclusively righteously, as the story of Adam recounts, yet there is always at least one person who lives more righteously than unrighteously, as the story of Noah recounts. Neither has to be the case, both could be otherwise: humans *could* live righteously (as Gen 1 and 2 show) and humanity *could* entirely drown in unrighteousness (as Gen 6 intimates). In fact, however, neither the one nor the other is the case. There are always just people and unjust people (even if there are many more unjust ones than just ones) and hence there is always both good and evil in the history of humanity (even if there is much more evil than good). An entirely just and an entirely unjust humanity are positive and negative points of orientation, but they are not realities of human life: they are limit concepts of human existence, not impossible but factually not the case.

This contingent facticity, however, has different reasons. While there is factually no entirely good world because humans are the way they are (wannabes and gluttons), there is factually no entirely evil world because God is the way he is (a just creator of a good creation). Neither is self-evident, both are traced back to God in the cycle of the biblical primordial history. God thus in the covenant with Noah restricts the consequences of evil in the wake of the unjust in such a way that they can never go so far as to entirely suspend the good order of creation: drawing that conclusion would entirely and exclusively be up to God himself and to nothing and no one else. And according the story of Noah, God has determined himself not to draw it but to be and remain what he has made himself: the just creator of a good creation. Yet—this is the second aspect—the good order of creation does not exclude but rather includes that because of their ambivalent position between animal and God, humans can act not only justly but unjustly as well: doing the latter is entirely and exclusively up to them, and they do in fact do it time and again.

God's experiment of creation thus has not led to human beings enjoying God's good deeds among the other creatures and actualizing their possibilities in his presence. Yet even in their lives at a distance from God, outside the garden, God in the connection of action and predicament has given them life-promoting basic rules and basic guidance by which they can reliably orient their lives: *unjust people are being punished by God, just people by contrast are rewarded*. Those who are doing well in life thus have God to thank for it, and those who are not doing well have only themselves to blame. God's justice allots to everyone what they deserve: to the unjust Evil, to the just the good, both according to the measure that serves the preservation of creation, by God ensuring that Evil does not get the upper hand in a way that would endanger all of creation and that the good is not misunderstood in a way that would blur and obscure the distinction between creator and creature.

12. The Questionability of the Connection between Action and Predicament

According to the Priestly Source, God's order of justice is reliable because God has committed himself to being and remaining the just creator of a good creation, that is, to not (or no longer) allowing human misconduct to put all of living creation and thereby also his own being-creator in question. Because he has declared creation—that is, *this* present world, not any other possible world—to be good, he cannot abolish it again, despite continued human misconduct, without placing himself in the wrong. In explicitly excluding this possibility, God determines himself as *just creator* (who he does not have to be but who he is because he decides to),[63] and he thereby simultaneously marks the order of this

---

63. It is not possible to speak of a *decision* of God's to be creator already on the basis of the creation

world as *contingent* (it could be otherwise or come to an end) yet *reliable* (it will not be otherwise or come to an end).

This reliability expressed in the regulated connection of action and predicament, however, can only to some extent be claimed for the way justice works in human life: injustice is by no means always punished, and justice is by no means always rewarded. Adam and Noah mark possibilities that by no means seem to be the norm of human life. Often, unjust people fare well and just people badly, often Noah seems to be punished and Adam rewarded. Or, as Ecclesiastes will put it much later, "there are righteous people who perish in their righteousness, and there are wicked people who prolong their life in their evildoing" (7:15). This does not simply suspend the basic rule, but it does give voice to considerable doubt concerning its comprehensive application.[64]

Given such experiences, we can try several things:

1. We could declare the rule to be wrong and abandon it, but that would amount to renouncing the orientation by God and would leave all religious, ethical, and life-practical questions open.

2. We could leave the rule intact but declare it to have no meaning for living our lives because God does not observe it and does whatever he wants: "It is all one; therefore I say, he destroys both the blameless and the wicked" (Job 9:22). The rule is not contested but declared to be meaningless for human beings' factual life and predicament.

3. We could hold on to the validity of the rule for human life and look for or suspect a deeper meaning or higher purpose in the deviations: *in this case* the unjust fare well or the just fare badly because God has a reason for it that we do not know or cannot understand. Even if that were accepted in some cases (Eccl 7:16–18), it must not happen too often, or else the rule would be dissolved by exceptions and orienting our practical lives by it be rendered impossible.

4. We could also try and solve the problem in the schema of time. The unjust are faring well *only for the moment* or *seemingly*, and the just are faring badly *only for the moment* and *not permanently*: sooner or later God's justice will catch up with the unjust and with the just, as Job's friends never tire of stressing (Job 8:13–19, 18:15–21, and 20:4–29). But often that is by no means the case. The unjust are doing well until the end and the just are doing badly their entire lives. Why is it the unjust who live a long life in prosperity with numerous progeny (Job 21:7–16) and who are treated preferentially even in death, being given grand funerals (21:32–33), while inversely, just people such as Job are prosecuted in the worst possible way for no reason at all?

5. To avoid throwing the rule into doubt this way, we might defend its validity against appearances by arguing, as Ben Sira does, that God will repay each human in the

---

of the ordered world recorded by the Priestly Source in Gen 1 but only on the basis of God holding on to his creation despite the near-failure of the humanity experiment and of his commitment, in the covenant with Noah, to continue holding on to it in the future and for all time. Only this free decision of God makes—in the terms of the narrative—his original creation a free creation as well.

64. See Krüger, *Theologische Gegenwartsdeutung im Kohelet-Buch*, 337.

hour of their death depending on how they have lived, for the hour of death balances out an entire life (Sir 11:25–28). Even if no one else might notice, God will, in the hour of death, do justice for the just and punish the unjust, for there is only this life and this death (cf. Sir 41:4).

6. Inversely, we could, to save the rule, drop the strict rejection of a beyond and postulate that given such cases, God's justice cannot be restricted to this life but will reach its goal only in a future, a different life: the unjust may be faring well *here*, but *there* they will be overtaken by God's judgment; and the just may be faring badly *in this life*, but *in the next life* they will be rewarded all the better. The religious sense and theological thinking of Israel reached this eschatological solution in later times. But that was possible only once the individual had acquired such weight that God's justice had to prove itself not only in the life of the people as a whole but in each individual life: if God's justice applies without wavering, then it also becomes manifest, and if that cannot be discerned in the current life of the just and the unjust, then there is every reason to hope for the actualization of God's justice in another life.

7. This can even be underscored, namely by concluding from the manifold exceptions, not that they abolish the connection of action and predicament because this connection is irrevocably founded in God's justice but, rather, that not only some but all human beings are incapable of being righteous before God. It is not that God is unwilling to observe the rule and does whatever he wants, it is the human beings who are incapable of living in accordance with it even if they wanted to: "Can mortals be righteous before God? Can human beings be pure before their Maker?" (Job 4:17). The exception from the rule that requires explanation, then, is not that in our experience, the connection often does not exist, but, on the contrary, what needs explaining is the curious fact that some people think that the connection sometimes exists: are not "the hearts of all . . . full of evil"? Is not "madness . . . in their hearts while they live, and after that they go to the dead" (Eccl 9:3; cf. Gen 6:5)? If we think this way, then we must consider Job's insistence on his own righteousness and on the, in his view, entirely unjustified and unjust abuse by God to be simple pretension and arrogance: "What are mortals, that they can be clean? Or those born of woman, that they can be righteous?" (Job 15:14). Every division of human beings into just and unjust, however, then becomes absurd because we are in no position to demonstrate this distinction in any concrete human being.[65] There is no one who is righteous, not one.

8. Yet in that case, we cannot be sure even when it comes to God. For if the human cannot be just, does God's justice at least apply unwaveringly? Could God not once again revise and abolish the basic rule that he punishes injustice and rewards justice? The rule is contingent, that is, it does not have to be the way it is, because life could work out differently without contradicting itself and does in fact seem to work out differently only all too often. Yet God would then be other than just, or his justice would be something entirely different from what we thought, and that

---

65. Forster, *Begrenztes Leben als Herausforderung*, 226–27, 235.

would amount to completely blurring the image of God and fundamentally shaking certainty about God.

9. If we want to avoid that, we might still suspect that we were wrong—not about our conception of God but about how we conceived of our own life experience. Perhaps the unjust are *better* than we thought after all, and perhaps the just are *not as just* as they appear: there might be an Adam in Noah, even if it is hidden well from God and from humans. Yet that, too, comes up against its limits when no hidden injustice can be found and the just refuses having his justice be thrown into question.

13. God as Enemy

That is what happens emphatically in the despairing accusation of God in Psalm 88.[66] Here, God has become the greatest enemy of the praying speaker. Other psalms may speak of God's oppression (Pss 90:15; 102:24; 119:75) and address God as the author of human transitoriness (90:3–6) and concrete distress (90:7–9).[67] And prophets like Deutero-Isaiah, too, are aware of the dark sides of God's actions (Isa 40:2; 42:24–25; 43:27–28; 45:7). But no psalm is as desolate an expression of a gravely ill person's despair and desertedness as Psalm 88.

The praying speaker leaves no doubt that it was God and no one else who has struck him down this way: "You have put me in the depths of the Pit, in the regions dark and deep" (88:6). God's fury weighs down on him (88:7), God's terror and anger destroy him (88:16). Nor does he leave any doubt that he has done nothing wrong: he has been miserable and ailing since his youth (88:15) and has never even been in a position to behave justly or unjustly. And he leaves no doubt that in his suffering, he has conducted himself toward God (unlike God toward him) as is to be expected of someone who is just: although he sees himself struck and mistreated by God in a wholly unjust way, he has beseeched God for help, turning to him in prayer every day, already early in the morning and still late at night (88:2, 9, 13), that is, he has done everything to be expected of a pious person in his distress. But God has not reacted. God not only torments him against all that is just and proper, he also cannot be moved to respond to any kind of supplication (88:2) such that the speaker is worn out and without hope (88:15) and, abandoned by friends and companions, only waits for his ultimate demise (88:5) in desolate darkness (88:18).

God not only has punished someone who has done nothing wrong with illness and infirmity from adolescence in, as the psalm drastically portrays it, an entirely unjust way, he also does not react, as would be right and proper, to the innocent man's entreaties to deliver him from his unjust suffering. God is unjust in what he inflicts on the speaker, and he is unjust in leaving him alone in his distress and ignoring his cries for help. In

---

66. See Lindström, *Suffering and Sin*, and "Theodicy in The Psalms," 266–68; Groß and Kuschel, *"Ich schaffe Finsternis und Unheil!,"* 46–59; Groß, "Zorn Gottes: Ein biblisches Theologumenon"; Zenger, *Dein Angesicht suche ich*, 72, and "Psalm 88"; B. Janowski, "Die Toten loben JHWH nicht" and *Arguing with God*, 218–35; Lescow, "Psalm 22,2–22 und Psalm 88," 226–31; and Schlegel, *Psalm 88 als Prüfstein der Exegese.*

67. Forster, *Begrenztes Leben als Herausforderung*; see also Luther's interpretation of this psalm in *Ennaratio Psalmi XC* (WA 40.III, 484–594) as well as Volkmann, *Der Zorn Gottes*, 87–91.

one and the same person, the speaker makes the experience that God does wrong to someone who has done nothing wrong and does not bestow justice on someone who has incurred no guilt. God not only is no helper in distress, he is the author of the distress, and in both he acts entirely unjustly. The lamentation before God, that the speaker is like one of the dead whom God no longer remembers (88:5), turns into an accusation of God, that all of this is entirely God's fault (88:16). Yet where God's goodness and faithfulness is no longer mentioned (88:11) and where there can be no talk of the miracle of his justice (88:12), there God himself has disappeared.[68]

With this abandonment by God and despairing of God, there is no trace of hope in this psalm. The only thing that might still surprise us is that this desperate man still addresses his accusation, abandonment, and despair to the one whom he considers the unjust author of this distress.[69] Even the indication that "it belongs to the *human dignity* of the poor, which Amos fought for, that, as a *legal subject*, he may *sue for* his life and in doing so has the right even to accuse God"[70] does not speak to the fact that God here functions only as the addressee of the accusation but no longer functions in any way as reason for hope: the praying speaker has put his life behind him, he expects nothing from this God anymore. But this he screams at him. And thereby he does not release God from his responsibility for the ill he inflicts on him.[71]

14. The Experiment of Justice: Job

What is given voice in Psalm 88 becomes, in the book of Job, the central topic of a theological reflection.[72] According to the biblical narrative, Adam's suffering was deserved because he conducted himself unjustly toward God whereas God proved to be just, and because of the way in which he reacted to Adam's injustice: he did not punish him with the death he had threatened but with removing him from his presence and with the suffering of living a life far from God, and he restricted the consequences of this suffering by not letting them get out of hand and by imposing limits on but not destroying human life.

Noah's not suffering, too, was deserved because he lived righteously, and God conducted himself justly toward him, too, by excepting him from the destruction of unjust humanity and ensuring that the animals of the land and of the air were not destroyed along with human injustice. But whereas Adam suffered deservedly and Noah deservedly did not suffer, Job is presented as someone who suffers not deservedly but unjustly. Against all attempts on the part of his friends and of his wife at interpreting his suffering in the traditional way as just punishment for an injustice, Job insists that he has committed no injustice and does not deserve this suffering. The one who is suffering here is

---

68. See Lescow, "Psalm 22,2–22 und Psalm 88," 230–31.

69. That is why Janowski wonders, "Can this psalm still be called a prayer?" (Janowski, *Arguing with God*, 222).

70. Lescow, "Psalm 22,2–22 und Psalm 88," 231; see also Lescow, *Theodizee*, 23–25.

71. On how the Rabbinic tradition took up this theme, see Thoma, "Gott im Unrecht."

72. See Müller, *Das Hiobproblem*; Gese, "Die Frage nach dem Lebenssinn"; Hermisson, "Notizen zu Hiob"; and Illman, "Theodicy in Job."

not an unjust man but a just one, and God not only allows this unjust suffering, he is the one who causes it.

This is made unambiguously clear by the framing narrative of the book of Job (1:1–2:13 and 42:10–17).[73] It is known to readers of the book but not to the actors of the dialogue (3:1–42:9), in which Job and his friends try to fathom the for them incomprehensible meaning of the evil that has overtaken the just Job because of the agreement between God and Satan.[74] Although he does not know why all of this is happening to him, Job refuses to have his justice questioned. He knows himself to be in the right, he does not let himself be swayed in the least by his friends' objections, and again and again, he begs God to give him an answer (13:22; 19:7; 23:5). Finally he challenges God to enter litigation: "Here is my signature! Let the Almighty answer me! O that I had the indictment written by my adversary!" (31:35).[75] Job insists on his righteousness. He suffers unjustly, and if God lets this unjustified suffering happen to him or even lets him suffer because of his righteousness (as the prologue in chs. 1 and 2 suggests), then it is God and not he who is in the wrong.

This unsettles the entire traditional image of God, even if the friends seek to hold on to it with ever new arguments.[76] What about God's justice when not the unjust but the just person suffers? When the righteous person suffers not although but because he is righteous? When his suffering goes back not to other people or to other things but to God himself? What remains of God's justice when it allows the just to suffer unjustly? What are we to orient ourselves by when God's justice itself becomes the cause of injustice? Are we to conclude, as Job's friends do, that no one can be just anyway, that all human beings are incapable of living righteously before God (4:17, 15:14)? Or are we to draw the consequence, as Job does, that what we do and how we live is all one, since God acts arbitrarily toward the just and the unjust equally (9:22)?

Either way, orientation by God seems to become meaningless for human life. If it is not possible anyway to live in a way that would be righteous before God, then there is no need to even try. And if there is no recognizable connection between justice and a good life or injustice and suffering, then why not live as we please? Job avoids drawing

---

73. With arguments worth pondering, Schmid, in "Der Hiobprolog und das Hiobproblem," makes a plausible case that the framing narrative is not older than the dialogic part, as has long been suspected. See also Köhlmoos, *Das Auge Gottes*, and Fyall, *Now My Eyes Have Seen You*, 18–20.

74. Gerhard von Rad interprets the narrative structure of these two levels of the plot, which stand in an epistemically asymmetrical relationship with each other, in realistic terms: "behind the curtain that conceals history there are no solutions but many much darker problems about which men have no inkling" (Rad, *God at Work in Israel*, 171). Yet greater circumspection seems advisable here to avoid confusing narrative operations with phenomena of reality. This applies not only with regard to the "sons of God" and the heavenly council but also with regard to Satan who acts as "prosecutor" in the heavenly court. See also Haag, *Vor dem Bösen ratlos?*, 75–78.

75. In *Putting God on Trial*, Robert Sutherland tries to show that on the basis of 23:1–7 and 27:2–6 the entire book of Job is to be read as a "lawsuit drama" (12) in which Job, by means of an "Oath of Innocence" (54), challenges God to enter into the boundaries of an informal legal process in which he himself will prove his innocence before God and prove God's guilt. See also Scholnick, *Lawsuit Drama in the Book of Job*; Laytner, *Arguing with God*; Fuchs, *Mythos und Hiobdichtung*; and Hartley, "From Lament to Oath."

76. There are thus good reasons for the difficulty Jewish interpreters have had in accepting Job as a figure of Jewish piety; see Mangan, "Interpretation of Job in the Targums," and Weinberg, "Job versus Abraham."

these conclusions. He refuses being unjust or acting ungodly (1:21–22; 2:9–10; 9:21; and elsewhere). Yet he also no longer counts on the validity of the action–predicament connection. If no human being is righteous, as Job's friends think, don't we have to wonder why not everyone is faring badly? And if the just are faring badly and the unjust faring well, don't we have to conclude that the one has nothing to do with the other, that there is no relation between justice and injustice on the one hand, and suffering and well-being on the other?

Job, in any case, does not know how his righteousness is supposed to deserve all that overtakes him. Even the hypothetical supposition that he has sinned (7:20) does not offer a way out because God's reaction in the suffering that has come down on him would be completely exaggerated. For Job, God is thus no longer a haven of hope but has become his "enemy" (16:9; 19:11; and 27). The worst thing is not that God does not care about him but, quite the inverse, that God does not leave him alone (7:19). Job can no longer flee to God, all he wants is flee from God, although he knows that to be impossible. At the very latest in death, he, who after all is righteous and therefore suffers unjustly, will see God as his "redeemer" and no longer as enemy (19:25–27), and God will have to admit his righteousness.[77] And that is how, indeed, the book of Job ends: after Job has recognized the creator in his great works (38–41) and has seen God in his own life with his own "eye," that is, no longer knows him only "by the hearing of the ear" (42:5) but knows God the way God knows him, God restores everything that had been taken "twofold" (42:10–17).

15. The Theological Problem and Job's Insight

The issue is thus not Job's righteousness. The question is whether and how this righteousness is connected with his great fortune and well-being on the one hand and his outsize suffering and misery on the other. The answer of the novella is: not at all. God decrees well-being and misery in his free power as creator (40–41), and no one has the right to confront God by appealing to their own righteousness and to demand certain consequences for their lives, as Job comes to understand at the end (42). This suspends the traditional answer that invoked the action–predicament connection, which Job's friends, not by coincidence, keep recalling at length. Yet if this connection is no longer to be valid, then the book of Job puts not only this connection but God's justice and thereby the justice of the entire order of creation to the test. For what is there left in life for humans to rely on? What are they to orient themselves by in their lives? How can they still understand fortune and misfortune, well-being and suffering in life as just or unjust, justified or unjustified?

Unlike what earlier times thought, the orientation by God does not offer an answer to this question because God decrees both in his free power, as the book of Job demonstrates. What happens, happens, and there is no sense in asking whether what happens is just or unjust: good and evil in life cannot be traced back in a regulated manner to

---

77. See Kessler, "Ich weiss, dass mein Erlöser lebet." In interpreting this text, we must take into account that according to the old Israelite view, Job in his miserable situation is already "in death"; see Hermisson, "Gott und das Leid," 12–13 and 13n19, as well as Krieg, *Todesbilder im Alten Testament.*

humans' being just or unjust. On the other hand, however, unlike later times, the book of Job does not refrain from bringing God into play with regard to both good and evil, as well as life and humans' being just or unjust. God is the creator of everything, there is nothing good or evil without him. Only, this knowledge does not help (anymore) in trying to understand the contingencies of human life. Human beings ought to be just because that is better for their living together than the opposite, but there is no reason to consider God to be just or to expect justice from him. God is the creator, not the guarantor of justice. He is unmistakably active in his works, to be sure, as God's speeches at the end of the book explicitly recall in invoking the wonderful orders of creation (38–41).[78] Yet humans are overstepping when they think this justifies them in demanding specific things for their lives. Those who try and make such claims count on the illusory certainties of the stories and traditions about God instead of paying attention to how God manifests in their own lives (42:5). And those who think they can trace well-being or not-well-being, their own or that of others, back to being just or not being just before God do not speak of him "what is right," as God admonishes Job's friends (42:7), because it demotes God to being the guarantor of a regulated connection of justice and well-being or injustice and suffering evil and thereby surrenders him to human demands.[79] Yet creatures are seriously wrong when they think they can instrumentalize the creator for their purposes: "Where were you when I laid the foundation of the earth? Tell me, if you have understanding" (38:4). God is wholly different from what this kind of thinking takes him to be.

From beginning to end, the book of Job takes this image of God and the misguided expectations it entails apart by sketching at every point the opposite of what is generally expected of God.[80] In Hermann Spieckermann's words:

> God as enemy of the human being, God who without reason, arbitrarily, destroys the order he himself founded on right and justice. And the human being surrendered to this God before whom right and blamelessness no longer count for anything. The human being who nonetheless has no one else to complain to, accuse, and place his hopes in than precisely this God.[81]

Job at the end comes to see that it is not possible to invoke the traditional image of God. We only know who, what, and how God is when we do not talk about God but with him, more precisely: when he speaks to us.[82] Job had known God "by the hearing of

---

78. It is no coincidence that the enumeration of the phenomena of creation that evince God's power and glory does not include human beings: these phenomena are pregivens for them, they are that in which they could recognize God's justice—if they were not fixated on themselves and their own fate. See Keel, *Jahwes Entgegnung an Ijob*.

79. The book of Job opposes this platitudinous instrumentalization of God with the explicit reference to the creator's inscrutable omnipotence. Saskia Wendel overlooks this critical point when she laments the resolution of the tension between transcendence and immanence in favor of mere inscrutability (Wendel, "Den Allmächtigen ergründen wir nicht. . .," 426 and 428n26).

80. See Thomason, *God on Trial*.

81. Spieckermann, "Die Satanisierung Gottes," 439.

82. Rüdiger Lux rightly underlines the decisive nature of this switch from the stychomythia *about* God in the conversation between Job and his friends to *God speaking to* Job (Job 38–41; see Lux, "Das Böse–warum lässt Gott das zu?," 42–48).

the ear" (42:5), but it was an error to think that God is the way he is being talked about. Thinking this way, as Job did, leads to talking "without knowledge" about things one does not understand (42:3). What is decisive is not what others say about God but only what he himself says to us: "Hear, and I will speak; I will question you, and you declare to me" (42:4). How God really is is something we know only once we have not just heard about him but seen him with our own eyes (42:5), experienced him in our own lives.[83] Only then do we really know God, because we then know God as we are known by him.[84]

16. Reconceiving the History of Creation

This is the constellation of the problem in the book of Job and its resolution on the narrative-dramatic level. As the framing plot of the first chapter and the conclusion make clear, the following starting conditions apply throughout; taken together, they can be read as guidelines for reconceiving the history of creation:[85]

1. *Job is and remains righteous* (and does not become unjust, as Adam does). The opening scene of the book describes a new paradise and a new Adam: a life in almost ungraspable abundance and richness in goods and possessions, animals and servants, sons and daughters, and a person who unites in himself all the good humanity has to offer. Job is the successful counterpart to the unsuccessful Adam, he conducts himself righteously in all life situations. No one questions this righteousness, neither God nor Satan nor Job himself. It is the base line of the drama.

2. *The suffering that happens to Job goes back to God himself* (and not to Job's own misconduct, as in the case of Adam). Precisely because Job is undisputedly righteous, the calamity that strikes him is traced back not to him but to an experiment of justice that God and Satan conduct on him. Job becomes the object of this experiment precisely because of his justice, not because of some injustice, even if that is all Job's friends are able to suspect: Job must have incurred guilt for an injustice, they say, and be it only because no human being is able to live righteously and without guilt before God. Given their premises, this is not a wrong inference but, as God himself notes at the end (42:7), their premises are false.

3. *Death is the definitive boundary of human life* (7:8, 21; 14:10–12; 16:22) such that an answer to the question of the just man's unjust suffering must be sought in his *own* life (and not in the succeeding generations of human life) and in *this* life (and not beyond it; 2:6). The way out taken in the story of Genesis—letting Adam die but having the Adamite lineage survive—is not an acceptable solution for the narrative of Job, and neither is the later eschatological form of thinking according to which the justice of the just will be rewarded if not in this life then at least in a life to come.

---

83. Job's desire to see God (19:26–27) is not just "his most ardent wish," a wish in fact fulfilled before his death, as Ebach, *Streiten mit Gott*, 156, thinks: it is the real point of the answer that the Book of Job gives to Job's plea for an answer to his questions.

84. See Janowski, *Arguing with God*, 90–96.

85. See Sutherland, *Putting God on Trial*, 19ff.

4. *God is and remains the creator of everything.* Life is not comprehensible without him, but neither is it comprehensible through him. It is unrealistic to deny the creator and ignore the reality of creation, or to pretend being unable to know anything about the creator and creation (as later skepticism and agnosticism did). Yet it is equally unrealistic to think that the traditional "hearsay" about God could offer a reliable basis for a correct understanding of God. With respect to God, no one can invoke others or tradition, everyone must reach in their own lives an answer for which they take responsibility.

On these four conditions, the book of Job seeks to find a solution the problem of the unjustly suffering just man, and it finds it in an entirely different way from what one might have expected.

17. The Point of Job for the Theory of Justice

Related to the theological problem just sketched and its solution is a consequential point that pertains to the theory of justice and warrants explicit emphasis. The novella uses the unjust suffering of the just Job to conduct a thought experiment that is concerned not only with the validity of the action–predicament connection but, quite fundamentally, with the *meaning of being just as such.*[86] The traditional rule might and did suggest that we fare well when we live justly and badly when we do not. In that case, it is prudent to practice justice and avoid injustice if we seek to have a good life.

The story of Job thoroughly destroys this rule of prudence. Justice, so the lesson it teaches, exists only *without meaning and purpose.* It is not a means by which to achieve something else; it can be lived only for its own sake or not at all. Justice bestows *no right to anything* on us, it is *without a what-for* or it is not at all. Those who are just to please God are not just and do not please God. Rather, only those are just who are just without wanting thereby to please God. Justice has its meaning *in itself alone,* and only if it is lived in this way, that is, without regard to its effect or absence of effect on God or in life, is it in fact being lived. The just live justly *without thinking of God.* They fear God *without expecting anything from God in return.* They love God *for God's sake* and not for some purpose. And they do not fight Evil to obtain the good but to put an end to Evil.[87]

These are new and unusual notes in the theological thought of Israel.[88] Yet the story of Job draws its consequences without compromise. Those who live justly *in order to* fare

---

86. This question of the *sense of (God's) justice* is, for me, the theological point of the Book of Job, not the theme of the *excess of Evil* highlighted by Philippe Nemo in *Job and the Excess of Evil,* for whom Evil in Job is excessive as a matter of principle: it cannot be inserted, neither in being nor in thought, into any social, cosmic, or metaphysical order but always exceeds them. Yet in the Book of Job, Evil or ill is the *means,* not the topic, of the narrative; Evil is not that for the sake of which the story is told, it is that with whose help the fundamental question concerning the sense of divine and human justice is discussed via the exemplary fate of Job.

87. The thesis, therefore, is *not* that justice as such is without meaning and purpose but rather that it is to be sought *for its own sake* and not for the sake of *some other sense or purpose* allegedly associated with it. We ought to be just *for the sake of justice* and not in order to reach something with its help that we hope to obtain thereby. Justice is a good, but it is not a good for something.

88. See, however, Sir 8:12–14 and Gen 4:7, which also intimate that to be just is to have no purpose

---

well must be prompted by Job's story to despair of God and of his justice. It is precisely the unjust who are faring well here and the just who are faring badly, both without sense or reason. The conclusion that it does not matter how one lives suggests itself. Job considers it. But it is not what the story as a whole aims for. Its conclusion, rather, is that only those who are just *without being just for the sake of something else* will receive good from God. The end of the story, often decried as rendering the whole account harmless in giving Job twice as much of all the goods that were taken away from him at the beginning (42:10–15), is thus anything but harmless: it is the narrative confirmation that only those fare well who do not live justly and fear God *in order* for them to fare well but who live justly and fear God no matter how they fare, that is, those whose justice is independent of their predicament in life. God does not reward purpose-oriented justice, only purpose-free justice. To be sure, we do not live justly if we do not want to live justly: to be just, we must want to be just. But when we want to be just for the sake of something else, we do not want to be just: we are mistaken about what we want and consider to be just what is not just.

That the issue is purpose-free justice is apparent not only in the concluding chapter but already in the opening chapters, where God and Satan negotiate the testing of Job. The debate is not whether Job is just or whether being just is something good—that is taken for granted. The question is: "Does Job fear God for nothing?" (1:9). Is Job just only *in order to* be rewarded by God with good, as Satan insinuates, is his fear of God only a means to win God's favor, or does it suffice itself? This is the hypothesis that is subsequently tested in a divinely staged experiment of justice in which Job is showered with the worst sufferings and ills—not only are all his possessions destroyed (1), his health, too, is inverted into sheer and utter suffering (2). If Job's justice were oriented by a purpose, these consequences would have to make him back off his being just: given these blows of fate, his friends try to convince him in long speeches, he should realize that he cannot be just but must somehow and somewhere be unjust.[89] And he should stop insisting on his being just, and if he did not do any wrong before, he should do so now, curse God and then at least die rightly for doing so and thereby put an end to his suffering, as his wife suggests to him (2:9).[90] Job, however, rigorously rejects all of this, no matter how hard his friends and his wife, seeing the suffering that has overtaken him, try to get him to distance himself from the certainty of his justice. He does not back off this certainty, even if he does not understand and grasp why he is faring ill.[91] He knows that he is just, he refuses being anything else, and challenges God to justify himself for letting him suffer so unjustly.

In rigorously and resolutely refusing to understand his suffering to be a consequence of an injustice, Job drives a wedge between the reality of life and humans' being just or unjust posited as the cause of this reality, even if this means that he can thereby

---

and thus has a value of its own. (I would like to thank my colleague Thomas Krüger for pointing this out to me.)

89. See Wahl, *Der gerechte Schöpfer*, as well as Witte, *Vom Leiden zur Lehre* and *Philologische Notizen zu Hiob 21–27*.

90. See Müller, *Hiob und seine Freunde*, 17–21; Penchansky, "Job's Wife: The Satan's Handmaid"; and Oeming and Schmid, *Hiobs Weg*, 42–45.

91. See Garrett, "The Patience of Job and the Patience of Jesus."

no longer understand his earlier well-being. How we fare in life has nothing to do with whether we live justly or unjustly, and living justly is not associated with any claim to faring well in life. This, however, means that a just life can be claimed to be such not with reference to the hoped for gain in goods and fortune in life but only when it is just without and free of any purpose: those who live justly do so for the sake of justice alone and not for the sake of anything else, and only those who live this way live justly. How they fare in fact is an independent question and must be explained another way. Justice is not a cause of people faring well and injustice not a cause of their ills and suffering. Only those who understand this and know that well-being cannot be bought with justice, and suffering and ills not be avoided through justice, will be able—if they so will and act—truly to live justly, namely for the sake of justice alone. And only those who live this way live justly before God as well—and in precisely so doing honor God.[92]

The result is not that God is unjust but that God's justice is entirely different from what had been supposed. The discovery of God's justice leads to the insight that God does not will human justice as a means to something else but as a good in itself: humans are not to be just in order thereby to obtain something (divine knowledge, eternal life, possessions, riches, and success in life) but for no other reason than, precisely, being just. Justice before God is not a means but an end in itself. In justice before God, the sense of human existence is fulfilled, whatever one's life may look like.[93]

92. It is especially in the light of the Job prologue that only justice that is practiced "for nothing," which does not have its eye on being rewarded by God, is really *justice before God*, that is, a justice that does not embarrass God before Satan but serves to glorify God. That human beings ought to be just without purpose does not exclude but includes that this *purpose-free justice*, precisely, *serve the purpose of honoring God*: God is not being glorified and honored by being just *for his sake*, but only *by being just for the sake of being just alone* do humans also honor and glorify their creator as well.

93. Of course purpose-free justice is *justice*, too, that is—in the context of the Old Testament and of the ancient world—that which does not favor chaos but strengthens order, what promotes life and serves the community. That is why humans are to strive for *justice* and not for its opposite or for something else. Yet they are to practice it *free of purpose*, that is, for its own sake and not for the sake of other (economic, political, religious, etc.) purposes thereby attainable. Only a justice practiced for its own sake can achieve what is hoped it will achieve: that thanks to a life oriented by justice, the chances of the good in the coexistence of human beings become greater than those of evil, and that the suffering of human and other living beings is restricted and reduced rather than intensified and promoted. That this does not always succeed is no reason not to live justly: every alternative would be even worse, not necessarily in each individual case (as the free-rider problem shows) but for the whole. Even if we suppose the extreme case that a just life does not in any recognizable way promote community and a human coexistence worth living or even damages it in a concrete case, that does not prove that living justly makes no sense; it only proves that the distinction between justice and injustice cannot be established on the basis of their correlate factual consequences because these consequences cannot tell us what to understand by "just" and "unjust." Indeed, it is the very point of a justice practiced free of purpose, for its own sake alone, that it does not help manifest a certain sense of "just" and "unjust" but instead creates a place for this life-promoting difference in human life in the first place by living "justly" in one's contemporary sense without reducing the sense of "just" to the factual effects such a life has. What is called "just" always has an excess of sense beyond the given practice and situations which triggers and maintains a history of discovering what justice could and ought to contain and mean for human beings and for human life. It first had to be arduously discovered in the course of human history that living justly can mean standing up for order and against disorder, for the community and against the uncommunal, for equal rights for everyone and against legal arbitrariness, for preserving the earth's ecological balance and against the shortsighted exploitation of its resources, and so on; and each of these conceptions of justice then had

18. The Challenge for Human Beings:
To Be Responsible (for) Themselves

Some have even gone a step further. The book of Job, on their reading, not only makes it clear that humans are to be just for the sake of justice and not with regard to goods in life they could thereby attain but also that "God expects human beings to stand up to him" and "challenge him for the creation of such a world." Human beings "have a moral duty to challenge God for such evil. They have a natural need to know and a natural right to receive the explanation for evil in the world."[94]

But there can be no question of that. Human beings might want to know why they are faring well or faring badly in life. Yet any kind of "natural right" to demanding an answer from God for the ill and evil in the world is precisely what the book of Job rigorously rejects. God, the omnipotent creator, is not accountable to anyone. Just as human justice is no foundation for any right of the human to receive from God what is good in life, so ill cannot inversely be interpreted as a divine institution oriented toward a purpose, namely to bring humans to love God without purpose: "God created a world of undeserved and unremitted suffering in order to make the highest form of human love possible: a completely selfless love of men and women for God."[95] Establishing this connection between ill and justice is as absurd as the connection of justice and welfare or injustice and misery, which the book of Job so resolutely repudiates. If we take the framing narrative seriously, then there can be no question of God bringing immeasurable ill over Job *in order for* Job to learn to be just entirely for nothing and to love God entirely selflessly. In the justice experiment negotiated with Satan, the ills, rather, serve to demonstrate *that* Job is just entirely for nothing and loves God entirely selflessly. Just as Job's justice cannot be instrumentalized for a claim to a good life, so the misery God sends him cannot be justified as a means of prompting him to purpose-free love of God and justice.

This is not the only untenable over-interpretation on Sutherland's part. There is also no indication in the text for the claims that "God is causally responsible for the evil in the world, but not morally blameworthy for it," that he will give humans the answer they seek to the question of unjust ills "on the Day of the Final Judgment" when he "will resurrect all human beings to give them that answer," or that "God will then judge all

---

once more to be criticized as one-sided, insufficient, or in need of being supplemented in order not to stop there but continue the process of concretizing. In this sense, the point of the purpose-free "just" life is to keep the orientation factor "justice" virulent in human life in such a way that, time and again, in ever further attempts, it can and must be discovered and established what deserves being called "just" for a human life and what does not. The dynamic the search for justice has developed in the course of history springs precisely from the fact that the orientation by justice brings an excess into play that experience cannot catch up with, that prevents people from settling for any state of justice in their lives but time and again pushes them to develop and reshape human life toward a more just state—without really knowing what that means exactly or where this process will ultimately lead. The history of humanity shows how the conception of justice became ever more profound and ever more defined without there being an end to this process in sight. It also makes clear, however, that human coexistence is still far from where it could be called "just" for everyone and without restriction.

94. Sutherland, *Putting God on Trial*, 10.
95. Sutherland, *Putting God on Trial*, 10.

human beings on the selflessness of their love for God."[96] All these references to a final judgment are being introduced to and have no basis in the text itself.[97] The text is being read here too quickly through the lens of later figures of thought. In the book of Job, the entire problem, including the litigation between Job and God, plays out in the life of the suffering just man between birth and death, not in an apocalyptic beyond this narrative is unaware of.[98] Yet that there is no connection between justice and a good or miserable life, as the book of Job highlights, does not mean that God deploys misery as an instrument to move humans to selfless love for God. Such a claim asserts once more the kind of connection between the two that the book of Job takes apart so emphatically.

Just as justice cannot be theologically instrumentalized for something else, so evil cannot be theologically instrumentalized for something else. It is not a pedagogical tool of God's that would acquire a good meaning by doing two things, namely "offer[ing] an explanation for the existence of undeserved evil in the world" and "offer[ing] an explanation for God's general practice of nonintervention in the world to prevent evil."[99] The point of the book of Job, on the contrary, is to bar any instrumentalization of evil as well as any instrumentalization of justice: the misery of the just is as devoid of sense as it is experienced to be, and it is entirely absurd to try and found being just on a reference to the good life it is said to effect or the miserable life it is said to prevent. There is no causal and there is no theological connection between the two. If a just person fares well, she owes it to God, not to her justice, and if she fares miserably although she is just, then she ought to accuse God but not question his justice (or let others question it). The accusation of God, however, must not reproach him with not preserving the connection of justice and the good life but only and exclusively with allowing people to suffer in misery. The sense of this lament is not to obtain a justification and explanation of the ills but to plead for rescue from the ills—and this rescue can in no way be justified as a right on the basis of one's justice, it can only be pleaded for as a freely given gift of God's.[100]

19. The Disjoining of Justice and Happiness

The discovery of God's justice in the biblical tradition thus cannot be detached from the discovery that human justice exists thanks to God's groundless care, which makes those

96. Sutherland, *Putting God on Trial*, 10.

97. This is true also of Job 19:25–27. The passage does not speak of a resurrection of the dead Job but says—as Hermisson, "Gott und das Leid," 13n19, rightly emphasizes—"that at least 'in death' he receives what in life he was denied."

98. John R. Schneider recognizes this but considers it a defect that "Israel had not yet developed a notion of the afterlife consistent with its intensely material anthropology—bodily resurrection would emerge as the solution in years hence" (Schneider, "Seeing God Where the Wild Things Are," 204).

99. Sutherland, *Putting God on Trial*, 11.

100. It is in this sense alone that Philippe Nemo is correct to say that in what happens to him, Job is confronted with his humanity: "In the very malice of God's, Job has perceived his all-weakness, thus his humanity, thus his compassion, his love, thus our divinity" (Nemo, *Job et l'excès du mal*, 142). [This sentence is not included in the English translation.—Trans.] To interpret this humanity as our "divinity" is not absurd only if it is clear that it consists in nothing but human beings' dependency on God for being just because they cannot give justice to or guarantee justice for themselves. If there is justice, it is entirely due to God because he alone ensures justice and creates situations in which human beings can live justly.

just who are not just, and that this means for human beings that justice in their lives is to be striven for and lived without intention and free of purpose and for its own sake alone. One must indeed be just to live up to God's care. But those who try to be just *in order to . . .* have from the outset gambled their justice away. As the recourse to God's justice does not explain why the ones are just and the others are not just, so it does not explain why the just fare badly and the unjust fare well. Everyone is responsible for their own being just, but that means, simultaneously, that there must be no associated expectation of the just being rewarded and the unjust punished. Whether that and what will be the case God reserves for himself. It belongs to God's sovereignty that he leaves it open.

If that were all, then of course God would become an arbitrary God no one can rely on and no one can orient themselves by. If the way we live our lives and happiness or unhappiness in life are completely disjoined, then how can we know what we owe and do not owe to God, what is to be expected from God and what is not? Does it not matter how we live because good and evil are allotted independently of that? And is there any significance, then, to the recourse to God, since it happens the way it happens no matter how we live? Evidently, the disjunction of striving for justice in life from the expectation of good in life leads to making the orientation by God superfluous or even impossible. If God is not the one who rewards the just and punishes the unjust, and be it at least in a life to come, then it is irrelevant to orient ourselves by him and his will because good and evil in life are being allotted to us independently of how we live. And the insistence that this does not take place independently of God seems meaningless when we can no longer say what we can really expect and not expect from God. If everything goes back to God and orientation by his will to justice no longer leads us to expect experiencing good or ill in our lives, then what sense does it still make to orient ourselves by him?

This very consequence suggesting itself is what the biblical tradition seeks to exclude. This happens in part by reaffirming the connection between the just life and the good life and rethinking it with an eschatological solution in mind: what does not seem to be the case in this life is to be hoped for from the life to come. But this hope is unfounded unless it is possible to exclude that the same ambivalence repeats itself in the next life, and that can be excluded only with reference to God's unequivocal will. The history of the discovery of God's justice thus has another central strand whose point is not religiously to moralize human life but to work on the notion of God and to clarify the character and reliability of God's will.

On the one hand, the human effort at justice is thereby disjoined from the expectation that the just will be rewarded and the unjust punished. Any kind of mechanism between human justice and happiness in life or human injustice and unhappiness is rejected on the basis of experiences in life that are incompatible with such a mechanism. That does not mean, however, that humans' being just and their ability to be just is not being traced back to God, on the contrary: without God's justice-creating caring turn toward them, humans cannot and will not be just. Yet it also does not mean that happiness and unhappiness are being allotted completely arbitrarily. Those who experience happiness and those who experience unhappiness are well advised to turn to God in gratitude and in lament, since nothing happens in life that God would be simply unaffected by or with which he would have nothing to do.

One thing, though, is not acceptable: invoking our own justice vis-à-vis God when we thank him for our happiness or lament our unhappiness. No one has a right to happiness, yet our unhappiness is nothing to reproach God with either, because God gives and effects what is good, not what is evil. No one can avoid becoming entangled in and being affected by evil in their lives. But neither can they rely on it not coming from him. God is the one who gives what is good in life, but he does not give it *because* someone is just but *because he is good* and wills to make others and other things good. The disjunction of striving for justice and justified expectation of happiness in human life thus corresponds to the discovery, in the biblical history of discovering God's justice, of God's willing to be unambiguously and exclusively good and just. Humans of course cannot prompt or compel or enforce a legal claim against him to have him do good in their lives because they live justly. Yet when they are allotted what is good, then they ought to thank God because God is the one to whom all that is good is due. And even if they are not allotted anything good, they ought nonetheless to live justly because in so doing they live up to their true humanity as being created in the image of God. In either case, they may hope that God wills good for them and therefore turn to God in gratitude and lament. That, however, presupposes that there is a reason to hope that God wills good for us. And how are we to have such reason when it is no longer possible to say that God rewards a just life and punishes an ill life?

The history of the discovery of God's justice would thus be insufficient and underdetermined if it were told only as a history of deinstrumentalizing human efforts at justice, a justice to be lived and practiced for its own sake and not for the sake of some external purpose. It would lead to rendering the orientation by God inconsequential if it were not at the same time a history of God's ever-clearer commitment to be the one who does and wills to do what is good, and not because he would be compelled to do so by humans but freely and entirely on his own.

That God can and must in fact be understood such that he wills and does the best for each and every one even though life often seems to be experienced in entirely different ways, however, was itself a discovery that took a long time to make and was difficult to hold on to. If by our own being just we do not have a claim to experiencing good from God, how can we still count on God being willing to grant and give what is good at all? How can we, how ought we to orient ourselves by God in our lives at all when the experiential connection between our own justice or injustice and divine reward and punishment is abolished? That was the question pondered in a third central strand of the biblical tradition.

B.3

Outdoing Evil: The Discovery of God's Love

THE DISCOVERY THAT GOD is not only himself good and has nothing to do with Evil but rather actively fights evil advances the knowledge of God.[1] Yet that God fights Evil is a message of consolation only if we can count on this fight being won. If the good is not just the opposite of Evil but the counterforce to Evil, then Evil is not only the other of the good, it is its enemy. Yet by what right can we say that the good and not Evil will win? Given the realities of life experience, the outcome of the conflict seems to be open at least, if not already decided negatively. The reality of *malum* in all its variety cannot be contested. Those who hope for its overcoming count on the greater power of the counterforce of the good. But by what right?

1. Hoping for God's Greater Power

The biblical tradition has asked this question again and again and answered it in more than just one way.[2] In so doing, its main currents have moved within certain parameters

---

1. That is, God works in an effective way in order for human and other living beings not to experience what they or others would rightly have to judge to be evil. This does not only include what I myself experience this way, it can also affect happenings that I would not myself judge to be *malum*. And it does not have to include everything I judge to be *malum* because it seems in some sense unpleasant or disruptive to me. That is why the question must be kept critically open whether what I experience as *malum* belongs to what God fights as *malum* and whether what I do not judge to be *malum* does not belong to it. Our standards are not just simply God's standards; not because what we experience as *malum* were no *malum* but because not every *malum* has the effect on us that it separates us from God and God from us, that is, that it hinders, obstructs, or obscures God's effective presence in a human life. See Dalferth, *Contingency of Evil*.

2. The term "biblical tradition" is not meant to designate any uniform homogeneous whole but rather the collection of various different testimonies of the Old and the New Testaments that have become the Bible. There, the engagement with question concerning God with respect to the reality of Evil has become manifest, in a way that has become determinative for Judaism and Christianity, in many, partly illuminating, partly aporetic, partly advancing experiences, explorations, essays, prayers, stories, songs, poems, reflections, collections of rules, and treatises.

that excluded a number of options and strategies for solutions that have come to determine other religious traditions.[3] Thus,

1. unlike Hinduism and Buddhism in the theory of karma, the biblical tradition has never conceived of an individual life's fate as the causal consequence of an earlier existence. It has always held on to the orientation by God, that is, never denied or rejected the notion of God (no a-theological solution strategy).[4]

2. Yet unlike polytheisms or Zoroastrianism, its main currents also have not looked for solutions in a confrontation of gods and demons, God and gods, or good God and satanic counter-god (no pluralist or dualist solution strategies).

3. Moreover, it has not renounced ascribing to God central attributes such as justice, goodness, or power even if in the course of history, it has defined these in significantly differing ways (no solution strategies that would empty the notion of God of its contents).

4. And finally, unlike some Indian religious, it has not denied the reality of suffering (no solution strategies that deny the reality of Evil).

This last point is of special importance for the biblical solution strategies. While over the course of centuries, there are significant changes in the image of God, this base line is maintained unwaveringly across all transformations: the reality of Evil is not questioned; rather, the hope that God will overcome Evil presupposes its reality throughout:

> The Bible *knows* about the threat to humanity and does not depict a "perfect world" alone. It *knows* about catastrophes: about hunger, plague and war, earthquakes and the sun going dark, smoldering fires and the sea turning into blood, the darkness and death of stars, or "only" about the "apocalyptic riders" (Rev 6) as symbols of hunger, war, disease, and death on the earth.

But it does not consider them to be the last word. What is being experienced in the catastrophes of a given present is not the end but the deliverance of humanity, "a deliverance that, evidently, does not appear as the goal of a straight and continuous upward path but as a leap and deliverance from the greatest of dangers."[5]

This also endows the recourse to God in situations of being affected by *malum* and of suffering from Evil with a particular character. It is not only a recourse to the one who himself is good and not evil and who because he is "good cannot act maliciously," as Luther emphasizes in his reply to Erasmus.[6] Nor is it only the recourse to the one who is good because he fights Evil, that is, the one who is actively good in working against Evil.[7] It is, rather, the recourse to the one who puts an end to the *malum* and turns evil

---

3. Compare Laato and Johannes C. de Moor ("Introduction," xx–liv, esp. xxx), who distinguish between six types of theodicy: retribution theology, educative theodicy, eschatological theodicy, the mystery of theodicy, communion theodicy, and human determinism.

4. See Doniger, *Origins of Evil in Hindu Mythology*; Meisig, "Leiden im Hinduismus"; and Meier, "Die Haltung des Buddhismus zur Leidensfrage."

5. Fritzsche, *. . .und erlöse uns von dem Übel*, 37.

6. Luther, *Bondage of the Will*, 224.

7. Karl Barth's correct attempt, too, to conceive of God's power not as "neutral force or omnipotence"

into good—not by revealing it, against all experience, to be good but by overcoming it through good. The decisive insight of the biblical tradition is not only that "God is good and not evil," nor only that "God is good because he fights Evil," but that "God is good because he overcomes what is evil through what is good."[8]

But given the experiential reality of *malum*, this, precisely, seems to be an insight based on hope. Does not everything or at least a lot oppose it? If life is not as good as it could be and ought to be, then how can we be certain that that will change when and because God works against Evil? Would not the world, then, have to be better than it is? If God works against Evil, then has he not always done so already, without it changing anything about the reality of evil? Are there reasons why God does not put an end to it although he could?[9] Or is he unable to put an end to it although he wills to, be it because he is himself incapable of doing so, be it because that could happen only in a way that depends not on him alone but on others as well? Yet in that case, what reason is there to hope that God will obtain the definitive victory of Good over Evil? The hope that God will impose himself has little evidence to support it in factual reality. Given experiential reality, it can invoke God only counterfactually, and this requires the certainty that God *wills* to do so, that he *can* do so, and that he therefore *will* do so.[10]

This certainty is not obvious. That God wills to, can, and will overcome *malum* is something that first had to be discovered, as the biblical tradition proves. The hope for the overcoming of Evil through God is founded on entirely contingent discoveries, not on eternal truths that are accessible at any time, in any place, and for anyone under any and all circumstances. To understand the foundation and content of Christian hope, it is indispensable to go back to this contingent history of discovery. This path cannot be shortened or avoided by turning its dogmatic result into one's starting point and invoking God's omnipotence and goodness, stating that God's *omnipotence* consists in God being able to do what he wills to and in him willing what he is able to do but that, as *God's* omnipotence, it is limited by God willing *only what is good* and thereby being *not* able to

---

but as "omnipotence of mercy—not quiet and passive mercy, but a mercy which is active, and thereby hostile to that power on behalf of poor man" (Barth, *Church Dogmatics*, IV.2, §64:232), really makes its point only because what is at issue is not only a "hostile" mercy that may or may not reach its goal and where it is unclear whether it fights Evil with evil or in some other way. At issue, rather, is a merciful hostility toward something that *is already* overcome and outdone: the *bonum* is not to be fought for in the first place, it has already been won, and it is not just to be deployed in the fight against the *malum* but to be deployed in such a way that the *malum* is not just being limited by another *malum* but brought to an end and outdone by *bonum*.

8. As Augustine notes: "God is so good that he makes good use even of the evils which his omnipotence would not have allowed to exist if he could not make good use of them by his supreme goodness" (Augustine. *Unfinished Work in Answer to Julian*, 5.60:586). Luther would later take up this quotation (Luther, "Vorrede zu Wider die gottlosen blutdürstigen Sauliten und Doegiten," 575, ll. 10–11).

9. Cited as such reasons, time and again, are: *God's compensatory justice*—God's divinity and justice, but also the dignity of the victims, do not allow that ill doing and evil go unpunished (the enduring reality of *malum* is an expression of *poena* and *culpa*: divine punishment for sin or self-produced consequence of misdoing and guilt)—and *God's pedagogical intention*—suffering because of an evil is an indispensable means, or at least an instrument more effective than others, to bring human beings closer to God. See Isa 53; Heschel, *Prophets*; and Talbert, *Learning through Suffering*.

10. That is why this certainty cannot indeed be asserted "triumphalistically" but "only ever cautiously and circumspectly" (Bauke, "Gottes Gerechtigkeit?," 349).

will and do *anything evil*. It would thus be self-contradictory just to try and think God as the author of evils.[11] That trying to think God that way does not think anything or at least does not think God is something that can be said only once the notion of God has, in light of the biblical tradition, been given a specific theological content.

This tradition, however, is not interested abstractly in God's ability or willing or in the metaphysical logic of these divine attributes but is interested concretely in the way in which the *bonum* and *malum* that unexpectedly, surprisingly, and toppling everything break into human life go back to God or call God to the scene. The central topic of the biblical tradition is not the question whether God wills good and is able to overcome evil through good at all but the memory of the good that God has done for specific people in concrete life situations by allotting *bonum* and overcoming *malum*.[12] This does indeed raise the question whether God also wills the good he is doing here for others or all others and whether he also wills to, can, and will overcome what for us is evil through what for us is good. This question, however, must be given a differentiated answer.

First, what God does and effects reacts not only to what humans experience as evil, it defines anew and differently what deserves to be called "evil" and "good" before God in the first place: the biblical narratives of deliverance and salvation are almost always and above all also narratives of redefining what is being overcome by this salvation and from what divine deliverance delivers; and what people plead with God to deliver them from is not always also what God delivers them from.

Second, this question is always already answered, to a certain extent, by the fact that what the biblical texts recall as God's good deeds toward specific people is being narrated in paradigmatic stories about representatives of the people (Abraham, Moses, David) or of all humanity (Adam, Noah, Jesus), that is, it expresses God's attitude toward the totalities thereby represented according to the narrative logic of these stories.[13]

Above all, however, this question concerning the validity of the biblical memory for others always presupposes that these narratives are concerned with recalling the good

---

11. Luther, *Luther on the Creation*, 278; see also Delius, *Die Quellen von Martin Luthers Genesisvorlesung.*

12. When the biblical tradition conceives of God as the God of specific people, as *their God*, as *God for them*, or as *deus pro nobis*, this always means that he is a God who is concerned with these people's situation, who allots them the *bonum* that enriches their lives and opposes the *malum* that damages them, who becomes involved with their misery and their distress and helps them bear what they themselves are unable to bear. Karl Barth has articulated this point in precise dogmatic terms: God not only practices solidarity with human beings, becomes involved with and shares their distress, he becomes human *for their benefit* (Barth, *Church Dogmatics*, IV.1, §59.2:215–16). *God's being God* consists in his *fighting and taking responsibility for others* who benefit from it—in allotting of *bonum* they could not have counted on, in putting an end to *malum* that has happened to them, and in his outdoing *malum* through *bonum*, which is possible for him alone. God is God in becoming that which does others good and in doing what benefits others. That he *does* what he does evinces his being God as love; that he *wills to do* what he does evinces the freedom of his love; and that he *is able to do* what he does evinces the power of his love.

13. Even if these narratives are vehicles for the historical memories of individual people, they are never only about their individual fates but concerned with the insights they can yield about God's will and willing with regard to the entire people of Israel or to all of humanity. The reason for transmitting these stories lies not in an individual human fate but in God's conduct toward the represented community manifest in this fate.

God has done and the evil he has overcome. The starting point is the remembered happening of *bonum* in human life, be it as the enhancement of a good, be it as the overcoming of an evil.

2. Election and Promise

It is not by chance that theological reflection on these biblical memories has led to the elaboration of two characteristic theoretical contexts.

On the one hand, the experience that God wills and effects what is good *concretely for specific people* has been symbolized in the notion of *election*.[14] Because the *bonum* enters human life from God without humans by themselves being able to make a significant or indeed any contribution, it is being conceived of as a distinction bestowed by God himself that is entirely undeserved, that cannot in any way be deduced or derived, and that can be grounded in nothing but God's free care. Those who experience *bonum* from God have been freely elected and created by God as addressees of his *bonum*: on the part of those elected, *election* can be developed only ever in categories of *strict passivity*, whatever the active consequences of such an election may be in the lives of the selected (mission, covenant, obedience, gratitude).[15] And accordingly, on the part of the one electing, *election* can be developed only ever in categories of *strict freedom* and *unconditional care* for the other of himself—a freedom that commits itself to working for the well-being of the other and a care that does make itself depend on anything about the other but turns to them in an originarily and unconditionally beneficial way, that— thought rigorously—elects only those but also all those whom it brings forth through this election in the first place such that they permanently depend, in that they are and in the way they are, on the one who elects and on his electing them.[16] Both—the originary freedom and the unconditional creative and beneficial care—are thought together in the

14. In connection with the Old Testament, the primary linguistic references are the topoi of the election of a king (2 Sam 6:21; 16:8), of a place or sanctuary (Deut 12:5, 11; 14:23), or of Israel (opening address of Deuteronomy, Isa 40–55), and the central theological references are the choice of Abraham (Gen 12:1–3) and, in a different tradition, the deliverance in the sea of reeds and the conclusion of the covenant on Mount Sinai (Exod 14ff and 33ff; Deut 7:7–8). Different texts place different emphases. While Deuteronomy associates the election with the First Commandment, grounds it in Jehovah's free love, and situates it during the Exodus, not with the patriarchs, Deutero-Isaiah, the prophet of the exile period, sees it with the patriarchs, for it would hardly have been possible to explain the enduring election to a people in exile by referring to the exodus and the granting of land. On the history of the notion in Judaism, see, among others, Ben-Chorin, *Die Erwählung Israels*. In connection with the New Testament, theological elaborations of the notion of election primarily take up Rom 8:29, 9:11, and Eph 1:4–11.

15. The mistake of the Arminian conception of "conditional election" is to mix up the aspects of the passivity of being elected and the activity of the elected and thereby to ignore the difference between the problems at issue in each. See Hanko, "Unconditional Election," ch. 2. On the variety of Old Testament conceptions of the Covenant (as an obligation imposed on oneself; an obligation imposed on someone else; the acceptance of reciprocal obligations; an obligation set for two parties by a third), see Gross, *Zukunft für Israel*.

16. It is for this reason that election has time and again been thought not only in terms of creation but also as corporate election; see Klein, *New Chosen People*, and Shank, *Elect in the Son*.

notion of *God's love*, which has, not by chance, become the central notion of Christian faith in God.

On the other hand, the discovery that God *wills to* overcome Evil is being symbolized centrally in the notion of the *promise*: that God *wills to* overcome Evil is shown by his *promise* to do so, and that God *can* overcome Evil is shown by the fulfillment of this promise, that is, by his delivering people from the distress and misery of *malum*. Both are recalled as happenings that intruded into the lives of certain people against their expectation and often—think of the prophets—also against their will and gave new and different directions to these lives. This experience opens up a *space for hermeneutic superimposition*,[17] insofar as events are being experienced and understood retrospectively or prospectively in light of other events—the overcoming of a *malum* as the fulfillment of a promise, or being overpowered by a *bonum* as God's obligating himself in a promise whose fulfillment can be counted on even if it seems not to have been fulfilled yet but which is also not being exhausted by its being fulfilled and instead comes with an excess of *bonum* that can never be compensated for. Not only do experiences of *bonum* acquire a surplus value of meaning by being understood as *God's promises*;[18] God's promises acquire a surplus value of *bonum* that is not exhausted by any concrete fulfillment but refers us to an open future of the overcoming of what is evil through what is good and to the enhancement of what is good in what is better, which can always be further outdone.

That is why it makes sense to ask God for deliverance from Evil and for the definitive imposition of his good will not only in heaven but on earth as well. For if God does what is good, then he wills to and can do what is good; if God can and wills to do what is good, then we may rely on God doing the good he has promised; and if God promises to and wills for someone that which is the best for that particular life, then we may rely on his being able to achieve it and on his actually achieving it, whatever experience to the contrary might try and impose itself. That God has done what is good, does what is good, and will do what is good, by himself and long before we ask for it and even after we are no longer able to ask him for it, in creating the world and in preserving life, in delivering us from illness, distress, and perdition, in liberating us from imprisonment and delivering us from enemies, in providing our daily bread, in his law for the good order of human life, in freeing us from guilt and sin, in fighting for justice for those deprived of rights, in caring for those whom no one cares about, in turning to those who have turned away from him, in taking mercy on those whom no one has mercy on—that is the *cantus firmus* of the biblical message.

Because it has its origins in these positive experiences of deliverance, healing, and salvation, the biblical tradition brings up the most profound challenges where the

17. *Superimposition* is the name I use for the hermeneutic procedure that consists in describing and understanding an event—which can be located more or less unambiguously in a series of events organized according to *earlier than*, *later than*, and *simultaneously with*—from different points of view, within different perspectives, and under different aspects, that is, to give a complex definition by means of a superimposed network of ways of seeing.

18. To experience a happening as God's promise, we need not experience it *as* God's promise. In the weak or hermeneutically implicit sense, something is experienced as *something* in being *experienced* in this way; in the strong or hermeneutically explicit sense, it is experienced as something in being experienced *as* something.

reliability of God's good will itself is being questioned. If, given the reality of *malum*, all we can do is hope that God will overcome it, then there are no grounds for this hope where God seems no longer to stand by his assurances: when God's reliability becomes questionable, hope for Evil being overcome through God becomes untenable.

This is precisely what the biblical tradition reflects in two stories of great theological volatility, which not by chance are of central importance in Jewish and Christian theology: *the testing of God by Abraham* and *the testing of God by Jesus*. Both narratives paradigmatically focus central experiences of the Jewish and the Christian faith by reporting how, in decisive situations, the very people who in an exemplary manner have bet everything on God's reliable promise no longer knew what they could and ought to rely on because God's will had become obscure and impenetrable to them. In both cases, however, this is narrated and handed down not to demonstrate the failure of the faith of even the "fathers of the faith," but to remind listeners that it is precisely in these situations that insights into God's willing and working emerged without which the Jewish and Christian conception of God can no longer be thought.

3. The Experiment of Reliability: Abraham

One of the most powerful stories of the Old Testament is the narrative of Abraham's testing of God in Gen 22.[19] It would be hermeneutically naive to think it possible to approach this story as if it had never been read before. Such a reading of one's own might be attempted only on the highly reflective path of methodically ignoring and willfully suspending the long and complex history of its interpretations. No one turns to this story without an emphatic prior opinion. Often, this is already apparent in the headings chosen, such as "the sacrifice of Isaac," "Abraham's temptation," or "the binding of Isaac." It is, after all, a key story of the biblical tradition that Judaism and Christianity have responded to in many, albeit many markedly different, ways.

While the Jewish tradition interprets Gen 22 as the revelation to Abraham that God does not want human sacrifice, as a testing of Abraham, or as a consolation story for Israel, it is read in Christianity usually as an example of Abraham's unconditional obedience and faith and thus as a typological model for Jesus Christ.[20] Both interpretations lead to a theological dilemma: How can God, flagrantly contradicting everything to be expected of God, order Abraham to sacrifice his own child, and how can Abraham accept without uttering a word?[21] The rabbinic interpretation seeks to avoid the dilemma by conceiving of the *aqeda* as the tenth and highest test of Abraham's faith and of his

19. The emphasis is usually placed the other way around: Abraham is being tested by God, not God by Abraham. See Volgger, "Es geht um das Ganze." As I will show, however, the real point of the text runs in the opposite direction.

20. For Jewish interpretations, see Levenson, *Death and Resurrection of the Beloved Son*; Caspi and Cohen, *Binding (aqedah) and its Transformations in Judaism and Islam*; McElwain, "Genesis 22, Judaism, Islam and the Sacrifice of Isaac"; Kundert, *Die Opferung/Bindung Isaaks*; Noort and Tigchelaar, *Sacrifice of Isaac*; and Houtman, "Theodicy in the Pentateuch," 166–67. For Christian readings, see Moberly, "Christ as the Key to Scripture" and *Bible, Theology, and Faith*, as well as Mays, "Now I Know."

21. See Boehm, "Binding of Isaac: An Inner-Biblical Polemic"; Brandscheidt, "Das Opfer des Abraham"; and Kaiser, "Deus absconditus and Deus revelatus."

readiness to sacrifice his only son Isaac as the highest expression of his piety. This may seem barbaric to us but in antiquity, Philo, for example, "had to defend against pagan slanderers who maintained that the act was not so uniquely praiseworthy since others in the ancient world had acted similarly."[22] Where that did not (or no longer) apply, Abraham was said—by the great Jewish commentator Rashi in the eleventh century, for example, or by Kierkegaard (albeit in a different way) in the nineteenth[23]—to have possessed prophetic foreknowledge that it would ultimately not come to the sacrifice of his son. Different traditions and different times thus consider quite different things to constitute the challenge and the problem of the story.[24] Yet it is unlikely that the story ever existed outside of contesting understandings and interpretations. That is also why it cannot be approached without getting involved in these controversies.

4. Abraham's Silence

It is well worth it to begin by taking a look at what the story does *not* narrate. Abraham does not speak, Isaac does not protest, Sarah does not appear at all, nor is Ishmael mentioned. Neither does Abraham manifest any ambivalent feelings toward Isaac, and Isaac does not say a word about anything that happens, indeed, he remains completely vague as a figure. After the sacrifice of the ram, Isaac disappears from the story and Abraham, along with his servants, returns to Beersheba. All this has time and again given rise to a great variety of interpretations and continuations of the story that eloquently make Abraham's silence speak, picture Sarah's shock at Isaac's alleged or actual killing, elaborate Isaac's role in the story in great detail by not having him endure his binding and sacrifice in silence but rather having him strive and ask for it, and so on. All these interpretations and continuations, which go back to pre-Christian times,[25] show just how open and mobile the history of the text has been for a long time, yet there is little for them to go on in the narrative in its current biblical form: they fill in what they experience as a lack because it is not being said and narrated there.

Yet when we stick to the explicit telling of the story in Gen 22, we must indeed ask whether it is really a story about Abraham *and* Isaac and not rather one only about *Abraham*, in which Isaac also figures—just as the story of William Tell, despite the apple-shot, is not really about the son or about the relationship between father and son. The *dramatis personae* and the possible relationships this configuration sets up, in any case, do not suffice as a key to understanding the story. To do that, we must keep to what is actually being recounted, that is, enter the narrative process and its dynamic and drama.

22. Anderson ("Abraham III.1," 14). On Philo's engagement with this entire set of problems, see Runia, "Theodicy in Philo of Alexandria."

23. See Levenson, *Death and Resurrection of the Beloved Son*, 130, and Kierkegaard, *Fear and Trembling*.

24. See Crenshaw, *Defending God*, 57–65.

25. See Vermès, "Redemption and Genesis xxii," and Fitzmyer, "Sacrifice of Isaac in Qumran Literature."

5. The Abraham Cycle

Genesis 22 is not an isolated story. It is part of the cycle of stories about Abraham that stretches from verse 27 in chapter 11 to chapter 22 or to the narration of Abraham's death in chapter 25. The entire cycle presupposes the existence of Israel, that is, it retrospectively recounts something of significance to contemporary Israel. Hermeneutically, therefore, these stories are not to be interpreted with a view to an Israel yet to come but as narratives of Israel, which, in a situation where that was not (or no longer) self-evident, sought to reassure itself of its own history and identity. As the genealogical lists and the names of peoples make clear, the cycle in the form we have it offers an "etiological history of the origin of Israel and its environment," that is, "an ethnogenesis, which provides the Israelite addressees with aids to basic orientation and identification."[26] Whether the narration allows for detailed historical inferences concerning a prehistoric "patriarchal age" is a matter of contention, but it is not of much significance for understanding the point of this cycle.

On the formal level, the Abraham cycle is conspicuously organized into episodes, that is, it offers a sequence of individual narratives with, in part, recurrent characteristics that have been composed together according to certain guiding aspects. It is likely that these narratives, beside originally oral traditions, also include new material, as the conspicuous "double traditions" suggest, which talk, for instance, about Sarah as the concubine or almost-concubine of foreign rulers (of Pharaoh at 12:10–20, of Abimelech in chapter 20). From the point of view of literary criticism, then, the cycle in its present form likely emerged in different stages that can be understood partly as inclusions of older narratives in a literary context, partly as literary creations, but partly also as additions and emendations of existing texts.

Unlike some of the individual narratives, the cycle as a whole is composed theologically. Its central motif is God's promise of land and the assured blessing of Abraham's numerous offspring and their becoming a people (Gen 12:1–3 and 13:14–17). The emphasis put on these points is probably best understood as a reflex to their actually being questioned in the experience of exile since 568/567, the time this cycle was most probably composed. Yet the cycle continued to be written after the exile period, when God's promises are intensified in Gen 15 and 17 as God's covenant with Israel (see also 22:15–18). In any event, the genesis of the traditional form of the Abraham cycle is complex, and this must be taken into account in interpreting the individual stories.

For the story told in Gen 22, this means that, hermeneutically, it can be read on different levels or from different perspectives, namely at least under the aspect of (1) the original story it is based on; (2) that story's inclusion in the cycle of stories about Abraham; (3) that cycle's inclusion in the wider context, ultimately the context of the Bible as a whole; and (4) the interpretations that pick up on it, both theological (in Judaism and Christianity) and non-theological (in philosophy as well as in the history, sociology, psychology, etc., of religion).

Under the first aspect—as clues such as the otherwise unknown "land of Moriah" and the absence of details about the place of sacrifice suggest—it is likely that there were

26. Blum, "Abraham I," 11.

older versions of the narrative that were not yet dominated by the theological theme that shapes the Abraham cycle.[27] Under the second aspect, the story is tied into a theological context that gives it a new point and thereby provokes the hermeneutic question whether there are reasons why it was this story precisely that was chosen to make this specific point. Under the third aspect, we must inquire into the function of the story within its more narrow (Old Testament) and its wider (New Testament) biblical contexts, that is, into its relationships with other texts in these traditions. Under the fourth aspect, finally, we must ask about its reverberations in later religious, theological, scientific, literary, and artistic interpretations. Differentiating these aspects in this way, on the one hand, is by no means to suggest a progress of interpretation but a hermeneutic focusing of different text–context constellations and traditions. On the other hand, such a differentiation is quite important from a methodological and hermeneutic point of view: interpretation must not unwittingly switch from one aspect to another.

Under the first aspect, the story seems not to have had anything to do with Abraham and Isaac at all. It may have been a sanctuary's "ancient cultic legend" that served to "legitimize . . . redeeming the sacrifice of a child, actually demanded by God, with the sacrifice of an animal." Whatever this story may have recounted, "this idea is quite foreign to the present narrative."[28] Under the second aspect, it is tied into the Abraham cycle's nexus of promise and blessing and thereby acquires a new, namely a theological point. Under the third aspect, this story with its new theological point can enter into relations of analogy and contrast with other narratives in the Old and New Testament,[29] all the way to the "parallel" that has decisively shaped the history of interpretation between the near-sacrifice of Isaac and Jesus's death on the cross confessed as the ultimate sacrifice (a closer look, though, shows such a parallel to exist only if the roles in the story are completely redefined).

Under the fourth aspect, finally, there is a methodological differentiation with significant consequences, which urges a distinction between on the one hand religious interpretations of the story in narrative and theological continuations and on the other hand non-religious interpretations. Drawing this line with precision may in each case be as difficult as drawing the line between day and night. But that does not change anything about the fact that both are to be kept distinct and not to be confused. Thus, in the one case, there is direct speech about Abraham, Isaac, God, and angels, whereas in the other case, they can be spoken about only indirectly, with reference to the given narrative texts

27. See Westermann, *Genesis 12–36*, 354 and 357–58. In the only other place where the name "Moriah" can be found in the Old Testament (2 Chr 3:1), it designates the hill on which God is said to have appeared to David and where Solomon builds the temple. According to Gunkel, *Genesis*, 234, this is the original use of the name "Moriyya" that was then retroprojected into the narrative of Genesis. Kilian, *Isaaks Opferung*, 45–46, makes a similar case.

28. Rad, *Genesis: A Commentary*, 242–43. The supposition of a ransoming, of course, is not without problems, if only because the text in the current form does not offer a real etiology of replacing child sacrifice with animal sacrifice: God at most accepts the sacrifice of the ram in the place of Isaac, he does not command it. If there is an older cultic legend behind this version that was in fact about replacing human sacrifice with animal sacrifice at a specific sanctuary, then the location of this sanctuary remains completely obscure. See also Levenson, *Death and Resurrection of the Beloved Son*, 118–19.

29. See Steins, *Die "Bindung Isaaks" im Kanon*.

and its figures and narrative actors. They are protagonists of the story, whose narrative drama, focus, style, and so on, shapes them. Certain questions thus do not make sense when the narrative point of the story is left aside. Just as we cannot expect an answer to the question where the snake learned to speak, so we may not expect in the present case an answer to the question whether Isaac screamed when he was being tied up, whether this treatment caused life-long trauma, or whether he developed feelings of revenge toward his father. The questions are not impossible, prohibited, or meaningless in their own right—but if the methodological decision is made to base the interpretation not on Abraham, Isaac, and God but only on the figures of this narrative as they appear in this version of the text, these questions become hermeneutically meaningless because this narrative does not allow for answering them one way or the other. The story does not have to say anything on these points because that is not what it is about. What, then, is it about?

6. The Dramatic Point of Gen 22

As a consequence of distinguishing between different interpretational aspects, there cannot be just one answer to this question. If we keep to the traditional narrative context of the Abraham cycle, however, the answer is given in fairly precise terms within the horizon of the second interpretational aspect. The drama unfolding in the story does not take place between Abraham and Isaac but between *God and Abraham*. It is thus not a father–son conflict between Abraham and Isaac but a *conflict with God* on the part of Israel, represented by its progenitor, Abraham.

That is why the dynamic of the narrative's action does not unfold in such a way that God at Gen 22:1 would "initiate" "events in the form of an imperative to engage in dialog," thereby establishing a "horizon of expectation" "between two protagonists in an asymmetrical relationship and of different existential constitutions" (mortal human being vs. immortal, sacred God).[30] That, rather, is already the second act in the story's drama. The decisive first act is the promise and the assurance of future blessings stated programmatically at the beginning of the cycle: "I will make of you a great nation, and I will bless you, and make your name great, so that you will be a blessing" (Gen 12:2). It is not a coincidence that a post-exilic continuation of the story explicitly repeats this assurance at its end (22:15–18). Nor is it a coincidence that this promise is explicitly narrowed down to Isaac just before the beginning of the *adeqa* narrative: God assures Abraham that it is not through Ishmael but "through Isaac that offspring shall be named for you" (21:12).

The decisive conflict thus consists in the narrative construction between a God who promises great things in and through Isaac and *the same* God who commands Abraham to perform a deed concerning Isaac whose execution would make actualizing this promise entirely impossible.[31] Jewish interpreters such as Rabbi Hillel Goldberg have spoken

---

30. Boothe, "Abraham schweigt," 8.

31. To try and derive from this a paradoxical, non-syllogistic "logic of God's" to which Abraham's syllogistic thinking had to defer is a not very convincing attempt at deescalating the fundamental conflict that manifests itself here. See Ellis, "Human Logic, God's Logic, and the *Akedah*."

of a dual irresolvable tension Abraham thus finds himself in: the philosophical-logical tension of God demanding something that contradicts everything God has promised; and the psychological tension that he is supposed to kill his own son and thereby violate the very ethics he has taught in God's name.[32] But as much as it may occupy interpreters, there is no such psychological tension that would play a narrative role in this story. There is no moral doubt "that the command to immolate Isaac . . . should be regarded as a law that is other than good. Indeed, the very angelic address that calls off the commanded sacrifice commends Abraham for his willingness to carry it out."[33] Nor is the story about Abraham's psychological problems with killing his son—nothing of the sort is even just suggested, and it is not by chance that the figure of Isaac is only roughly sketched. The only one to be narratively relevant is the tension given expression in the command to kill, the tension between *God's promise* and *God's making this promise impossible to keep*. That is the contradiction that defines the narrative: Does God give Israel with one hand what with the other he takes away again? Is it possible to rely on someone who can take back again everything he promised, at any time and without cause or reason? Is it still possible to count on God's faithfulness, indeed, to count on God at all?

The narrative unmistakably ascribes both, the promise and the command to make the promise impossible to keep, to *the same* God, that is, it does not afford the way out that consists in assigning the promise to God and the questioning of the promise to someone other than God, as continuations of the *aqeda* story that borrow from the prologue to Job try to do.[34] Abraham is thus portrayed in a conflict situation in which there is literally nothing left for him to say because God seems to be mired in self-contradiction. Talking to others about God does not lead anywhere; talking to God himself has become impossible because God has become so ambivalent for Abraham that he is no longer addressable as a specific God, as "my God."

Where there is nothing left to say, life decides. The conflict cannot be settled by discussion because God has become unreachable and unaddressable as an interlocutor. It can be settled only by Abraham taking one side of the contradictory and thus self-defeating divine will at its word and acting on it until the question of God either sorts itself out on its own or God himself—and this is the solution of the story[35]—abolishes the ambivalence in his relationship with Abraham/Israel and commits himself to his promises. Put bluntly: it is not Abraham who is being tested by God here, it is God who is being tested by Abraham, by Abraham no longer talking but acting: Abraham practically compels God either to take leave, as God, of the life of his people or to prove himself to be God and stand by his promises for his people. He dares to test God and he

32. Goldberg, "Abraham and Isaac: 'The Test.'"

33. Levenson, *Death and Resurrection of the Beloved Son*, 113; see also Crenshaw, *Defending God*, 62–65.

34. See for example the versions of the story found at Qumran, in which "Prince Mastema" and his evil angels scheme against Abraham (4Q225 2 i and ii; WQPS-Juba 2 i 7–14, 2 ii 1–14). See Fitzmyer, "Sacrifice of Isaac in Qumran Literature," 216–27.

35. The angel appearing in verse 11 cannot be mobilized against God, even if this difference has been particularly stressed and interpreted in the long exegetical tradition.

wins—wins not only clarity (which would have been the case as well had the result been negative) but certainty that God stands by his promises.

Why is this testing of God, this playing out of the conflict in Israel's relation to and conception of God theologically represented by, precisely, the story of Abraham's offering of his beloved son? Because, in a way difficult to surpass, it is able to express this conflict in Abraham's conception of and trust in God. It does not hinge on the "killing of the son contradicting the father's interest in the survival of his child"[36] but on the fact that Israel's certainty about God depends on it: the narratively decisive point is not that it is *his beloved son* whom Abraham is supposed to kill but that his beloved son is *the only reliable pledge of God's promise*. Abraham's setting about destroying this pledge of God's promise on the command of God himself brings out the extreme existential situation in which he or Israel finds itself vis-à-vis God: either this is the end of all stories of Israel with God or God must definitively shed his ambivalence in the history of Israel.

It is for representing this testing of God alone that the Abraham cycle takes up the cultic legend of the replacement of child sacrifice with animal sacrifice and retells it with God, Abraham, and Isaac as its protagonists. The story is unsuitable for describing God himself or his relationship with Israel, that is, for making inferences about God's bare arbitrary will or an allegedly demanded blindly obedient faith going all the way to the faithful's moral self-destruction. All this is not at issue. The one and only issue is putting an end to the dubiousness of a God who in his turning toward and turning away from his people is being experienced as pure self-contradictoriness and is thus unsuitable for giving orientation in life.[37] Such a God cannot be relied on. He is superfluous as a point of reference and of orientation in human life.

7. Ridding the Conception of God of Its Ambiguity

This may be put in the more general terms of a theology of experience: in a world in which we never know what to make of God because there are always life-experiences that can be cited in his favor and experiences that can be cited against him, life-orienting clarity can be attained only in an extreme situation where the confrontation is not merely between faith and unfaith but where faith in God confronts faith in God in such a way that it either negates itself (and thereby brings clarity in a negative way) or clarifies where one can count on God and where one can certainly not count on God (thus understood) and ought therefore not to seek him out and may not evoke him.

The result of this clarification is not a proof of God's existence but a sharpened, more precise, and more defined conception of God and a relationship with God that will no longer seek God, and does no longer see God, undifferentiatedly in everything

36. Boothe, "Abraham schweigt," 5.

37. This point is clearly grasped in the twin parables of Bereishit Rabbah 56 that interpret Gen 22:15–16. It is Abraham who, thanks to the strength of his faith, prevents God from becoming entangled in a fatal self-contradiction and from shattering the promise he has himself given. And according to the second parable, it is not God who has Abraham swear but Abraham who has God swear never to do something similar again: "swear to me not to test me ever again." This divine oath commits God to his promise; God from now on is reliable. See Thoma and Lauer, *Von der Erschaffung*.

but only in certain experiences, a conception that will no longer understand, accept, and practice everything as a human living and acting that corresponds to God's will but only a specific living and acting. This is the basic point and the starting point of all of Jewish ethics culminating in the Torah, and also of Christian ethics concentrated in the commandment of love: it is now possible to say with certainty that nothing can be ascribed to God or God's will that would make God contradict his promises or make humans contradict God's promised will. This is not a matter of course, for why should a freely given promise not be freely revoked? This possibility, precisely, is what the *aqeda* narrative excludes by turning the actualization of this possibility into a self-contradiction and into God's self-abolition and thereby declaring it to be, in fact, impossible. *God's promises are certain, even if within the horizon of our own life-experiences, we may not know what to make of God*—this is one way to summarize the point this story in the Abraham cycle is making about practical life.[38]

The biblical tradition has shown this reliability of the promise time and again, not only in the story of Abraham but also and differently in the story of Jesus by describing the possibility of revoking the promise as God's self-abolishment and thereby rendering it an impossibility: God would abolish himself and become superfluous for human beings if the ambivalence of their (not) experiencing God is not overcome by a God who can still be unequivocally addressed and appealed to as a God committed to his promises even when he is not being experienced as God, as obscure and withdrawn. Where being abandoned by God can no longer be brought before God ("My God, why have you forsaken me?"), one cannot even meaningfully call oneself abandoned by God. God then does not just have no more role to play; it is no longer even clear what role he could have played. Inversely, precisely because he cannot be seen as distinct from his promises or thought as arbitrarily willing despite them, God can no longer be claimed for everything but only for very specific things.

In short, Gen 22, by means of an old legend about replacing child sacrifice with cultic animal sacrifice, tells a new story with extraordinary consequences for religious thinking and living: the story of ascertaining the reliability of God's promises through Abraham's testing of God. In silently taking God, of whom Israel no longer knows what to make, at his word and acting, Abraham provokes a situation of decision in which God either proves himself to be entirely superfluous for human beings or shows himself to be the one who absolutely does not contradict his promises because he could revoke them only at the price of abolishing himself. God thereby excludes as impossible for himself what is in itself possible and seems, in human experience, to be the case, and he thereby puts human experience as an authority for judging him in its place: either there is no God or God's promises cannot be revoked even by God. *Tertium non datur.*

This experiment reliably inscribes the promise in the notion of God. God becomes inseparable from what he has promised Israel. That is why recourse to God in situations

---

38. From this perspective, it also becomes possible to appreciate Kant's moral-theological point that "Abraham should have replied to this supposedly divine voice: 'That I ought not to kill my good son is quite certain. But that you, this apparition, are God—of that I am not certain, and never can be, not even if this voice rings down to me from (visible) heaven'" (Kant, *Conflict of the Faculties*, in *Religion and Rational Theology*, 233–327, here 283n [AA 7:63]).

in which a *malum* intrudes in human life becomes recourse to someone whom we can rely on to be more powerful than the Evil he works against. That does not put an end to the *malum*. But it prompts the justified hope that the *malum* will not have the last word.

8. Strategies for Orienting Contested Hope

Yet this very hope becomes doubtful in each concrete case where the *malum* in a person's life is not being overcome but destroys this life to the point where it becomes unrecognizable and annihilates it. Given this reality, how is it possible to hold on to the reliability of God's promise to overcome Evil?

If we do not abandon hope, there are formally different strategies to orient ourselves in such situations of contested hope. Among the most important of these, which can be combined in various ways, are:

1. *the pattern of individual and whole*: God's promise does not apply to each individual case but to the history of the people as a whole; or it does not apply to some but to others. In this case, God does not stand in the same relationship with all human beings but is closer to some than he is to others: closer to his people than to the heathens, closer to the faithful than to those without faith. This may correspond to human life-experience, but it leads to difficulties regarding God's will and self-commitment: What is God's will to salvation worth when it aims at only a few and ignores the majority? How can he will only the well-being of the few and accept or even will the annihilation of the many without it becoming necessary to call him not a good but a terrible God, not a just but an unjust God?[39]

2. *the pattern of place*: God's promise is actualized not here but there, not with these people but with those. This orienting strategy is similarly efficient as the first and leads to similar problems. If God's promise applies not to all places but only to some and if it is fulfilled not here but only in some places, this amounts to depriving the notion of promise of its content.

3. *the pattern of horizons of reference*: Even if a life is damaged by *malum* in such a way that the *bonum* promised by God does not prove itself *in this life* and *for this life*, it can still show itself *for another life*. Not the one suffering the *malum* but the one suffering with her or even the one profiting from it can become the place where the *malum* is shown not to have the last word. There are many examples of this, and in one way or another, everyone or at least many people profit in their lives from

---

39. Those who argue, in line with Calvin and strict Calvinism, that election necessarily implies rejection because to elect the ones always means rejecting the others, rightly see that with view to God's election, there is no neutral ground: if God elects freely, then there is no human being who would be neither elected nor not elected. Their argument, however, requires the actuality of what needs only be thinkable as a possibility. For it to make sense to say that someone is elected, it must be *possible* that this person or another could also not have been elected, but it does not follow that this person can be elected only if someone else *is* not elected but rejected. God does not have to reject to be able to elect. Rather, God could not elect if it were impossible to reject. Yet it does not follow that he in fact does or must reject: electing *everyone* when everyone could also have been rejected also fulfills the condition that with regard to divine election, there is no neutral ground.

the *malum* of others. Yet we do need to distinguish here between two cases, that of *another human life* and that of *divine life*.

If all that is at issue were that *others* learn from the evil in the life of a human being, then such a hope would lead to a *bonum* in their lives but not in hers. And if all that was being hoped for was that the *malum* of a life would have as its consequence a *bonum* in the life of another, then the place of Evil and the place of the overcoming of Evil would have to be sought in different lives. This includes the hope for the divine surpassing of Evil through Good, but this overcoming cannot be understood in this way alone if it is not to be deprived of its essential point. A salvation that *always only* actualizes for another is not a salvation one can hope for. The hope, rather, is that *at the same place* that the evil occurs, this outdoing good will be found as well and that *for the same person* who is damaged by the *malum*, the *bonum* goes into effect. Salvation must be actualized in the life of those who suffer, not only in the lives of others.

This also applies if at this point the *other* life is understood to be the *divine life*. This does not mean shifting the good to another (human) life in the here and now or to another (divine) life in the beyond, but divine life is precisely that which overcomes Evil here and now with good and does so at the place of the Evil and not in some other place. Those who are *evil* must be delivered from evil, not those who are not evil. More than that: the hope is not only directed at evil being outdone in the place of the evil, such that Job, and not someone else, is again blessed with all the goods that were taken from him. Rather, Evil is to be outdone by Good in such a way that not only the wrong life is brought to rights, but the inversion of life into wrong life is brought to an end. The hope is directed not only at correcting and repairing Evil in the specifically affected life but at Evil being ended and eliminated for each and every life in being outdone by Good: Evil is to be overcome not just *here* and *for this person* but *for everyone* and *permanently*. For this very reason, the point of hoping for *malum* being outdone by *bonum* is not the confidence that somehow, Good will win out, but that *God* will bring this about, by on the one hand continuing and outdoing each life affected by *malum* in the way that is best for it (God's saving action) and on the other ensuring that avoidable and unjust *malum* is definitively replaced and outdone by *bonum* (God's perfecting action).

4. *the pattern of concealment*: The actualization of God's promise does not (in every case) take place in a way that can be experienced but also always in a concealed way. When it is not being experienced and perceived, it is not possible to infer that it is not being fulfilled, only that the fulfilment is not being experienced. This, too, is an evidently absurd strategy, since a good that those affected do not experience as a good does not represent a good for them. If God's promise were not furthermore fulfilled somewhere in an experienceable way, there would be no reason to consider it to be concealed. It must be possible to distinguish concealment, like absence, from non-presence or non-existence. And that is possible only if there is good reason to say that that which could in principle be present and evident is in fact (still)

concealed and absent; and such good reason can exist only in the reference to a factual actualization of God's promise.

5. *the pattern of growth*: God's promise does not actualize all at once but gradually, its actualization grows from imperceptible beginnings to its final perfection. For a long time, we might not notice anything, but sooner or later, it will be actualized in an experienceable way. For individual life, this seems to be a defensible view only until death; for the whole life of a people or a community, it represents more than just a deferment to a later point in time never attained only if signs and traces of its being actualized can be perceived already now.

6. *the pattern of time*: God's promise does not actualize now but then, not in this life but in a life to come. This pattern can be a continuation of the pattern of growth. Often, however, it manifests in two other variants.

The first is the *apocalyptic pattern*, according to which God's promise will be actualized not in this but only in a new world. Actualizing it requires not just a changed but a new world, spatially discontinuous with the old world and temporally either continuous or discontinuous with it. In the case of temporal continuity, the end of the old world becomes the necessary precondition for the new world that can rise up only from the rubble of the old. In the case of temporal discontinuity, the new world can begin or already have begun even while the old one still exists. The actualization of the promise is then thought as a changing of worlds, be it as a transition to another world, be it as the parallel existence of the old and the new world.

The *eschatological pattern* thinks this in concrete terms. God's promise will not actualize in this world, but neither will it actualize only in a world yet to come. Its actualization has already begun in this world but will continue beyond it in the new world that actualizes as it grows. Time is thus differentiated into two phases, which, on the one hand, stretch between the time of the *promise* and the time of the *fulfillment* and, on the other hand, have the time of fulfillment extend between the *already now* and the *not yet*, between the *beginning* and the *perfection* of the fulfillment. Not only is life being thought dynamically from promise toward fulfillment, the fulfillment, too, is thought dynamically as capable of enhancement and in the direction of an as-yet unattained perfection. The goal of the promise is not only the actualization of salvation but the perfection of salvation in a life that as a new life not only differs fundamentally from the old life but differentiates into a beginning that is experienced and a perfection that is hoped for.

This eschatological orientation strategy experiences the present good as doubly determined. On the one hand, this good is the hoped-for fulfillment of the divine promise; on the other, it is the reason for hoping for the perfection to come. The eschatological *bonum* thus urges us to look from the present in a differentiated manner, both retrospectively to the past and prospectively to the future.

In the first regard, it has behind it a promise whose fulfillment in this good allows for a retrospective definition and concrete description of the promise: God's promise contains that which is taking place here and now and is being experienced as *bonum*. This in turn clarifies what *malum* really is and what must be overcome as evil: not only that is evil which is being experienced and lived as evil but also that, precisely, which is not being experienced and lived as evil but comes to be seen in the light of the eschatological *bonum* as that which prevents, impairs, damages this good. The look back therefore urges us to subject the life of those affected by this *bonum* but also, from the perspective of this life, the entire individual and communal past to a differentiated hermeneutic rereading that identifies and highlights that which the eschatological *bonum* takes up, amplifies, and continues as well as that which thereby becomes identifiable as *malum*, including in its still-effective previous shapes. The eschatological opposition of *bonum* and *malum* thereby sheds a differentiated light on the past as well, just as it does on the present.

In the second regard, the eschatological *bonum* in the present opens up a view onto the future, which allows for seeing two things as well. On the one hand, this present *bonum* will increase to perfection, since it is due solely to the self-actualization of the divine promise and since the surplus and excess of this promise leads those affected into an ever-advancing, extensive (ever more) and intensive (ever better) process of enhancing the good: the *bonum* God's promise promises is always even more and even better than what is actualized at any time. On the other hand, this includes as its flipside that the present and future *malum* is being restricted, overcome, outdone, replaced, marginalized, ended by the *bonum*. The prospective view from the present *bonum* into the future opening up thus is a view onto a twofold process of the unforeseeable enhancement of the *bonum* and the incessant outdoing of the *malum*. This process, however, is open—not because its issue were uncertain but because its issue in the *bonum* is such that the fullness of the *bonum* urges an ever-further actualization of the fulfillment of God's promise. The *bonum* does not end in the optimum; the optimum is the open process of enhancing the good in the direction of the ever-better.

9. The Word of the Cross

In Christianity, the eschatological orientation strategy just sketched is decisively founded on the "word of the cross" to which, according to Paul, Christian faith owes its existence. The cross of Jesus Christ is the key not only to a specific *order* of life, insofar as the world is understood as being instituted by God for the presentification of the *bonum* that he has intended for the human being and for all of creation but also to a specific *locating* of the human being within this order, which is defined, in accordance with how a human life is to be assessed under the aspect of God's gift, either as unfaith or as faith.

The cross of Jesus Christ is thus the central eschatological *bonum*[40] that in the word of the cross is understood—in multiple superimpositions—vertically and horizontally, and each time in a twofold sense. Vertically it is being understood, guided by the

40. It is a *bonum* because it marks the salvation happening to human beings from God and it is *eschatological* because it happens to them in such a way that their lives are irreversibly differentiated into the passing old life and the coming new life.

difference *creator–creature*, as an event that is simultaneously *historical* (it tells of Jesus) and *divine* (it tells of God); horizontally as a historical event that, guided by the eschatological difference *old life–new life*, is to be read simultaneously *retrospectively* and *prospectively*.

Taken together, this yields the characteristic superimposed, vertical and horizontal, multiple determination of the cross that is being commemorated and presentified in the word of the cross.[41] Vertically, the cross is thus, on the one hand, the historical event in which the life of Jesus of Nazareth is ended; it is the *cross of Jesus Christ*. On the other hand, *as resurrection of the crucified Christ*, it expresses God's committing himself, through the way God acts toward Jesus, to declaring what Jesus has announced about God to be binding for how God wills to and will act toward all human beings. The one (the cross of Jesus Christ) is commemorated by Christians on Good Friday, the other (resurrection of the crucified Christ) on Easter. Yet if the word of the cross is not to be emptied of its content and deprived of its point, both can be commemorated by Christians only together: without Good Friday, there would be nothing to be commemorated on Easter, and without Easter, there would be nothing to be commemorated on Good Friday.

For this very reason, however, the cross of Jesus Christ is also to be understood, guided by the word of the cross, horizontally within history, in a differentiated way, retrospectively and prospectively. On the one hand, the cross is that from the perspective of which the life of Jesus, Jesus's proclamation, in words and deeds, of the commencing kingdom of God, and the divine history of Israel thereby updated and brought to a head, come into view. This is made clear by the rereading of Jesus's life and actions in the gospel and the differentiated references to the theological traditions of Israel set up there (some things are taken up especially and amplified, others are sidelined and ignored).[42]

---

41. That is why the cross as used by Christians is a semantically dense symbol that is regularly being foreshortened when it is being reduced to just one aspect (historically, politically, social-historically, Christologically, soteriologically, theologically, and so on) or when one such aspect is declared to be fundamental. In different respects, and depending on the question and the guiding interest, different elements of the complex superimposition of the cross can become the central aspect. That is why we must always be clear as to which interest guides the practical context in which or out of which we seek to understand the cross.

42. The tension-filled process of tradition formation set up in the Jewish theological tradition thus continues, via Jesus, in Christianity. Already within the Torah, there was from the beginning a tension between "texts that sought to give legal, social, and liturgical order to the life of the Israelites and texts that, in narratives, put the themes of God's promise and protection in distress front and center." This is amplified in the tensions between the Torah and the prophetic writings, where it was especially those largely rejected in the preexile period, the prophets of judgment, who not only became "decisive aids . . . in working through the catastrophe of exile" but also "the canon's most important interpreters of Torah" (Jeremias, "Alttestamentliche Wissenschaft im Kontext der Theologie," 16; see also Dohmen and Oeming, *Biblischer Kanon, warum und wozu?*, 68–89). Jesus brought Torah and prophets to a head, characteristically in his proclamation of the commencing kingdom of God. And this in turn becomes the key to understanding his life and its ending on the cross, and it manifests itself in the formation of the New Testament's theologies. Each of these junctures (which I can only quickly hint at here) selectively take up, refine, restructure, expand, modify, interpret, continue, and reaccentuate what came before and precisely in so doing develop a simultaneously differentiating and time and again resynthesizing history of the impact of traditions that are becoming canonical, those which have not been included in a (given) canon, and those which no longer stand at the center of or have even been excluded from such a canon.

On the other hand, it is that from the perspective of which the present and the future are seen as the time of Christ resurrected by God, of the action of his Spirit sent by God, of assembling God's congregation from all nations, of expecting the perfection of the kingdom of God in the enactment and actualization of God's love of all human beings as proven in Jesus on the cross. This, too, is an occasion to experience the history lived individually or communally in a differentiated way under the aspect of how the *bonum* of God's love comes to act in the world and how thereby that is being discovered, fought, overcome, and outdone which is thus disavowed as *malum*. This is reflected theologically in the differentiating aspect sin–grace, and Christians commemorate it in baptism and communion, which celebrate the beginning of the new life under the conditions of the passing old life (baptism) and the living community of this life with God and with each other (communion) in the hope for the perfection of the *bonum* in the overcoming and outdoing of the *malum*.

10. The Experiment of Life: Jesus

The eschatological orientation of life in the Christian faith thus outlined cannot be thought without reference to the life, action, suffering, and death of Jesus and the life, doing, and willing of God for humanity manifest in them. Yet it is not obvious that Jesus's life and death manifest God's doing and willing the *bonum* of human beings. To be sure, according to the reports of the Gospels, Jesus in his message and in his healing actions immediately associated the beginning of God's good kingdom with his person and his actions (Matt 11:5–6), and in the short years of his activity, he was able to convince a number of people, as the gathering of the apostles shows. Yet at the end of his life, not even he himself was convinced by this association anymore. According to the oldest Gospels, Mark and Matthew, Jesus's last words before he died uttering a loud scream were a cry of being abandoned by God: "My god, my god, why have you forsaken me?" (Mark 15:34; Matt 27:46). The quotation from Ps 22:1 at this point is not a disguised sign of hope in God but an expression of despair. It is a lament and an accusation by the one who experiences himself, unjustly and against all that is fair, as abandoned by God, someone whom God does not assist and help in his distress and suffering, who is dying abandoned by God and by the world, without the trust in God Luke attributes to him (Luke 23:46) and without the confidence John ascribes to him of having fulfilled the task he was charged with (John 19:30).

God here is no longer just the one to whom one turns in the happening of *malum*. God is the one whose silence and refusal of help is the real *malum*: for Jesus on the cross, God himself has become a cross that drives him to despair. God certainly is also still the one whom Jesus accuses of this. Jesus is not plagued by modernity's doubt about the existence of God but by practical despair about the concealment, the withdrawal, the inaction of God in the moment of life's greatest distress. God, by whom his life was oriented in the most intimate intensity ("my father"), has turned away from him and no longer offers help and orientation.

This contradicts everything that Jesus, according to the testimony of the New Testament, has announced, in his teachings, in his life, and in his allegorical actions, as

"God's good news":[43] the time of God's salvation is beginning and ends and eliminates the *malum* of those human beings who change their lives and believe the gospel (Mark 1:15). According to all we know, Jesus taught this and lived this in the conviction that he thereby asserted God's will. For this very reason, God's absence and concealment at the cross for Jesus is a breach of promise, an injustice and lack of mercy toward him who has bet everything on God's mercy and justice, aid denied to his creature, the father incurring guilt toward his son, a contradiction of everything he announced about God's good will and action for humanity in the parables of the lost son, the good Samaritan, in healing the sick, in working signs, and in forgiving sins. Because he hangs on the cross not just as a Jew from Galilee but as God's representative, Jesus's cry of being abandoned by God is not only a lament about undeserved ills but an accusation of God. To accuse means to think one deserves better, to think that what is happening is injustice and not justice. It would have been justice if God had helped him, if he had not let him suffer and die this way, if the *bonum* of his commencing kingdom had put the *malum* of the forces opposing it in its place. Yet at the cross, God seems to have become unfaithful to himself, and according to the oldest reports in the Gospels, Jesus died in this despair.

The story of Abraham in Gen 22 and the story of Jesus in Mark thus both present their protagonists conducting an experiment concerning God, his faithfulness, and the reliability of his promise, yet the development and the outcome markedly differ in the two cases. Abraham, according to the story, puts God to the test when, confronted with God's contradictory assurances and commandments, he no longer knows what to make of God. At the end of the story, God has proven to be the one who can no longer be separated from his promises because he has committed himself to them: God is the God of the promise, and because he cannot and does not will to be different, his promise to Israel can be relied on even where this is no longer discernible in a concrete life situation. According to the story of the gospel, Jesus, by contrast, in all of his "professional life," as it were, has bet everything on God's assurance and counted on God's faithfulness and reliability, yet in the end he dies despairing of God.

On the narrative level, the first story has a positive ending, the second a negative one. The narrative logic of the *aqeda* story presents the abolition of God's ambivalence itself, and namely as the result of Abraham's actions that lead God into a situation in which he must decide for or against himself and is therefore compelled to commit to what he as God wants to be for Israel. The decision about God's divinity is made in the story and the result is presented in the story as well. In the Gospel according to Mark, by contrast, the ambivalence is heightened to the extreme of Jesus being abandoned by God on the cross and is precisely not resolved (or its resolution presented) narratively. The narrative logic of the story of the Gospels lets the story end with the report of Jesus's death on the cross, at the opposite pole of what Mark 1:15 names as the content of the good news and of what the presentation of Jesus's workings elaborates narratively. The one story thus results in a clarified notion of God, the other leads to the point where nothing clear can be associated with the expression "God" any longer. Where the narrative slope in the Abraham story leads from uncertainty about God to certainty about

---

43. In his *Jesus and Gospel*, Graham N. Stanton traces the concept of the "good news" back to Jesus himself, citing Isa 61, Luke 4, and the Q passage Luke 7:19–23/Matt 11:2–6.

God, the narrative slope of the story of the Gospels leads from certainty about God to a loss of God.

Yet this holds only if we look at the stories in isolation and disregard their continuations in other contexts. In the Abraham story, everything that is to be said is being said *in* the story. Mark's story of Jesus, by contrast, sets up a dramatic contradiction between the conception of God of the gospel announced by Jesus and the loss of God of the announcer of the gospel perishing on the cross, a contradiction that—as the secondary conclusion to Mark (16:9–20) confirms—is no longer resolved narratively-semantically in the life story of Jesus but only pragmatically in the life story of those who experience the crucified Jesus as the resurrected Christ. The obscurity that the conception of God enters into on the cross is abolished and eliminated not in the life story of Jesus and thus for Jesus himself but in the life story of those who believe in him as Christ.[44]

This of course can itself be recounted and it has been—not only in the later ending to Mark but in the other Gospels as well, which do not have Jesus's life experiment end with the cross but continue it in the stories of the discovery of the resurrection on Easter, the appearances of the resurrected Christ, and his ascension to God in heaven. Yet as is evident in Luke in particular, it urges continuing the story of Jesus in the story of the congregation of Christ, that is, having the Gospel be followed by the story of the apostles. This continuation can take different forms. It occurs not only, as it does in Luke, as a continuation of the story of Jesus by an additional story of the apostles but also as a superimposition of the story of Jesus and the story of the congregation. Thus Mark, Matthew, Luke, and John present the view of the developing Christian community in their markedly differing rereadings of the events of Jesus's life, teaching, and death: they are writing *Christian* Gospels that testify that the theological point of the story of Jesus is not to be sought in this story itself but in the life of those who confess Jesus as Christ and that it can be represented only if they are included. From the autobiographical perspective of *Jesus himself*, his history with God ends in the cry of abandonment. Only from the biographical perspectives of *others* onto the story of Jesus does it become clear that this is not the last word on God's divinity.

Theologically, too, it has from the very beginning been possible to read this in two ways. The life story of Jesus was either seen (if it was taken notice of at all) as a short episode that did not essentially change the course of things or God's history with Israel and the world but represented a marginal phenomenon in the greater whole, largely untouched by it, of the religious history of Israel and Rome. The crisis of God on the cross then remains restricted to Jesus and has nothing to say about God, only about Jesus. Or it was seen as a story that irrevocably changed the conception of God because it inscribed itself in God's very own life story and irreversibly readjusted God's relationship with his creation. In this case, the ambivalence of God breaking through on the cross is overcome in the continuation of the history of God after the story of Jesus precisely in that the conception of God is entirely shaped by this story of Jesus. The abysmal aporia

---

44. In *The Glass of Vision*, Austin Farrer correctly concludes that the category of revelation cannot mean the life, teachings, and death of Jesus but the apostolic preaching of this life as the life of the Christ: the site of God's revelation is not the cross but the word of the cross. And that is why revelation does not take place somewhere in the past but always wherever the word of the cross moves people to believe in Jesus as God's Christ.

between Jesus's proclamation of God and the ending of his life is inscribed as a dialectic in the conception of God, which thereby, precisely, does not remain simply Jesuanic but becomes *Christian*.

In the process, certain traits of the Jesuanic image of God are amplified and new ones acquired, not in an arbitrary recasting but as an expression of how God was seen to reveal himself in these events. It is thus—to put it in the terms of the developing Christian community—*God himself alone* who abolishes his ambivalence manifest on the cross in the action of the *Spirit*, moving people to have faith in Jesus as the Christ. And it is precisely the reference to the story of Christ culminating on the cross, which is being recounted as Jesus's life experiment with God, that is inscribed as a permanent de- terminacy in the conception of God. Narratively, this takes place in the story-metaphors of the resurrection, the ascension to heaven, and the seat at God's right hand, which all and each in its own way highlight that God henceforth is no longer to be understood and thought without heeding a double reference: the reference to the life story of Jesus and the reference to the life story of those who believe and confess Jesus as Christ.

The further formation of the Christian tradition in Roman-Hellenistic culture takes this up. It thinks the conception of God being shaped by the life story of Jesus in the narrative focus of the *father–son metaphor* and doxologically primarily in the *logos metaphor*. This has a retroactive hermeneutic effect: it makes clear that and how the particular, almost absurd story of Jesus was able, through the conception of God it shaped, to become relevant to others, indeed to everyone and everything else: any speech about "God" is specified in light of the conception of God shaped by the story of Jesus. This is apparent both in the doxological address of God as "heavenly father" and in the homological address of Jesus as son of God. Neither expresses a patriarchal re- mythologization of God or a deviation from monotheism; on the contrary, they express the concretization of monotheism by the determination of God through the story of Jesus. The shaping of the conception of God through the experiences of the commu- nity, in turn, is being thought in the *metaphor of the Spirit*, which expresses that and how the conception of God becomes concrete in defining an individual and communal life practice. The conception of God is not the result of abstract conceptualization but the expression of a concretely lived and experienced relationship with God: any speech about "God" is specified with reference to the practice in which we, together with others, orient our lives by God.

Both concretizing references have become determinative for the Christian concep- tion of God, as the developments of Trinitarian theology in the first century and their concrete focus on the notion of love show. They ensure that the conception of God ac- quires a definite shape without which it would be impossible in the concrete living of life to orient oneself by God. And in the definition of God as love, they articulate it in such a way that God's love is from the outset being understood as the eschatological shaping of human life in the love of God and among the community: it is the *bonum* in which God is present in human life and coexistence and through which the past human life is integrated into God's eternal life. As the mode in which God is effectively present, it is what is permanent in what is transitory, and it will remain even where faith is no longer being lived hopefully by human beings.

That the dramatic theological point of Jesus's life experiment is manifest not in his own life story but in the life story of those who profess him as Christ is not a merely external-arbitrary connection. The life story of Jesus and the life stories of the faithful, rather, are mediated by the reference to the image of the same God thus being specified. The process of interpretation manifesting here unfolds—simply put—in three different stages, that of a Jewish, a Jesuanic, and a Christian conception of God.[45] The teachings and the life of Jesus take up and focus the conception of God in the prophetic and theological traditions of Israel he was familiarized with in a specific way: Jesus's conception of God as the "Father in heaven" is a concentration and life-practical articulation of Israel's traditional conception of God. This Jesuanic conception of God, which Jesus announced and lived, enters into crisis on the cross. This could have been the end of this Jesuanic focusing of the theological tradition of Israel. But the exact opposite has been the case insofar as that which seemed to have come to an end there became the framework for understanding even this very ending. In that the followers of Jesus experience, understand, and interpret the cross in light of his conception of God, the Jesuanic image of God's crisis of the cross is being worked through within and by means of this very image and this image is thereby further specified to become the Christian image of God. The Christian conception of God thus grows from the Jewish tradition via the stages of its Jesuanic focusing, the crisis of the Jesuanic conception of God on the cross, and the further specification and reshaping of this conception of God in the interpretation of the crisis of the Jesuanic conception of God by means of this conception itself.

At the center of the whole story, then, is the *relationship toward God* and the dynamically self-specifying *conception of God* as the decisive point of reference of an eschatological orientation of life. In this dynamic relationship with and conception of God, Christian faith emerges and develops; in Christian faith, the superimposition of the story of Jesus and the experiences of the Christian community manifest in the Gospel takes place; and the introduction into this dynamic is, to this day, what Christians are interested in in the story of Jesus. To illustrate the point, let's look at some basic traits of this story in more detail.

11. The Gospel Accounts of Jesus

From the perspective of current historical approaches to the past, it is surprising how much the first Christians were *not* interested in Jesus and how little reliable information about Jesus has been passed down. There are, of course, several biographical clues in the New Testament. There are indications concerning his family, his background, his speaking and acting, which made him a public figure, the end of his life in Jerusalem, the appearances that brought his followers to announce his resurrection by God. But there are no entries in a Nazareth or Capernaum village chronicle, no transcripts of his speeches, no diaries of his wanderings and travels, no documentation of his deeds, no letters written or received by Jesus, no texts dictated by him to his disciples, no written

45. These are all given only in pluralistic variety, including Jesus's conception, which is accessible only through the refractions of the several Gospels.

testimony from his lifetime. What appeared to be remarkable and important about him, his public speaking and acting, his preaching before modest people in Galilee, his symbolic acts, his journey to Jerusalem, his death at the hands of the Romans, all that was handed on and recounted in the form of composed sayings and exemplary stories, in stylized episodes of his actions and typical parables from his proclamation, in accounts of his miracles and of the end of his life. All this was written down only years after his violent death in Jerusalem (in a collection of disputes, parables, and miracle stories known as Q source) and given an order of events in the Gospels (an order that differs among the Gospels) that culminate in Jesus's death on the cross. But we do not have a firsthand or secondhand life story of Jesus. Christians wrote Gospels, but they did not write a biography of Jesus. They were interested not in a detailed life story of Jesus but in what they called the *good news*: the message of God's caring for those who are poor, disenfranchised, hopeless, and lost. Only because Jesus indissolubly belongs to this gospel is he significant for Christians: he was and is of interest to them only as the symbol of this gospel, as this gospel in person.

All this is nothing special. Jesus did not live in a culture where everything was written down. Neither "Jesus nor one of Jesus's followers, nor his family or his contemporaries collected written material for a biography of Jesus." What was considered to be remarkable was recounted orally.[46] And what was remarkable was not some kind of biographical detail from Jesus's life but what impressed the people around him as important and significant for them: not his early childhood experiences and the influence of his family, not his sleeping and eating habits, his inner feelings, his mode of experience, the biographical development of his character, or his formal education but that which concerned his *public role and his actions*, his insights and his deeds, which showed something to others, made something clear to them, benefitted them. That was what people were interested in; that is what they told others about.

In antiquity generally, this was the reason why people told others things about other people. What was of interest about other people was not their private personality, their private life and private views, opinions, and feelings but *their significance for others*—that is, what they did and brought about for the city (like Pericles and Hannibal), for their people (like Moses or David), for philosophy and science (like Socrates and Archimedes), or for religion (like the prophets or Jesus). What was being recounted about someone concerned primarily their public role and public action, their discoveries, achievements, and deeds that left—positive or negative—traces in the lives of people: they were remembered as legislators and conquerors, kings and men of God, wise men and war heroes—but not as people who had parents and siblings, went to school, learned a profession, were exposed to the most varied influences, fell in love when they went through puberty, more or less did or did not get along with their wives or husbands, who constantly struggled with real or imagined illnesses, or whatever. What was of interest was *their public lives*, not their private, never mind their inner lives. Even in the case of well-known personalities from antiquity, we usually know little or nothing of these latter. Given this situation, we even have to say that compared with what we know about other people back then, including people around Jesus such as Pontius Pilate, John the

46. Becker, *Jesus von Nazareth*, 22–23.

Baptist, Peter, or Mary, his mother, our "knowledge about Jesus is still relatively good." However: it is largely restricted to the time of his public appearances, his words, deeds, and destiny "from his baptism by John the Baptist to his crucifixion by Pilate." Even if only approximate dates can be given, this was only a very short time, from around 28 to around 30 AD.[47] In this time, something happened that changed the world. That, above all, is what people wanted and had to tell others about. What was it? What happened in these few months such that people to this day have not stopped talking about Jesus?

12. Christian Interest in Jesus

The answer is: almost nothing, yet something very important that changed everything from the ground up. If one is looking for sweeping political events, great feats of war, a social revolution, or a rousing religious revival, then almost nothing happened. Jesus's short activity left many of his contemporaries entirely unimpressed, some likely hardly took notice of it, and those who did take notice did not take it very seriously. Jesus was not the only religious miracle worker in his day, not the only preacher to speak of repentance, not the only one wandering the land with a group of followers. There were others, John the Baptist, the community at Qumran, the wandering philosophers in the Greek cities of Palestine. The insignificance expressed in the Christmas story by his being born in a stable, in a feeding trough, also characterizes his life insofar as we know about it: if the world was changed, then it was certainly not by the earth-shattering significance of Jesus of Nazareth and his appearance on the stage of world history. On that stage, he was noticed only long after his death.

Yet the world was changed, and it was changed in that, through Jesus and in Jesus, first to some and then to ever more numerous human beings something dawned about *God* that changed their own lives and their conception of this world from the ground up. The significance of Jesus for the Christian faith is that he interpreted *God* in a way that taught his followers to understand their own lives, Jesus's life, and the entire world in a whole new way. Because through Jesus they understood *God* in a new way, they understood everything in a new way. Understanding everything in a new way had effects in their lives. And these effects have changed the world. Christians are interested in Jesus *solely* with regard to what in him and through him became clear *about God* because *that alone* makes Jesus interesting, including for us today, as not just a historical figure in an ever more distant past. Christians are not interested in Jesus the way we can be interested in Charlemagne or Napoleon or Pilate, as more or less influential figures of the past. They can do that, too, of course, but that does not make them Christians. *As Christians* they are interested *in God* when they engage with Jesus—everything else one might also be interested in about Jesus, the way he looked and the color of his hair, his eating habits and his knowledge of languages, are questions they leave to historians or the tellers of fairy tales. Only because and insofar as they are interested *in God* and look at Jesus *with regard to God* do they catch sight of something that is relevant to us here as well: a *direct* significance of Jesus for the Christian faith, a significance assigned to Jesus *without God*

---

47. Becker, *Jesus von Nazareth*, 23–24 and 26–27.

being mentioned is always a foreshortening. Christian life in that case is oriented by an ideal of Jesus that usually does not stand up to scrutiny. Every attempt at talking about Jesus's significance for us and for other people without talking about the *God* of Jesus Christ on whom the Christian faith depends paints an image of Jesus—however impressive it may be—that fails to capture the significance of Jesus for the Christian faith: Jesus would not be significant for the Christian faith if he were not of central significance to the God in whom the faith believes.

The New Testament texts are very clear that they are not just about Jesus but, in being about Jesus, about *God*. When the childhood stories in Matt 1–2 and Luke 1–2, for example, tell about Jesus's birth and childhood and report his family tree, they do not represent reliable historical sources and guides to Jesus's early childhood; they are popular tales and theological judgments that already put the young Jesus into the true light as the one who would later put God into the true light for humanity. Jesus's genealogical tree at Matt 1:1–17, for instance, is characterized by the "intention to associate Jesus with the main bearers of the messianic promises, Abraham and David, and with David's descendants."[48] Jesus is the one in whom the promise to Abraham and the promise of Zion have been fulfilled. The genealogical tree at Luke 3:23–38 is more universalist and goes back to Adam, the head of all humanity, and via him back to *God*; and what this is meant to say becomes clear when we notice that Luke inserts this genealogy after the story of Jesus's baptism—as an explanation, as it were, of the voice from heaven: "You are my Son, the Beloved; with you I am well pleased" (Luke 3:22). Jesus is the *new Adam*, with him, a *new humanity* begins—a notion Paul, too, explicitly takes up and develops in Rom 5:12–21. Just as through Adam, sin comes into the world, so through Jesus, mercy comes into the world. The birth and childhood stories in Matthew and Luke (and the same is true for the prologue in John) are thus *prehistories for the real story of Jesus*, they prefigure what the Gospels are then really about: the *proclamation of the kingdom of heaven* (Matt 3ff.) and about *Jesus's activity in public* (Luke 4:14–41). The Gospel according to Mark begins with just that, without a prehistory (Mark 1). These stories are thus in a way like advent, the light shining from Christmas—and like advent, their significance lies in pointing toward and leading toward this real event. In short, what the stories of the New Testament are interested in about Jesus and the reason why they tell of him lie in what he means *for God* and in how he interpreted *God* for those around him. They are always and primarily concerned with God, and they are about Jesus and about everything else only insofar as these relate to God.

There is good reason for this. Faith is directed always only *at God*. That is why Jesus is significant for Christian faith not because he was such an impressive personality, an exemplarily selfless human being, a pious social revolutionary, a committed critic of the religious establishment of his time, a visionary of a new humanity, or whatever other images of Jesus there might be. Instead, Jesus is fundamentally and unrepealably significant for Christian faith solely because without Jesus, the God at whom faith is directed would not be the God at whom the faith could be directed.

This faith would then not exist, and if there still were something like Christians, they would not need to be interested in Jesus. Only because Jesus has unrepealable

48. Deissler et al., *Neue Jerusalemer Bibel*, 1377.

significance for God does he have an unrepealable *significance for the Christian faith*. For why should one be interested in someone who died so long ago, an artisan's son from a peripheral Roman province who ran away from home and whom his family declared to be crazy? Why should he interest us more than Caesar or Augustus or Hannibal or Paul or John or Augustine or Luther or whoever else? If Jesus were not of fundamental significance for God, he would have no significance for faith.

Therefore, everything about Jesus and about what has come down to us concerning him that does not contribute to understanding *God* is without interest for the understanding of faith—whatever else we or others might find interesting about Jesus. All these other, quite respectable questions about Jesus are not what makes Jesus significant for faith. Nor does it help the understanding of faith to answer questions about Jesus that are not concerned with a better understanding *of God*. Christians are interested in Jesus not in order to imitate Jesus but in order to understand God and themselves. We do not come closer to the mystery of faith by wearing linen clothes woven in one piece or by letting our hair grow and wearing nothing but sandals. Instead, it is a telling historical fact that, unlike what happened with so many other so-called founders of religions, "Jesus' way of life . . . did not occasion an imitation of his mode of existence." What was "understood as model for imitation" was not the figure of Jesus.[49] What was taken up and accepted, rather, was his conception of God and the view and interpretation of the reality of our world and our life it entailed.

In short: Jesus has been, and is to this day, of interest to believers as a *sign for God*, a sign for an image of God and a conception of God whose point we cannot understand without understanding ourselves and our world in an entirely new and different way. For the Christian faith, Jesus is the decisive sign for God's caring for the godless human being, the human not interested in God. The interest of faith is in God, and Jesus is of interest to faith because he interprets God in such a way that it is possible to believe in him: as the presence of the unfounded and unfathomable love to whom not only all life is due but the overcoming of all barriers, too, that humans put up between God and themselves.

13. The Fundamental Christian Confession

That it is *God* and that from the beginning it has been God with whom Christians were concerned when they took an interest in Jesus is evident in the first and fundamental *confessional statements* with which a group of people within Judaism spoke up that would later be called Christians. *God*—this was their message—*has resurrected Jesus from the dead* (Rom 4:24; 8:11; 10:9; Gal 1:1; 1 Cor 6:14; etc.). They did not talk about a different God than the Jews, to whom they themselves belonged. Yet they made a fundamentally new confessional statement about him: *this God has resurrected from the dead Jesus who died on the cross.*

For us today, this paschal confession of the early Christians is so provocative because we have problems with the notion of the resurrection of the dead. To be sure, even

---

49. Becker, *Jesus von Nazareth*, 444.

then the statement was not self-evident. Some contested that it made any sense at all (the dead stay dead). Others were hoping for it, at least for the righteous, in a (distant) future when the world comes to an end, is destroyed, and God's kingdom finally dawns powerfully in a new world. Yet to the ears of Jewish contemporaries, the real sting and provocation of the early Christians' paschal confession lay not in confessing the resurrection of the dead as such but above all in what was thereby being said about *God*: that he had *already taken* the saving action at the end of time that some had hoped for at the end of the world in the future, that is, that world had already reached its end.

This was outrageous not only because the Christians were talking about the end of the world and nobody had noticed it. What was scandalous to Jewish ears above all was that Christians opposed the traditional Jewish confession of God as *the one "who brought the people of Israel up out of the land of Egypt"* (Deut 8:14; Jer 16:14) with their new confession of God as *the one who resurrected Jesus, as the first, from the dead.* For just as Israel in confessing God to have led Israel from Egypt holds on to and recalls again and again "which divine salutary act forever turned Israel into the people of God,"[50] so the first Jewish Christians in their confession of God say that the experience of Easter is to be granted the same fundamental salutary status as Israel's being guided out of Egypt.

This had consequences: where previously it was said that God counts among his people all those who belong to the Israel he has led out of Egypt, it is now said that God counts among his people all those who belong to this resurrected Jesus. Yet one does not belong to this resurrected Jesus by way of family ties and natural descendance from the same people but—as Paul especially makes clear later—through the *faith* worked by God's Spirit, which leads Jews and heathens into an *entirely new community*, into the community with Christ, the "body of Christ." That is why in this nonnatural *new* community of human beings—as Paul says (Gal 3:28)—all natural, social, cultural, religious, economic, political, other differences between Jews and Greeks, servants and masters, men and women, rich and poor, powerful and dependent are theologically abolished: in the Christian community, all that counts is belonging in faith to the resurrected Jesus Christ.

The question thus raised, which still today weighs down on and is debated in the relationship between Jews and Christians, whether this new confession of God and its statement about salvation abolishes the old one was answered, vehemently, in the negative already by Paul: *Jesus himself*, after all, belonged to the *Israel* whom God had chosen as his people and whom he had given his salutary promise. Those who *in faith belong to the resurrected Jesus* are thus *included in God's promise of salvation to Israel in, with, and through Jesus*, as it were. They are, as Paul's image has it, grafted like a branch from a wild olive tree onto a noble one (Rom 11:16–24). They live on the same root, and they should not forget that. The new confession of God thus does not abolish the old but *expands* and *opens it up* in such a way that *all human beings* are included in God's promise of saving his people—through the faith worked by God's Spirit itself.

When Christian faith is interested in Jesus, it is thus entirely and exclusively concerned with *God*. Faith interprets and understands Jesus as the *sign of God's irrevocable care for human humanity*, and with regard to Jesus, it is interested precisely in what Jesus

50. Becker, *Jesus von Nazareth*, 442.

allows us to understand about God. Yet: not everyone interprets and understands Jesus in this way or must interpret and understand him in this way. When we speak of *signs*, we must always keep three things in mind.

First, we must notice *that something is a sign*, that the scratch on the tree is an arrow pointing the way, say, or that traces of chalk on the board are letters. We must also notice that Jesus is a sign, and not everybody notices and sees this. On the contrary, the Christian faith emphasizes explicitly that we do not perceive and notice Jesus as a sign of God's care and closeness if God's Spirit does not open our eyes for it. It is thus by no means self-evident and obvious for everyone that Jesus is a sign.

But—and this is the second thing—noticing that something is a sign is not enough. We must also understand *what it signifies*. When I notice that the scratch on the tree is meant to point the way but do not understand whether it points left or right, it does not help me. And when I recognize the signs on the board as letters but do not understand the language they are written in, they do not tell me anything. That is why it is decisive for the Christian faith not only *that* Jesus is a sign; what is decisive as well is *what this sign signifies and what it gives us to think*.

And—this is the third thing—for a sign to signify something, there must be someone who uses, employs, and understands it that way. Signs do not grow like trees in nature. They exist only where they are being *used, employed, and understood as signs*. To every sign thus belongs a community of people that understand and speak this sign and this language. That is why it is not possible to talk about Jesus as a sign without also talking about those who interpret and understand him as sign, that is, about the Christian faith and about the Christians who see in him the crucial sign of God's love for us.

Because Christians understand him that way, their interest is directed not at Jesus as such but at what through him becomes understandable about God. Signs usually do not interest us as such but as indications of that toward which they seek to guide us. We usually do not read a book to look at the letters, words, and sentences we find there but to understand what they are talking about. Even a simple sign like a signpost fulfills its function not when we stop in front of it but when we go in the direction in which it is pointing us. That is the case with Jesus, too. Because everything lies in what he refers us to, we must and ought not to cling to and stop with him—more precisely: we ought to perceive him only as someone who seeks to refer us *to God*.

There is a whole series of indications that this is the way Jesus himself conceived of his work. In his proclamation, he did not foreground himself but that which he announced, the coming kingdom of God. In his symbolic actions, he did not seek to demonstrate his miraculous powers, and he rejected requests of that kind as impertinent (Mark 8:11–13). Rather, he sought to draw attention to this kingdom beginning: they are not signs of his miraculous power but of the commencing divine rule and its radical power to create the new. He did not gather disciples around him to flatter his own ego as the head of a school or leader of a religious community or group but to symbolically represent in the twelve apostles the entire people of Israel with its twelve tribes gathering at the commencement of the rule of its God and readying for it (see the mission of the twelve Mark 6:6–11; Matt 10/Luke 9). With what he said and with what he did Jesus thus *pointed away from himself* and *toward God, God's presence, and his commencing kingdom*:

he did not put himself front and center but God. And in this, precisely, he has become for the Christian faith a crucial sign for God.

14. Signs of God

It is thus not entirely arbitrary and unfounded for the Christian faith to understand Jesus as *the sign of God's irrevocable and unconditional care for us*. It thus repeats and simply states explicitly what Jesus, although he did not say it about himself, expressed in his speaking, acting, living, and dying. In this respect, faith interprets explicitly how and as what Jesus interpreted God, the world, and human life. It moves Jesus himself into that light into which Jesus moved God and the life of this world: the light of the commencing kingdom of God.

This is apparent in many ways. Jesus in his proclamation interprets entirely quotidian human *life* in this world as the place in which God's welfare, closeness, and love are present and experienceable. His parables about the kingdom of God do not talk about special religious or mystic states of exception but about everyday scenes in the field, at home, in the vineyard, at the merchant's—everyday scenes from the life of his listeners, and these precisely are described as the place in which God's presence becomes noticeable.

Similarly, his symbolic actions make it clear how—entirely quotidian—life changes when it is being changed by God's presence: from sickness to health (healings of the sick), from lack to plenitude (feeding of the five thousand), from conflict about particular rights to overflowing justice that gives plenty to all (workers in the vineyard). In all this, Jesus interprets *God* as the one who intervenes even in the trivial matters of the everyday, in the highs and lows of human life, in order to be close to those who do not want to know him, be close to them as the one who brings them love, mercy, justice, health, and life: not a distant God but the close God. Not an obscure God but a God who opens up and turns toward the human, and who does so not only when people seek him and ask for him but on his own initiative, out of love.

And in this, precisely, Jesus in person—without highlighting it himself—has become significant for his listeners and followers as the one who has pointed them to this presence of God's and thus brought God closer to them: he has become for them the *living sign* of God's unconditional care for them and for all human beings.

This becomes clear when we look at *Jesus's proclamation*. Jesus did not call himself the sign for God's closeness. But what he said and did, how he lived and died made him for Christians the sign for the closeness of God's love. The Gospel according to Mark summarizes this in the concept of the "good news."[51] Jesus is said to have proclaimed: "The time is fulfilled, and the kingdom of God has come near; repent, and believe in the good news" (Mark 1:14–15). Jesus is thus said to have announced, in word and deed and life, the *commencing of God's good rule*: God is coming *now*; when God is coming, it is a *time of salvation*; and that is why *now is the time of salvation*, now, not some point in a

---

51. For good reason, as Graham Stanton has shown, who traces the motif all the way back to Jesus himself; see his *Jesus and Gospel*.

future that never becomes a present; and if the time of salvation is now, then it is sheer stupidity to act as if it were not so, then human beings ought to open their lives to this salutary presence of God or, better: let themselves be opened up by it and let themselves be drawn into this salvation of God's.

This summary by Mark of Jesus's proclamation thus explicitly stresses that what is decisive is happening *now*; that it consists in the *commencing of the Kingship of God*; that this commencing is a *salutary event* that can be spoken of only as a *good news*, as a message of joy; and that this joy is so contagious *that it changes life*, that it does not and cannot leave life as it is.

Mark thereby captures exactly what the New Testament reports of Jesus's proclamation elsewhere as well. Let me cite six central characteristics:

1. The Kingship of God is the *time of salvation*, its commencing makes everything new. Jesus makes clear what that means when he defines the content of this rule as the overpowering fatherly love of which he speaks in the parable of the lost son and for whose coming he teaches us to pray in the Lord's Prayer. When this love comes to rule, God's justice and mercy will be erected and his good will be asserted in full. The Kingship of God is therefore not a heavy yoke; it comes unconditionally and without expecting preparations, especially to the poor, ostracized, despised, and those who have incurred guilt. For them, it is the beginning of the time of salvation in which their present distress is eliminated from the root. That is why they are praised as blessed (Luke 6:20–21; Matt 5:3–11)—not because they are poor but because for them, the coming of the Kingship of God means the end of their misery and the beginning of salvation.

2. Because the Kingship of God makes everything new, it does not come about without a comprehensive, *radical change in the lives of individuals and of peoples*. Jesus's proclamation speaks neither "of the godless world power [Rome—IUD] nor of the coming rule of Israel . . . on the contrary: heathens and Samaritans are presented to the obstinate people of God as examples of true reversal and love."[52] When the Kingship of God comes, it comes without conditions, not tied to any (ethnic or religious) preconditions, and that is why it comes to everyone in the same way.

3. This does not, however, mean in any way that it also has the same consequences for everyone, works the same for everyone, or means the same for everyone. *It comes as the same to everyone, but it affects each person in their own way.* How the Kingship of God affects us crucially depends on how it encounters us, and what it works depends on how it finds us. It always works a fundamental change, but this radical change changes the life and the situation of those affected in different ways. For the poor, the ostracized, the despised, and for those who have incurred guilt, the Kingship of God means the end of their misery. For many others, by contrast, for the ruling circles of Israel, for the big landowners of the feudal upper class that put more store by money than by God (Matt 6:24), for the Sadducean priestly hierarchy at the temple who had turned God's house into a robber's den (Mark 11:17), for the

52. Hengel, *Christus und die Macht*, 17.

scholars and Pharisees who in their fastidious interpretation of the Torah in in-numerable individual commands covered over and obscured the heavenly father's simple, clear, and unlimited will to love, for all of them, the coming of the King-ship of God means the end of their own rule, advantages, and privileges. In Luke (6:24–26) the beatitudes are thus sharply contrasted with curses directed at those who, thanks to their religious, social, or economic advantages, have made them-selves comfortable in this God-less time of the world and made their peace with its injustice, ruthlessness, and lovelessness. For them, the coming of the Kingship of God does not mean salvation but criticism, correction, and judgment, because self-righteousness, lack of mercy, and lovelessness have no place in God's kingdom.

4. The commencing of the Kingship of God is therefore a *time of separation and deci-sion*. While the Kingship of God always advenes as merciful fatherly love, it does not encounter everyone such that they let themselves be affected and defined by it. That is why Jesus in his parables time and again emphatically calls on listen-ers to adjust to God's coming and to take his arrival into account: God can come as unexpectedly as the traveling master, whose sudden return his servants must always be prepared for (Mark 13:33–37; Luke 12:36–38), or like the thief breaking into a house (Matt 24:43–44; Luke 12:39–40), or like the bridegroom whose arrival the ten bridesmaids are awaiting (Matt 25:1–13). Yet it is not enough to be awake, one must also react to the arrival of the Kingship of God in the right way. Mark conceptualizes this as *repentance* (see also Matt 11:21; 12:41; Luke 10:13; 11:32; 13:3, 5; 15:7, 10; 16:30). Yet unlike the Baptist, who also calls for repentance, Jesus is not thereby urging a purifying baptism but calls on his listeners to become *follow-ers*—not to become a follower of Jesus but *to become, like Jesus, a follower of God*. This following consists in fully making oneself available to God's dawning rule, and that is impossible without renouncing all family, social, and economic ties to the passing world and its structure. Those who come to deal with the Kingship of God cannot go on living as before. Like the lost son (Luke 15:17), they must change their lives from the ground up and reorient them.

God does not compel this repentance and reorientation. It must be undertaken voluntarily on one's own insight because God's fatherly love attains its goal only in freely requited love. Even in the encounter with the Kingship of God and his love, this repentance does not take place by necessity and as if by itself. It happened in the case of Zacchaeus (Luke 19:8); in the case of the rich man, it did not, because he could not and did not want to give up his riches (Mark 10:17–22). That is why it is so much harder for the rich, the wealthy, and the privileged than for the poor who have nothing to lose. This fundamental reorientation of life can basically only happen, as Jesus explains, when we meet the Kingdom of God with the impartiality, openness, and spontaneous joy with which children react to gifts, without asking whether they are entitled to them or worthy of them, and without counting or in-sisting on their own greatness or significance (Mark 10:14; Luke 18:17; Matt 18:3).

5. The Kingship of God thus can only be accepted like a gift that we can neither pro-cure ourselves nor claim for ourselves. *It comes when and in the way God wills it.*

It cannot be compelled by a messianic insurrection; it comes in its own way and at the time God determines by himself. Human beings can and should recognize the signs of the times (Luke 12:54–56; Mark 13:28–29) and prepare for God's kingship by repenting and changing their lives, but they can neither accelerate nor postpone the beginning of his kingship. They can accept it and prepare for it (have faith) or they can reject it and ignore it (not have faith), but they cannot actualize it through their actions. In light of God's closeness and love opening up to them, they can change their lives from the ground up or they can ignore the chance at salvation they are being offered and hold on to their present privileges and advantages, but they can neither obstruct nor facilitate the coming of God's kingship. They can tie their lives to the passing old times or the commencing new times, but they cannot influence the end of the old and the dawning of the new age.

6. In Jesus's proclamation, all this is not a statement about a future expected at some indeterminate time but a proclamation about events in the present: God's kingship is coming *now*, it is *very close*, it is *already commencing*, the time of salvation *has begun* and unmistakably makes itself felt in Jesus's actions and proclamation: "Blessed are the eyes that see what you see! For I tell you that many prophets and kings desired to see what you see, but did not see it, and to hear what you hear, but did not hear it" (Luke 10:23–24; Matt 13:16–17). In Jesus's proclamation, God's kingship is not a distant, future reality, but *is* already (Luke 17:20–21). Its reality is evident in its efficacy, in Jesus's exorcisms and expulsions of demons (Luke 11:20; Matt 12:28); in his depriving Satan of his power (Luke 10:18); in his curing and healing. They all show: the time of salvation has begun; the time of waiting has come to an end. What counts is not to hesitate any longer but to depart unconditionally and without consideration for existing ties. Those who do not let themselves be swept up by the commencing kingship of God are not for it but against it. Pious duties toward the dead (Matt 8:22), one's family, and, indeed, one's very own life (Luke 14:26–27) are no argument for dodging the call to followership. In light of the good of God's kingship, which transforms everything and outdoes everything, they are just as inappropriate as worries about securing one's livelihood (Luke 12:22–34). Now there is only one duty and one care: "strive for his kingdom, and these things will be given to you as well" (Luke 12:31). In its coming, God's kingship fills the entire present, and it is the one and only reality to count. Yet because it is not a violent rule but the presence of God's inexhaustible love, it does not bear down on and overpower humans. It takes care of everything they need. It is the time of peace, of justice, of plenitude, the time of salvation that is commencing now, in Jesus's very actions, and prompts everyone, men and women from all classes and by no means just from Israel, to reorient and remake their lives.

This focusing and determinacy is what makes Jesus's proclamation special: *salvation is taking place here and now*. Whereas John the Baptist announced the imminent beginning of the time of judgment (Matt 3:10), Jesus announced the dawning of God's salutary kingdom in the present (Matt 12:28). And while John in light of the imminent judgment calls for repentance, for penance, and for baptism, Jesus proclaims the dawning of God's good kingship that brings justice to those deprived of their rights (Luke 1:46–55). Human lives are being changed from the ground up by God's very presence, which orients humans entirely toward God and thus turns their very lives, beyond all religious rules, regulations, and traditions, into the place where God's salutary will is actualized.

It is thus for good reason that Mark does not summarize Jesus's proclamation as a preaching of judgment but as good news, as *gospel*. Jesus's proclamation already is a sign for what was then shown by the resurrection of the crucified: that God will not be hindered by anything in asserting his salutary will for us human beings. We might even say: just as the childhood stories represent a foreshadowing of Jesus's message proper in his public work, so the testimony of Jesus's life, his proclamation of the kingdom of God, and his symbolic actions represent a foreshadowing of what was demonstrated on Easter: that God confirmed, in the one who proclaimed his closeness and love, precisely what had thus been proclaimed about him: God's closeness and love.

That is also why all the texts we have in the New Testament are written from the perspective of Easter. And precisely from the perspective of Easter does Jesus, do his proclamation, his deeds, his suffering and dying have enduring significance. For it was his proclamation of the commencing rule of God's merciful love that also offered the women and men who followed him *the key to understanding the death on the cross of Jesus*, whose life had ended so differently from what they had hoped for and expected. In light of Jesus's proclamation of God, they could also conceive of his death on the cross as the taking place of the rule of God's love for us human beings. Not immediately, not without difficulties, and not just in one way. And yet in such a way that Jesus, his person, became for them the powerful example for and evidence of this love of God's. Through his proclamation, "Jesus himself [had] become a lost, miserable figure. This figure, precisely, God had cared for in paschal action."[53] Jesus, in person, thus became for Christians the divine sign and seal for the truth of the conception of God he had proclaimed: God is indeed the creative love that brings salvation and life even where humans do not expect it or can no longer do so.

15. God's Love

Because it is this truth that is at issue, there is no Christian faith that could leave Jesus aside. If *God and God's kingship* are the way Jesus proclaimed them in word and deed and in his entire life, if this kingship *has effectively asserted itself in Jesus's speaking and acting*, and if Jesus's message of the commencing of God's kingship always already offered the *horizon of meaning for understanding his death on the cross and the appearances of the crucified Christ as definite salutary action, overcoming death itself*, as Christians expressed it in confessing God's resurrection of the crucified Christ, then Christian faith could not and cannot be lived without keeping all this in mind by remembering Jesus's teachings, life, and death.

Because the faith is entirely directed at this *God of salvation*, Christian faith is unrepealably oriented toward Jesus. It is *faith in Jesus Christ* because it is *faith in God*, who

---

53. Becker, *Jesus von Nazareth*, 443.

revealed his true essence in the teaching, the life, and the death of Jesus: that he is not an obscure, concealed, dangerous God but life-creating, merciful, omnipotent love—a love that is not stopped by or ignores misery, suffering, and death but through them and precisely in them proves to be love that is stronger than death.[54]

The faith that Christians confess as the God-effected beginning of a new life starts from the reality of this love. That is why they do not stop interpreting Jesus as the one who interpreted God in such a way that it is possible to have faith in him. God is not to be feared as a blind power of fate; rather, he is the one on whom we can rely, despite everything that contradicts it, to be the one who works salvation and life, justice, freedom, and peace—all, that is, that comes together in the central Christian symbol of *love*: "God is love," as the author of 1 John succinctly puts it, "and those who abide in love abide in God, and God abides in them" (1 John 4:16).

This is the God Jesus in his life bore witness to, this is the testimony that his death, against Jesus's own experience, confirmed for others who experienced that the merciful love Jesus proclaimed God to be continued to be active where Jesus himself could no longer be active. That is why, for Christians, Jesus is the place and the sign of a fourfold discovery whose four aspects all take up and pointedly develop earlier experiences Israel had of itself and of God:

1. *the discovery of God's love, humanity, grace, and care for human beings*: God's committing himself to loving the other of himself, which always anticipates any human turn to God and which is solely and exclusively initiated by God and therefore irreversible,[55] a love precisely of that which ignores him, does not want to hear about him, turns against him, is hostile to him: *God loves those who are hostile to him*;

2. *the discovery that humans are destined to be in communion with God*: that is, the superimposition of human self-conceptions with the discovery that and how they are being defined and understood as addressees of God's love: *human beings are destined, and therefore capable and able, to love God*;[56]

3. *the discovery that the actualization of this destiny is not merely a future possibility but a present reality* because God does not wait for humans to come to meet him,

54. "Jesus is the perfect expression of God's thought, character and will. He is God's self-definition to us . . . in Christ, God defines and expresses himself as a God of outrageous love" (Boyd, *Is God to Blame?*, 39). It does not at all follow, however, that Satan and legions of fallen angels acting against God's love are responsible for all ills in the world. See Boyd, *Satan and the Problem of Evil*.

55. It is irreversible because reversing it would be a self-contradiction and therefore mean God's self-destruction.

56. That is why an extreme Calvinism that holds, as W. E. Best does, that speaking of God's love means that "God loves some and hates others . . . God does not love everybody" (Best, *God Is Love*, 39) is entirely absurd. *Extra amore dei nulla existentia*. If God's love is God's essence, then it cannot be actualized as its own opposite without turning God into a demon. For logical and theological reasons, then, it is necessary to maintain that, as the creative love that makes loveable that which without it is not just not loveable but would not exist at all, God's love cannot hate anyone but loves all those whom it makes since no one and nothing would exist if the creator's love did not will it and effect it. See Lake, "He Died for All"; Oden, *Transforming Power of Grace*, 84–87; and Talbott, "Love of God and the Heresy of Exclusivism."

but by himself comes toward them. It is not as if humans as such or naturally had the capacity for loving God even if they did not (yet) practice it, such that among all the creatures, they would be the ones who could love God even if they factually did not. Rather, the capacity for loving God (love for God) comes to them in the reality of God's love for them (love by God), not only in that what they do not have (the capacity to love God) is being allotted to them but because God's creative love turns them into what they, despite all their capacity, cannot by themselves become: creatures who freely love their creator because they live in a situation in which they can love God, and this in the double sense of God becoming loveable for them because he loves them (God becomes loveable) and of their becoming capable of loving God because God turns them into what he does with them (they become able and willing to love). Or, as 1 John says: "In this is love, not that we loved God but that he loved us" (4:10); and finally,

4. *the discovery that God's love for human beings cannot be actualized in humans' love for God if humans do not love each other as God loves them*: If God is the one who makes everyone close to him by loving them, then God cannot be loved without also loving those whom God loves: oneself and everyone else. Love of God (as love by God and love for God) exists only if there is also love of oneself, love of one's neighbor, and love of one's enemies—if, that is, everyone, no matter how distant, is appreciated as someone who is just as much God's neighbor and addressee as oneself.

To the discovery of love as the core of the conception of God thus correlates the discovery of love as the core normative determination of the human conception of self and of life. Both concur in the place where this conception of God and the human conception of life become manifest. That is why Christians confess Jesus as *Christ*, as the God-anointed savior, because for the Christian faith, he is both: the decisive sign of God's humanity and reliability *and* the definitive sign of humans' destiny to live in communion with God.

16. Love, the Cross, and the Conception of God

Considering the experience of *malum* in our lives, God's love working in the world and in human life is not exactly obvious. To see it, it takes the gaze of faith, which comes from the *bonum* of God's love, revealed in the word of the cross. From there, it becomes clear what God is and wills, where God is at work and where he certainly is not, and that God's love can be at work where we do not see it and are unable to see it, just as Jesus himself did not see it when he died on the cross with the cry of being abandoned by God. The word of the cross is thus the permanent objection to the theological and epistemic inclination not to grant greater weight to the view of the others and above all to the view of God, who is other vis-à-vis everyone else.

For Christians, Jesus is the permanent reminder that we do not and cannot everywhere notice that and how God is at work but also that we do not have to know and notice it for it to be the case. Even if in our own lives, we often do not see or pay attention to it—others may notice it, and sometimes we only notice it when we look back at our lives. Thus Christians noticed it with regard to Jesus in the light of Easter. From there, as the Gospels show, they saw God to be at work everywhere in Jesus's life, even there where Jesus himself no longer saw, noticed, and found anything: in his death. They concentrated this insight and experience in the *good news* that—as Paul says—there is nothing, "neither death, nor life, nor angels, nor rulers, nor things present, nor things to come, nor powers, nor height, nor depth, nor anything else in all creation [that] will be able to separate us from the love of God in Christ Jesus our Lord" (Rom 8:38–39). Not only according to Paul, Jesus unrepealably belongs in this gospel as the Christ who revealed to humanity God's love and God as love and made him present to them in what he taught and did but also in how he lived and died. He is the place where God's love—also for those who do not love him—has revealed itself as the last and definitive reality of human life.

Hermeneutically, the discovery of God's life on the cross of Jesus takes place as the twofold process of defining the cross in light of Jesus's conception of God and of defining the conception of God through the crisis of the Jesuanic conception of God on the cross.

From the first perspective, the *failure* of God's love on the cross (from Jesus's pre-paschal perspective) is understood as the *enactment* of God's love (from Christians' postpaschal perspective) and defined as *self-emptying, self-debasing, self-sacrificing love*: the cross does not prove that Jesus wrongly hoped for God's merciful love but just the contrary, that this hope is reasserted because God's love remains merciful love to the point of self-sacrifice. God's love is not refuted by the *malum* of suffering and death but identifies with the *malum* of the cross, and it does so in such a way that the *malum* does not put an end to God's love, but God's love puts an end to the *malum* as expressed in the confession of the crucified Christ's resurrection by God.

From the second perspective, this very point is inscribed in the conception of God as its core definition, that is, God's love is defined as that which, even in its most extreme opposite, becomes what it is in working for the best of the affected others in such a way that it is not death that puts an end to their lives, but life puts an end to their deaths. God's love proves its creative efficacy in that the *malum* does not cause the *bonum* to fail, but the *bonum* outdoes the *malum*. Just as the first perspective sees the debasement of love all the way to its own opposite, so the second perspective sees the outdoing of even the most extreme opposite of love by this love.[57]

---

57. That is why the issue is not just to think God's love as com-miseration, limiting it to God not remaining distant from Jesus's suffering, but as being affected by it in suffering with him. See Surin, *Theology and the Problem of Evil*, 112–41; Fiddes, *Creative Suffering of God*; Steen, "Theme of the 'Suffering' God"; Koslowski, "Der leidende Gott"; and Whitney, *Theodicy: An Annotated Bibliography*, appendix C, 317–38. Nor is the issue that of turning the "ancient theopaschite heresy that God suffers" into the "new orthodoxy," as Goetz, "Suffering God," 385, thinks. The point of Jürgen Moltmann's attempt, in *Der gekreuzigte Gott*, at describing the suffering of the father as suffering with the suffering of the son, too, is not that the sum total of those suffering is thereby only being increased (see Adams, *Horrendous Evils*, 175–77). The point, rather, is that the suffering of *malum* is being sublated into a suffering-with of a love in which it is neither overwritten and downplayed nor eternalized as suffering but determined as something that will not have the last word. And thereby the issue, inversely, is a divine love that even at its most extreme opposite pole asserts itself as love for the benefit of the other. Insofar as this is what is meant by the emphasis on God's eschatological solidarity with those who suffer, and insofar as the formula of God's absolute willingness and power to establish relationships does not simply articulate the

By superimposing the two perspectives on each other in the reference to the cross, God's love is defined as that which even in its most extreme opposite is and remains that which can be surpassed and outdone only by itself: there is no place, however distant from it, where it would not also be, and there is no place higher than it where it could be outdone by something other than itself. It stretches all the way to its own most extreme opposite (in the metaphor of *emptying* or *debasement*), and it is the dynamic of its own outdoing. Extensively and intensively, there is no beyond of this love, such that everything is in and through it, but nothing is and can be without or durably against it.

In that the failure (from Jesus's perspective) of God's love on the cross does not let the hope placed in it fail but rather integrates it (from the perspective of faith in Christ) in the definition of God's love in such a way that in failing, this love overcomes its own failure through love, it not only becomes possible, it becomes indispensable to address God *comprehensively and unrestrictedly* as love. For—and this is the basic alternative posited by the cross—either the God of love Jesus claimed to make present does not exist or God can truly be God only as a love that even in its own failure still works as love for the best of the other. *Tertium non datur.* Had the cross been the last thing to be recounted about Jesus, had there not been the possibility and necessity of recounting what is being recounted in the developed metaphors of the resurrection by God and the ascension to heaven, then the question concerning God and the orientation of life by God would be settled. Inversely, nothing can separate God and love anymore once, in keeping with the New Testament, the autobiographical perspective of Jesus, in which the cross is experienced as the aporia of the hope in God's love, is superimposed on the biographical perspective of believers in Christ, who experience the cross of Jesus as the ultimate concretion of God's love insofar as there, any and all outside of love is integrated into love itself.[58]

This, then, makes it possible for Christians to talk about every experience of *bonum* and every overcoming of *malum* as an experience of God's love, because there is nothing that would not fall within its domain. And inversely, it becomes possible to talk about God's love in all the concretions in which *bonum* and the overcoming of *malum* are experienced in human life: as *liberation* from imprisonment, as *redemption* from Evil, as *overcoming* of everything that stands against God's goodness as creator. God's love is not only the other of *malum* (like the Platonic Good) nor only what works and fights against *malum* (as in large parts of the biblical tradition), he is that which in overcoming *malum* proves itself to be what overcomes Evil with Good and asserts what is good even in what is evil.

---

notion of God in relational terms but understands the content of God's relating to the other of himself qualitatively in such a way that it is not exhausted in a merely accompanying being-with with human beings but aims at overcoming their *malum* through the *bonum* worked by God, we have to agree with Jürgen Werbick (*Von Gott sprechen an der Grenze zum Verstummen*, 74, 129–30, and elsewhere).

58. That is why the Christian experience of salvation expresses itself, also and especially with respect to the experience of *malum*, as being integrated in this love of God's, which is without ground and reason and from which nothing can separate believers (Rom 8:31–39). See Holmén, "Theodicean Motifs in the New Testament," 626–36, and Bieringer, "Aktive Hoffnung im Leiden."

Because God's love, understood against the background of the cross, is not only the other or the counterforce to *malum* but is the *means* with which *malum* is overcome and the *goal* toward which it is overcome, it is not only the *overcoming* of Evil but the overcoming of Evil *through what is good*. It therefore takes all the forms in which a given *malum* is put an end to and outdone in such a way that in the specific context, no new *malum* is being produced: the forms of *dedication, sympathy, commiseration, sacrifice for others, substitution, taking over the ill that affects them*, and so on. None of these figures can be absolutized or generalized across contexts because their point is always to react to *specific malum* in such a way that this *malum* is outdone by a working of God's love to be understood in *this* context as a *bonum*.[59]

Because God's love is tied back to the cross on the level of content, the notion of God's love does not run the risk of losing any definite sense by thus being tied to an inexhaustible number of concretions. On the cross, in the superimposition of the perspectives described, we can definitively read what God's love is and how it works and therefore also what it is not and how it does not work. In metaphorical terms, two traits in particular are to be highlighted. On the one hand, this love unfolds as *self-sacrifice*, that is, not as self-assertion over against Evil but as an entering into the *malum* that leaves the *malum* unable to resist the love, that removes its "sting." The negative power of the *malum* is neutralized, invalidated, and brought to nothing by self-sacrificing love. On the other hand, therefore, this love unfolds as a *process of invalidating Evil* that takes time.[60] That is to say, it does not take place all at once but leads into the tension between the *already now* commemorated in the reference to the cross and resurrection of Christ and the *then fully and entirely* represented in the hope for Christ's ultimate return.

To this process corresponds a different *conception of the world*: the now-world is not, as in apocalyptics, the old world coming to an end; it is the new world already

59. That means, however, that this *bonum* does not have to be or remain addressable as a *bonum* outside the context of its concrete use to outdo a specific *malum*. Just as every *malum* is not always, everywhere, and for everyone a *malum*, so that which in a specific context is a *bonum* is not always, everywhere, and for everyone a *bonum*. The working of God's love is always very concrete and not stereotypical and for that reason infinitely varied: it is always a question of putting an end to and over-coming that which *in this case* is a *malum* by means of what *in this case* is the best.

60. Both have to be kept in mind when the emphasis is placed, correctly, on the cross showing not only what God's love but also what his anger is. See Carson, "God's Love and God's Wrath," 390, and my "Der Zorn Gottes: Grundlinien einer Gottesmetapher." The cross not only shows under the guise of its opposite what God's love and anger are and what they are directed at (respectively, at the life that con-nects us with God and against the sin that entails death, that is, the permanent separation from God), it also shows how God's love and anger work: love works by having mercy on the sinner, anger works by distinguishing that which it is directed against (the sin) from the one to whom it would have to be attributed (the sinner). In just this way, God's anger proves to be a way in which his love manifests, not its opposite, as Härle rightly emphasizes: "God's anger is a *reaction to the sin of human beings*. . . . It is precisely God's *love* that is hurt by human sin and summons his anger" (Härle, "Die Rede von der Liebe und vom Zorn Gottes," 55). More than that: insofar as, in Luther's words, "God's love does not find, but creates, that which is pleasing to it" (Luther, *Heidelberg Disputation*, 85, 104–5), God's anger is an essential moment of God's effective love creating the one whom God loves by distinguishing between sinner and sin and thereby separating the sinner from his sin. Put differently, anger is that side of divine love that puts an end to what is old in creation and separates us from God in order that what is new and open to God can come into being: the one whom God loves and who in turn and on her own initiative loves God.

having commenced and in the process of outdoing Evil through good, which thereby marginalizes Evil and pushes it out. To this process also corresponds a different *conception of God*: to understand God from the perspective of the cross as love means to understand God to be the one who in suffering works against evil and is good precisely in that he not only *makes* good but makes good *through good*, that is, in that he does not outdo evil with evil but with self-sacrificing love. And to this process corresponds, finally, a different *self-conception* that leads to a different *relationship to God and to the world*: those who understand themselves to be addressees of God's love find themselves taken up in a process in which it is a matter of course that—as the commandment of love, in an objectively misleading but life-practically comprehensible imperative manner puts it—relate to the other, to the neighbor, to the enemy the way God relates to us and to all others: we do not resist hostility with hostility but seek to invalidate it through a devotion that deprives the other of the chance to be hostile. For like us, they too are the addressee of God's love and thereby deserve to be treated as someone whom God's love seeks to make good, whom, indeed, it has made good.[61] The conception of oneself as addressee of God's love thus has as its correlate the *relationship to the world* of an attitude in life, of a love that fully devotes itself to what is other, foreign, evil, hostile with the goal—as the case may be, and insofar as it is *malum*—of putting an end to it, replacing it, or outdoing it with the *bonum* of love.

The new world hoped for is not simply the other of the present world; the present world, rather, is the place where the old and the new world separate. That is why it is decisive which world we count ourselves or let ourselves be counted to belong to and which world we are being counted to belong to: to the *passing old* or the *commencing new*. Neither excludes experiences of *malum*. But in the one case, the *malum* expresses the reality of the world, in the other it refers to the greater reality of the *bonum* that urges the distinction of the world into *old* and *new*—a distinction not made about the world as such but made in the attitude of humans toward the world: that world is *old* that is recognized to be *malum* for oneself or for others, and that world is *new* that is experienced as the *bonum* we owe to the presentification of God's love that makes new and good. That is why the correlate of this eschatological difference in the relationship to the world and to God is the fundamental theological difference between *faith* and *unfaith*. For *faith* is orienting one's life by God's love specified through the cross; *unfaith* by contrast is any mode of living that does not do so.

17. The Diversity of Suffering and Evil and God's Renewing Creativity

Despite the diversity of its assessments of evil and of ways of dealing with it, the biblical tradition leaves no doubt that it is God who fights *malum* and who proves to be good, just, and loving precisely in overcoming *malum* through *bonum*. Even in the face of experiences of extreme uncertainty and contestation that render God obscure and

---

61. In this sense, it is possible to say that the "point of Jesus' instruction" at Matt 5:44 to love our enemies does not lie "in treating enemies like friends but in confronting enemies *as enemies* with love," that is, in seeing them as someone in whom God does not see enemies (Dietrich et al., *Gewalt und Gewaltüberwindung in der Bibel*, 208).

questionable, it asserts time and again that God does not let *malum* have the last word in the lives of his creatures but rather proves to be their God precisely in willing the best for them and working good for them even from evil.

What that consists in and how that happens, however, depends not only on the concrete kind of *malum* and the particular circumstances of a given life but also and decisively on which *bonum* God effects and what he thereby puts an end to and overcomes as *malum*: God's *bonum* defines what *malum* is, not the other way around. What we experience as *malum* does not decide what *bonum* we are to hope and ask for from God—the *bonum* that God by himself works and does uncovers what the *malum* is.[62] Faith's detour in dealing with evil via God leads to a reorientation of one's entire life precisely because a revaluation of all values is called for: from the perspective of the *bonum* God does, it becomes clear that by no means everything we experience and designate as *malum* belongs to the *malum* in the sense thus overcome by God's *bonum*, yet also, inversely, that this *malum* is also to be found where we would never have expected it. In the end, what decides what is to be feared in human life is not our experience but what God through his *bonum* abandons to the old and declining.

This is the central point of the way faith deals with the reality of Evil in the detour via God. This detour begins with the reality of Evil in all its nonsensical and repulsive diversity and it seeks, on the detour via God, to reorient the life thereby thrown off course and to set it onto a path that allows for living with the absurdity of Evil and its incomprehensibility. Yet this does not presuppose giving Evil a sense it does not have; it means attaining a different attitude toward it that moves it, as something incomprehensible and nonsensical, into a different light and thus into a different context. This, precisely, is enabled by the detour via God, if it succeeds, because inquiring into God's creative and new-creating judgment about the evil that has happened and been experienced sheds new light on this evil and thereby allows for assuming a new attitude toward it. Yet from this point, precisely, the perspective changes. While initially, the path begins with the reality of Evil and takes the detour via God in order to establish a relationship with this reality that allows us to go on living, the orientation by God's creative judgment shows that God does not in every case remove what has been experienced as a *malum* through a *bonum* but does something entirely different. The paralytic is not liberated of his paralysis but first his sins are being forgiven (Mark 2:1–12). The sick are not all cured but declared to be God's children and inheritors. Death is not prevented but deprived of the sting of representing a definitive separation from God. Thus it is not the *malum* experienced that defines what the *bonum* to be hoped from God is but the other way around. It

---

62. The central weak point of Jürgen Manemann's reflections is that he does not heed this difference but short-circuits our view of ill and good with God's view. It manifests in his inability to understand the notion of justification in any other way than moralistically. See Manemann, *Rettende Erinnerung an die Zukunft*; "If the Good becomes the Evil," 167–72; and "In Response to Dider Pollefeyt and David Patterson," 186–88. That speaking of God's love is "idolatry" unless it is possible to "show how it transforms us into better human beings" ("In Response to Dider Pollefeyt and David Patterson," 187) would be the case only if "being better human beings" were not moralized in an absurd manner and thus deprived of its theological point, which is to let oneself be made into a new human being *by God*, a being who does not already know in advance what God will make her into but lets herself be surprised by it because she and her ideas and expectations are not the "all-determining reality."

is the *bonum* gifted by God that shows what the real *malum* is, the decisive *malum* in the relationship with God, others, and oneself: *malum* is not always and everywhere what we experience as such and what is such for us but above all and throughout, *malum* is *what would separate human beings from God's love and life*. Not everything that harms life and ends life is also *malum* in the religiously relevant sense, only that which would separate us from the source of life, God's love. This can be many things people do not even experience as *malum* because they do not understand themselves and their lives in reference to God. Yet there are also many things that are experienced as *malum* that are unable to harm and endanger the relationship with God and God's relationship with the human. The answer given in the recourse to God is thus, in important respects, not only an answer to open questions concerning life; the answer God gives makes clear in the first place what the truly important questions were and what the truly problematic *malum* for human life consists in.[63] Human beings turn to God in the distress of the *malum* that happens to them. Yet they do not turn to God the way they turn to a physician, a judge, or a technician who is to set right what has gone wrong. They do not only seek to understand the *malum*, they seek to understand *themselves* in the face of the *malum*, for only then can they attain a different attitude toward it. According to the experience of the Christian faith, this succeeds thanks to God giving them a *bonum* that shows what the real *malum* they should worry about consists in; shows that this *malum* from God's perspective does not exist (anymore); and shows that, for this reason, it is not what they experience as *malum* but what God works as *bonum* that has the last word in their lives.

The real *malum* is not always what people seek to understand and hope to have eliminated when they turn to God. When what people think of as a *malum* is not eliminated and put an end to, that does not mean that God is ignoring the pleas of the sufferers. Rather, we have to take the possibility into account that God reacts in a different way, that instead of answering or not answering the question posed to him, he revises the starting point of the questions and pleas by giving an answer that differs from the one expected or hoped for or feared. What God does is a *bonum* not because it puts an end to or eliminates a specific *malum* in human life but *because God does it* and thereby overcomes that which would have permanently prevented God's living together with

---

63. This contradicts the already quite old rationalizing attempts that seek to find the reason for the "universality of sin" and of Evil in human life in the finitude and transitoriness of this life. "The human being is already created as a deficient being—in the moral sense as well. Nothing can remedy this deficiency, not even an intervention by God" (Pfeiffer, "'Ein reines Herz schaffe mir, Gott!,'" 309–10). Those who think and argue this way—as Job's friends already do (Job 4:17–21; 15:14–16; cf. Sir 17:26–32)—do not even see that we can and must ask whether the *mala* deriving from finitude are really the ones that count as *malum* before God and that, according to the Christian faith, are eliminated and overcome through God's caring for and being present to human beings. They suppose that the life of human beings defines what the *malum* is that God's salutary action liberates us from, that is, that we always already know what our *malum* and thus *e negativo* also know what the *bonum* for us is. They do not consider the possibility that what *we* experience as *malum* may not be what stands as *malum* between humans and God, and that *this malum* is discovered only by the fact that and by how God reacts to it. On this view, it is not the anthropology of deficiency of the finite human being but the anthropology of excess of the human being on whom God lavishes his goodness that constitutes the appropriate horizon for thinking the universality of sin and of Evil: as that which in every human life and for every human life is righted by God's greater love.

humanity and made it impossible. What we consider to be such a *malum* does not have to be such. Yet nothing we experience as *malum* for ourselves is of such a kind either that it could separate us from God's love when everything that might be able to do so is overcome by the *bonum* that God effects and does.

The detour via God in dealing with the reality of Evil is thus, in a decisive respect, a process of discovering what the *malum* in the relation between God and human beings and thus also in human interaction is. The better we recognize this, the more serenely we can deal with the various *mala* of life and their incomprehensible nonsensicalness, and the more differentiated our attitude toward them can be. For even if usually, there is no doubt that the *malum* is what is being suffered and experienced as such, not every happening is experienced in every life in the same way as *malum*, and not everything that is experienced this way also separates us from God. Not only is not every *malum* in life a *malum* in living with God; only that is which would damage this relation and make it impossible. Every kind of *malum* of life demands an appropriate approach—illness a different one from unfreedom, crime a different one from stupidity, wars a different one from natural catastrophes. Significant cultural progress in engaging *malum* was and is being made by developing the medical, political, legal, pedagogical, technological, moral, and also religious means and procedures for dealing with specific kinds of evil.

Yet in the special domain of dealing with *malum* religiously in the detour via God, there is great differentiation in dealing with different kinds of *malum* in the lives of different people and groups of people. *Malum* is always experienced in suffering, but what is thus experienced is assessed in very different ways. For not every suffering is *malum*; not every suffering experienced as *malum* is *malum* in the same way; not every *malum* can be made sense of; not every *malum* allows for living with it despite its senselessness and irrationality, in the reference to God; and not everything others experience as *malum* is experienced by believers in the exact same way. Grief, fear, persecution, hunger, nakedness, danger, sword are *mala* for all human beings, but according to Paul (Rom 8:35), believers suffer them in a special and different way because for them, they are signs of the end times: "For your sake we are being killed all day long" (Rom 8:36). Their suffering is a sign of the community with God's love, not of the separation from it (Rom 8:38–39).[64]

That is why the biblical tradition, in dealing with *malum*, does not proffer wholesale answers, and later theological thinking turns into unclear and absurd oversimplification when it tries to describe or render comprehensible the entire vast and unclassifiable diversity of *malum* in one single manner. Even if no theoretical approach can do without simplifications and any approach can therefore be judged in concrete instances to be oversimplifying when it thinks what is experienced in suffering as *malum*, not all suffering of human beings is to be described as an experience of *malum* and not every experience of *malum* is an indication of human beings' separation from God. There is—to name but a few examples—

64. Not just Paul, 1 Peter, too (1 Pet 2:19–24; 4:1, 12–14, and elsewhere), emphasizes that it is part of the life of believers especially to suffer with Christ and like Christ for the sake of their belonging to God's love. See Osborne, "Guide Lines for Christian Suffering."

1. suffering that results from ill doing, that is comprehensible as *malum* without referring to God, and that is being ended by interrupting and not continuing it, even if in its facticity and its consequences, it cannot be undone. There is

2. suffering that results from accidents or catastrophes whose *malum* character is undisputed without there even being the possibility of meaningfully looking for someone responsible. Yet there is also

3. suffering that intrudes into lives inexplicably and incomprehensibly yet behind which it is possible or necessary to see God, even if God—as in the book of Job— evokes his power as creator for the use of which he is not accountable to anyone. There is

4. suffering that as *malum* is not inexplicable or incomprehensible because it is the— albeit not causal but moral or legal—consequence of an ill deed for which one is rightly being punished.[65] There is

5. suffering that even if it is *malum* is not judged by those affected to be such or although it is judged to be such, it is not lamented because they experience it as voluntarily or involuntarily suffering for others (a person or God).[66] There is

6. suffering that is commiseration with others who are affected by a *malum* and with which, according to the biblical tradition, God, distressed by the suffering of his people or his prophets, is familiar as well. There is

7. suffering that is being accepted, not avoided, or even sought out because it comes with belonging to Christ and therefore is a sign not of the separation and distance from God but of the *simil iusti et tentati* participating in God's love by participating in the suffering, death, and resurrection of Jesus.[67] Such

8. suffering for the sake Jesus exists especially as the mark of apostolic existence, as Paul outlines at 1 Cor 12:7–10.[68] There is

9. suffering that is *malum* because it suffers from God's concealment, inaccessibility, or absence. Yet there is also

10. suffering that is *malum* because it suffers from God himself, in which, that is, God himself is or seems to be the *malum* or the reason and occasion of the *malum* such that he is addressed and must be addressed not only with laments but with accusations. And there is

11. suffering that is suffering for God's sake, which those affected can experience as *malum* or not as *malum*.[69]

65. On the traditional distinction between *deserved* and *undeserved* suffering this entails, see Reichenbach, *Evil and a Good God*.

66. See De Villiers, "Joy in Suffering in 1 Peter"; Satake, "Das Leiden der Jünger 'um meinetwillen'"; and Wolter, "Leiden III: Neues Testament," 685.

67. Holmén, "Theodicean Motifs in the New Testament," 630; see also Heckel, "Gottes Allmacht und Liebe."

68. See Güttgemanns, *Der leidende Apostel und sein Herr*, 162–65; Wolter, "Der Apostel und seine Gemeinden"; and Hotze, "Gemeinde als Schicksalsgemeinschaft mit Christus."

69. In this sense, the New Testament does not emphasize "that in Jesus God has undertaken to suffer

This list is neither complete nor finished, but it sufficiently signals the differentiation in which suffering and *malum* that is or is not experienced in or through suffering must be theologically focused if thinking is not to become entangled in hasty oversimplifications. The biblical tradition not only is unfamiliar with any uniform sense of suffering;[70] it does not even suppose that all suffering can yield a sense or that all *malum* can be understood and divested of its absurdity.[71] In wide swaths of life, the reality of Evil is the reality of the nonsensical that evades and refuses all efforts at understanding. The recourse to God is not a way of turning this nonsensicalness into sense but, quite the inverse, it is the attempt at living nonetheless in the face of the senselessness of much evil and at not losing confidence in God's promise to overcome Evil through Good, not just as a matter of principle but also for one's own life and for the others whose life is being destroyed by *malum*.

18. God and Nothingness

On the semantic level, *malum* and *bonum* are contrast concepts, but on the level of content, their contrast is asymmetric. While there is no *malum* without there also being a *bonum*, the inverse is not true. Semantically, to be sure, what is evil always is not what is good and what is good is not what is evil, yet while no evil can exist if no good exists either, something that would deserve being called "good" can exist even if there were nothing that would have to be called "evil." For it to be possible that it be called good, there must be only the possibility, not the reality, that something be called "evil." Yet for something to be called "evil," good must exist, not just possibly but actually.

This train of thought must be kept in mind when in confronting the reality of Evil we ask how it is possible that there is *malum* when God creates good and overcomes and outdoes evil through good. Karl Barth's answer that evil exists *because* God rights it and fights it interprets the reality of the evil God is fighting as implied by, or at least

---

with the suffering world," as for example Gerhard Barth (*Der Tod Jesu Christi im Verständnis des Neuen Testaments*, 162–63) and Martin Karrer (*Jesus Christus im Neuen Testament*, 168) argue but, quite the inverse, that "those who follow him are 'called' to be *his* fellow-sufferers" (Holmén, "Theodicean Motifs in the New Testament," 649–50). The New Testament does not a suggest a Christology of commiseration (Christ is suffering with us) but a soteriology of commiseration (suffering with Jesus is part of faith) because the point is to stand with him before God in the place where, entirely gratuitously, one receives good from God. The point of the exhortation to commiserate is thus not to participate in Christ's work of salvation but to put ourselves with him in his place before God and to let our lives be drawn into the salvation he actualized and understand them from that perspective. It is not the case that *our suffering* defines what as *malum* we are being delivered from; what the *malum* we are being delivered from becomes clear when we understand our lives and suffering in light of the suffering of Jesus Christ.

70. See Klaus Berger (*Wie kann Gott Leid und Katastrophen zulassen?*, 180–83) who dresses a somewhat different list. Tom Holmén, too, stresses the variety of attempts at understanding Jesus's suffering. He distinguishes six main types ("Theodicean Motifs in the New Testament," 647–48), but above all, he highlights that "the death of Jesus has, in the New Testament, no explicit theodicean foundation" and asserts that the focus of its reflections is not suffering as such but Jesus's death on the cross (646).

71. The New Testament generally thus does not refer God's love proving itself on the cross to human experiences of suffering and *malum* as such but to what separates them from God's love, and that does not have to be what they are suffering from. See Baudler, "El-Jahwe-Abba," 250.

as a correlate of, God's action against it.[72] Barth thus runs the danger of turning the contingency of Evil into the necessary concomitant and flipside of divine action and thereby of declaring its reality, which could also not be, to be a necessity conditioned by God's action, a necessity which cannot not be even if, taken by itself, it would not have to be. Theologically, something that does not have to and ought not to be thus becomes, surreptitiously, something that cannot not be because God is turning against it.[73] Yet it is one thing to say "because evil exists, God turns against it," another thing to say "because God turns against it, evil exists."[74] The first is a statement of "biblical realism," which starts from the reality of *malum*, the second an absurd misinterpretation on the part of a rationalization that thinks it can do justice, theologically, to the reality of Evil only if it is "explained" or "justified" starting from God. Yet in many cases *there is nothing to be explained* here. It is to misunderstand the work and achievement of faith and theology when it is passed off as a *religious explanation* of what cannot be explained scientifically, medically, politically, legally, morally, and so on, rather than understood as a *rejection* or *renunciation of explanation* and as an *instruction and aid in living and dying humanely with what it is inexplicable, irrational, senseless, obscure, unfathomable.*

The task of theology is not to show what is senseless to have sense after all and to of-fer explanations for what cannot be explained otherwise. The questions of those affected by Evil *Why? Why me? Why them? Why already now?* are not thereby settled and set aside. But it will not always be possible to answer them in the same way, and sometimes it will be impossible to answer them at all. To avoid trying to do too much, theologically and practically, and thus to avoid doing something wrong, we must keep important dis-tinctions in mind: between *avoidable* evil that does not have to be and *unavoidable* evil that cannot not be if there is anything at all (for instance, life exists only at the expense of and in consuming other life); between evil that *can be justified*, be it with reference to a good that would not otherwise be possible, be it as punishment for something evil, and evil that *cannot be justified* because it goes beyond the dimensions of what can be justi-fied as such or as a means for a higher purpose;[75] between evil that despite its irrational-ity can be understood at least in its facticity because there are reasons why it came to be (for instance, cardiac insufficiency resulting from an untreated viral infection) and evil

72. Barth, *Church Dogmatics*, III.3, §50: "God and Nothingness," 289–368.

73. See Dierken, "Karl Barth (1886–1968)," 246.

74. See Barth, *Church Dogmatics*, III.3, §50.4:353, where he writes about nothingness: "It 'is' only in virtue of the fact that God is against it." This of course can mean different things. Read ontologically (as in Härle, *Sein und Gnade*, 230–46), it must be misunderstood as stating that because of grace, sin is necessary. Read *hermeneutically*, in contrast (and indeed as correcting some of Barth's statements in the doctrine of divine properties especially), the emphasis is not on explaining the *actuality* of nothingness but on indicating *the theologically appropriate way of dealing with* its reality: theologically, "nothingness may be understood *only* as something that is and ought to be negated," as Wolf Krötke rightly stresses (*Sin and Nothingness in the Theology of Karl Barth*, 119). It has no ontological valence of its own and it most certainly cannot be characterized as an ontological counterprinciple to God's grace.

75. Adams, *Horrendous Evils*, 26, defines these "horrendous evils" as "evils the participation in which (that is, the doing or suffering of which) constitutes prima facie reason to doubt whether the participant's life could (given their inclusion in it) be a great good to him/her on the whole." See also Adams, "Theod-icy without Blame" and "Horrors in Theological Context," as well as Placher, "Engagement with Marilyn McCord Adams's *Horrendous Evils.*"

that is not only irrational as such but whose very occurrence or happening goes beyond comprehensibility (such as child abuse, sociopathic serial killings, "the rape of a woman and axing off her arms").[76]

Yet suppose all explicable evil were explained, all evil capable of justification were justified, and all evil whose occurrence, at least, can be understood were understood: How is all the Evil that still remains to be treated theologically? Barth's reflections on *nothingness* furnish important indications in this regard. In what follows, I read them not as an absurd theometaphysical "ontology of evil," which Barth for good reason always emphatically rejected (even if he not always fully avoided it),[77] but as a *hermeneutic attempt* at drawing the conclusions of God's grace, revealed in all its profundity on the cross, for theologically dealing with the indisputable reality that Evil has even *post Christum crucifixum et resurrectum*. The issue for theology is not explaining something that *is* (namely "nothingness") but, inversely, making comprehensible something that is *not*, that *cannot be explained or justified* because it does not meet the minimum requirement for it, namely *to be* something. Yet since this, in turn, does not mean that evil *would not be real*, the theological task, in clear-cut terms, consists in showing how to deal with evil whose *reality* is not being denied but whose *being* is. Barth's concept of "nothingness" is meant to designate just that.[78]

Barth's hermeneutic principles for theologically dealing with nothingness first of all stress two moments to be considered: nothingness must not be *overestimated*, but it must also not be *played down*. It must not be overestimated because it is neither a counter-God nor a principle of being of its own, as if good could be explained by recourse to the

---

76. Adams, *Horrendous Evils*, 26.

77. In his exegesis of Gen 1, for example, Barth unambiguously notes that nothingness "is that which God as Creator did *not* elect or will, that which as Creator He *passed over*, that which . . . He set behind him as chaos, not giving it existence or being." Nothingness "is that which is actual only in the negativity allotted to it by the divine decision, only in its exclusion from creation, only, if we may put it thus, at the left hand of God. But in this way it is truly actual and relevant and even active after its own particular fashion" (Barth, *Church Dogmatics*, III.3, §49.1:73–74; my emphases). All these statements become questionable, however, when we read them in the sense of an absolutist logic of action, choice, and decision that knows nothing *but* actions based on decisions and thereby construes even nondecisions as decisions. Not choosing something is then conceived of as choosing not to choose, a choice that as such endows what has not been chosen with a precarious status in reality: choosing not to choose something then does not mean that we do not choose because there is nothing to choose but that there is something we do not choose. Not-doing then becomes doing, and omitting to do something becomes permitting something we omit doing. Barth himself is ambivalent on this point and goes off track when in the doctrine of properties, unlike in the doctrine of reconciliation, he speaks of God's permission and operates with the non-notion of a *voluntas permittens*, a "mighty not-willing of evil," a "mighty permission," precisely not a *voluntas inefficax* but *efficax* (Barth, *Church Dogmatics*, II.1, §31.2:594–97, quotes on 596). In the recourse to God's "permission," Barth thus proffers an explanation of the reality of *malum* after all, rather than just making a soteriological statement about God not willing and doing Evil but fighting and defeating it. For criticism, see Härle, *Sein und Gnade*, 266–69; Kress, *Gottes Allmacht angesichts von Leiden*, esp. 217–23; and Wüthrich, *Gott und das Nichtige*.

78. It has repeatedly been noted that Barth is not as clear on this point as might be desired. In bringing together "God and Evil within one ontological framework," he offers, in the form of a negative explanation of what God does not will, an explanation of Evil after all. See Jüngel, "Revelation of the Hiddenness of God," 142. Any attempt at taking up Barth's reflections on nothingness in a theologically fruitful way must avoid *any semblance* of sketching a theological "ontology of Evil."

principle of the Good and evil by recourse to the principle of Evil. We saw earlier that and how this is absurd. Nor can it be integrated in the good creation as a negative aspect to enhance the harmony and beauty of the whole, as if the creator's judgement in Gen 1, "It is good," somehow meant Evil as well. Evil does not belong to Good *in negative form*, and nothingness is not a good that is not; nothingness is that which not only is not, it is that which *nihilates* and *annihilates*, that which *ruins* and *destroys what is good*.

This has the epistemic consequence that nothingness can in no way be accessed or recognized via that which the reality of creation excludes. It is not an aspect of the reality of creation that could be obtained *e negativo* from this reality. The principle of knowing nothingness, rather, is solely *what God does not will and effect*, and the place where this becomes noticeable for human beings, according to Barth, is the reality nexus designated by the name "Jesus Christ." For only where it becomes clear "positively what He is and wills" does it also become clear what God "is not and does not will."[79] Knowledge of the ontologically deficient reality of nothingness, according to Barth, can thus be had solely in a Christological perspective.[80] In regard to Jesus Christ it becomes clear what God is and wills because this regard itself is due to God's working in the Spirit here and now: only God's Spirit opens our eyes to seeing God at work in Jesus Christ, and only in Jesus Christ do we thereby see God at work in such a way that it becomes clear, definitively and bindingly, what God is and wills and therefore also what he is not and does not will. God's Spirit opens our eyes for *God's presence* in the world. That this Spirit of God's is the *Spirit of Christ* and that God's presence in the world is the *presence of God's love* to the other of himself, however, that becomes unmistakably clear only with regard to Jesus Christ because it is there that who and what God truly is, God who is present in the world in his Spirit, is being revealed to the gaze of the Spirit: God is love, unlimitedly free, inexhaustibly creative, making everything new.[81]

Yet from this perspective, nothingness, that is, all that opposes and could oppose this divine love, comes into view only ever "as something which has already been overcome, something which yields," that is, as something that God's action has deprived of the ground of its reality.[82] It has no being of its own but "exists" in an entirely parasitic manner: it is a reality that *ought not to be* and *will not be* in the long run because on its

79. Barth, *Church Dogmatics*, II.2, §33.1:141.

80. Berner, *Theorie des Bösen*, 183–249, is thus correct to develop his presentation of Barth's position starting from this point.

81. This not only takes up the old figure of thought that God can only be known through God (the Spirit) and by way of God (Christ); it also overcomes the theological indeterminacy of a concept of the Spirit not qualified by the reference to the Father and the *filioque* and of a consideration of Jesus not qualified with regard to the Spirit and with reference to Father and Son by means of a trinitarian definition of the Spirit in the relationship with Father and Son and of the Son in the relationship with Father and Spirit. Knowing God through God by way of God is the reciprocal definition of a process of reality in which Father, Son, and Spirit make each other recognizable and accessible, through each other and with each other, as the one merciful and loving God: the Father as the loving Father of the Son through the Spirit; the Son as beloved Son of the Father who out of love sends the Spirit; the Spirit as the form of the presence of God's love in which God opens himself up and communicates himself to himself and to others as the God who is, wills, and works love and nothing else.

82. Barth, *Church Dogmatics*, II.2, §33.2:172.

own and coming from God, *it cannot be.*[83] Barth, to be sure, in a seemingly paradoxical way, says that "[t]he possibility of existence which evil can have is only that of the impossible, the reality of existence only that of the unreal."[84] But this is not an elaboration of an ontology of the negative. It is an unfortunate (because it lends itself to misunderstanding) way of saying that it is *not* possible that evil is an autonomous reality, and that it actually is *not* in that way. It is *not* part of God's good creation that it would *have to* always also feature evil or at least possess the *possibility* of evil because only then—as is often argued—human freedom as choosing the good and not choosing Evil would be possible.[85] Evil is said to be the "price of freedom," and if God wants a creation in which there is finite freedom, it cannot exist without the possibility of evil. Sin is then seen as a "creaturely possibility" of the human grounded in the human freedom to self-determination, and the human being, accordingly, is attributed a "capacity for sinning."[86]

That, however, is exactly what Barth's analysis contradicts. For him *Evil* is strictly that which God denies, and *nothingness* is that which God explicitly does not will and work, neither as reality nor as possibility. Nothingness is neither God (or God-like) nor creature (or an analogue to creation). It is not a countergod and not an *opus dei* but (and this, too, is a formula that lends itself to misunderstanding) God's *opus alienium*, his "work to the left."[87] It lends itself to misunderstanding because it refers nothingness yet again to God's creative action in a quasi-ontological way when it must be referred to it strictly and exclusively *hermeneutically* as that which *from the perspective of this creative action* appears as and must be discussed as excluded, outmoded, not willed, and not effected. It is not impossible *as such* because it would, for example, involve a self-contradiction. As such, rather, it is indeed possible, as its reality attests. Yet this reality is not what God wills, and in this respect, seen *from God's perspective*, it comes into view as something that ought to be *impossible, not real, not possible, not effective.* If this detour via God ("from God's perspective") is ignored, evil does not come into view, at least not as evil or nothingness; what is seen will be something beside something else (an event among others).[88] Yet this means, inversely, that nothing that occurs or can occur

83. Yet if God's willing and not willing is construed abstractly and, in parallel, effectively as effecting or not effecting something, this does indeed lead to misunderstanding not effecting something as effecting nothing and to seeing in the difference between effective divine willing and not willing merely a verbal distinction. See Hick, *Evil and the God of Love,* 149–50; Davaney, *Divine Power;* and *Härle, Sein und Gnade,* 230–46.

84. Barth, *Church Dogmatics,* II.2, §33.2:170.

85. That is why it is also not possible to speak, as John C. McDowell does, of a "certain *thereness-*of-evil anterior to, and even regulative of, subsequent sinning" ("Much Ado about Nothing," 333). This amounts to prolonging the perversion of sin in the notion of creation, that is, to perverting creation itself.

86. See Härle and Herms, *Rechtfertigung,* 191 and 95, as well as my "Fähig zur Sünde?," 3–12.

87. This distinction can be found already in Luther (*Dictata super Psalterium,* in WA 3, 246, ll. 19–20; see Bandt, *Luthers Lehre vom verborgenen Gott,* 54–82). Jüngel tries to solve the problem theologically with regard to Luther's discussion by distinguishing between *deus absconditus* and *opus dei absconditum:* "There is no *terrible deus absconditus who incites terror* but only an *opus dei absconditum*" (Jüngel, "Revelation of the Hiddenness of God," 137). He thereby, however, distinguishes between God's being and God's work in a way that has problematic consequences.

88. That is why Barth's point is not captured by saying that nothingness is the chaos the creator's

as event among others, and this includes the negation of events, is, taken by itself, evil or nothingness. *Nothingness* is not identical with what is *not* because the negative alternative of something is the negation or "the legitimate 'not'" of the created.[89] It is evil only if it comes into view and is to be judged as evil *from God's perspective*, and this applies to something being posited as much as for it being negated.

That is why Barth correctly says that nothingness is neither a *nihil pure negativum* nor a relative not-being as opposed to being but a reality not willed and not worked *from the perspective of God*. The crucial point, also and especially vis-à-vis the *privatio boni* tradition, is that nothingness is not an opposite of being nor is it only a lack of being but, we might say, it is the opposite of the opposition between being and not-being: nothingness as it were stands *before* the parenthesis in which being and not-being are distinct from and opposed to each other, and in this before, nothingness is in opposition both to creation (to the totality of what is created, including its negations) and to God. Through this opposition, it is defined as that which God *does not will* as distinct from that which God wills and works. The latter is what is called "creation," the former is nothingness. In other words: nothingness is not an ontological reality beside or behind creation (in position and negation) or beside God, but it is—once more put in hermeneutic terms— that which *from God's perspective* is never willed and worked in creation: it is the *divine judgment* of all that in creation which *ought not to be* if creation is good and is rightly to be called good.

No investigation of the world and its phenomena can therefore lead to what theologically deserves being called evil or nothingness. What happens to us and what as happening can be examined as to its causes and effects is not evil independently of its being evil *for someone* and its rightly being judged to be such. What is being judged by someone to be evil, however, is not readily also what *theologically* deserves being called evil. That can *only ever be determined as such in taking recourse to God's nihilating judgment*, and what this judgment comprehends, what it is directed against and what not, that becomes clear definitively, Christians are convinced, from the perspective of the place where God revealed his judgment of all of creation: from the cross of Jesus

---

ordering action has pushed to the margins of creation, a chaos that time and again erupts in creation, occurring in the form of "natural disasters" such as "earthquakes, tornadoes, hurricanes, blizzards, droughts, floods, forest fires, volcanic eruptions, mountain slides," as Tupper interprets Barth (*Scandalous Providence*, 138). This interpretation is misguided because not only negative but also (ostensibly) positive phenomena and events in life may be forms in which nothingness manifests. What, concretely, belongs among these is decided not in what we experience as ill but solely in God's nihilating judgment that it ought not to be. Boyd, too, misunderstand this crucial point of Barth's argument (Boyd, *Satan and the Problem of Evil*, 284–90). That is why he can take up Barth's notion of nothingness only by associating it, against Barth's stated intention, with his own free will defense and rearticulating it as that which God negates but which we, because of our freedom, both are able to choose and do and in fact choose and do (339–47). Doing what pertains to nothingness is thus said to be the great and indispensable good of creatures, and Boyd, citing Richard E. Creel (*Divine Impassibility*, 141–43), explicitly speaks of "the enduring good of free will, even when it has irrevocably chosen evil" (Boyd, *Satan and the Problem of Evil*, 343n5). This reduction of the notion of nothingness to the traditional free-will defense and to what humans freely choose and do although God does not will it downplays and misses the point of Barth's theory of nothingness.

89. Barth, *Church Dogmatics*, III.3, §50.4:350.

Christ.[90] No phenomenon is evil *per se*; every phenomenon *can* be evil, even those that under different aspects we might call good; yet only that is in fact evil which is not being willed and effected by God, that is thus subject to his judgment that it ought not to be, that it would be better if it were not, and that it will not be when the world is what it is becoming: God's good creation.

19. Overcoming and Outdoing Evil

Then, however, the *overcoming and outdoing of Evil* can no longer be approached as the elimination of every *malum* experienced by someone, every ill happening to someone in their lives, every malice one encounters. It can only ever be about what ought not to be *from God's perspective*. And that is not to be read off the phenomenon but off God's judgment about this phenomenon.

This judgement, though, is not a summary judgment about everything all at once but a judgment concretely referring to each specific case, a specific life, a life's specific event, happening, or doing. This judgment can define every life phenomenon as *malum*, whichever way it may be experienced and understood by those affected themselves. That is why in dealing with evil in practical life, the path of faith is always the detour via God's judgment, and the concrete traits of this judgment, according to the conviction of the Christian faith, have found expression in Jesus Christ as judgment about every human life: that is evil which God shows to be not willed by putting an end to and outdoing it through good—through that which is the best for a given concrete life and which thereby also brings out what is truly evil for this life. Thus the paralytic seeking a cure first and above all is being forgiven his sins (Mark 2:5), that is, the damage undone is not one in his life but a damage in the relation of his life to God. And in Jesus's case, too, what is prevented is not the physical death on the cross but the "theological death (the separation from God)."[91] God counters this fatal separation by resurrecting the crucified Christ. The separation, not the physical death, is the *malum* that God thwarts and overcomes in the working of his love.

The *bonum* God allots a life can thus deviate significantly from what we might ourselves imagine it to be. It is a *bonum* that not so much compensates for *malum* experienced than it surpasses everything that can be expected and experienced by us. In this sense, the *bonum* at which Christian hope is directed is not a compensation for *malum* suffered and not a replacement of *bonum* not gained in this life such that it would be possible to imagine *e negativo* what it might be. Rather, it is an excess of the good that surpasses everything imaginable and can only be outlined as a new beginning of eternal life with God, instituted by and coming from God. Not what human beings imagine but what happens to them coming from God is the content of Christian hope. Because it is entirely and exclusively directed at God, from whom it hopes all that is good and only what is good, Christian hope does not bet on a good eschaton and eschatic good, a

---

90. In his own way, C. S. Lewis makes this point when he notes that "hell is hell, not from its own point of view, but from the heavenly point of view. . . . It is only to the damned that their fate could even seem less than unendurable" (Lewis, *Problem of Pain*, 112).

91. Kessler, *Gott und das Leid*, 109n49.

paradise at the end of times or heaven on earth that is being missed so much right now and therefore imagined to be all the more dazzling, but rather bets entirely on the eschatos it trusts to do everything for the best. In that regard, Christians precisely do not know what they may hope, as Kant put it, and they cannot even imagine it; all they know is *who they may hope for*—and that is enough. Christian hope is not merely hope for what is good but hope for the God whom it trusts to make the fragments of human life not just whole but, in an unforeseeable way, good and luminous in the splendor of his life.[92]

20. Ethical Overcoming

The overcoming of evil that comes to be seen as such in the detour via God is thus to be understood as two-step process with an *ethical* and an *eschatological* component. First, *ethically*, the theological definition of *malum* opens up a critical difference between what in the biological, human, and personal contexts of life we consider to be evil and experience as evil, and what is to be judged as evil from God's perspective. For not everything that happens to humans in such a way that they rightly judge it to be evil is for that reason alone also evil in the sense of theologically defined *malum*, that is, something that according to the divine judgment ought not to be because it separates those affected by it from God's presence and love.

The detour via God's judgment thus draws attention to a difference between what we experience as *malum for us* and what is *malum according to divine judgment*. The difference is important because what God judges to be and rejects as *malum* does not even have to be experienced by humans as *malum* and is almost by definition not experienced as such by sinners: both what human beings experience as *malum* and what they consider *bonum* can be *malum* in light of God's judgment—an expression, that is, of a life that ignores the one to whom it owes itself and who makes it possible and maintains it. This means on the one hand that we must be critical even toward what we experience as *bonum* and that not everything that is pleasant is always already to be considered good. And it means on the other hand that in practical life, humans can assume a different attitude toward the evil that affects them in life because it does not *ipso facto* have to be something that separates them from God and thus cuts them off from the source of life.

To that extent, it also possible to say that Christians suffer evil in their lives like other people do but that they suffer it differently, namely with a different attitude toward it, because they judge it to be something that will not have the last word. Thus they see theologically relevant evil (evil in the sense of God's judgment) even where others are not (yet) able to perceive *malum*, and the history of Christianity, in its best parts, is a history of developing a sense of life phenomena that in this sense are not simply to be accepted but to be judged as *mala*: that is the contribution of Christianity to the humanization of the world.[93] Yet on the other hand, they also do not see a lot of things people

92. What Gestrich, in *Die Wiederkehr des Glanzes*, with regard to the forgiveness of sin aptly calls the "return of splendor in the world" is, articulated as eschatological hope, the entry of fragmented human life into the splendor of the divine life, which, through incomprehensible good, outdoes what incomprehensible evil kept open and uncompleted in human life. See also the studies in Gestrich, *Peccatum*.

93. It hardly needs to be specially emphasized that time and again and in partly unimaginable ways,

might judge as *malum* as something that would have to be judged as *malum* religiously or theologically as well because it has the effect of damaging the relationship of creature and creator and separating us from God's love. Becoming sensitive to the forms and phenomena of evil relevant from the point of view of faith on the one hand, and serenity in confronting evil that damages life but is unable to separate human beings from God because God does not let his relationship with them be damaged by it on the other, are thus the two modes in which a different attitude toward experiences of evil in the life of human beings is being assumed in light of the divine judgment of Evil.

21. Eschatological Outdoing

This attitude, however, and this is the second component, is guided by the hope that God will actively overcome what affects humans as *malum* and do so in such a way that human life is not permanently separated from God's life but instead is lived, in its finite manifestations, transparent to the presence of creative love and in community with God.

Without this *eschatological* component, the Christian attitude toward Evil would be insufficiently understood. The ongoing present of what is made past through God's effective presence, according to the judgment of faith, is a state whose end Christians hope for and whose being ended they petition for.[94] The petition for deliverance from Evil in Jesus's prayer is thus not only betting on God's being with and his solidarity with those who suffer.[95] It is a petition for God's good kingship, which has commenced but has not yet become manifest for everyone and broken through everywhere, to become public. In that regard, Christian hope is the hope that that which is also comes to be in the lives of those who are still being affected by what no longer is.

The present, too, in which human beings live is thus understood in a qualified way, namely in a differentiating qualification: it is a present that is still defined by the presence of the past *malum* that God has overcome through the good he does. Yet it is also a present in which that manifests and becomes effective to which God has promised a future. That is why time is always to be differentiated into that which does not deserve to remain and that which will remain. And this distinction will be able to orient itself, in a theologically relevant respect, solely by God's judgment to put an end to sin and to open up a life for the sinner in which sin is only past and no longer still present as past.[96]

Christianity has also contributed to inhumanity in the world. As a historical phenomenon, Christianity is to be seen as no more ambivalent than other phenomena: identifying its history with the history of salvation is misleading already because the view faith has of human history—in light of God's judgment and in light of its distinction between Law and Gospel—also and especially urges counting the historical realities of Christianity itself among what is to be judged as *malum*. It is not Christianity that must be critically recalled, it is God's effective present, of which Christianity reminds itself and the world in its services, that must be critically recalled time and again also against the real figures of Christianity. This is the aim of the *semper reformanda*, which urges Christian life in all its individual and communal (church) aspects to reorient itself ever anew by God's judgment.

94. In that respect, we ought indeed to emphasize that "so long as horrors and vulnerability to horrors persist, God's work is not yet done" (see Adams, "Horrors in Theological Context," 473).

95. See Werbick, *Von Gott sprechen an der Grenze zum Verstummen,* 74–77.

96. See Dalferth, *Leiden und Böses,* 201–6.

The attitude of hope that corresponds to this orientation is not aimed at a specific expected state of the world and of life but at God whom it trusts to arrange what is best for oneself and for all others in each case and to allow it to become actual. Christian hope is hope for God's self-actualizing love, which through loving, that is, through good, overcomes, continues, rights, and perfects everything that resists or ignores it. Looking at the world we live in, therefore, the attitude of hope judges neither that everything that is is good or very good nor that everything will be good or very good but that God as creator, redeemer, and perfecter of this world will also ensure that what was and is *malum* for the creatures will be replaced and outdone by what is *bonum* for them. Formally, this *bonum*, for every human being, is the unbroken and unhindered living communion with God, which is not what it is once and for all but is able infinitely to enhance itself because God's love can surpass itself unimaginably and can become both intensively more profound and extensively more comprehensive.

What that means concretely in each case depends on the specific life whose concrete *mala* will be overcome by God's infinitely enhanceable *bonum*. All creaturely life thus leaves its own unmistakable trace in God's life, and because the effect of the effective presence of God's love lies not in rendering everything indifferent but in infinitely enhancing the particularity of each and everyone, the appropriate image of the hoped-for living communion is not that of the drop merging with the infinity of the ocean but that of the crystal which ever more clearly refracts and mirrors the totality of the universe in an unmistakably unique way. God will be all in all because in his love for every individual he becomes everything and makes every individual a unique image of his infinite love for everything. In this sense, the Christian hope for the overcoming of *malum* through God's *bonum* aims not at the eschaton but at the divine eschatos which, in light of Christ, it understands to be the transformative power of an infinite love that makes everything new.

III

ORIENTING STRATEGIES
FOR DEALING WITH EVIL

CHRISTIAN STRATEGIES FOR ORIENTATION in dealing with the experiences of *bonum* and *malum* in human life are elaborated in critically and pointedly engaging with whatever religious and nonreligious modes of orientation Christians encounter in their particular cultural environment. They never begin at some historical or cultural point zero but always in situations shaped by contingent forms of living and thinking the incomprehensible, which they transform into new forms of living and thinking for dealing with what goes against and what goes beyond sense, sense-destroying *malum* and sense-exceeding *bonum*.[1]

The strategies developing to this end in Christian life and thinking by no means take up only religious orientation procedures in human life but non-religious ones as well, which they critically transform and elaborate. It is not surprising that this leads to a great variety of similarities and points of contact. It would be surprising if that were not the case. Yet when we seek to understand the point of Christian orienting strategies, it is not the similarities but the differences that are theologically instructive. And that, precisely, requires the hermeneutic acknowledgement of the concrete starting situations and historical lines of development of the Christian transformation processes.

Thus the orienting procedures of ordering and locating, of emotionally, cognitively, and imaginatively structuring the world as the shared living space of human beings, and of practically locating human life in the world thus structured are not completely new. Rather, they continue given modes of orientation in new ways by practicing them from a different point of view, within a different horizon, and thus also with different aims.[2] Thus they develop, starting from faith in Jesus Christ, a perspective on human life in this world in which everything is viewed and judged within the eschatological

1. See Dalferth, *Das Böse*.

2. Presenting Christianity and its message of the God of love only in purely contrasting terms as what is entirely other than everything that preceded it is a Marcionite opposition that is not just abstract and ahistorical but also hermeneutically and theologically dubitable: it primarily or exclusively restricts what is new about the Good News to its negation of what came before or at least understands it mainly in terms of this negation. See Schmid, *Marcion und sein Apostolos*, and May et al., eds., *Marcion and His Impact on Church History*.

horizon of God's effective presence and his action that creates the new. Everything given and handed down is thus discriminately assessed as to what has come to an end as the old and what can be taken up and continued in the new. This applies to the modes of orienting of pre- and non-Christian life as well. Christian living and thinking amplifies and changes them, modifies, intensifies, and renovates them, that is, it does not linearly continue them or simply break them off and replace them but recasts them in a hermeneutically highly complex manner. In this way, adoption and delimitation, continuation and reformation create a new practice of orientation into which many things that can already be found earlier are being merged.

This is particularly evident in the Christian adoption and reformation of religious orienting practices. The turn toward God, gods, or the divine with thanks and petitions, lamentation and praise belongs to the basic religious modes in which human beings seek to orient or reorient themselves when they experience good and evil. They thereby react to happenings to which they experience themselves to be passively exposed and which they can control neither as to their origin nor as to their course. What happens to them is beyond their control and influence, incomprehensible and unintelligible, both as good that surprises them and as evil that happens to them.

1. Orienting Concepts

Both designations do not name phenomena that as such are something good or something evil but they express assessments and evaluations of phenomena that human beings define as something good or evil based on the effects these phenomena have in their own or someone else's life. There are no *bona* and *mala* in the world; processes in the world become *bona* or *mala for us* that represent, for our life or for someone else's, a gain or a loss, an increase of possibilities or a decrease of opportunities, acknowledgement of its particularity or contempt for its dignity. The expressions *something good* and *something evil* thus do not designate empirical concepts for classifying phenomena or categorial concepts for classifying empirical phenomena via the epistemological aspects of the true and the false; they name pragmatic and transcategorial orienting concepts with whose help human beings assess and evaluate phenomena with regard to what is good or evil for life, for being human, or for being a person in order to orient themselves in their world and to be able to live and act in this world with some degree of reliability.

The distinction between what is good and what is evil thus does not designate phenomena or classes of phenomena but brings out an assessing and evaluating attitude that is virulent in experience itself, an attitude humans assume toward the phenomena that affect their lives in its basic biological, specific human, or particular personal manifestations.[3] The sense of this distinction lies in the orientation it allows for in the living of

---

3. That does not mean, to repeat, that this attitude is only added to the phenomena secondarily, as a subjective supplement, in an explicit judgment or evaluation. On the contrary, it means that the phenomena *are being experienced this way*. There is no initial descriptive experience that would subsequently be assessed or evaluated this way or that; the happening in question is experienced as evaluating from the outset, that is, experienced as *bonum* or *malum*. The two aspects (descriptive and evaluative) can be distinguished only in an analytic attitude and then in different ways according to one's point of view (as someone affected or someone observing).

human life in the world; its concrete content, in contrast, depends on the aspect under which the distinction is made. As we saw, the concrete figuration of this distinction depends on one's discriminating standpoint as observer or as someone affected and on how the sense of "good" and "evil" can be defined differently with respect to life's biological, human, and personal dimensions: as mere contrast, as conflicting with each other, as overcoming or destruction of the other side, as functional contrast, as moral opposition, as religious distinction, and so on.[4] For all these reasons, the distinction is unsuitable for differentiating the world into what is good and what is evil by merely listing phenomena. Using this distinction does not yield insight into the structure of the world but information about the way in which human beings evaluate and assess what affects their lives in their various dimensions as what is good or evil.

2. The Unwanted Probability of Evil and the Normal Improbability of the Good

In this connection, two things can be regularly observed. On the one hand, there is a conspicuous asymmetry in the human self-perception of life between the experience-conditioned *improbability of the good* and the inverse *probability of evil*: that evil happens to us is the unwanted norm, that good things happen is the exception counterfactually desired to be the norm. Of course our wishes for our own lives and usually also for the lives of others aim for increasing the good and minimizing evil. Yet since both essentially are happenings whose occurrence we cannot influence or influence only indirectly and imprecisely, directing the living of one's life toward making *bonum* the norm and *malum* not the norm depends on factors over which we have little or no control. Who would not rather have their life be determined by what they see as *bonum* than by what they judge as *malum*? Yet time and again, *malum* is experienced to be more probable, *bonum* to be more improbable. And although the wish for what is good also always arises from the experience of good, it is the normal probability of Evil that amplifies the counterfactual hope for the good.

On the other hand, however, *bonum* and *malum* are not given in the processes of life as such, independently of how human and other organisms are affected by them. The normal improbability of *bonum* and probability of *malum* appear only within the horizon of humans perceiving themselves and others. Whether what affects humans is something good or evil cannot be read off the phenomena themselves, it is decided by what these phenomena make of the life they affect. In the moment of being affected, this is often as difficult to decide for those affected as the question whether we have touched something very hot or something extremely cold. That is why it takes distance, time, and detours via a third to relate to and engage with what has happened in such a way that it becomes possible to understand it as something ungraspable in its ungraspability and to judge it as good or evil based on the effects it has on the life it affects. The improbability of the *bonum* cannot be diminished by articulating the probability of the *malum* as a rule that allows for practical orientation. Rather, the opposite is the case: with regard

4. See also Dalferth, *Das Böse*.

to both, a reliable orientation of our lives becomes possible only if we learn to live with the essentially unrepealable ungraspability of *bonum* and *malum*. This is what religions specifically contribute to.

3. Religious Orientations

The particularity of religious orientation strategies is that they react to the ungraspable that has happened to a life by relating it to another ungraspable from whose perspective they locate it, in its ungraspability, in life and inversely understand life vis-à-vis the ungraspable that time and again intrudes into life and, as a *bonum*, unexpectedly enhances it or, as a *malum*, nonsensically destroys it.

The goal of religious orientation strategies thus lies precisely in preserving the incomprehensibility and enhancing the ungraspability of what has happened and not in rendering what is incomprehensible comprehensible and what is ungraspable graspable. Attempts at doing the latter regularly result in dubious mythologemes that provoke no less dubious naturalizations in reaction. The world is then described as the battlefield of good and evil spirits and all processes in nature and history are described as the actions of suprahuman agents in conflict with each other.[5] Or, in opposition, the world and life are presented as purely naturalist processes of evolution in which the brain is the epitome of what can be said about the mind because this is thought to be the only way to defend against the gnosticizing hypostasizations and Manichean principilizations of Good and Evil—without noticing that this just amounts to succumbing to another version of dualist hypostasization.

The simple objection to what is wrong is not *ipso facto* what is correct, and not every form of religion is attained by the same kind of criticism. Thus, current forms of neomysticism and neognosticism,[6] even if they appear within Christianity, must not be confused with the Christian faith, which from the beginning disenchanted and secularized the world because it taught experiencing the world exclusively as God's creation and domain and no longer as the battlefield of demons. This view of the world imposed itself only slowly, not unilinearly, and never comprehensively. Even within Christianity, this debate must be had time and again to advance from the syncretisms of the age to the clarifications of the faith. Similar things can be said of the other monotheistic religions.

The naturalistic dismissal of all religion will thus not yield an answer to move us forward because it ignores the tasks of orientation to which religions respond. A dispute, rather, must take place within religions about what they could be, given their many and varied aberrations and follies. All religions could be better than they are. Yet they will become better only if they are not lumped together without distinction, only if attention is paid to the different developments and possibilities set up in them that can be

5. See Boyd, *God at War* and *Satan and the Problem of Evil*.

6. King, *What Is Gnosticism?*, esp. chs. 3–5, has shown with good arguments that and how using the category "gnosis" historically is a dubious enterprise. That does not mean, however, that it cannot be used or even that it could be dispensed with as a descriptive category to address and interpret certain modern and contemporary developments in religious and intellectual history as "gnostic" or "neognostic."

strengthened or weakened. Life is not better without religion; it becomes better when religions become better.

In this sense, when religious orientation strategies worth discussing engage—in an age methodically aiming to explain everything and unwilling to accept anything incomprehensible—the questions raised by the intrusion of good and the happening of evil in a life, they are not concerned with rendering comprehensible what is incomprehensible or making what is ungraspable graspable. Their goal, rather, is the inverse, to address the question how humans exposed to the ungraspable can live with and despite the incomprehensible. Religious effort aims not at eliminating what is incomprehensible and ungraspable but at reorienting those to whom it happens. How is it possible to experience good in life without putting others down and thus becoming evil? How is it possible to fight evil without being infected by it? How is it possible to live with and despite incomprehensible evil without leaving the field clear for evil or becoming evil oneself?

These and similar questions show that religions are concerned with something different from what the sciences aim to do. The religious attempt at orientation, making what is ungraspable comprehensible in the detour via an ungraspable, is obviously unsuitable for explaining something in a scientific or science-like way. If properly understood, though, it does not even seek to do so, for all explanation of experiences of *malum* refers to their descriptive (*what?*) and not their evaluative (*how?*) component and therefore does not explain evil but only that which occasions experiences of *malum*.[7] Compared to scientific attempts at explaining and technological attempts at shaping the world, religious strategies for confronting evil have a different point. They do not seek to resolve the ungraspability of what happens, try and explain it after the fact in order, prospectively, to be able to promote it (in the case of good) or prevent it (in the case of evil). Instead, they suppose its incomprehensible reality in life and ask how it is possible to establish a constructive life relationship toward it as what is ungraspable: the issue is finding a way back into life from the interruption of life by something ungraspable and incomprehensible, a path that does not negate, minimize, and dissolve the ungraspable and incomprehensible but allows for living with it and face to face with it.

That is only possible because and insofar as we do not try, once all that can be explained scientifically has been explained, *per impossibile* to also try to explain and understand the ungraspable and incomprehensible in religious terms[8] but rather learn

---

7. As noted, I speak of a descriptive and an evaluative component because analyses of experiences of *malum* can and must always thematize *what* is being experienced and *how* it is being experienced. The first can be articulated in a judgment of fact (*this or that* is evil), the second in a judgment of value (this or that *is evil*). Yet that does not mean that a *malum* would exist only once a cognitive judgment of value is being made; such a judgment, rather, can be made in the first place, justly or unjustly, only because what is being experienced is always experienced and assessed within an evaluating perspective. Already the perception of what is being experienced is evaluative, not just the judgment concerning it. For nothing is perceived without being perceived in a specific way: there is no experiencing of something that would not take place in a specific mode.

8. That would only amount to drawing religion and faith into the one-dimensional worldview of modernity, which translates all vertical transcendences into horizontal sequences, that is, arranges everything on the horizontal plane in ever new and different ways, but methodologically no longer knows anything that does not fit the sequence. Faith thus becomes "religious belief" and joins other kinds—scientific, moral, aesthetic, etc.—beliefs. Yet it is thereby inserted into the domain of a concept of

to understand *ourselves* in new and different ways in confronting the ungraspable and incomprehensible. This, precisely, is what religion and faith crucially contribute to. They do not explain what cannot (yet) be explained scientifically, but they provide guidance in understanding oneself, in the face of ungraspable happenings of incomprehensible good or evil, in such a way that the interruption does not block the way back to life but is able to become the beginning of a new and differently understood life. They allow human beings to understand the world they live in and their lives in this world differently by opening up to them, thanks to including them in practices of living and orienting guided by God, gods, or the divine, a different conception of self, world, and life than modernity's secular experience of life and the sciences' methodologically restricted access to the world allow for. And they do so not arbitrarily and pre-rationally but by continuing the practices of the lifeworld (from which scientific explanation starts as well) differently, precisely by taking up the orienting procedures practiced there and elaborating them into specific orienting practices.

4. Science and Religion

Science and religion have shared roots in the concrete life practice of human beings who ask *why?* when they no longer understand something and *what is that for?* or *why me?* when they no longer know what to do. Yet in the course of history, both have developed different strategies for dealing with such questions. This has led to an ever more defined differentiation of what in concrete life is often quite close and barely distinguishable. In the European tradition, science and religion have often taken opposing paths. While since their pre-Socratic beginnings, the sciences have depersonalized the explanatory way of dealing with the world and drawn not on gods and powers but on elements, forces, and laws, Judaism, Christianity, and Islam within the framework of their theologies of creation and of history have developed markedly personal conceptions of orientation in the world. To systematically answer explanatory questions, the sciences theoretically generalized a practical model of explanation obtained from human doing and acting—as is particularly evident in Aristotle—and expanded it as a model of causal explanation to include all worldly phenomena. To systematically answer questions of orientation, the great monotheistic religions, in contrast and as it were inversely, developed a system of personal references and relationships that described the ordering and locating tasks of orientation in the world as interactions between divine and created agents. The world here is understood not as a rule-governed nexus of events but as an interactive nexus of actions, and accordingly, the answers to the questions of *why* and *what for* differ as well.

Human beings to whom inexplicable evil happens, who are affected by evil happening to others, or who fear such evil for themselves and others, turn to God, gods, or the divine with petitions and pleas, laments and accusations. God, gods, or the divine of course are as fundamentally beyond their control as the Evil they fear. But they suppose

---

belief that no longer knows of any vertical but only of horizontal variation: there may be other kinds of faith but there can be no faith that does not allow for representation and expression as a kind of belief. A look at the (common) naturalization of the concept of belief suffices to see what foreshortening this inevitably leads to.

them to have, unlike humans, the capacity and power not to be helplessly exposed to the intrusion of Evil but to defend themselves and, if they so choose, help humans do the same. That is why people turn to them, because from this divine, they expect and hope to obtain unconditioned and incomprehensible help in the face of the incomprehensible and uncontrollable that has happened. This hope is centrally directed at attaining a view of what has happened or what is feared that does not correspond to our own experience but to that of the divine counterpart. We seek a new selfconception in the face of the incomprehensible evil, we seek it in the reference to a counterpart whose judgment is reliable because it posits reality, and by understanding ourselves in light of this judgment, we can attain a different attitude even toward what we do not comprehend and understand by trusting that the last word will lie not with the Evil we experience but with the divine counterpart from whose perspective we experience ourselves differently.

In the recourse to an uncontrollable divine, we thus thematize uncontrollable evil in such a way that we do not try to obtain a sense from nonsensical Evil but in facing this nonsensicalness learn to understand *ourselves* in a new and different way. The recourse to God, biographically and historically, might begin as a search for an explanation for what cannot be explained and thus not differ profoundly from scientific efforts. But unlike scientific attempts at explanation, it sooner or later turns into a recourse to that counterpart of everything that does not explain the inexplicable but allows the human beings affected to assume a new and different attitude to what they experience as incomprehensible. With God and on God's side, they can object to all evil happening that it is neither the first nor the last reality. And that is why a religion's deepest crises are those in which God, the gods, or the divine becomes indistinguishable from or even the origin of Evil.

5. Living with Gods

In the face of impenetrable life experiences, human beings take recourse to what affords them orientation and continued life in their particular situation. When they turn to the gods, they do so because as powers of order, the gods inscribe reliable structures in the threatening chaos of life and thereby structure, in an always precarious and threatened manner, a living space in which humans can live more or less reliably in orienting themselves by the gods who confront and hinder them or stand by their side and assist them. Gods are the power centers of human living spaces to which one must refer if in these spaces one is affected by what is incomprehensible.

These power centers mark both the reliability of the ordinary and the ecstasy of the extraordinary. Gods guarantee order, but it is they, too, who time and again manifest the extraordinary within the order: Apollonian and Dionysian dimensions constitutively belong to the life of polytheistic religions. But that is not all. The pluralism of living spaces and their gods requires familiarity with the relationships between them to avoid becoming entangled in irresolvable aporia when one tries to orient oneself by them. Where gods work in different spaces or even fight each other over the same domains, the power hierarchies among the gods decide who is really able to help humans in their different life situations and whom humans should therefore turn to with thanks and petitions.

In this regard, polytheism urges an order among the divine organizers of human living spaces, genealogical dependencies, and functional hierarchies among the gods. Human beings must be familiar with these if they do not want to expose themselves, in addition to the dangers of life, to dangers from the gods. To gain certain orientation in life, it is necessary to turn to the god who is competent and influential in a given matter. It is thus not an accident that many mythological polytheisms feature a trend toward henotheism.

6. The Good God

This henotheism becomes a monotheism where the variety of the nonsensical is confronted with the uniqueness of the good, that is, where the question is raised to what extent and in what sense God can become good and God's good can become the decisive point of reference in orienting oneself within the incomprehensible. The semantics of the expression "God" is then defined in such a way that it balks at plural formation, that is, the good is conceived of in the singular and can in all situations be thematized as the same good. Any and all differences between God and good are removed, and only thereby does orientation by God always and everywhere become orientation by the good or, inversely, orientation by the good also always is orientation by God, consciously or not.

It is human beings' need for orientation in the face of impenetrable experiences both of the good that overwhelms them and of the evil happening to them that liberates religious and cultural processes, which in ever more detail clarify the work the notion of God performs in ordering life and locating the human within this order. The recourse to God becomes a religious form of thinking and living that affords practical life orientation in the face of incomprehensible good and incomprehensible evil. This exemplarily includes the prophetic effort at defining the divine will unambiguously as salutary will but also the parallel Platonic operation of assigning all that is good to God and all that is not good to something other than God.

To this end, the notion of God must be cleansed and defined in such a way that orientation by God is orientation by the one to whom only what is good and not also what is evil and ill is due. The notional operations in which this takes place follow an ever-recurrent pattern:

1. *the absolutely good God*: In a first phase, the attempt is made to distinguish God from all *malum*, that is, to establish as unambiguous a difference between God and everything else by defining God, in distinction from all else, as entirely and exclusively good.

2. *God loses relevance*: This can increase the difference between God and the experiential world of life to such an extent that God no longer seems relevant to anything in concrete life with its different problems of *bonum* and *malum*. The result is an Epicurean side by side of the entirely good life of God and the entirely-not-only-good life of human beings, which do not refer to each other in any real sense. In all the concrete cases of life, orientation by God thus becomes fruitless, unnecessary, and

impossible: there is nothing to be learned from God for human life; all problems, rather, can be solved without recourse to God.

3. *God of Good and Evil*: When the attempt is made to avoid this, when one insists like Lactantius that the entirely good God must be related above all also to the *mala* of life, without thereby dissolving the difference between the divine creator and the earthly creation, there are two possible options:

4. *differentiating the conception of God*: Either a perspectival difference is introduced into the conception of God by understanding God not just as reason and cause of the good but also of evil and ill in order to be able to speak of God's love and God's anger.[9] This entails the danger of dualizing the image of God, be it by distinguishing a good God of Love and a demonic God of the Law, be it by inscribing a distinction between *deus absconditus* and *deus revelatus* in the conception of the one God to which corresponds, on the human side, the distinction between fear of God and love of God. Yet both solutions come at a price. In the first case, there is a tendency, on the Manichean model, for the counterimages of God to develop a life of their own to become independent gods that fight each other and for an abstract dualism to dominate the orientation by God. In the second case, by contrast, the recourse to God under the two differing aspects of fear and love is constantly threatened by the possibility that the background or underground of God's dark sides might question or abolish the reliability of his good sides. All certainty of orientation then sinks into the experience of contestation in which God withdraws his presence and seems himself to be the reason for the helpless loss of orientation of human life in the face of the reality of Evil.

5. *obscuring the conception of God*: Or one renounces introducing such a difference into the image but thereby accepts the danger that, in the face of experiences of *mala* God seems to be responsible for, the conception of God becomes entirely ambiguous: it can no longer be determined whether God is a loving father or a merciless demon. In this situation, the paths diverge.

6. *paths leading out of faith*: The anti- or areligious path out of faith consists in stopping to orient one's life by God in the face of his ambiguity and trying to obtain nonreligious possibilities for orientation in life. Where in the light of ambiguous life experience, the conception of God becomes ambivalent, it is no longer possible to orient oneself by God. People accept that and begin therefore to settle into life without God and radically to secularize life.

7. *paths within faith*: The other or religious path within faith, in contrast, is the attempt to chase ambivalence from the conception of God in order to hold on to orientation by God. In the face of pressing experiences of Evil, that cannot be achieved by privileging one view of God over another without giving further reasons than just the wish to believe in a good God. The counterposition could always do the same thing, and the ambivalence in the conception of God would not be abolished.

---

9. See Härle, "Die Rede von der Liebe und vom Zorn Gottes"; Miggelbrink, *Der Zorn Gottes*; and Volkmann, *Der Zorn Gottes*, 263.

The historically momentous decisions of the great religious traditions were made in a different way and would be entirely misunderstood if they were seen merely as a stubborn, headstrong, or unreasonable holding on to God under adverse circumstances. When Judaism, Christianity, and Islam appeal to God's goodness, mercy, reliability, and faithfulness, then this is not an arbitrary orientation by just one side of an equivocal conception of God but a reminder that the confession of God's goodness is due to the overcoming of the equivocations of experience-based conceptions of God by God himself: for them, "good" in connection with God is not just a word marking a contrast but a word marking *success* that brings out God's own decision not to remain obscure and equivocal for humanity but to exclusively and unambiguously be good. This stresses not only God's contrast with Evil but also the overcoming of Evil and the resolution, by God himself, of the ambiguity of a divine being good or evil in favor of his unambiguous being good for human beings. God is good because he wills not to remain ambiguous and puts an end to and overcomes Evil through good.

8. *life experiments:* This remains a merely abstract claim on the part of religions if we ignore that they have reached this insight by way of a kind of *experimentum crucis* that they commemorate in rituals and teachings as the central event of their history. Especially in the face of God's becoming ambiguous in the experiences of life and the loss it entails of the capacity to orient one's life individually and communally by God, the conception of God is systematically being rid of its ambiguity by a "life experiment" that clarifies the character of God's divinity and commits God to the good. The decisive point of this life experiment is that it is not a conception of God that is being tested here by way of experiences as to whether it is more likely or not to be tenable. Instead, human living and acting brings about a situation characterized by a rigorous and complete alternative: here it either turns out that God remains wholly unpredictable, obscure, and ingraspable because it is not possible to see what he wills and does since good and evil are to be associated with him in impenetrable ways. Then there is no use trying to orient human life by God because there is nothing to be seen by which one could orient oneself (in the case of God's obscure ambivalence) or because it becomes very clear that God deserves to be called not God but devil (in the case of the indistinguishability of God from Evil). Or he proves not to be obscure or evil but so good that he can be identified with his goodness, not just in this but in every situation. Then it is possible to orient human life by him even if in concrete experiences it remains obscure how and where God is to be sought in them. For it is not they that define whether God is good, but God defines what is good.

9. *tensions between faith in God and life experience*: This, too, comes at a price, of course, namely at the price of permanent conflict between faith in God and life experience. The two are never without tension but are only ever to be referred to each other dialectically. For on the one hand the goodness associated with God is never fully congruent with the realities of life, while on the other hand the connection between God and the realities of life must not become so vague that orientation

by God no longer yields orientation in life. If the former is not observed, the result is an enthusiastic, foreshortened, and one-sided faith that characteristically fails to perceive the realities of life. If the latter is not observed, faith and life remain without consequence for each other, and there is thus no more faith. Yet even if these extremes are avoided, fundamentally two possibilities remain.

10. *theodicy conflicts*: On the one hand, this can lead life experience to become a permanent objection to faith in God and lead Evil to become the basic touchstone of the conception of God. This happens in the theodicy debates of modernity. There the conception of God's goodness, omnipotence, and omniscience is no longer seen and understood against the background of what these "words of success" commemorate as the overcoming of ambivalences of the notion of God that are rooted in experience. The content of these attributes is then no longer developed from the stories and memories they summarize. Instead, the attempt is made to explicate this content directly by taking recourse to the life experience thematized in each case. The effect throughout of this approach is that the evil experienced in each case triumphs over the believed goodness of God because it is of greater experiential evidence than a conception of God in faith that has been emptied of its origins and turned into a formula.

11. *alternative realities*: On the other hand, however, it can also lead not to a revision of faith in God in the face of irreconcilable life experiences but to a mobilization of faith in God against the reality experienced. In the orientation toward God, who, excluding other possibilities, has bindingly and reliably committed himself to willing and working the best for each of his creatures, faith in God is asserted as permanent objection to the insufficiencies of life experience and of the world of experience. That faith in God's goodness cannot be made congruent with life experience does not result in dismissing faith in God but in hope for a different and better life. The recourse to God becomes the definitive objection to Evil in life; Evil in life does not become an irresolvable contradiction of the orientation by God. And that means that religious life takes place no longer primarily or exclusively in the mode of believing and knowing but of hoping and loving. In the Christian case, faith in God's presence in Jesus Christ and his Spirit is then not a theoretical conviction of faith foreign to life, which in the best of cases results in a life according to the double commandment of love and, in many cases, is completely abandoned in the face of the experienced adversities of life, but the exact opposite: the faith in the world-changing and life-renewing reality of the trinitarian God expresses a life of hope for God's goodness and love that make everything new, a life according to the double commandment of love. The hope for God does not teach us to bear the reality of Evil in life but on the contrary makes us sensitive to the fact that it is entirely unbearable.[10] "God is good" is thus the permanent objection to a reality that is not the way it could be and ought to be. And this is why the standard for faith in God is not reality but this critical objection to resigning oneself to it.

---

10. See Hebblethwaite, *Evil, Suffering and Religion*, 95–106.

7. Matter and Evil Deed

All this, of course, does not even touch on a decisive point: If the *malum* experienced in this life is not to be traced back to God, then to whom? *Si deus, unde malum?* All (as Herms says, "nonheretical") theological answers in the creation-theological religions that are Judaism, Christianity, and Islam suppose that the answer must be given via recourse not to the creator but to creation.[11] The Christian tradition has developed two main strategies for a solution that are interlinked at many points and not limited to this tradition alone.

The first is the *ontological-cosmological solution* that sees Evil to result from the insufficiency of what has been created, that is, from that which allows and makes it possible for creatures to be not as good as they could be and ought to be. The guiding concept of this attempt at a solution is *matter*, which represents the potential of what has been created to become and to change. Because all that is created is capable of and stands in need of betterment, it is not as good as could be; instead, it is a combination (to be determined in detail for each case) of *malum* and *bonum*, of what causes its deficits (matter) and what grounds its reality (form). The difficulties of this attempted solution are not just that it moves within the framework of the problematic metaphysics of an ontological hylomorphism: as the dominant categorial horizon of the thinking of an age, that is by no means an inappropriate frame of reference for a theological treatment of the problem. The difficulty is above all that within this intellectual framework no solution can be found that would not raise even greater theological problems. The path to a solution thus taken either leads to a theologically unacceptable dualism of matter and form that the *privatio boni* theory keeps at bay only with great effort. Or it results in the theologically no less unacceptable thesis that the matter created by God and, like everything created, declared to be good is what makes other things not good but evil and bad. This would send responsibility for *malum* in creation directly back to God and the problem to be solved would, precisely, not be solved.

That the problem did not go unnoticed is evident in the reflections of many early Christian theologians. According to Origen, for instance, matter cannot simply be designated as *causa mali* but is doubly coded: it is the creator's first institution for saving creation.[12] For if God had not created the visible universe to save them from this fate, the souls created from eternity would have fallen from the presence of the origin of being into nothing. "The present constitution of the world is thus the result of the special care of divine providence."[13] Material-sensible existence is not *ipso facto* ill or evil, it is the first step toward redemption whose second step consists in being liberated from this stopgap of materially ensuring life and being restituted to a full life in the reality of God.

Yet the reason for *malum* can then no longer be sought and found in matter as such, since matter is already a helping reaction on God's part to the *malum* of creatures' turning away from their creator. That is why for Christian thinking, this first, ontological-cosmological attempt at a solution has always been and has always remained insufficient.

11. See Herms, "Das Böse: Systematische Überlegungen," 238, 244–56.

12. See Roukema, "L'Origine du mal selon Origène."

13. Geyer, "Das Böse in der Perspektive von Christentum und Neuplatonismus," 242.

The second path is *the solution of the theology of action*, which attempts to think Evil as expression and consequence of evil acting, that is, to think *malum* as sin. It whole-heartedly takes up the basic assumption of a creation-theological view of the world: all that differs from God, that is, all that is becoming and can become, is due to the decision on the part of the creator that it be and can become and not rather not. Nothing is that is not willed by God, and nothing is willed by God of which it is not true that it is good because God wills it. Yet how can *malum* arise in what God wills as good? How, under the conditions of God's being the creator, can there be something "that strives against and works against the creators willing and working," that is, something that is *evil*?[14] Only in one way, according to the central thesis of this tradition, namely that among the things God wills and creates, there are also creatures who, thanks to their horizon and capacity, are able to decide between *malum* and *bonum* themselves. For there would be no *bonum* in creation if it could not be distinguished from *malum*, and since that is possible, there must at least be the possibility of *malum*: only where there can be *malum* there can also be *bonum*.

When this notion is connected with a central series of arguments of Aristotelianism according to which all that and only that is possible that either was actual, is actual, or will be actual, then the reality of *bonum* is to be had only at the price of the possibility of *bonum or malum*, but this possibility only at the price that what can be sooner or later is: where *malum* is possible, it will sooner or later be actual. That it is *possible* is due to God who wills there to be good in his creation and therefore creates the possibility of good or evil. That, in contrast, it becomes *actual*, i.e., in fact, a *malum*, and that what is being actualized is not always only *bonum*, that is due exclusively to the creatures who bring it about with their decisions. As creator, God is responsible solely for the *possibility of Evil or Good* in created life; for the *reality of Evil* sole responsibility lies with the creature who has thus decided.

On the one hand, then, God creates creatures that are not simply what they are but that are to make themselves into what they can make themselves: God makes creatures make themselves. On the other hand, the creatures who are able to do so are characterized by two things. First, they differ from all other creatures in being able to choose and decide between *malum* and *bonum*. The tradition considered this to be what distinguishes human beings (and angels) from all other creatures. Second, they differ from God, their creator, in that unlike him they also must decide between the two, that they cannot *not* choose between *malum* and *bonum*. Yet if it is true that they both can and must choose, then there is nobody who lives and does not decide this way or that; and if *malum* is possible only because it is or will be actually true, then there can be a decision for a *bonum* only because and insofar the *malum* is chosen as well.

This, however, has consequences. For if someone decides in favor of *malum* just one single time, a state of affairs is created that cannot in any way be reversed. Because no one can act retroactively, but everyone only ever can and must act prospectively, evil that has happened cannot be abolished, eliminated, or reversed by any good that is done now or in the future. It will instead always be true and remain true that a *malum* has happened, and no future conduct or action of this or any other creature can reverse that.

14. Herms, "Das Böse: Systematische Überlegungen," 238.

That is why all *malum* in creation has the form of *malum facere* or *malum pati*, of doing or suffering evils; and all *malefecere* presupposes a *male velle* or *bene nolle*, a willing of evil or not willing of good, if acting is always to be understood as *facere* in the sense of deciding between Good and Evil. Insofar as there is evil, it is thus done by someone who did not have to do it, and it is suffered by someone who did not have to suffer it. When a *malum* is inflicted on someone, it must be assessed in a differentiated way. It happens unjustly when they have done nothing wrong and have not deserved the *malum*. It happens justly, in contrast, when that is not the case, when the *malum* inflicted, rather, is a reaction to *malum* done to others or to oneself. There is much leeway here for considerations concerning the appropriate or inappropriate scope of the ill that can, may, or must be returned to an ill doer for an ill deed. Yet it is clear that judges or police officers are not ill doers, even if they inflict ill on a human being because this ill is punishment for injustice committed. This figure of thought finally also allows for assessing God's action: when God inflicts *malum* on a creature, then it is never anything other than punishment for the creature's transgression, it is nothing that would be *malum* in the sense that it would be due to a *male velle* or *bene nolle* on God's part. Rather, God's punishing, too, is an expression and manifestation of his goodness and justice, not because it would have to be good for the punished perpetrator (although that could be said as well) but above all because in this way, justice is done for the victim of the perpetrator's ill deed. God when he punishes is good because he thereby brings the victims justice. And whatever one might think theologically about this entirely classic model of thought: any theologically acceptable solution to the problem will have to hold on to that notion.

8. Fortune and Misfortune in Life

Yet the question where Evil comes from in a creation that is good in principle because it is willed by God is not the only and probably not the most important problem for Christian faith. For whatever the answer given may be, what is decisive is that evil is not just possible but actually real. There is evil, and humans and other organisms suffer from it. Believers start from this reality when they turn to God with laments and petitions. If it cannot in principle be prevented and changed that evil exists in the variety of ills, how can we prevent or avoid on occasion becoming entangled in and being affected by evil? Is there a connection between the way we live our lives and happiness in our lives, between being affected by evil and the lives we lead? And can this connection be clarified via recourse to God?

In ever-new attempts, the biblical tradition has tried to answer these questions and in so doing has succeeded in clarifying and specifying the conception of Evil and the conception of God. Central here is the question if there is a regular connection between human conduct and happiness or unhappiness in life, an order by which we can and must orient our conduct to avoid experiences of *malum* and to have experiences of *bonum*. The orienting basic contrast, accordingly, is the one between *just* and *unjust*, where those are just who live in accordance with God's will and those are unjust who in fact or intentionally do not do so. Can those who live justly also count on a good and happy life? And will those who do not live justly also have no good and happy life?

The precondition for being able to make this distinction is the recourse to God's will from whose perspective the decision is made what a just life and an unjust life is. From the point of view of this problem, God is thus seen concretely and explicitly as *will*, as *divine will*.[15] The point of this will is that through it, the relationship between this will and everything else is organized in such a way that created life is possible and human beings can lead a good life in orienting themselves by God's will.

To this end, it does not suffice that a divine will orders everything in a good way, that there is thus a divine will that can posit and preserve a good order because it has the capacity and the power to do so, and that, although it would also be possible not to will so and not to do so, does not not will so and not not do so such that his faithfulness can be relied on: in order to orient oneself by this will in the world thus ordered and adopt specific modes of conduct, it must also be possible to recognize this will. The necessary recourse to God's will would become impossible if this will were unknown. To be sure, a life is just or unjust even if it does not explicitly know God's will but factually accords or does not accord with it; and that is precisely what is supposed of every human life because the will of God applies without restrictions to everyone,[16] such that there is no one who would not factually live justly or unjustly. No one is not either just or unjust because there is no situation of life that would not be subject to the standard of God's will. But it is part and parcel of the logic of this train of thought that it would be downright unjust if God's will would remain concealed in principle and not be accessible in such a way that human beings could explicitly know it and orient their lives by it. God would be unjust if he withheld from humanity that which decides the justness or unjustness and thus also the happiness or unhappiness of their human lives. God, accordingly, is confessed to be just not only because his will for humanity is just but because it is right and just that in the Law, he explicitly reveals his will to them: *what* God is and wills and *that* God declares to human beings what he wills are both basic traits of his justice. God's will would not be just if it were not revealed to humans as a will posited for them. God's justice essentially stands and falls with the revelation of his justice to humanity.

God's will becoming known is thus the precondition for measuring the justness or unjustness of human life by the standard of the will of God: without the *law* given by

15. The question, however, is not "whether there is will in God," as Aquinas asks and answers in the affirmative by pointing out that every being that has an intellect also has will (*Summa Theologiae*, I q19 a1). The question continues to be debated in this manner to this day; see for example Weingartner, "Kommentar zu Thomas von Aquin" and *Evil*, 77–95. When in the context of evil and good that are being experienced, the question of God's will comes up, the issue is not whether God has a will but *that* and *which* will God *is*: whether his effective presence among his creatures is a *bonum* or *malum* for them generally and in the concrete case being discussed, such that one must thank him or rail against him.

16. This, too, must be expressed in a historically and objectively differentiated way. The discovery of the universal validity and at the same time of the different scope of different dimensions of God's will (as creator, as redeemer, and as perfecter) was itself a historical discovery that was made only gradually. The will of God applies to everyone but not for everyone in the same way, as the bond with Israel highlights, and that is why not everything attributed to God's will applies to everyone in every respect and in the same way. The content and scope of the will of God can be determined in different ways, and it was once again in a process that must be traced historically that the core content of God's will was concentrated in the Torah; that the Torah, in turn, was concentrated in what Christians capture in the double commandment of love; and that what initially seemed to oblige only a few came to be seen to be binding for others or for all others, that is, Yahweh's henotheistic will for his people became God's monotheistic will for all.

God to humanity, that is, the revelation of God's good will for his creatures, for humanity, and for his people, there would be no orienting standard for a just life and thus no possibility to codetermine the happiness of our life through the conduct of our lives. The following typical sets of problems have been particularly important and consequential in this context.

1. *The Adam paradigm*: An elementary connection is said to exist between human doing and the suffering of evil: those who do evil will suffer evil, and those who suffer evil can be supposed to have done evil. This is a widely shared conviction, not just in religions. Where the life of people is damaged, weighed down, or destroyed by *malum*, it is a consequence of their evil action.

Here already, however, a fundamental problem appears that in the course of developing the religious interpretation of this maxim via the recourse to God's will comes out ever more clearly: the question whether the evil that we do and the evil that we suffer is *evil in the same sense*. From the religious point of view, *evil* is always that which violates God's will, not necessarily on purpose but factually. Accordingly, the *malum* happening to humans, too, is usually seen as something that according to God's will ought not to be, such that both, evil done and evil suffered, are evil by virtue of contradicting the will of God.

This, however, contains a supposition that the experienced reality of life such as the biblical texts reflect it increasingly renders doubtful: the supposition that what happens to humans as *malum* in their lives is *ipso facto* something that according to God ought not to be. Is what is evil *for us* to be equated in a uniform manner with what deserves to be called evil *from God's perspective*? Is the *malum* humans suffer *malum in the same sense* as the *malum* they commit in intentionally or unintentionally violating the will of God? Could it not be the case that some things that are *evil for us* are not for that reason alone something that is to be defined as *malum from God's perspective*, that is, contradicts his will? And is the situation of the reality of evil in human life not to be described more precisely such that human experiences of *malum* and the divine judgment of *malum* are always in tension with each other and are to be related to each other without from the outset being congruent or ever becoming congruent? Only on this precondition does it make sense to ask whether *this specific malum* with which a human being has to deal concretely in her life is also a *malum* in God's sense, that is, to inquire into God's will with regard to a concrete happening in life. Otherwise, the mere fact that a *malum* happens to human beings would simply by itself justify the conclusion that God does not will this to happen. Then it would be human experience that would decide what contradicts the will of God but not God's will that would decide what *malum* is in human life. And then the false judgment suggests itself that the mere fact that something is not experienced as *malum by us* also proves that it is not a *malum coram deo*.

Yet if this is recognized to be a problem because we do not have to experience and judge the evil we do to be evil ourselves, as sinners exemplarily demonstrate, then a twofold possibility must be taken into account. On the one hand, even people's seemingly good conduct and experience before God might have to be classified and assessed as *malum*. On the other, it is true with regard to human life that between what we experience as *malum* and what is a *malum* before God, a difference opens up such that it not only makes sense but becomes necessary to ask in each case whether the *malum* experienced as such in the human (experiential) sense is also a *malum* in God's (judging) sense or not. What seems evil to us because it affects our life as evil is not inevitably evil in God's sense as well. And what does not seem evil to us because it does not seem to damage our lives or that of others is not inevitably not evil or even good in God's sense.

Religious experience and religious thinking did not encounter these questions and distinctions from the outset. Instead, we can observe how most of the time, the identity of the two senses of Evil is supposed in a downright self-evident manner when life is lived according to the rule that those who do evil will also suffer evil and those who suffer evil must also have done evil. In the biblical tradition, this is presented exemplarily in Adam and Eve who, according to the story of Genesis, owe their hard life and the ill lot they suffer from to their own misconduct toward God. The reality of evil in life is self-incurred. The point is not made without differentiation: it is possible to be defrauded of what is good without being responsible for it, such that one does not have the happiness in life one would be entitled to. The biblical tradition has thought this through exemplarily in the story of Esau, who was cheated by his brother Jacob out of the blessing of his father Isaac, which he would have been entitled to as the firstborn son, without in any way being responsible for being cheated (Gen 27). Not everyone in their lives receives what they would actually be entitled to. In that sense, life is by no means just. Yet good we are entitled to but do not receive is something different from evil we incur. According to the Adam paradigm, we are ourselves responsible for such evil, or otherwise it would not affect us.

Evidently, the boundaries between the good we do not receive although we would be entitled to it and the evil we are said to have incurred ourselves are fluid. The development, of course, did not end with this overly simple model because it all too obviously fails in the encounter with reality. By contrast, the biblical tradition emphatically rejects the widespread notion of inflicting evil through magical action: those affected by evil cannot talk their way out by claiming it to have been pinned on them by someone else without being at fault themselves. Having been bewitched is no explanation for evil happening to them. In all events, the Adam paradigm stresses that it is not God who is responsible for Evil in the lives of human beings but they themselves. God is just because he punishes evil with evil. But he is also just—and this is the second point—because he rewards good with good.

2. *The Noah paradigm*: The Adam paradigm, according to which evil in life is the consequence of evil action, has a correlate in the Noah paradigm, according to which good in life is what someone who acts well can and may expect. Because Noah was the only one to live piously and righteously, he and his family are spared God's wrath. This does not change anything about the fact that humans do not renounce evil actions, as the continuation of the story shows. But God is just because he rewards good with good, and the covenant with Noah underscores that God no longer wills to punish Evil by destroying those who are evil but becomes reliable and predictable in his goodness: he helps those who are good and punishes those who are evil, but he does not destroy all life for the sake of those who are evil.

3. *The Job paradigm*: The unequivocal connection the Adam and Noah paradigms describe between evil deeds and evil consequences and good deeds and good consequences stands up to real life only so much. On the contrary, ill doers are faring well, as the psalmist knows, and the good are faring ill. We find this in the biblical story of Cain and Abel, which expresses both the spreading evil and God's attempt at containing it with good: Abel is unjustly killed by Cain, but God ensures that the perpetrator does not suffer the same fate. The evil strikes the one who is just, and if God did not protect the unjust from the consequences of his evil doing, all would die in the affair.

The Job novella reflects in detail on the problem thus sketched. How are we to deal with good and just conduct not being followed by the expected good life but by an entirely miserable and evil life? The book rigorously rejects the explanation that suggests itself, namely that God is responsible for the good and someone other than God, the tempter, is responsible for Evil. Both, the good and the evil in life go back entirely to God, both are the work of the creator, even if by means of the evil he seeks to test and prove Job's justness and piousness. That, however, means that the regulated connection that Job's friends evoke again and again, between good actions and a good life or between evil actions and an evil life, is being dissolved. It is not possible to deduce from the good or the evil in a person's life that he is good or evil and has acted in a good or evil way. Job is steadfast in insisting that he has done nothing wrong before God. He is thus in no way responsible for the evil that has affected him. He no longer accepts the traditional figure of thought, not because he rebels against God but precisely because he appeals to the justice attributed to God: if God is responsible for all the ills in his life, then God must justify himself. The consequence is not just that the legal process becomes the model, in which it is not God who calls the human but the human being who calls God to the bar. It is also that the happiness experienced in life is being disconnected from religiously and morally good conduct: the justification for leading a good and just life can no longer be that one will then also do well in life. Those who live a good and just life cannot justify doing so by eyeing the happiness in life this might procure, they must consider doing so worth doing as such and for its own sake. Then—as the end of the Job novella shows—they may hope that God will do good for them. That, however, is never a direct consequence of our own doing but always the free gift and grace of God, not a happiness to be achieved but always a gift we owe to God.

There is thus no demonstrable and regular connection, either in good or in evil, between the conduct of our lives and happiness in our lives. This has three important consequences.

1. It increases humans' responsibility for doing good: they must do it for its own sake and cannot justify it with the consequences to be obtained.

2. It also relieves humans of the responsibility for the ill and evil that strikes them: they do not have to look for the causes of all the ill that affects them in their lives in themselves, and the same is true with regard to others. Not everyone to whom ill happens is an ill person. Only where that is understood can an attitude of commiserating with the suffering of others develop because they are not regularly to be held responsible for the ills they suffer.

3. God more than ever becomes the one who is to be thanked for all that is good in life: he, not humans and their behavior, are responsible for it. But God also becomes the one to whom ultimately all that is evil in life must be traced back.

The Job solution, therefore, on the one hand, leads to a liberating relief for humans as regards responsibility for the ill that strikes them, yet simultaneously, on the other hand, it corrodes the approach of seeking to understand evil in life starting from the creature, not from the creator. It now seems to be the creator after all who, in his impenetrable power, is ultimately responsible for everything. It is no coincidence that the book of Job ends by emphasizing God's power as creator. Yet this is a rejection of the question concerning the origin of evil more than it is an answer. By disconnecting mode of life and happiness in life, the theological search for the one who is responsible for Evil leads to a dead end.

9. The End of Ambiguity

As a consequence, the orientation by God itself becomes questionable and does so in different respects. First, it is no longer possible to claim that orienting our lives by God will also lead to a life that by the standards of human experience deserves being called good. Neither wealth nor success nor happiness may be cited as purposes for the sake of which a life is to be oriented by God. All that can, but it does not have to occur. Pious people are not faring better than non-pious people, often they are even faring worse. It will thus be no more possible to justify orienting our lives by God with reference to purposes thereby attainable than it is to justify leading a morally good life in this way. It must be striven for as a value in itself, not as a means to another end. Those who love God love him without any other sense and purpose than for the sake of the love of God alone. Only in this way do we live up to God's disinterested love for the other of himself. And only in this way can the love of God become the basic orientation of a life that shapes and defines all purposes pursued and means employed there.

Important strands in Judaism, Christianity, and Islam did, of course, see this differently and some still do. If orientation by God does not yield anything positive in this life—this is already the argument in the late writings of the Old Testament and in early Rabbinic Judaism—then it must "pay off" in a later life.[17] This does not alter the rule but the domain where it applies. It thinks according to the same schema the Job novella had thrown into question: the connection between doing good and faring well, which is empirically untenable, is installed eschatologically. Criticism of religion does not fully grasp this when it sees it as consoling postponement to a beyond because its point lies in life here and now: conduct here decides the goodness of life there. Because we want our lives there to be better than our lives here, we live (morally) good lives here. Yet that, precisely, means that we live *in order to. . . .* We practice morality not for its own sake but as a means to an end. And God, too, is not being loved for his own sake but as a means to an end. This "natural eschatology," which expects from another life what cannot be obtained in this one, thinks the relationship between these two lives in entirely

---

17. Berger, *Wie kann Gott Leid und Katastrophen zulassen?*, 18–19.

traditional terms and thus includes all the questionable issues the biblical paradigms of Adam, Noah, and Job deal with: those who lead a good and just life here will fare well and justly there. And those who lead an ill and evil life here will fare ill and evil there. Heaven and hell are the eschatological correlates of a hope that counts not on God's love but on the effects of what we do and do not do ourselves.

This precisely is what those versions of Christian eschatology omit that do not start from the good or evil actions of humans in this life but from the surprisingly allotted good God grants a life. We will then expect good in the next life not because we count on a reward for good actions in this life and on evil actions being punished but because we hope for God's goodness. The hope is directed at God's unconditional grace and mercy, not at the eschatological tenability of an empirically untenable rule. The object of this hope is not the happiness of the good and the unhappiness of the evildoers in the beyond but the God of whom we know and confess that he has unconditionally and without constraint committed himself to love for his creatures. God is good and that is why he will arrange things for the good—that is the Christian hope, not that we will fare well because we have led a good life.

This, however, has one important precondition: we can say and confess that God is good and reliable in his goodness only if God has not become entirely obscure and ambiguous in our life. And that is why this, precisely, is the great danger that the biblical texts note and try to exclude again and again. Yet without recourse to the experiences of others, it cannot be excluded: precisely because in our own experience, God time and again threatens to become obscure, it is indispensable for us to be able to refer to the experience of others. Our own life is too narrow ground to found a definitive judgment about the faith on it. That is why there is no great religion without a tradition, and the tradition always says more than our own experience can live up to and confirm. Indeed, it is essential to the tradition that it resists this: it goes beyond a given individual life and reminds us that each life is embedded in the lives of others and the history of the world in complex ways. In the individual, the questions erupt that go beyond the individual; and in the whole, the decisions are made concerning what is valid in the individual.

According to central biblical traditions, God's unambiguous reliability, too, is not always and everywhere conspicuous for everyone in their own lives. As the paradigmatic story of Abraham shows, God proves to be reliably good to those who unflinchingly count on his being just that and live and act accordingly. Even if we might not experience it that way in our concrete life, God is good and just and reliable because God has committed himself to it, as the *aqeda* story reminds us. And that applies, as the paradigmatic story of Jesus shows, even when we do not experience God's goodness and reliability ourselves. That is the moment of universalization inscribed in Christian faith and hope: it always pushes beyond itself because extensively and intensively, it hopes for more from God than it experiences or does not experience.[18]

18. This is the starting point for thinking God himself as a theogonic process, as Schelling attempted to do: "because God is a life, not merely a Being," yet all life "is subject to suffering and becoming," "the time when God will be all in all things, that is, when he will be fully realized" must be "posit[ed] as a distant future" (Schelling, *Philosophical Investigations into the Essence of Human Freedom*, 66). See Rosenau, "Theogonie." This is the very notion also taken up and developed by Whitehead, *Process and Reality*, and process philosophy. A God thus thought as a process of actualization is comprehensible as the correlate

The price to be paid, of course, is that there is no (more) direct inference from concrete life experience to God's character. No life experience taken by itself can as such serve to prove the reliability of God's goodness or to throw it into doubt. This suggests two possible reactions.

The first is that of *indifference*. If experience no longer reliably shows that orientation by God makes life good or at least better, then this orientation can be dispensed with. The orientation of life by God must manifest in a noticeable increase of happiness in life, or otherwise one can do without it. In that case, thinking in terms of means and ends governs religious life as well.

The second is the *eschatological hope for God*. The fact that God's goodness is not being experienced in life unambiguously and by everyone can strengthen faith in God or problematize it, but it cannot problematize that which makes it true: what and how God truly is. That is why faith always features a counterfactual trait expressed in the objection to a reality of life that never unambiguously manifests God's goodness. And accordingly, the eschatological hope is aimed at the reality of life becoming such that it no longer stands in contrast but in correlation with faith in God's reliable goodness. The world must change, not God, and the world changes for the good when it becomes the mirror of God's goodness.

The two options of indifference toward God and the eschatological hope for God are at the same time alternative attitudes toward the moral instrumentalization of faith. Both suppose that faith demonstrably does not morally improve human beings. Yet they draw opposite conclusions from this. One side therefore considers faith to be superfluous and dispensable, the other side considers it for that very reason to be more than necessary: faith does not solve any problem of life in a better way, but it gives life a horizon within which it is possible to live trusting that God will assert his goodness in remaking every life into a mirror of his goodness. Nothing is as good as it could be and ought to be before God, yet every human being is such that God makes the fragment of life of this human being into the place where his goodness will eschatologically appear. Hope for God thus does not change anything in life, it changes the human attitude toward life in that human beings in this hope refer to God in such a way that they distance themselves from their immediate experience and are able to view this experience from the perspective of God and in light of his work in creation.

10. Consequences for Life

The consequences of this change of attitude for life are more incisive than a merely partial revision of a partial aspect because they affect everything. For how do we live and how should we live if we orient ourselves in this sense by a God who is not ambiguous and obscure but who clarifies himself?

---

of the Christian hope for God that time and again pushes beyond any concretion. If this dynamic of hope is disregarded, though, and God is conceived of as a theogonic-cosmological process, the image of God of Christian hope is being ontologized in a problematic way because it is being detached from the relation of hope central to the life of the Christian faith.

The answer of Job is that we ought not to make our moral and religious life depend either on one another or on a third: we are urged to live a morally good life not only when we may thereby gain happiness in life, respect, security, and reputation but also when these do not come to pass. And it is worth living religiously not only when we will profit from it, if not in this life, then in the next. Just as the morally good is to be chosen and done *for its own sake*, so the religiously good is to be chosen and lived *for its own sake*. We are not good *in order to . . .*, even if there is no need to balk at or protest against faring well. And we also do not live oriented by God *in order to . . .* but because in the attitude toward the world and toward life thus assumed and thereby to be obtained, we live more serenely by taking that distance and live more intensely in the relationship. Those who relate to themselves, their lives, and their world via God differ from themselves in such a way that they become free from the ties of their history, their lives, their world. And at the same time, they thereby refer to the world thus coming into view as creation and as the world of their neighbors in such a way that from the freedom gained, the commitment of love on behalf of the other is released and arises. That is why it is no coincidence that freedom and love are the basic ethical figures by which to describe the life of faith: as a *freedom from everything* that could tie us down and distract us from God and as a *love for everything* that is due to freedom and is therefore a bond that cannot be demanded from anyone but can only be freely rendered.

This also applies to the living of life vis-à-vis God, that is, to actively and explicitly religious life. Because in faith, we live in a different attitude to everything than without faith, everything comes into view from the differentiating perspective of freedom and love. And that means that everything is not viewed in the same way but that life in the multitude of its situations is viewed in a differentiated manner and related to God: we are grateful for what is good, lament what is ill, and accuse where we are affected by evil we can assign to someone responsible. It is thus no coincidence that religions offer a highly differentiated cultic repertoire that cannot be reduced to one basic attitude toward everything. Those who see themselves as creatures and the world as God's creation perceive it in the entire infinite diversity in which it exists before God. And they refer to what affects them as *bonum* or *malum* in the differentiated diversity appropriate to it.

Accordingly, dealing with evil in life is not a simple but a differentiated undertaking. A first differentiation refers to what affects us and to the way in which it affects us, that is, to the descriptive and the evaluative component of Evil. It is necessary to make this distinction in order to be able to distinguish more precisely between the different respects in which we can and must engage with the reality of Evil and to be able to define the tasks that thereby arise with more precision.

The second differentiation concerns the different descriptively distinguishable domains in which something that affects us as evil can occur: medicine, law, morality, technology, and so on. In the differentiating development of the sciences, each discipline has found the forms that allow it to explain and shape what is happening in these domains. Scientific and technological labor here does not directly engage evil but works on reducing the occasions of experiences of evil and thus works to restrict evil.

In the domain of religion, the special concern is not with controlling and eliminating evil in life but with gaining a new attitude without which there is no sober way of dealing with what can be done or not be done, with what would have to be and ought to be done, and with what need not be done. A religious life is the gift of a life attitude and its active intensification, in which everything comes to be seen in the light of what God does for human life and for his creation as a whole.

This includes the insight that much remains nonsensical and cannot be resolved and rendered comprehensible. Living with this and being able to live with it is what faith offers guidance on. It does so precisely not by promoting and maintaining the illusion of a definitive abolition of all nonsensicalness and all destruction in life but by guiding a life of hope that counts on God and on nothing else. For this not only keeps in mind that the nonsensical and evil is not all there is in life (this can also be achieved by recalling what came before and what other possibilities there are in the evil reality) but also that it is not the last and decisive thing, because God in his conduct toward humanity does not let himself be defined, stopped, or hindered by it. The hope faith places in God is the hope and confidence that nothing is so evil and no *malum* so great that it could separate human beings from God's love, that it could make them immune and inaccessible to this love. Those who hope have faith in the greater power of God's love over against all evil, a power that does not consist in the levelling of evil but in distinguishing and saving the human beings affected from what affects them as evil in their lives. God's love is love for human beings in their suffering from the ills of their lives, even when suffering from them seems to destroy their lives. Saying that God's love is always greater does not minimize Evil; on the contrary, it praises the power of the divine love, which does not come up against its limits where not only human beings' capacities but their very imagination fails. God loves the creature into life—into his life. And no ill that affects it and no evil that seems to destroy it can make it fall from this life.

Bibliography

Abel, R. Christopher, and William O. Hare. *Hermes Trismegistus: An Investigation into the Origin of the Hermetic Writings.* Edmonds, WA: Alexandrian, 1997.

Adams, Marilyn McCord. *Horrendous Evils and the Goodness of God.* Ithaca, NY: Cornell University Press, 1999.

———. "Horrors in Theological Context." *Scottish Journal of Theology* 55, no. 4 (2002) 468–79.

———. "Theodicy without Blame." *Philosophical Topics* 16, no. 2 (1988) 215–45.

Adams, Marilyn McCord, and Robert Merrihew Adams, eds. *The Problem of Evil.* Oxford: Oxford University Press, 1990.

Aeschylus. *Agamemnon.* Translated by Herbert Weir Smyth. New York: Putnam, 1926.

Ahern, M. B. *The Problem of Evil.* New York: Schocken, 1971.

Alston, William P. "The Evidential Argument From Evil." In *The Inductive Argument from Evil and the Human Cognitive Condition*, edited by Daniel Howard-Snyder, 97–125. Bloomington: Indiana University Press, 1996.

Alt, Karin. *Weltflucht und Weltbejahung: Zur Frage des Dualismus bei Plutarch, Numenios, Plotin.* Mainz: Akademie der Wissenschaften und der Literatur, 1993.

Ammicht-Quinn, Regina. *Von Lissabon bis Auschwitz: Zum Paradigmawechsel in der Theodizeefrage.* Freiburg: Herder, 1992.

Anderson, G. A. "Abraham III.1." In *Religion Past and Present*, edited by Hans Dieter Betz et al., 1:13–14. Brill: Leiden, 2008.

Anselm of Canterbury. *The Major Works.* Edited by Brian Davies and G. R. Evans. Oxford: Oxford University Press, 1998.

———. *Opera Omnia.* Edited by Franciscus Salesius Schmitt. Stuttgart: Frommann, 1968.

Antommarchi, François Carlo. *Mémoires du docteur F. Antommarchi, ou les derniers moments de Napoléon.* Vol. 1. Paris: Barrois L'Aîné, 1825.

Aquinas, Thomas. *Summa contra gentiles.* Translated by the English Dominican Fathers. London: Burns, Oates, and Washbourne, 1934.

———. *Summa Theologiae.* Translated by the English Dominican Fathers. New York: Benziger, 1947–48.

Arendt, Hannah. *Eichmann in Jerusalem: A Report on the Banality of Evil.* New York: Viking, 1963.

———. *Ich will verstehen: Selbstauskünfte zu Leben und Werk.* Edited by Ursula Ludz. Munich: Piper, 1996.

———. *Men in Dark Times.* New York: Harcourt, Brace and World, 1968.

———. *On Evil.* Translated by Jean T. Oesterle and John A. Oesterle. Notre Dame: University of Notre Dame Press, 1995.

———. *On Revolution.* London: Penguin, 1990.

Arendt, Hannah, et al. *Nach Auschwitz.* Berlin: Tiamat, 1989.

Aristotle. *Aristotelis ethica Nicomachea.* Edited by Ingram Bywater. Oxford: Clarendon, 1984.

———. *Aristotelis Metaphysica.* Edited by Ingram Bywater. Oxford: Clarendon, 1984.

———. *The Complete Works of Aristotle: The Revised Oxford Translation.* Edited by Jonathan Barnes. 2 vols. Princeton: Princeton University Press, 1984.

Arnold, Clinton E. *Powers of Darkness: Principalities and Powers in Paul's Letters.* Downers Grove: InterVarsity, 1992.

Assmann, Jan. *Politische Theologie zwischen Ägypten und Israel*. 3rd exp. ed. Munich: Carl Friedrich von Siemens Stiftung, 2006.

Auffarth, Christoph, and Loren T. Stuckenbruck, eds. *The Fall of the Angels*. Leiden: Brill, 2004.

Augustine. *The City of God Against the Pagans*. Translated by Philip Levine. Cambridge: Harvard University Press, 1966.

———. *Corpus Augustinianum Gissense* [CAG]. Edited by Cornelius Mayer. Basel: Schwabe, 1995.

———. *On the Holy Trinity; Doctrinal Treatises; Moral Treatises*. Edited by Philip Schaff. Nicene and Post-Nicene Fathers I.3. Buffalo: Christian Literature Company, 1887.

———. *On the Literal Interpretation of Genesis*. In *On Genesis: Two Books on Genesis Against the Manichees and On the Literal Interpretation of Genesis*, translated by Ronald J. Teske, 143–88. Washington, DC: Catholic University of America Press, 1991.

———. *The Works of Saint Augustine: A Translation for the 21st Century*. Edited by John E. Rotelle. New York: New City, 1990–2001.

———. *The Writings Against the Manichæans, and Against the Donatists*. Edited by Philip Schaff. Nicene and Post-Nicene Fathers I.4. Buffalo: Christian Literature Company, 1887.

Balz, Horst Robert, et al., eds. *Theologische Realenzyklopädie*. Berlin: De Gruyter, 1977.

Bandt, Hellmut. *Luthers Lehre vom verborgenen Gott: Eine Untersuchung zu dem offenbarungsgeschichtlichen Ansatz seiner Theologie*. Berlin: Evangelische Verlagsanstalt, 1958.

Barrera, Albino. *God and the Evil of Scarcity: Moral Foundations of Economic Agency*. Notre Dame: University of Notre Dame Press, 2005.

Barth, Gerhard. *Der Tod Jesu Christi im Verständnis des Neuen Testaments*. Neukirchen-Vluyn: Neukirchener Verlagshaus, 1992.

Barth, Karl. *Church Dogmatics*. 4 vols. Edinburgh: Clark, 1956–67.

Bartholomew, David J. *God of Chance*. London: SCM, 1984.

Basinger, David. *The Case for Freewill Theism: A Philosophical Assessment*. Downers Grove: InterVarsity, 1996.

———. "Simple Foreknowledge and Providential Control." *Faith and Philosophy* 10, no. 3 (1993) 421–27.

Battaglia, Vincent. "Si Deus, Unde *Malum*? A Critical Evaluation of Augustine's Theodicy." *Australasian Catholic Record* 83, no. 1 (2006) 38–53.

Baudler, Georg. "El-Jahwe-Abba: Der biblische Gott und die Theodizeefrage." *Theologie der Gegenwart* 41 (1998) 242–51.

Bauke, Jan. "Gottes Gerechtigkeit? Hinweise zur Theodizeeproblematik." *Zeitschrift für Theologie und Kirche* 102, no. 3 (2005) 333–51.

Baum, Wolfgang. *Gott nach Auschwitz: Reflexionen zum Theodizeeproblem im Anschluss an Hans Jonas*. Paderborn: Schöningh, 2004.

Baumeister, Roy F. *Evil: Inside Human Cruelty and Violence*. New York: Freeman, 1997.

Baumeister, Theofried. "Montanismus und Gnostizismus: Die Frage der Identität und Akkomodation des Christentums im 2. Jahrhundert." *Trierer theologische Zeitschrift* 87 (1978) 44–60.

Bayle, Pierre. *The Dictionary Historical and Critical of Mr. Peter Bayle*. 5 vols. 2nd ed. London: Knapton, 1739.

Beck, Martin. *Elia und die Monolatrie: Ein Beitrag zur religionsgeschichtlichen Rückfrage nach dem vorschriftprophetischen Jahwe-Glauben*. Berlin: De Gruyter, 1999.

Becker, Jürgen. *Jesus von Nazareth*. Berlin: De Gruyter, 1996.

Beckermann, Ansgar. "Neuronale Determiniertheit und Freiheit." In *Willensfreiheit als interdisziplinäres Problem*, edited by Kristian Köchy and Dirk Stederoth, 289–304. Freiburg: Alber, 2006.

Beilby, James K., et al., eds. *Divine Foreknowledge: Four Views*. Downers Grove: InterVarsity, 2001.

Beinert, Wolfgang, ed. *Gott—ratlos vor dem Bösen? Mit einer Stellungnahme Kardinal Ratzingers zum motu proprio "Ad tuendam fidem."* Freiburg: Herder, 1999.

Ben-Chorin, Schalom. *Die Erwählung Israels: Ein theologisch-politischer Traktat*. Munich: Piper, 1993.

Berger, Klaus. *Wie kann Gott Leid und Katastrophen zulassen?* Gütersloh: Gütersloher Verlagshaus, 1996.

Berner, Knut. *Theorie des Bösen: Zur Hermeneutik destruktiver Verknüpfungen*. Neukirchen-Vluyn: Neukirchener Verlagshaus, 2004.

Berthold, Fred. *God, Evil, and Human Learning: A Critique and Revision of the Free Will Defense in Theodicy*. Albany: State University of New York Press, 2004.

Best, W. E. *God Is Love*. Houston: South Belt Assembly of Christ, 1985.

Betz, Hans Dieter, et al., eds. *Religion Past and Present: Encyclopedia of Theology and Religion.* Leiden: Brill, 2007.

Beuken, Wim, ed. *The Book of Job.* Leuven: Leuven University Press, 1994.

Bieri, Peter. *Das Handwerk der Freiheit: Über die Entdeckung des eigenen Willens.* Munich: Hanser, 2001.

Bieringer, Reimund. "Aktive Hoffnung im Leiden: Gegenstand, Grund und Praxis der Hoffnung nach Roem 5, 1–5." *Theologische Zeitschrift* 51, no. 4 (1995) 305–25.

Bierl, Anton. *Dionysos und die griechische Tragödie: Politische und "metatheatralische" Aspekte im Text.* Tübingen: Narr, 1991.

Billicsich, Friedrich. *Von Platon bis Thomas von Aquino.* Vol. 1 of *Das Problem des Übels in der Philosophie des Abendlandes.* Vienna: Sexl, 1952.

Bloom, Howard K. *The Lucifer Principle: A Scientific Expedition into the Forces of History.* New York: Atlantic Monthly, 1995.

Blum, Erhard. "Abraham I. Old Testament." In *Religion Past and Present*, edited by Hans Dieter Betz et al., 1:111–13. Brill: Leiden, 2008.

Blumenberg, Hans. *Wirklichkeiten in denen wir leben: Aufsätze und eine Rede.* Stuttgart: Reclam, 1981.

Blumenfeld, David. "Leibniz's Ontological and Cosmological Arguments." In *The Cambridge Companion to Leibniz*, edited by Nicholas Jolley, 353–81. Cambridge: Cambridge University Press, 1995.

Blumenthal, David R. *Facing the Abusing God: A Theology of Protest.* Louisville: Westminster John Knox, 1993.

———. "Theodicy: Dissonance in Theory and Praxis." *Concilium*, no. 1 (1998) 95–106.

Böcher, Otto. *Christus Exorcista: Dämonismus und Taufe im Neuen Testament.* Stuttgart: Kohlhammer, 1972.

Boehm, Omri. "The Binding of Isaac: An Inner-Biblical Polemic on the Question of "Disobeying" a Manifestly Illegal Order." *Vetus Testamentum* 52, no. 1 (2002) 1–12.

Böhlig, Alexander, and Christoph Markschies. *Gnosis und Manichäismus: Forschungen und Studien zu Texten von Valentin und Mani sowie zu den Bibliotheken von Nag Hammadi und Medinet Madi.* Berlin: De Gruyter, 1994.

Bolzano, Bernard. *Wissenschaftslehre.* Edited by Jan Berg. Stuttgart: Frommann, 1985.

Boothe, Brigitte. "Abraham schweigt: Eine Zerreissprobe." Lecture, Zurich, October 10, 2005.

Boyd, Gregory A. *God at War: The Bible and Spiritual Conflict.* Downers Grove: InterVarsity, 1997.

———. *God of the Possible: A Biblical Introduction to the Open View of God.* Grand Rapids: Baker, 2000.

———. *Is God to Blame? Moving Beyond Pat Answers to the Problem of Evil.* Downers Grove: InterVarsity, 2003.

———. *Satan and the Problem of Evil: Constructing a Trinitarian Warfare Theodicy.* Downers Grove: InterVarsity, 2001.

Bracht, Kathrin. "Freiheit radikal gedacht: Liberum arbitrium, securitas und der Ursprung des Bösen bei Augustin." *Sacris Erudiri* 44, no. 1 (2008) 189–217.

Brandscheidt, Renate. "Das Opfer des Abraham (Genesis 22, 1–19)." *Trierer theologische Zeitschrift* 110, no. 1 (2001) 1–19.

Brandt, Reinhard, and Steffen Schmidt, eds. *Mythos und Mythologie.* Berlin: Akademie Verlag, 2004.

Bremmer, Jan N. *The Early Greek Concept of the Soul.* Princeton: Princeton University Press, 1983.

———. *Greek Religion.* Oxford: Oxford University Press, 1994.

———, ed. *Interpretations of Greek Mythology.* London: Croom Helm, 1987.

Bremmer, Jan N., and Kai Brodersen. *Götter, Mythen und Heiligtümer im antiken Griechenland.* Darmstadt: Primus, 1996.

Brooks, Robert E. *Free Will: An Ultimate Illusion: Problems and Opportunities.* Lake Oswego, OR: CIRCA, 1986.

Bruit-Zaidman, Louise, and Pauline Schmitt-Pantel. *Religion in the Ancient Greek City.* Translated by Paul Cartledge. Cambridge: Cambridge University Press, 1992.

Bründl, Jürgen. *Masken des Bösen.* Würzburg: Echter, 2002.

Burkert, Walter. "Griechische Religion." In *Theologische Realenzyklopädie* 14 (1985) 235–53.

———. *Savage Energies: Lessons of Myth and Ritual in Ancient Greece.* Translated by Peter Bing. Chicago: University of Chicago Press, 2001.

Card, Claudia. *The Atrocity Paradigm: A Theory of Evil.* Oxford: Oxford University Press, 2002.

Carson, D. A. "God's Love and God's Wrath." *Bibliotheca Sacra* 156 (1999) 387–98.

Caspi, Mishael, and Sascha Benjamin Cohen. *The Binding (Aqedah) and Its Transformations in Judaism and Islam: The Lambs of God.* Lewiston, NY: Mellen Biblical, 1995.

Chilton, Bruce D. "Theodicy in the Targumim." In *Theodicy in the World of the Bible: The Goodness of God and the Problem of Evil,* edited by Antii Laato and Johannes Moor, 728–52. Leiden: Brill, 2003.

Cioran, Emil. *On the Heights of Despair.* Translated by Ilinca Zarifopol-Johnston. Chicago: University of Chicago Press, 1992.

Claret, Bernd J. *Geheimnis des Bösen: Zur Diskussion um den Teufel.* Innsbruck: Tyrolia, 1997.

Clark, Gordon H. *Religion, Reason, and Revelation.* Philadelphia: Presbyterian and Reformed, 1961.

Clarke, Randolph. "Toward a Credible Agent-Causal Account of Free Will." In *Agents, Causes, and Events: Essays on Indeterminism and Free Will,* edited by Timothy O'Connor, 201–15. Oxford: Oxford University Press, 1995.

Clendinnen, Inga. *Reading the Holocaust.* Cambridge: Cambridge University Press, 1999.

Cohen, Hermann. *Ethik des reinen Willens.* Vol. 7 of *Werke.* Edited by Helmut Holzey. Hildesheim: Olms, 1981.

Colpe, Carsten, and Wilhelm Schmidt-Biggemann, eds. *Das Böse: Eine historische Phänomenologie des Unerklärlichen.* Frankfurt am Main: Suhrkamp, 1993.

Confessio Augustana/The Augsburg Confession. Translated by Charles P. Krauth. In *The Creeds of Christendom: The Creeds of the Evangelical Protestant Churches,* edited by Philip Schaff, 3:3–73. 4th ed. Grand Rapids: Baker, 1977.

Copenhaver, Brian P., ed. and trans. *Hermetica: The Greek Corpus Hermeticum and the Latin Asclepius in a New English Translation.* Cambridge: Cambridge University Press, 1992.

Corey, Michael A. *Evolution and the Problem of Natural Evil.* Lanham: University Press of America, 2000.

Corrigan, Kevin. *Plotinus' Theory of Matter-Evil and the Question of Substance: Plato, Aristotle, and Alexander of Aphrodisias.* Leuven: Peeters, 1996.

Creel, Richard E. *Divine Impassibility: An Essay in Philosophical Theology.* Cambridge: Cambridge University Press, 1986.

Crenshaw, James L. *Defending God: Biblical Responses to the Problem of Evil.* Oxford: Oxford University Press, 2005.

———. "The Problem of Theodicy in Sirach: On Human Bondage." *Journal of Biblical Literature* 94, no. 1 (1975) 47–64.

———. *A Whirlpool of Torment: Israelite Traditions of God as an Oppressive Presence.* Philadelphia: Fortress, 1984.

Cress, Donald A. "Augustine's Privation Account of Evil: A Defense." *Augustinian Studies* 20 (1989) 109–28.

Curtius, Ernst Robert. *European Literature and the Latin Middle Ages.* Translated by Willard Ropes Trask. New York: Pantheon, 1953.

Dalferth, Ingolf U. "Alles umsonst: Zur Kunst des Schenkens und den Grenzen der Gabe." In *Le don et la dette,* edited by Marco M. Olivetti, 53–76. Padova: CEDAM, 2004.

———. *Auf dem Weg der Ökumene: Die Gemeinschaft evangelischer und anglikanischer Kirchen nach der "Meissener Erklärung."* Leipzig: Evangelische Verlagsanstalt, 2002.

———. "Becoming a Christian According to the 'Postscript': Kierkegaard's Christian Hermeneutics of Existence." *Kierkegaard Studies Yearbook* (2005) 242–81.

———. *Becoming Present: An Inquiry into the Christian Sense of the Presence of God.* Leuven: Peeters, 2006.

———. "Christian Discourse and the Paradigmatic Christian Experience: An Essay in Hermeneutics." *New Studies in Theology* 1 (1980) 47–73.

———. "The Contingency of Evil." *Archivio di filosofia* 75, nos. 1–2 (2007) 251–74.

———. *Crucified and Resurrected: Restructuring the Grammar of Christology.* Translated by Jo Bennett. Grand Rapids: Baker, 2015.

———. *Das Böse: Essay über die kulturelle Denkform des Unbegreiflichen.* Tübingen: Mohr Siebeck, 2006.

———. "Der Zorn Gottes: Grundlinien einer Gottesmetapher." In *Gefühle zeigen: Manifestationsformen emotionaler Prozesse,* edited by Johannes Fehr and Gerd Folkers, 11–47. Zurich: Chronos, 2009.

———. "'Die Sache ist viel entsetzlicher': Religiosität bei Kierkegaard und Schleiermacher." In *Schleiermacher und Kierkegaard: Subjektivität und Wahrheit,* edited by Niels Jørgen Cappelørn et al., 217–64. Berlin: De Gruyter, 2006.

———. *Die Wirklichkeit des Möglichen: Hermeneutische Religionsphilosophie.* Tübingen: Mohr Siebeck, 2003.

———. *Evangelische Theologie als Interpretationspraxis: Eine systematische Orientierung.* Leipzig: Evangelische Verlagsanstalt, 2004.

———. *Existenz Gottes und christlicher Glaube: Skizzen zu einer eschatologischen Ontologie.* Munich: Kaiser, 1984.

———. "Fähig zur Sünde?" *Theologische Fakultät der Universität Zürich* 1 (1998) 3–12.

———. *Gott: Philosophisch-theologische Denkversuche.* Tübingen: Mohr Siebeck, 1992.

———. "How Is the Concept of Sin Related to the Concept of Moral Wrongdoing?" *Religious Studies* 20, no. 2 (1984) 175–89.

———. *Jenseits von Mythos und Logos: Die christologische Transformation der Theologie.* Freiburg: Herder, 1993.

———. "Leben angesichts des Unverfügbaren: Die duale Struktur religiöser Lebensorientierung." In *Orientierung: Philosophische Perspektiven*, edited by Werner Stegmaier, 245–66. Frankfurt: Suhrkamp, 2005.

———. *Leiden und Böses: Vom schwierigen Umgang mit Widersinnigem.* Leipzig: Evangelische Verlagsanstalt, 2006.

———. "Mere Passive: Die Passivität der Gabe bei Luther." In *Word—Gift—Being: Justification—Economy—Ontology*, edited by Bo Kristian Holm and Peter Widmann, 43–71. Tübingen: Mohr Siebeck, 2009.

———. *Religiöse Rede von Gott.* Munich: Kaiser, 1981.

———. *Theology and Philosophy.* Oxford: Blackwell, 1988.

———. "Umsonst: Vom Schenken, Geben und Bekommen." *Studia Theologica* 59, no. 2 (2005) 83–103.

Darwin, Charles. *The Autobiography of Charles Darwin, 1809–1882: With Original Omissions Restored.* Edited by Nora Barlow. London: Collins, 1958.

———. "Letter to Asa Grey, 22 May 1860." In *The Correspondence of Charles Darwin*, edited by Frederick Burkhardt et al., 8:223–24. Cambridge: Cambridge University Press, 1993.

Davaney, Sheila Greeve. *Divine Power: A Study of Karl Barth and Charles Hartshorne.* Philadelphia: Fortress, 1986.

Davies, Nigel. *Human Sacrifice in History and Today.* New York: Morrow, 1981.

Day, Peggy Lynne. *An Adversary in Heaven: Satan in the Hebrew Bible.* Atlanta: Scholars, 1988.

Decher, Friedhelm. *Verzweiflung: Anatomie eines Affekts.* Lüneburg: Zu Klampen, 2002.

Decker, Bruno. *Die Entwicklung der Lehre von der prophetischen Offenbarung von Wilhelm von Auxerre bis zu Thomas von Aquin.* Breslau: Müller & Seiffert, 1940.

Deigh, John. "Cognitivism in the Theory of Emotions." *Ethics* 104, no. 4 (1994) 824–54.

Deissler, Alfons, et al., eds. *Neue Jerusalemer Bibel: Einheitsübersetzung mit dem Kommentar der Jerusalemer Bibel.* 13th ed. Freiburg: Herder, 2001.

Delius, Hans-Ulrich. *Die Quellen von Martin Luthers Genesisvorlesung.* Munich: Kaiser, 1992.

Deme, Daniel. "The 'Origin' of Evil according to Anselm of Canterbury." *Heythrop Journal* 43, no. 2 (2002) 170–84.

Descartes, René. "Author's Replies to the Sixth Set of Objections." Translated by John Cottingham. In *The Philosophical Writings of Descartes*, edited by John Cottingham et al., 2:285–301. Cambridge: Cambridge University Press, 1984.

Deutscher Evangelischer Kirchenausschuss, ed. *Bekenntnisschriften der evangelisch-lutherischen Kirche.* 11th ed. Göttingen: Vandenhoeck & Ruprecht, 1992.

De Villiers, Jan Lodewyk. "Joy in Suffering in 1 Peter." *Neotestamentica* 9, no. 1 (1975) 64–86.

Dexinger, Ferdinand. "Alttestamentliche Überlegungen zum 'Erbsünde'-Problem." In *Ist Adam an allem schuld? Erbsünde oder Sündenverflochtenheit?*, edited by Ferdinand Dexinger et al., 24–115. Innsbruck: Tyrolia, 1971.

Dierken, Jörg. "Karl Barth (1886–1968)." In *Klassiker der Theologie*, edited by Friedrich Wilhelm Graf, 2:223–57. Munich: Beck, 2005.

Dietrich, Walter, and Christian Link. *Die dunklen Seiten Gottes.* Vol. 1 of *Willkür und Gewalt.* 6th ed. Neukirchen-Vluyn: Neukirchener Verlagshaus, 2015.

Dietrich, Walter, et al., eds. *Gewalt und Gewaltüberwindung in der Bibel.* Zurich: Theologischer Verlag Zürich, 2005.

Dietz, Bettina. *Utopien als mögliche Welten:* voyages imaginaires *der französischen Frühaufklärung 1650–1720.* Mainz: Von Zabern, 2002.

Dohmen, Christoph, and Manfred Oeming. *Biblischer Kanon, warum und wozu? Eine Kanontheologie.* Freiburg: Herder, 1992.

Domning, Daryl P., and Monika Hellwig. *Original Selfishness: Original Sin and Evil in the Light of Evolution.* Burlington, VT: Ashgate, 2006.

Doniger, Wendy. *The Origins of Evil in Hindu Mythology.* Berkeley: University of California Press, 1976.

Dore, Clement. *Moral Scepticism.* New York: St. Martin's, 1991.

Dorner, Isaak August. *Divine Immutability: A Critical Reconsideration.* Translated by Claude Welch and Robert R. Williams. Minneapolis: Fortress, 1994.

Dörrie, Heinrich. "'Hypostasis': Wort- und Bedeutungsgeschichte." In *Platonica minora,* 13–69. Munich: Fink, 1976.

———. *Leid und Erfahrung: Die Wort- und Sinn-Verbindung* pathein—mathein *im griechischen Denken.* Wiesbaden: Steiner, 1956.

Double, Richard. *The Non-Reality of Free Will.* Oxford: Oxford University Press, 1991.

Draper, Paul. "More Pain and Pleasure: A Reply to Otte." In *Christian Faith and the Problem of Evil,* edited by Peter van Inwagen, 41–54. Grand Rapids: Eerdmans, 2004.

———. "Pain and Pleasure: An Evidential Problem for Theists (1989)." In *The Evidential Argument from Evil,* edited by Daniel Howard-Snyder, 12–29. Indianapolis: Indiana University Press, 1996.

———. "Probabilistic Arguments from Evil." *Religious Studies* 28, no. 3 (1992) 303–17.

Ebach, Jürgen. *Streiten mit Gott: Hiob.* Vol. 2. Neukirchen-Vluyn: Neukirchener Verlagshaus, 1996.

Ebbinghaus, Julius. "Die Formeln des kategorischen Imperativs und die Ableitung inhaltlich bestimmer Pflichten." In *Gesammelte Schrifte,* edited by Georg Geismann and Hariolf Oberer, 2:209–29. Bonn: Bouvier, 1988.

Ebeling, Gerhard. "Theologie zwischen reformatorischem Sündenverständnis und heutiger Einstellung zum Bösen." In *Wort und Glaube,* 3:173–204. Tübingen: Mohr Siebeck, 1975.

Eckstein, Hans-Joachim. "'Denn Gottes Zorn wird vom Himmel her offenbar werden': Exegetische Erwägungen zu Röm 1,18." *Zeitschrift für die Neutestamentliche Wissenschaft und die Kunde der Älteren Kirche* 78, no. 1–2 (1987) 74–89.

Eichinger, Werner. *Erbsündentheologie: Rekonstruktionen neuerer Modelle und eine politisch orientierte Skizze.* Frankfurt: Lang, 1980.

Ellis, Richard S. "Human Logic, God's Logic, and the *Akedah.*" *Conservative Judaism* 52, no. 1 (1999) 28–32.

Embry, Ray. *The Enigma about Divine Love and the Creation of Evil: The Lost Belief among Early Christians about a God of Total Compassion.* San Jose: Writers Club, 2000.

Emmendörffer, Michael. *Der ferne Gott: Eine Untersuchung der alttestamentlichen Volksklagelieder vor dem Hintergrund der mesopotamischen Literatur.* Tübingen: Mohr Siebeck, 1998.

Epicurus. *Epicurea.* Edited by Hermann Usener. Leipzig: Teubner, 1887.

———. *Epicurus: The Extant Remains.* Edited and translated by Cyril Bailey. 2nd ed. Oxford: Clarendon, 1926.

Evans, G. R. *Augustine on Evil.* Cambridge: Cambridge University Press, 1982.

Farley, Edward. *Good and Evil: Interpreting a Human Condition.* Minneapolis: Fortress, 1990.

Farley, Wendy. *Tragic Vision and Divine Compassion: A Contemporary Theodicy.* Louisville: Westminster John Knox, 1990.

Farrer, Austin Marsden. *The Glass of Vision.* London: Dacre, 1948.

———. *Love Almighty and Ills Unlimited.* London: Collins, 1962.

———. *A Rebirth of Images: The Making of St. John's Apocalypse.* London: Dacre, 1949.

Ferguson, Everett. *Demonology of the Early Christian World.* New York: Mellen, 1984.

Fiddes, Paul S. *The Creative Suffering of God.* Oxford: Clarendon, 1988.

Fishbane, Michael A. *Biblical Myth and Rabbinic Mythmaking.* Oxford: Oxford University Press, 2003.

Fitzmyer, Joseph A. "The Sacrifice of Isaac in Qumran Literature." *Biblica* 83, no. 2 (2002) 211–29.

Flasch, Kurt. *Augustin: Einführung in sein Denken.* Stuttgart: Reclam, 1980.

Flew, Antony. "Divine Omnipotence and Human Freedom." In *New Essays in Philosophical Theology,* edited by Antony Flew and Alasdair C. MacIntyre, 144–69. London: SCM, 1955.

Flint, Thomas P. *Divine Providence: The Molinist Account.* Ithaca: Cornell University Press, 1998.

Fontenelle, Bernard de. *Conversations on the Plurality of Worlds*. Translated by H. A. Hargreaves. Berkeley: University of California Press, 1990.

Forster, Christine. *Begrenztes Leben als Herausforderung: Das Vergänglichkeitsmotiv in weisheitlichen Psalmen*. Zurich: Pano, 2000.

Freedman, David Noel, ed. *The Anchor Bible Dictionary*. New York: Doubleday, 1992.

Freund, Gerhard. *Sünde im Erbe: Erfahrungsinhalt und Sinn der Erbsündenlehre*. Stuttgart: Kohlhammer, 1979.

Fries, Heinrich. *Fundamental Theology*. Translated by Robert J. Daly. Washington, DC: Catholic University of America Press, 1996.

Fritzsche, Hans Georg. *. . . und erlöse uns von dem Übel: Philosophie und Theologie zur "Rechtfertigung Gottes."* Stuttgart: Calwer Verlag, 1987.

Fritzsche, J. "Privation." *Historisches Wörterbuch der Philosophie* 7 (1989) 1378–83.

Fuchs, Gisela. *Mythos und Hiobdichtung: Aufnahme und Umdeutung altorientalischer Vorstellungen*. Stuttgart: Kohlhammer, 1993.

Fyall, Robert S. *Now My Eyes Have Seen You: Images of Creation and Evil in the Book of Job*. Downers Grove, IL: InterVarsity, 2002.

Garrett, Susan R. *The Demise of the Devil: Magic and the Demonic in Luke's Writings*. Minneapolis: Fortress, 1989.

———. "The Patience of Job and the Patience of Jesus." *Interpretation* 53, no. 3 (1999) 254–64.

Gassendi, Pierre. "Exercises against the Aristotelians, 1624." In *The Selected Works of Pierre Gassendi*, 15–108. New York: Johnson Reprint, 1972.

Geach, Peter Thomas. *Providence and Evil: The Stanton Lectures 1971–2*. Cambridge: Cambridge University Press, 1977.

Geismann, Georg. "Die Formeln des kategorischen Imperativs nach H. J. Paton, N. N., Klaus Reich und Julius Ebbinghaus." *Kant-Studien* 93, no. 3 (2002) 374–84.

Gert, Bernard, and Timothy J. Duggan. "Free Will as the Ability to Will." *Noûs* 13, no. 2 (May 1979) 197–217.

Gesang, Bernward. *Angeklagt: Gott. Über den Versuch, vom Leiden in der Welt auf die Wahrheit des Atheismus zu schliessen*. Tübingen: Attempto, 1997.

Gese, Hartmut. "Die Frage nach dem Lebenssinn: Hiob und die Folgen (1982)." In *Alttestamentliche Studien*, 161–79. Tübingen: Mohr, 1991.

Gestrich, Christof. *Die Wiederkehr des Glanzes in der Welt: Die christliche Lehre von der Sünde und ihrer Vergebung in gegenwärtiger Verantwortung*. Tübingen: Mohr, 1989.

———. *Peccatum: Studien zur Sündenlehre*. Tübingen: Mohr Siebeck, 2003.

Geyer, Carl-Friedrich. "Das Böse in der Perspektive von Christentum und Neuplatonismus." *Philosophisches Jahrbuch* 98, no. 2 (1991) 233–50.

———. *Leid und Böses in philosophischen Deutungen*. Freiburg: Alber, 1983.

———. "Theodizee oder Kulturgeschichte des Bösen? Anmerkungen zum gegenwärtigen Diskurs." *Zeitschrift für philosophische Forschung* 46, no. 2 (1992) 238–56.

Geyer, Christian, ed. *Hirnforschung und Willensfreiheit: Zur Deutung der neuesten Experimente*. Frankfurt: Suhrkamp, 2004.

Gilbert, Maurice. "God, Sin and Mercy: Sirach 15:11–18:14." In *Ben Sira's God*, edited by Renate Egger-Wenzel, 118–35. Berlin: De Gruyter, 2002.

Glei, Reinhold. "Et invidus et inbecillus: Das angebliche Epikurfragment bei Laktanz, De ira Dei 13,20–21." *Vigiliae Christianae* 42, no. 1 (1988) 47–58.

Goetz, Ronald G. "The Suffering God: The Rise of a New Orthodoxy." *Christian Century* 103, no. 13 (April 1986) 385–89.

Goldberg, Hillel. "Abraham and Isaac: 'The Test.'" *Torah.org*, 1996. http://www.torah.org/projects/genesis/topic7.html.

Goldie, Peter. *The Emotions: A Philosophical Exploration*. Oxford: Clarendon, 2000.

Goldstain, Jacques. *Création et péché*. Paris: Desclée, 1968.

Gordis, Robert. *The Book of God and Man: A Study of Job*. Chicago: University of Chicago Press, 1965.

Graves, Robert. *The Greek Myths*. 2 vols. Rev. ed. Harmondsworth: Penguin, 1960.

Greenstein, Edward L. "The Wrath of God in the Book of Lamentations." In *The Problem of Evil and Its Symbols in Jewish and Christian Tradition*, edited by Henning Graf Reventlow and Yair Hoffman, 29–42. London: Continuum, 2004.

Griffin, David R. *Evil Revisited: Responses and Reconsiderations.* Albany: State University of New York Press, 1991.

———. *God, Power, and Evil: A Process Theodicy.* Louisville: Westminster John Knox, 2004.

Griffin, David R., et al., eds. *Searching for an Adequate God: A Dialogue between Process and Free Will Theists.* Grand Rapids: Eerdmans, 2000.

Groß, Walter. "Zorn Gottes: Ein biblisches Theologumenon." In *Gott, ratlos vor dem Bösen?*, edited by Wolfgang Beinert, 47–85. Freiburg: Herder, 1999.

———. *Zukunft für Israel: Alttestamentliche Bundeskonzepte und die aktuelle Debatte um den Neuen Bund.* Stuttgart: Katholisches Bibelwerk, 1998.

Groß, Walter, and Karl-Josef Kuschel. *"Ich schaffe Finsternis und Unheil!" Ist Gott verantwortlich für das Übel?* Mainz: Grünewald, 1992.

Gunkel, Hermann. *Genesis.* Translated by Mark E. Biddle. Macon: Mercer University Press, 1997.

Güttgemanns, Erhardt. *Der leidende Apostel und sein Herr: Studien zur paulinischen Christologie.* Göttingen: Vandenhoeck & Ruprecht, 1966.

Haag, Herbert. *Vor dem Bösen ratlos?* Munich: Piper, 1978.

Häberlin, Paul. *Das Böse: Ursprung und Bedeutung.* Bern: Francke, 1960.

Haggard, Patrick, and Martin Eimer. "On the Relation Between Brain Potentials and the Awareness of Voluntary Movements." *Experimental Brain Research* 126, no. 1 (1999) 128–33.

Hall, Douglas John. *God and Human Suffering: An Exercise in the Theology of the Cross.* Minneapolis: Augsburg, 1986.

Hanko, Herman C. "Unconditional Election." In *The Five Points of Calvinism*, edited by Herman C. Hanko, et al., 27–42. Grand Rapids: Reformed Free Publishing Association, 1976.

Hanson, Anthony Tyrrell. *The Wrath of the Lamb.* London: SPCK, 1957.

Happ, Heinz. *Hyle: Studien zum aristotelischen Materie-Begriff.* Berlin: De Gruyter, 1971.

Häring, Hermann. *Das Böse in der Welt: Gottes Macht oder Ohnmacht?* Darmstadt: Primus, 1999.

———. *Das Problem des Bösen in der Theologie.* Darmstadt: Wissenschaftliche Buchgesellschaft, 1985.

———. *Die Macht des Bösen: Das Erbe Augustins.* Gütersloh: Mohn, 1979.

Härle, Wilfried. "Die Rede von der Liebe und vom Zorn Gottes." *Zeitschrift für Theologie und Kirche*, supplement 8 (1990) 50–69.

———. *Sein und Gnade: Die Ontologie in Karl Barths kirchlicher Dogmatik.* Berlin: De Gruyter, 1975.

Härle, Wilfried, and Eilert Herms. *Rechtfertigung, das Wirklichkeitsverständnis des christlichen Glaubens: Ein Arbeitsbuch.* Göttingen: Vandenhoeck & Ruprecht, 1979.

Hartley, J. E. "From Lament to Oath: A Study of Progression in the Speeches of Job." In *The Book of Job*, edited by W. A. M. Beuken, 79–100. Leuven: Peeters, 1994.

Hartshorne, Charles E. *Omnipotence and Other Theological Mistakes.* Albany: State University of New York, 1984.

———. *Reality as Social Process: Studies in Metaphysics and Religion.* New York: Harner, 1971.

Hasker, William. "A Philosophical Perspective." In *The Openness of God: A Biblical Challenge to the Traditional Understanding of God*, edited by Clark Pinnock et al., 126–54. Downers Grove: InterVarsity Academic, 1994.

———. *Providence, Evil, and the Openness of God.* London: Routledge, 2004.

Hasker, William, et al., eds. *Middle Knowledge: Theory and Applications.* Frankfurt: Lang, 2000.

Haught, John F. *God After Darwin: A Theology of Evolution.* 2nd ed. Boulder: Westview, 2008.

Hebblethwaite, Brian Leslie. *Evil, Suffering and Religion.* New York: Hawthorne, 1976.

Heckel, Ulrich. "Gottes Allmacht und Liebe: Paulinische Überlegungen zur Theodizee—Problematik." *Theologische Beiträge* 31 (2000) 237–42.

Heimsoeth, Heinz. "Zum kosmotheologischen Ursprung der kantischen Freiheitsantinomie." *Kant-Studien* 57 (1966) 209–29.

Heine, Heinrich. *Sämtliche Schriften.* Edited by Klaus Briegleb, et al. 2nd ed. Munich: Hanser, 1985.

Heinekamp, Albert. *Das Problem des Guten bei Leibniz.* Bonn: Bouvier, 1969.

Held, Klaus. "Ethos und christliche Gotteserfahrung." *Veritas* 45, no. 1 (2000) 67–82.

Helm, Paul. *The Providence of God.* Downers Grove: InterVarsity, 1994.

Hengel, Martin. *Christus und die Macht: Die Macht Christi und die Ohnmacht der Christen: Zur Problematik einer "politischen Theologie" in der Geschichte der Kirche.* Stuttgart: Calwer Verlag, 1974.

Henrix, Hans Hermann. "Machtentsagung Gottes? Ein Gespräch mit Hans Jonas im Kontext der Theodizeefrage." In *Landschaft aus Schreien,* edited by Johann Baptist Metz, 118–43. Mainz: Matthias-Grünewald-Verl, 1995.

Herion, Gary A., et al. "Wrath of God (OT)." In *The Anchor Bible Dictionary,* edited by David Freedman, 6:989–96. New Haven: Yale University Press, 1992.

Hermanni, Friedrich. *Das Böse und die Theodizee: Eine philosophisch-theologische Grundlegung.* Gütersloh: Gütersloher Verlagshaus, 2002.

———. "Die Positivität des *Malum*: Die Privationstheorie und ihre Kritik in der neuzeitlichen Philosophie." In *Die Wirklichkeit des Bösen,* edited by Friedrich Hermanni and Peter Koslowski, 49–72. Paderborn: Fink, 1998.

Hermanni, Friedrich, and Peter Koslowski, eds. *Die Wirklichkeit des Bösen: Systematisch-theologische und philosophische Annäherungen.* Munich: Fink, 1998.

Hermisson, Hans-Jürgen. "Gott und das Leid: eine alttestamentliche Summe." *Theologische Literaturzeitung* 128, no. 1 (2003) 3–18.

———. "Notizen zu Hiob." In *Studien zu Prophetie und Weisheit: Gesammelte Aufsätze,* edited by Jörg Barthel, et al., 286–99. Tübingen: Mohr Siebeck, 1998.

Herms, Eilert. "Das Böse: Systematische Überlegungen im Horizont des christlichen Wirklichkeitsverständnisses." In *The Fall of the Angels,* edited by Christoph Auffarth and Loren Stuckenbruck, 236–60. Leiden: Brill, 2003.

Herms, Eilert, ed. *Leben: Verständnis, Wissenschaft, Technik: Kongressband des XI. Europäischen Kongresses für Theologie, 15.-19. September 2002 in Zürich.* Gütersloh: Gütersloher Verlagshaus, 2005.

Herodotus. *History.* Edited and translated by A. D. Godley. Vol. 2. Cambridge: Harvard University Press, 1946.

Heschel, Abraham Joshua. *The Prophets.* Philadelphia: Jewish Publication Society of America, 1962.

Hick, John. *Evil and the God of Love.* Basingstoke: Palgrave Macmillan, 2007.

Hödl, Ludwig. "Die metaphysische und ethische Negativität des Bösen in der Theologie des Thomas von Aquin." In *Das Böse: Eine historische Phänomenologie des Unerklärlichen,* edited by Carsten Colpe and Wilhelm Schmidt-Biggemann, 137–64. Frankfurt am Main: Suhrkamp, 1993.

Hoffman, Yair. "The First Creation Story: Canonical and Diachronic Aspects." In *Creation in Jewish and Christian Tradition,* edited by Henning Reventlow and Yair Hoffman, 45–66. London: Sheffield Academic Press, 2002.

———. "Jeremiah 50–51 and the Concept of Evil in the Hebrew Bible." In *The Problem of Evil and Its Symbols in Jewish and Christian Tradition,* edited by Henning Reventlow and Yair Hoffman, 14–28. London: Clark, 2004.

Hollatz, David. *Examen theologicum acroamaticum universam theologiam thetico-poelmicam complectens.* Darmstadt: Wissenschaftliche Buchgesellschaft, 1971.

Holmén, Tom. "Theodicean Motifs in the New Testament: Response to the Death of Jesus." In *Theodicy in the World of the Bible,* edited by Antii Laato and Johannes Moor, 605–51. Leiden: Brill, 2003.

Homer. *Iliad.* Translated by A. T. Murray. Cambridge: Harvard University Press, 1924.

Hoping, Helmut. "Abschied vom allmächtigen Gott? Anmerkungen zu einer aktuellen Diskussion." *Trierer theologische Zeitschrift* 106 (1997) 177–88.

Horst, Friedrich. "Teufel II: Im AT, Judentum und NT." In vol. 6 of *Religion in Geschichte und Gegenwart: Handwörterbuch für Theologie und Religionswissenschaft,* edited by Kurt Galling. 3rd ed. Tübingen: Mohr Siebeck, 1962.

Hotze, Gerhard. "Gemeinde als Schicksalsgemeinschaft mit Christus (2 Kor 1, 3–11)." In *Ekklesiologie des Neuen Testaments: Für Karl Kertelge,* edited by Rainer Kampling and Thomas Söding, 336–55. Freiburg: Herder, 1996.

Houtman, Cornelis. "Theodicy in the Pentateuch." In *Theodicy in the World of the Bible,* edited by Antii Laato and Johannes Moor, 151–82. Leiden: Brill, 2003.

Howard-Snyder, Daniel. "God, Evil, and Suffering." In *Reason for the Hope Within,* edited by Michael J. Murray, 76–115. Grand Rapids: Eerdmans, 1999.

———, ed. *The Evidential Argument from Evil.* Bloomington: Indiana University Press, 1996.

Hugh of Saint Victor. *On the Sacraments of the Christian Faith (De sacramentis)*. Translated by Roy J. Deferrari. Cambridge: Mediaeval Academy of America, 1951.

Hügli, Anton. "Die Instrumentalisierung des *Malum* in der Philosophie der Neuzeit." In *Die Wirklichkeit des Bösen*, edited by Friedrich Hermanni and Peter Koslowski, 159–83. Paderborn: Fink, 1998.

Hume, David. *Dialogues Concerning Natural Religion and Other Writings*. Edited by Dorothy Coleman. Cambridge: Cambridge University Press, 2007.

Hunt, David P. "Divine Providence and Simple Foreknowledge." *Faith and Philosophy: Journal of the Society of Christian Philosophers* 10, no. 3 (1993) 394–414.

———. "Prescience and Providence: A Reply to My Critics." *Faith and Philosophy: Journal of the Society of Christian Philosophers* 10, no. 3 (1993) 428–38.

Hunter, Cornelius G. *Darwin's God: Evolution and the Problem of Evil*. Grand Rapids: Brazos, 2002.

Hunter, Ian. *Rival Enlightenments: Civil and Metaphysical Philosophy in Early Modern Germany*. Cambridge: Cambridge University Press, 2001.

Illman, Karl-Johan. "Theodicy in Job." In *Theodicy in the World of the Bible*, edited by Antii Laato and Johannes Moor, 304–33. Leiden: Brill, 2003.

Inbody, Tyron. *The Transforming God: An Interpretation of Suffering and Evil*. Louisville: Westminster John Knox, 1997.

Inwagen, Peter van. "The Argument from Evil." In *Christian Faith and the Problem of Evil*, edited by Peter van Inwagen, 55–73. Grand Rapids: Eerdmans, 2004.

———, ed. *Christian Faith and the Problem of Evil*. Grand Rapids: Eerdmans, 2004.

———. "The Problem of Evil, the Problem of Air, and the Problem of Silence." In *God, Knowledge, and Mystery: Essays in Philosophical Theology*, 66–95. Ithaca: Cornell University Press, 1995.

Ishiguro, Hidé, *Leibniz's Philosophy of Logic and Language*. 2nd ed. Cambridge: Cambridge University Press, 1990.

Jaeger, Werner. *The Conflict of Cultural Ideals in the Age of Plato*. Translated by Gilbert Highet. Vol. 3 of *Paideia: The Ideals of Greek Culture*. Oxford: Oxford University Press, 1986.

Janowski, Bernd. *Arguing with God: A Theological Anthropology of the Psalms*. Translated by Armin Siedlecki. Louisville: Westminster John Knox, 2013.

———. "Die Toten loben JHWH nicht: Psalm 88 und das alttestamentliche Todesverständnis." In *Auferstehung—Resurrection: The Fourth Durham-Tübingen Research Symposium*, edited by Friedrich Avemarie and Hermann Lichtenberger, 3–45. Tübingen: Mohr Siebeck, 2001.

Janowski, J. Christine. *Ein Gott, der tötet? Der vernichtende Gott, der leidende Gott*. Frankfurt: Lang, 2003.

Janssen, Hans-Gerd. *Gott—Freiheit—Leid: Das Theodizeeproblem in der Philosophie der Neuzeit*. Darmstadt: Wissenschaftliche Buchgesellschaft, 1989.

Jeremias, Jörg. "Alttestamentliche Wissenschaft im Kontext der Theologie." In *Eine Wissenschaft oder viele? Die Einheit evangelischer Theologie in der Sicht ihrer Disziplinen*, edited by Ingolf U. Dalferth, 9–22. Leipzig: Evangelische Verlagsanstalt, 2006.

———. "Das Wesen der alttestamentlichen Prophetie." *Theologische Literaturzeitung* 131, no. 1 (January 2006) 3–14.

Jolivet, Régis. *Le problème du mal d'après Saint Augustin*. 3rd ed. Paris: Beauchesne, 1936.

Jolley, Nicholas, ed. *The Cambridge Companion to Leibniz*. Cambridge: Cambridge University Press, 1995.

Jonas, Hans. "The Concept of God after Auschwitz: A Jewish Voice." In *Mortality and Morality: A Search for the Good after Auschwitz*, edited by Lawrence Vogel, 131–43. Evanston: Northwestern University Press, 1996.

Jung, Leo. *Fallen Angels in Jewish, Christian, and Mohammedan Literature*. New York: Ktav Publishing House, 1974.

Jüngel, Eberhard. "Böse—was ist das? Versuch einer theologischen Begriffsbestimmung." In *Leben im Schatten des Bösen*, edited by Union Evangelischer Kirchen, 124–51. Neukirchen-Vluyn: Neukirchener Verlagshaus, 2004.

———. "Gottes ursprüngliches Anfangen als schöpferische Selbstbegrenzung." In *Wertlose Wahrheit: Zur Identität und Relevanz des christlichen Glaubens: Theologische Erörterungen III*, 214–42. Munich: Kaiser, 1990.

———. "The Revelation of the Hiddenness of God: A Contribution to the Protestant Understanding of the Hiddenness of Divine Action." In *Theological Essays II*, edited and translated by J. B. Webster and Arnold Neufeldt-Fast, 120–44. London: Bloomsbury, 2014.

Kadowaki, Takuji. *Das Radikal Böse bei Kant*. PhD dissertation, University of Bonn, 1960.

Kaiser, Otto. "Deus absconditus and Deus revelatus: Three Difficult Narratives in the Pentateuch." In *Shall Not the Judge of All the Earth Do What Is Right?*, edited by David Penchansky and Paul L. Redditt, 73–88. Winona Lake: Eisenbrauns, 2000.

Kane, G. Stanley. "Evil and Privation." *International Journal for Philosophy of Religion* 11, no. 1 (1980) 43–58.

———. "The Failure of Soul-Making Theodicy." *International Journal for Philosophy of Religion* 6, no. 1 (1975) 1–22.

———. "Soul-making Theodicy and Eschatology." *Sophia* 14, no. 2. (1975) 24–31.

Kane, Robert. *The Significance of Free Will*. New York: Oxford University Press, 1996.

Kant, Immanuel. "Attempt to Introduce the Concept of Negative Magnitudes into Philosophy." In *Theoretical Philosophy, 1755–1770*, edited and translated by David Walford and Ralf Meerbote, 203–41. Cambridge: Cambridge University Press, 1992.

———. *Critique of Pure Reason*. Edited and translated by Paul Guyer and Allen W. Wood. Cambridge: Cambridge University Press, 1998.

———. *Critique of the Power of Judgment*. Edited by Paul Guyer. Translated by Paul Guyer and Eric Matthews. Cambridge: Cambridge University Press, 2000.

———. *Lectures on Metaphysics*. Edited and translated by Karl Ameriks and Steve Naragon. Cambridge: Cambridge University Press, 1997.

———. "On the Miscarriage of All Philosophical Trials in Theodicy." In *Religion and Rational Theology*, edited by Allen W. Wood and George Di Giovanni, 19–37. Cambridge: Cambridge University Press, 1996.

———. *Practical Philosophy*. Translated by Mary J. Gregor. Cambridge: Cambridge University Press, 1996.

———. *Prolegomena to Any Future Metaphysics that Will Be Able to Come Forward as Science*. Translated by Gary Hatfield. In *Theoretical Philosophy after 1781*, edited by Henry Alison and Peter Heath, 29–169. Cambridge: Cambridge University Press, 2002.

———. *Religion and Rational Theology*. Edited by Allen W. Wood and George Di Giovanni. Cambridge: Cambridge University Press, 1996.

Kapitan, Tomis. "Providence, Foreknowledge, and Decision Procedures." *Faith and Philosophy* 10, no. 3 (1993) 415–20.

Karrer, Martin. *Jesus Christus im Neuen Testament*. Göttingen: Vandenhoeck & Ruprecht, 1998.

Kaulbach, Friedrich. *Immanuel Kants "Grundlegung zur Metaphysik der Sitten": Interpretation und Kommentar*. 2nd ed. Darmstadt: Wissenschaftliche Buchgesellschaft, 1996.

Keel, Othmar. *Jahwes Entgegnung an Ijob: Eine Deutung von Ijob 38–41 vor dem Hintergrund der zeitgenössischen Bildkunst*. Göttingen: Vandenhoeck & Ruprecht, 1978.

Keller, Isabelle, and Heinz Heckhausen. "Readiness Potentials Preceding Spontaneous Motor Acts: Voluntary vs. Involuntary Control." *Electroencephalography and Clinical Neurophysiology* 76, no. 4 (1990) 351–61.

Kerényi, Karl. *Griechische Grundbegriffe: Fragen und Antworten aus der heutigen Situation*. Zurich: Rhein, 1964.

———. "Theos: 'Gott' auf Griechisch." In *Antike Religion: Ein Entwurf von Grundlinien*, 207–17. Munich: Langen Müller, 1971.

Kermani, Navid. *Gott ist schön: Das ästhetische Erleben des Koran*. 2nd ed. Munich: Beck, 2003.

———. *The Terror of God: Attar, Job and the Metaphysical Revolt*. Translated by Wieland Hoban. Malden: Polity, 2011.

Kern, Walter. "Theodizee: Kosmodizee durch Christus." In *Geist und Glaube: Fundamentaltheologische Vermittlungen zwischen Mensch und Offenbarung*, edited by Karl H. Neufeld, 109–45. Innsbruck: Tyrolia, 1992.

Kessler, Hans. "Christologie." In *Handbuch der Dogmatik*, edited by Theodor Schneider et al., 1:241–442. 3rd ed. Düsseldorf: Patmos, 2000.

———. *Gott und das Leid seiner Schöpfung: Nachdenkliches zur Theodizeefrage*. Würzburg: Echter, 2000.

Kessler, Hans, ed. *Leben durch Zerstörung? Über das Leiden in der Schöpfung: Ein Gespräch der Wissenschaften*. Würzburg: Echter, 2000.

Kessler, Rainer. "'Ich weiss, dass mein Erlöser lebet:' Sozialgeschichtlicher Hintergrund und theologische Bedeutung der Löser-Vorstellung in Hiob 19, 25." *Zeitschrift für Theologie und Kirche* 89 (1992) 139–58.

Khoury, Adel Théodore, and Peter Hünermann. *Warum leiden? Die Antwort der Weltreligionen.* Freiburg: Herder, 1987.

Kierkegaard, Søren. *The Concept of Anxiety.* Vol. 8 of *Kierkegaard's Writings.* Edited and translated by Reidar Thomte with Albert Anderson. Princeton: Princeton University Press, 1980.

———. *The Sickness Unto Death: A Christian Psychological Exposition for Upbuilding and Awakening.* Vol. 19 of *Kierkegaard's Writings.* Edited and translated by Howard V. Hong and Edna H. Hong. Princeton: Princeton University Press, 1980.

Kilian, Rudolf. *Isaaks Opferung; zur Überlieferungsgeschichte von Gen. 22.* 2nd ed. Stuttgart: Katholisches Bibelwerk, 1982.

King, Karen L. *What Is Gnosticism?* Cambridge: Harvard-Belknap, 2003.

Kirk, Geoffrey Stephen. *The Nature of Greek Myths.* Harmondsworth: Penguin, 1974.

Kittel, Gerhard, and Gerhard Friedrich, eds. *Theological Dictionary of the New Testament.* Translated by Geoffrey William Bromiley. Grand Rapids: Eerdmans, 1972.

Kleffmann, Tom. *Die Erbsündenlehre in sprachtheologischem Horizont: eine Interpretation Augustins, Luthers und Hamanns.* Tübingen: Mohr, 1994.

Klein, William W. *The New Chosen People: A Corporate View of Election.* Grand Rapids: Academie, 1990.

Kluge, Friedrich, and Walther Mitzka. *Etymologisches Wörterbuch der deutschen Sprache.* 24th ed. Berlin: De Gruyter, 2002.

Knebel, Sven K. "Necessitas moralis ad optimum: Zum historischen Hintergrund der Wahl der besten aller möglichen Welten." *Studia Leibnitiana* 23, no. 1 (1991) 3–24.

Knierim, Rolf. *Die Hauptbegriffe für Sünde im Alten Testament.* Gütersloh: Gütersloher Verlagshaus, 1965.

Koch, Klaus. "Vom Mythos zum Monotheismus im alten Israel." In *Mythos und Mythologie,* edited by Reinhard Brandt and Steffen Schmidt, 89–121. Berlin: Akademie Verlag, 2004.

Köhlmoos, Melanie. *Das Auge Gottes: Textstrategie im Hiobbuch.* Tübingen: Mohr Siebeck, 1999.

König, Johann Friedrich. *Theologia positiva acroamatica (Rostock 1664).* Edited and translated by Andreas Stegmann. Tübingen: Mohr Siebeck, 2006.

Korpel, M. C. A. *A Rift in the Clouds: Ugaritic and Hebrew Descriptions of the Divine.* Münster: Ugarit, 1990.

Körtner, Ulrich H. J. *Wie lange noch, wie lange? Über das Böse, Leid und Tod.* Neukirchen-Vluyn: Neukirchener Verlag, 1998.

Koslowski, Peter. "Der leidende Gott." In *Theodizee: Gott vor Gericht?,* edited by Willi Oelmüller, 33–66. Munich: Fink, 1990.

———. *Gnosis und Theodizee: Eine Studie über den leidenden Gott des Gnostizismus.* Vienna: Passagen, 1993.

Köster, Helmut. "ὑπόστασις [hypostasis]." In *Theological Dictionary of the New Testament,* edited by Gerhard Kittel and Gerhard Friedrich, 8:572–89. Grand Rapids: Eerdmans, 1972.

Krämer, Hans Joachim. *Arete bei Platon und Aristoteles: Zum Wesen und zur Geschichte der platonischen Ontologie.* Heidelberg: Winter, 1959.

Kreiner, Armin. *Gott im Leid: Zur Stichhaltigkeit der Theodizee-Argumente.* 2nd ed. Freiburg: Herder, 1998.

Kress, Christine. *Gottes Allmacht angesichts von Leiden: Zur Interpretation der Gotteslehre in den systematisch-theologischen Entwürfen von Paul Althaus, Paul Tillich und Karl Barth.* Neukirchen-Vluyn: Neukirchener, 1999.

Krieg, Matthias. *Todesbilder im Alten Testament, oder. "Wie die Alten den Tod gebildet."* Zurich: Theologischer Verlag, 1988.

Krochmalnik, Daniel. "Das Böse in der jüdischen Tradition." In *Das Böse in den Weltreligionen,* edited by Johannes Laube, 13–62. Darmstadt: Wissenschaftliche Buchgesellschaft, 2003.

Krötke, Wolf. "Das Böse als Absurdes: Theologische Zuspitzungen." In *Leben im Schatten des Bösen,* edited by Union Evangelischer Kirchen, 63–81. Neukirchen-Vluyn: Neukirchener Verlagshaus, 2004.

———. *Sin and Nothingness in the Theology of Karl Barth.* Edited and translated by Philip G. Ziegler and Christina-Maria Bammel. Princeton: Princeton Theological Seminary, 2005.

Krüger, Thomas. *Theologische Gegenwartsdeutung im Kohelet-Buch*. Habilitation dissertation, University of Munich, 1990.

Kundert, Lukas. *Die Opferung/Bindung Isaaks*. Neukirchen-Vluyn: Neukirchener Verlag, 1998.

Kushner, Harold S. *When Bad Things Happen to Good People*. New York: Schocken, 1989.

Kutschera, Franz von. *Vernunft und Glaube*. Berlin: De Gruyter, 1990.

Laato, Antti, and Johannes C. de Moor. "Introduction." In *Theodicy in the World of the Bible*, edited by Antti Laato and Johannes C. de Moor, vii–liv. Leiden: Brill, 2003.

———, eds. *Theodicy in the World of the Bible*. Leiden: Brill, 2003.

Lacroix, Michel. *Le mal*. Paris: Flammarion, 1998.

Lactantius. *The Wrath of God*. In *Minor Works*, translated by Mary Francis McDonald, 59–116. Washington, DC: Catholic University of America Press, 1965.

Lake, Donald M. "He Died for All: The Universal Dimensions of the Atonement." In *Grace Unlimited*, edited by Clark H. Pinnock, 31–51. Minneapolis: Bethany Fellowship, 1975.

Laks, André, and Glenn W. Most, eds., trans. *Early Greek Philosophy*. Cambridge: Harvard University Press, 2016–.

Latacz, Joachim. *Einführung in die griechische Tragödie*. Göttingen: Vandenhoeck & Ruprecht, 1994.

Laytner, Anson. *Arguing with God: A Jewish Tradition*. Northvale: Aronson, 1990.

Leibniz, Gottfried Wilhelm. *Confessio philosophi: Papers concerning the Problem of Evil, 1671–1678*. Edited and translated by R. C. Sleigh. New Haven: Yale University Press, 2005.

———. "On Contingency." In *Philosophical Essays*, edited and translated by Roger Ariew and Daniel Garber, 28–30. Indianapolis: Hackett,1989.

———. "On First Truths." In *The Shorter Leibniz Texts: A Collection of New Translations*, translated by Lloyd Strickland, 29–30. London: Continuum, 2006.

———. *New Essays on Human Understanding*. Translated and edited by Peter Remnant and Jonathan Bennett. Cambridge: Cambridge University Press, 1981.

———. *Philosophical Papers and Letters*. Edited and translated by Leroy E. Loemker. Dordrecht: Reidel, 1969.

———. *Principles of Nature and of Grace*. In *Philosophical Papers and Letters*, edited and translated by Leroy E. Loemker, 636–42. Dordrecht: Reidel, 1969.

———. *Theodicy: Essays on the Goodness of God, the Freedom of Man, and the Origin of Evil*. Edited by Austin Farrer. Translated by E. M. Huggard. Chicago: Open Court, 1985.

Lenzen, Wolfgang. *Glauben, Wissen und Wahrscheinlichkeit: Systeme der epistemischen Logik*. Vienna: Springer, 1980.

Lescow, Theodor. "Psalm 22,2–22 und Psalm 88: Komposition und Dramaturgie." *Zeitschrift für die Alttestamentliche Wissenschaft* 117, no. 2. (2005) 217–31.

———. *Theodizee: Christa Wolf, Altes Testament, Neues Testament, Paul Celan*. Malente: Theodor Lescow, 2002.

Levenson, Jon Douglas. *Creation and the Persistence of Evil: The Jewish Drama of Divine Omnipotence*. San Francisco: Harper & Row, 1988.

———. *The Death and Resurrection of the Beloved Son: The Transformation of Child Sacrifice in Judaism and Christianity*. New Haven: Yale University Press, 1993.

Lewis, C. S. *The Problem of Pain*. New York: Simon and Schuster, 1996.

Lewis, Edwin. *The Creator and the Adversary*. New York: Abingdon-Cokesbury, 1948.

Libet, Benjamin. *Neurophysiology of Consciousness: Selected Papers and New Essays by Benjamin Libet*. Boston: Birkhäuser, 1993.

Lichtenberg, Hans P. "Über die Unerforschlichkeit des Bösen nach Kant." *Studia philosophica* 53 (1993) 117–31.

Limbeck, Meinrad. "Zürnt Gott wirklich? Anfragen an die Basis der paulinischen Rechtfertigungsbotschaft." *Bibel heute* 136 (1998) 220–22.

Lindström, Fredrik. *Suffering and Sin: Interpretations of Illness in the Individual Complaint Psalms*. Stockholm: Almqvist and Wiksell, 1994.

———. "Theodicy in The Psalms." In *Theodicy in the World of the Bible*, edited by Antti Laato and Johannes C. de Moor, 256–303. Leiden: Brill, 2003.

Lovejoy, Arthur O. *The Great Chain of Being: A Study of the History of an Idea*. Cambridge: Harvard University Press, 1964.

Löwith, Karl. "Knowledge and Faith: From the Pre-Socratics to Heidegger." In *Religion and Culture: Essays in Honor of Paul Tillich*, edited by Walter Leibrecht and translated by Harold O. J. Brown, 196–210. New York: Harper, 1959.

Luther, Martin. *The Bondage of the Will*. In *Word and Faith: The Annotated Luther 2*, edited by Kirsi I. Stjerna, 153–57. Minneapolis: Fortress, 2015.

———. *The Freedom of a Christian*. In *The Roots of Reform: The Annotated Luther 1*, edited by Timothy J. Wengert, 467–538. Minneapolis: Fortress, 2015.

———. *The Heidelberg Disputation*. In *The Roots of Reform: The Annotated Luther 1*, edited by Timothy J. Wengert, 67–120. Minneapolis: Fortress, 2015.

———. *The Large Catechism*. In *Word and Faith: The Annotated Luther 2*, edited by Kirsi I. Stjerna, 279–415. Minneapolis: Fortress, 2015.

———. *Luther on the Creation: A Critical and Devotional Commentary on Genesis*. Edited and revised by John Nicholas Lenker. Translated by Henry Cole. Minneapolis: Lutherans in All Lands Co., 1904.

———. *Martin Luther's Werke: Kritische Gesammtausgabe*. Weimar: Böhlau, 1883.

———. *Pastoral Writings: The Annotated Luther 4*. Edited by Mary Jane Haemig. Minneapolis: Fortress, 2016.

———. *The Small Catechism*. In *Pastoral Writings: The Annotated Luther 4*, edited by Mary Jane Haemig, 201–52. Minneapolis: Fortress, 2016.

Lüthi, Kurt. *Gott und das Böse: Eine biblisch-theologische und systematische These zur Lehre vom Bösen, entworfen in Auseinandersetzung mit Schelling und Karl Barth*. Zurich: Zwingli, 1961.

Lux, Rüdiger. "Das Böse—warum lässt Gott das zu? Hiobs Fragen an den Gott, der der Allmächtige ist." In *Leben im Schatten des Bösen*, edited by Union Evangelischer Kirchen, 26–49. Neukirchen-Vluyn: Neukirchener Verlagshaus, 2004.

Maas, Wilhelm. *Unveränderlichkeit Gottes: Zum Verhältnis von griechisch-philosophischer und christlicher Gotteslehre*. Paderborn: Schöningh, 1974.

Mackie, John Leslie. "Evil and Omnipotence." *Mind* 64, no. 254 (1955).

———. *The Miracle of Theism: Arguments For and Against the Existence of God*. Oxford: Clarendon, 1982.

Madden, Edward H., and Peter H. Hare. *Evil and the Concept of God*. Springfield: Thomas, 1968.

Mandouze, André. *Saint Augustin: L'aventure de la raison et de la grâce*. Paris: Études Augustiniennes, 1968.

Manemann, Jürgen. "If the Good becomes the Evil: Antimonotheism in Germany after Reunification and the Problems of the Doctrine of Justification." In *Fire in the Ashes: God, Evil, and the Holocaust*, edited by David Patterson and John K. Roth, 160–74. Seattle: University of Washington Press, 2005.

———. "In Response to Dider Pollefeyt and David Patterson." In *Fire in the Ashes: God, Evil, and the Holocaust*, edited by David Patterson and John K. Roth, 184–88. Seattle: University of Washington Press, 2005.

———. *Rettende Erinnerung an die Zukunft: Essay über die christliche Verschärfung*. Mainz: Matthias-Grünewald-Verlag, 2005.

Mangan, Céline. "The Interpretation of Job in the Targums." In *The Book of Job*, edited by W. A. M. Beuken, 267–80. Leuven: Peeters, 1994.

Markschies, Christoph. *Gnosis: An Introduction*. Translated by John Bowden. London: Clark, 2003.

Marquard, Odo. *In Defense of the Accidental: Philosophical Studies*. Translated by Robert M. Wallace. Oxford: Oxford University Press, 1991.

———. "Malum." In *Historisches Wörterbuch der Philosophie*, edited by Joachim Ritter, et al., 5:652–56. Basel: Schwabe, 1984.

Martinek, Manuela. *Wie die Schlange zum Teufel wurde: Die Symbolik in der Paradiesgeschichte von der hebräischen Bibel bis zum Koran*. Wiesbaden: Harrassowitz, 1996.

Mathewes, Charles T. *Evil and the Augustinian Tradition*. Cambridge: Cambridge University Press, 2001.

May, Gerhard, et al., eds. *Marcion und seine kirchengeschichtliche Wirkung = Marcion and His Impact on Church History: Vorträge der Internationalen Fachkonferenz zu Marcion, gehalten vom 15.-18. August 2001 in Mainz*. Berlin: De Gruyter, 2002.

Mays, James Luther. "'Now I Know': An Exposition of Genesis 22:1–19 and Matthew 26:36–46." *Theology Today* 58, no. 4 (2002) 519–25.

McCloskey, Henry John. *God and Evil*. Hague: Nijhoff, 1974.

McDowell, John C. "Much Ado about Nothing: Karl Barth's Being Unable to Do Nothing about Nothingness." *International Journal of Systematic Theology* 4, no. 3 (2002) 319–35.

McElwain, Thomas. "Genesis 22, Judaism, Islam and the Sacrifice of Isaac." *Christian Churches of God*, 2011. http://www.ccg.org/weblibs/study-papers/p244.html.

McFarlane, Adrian Anthony. *A Grammar of Fear and Evil: A Husserlian-Wittgensteinian Hermeneutic.* New York: Lang, 1996.

Meessen, Frank. *Unveränderlichkeit und Menschwerdung Gottes: eine theologiegeschichtlich-systematische Untersuchung.* Freiburg: Herder, 1989.

Meier, Erhard. "Die Haltung des Buddhismus zur Leidensfrage." In *Warum leiden? Die Antwort der Weltreligionen*, edited by Adel Théodore Khoury and Peter Hünermann, 44–73. Freiburg: Herder, 1987.

Meisig, Konrad. "Leiden im Hinduismus." In *Warum leiden?*, edited by Adel Théodore Khoury and Peter Hünermann, 9–43. Freiburg: Herder, 1987.

Melanchthon, Philipp. *Loci communes rerum theologicarum.* In *Loci theologici*, vol. 21 of *Opera quae supersunt omnia*, edited by Heinrich Ernst Bindseil, cols. 82–229. Braunschweig: Schwetschke, 1854.

———. *Lucubratiuncula.* In *Loci theologici*, vol. 21 of *Opera quae supersunt omnia*, edited by Heinrich Ernst Bindseil, cols. 11–48. Braunschweig: Schwetschke, 1854.

Menke, Karl-Heinz. "Der Gott, der jetzt schon Zukunft schenkt: Plädoyer für eine christologische Theodizee." In *Mit Gott streiten*, edited by Harald Wagner, 90–130. Freiburg: Herder, 1998.

Menne, Albert. "*Malum.*" In *Historisches Wörterbuch der Philosophie*, edited by Joachim Ritter, et al., 6:666–70. Basel: Schwabe, 1984.

Mettinger, Tryggve N. D. "Fighting the Powers of Chaos and Hell: Towards the Biblical Portrait of God." *Studia Theologica—Nordic Journal of Theology* 39, no. 1 (1985) 21–38.

Metz, Johannes Baptist. "Theodizee-empfindliche Gottesrede." In *Landschaft aus Schreien*, edited by Johann Baptist Metz, 81–102. Mainz: Matthias-Grünewald-Verl, 1995.

———, ed. "*Landschaft aus Schreien*": *Zur Dramatik der Theodizeefrage.* Mainz: Matthias-Grünewald-Verlag, 1995.

Miggelbrink, Ralf. *Der Zorn Gottes: Geschichte und Aktualität einer ungeliebten biblischen Tradition.* Freiburg: Herder, 2000.

Miller, Jeff, and Judy Arnel Trevena. "Cortical Movement Preparation and Conscious Decisions: Averaging Artifacts and Timing Biases." *Consciousness and Cognition* 11, no. 2 (2002) 308–13.

Miller, Patrick D. *The Religion of Ancient Israel.* Louisville: Westminster John Knox, 2000.

Moberly, R. Walter L. *The Bible, Theology, and Faith: A Study of Abraham and Jesus.* Cambridge: Cambridge University Press, 2000.

———. "Christ as the Key to Scripture: Genesis 22 Reconsidered." In *He Swore an Oath: Biblical Themes from Genesis 12–50*, edited by Richard S. Hess et al., 143–73. Grand Rapids: Baker, 1994.

Moltmann, Jürgen. *Der gekreuzigte Gott: Das Kreuz Christi als Grund und Kritik christlicher Theologie.* Munich: Kaiser, 1972.

Morton, Adam. *On Evil.* New York: Routledge, 2004.

Mugerauer, Roland. *Versöhnung als Überwindung der Entfremdung: Die Konzeption der Entfremdung und ihrer Überwindung bei Paul Tillich in der Auseinandersetzung mit anderen Konzeptionen.* Marburg: Tectum, 1996.

Müller, Hans-Peter. *Das Hiobproblem: Seine Stellung und Entstehung im alten Orient und im Alten Testament.* Darmstadt: Wissenschaftliche Buchgesellschaft, 1978.

———. *Hiob und seine Freunde: Traditionsgeschichtliches zum Verständnis des Hiobbuches.* Zurich: EVZ, 1970.

Murphy, George L. "Does the Trinity Play Dice?" *Perspectives on Science and Christian Faith* 51, no. 1 (1999) 18–25.

Murphy, Nancey C., and George F. R. Ellis. *On the Moral Nature of the Universe: Theology, Cosmology, and Ethics.* Minneapolis: Fortress, 1996.

Nagel, Thomas. "Death." *Noûs* 4, no. 1 (1970) 73–80.

Natterer, Paul. *Systematischer Kommentar zur Kritik der reinen Vernunft: Interdisziplinäre Bilanz der Kantforschung seit 1945.* Berlin: De Gruyter, 2003.

Neiman, Susan. *Evil in Modern Thought: An Alternative History of Philosophy.* Princeton: Princeton University Press, 2015.

Nemo, Philippe. *Job and the Excess of Evil*. Translated by Michael Kigel. Pittsburgh: Duquesne University Press, 1998.

———. *Job et l'excès du mal*. Rev. ed. Paris: Albin Michel, 1999.

Nestle, Wilhelm. *Die Nachsokratiker*. Vol. 2. Jena: Diederichs, 1923.

Neuenschwander, Ulrich. *Gott im neuzeitlichen Denken*. Vol. 1. Gütersloh: Gütersloher Verlagshaus, 1977.

Neuhaus, Gerd. "Theodizee: Abbruch oder Anstoss des Glaubens? Eine Annäherung von ausgewählten Beispielen der Literatur her." In *Landschaft aus Schreien*, edited by Johann Baptist Metz, 9–55. Mainz: Matthias-Grünewald-Verl, 1995.

———. "Theodizee und Glaubensgeschichte: Zur Kontingenz einer Fragestellung." In *Mit Gott streiten*, edited by Harald Wagner, 11–47. Freiburg: Herder, 1998.

Neuner, Peter. "Der Glaube als subjektives Prinzip der theologischen Erkenntnis." In *Handbuch der Fundamentaltheologie*, edited by Walter Kern, et al., 4:23–36. 2nd rev. ed. Tübingen: Francke, 1988.

Neusner, Jacob. "Theodicy in Judaism." In *Theodicy in the World of the Bible*, edited by Antti Laato and Johannes C. de Moor, 685–727. Leiden: Brill, 2003.

———. *The Theology of the Oral Torah: Revealing the Justice of God*. Montreal: McGill-Queen's University Press, 1999.

Newsom, Carol A. *The Book of Job: A Contest of Moral Imaginations*. Oxford: Oxford University Press, 2003.

Noort, Edward, and Eibert J. C. Tigchelaar, eds. *The Sacrifice of Isaac: The Aqedah (Genesis 22) and Its Interpretations*. Leiden: Brill, 2002.

Norris, Joel. *Serial Killers: The Growing Menace*. New York: Doubleday, 1988.

Nüchtern, Michael. *Warum lässt Gott das zu? Kritik der Allmacht Gottes in Religion und Philosophie*. Frankfurt: Lembeck, 1995.

O'Connor, Timothy. "Agent Causation." In *Agents, Causes, and Events*, edited by Timothy O'Connor, 61–79. Oxford: Oxford University Press, 1995.

———, ed. *Agents, Causes, and Events: Essays on Indeterminism and Free Will*. Oxford: Oxford University Press, 1995.

Oberdorfer, Bernd. "'Was sucht ihr den Lebendigen bei den Toten?' Überlegungen zur Realität der Auferstehung in Auseinandersetzung mit Gerd Lüdemann." In *Die Wirklichkeit der Auferstehung*, edited by Hans-Joachim Eckstein and Michael Welker, 165–82. Neukirchen-Vluyn: Neukirchener Verlagshaus, 2002.

Oberhänsli-Widmer, Gabrielle. "Schafft Gott das Böse? Schöpfung und Sündenfall biblisch, talmudisch und kabbalistisch gelesen." *Judaica* 59, no. 2 (2003) 129–43.

Obeyesekere, Gananath. "Theodicy, Sin and Salvation in a Sociology of Buddhism." In *Dialectic in Practical Religion*, edited by Edmund Ronald Leach, 7–40. Cambridge: Cambridge University Press, 1968.

Oden, Thomas C. *The Transforming Power of Grace*. Nashville: Abingdon, 1993.

Oeing-Hanhoff, Ludger, and Walter Kasper. "Negativität und Böses." In *Christlicher Glaube in moderner Gesellschaft*, edited by Franz Böckle, 9:150–75. Freiburg: Herder, 1981.

Oelmüller, Willi. *Die unbefriedigte Aufklärung: Beiträge zu einer Theorie der Moderne von Lessing, Kant und Hegel*. Frankfurt: Suhrkamp, 1979.

Oeming, Manfred, and Konrad Schmid. *Hiobs Weg: Stationen von Menschen im Leid*. Neukirchen-Vluyn: Neukirchener Verlag, 2001.

Olivetti, Marco M., ed. *Teodicea oggi?* Archivio di filosofia 56. Padova: CEDAM, 1988.

Omolade, Barbara. "Faith Confronts Evil." In *Christian Faith and the Problem of Evil*, edited by Peter van Inwagen, 277–313. Grand Rapids: Eerdmans, 2004.

Ormsby, Eric L. *Theodicy in Islamic Thought: The Dispute over al-Ghazālī's "Best of All Possible Worlds."* Princeton: Princeton University Press, 1984.

Osborne, Thomas P. "Guide Lines for Christian Suffering: A Source-Critical and Theological Study of 1 Peter 2:21–25." *Biblica* 64, no. 3 (1983) 381–408.

Otte, Richard. "Probability and Draper's Evidential Argument from Evil." In *Christian Faith and the Problem of Evil*, edited by Peter van Inwagen, 26–40. Grand Rapids: Eerdmans, 2004.

Otto, Eckart. *Mose: Geschichte und Legende*. Munich: Beck, 2006.

Otto, Walter Friedrich. *The Homeric Gods: The Spiritual Significance of Greek Religion*. Translated by Moses Hadas. London: Thames and Hudson, 1979.

Oz, Amos. "On Degrees of Evil." In *The Many Faces of Evil: Historical Perspectives*, edited by Amélie Oksenberg Rorty and translated by Maurie Goldberg-Bartura, 288–90. London: Routledge, 2001.

Pagels, Elaine H. *The Origin of Satan*. New York: Random House, 1995.

Pannenberg, Wolfhart. *Anthropology in Theological Perspective*. Translated by Matthew J. O'Connell. London: Clark, 2004.

Park, Kyungsook. *Das Schlechte und das Böse: Studien zum Problem des Übels in der Philosophie des Thomas von Aquin*. Frankfurt: Lang, 2002.

Parker, Robert. *Athenian Religion: A History*. Oxford: Oxford University Press, 1996.

Parkinson, G. H. R. "Philosophy and Logic." In *The Cambridge Companion to Leibniz*, edited by Nicholas Jolley, 199–223. Cambridge: Cambridge University Press, 1995.

Patzer, Harald. "Die dichterischen Formgesetze der Gattung 'Tragödie.'" In *Gesammelte Schriften*, edited by Rüdiger Leimbach and Gabriele Seidel, 470–502. Stuttgart: Steiner, 1985.

———. "Humanismus und griechische Tragödie." In *Gesammelte Schriften*, edited by Rüdiger Leimbach and Gabriele Seidel, 172–85. Stuttgart: Steiner, 1985.

Pauen, Michael. *Illusion Freiheit? Mögliche und unmögliche Konsequenzen der Hirnforschung*. Frankfurt: Fischer, 2004.

Penchansky, David. "Job's Wife: The Satan's Handmaid." In *Shall Not the Judge of All the Earth Do What Is Right?*, edited by David Penchansky and Paul L. Redditt, 223–28. Winona Lake: Eisenbrauns, 2000.

———. *What Rough Beast? Images of God in the Hebrew Bible*. Louisville: Westminster John Knox, 1999.

Penchansky, David, and Paul L. Redditt, eds. *Shall Not the Judge of All the Earth Do What Is Right? Studies on the Nature of God in Tribute to James L. Crenshaw*. Winona Lake: Eisenbrauns, 2000.

Penelhum, Terence. "Divine Goodness and the Problem of Evil." In *Christian Faith and the Problem of Evil*, edited by Peter van Inwagen, 69–82. Grand Rapids: Eerdmans, 2004.

Penrose, Roger. *The Emperor's New Mind: Concerning Computers, Minds, and the Laws of Physics*. Oxford: Oxford University Press, 1989.

Perru, Olivier. "Le mal a-t-il une réalité ontologique: Approche comparative chez Saint Thomas et le Pseudo-Denys." *Recherches de science religieuse* 86, no. 2 (1998) 171–200.

Peters, Dieter Stefan. "Biologische Anmerkungen zur Frage nach dem Sinn des Leidens in der Natur." In *Leben durch Zerstörung?*, edited by Hans Kessler, 27–37. Würzburg: Echter, 2000.

Petersen, Uwe. *Das Böse in uns: Phänomenologie und Genealogie des Bösen*. Horitschon: Novum, 2005.

Peterson, Michael L. *Evil and the Christian God*. Grand Rapids: Baker, 1982.

Petrik, James M. *Evil Beyond Belief*. Armonk: Sharpe, 2000.

Pfeiffer, Henrik. "'Ein reines Herz schaffe mir, Gott!' Zum Verständnis des Menschen nach Ps 51." *Zeitschrift für Theologie und Kirche* 102, no. 3 (2005) 293–311.

Phillips, Dewi Zephaniah. *The Problem of Evil and the Problem of God*. Minneapolis: Fortress, 2005.

Philo. "On the Unchangeableness of God." In *Philo*, edited and translated by F. H. Colson and G. H. Whitaker, 2:3–101. Cambridge: Harvard University Press, 198.

Pieper, Annemarie. "Das Böse: Verhängnis oder Schuld? Philosophische Annäherungen." In *Leben im Schatten des Bösen*, edited by Union Evangelischer Kirchen, 9–25. Neukirchen-Vluyn: Neukirchener Verlagshaus, 2004.

———. *Gut und Böse*. 3rd ed. Munich: Beck, 2008.

Pieper, Josef. *Begeisterung und göttlicher Wahnsinn: Über den platonischen Dialog "Phaidros."* Munich: Kösel, 1962.

Pierris, Apostolos L., ed. *The Empedoclean "Kosmos": Structure, Process and the Question of Cyclicity*. Patras: Institute for Philosophical Research, 2005.

Pike, Nelson. "Hume on Evil." In *The Problem of Evil*, edited by Marilyn McCord Adams and Robert Merrihew Adams, 38–52. Oxford: Oxford University Press, 1990.

Pilnei, Oliver. *Wie entsteht christlicher Glaube? Untersuchungen zur Glaubenskonstitution in der hermeneutischen Theologie bei Rudolf Bultmann, Ernst Fuchs und Gerhard Ebeling*. Tübingen: Mohr Siebeck, 2007.

Pinnock, Clark H. *Most Moved Mover: A Theology of God's Openness*. Grand Rapids: Baker, 2001.

Pinnock, Clark H., et al., eds. *The Openness of God: A Biblical Challenge to the Traditional Understanding of God*. Downers Grove: InterVarsity, 1994.

Pinomaa, Lennart. "Der Zorn Gottes: Eine dogmengeschichtliche Übersicht." *Zeitschrift für Systematische Theologie* 17 (1940) 587–614.

Placher, William C. "An Engagement with Marilyn McCord Adams's *Horrendous Evils and the Goodness of God.*" *Scottish Journal of Theology* 55, no. 4 (2002) 461–67.

Plantinga, Alvin. "Epistemic Probability and Evil." In *Teodicea oggi?*, edited by Marco M. Olivetti, 557–84. Archivio di filosofia 56. Padova: CEDAM, 1988.

———. "The Free Will Defence." In *The Philosophy of Religion*, edited by Basil Mitchell, 105–20. London: Oxford University Press, 1971.

———. *God and Other Minds: A Study of the Rational Justification of Belief in God.* Ithaca: Cornell University Press, 1990.

———. *God, Freedom, and Evil.* London: Allen & Unwin, 1975.

———. "Good, Evil, and the Metaphysics of Freedom." In *The Problem of Evil*, edited by Marilyn McCord Adams and Robert Merrihew Adams, 83–109. Oxford: Oxford University Press, 1990.

———. *The Nature of Necessity.* Oxford: Clarendon, 1974.

———. "The Probabilistic Argument from Evil." *Philosophical Studies: An International Journal for Philosophy in the Analytic Tradition* 35, no. 1 (1979) 1–53.

———. "Self-Profile." In *Alvin Plantinga*, edited by James E. Tomberlin and Peter van Inwagen, 3–97. Dordrecht: Reidel, 1985.

———. "Supralapsarianism, or 'O Felix Culpa.'" In *Christian Faith and the Problem of Evil*, edited by Peter van Inwagen, 1–25. Grand Rapids: Eerdmans, 2004.

Plato. *The Dialogues of Plato.* Edited and translated Benjamin Jowett. 4th ed. Oxford: Clarendon, 1953.

Plotinus. *Enneads.* Translated by Arthur Hilary Armstrong. Cambridge: Harvard University Press, 1988.

Pohlenz, Max. *Vom Zorne Gottes: Eine Studie über den Einfluss der griechischen Philosophie auf das alte Christentum.* Göttingen: Vandenhoeck & Ruprecht, 1909.

Polkinghorne, John C. *Science and Providence: God's Interaction with the World.* Boston: Shambhala, 1989.

Poma, Andrea. *The Impossibility and Necessity of Theodicy: The "Essais" of Leibniz.* Dordrecht: Springer, 2013.

Pope, Alexander. "An Essay on Man." In *The Major Works*, edited by Pat Rogers, 270–308. Oxford: Oxford University Press, 2008.

Primavesi, Oliver. "The Structure of Empedocles' Cosmic Cycle: Aristotle and the Byzantine Anonymous." In *The Empedoclean "Kosmos": Structure, Process and the Question of Cyclicity: Proceedings of the Symposium Philosophiae Antiquae Tertium Myconense, July 6th-July 13th, 2003*, edited by Apostolos L. Pierris, 245–64. Patras: Institute for Philosophical Research, 2005.

Prinz, Wolfgang. "Freiheit oder Wissenschaft?" In *Freiheit des Entscheidens und Handelns: Ein Problem der nomologischen Psychologie*, edited by Mario von Cranach and Klaus Foppa, 86–103. Heidelberg: Asanger, 1996.

Rad, Gerhard von. *Genesis: A Commentary.* Translated by John H. Marks. Philadelphia: Westminster, 1961.

———. *God at Work in Israel.* Translated by John H. Marks. Nashville: Abingdon, 1980.

———. "'Righteousness' and 'Life' in the Cultic Languages of the Psalms." In *The Problem of the Hexateuch and Other Essays*, translated by E. W. Trueman Dicken, 243–66. New York: McGraw-Hill, 1966.

Ramelow, Tilman. *Gott, Freiheit, Weltenwahl: Der Ursprung des Begriffes der besten aller möglichen Welten in der Metaphysik der Willensfreiheit zwischen Antonio Perez S.J. (1599–1649) und G.W. Leibniz (1646–1716).* Leiden: Brill, 1997.

Rasmussen, Josh. "On Creating Worlds without Evil: Given Divine Counterfactual Knowledge." *Religious Studies* 40, no. 4 (2004) 457–70.

Ratschow, Carl Heinz. *Lutherische Dogmatik zwischen Reformation und Aufklärung.* 2 vols. Gütersloh: Gütersloher Verlagshaus, 1966.

Reichenbach, Bruce R. *Evil and a Good God.* New York: Fordham University Press, 1982.

Reiner, Hans. "Vom Wesen des *Malum*: Positives zur Kritik des Axioms 'omne ens est *bonum.*'" *Zeitschrift für philosophische Forschung* 23, no. 4 (1969) 567–77.

Reinhardt, Karl. *Aischylos als Regisseur und Theologe.* Bern: Francke, 1949.

Reinhuber, Thomas. *Kämpfender Glaube: Studien zu Luthers Bekenntnis am Ende von De servo arbitrio.* Berlin: De Gruyter, 2000.

Repp, Martin. *Die Transzendierung des Theismus in der Religionsphilosophie Paul Tillichs.* Frankfurt: Lang, 1986.

Reventlow, Henning, and Yair Hoffman, eds. *The Problem of Evil and Its Symbols in Jewish and Christian Tradition.* London: Clark, 2004.

Ricœur, Paul. *Evil: A Challenge to Philosophy and Theology.* Translated by John Bowden. London: Continuum, 2007.

———. *Oneself as Another.* Translated by Kathleen Blamey. Chicago: University of Chicago Press, 1992.

Ringleben, Joachim. *Die Krankheit zum Tode von Sören Kierkegaard: Erklärung und Kommentar.* Göttingen: Vandenhoeck & Ruprecht, 1995.

Ritter, Joachim, et al., eds. *Historisches Wörterbuch der Philosophie.* 13 vols. Basel: Schwabe, 1971–2007.

Robinson, William. *The Devil and God.* Nashville: Abingdon-Cokesbury, 1945.

Rogozinski, Jacob. "Kant et le mal radical." *Kriterion* 39, no. 98 (1998) 7–21.

Rohls, Jan. *Geschichte der Ethik.* Tübingen: Mohr, 1991.

Rommel, Herbert. *Zum Begriff des Bösen bei Augustinus und Kant: Der Wandel von der ontologischen zur autonomen Perspektive.* Frankfurt: Lang, 1997.

Rorty, Amélie Oksenberg, ed. *The Many Faces of Evil: Historical Perspectives.* London: Routledge, 2001.

Rosenau, Hartmut. "Theogonie: Schellings Beitrag zum Theodizeeproblem nach seiner 'Freiheitsschrift' von 1809." *Neue Zeitschrift für systematische Theologie und Religionsphilosophie* 32, no. 1 (1990) 26–52.

Rosenberg, Shalom. *Good and Evil in Jewish Thought.* Translated by John Glucker. Tel-Aviv: MOD, 1989.

Ross, George MacDonald. *Leibniz.* Oxford: Oxford University Press, 1984.

Roth, Gerhard. *Aus Sicht des Gehirns.* Frankfurt: Suhrkamp, 2003.

Roth, John K. "A Theodicy of Protest." In *Encountering Evil: Live Options in Theodicy,* edited by Stephen T. Davis, 7–37. Atlanta: John Knox, 1981.

Rötzer, Florian, ed. *Das Böse: Jenseits von Absichten und Tätern oder: Ist der Teufel ins System ausgewandert?* Göttingen: Steidl, 1995.

Roukema, Riemer. "L'Origine du mal selon Origène et dans ses sources." *Revue d'histoire et de philosophie religieuses* 83, no. 4 (2003) 405–20.

Rowe, William L. "The Empirical Argument from Evil." In *Rationality, Religious Belief, and Moral Commitment: New Essays in the Philosophy of Religion,* edited by Robert Audi and William J. Wainwright, 227–47. Ithaca: Cornell University Press, 1986.

———. "Evil and the Theistic Hypothesis: A Response to Wykstra." In *The Problem of Evil,* edited by Marilyn McCord Adams and Robert Merrihew Adams, 161–67. Oxford: Oxford University Press, 1990.

———. "The Problem of Evil and Some Varieties of Atheism." In *The Problem of Evil,* edited by Marilyn McCord Adams and Robert Merrihew Adams, 126–37. Oxford: Oxford University Press, 1990.

———. "Ruminations about Evil." *Philosophical Perspectives* 5 (1991) 69–88.

Runia, David T. *Philo of Alexandria and the 'Timaeus' of Plato.* Leiden: Brill, 1986.

———. "Theodicy in Philo of Alexandria." In *Theodicy in the World of the Bible,* edited by Antti Laato and Johannes C. de Moor, 567–604. Leiden: Brill, 2003.

Russell, Bertrand. *A Critical Exposition of the Philosophy of Leibniz with an Appendix of Leading Passages.* Cambridge: Cambridge University Press, 1900.

Russell, Jeffrey Burton. *Satan: The Early Christian Tradition.* Ithaca: Cornell University Press, 1981.

Russell, Robert John. "Quantum Physics in Philosophical and Theological Perspective." In *Physics, Philosophy, and Theology: A Common Quest for Understanding,* edited by Robert John Russell et al., 579–95. Notre Dame: University of Notre Dame Press, 1988.

Rüterswörden, Udo. "Das Böse in der deuteronomischen Schultheologie." In *Das Deuteronomium und seine Querbeziehungen,* edited by Timo Veijola, 223–41. Göttingen: Vandenhoeck & Ruprecht, 1996.

Sack, Max. *Die Verzweiflung, eine Untersuchung ihres Wesens und ihre Entstehung.* Kallmünz: Lossleben, 1930.

Safranski, Rüdiger. *Das Böse oder das Drama der Freiheit.* Munich: Hanser, 1997.

Sala, Giovanni B. "Das Böse und Gott als Erstursache nach dem hl. Thomas von Aquin." *Theologie und Philosophie* 77, no. 1 (2002) 23–53.

———. *Kants Kritik der praktischen Vernunft: Ein Kommentar.* Darmstadt: Wissenschaftliche Buchgesellschaft, 2004.

Sanders, John. *The God Who Risks: A Theology of Providence.* Downers Grove: InterVarsity, 1998.

Sands, Kathleen M. *Escape from Paradise: Evil and Tragedy in Feminist Theology.* Minneapolis: Fortress, 1994.

Sarot, Marcel. "Theodicy and Modernity: An Inquiry into the Historicity of Theodicy." In *Theodicy in the World of the Bible: The Goodness of God and the Problem of Evil*, edited by Antii Laato and Johannes Moor, 1–26. Leiden: Brill, 2003.

Satake, Akira. "Das Leiden der Jünger 'um meinetwillen.'" *Zeitschrift für die Neutestamentliche Wissenschaft und die Kunde der Älteren Kirche* 67, no. 1 (1976) 4–19.

Scarre, Geoffrey. *After Evil: Responding to Wrongdoing.* Aldershot: Ashgate, 2004.

Schadewaldt, Wolfgang. *Die Anfänge der Philosophie bei den Griechen: Die Vorsokratiker und ihre Voraussetzungen.* Edited by Ingeborg Schudoma. Frankfurt: Suhrkamp, 1978.

Schäfer, Christian. *Unde malum: Die Frage nach dem Woher des Bösen bei Plotin, Augustinus und Dionysius.* Würzburg: Königshausen and Neumann, 2002.

Scharbert, Josef. *Prolegomena eines Alttestamentlers zur Erbsündenlehre.* Freiburg: Herder, 1968.

Scheiber, Karin. *Vergebung: Eine systematisch-theologische Untersuchung.* Tübingen: Mohr Siebeck, 2006.

Schelling, Friedrich Wilhelm Joseph von. *Philosophical Investigations into the Essence of Human Freedom.* Translated by Jeff Love and Johannes Schmidt. Albany: State University of New York Press, 2006.

Schepers, Gerhard. *Schöpfung und allgemeine Sündigkeit: Die Auffassung Paul Tillichs im Kontext der heutigen Diskussion.* Essen: Ludgerus, 1974.

Schiwy, Günther. *Abschied vom allmächtigen Gott.* Munich: Kösel, 1995.

Schlegel, Juliane. *Psalm 88 als Prüfstein der Exegese: Zu Sinn und Bedeutung eines beispiellosen Psalms.* Neukirchen-Vluyn: Neukirchener Verlagshaus, 2005.

Schleiermacher, Friedrich. *The Christian Faith.* Edited by Hugh Ross MacKintosh and J. S. Stewart. Translated by Hugh Ross MacKintosh. Edinburgh: Clark, 1928.

Schmid, Konrad. "Der Hiobprolog und das Hiobproblem." In *Hiobs Weg: Stationen von Menschen im Leid*, edited by Manfred Oeming and Konrad Schmid, 9–34. Neukirchen-Vluyn: Neukirchener Verlag, 2001.

Schmid, Ulrich. *Marcion und sein Apostolos: Rekonstruktion und historische Einordnung der marcionitischen Paulusbriefausgabe.* Berlin: De Gruyter, 1995.

Schmidt, Hans. *Gott und das Leid im Alten Testament.* Gießen: Töpelmann, 1926.

Schmidt-Biggemann, Wilhelm. "Böses und Psyche: Immoralität in psychologischen Diskursen." In *Das Böse: Eine historische Phänomenologie des Unerklärlichen*, edited by Carsten Colpe and Wilhelm Schmidt-Biggemann, 300–322. Frankfurt am Main: Suhrkamp, 1993.

———. "Vorwort: Über die unfaßliche Evidenz des Bösen." In *Das Böse: Eine historische Phänomenologie des Unerklärlichen*, edited by Carsten Colpe and Wilhelm Schmidt-Biggemann, 7–12. Frankfurt am Main: Suhrkamp, 1993.

Schmitt, Arbogast. "Wesenszüge der griechischen Tragödie: Schicksal, Schuld, Tragik." In *Tragödie, Idee und Transformation*, edited by Hellmut Flashar, 5–49. Stuttgart: Teubner, 1997.

Schmucker, Josef. *Das Problem der Kontingenz der Welt: Versuch einer positiven Aufarbeitung der Kritik Kants am kosmologischen Argument.* Freiburg: Herder, 1969.

———. *Das Weltproblem in Kants Kritik der reinen Vernunft: Kommentar und Strukturanalyse des ersten Buches und des zweiten Hauptstücks des zweiten Buches der transzendentalen Dialektik.* Bonn: Bouvier, 1990.

———. *Die Ontotheologie des vorkritischen Kant.* Berlin: De Gruyter, 1980.

———. *Die primären Quellen des Gottesglaubens.* Freiburg: Herder, 1967.

Schneider, John R. "Seeing God Where the Wild Things Are: An Essay on the Defeat of Horrendous Evil." In *Christian Faith and the Problem of Evil*, edited by Peter van Inwagen, 226–62. Grand Rapids: Eerdmans, 2004.

Scholnick, Sylvia Huberman. *Lawsuit Drama in the Book of Job.* PhD diss., Brandeis University, 1976.

Schönberger, Rolf. "Die Existenz des Nichtigen: Zur Geschichte der Privationstheorie." In *Die Wirklichkeit des Bösen*, edited by Friedrich Hermanni and Peter Koslowski, 15–47. Paderborn: Fink, 1998.

Schopenhauer, Arthur. *The World as Will and Representation.* Vol. 1. Edited by Judith Norman et al. Cambridge: Cambridge University Press, 2010.

Schrey, Heinz Horst. *Entfremdung.* Darmstadt: Wissenschaftliche Buchgesellschaft, 1975.

Schrödter, Hermann. *Privatio: Eine Untersuchung zu den Hintergründen der Ontologie des Mittelalters.* PhD disseration, University of Frankfurt, 1962.

Schüle, Andreas. "Der dunkle Gott: ein Gott des Glaubens: Zu Walter Dietrichs und Christian Links *Die dunklen Seiten Gottes*." *Evangelische Theologie* 61, no. 3 (2001) 241–49.

Schulte, Christoph. *Radikal Böse: die Karriere des Bösen von Kant bis Nietzsche.* Munich: Fink, 1988.

Schumacher, Thomas. *Theodizee: Bedeutung und Anspruch eines Begriffs.* Frankfurt: Lang, 1994.

Searle, John R. *Minds, Brains, and Science.* Cambridge: Harvard University Press, 1984.

Seltzer, Mark. *Serial Killers: Death and Life in America's Wound Culture.* London: Routledge, 1998.

Sereny, Gitta. *Cries Unheard: Why Children Kill: The Story of Mary Bell.* New York: Metropolitan, 1999.

Sextus Empiricus. *Outlines of Scepticism.* Edited and translated by Julia Annas and Jonathan Barnes. Cambridge: Cambridge University Press, 2000.

Shank, Robert. *Elect in the Son: A Study of the Doctrine of Election.* Minneapolis: Bethany, 1989.

Shuster, Marguerite. *The Fall and Sin: What We Have Become as Sinners.* Grand Rapids: Eerdmans, 2004.

Simon, Erika. *Die Götter der Griechen.* 4th ed. Munich: Hirmer, 1998.

Spieckermann, Hermann. "Die Satanisierung Gottes: Zur inneren Konkordanz von Novelle, Dialog und Gottesreden im Hiobbuch." In *"Wer ist wie du, Herr, unter den Göttern?": Studien zur Theologie und Religionsgeschichte Israels für Otto Kaiser zum 70. Geburtstag,* edited by Ingo Kottsieper, 431–53. Göttingen: Vandenhoeck & Ruprecht, 1994.

Stackhouse, John G. *Can God Be Trusted? Faith and the Challenge of Evil.* Oxford: Oxford University Press, 1998.

Stanton, Graham. *Jesus and Gospel.* Cambridge: Cambridge University Press, 2004.

Steel, Carlos. "Does Evil Have a Cause? Augustine's Perplexity and Thomas's Answer." *The Review of Metaphysics* 48, no. 2 (1994) 251–73.

Steen, Marc. "The Theme of the 'Suffering' God: An Exploration." In *God and Human Suffering,* edited by Jan Lambrecht and Raymond F. Collins, 69–93. Louvain: Peeters, 1990.

Stegmaier, Werner, ed. *Orientierung: Philosophische Perspektiven.* Frankfurt: Suhrkamp, 2005.

———. *Philosophie der Orientierung.* Berlin: De Gruyter, 2008.

Steins, Georg. *Die "Bindung Isaaks" im Kanon (Gen 22) Grundlagen und Programm einer kanonisch-intertextuellen Lektüre.* Freiburg: Herder, 1999.

Stocker, Michael. "Desiring the Bad: An Essay in Moral Psychology." *Journal of Philosophy* 76, no. 12 (1979) 738–53.

Stoellger, Philipp. "Die Vernunft der Kontingenz und die Kontingenz der Vernunft." In Stoellger and Dalferth, eds. *Vernunft, Kontingenz, und Gott: Konstellationen eines offenen Problems,* edited by Philipp Stoellger and Ingolf U. Dalferth, 73–116. Tübingen: Mohr Siebeck, 2000.

———. *Passivität aus Passion: Zur Problemgeschichte einer 'categoria non grata.'* Tübingen: Mohr Siebeck, 2010.

Stoellger, Philipp, and Ingolf U. Dalferth, eds. *Vernunft, Kontingenz, und Gott: Konstellationen eines offenen Problems.* Tübingen: Mohr Siebeck, 2000.

Stolz, Fritz. *Religion und Rekonstruktion: Ausgewählte Aufsätze.* Edited by Daria Pezzoli-Olgiati. Göttingen: Vandenhoeck & Ruprecht, 2004.

———. *Weltbilder der Religionen: Kultur und Natur, Diesseits und Jenseits, Kontrollierbares und Unkontrollierbares.* Zurich: Pano, 2001.

Streminger, Gerhard. *Gottes Güte und die Übel der Welt: Das Theodizeeproblem.* Tübingen: Mohr, 1992.

Stuermann, Walter Earl. *The Divine Destroyer: A Theology of Good and Evil.* Philadelphia: Westminster, 1967.

Stump, Eleonore. *Die göttliche Vorsehung und das Böse: Überlegungen zur Theodizee im Anschluss an Thomas von Aquin.* Frankfurt: Knecht, 1989.

———. "Evil and the Nature of Faith." In *Seeking Understanding: The Stob Lectures 1986–1998,* edited by Calvin College and Calvin Theological Seminary, 530–50. Grand Rapids: Eerdmans, 2001.

———. "Knowledge, Freedom and the Problem of Evil." *International Journal for Philosophy of Religion* 14, no. 1 (1983) 49–58.

———. "Narrative and the Problem of Evil: Suffering and Redemption." In *The Redemption: An Interdisciplinary Symposium on Christ as Redeemer,* edited by Stephen T. Davis et al., 207–34. Oxford: Oxford University Press, 2004.

———. "The Problem of Evil." *Faith and Philosophy* 2, no. 4 (1985) 392–423.

————. "Second-Person Accounts and the Problem of Evil." In *Perspectives in Contemporary Philosophy of Religion*, edited by Tommi Lehtonen and Timo Koistinen, 88–113. Helsinki: Luther-Agricola-Society, 2000.

Suchocki, Marjorie. *The End of Evil: Process Eschatology in Historical Context*. Albany: State University of New York Press, 1988.

Suda, Max Josef. "Psalm 51,7 als Belegstelle für Augustins Erbsündenlehre." In *Zur Aktualität des Alten Testaments: Festschrift für Georg Sauer zum 65. Geburtstag*, edited by Siegfried Kreuzer and Kurt Lüthi, 187–98. Frankfurt: Lang, 1992.

Surin, Kenneth. *Theology and the Problem of Evil*. Oxford: Blackwell, 1986.

Sutherland, Robert. *Putting God on Trial: The Biblical Book of Job*. Victoria: Trafford, 2004.

Swinburne, Richard. *The Existence of God*. 2nd ed. Oxford: Oxford University Press, 2004.

————. *Faith and Reason*. 2nd ed. Oxford: Clarendon, 2005.

————. "The Free Will Defence." In *Teodicea oggi?*, edited by Marco M. Olivetti, 141–67. Archivio di filosofia 56. Padova: CEDAM, 1988.

————. "The Problem of Evil" and "Postscript." In *Reason and Religion*, edited by Stuart C. Brown, 81–102, 134–39. Ithaca: Cornell University Press, 1977.

————. "The Problem of Evil [1994 lecture]." In *Jahrbuch für Philosophie des Forschungsinstituts für Philosophie Hannover*, edited by Perry Schmidt-Leukel, 6:17–28. Vienna: Passagen, 1995.

————. *Providence and the Problem of Evil*. Oxford: Oxford University Press, 1998.

Talbert, Charles H. *Learning through Suffering: The Educational Value of Suffering in the New Testament and in Its Milieu*. Collegeville: Liturgical, 1991.

Talbott, Thomas. "The Love of God and the Heresy of Exclusivism." *Christian Scholars Review* 27, no. 1 (1997) 99–112.

Taplin, Oliver. *The Stagecraft of Aeschylus: The Dramatic Use of Exits and Entrances in Greek Tragedy*. Oxford: Clarendon, 1977.

Tasker, R. V. G. *The Biblical Doctrine of the Wrath of God*. London: Tyndale, 1951.

Tattersall, Nicholas. "The Evidential Argument From Evil." *The Secular Web*, http://infidels.org/library/modern/nicholas_tattersall/evil.html.

Theile, Ursel. "Destruktion durch angeborene Fehlbildungen und Defekte." In *Leben durch Zerstörung?*, edited by Hans Kessler, 66–84. Würzburg: Echter, 2000.

Theunissen, Michael. *Das Selbst auf dem Grund der Verzweiflung: Kierkegaards negativistische Methode*. Frankfurt: Hain, 1991.

————. *Kierkegaard's Concept of Despair*. Princeton: Princeton University Press, 2005.

Thiel, John E. *God, Evil, and Innocent Suffering: A Theological Reflection*. New York: Crossroad, 2002.

Thiel, Winfried. "'Evil' in the Books of Kings." In *The Problem of Evil and its Symbols in Jewish and Christian Tradition*, edited by Henning Graf Reventlow and Yair Hoffman, 2–13. London: Continuum, 2004.

Thoma, Clemens. "Gott im Unrecht: Rabbinische und halakhische Deutungen des rätselhaft, hilflos und zerstörend wirkenden Gottes." In *Gott—ratlos vor dem Bösen?*, edited by Wolfgang Beinert, 86–108. Freiburg: Herder, 1999.

Thoma, Clemens, and Simon Lauer, eds. *Von der Erschaffung der Welt bis zum Tod Abrahams: Bereschit Rabba 1–63*. Vol. 2 of *Die Gleichnisse der Rabbinen*. Bern: Lang, 1991.

Thomas, Laurence. *Vessels of Evil: American Slavery and the Holocaust*. Philadelphia: Temple University Press, 1993.

Thomason, Bill. *God on Trial: The Book of Job and Human Suffering*. Collegeville: Liturgical, 1997.

Thorp, John. *Free Will: A Defence Against Neurophysiological Determinism*. London: Routledge and Kegan Paul, 1980.

Tilley, Terrence W. *The Evils of Theodicy*. Washington, DC: Georgetown University Press, 1991.

Tillich, Paul. "Das Neue Sein als Zentralbegriff einer christlichen Theologie." In vol. 8 of *Gesammelte Werke*, edited by Renate Albrecht, 220–39. Stuttgart: Evangelisches Verlagswerk, 1970.

————. *Systematic Theology*. 3 vols. Chicago: University of Chicago Press, 1951–63.

————. "The Two Types of Philosophy of Religion." In *Theology of Culture*, edited by Robert C. Kimball, 10–29. Oxford: Oxford University Press, 1959.

Toorn, Karel van der. *Sin and Sanction in Israel and Mesopotamia: A Comparative Study*. Assen: Van Gorcum, 1985.

Travis, Stephen H. "The Wrath of God (NT)." In *The Anchor Bible Dictionary*, edited by David Noel Freedman, 6:##–##. New York: Doubleday, 1992.

Trillhaas, Wolfgang. *Dogmatik*. 4th ed. Berlin: De Gruyter, 1980.

Tugendhat, Ernst. "Gedanken über den Tod." In *Philosophie in synthetischer Absicht = Synthesis in Mind*, edited by Marcelo Stamm, 487–512. Stuttgart: Klett-Cotta, 1998.

Tupper, E. Frank. *A Scandalous Providence: The Jesus Story of the Compassion of God*. Macon: Mercer University Press, 1995.

Twelftree, Graham H. *Jesus the Exorcist: A Contribution to the Study of the Historical Jesus*. Tübingen: Mohr Siebeck, 1993.

Union Evangelischer Kirchen in der Evangelischen Kirche in Deutschland, ed. *Leben im Schatten des Bösen: Eine Vortragsreihe im Berliner Dom*. Neukirchen-Vluyn: Neukirchener Verlagshaus, 2004.

Vermès, Géza. "Redemption and Genesis xxii: The Binding of Isaac and the Sacrifice of Jesus." In *Scripture and Tradition in Judaism: Haggadic Studies*, 193–227. Leiden: Brill, 1961.

Vernant, Jean-Pierre. *Mythe et religion en Grèce ancienne*. Paris: Seuil, 1990.

Verweyen, Hansjürgen. *Philosophie und Theologie: Vom Mythos zum Logos zum Mythos*. Darmstadt: Wissenschaftliche Buchgesellschaft, 2005.

Volgger, David. "Es geht um das Ganze: Gott prüft Abraham (Gen 22,1–19)." *Biblische Zeitschrift* 45, no. 1 (2001) 3–19.

Volkmann, Stefan. *Der Zorn Gottes: Studien zur Rede vom Zorn Gottes in der evangelischen Theologie*. Marburg: Elwert, 2004.

Wagner, Harald, ed. *Mit Gott streiten: Neue Zugänge zum Theodizee-Problem*. Freiburg: Herder, 1998.

Wahl, Harald-Martin. *Der gerechte Schöpfer: Eine redaktions- und theologiegeschichtliche Untersuchung der Elihureden, Hiob 32–37*. Berlin: De Gruyter, 1993.

Wakeman, Mary K. *God's Battle with the Monster: A Study in Biblical Imagery*. Leiden: Brill, 1973.

Waldenfels, Bernhard. *In den Netzen der Lebenswelt*. Frankfurt: Suhrkamp, 1985.

Walter, Henrik. *Neurophilosophy of Free Will: From Libertarian Illusions to a Concept of Natural Autonomy*. Trans. Cynthia Klohr. Cambridge: Massachusetts Institute of Technology Press, 2001.

Watts, Rikki E. *Isaiah's New Exodus and Mark*. Tübingen: Mohr Siebeck, 1997.

Weatherford, Roy. *The Implications of Determinism*. New York: Routledge, 1991.

Weber, Max. *Economy and Society: An Outline of Interpretive Sociology*. Edited by Guenther Roth and Claus Wittich. Translated by Ephraim Fischoff et al. Berkeley: University of California Press, 1978.

———. *The Protestant Ethic and the Spirit of Capitalism*. Translated by Talcott Parsons. London: Routledge, 1993.

———. *Wirtschaft und Gesellschaft: Die Wirtschaft und die gesellschaftlichen Ordnungen und Mächte: Nachlass*. In *Gesamtausgabe*, edited by Hans G. Kippenberg et al. Abt. I, Bd. 22 Tlb. 2. Tübingen: Mohr Siebeck, 2001.

Weinberg, Joanna. "Job versus Abraham: The Quest for the Perfect God-Fearer in Rabbinic Tradition." In *The Book of Job*, edited by W. A. M. Beuken, 281–96. Leuven: Peeters, 1994.

Weingartner, Paul. *Evil: Different Kinds of Evil in the Light of a Modern Theodicy*. Frankfurt: Lang, 2003.

———. "Kommentar zu Thomas von Aquin, Summa Theologica I,19,1 über den Willen Gottes." In *Kirche und Gesellschaft: Theologische und gesellschaftswissenschaftliche Aspekte*, edited by Erika Weinzierl, ##–##. Vienna: Geyer, 1979.

Weisberger, Andrea M. *Suffering Belief: Evil and the Anglo-American Defense of Theism*. New York: Lang, 1999.

Welzer, Harald, and Michaela Christ. *Täter: Wie aus ganz normalen Menschen Massenmörder werden*. Frankfurt: Fischer, 2005.

Wendel, Saskia. "'Den Allmächtigen ergründen wir nicht...' Zur Verhältnisbestimmung von Transzendenz und Immanenz angesichts von 'Ijobs Gott.'" *Concilium* 40, no. 4 (2004) 416–29.

Werbick, Jürgen. *Von Gott sprechen an der Grenze zum Verstummen*. Münster: Lit, 2004.

Westermann, Claus. *Genesis 12–36: A Commentary*. Translated by John J. Scullion. Minneapolis: Augsburg, 1985.

———. *Genesis 37–50: A Commentary*. Translated by John J. Scullion. Minneapolis: Augsburg, 1986.

———. *Lamentations: Issues and Interpretation*. Translated by Charles Muenchow. Minneapolis: Fortress, 1994.

Whitehead, Alfred North. *Process and Reality: An Essay in Cosmology*. Edited by David Ray Griffin and Donald W. Sherburne. Corrected ed. New York: Free Press, 1978.

Whitney, Barry L. *Theodicy: An Annotated Bibliography on the Problem of Evil, 1960–1991*. Bowling Green, OH: Bowling Green State University, 1998.

Wiertz, Oliver. "*Das Problem des Übels* in Richard Swinburnes Religionsphilosophie: Über Sinn und Grenzen seines theistischen Antwortversuches auf das Problem des Übels und dessen Bedeutung für die Theologie." *Theologie und Philosophie* 71, no. 2 (1991) 224–56.

Willnauer, Elmar. *Heute das Böse denken: Mit Immanuel Kant und Hannah Arendt zu einem Neuansatz für die Theologie*. Berlin: Rhombos, 2005.

Wimmer, Reiner. *Kants kritische Religionsphilosophie*. Berlin: De Gruyter, 1990.

Witte, Markus. *Philologische Notizen zu Hiob 21–27*. Berlin: De Gruyter, 1995.

———. *Vom Leiden zur Lehre: Der dritte Redegang (Hiob 21–27) und die Redaktionsgeschichte des Hiobbuches*. Berlin: De Gruyter, 1994.

Wolde, Ellen J. van. *A Semiotic Analysis of Genesis 2–3: A Semiotic Theory and Method of Analysis Applied to the Story of the Garden of Eden*. Assen: Van Gorcum, 1989.

Wolter, Michael. "Der Apostel und seine Gemeinden als Teilhaber am Leidensgeschick Jesu Christi: Beobachtungen zur paulinischen Leidenstheologie." *New Testament Studies* 36, no. 4 (October 1990) 535–57.

———. "Leiden III: Neues Testament." In vol. 20 of *Theologische Realenzyklopädie*, edited by Horst Robert Balz et al., 677–88. Berlin: De Gruyter, 1977.

Wolterstorff, Nicholas. *Lament for a Son*. Grand Rapids: Eerdmans, 1987.

Wright, Nigel Goring. *A Theology of the Dark Side: Putting the Power of Evil in its Place*. Carlisle: Paternoster, 2002.

Wüthrich, Matthias Dominique. *Gott und das Nichtige: Eine Untersuchung zur Rede vom Nichtigen ausgehend von §50 der Kirchlichen Dogmatik Karl Barths*. Zurich: Theologischer Verlag, 2006.

Wykstra, Stephen J. "The Humean Obstacle to Evidential Arguments from Suffering: On Avoiding the Evils of 'Appearance.'" In *The Problem of Evil*, edited by Marilyn McCord Adams and Robert Merrihew Adams, 138–60. Oxford: Oxford University Press, 1990.

Wynn, Mark. *Emotional Experience and Religious Understanding: Integrating Perception, Conception and Feeling*. Cambridge: Cambridge University Press, 2005.

Wyrwa, Dietmar. "Augustine and Luther on Evil." In *The Problem of Evil and Its Symbols in Jewish and Christian Tradition*, edited by Henning Graf Reventlow and Yair Hoffman, 124–46. London: Continuum, 2004.

Zagzebski, Linda. "An Agent-Based Approach to the Problem of Evil." *International Journal for Philosophy of Religion* 39, no. 3 (1996) 127–39.

Zenger, Erich. *Dein Angesicht suche ich: Neue Psalmenauslegungen*. Freiburg: Herder, 1998.

———. "Psalm 88." In *Psalmen 51–100*, edited by Frank-Lothar Hossfeld and Erich Zenger, 563–76. Freiburg: Herder, 2000.

Zimmermann, Bernhard. *Greek Tragedy: An Introduction*. Translated by Thomas Marier. Baltimore: Johns Hopkins University Press, 1991.